The Trumpet

Also available in the series

The Flute
Ardal Powell

Timpani and Percussion
Jeremy Montagu

The Oboe
Geoffrey Burgess and Bruce Haynes

The Trombone
Trevor Herbert

The Clarinet
Eric Hoeprich

THE YALE MUSICAL INSTRUMENT SERIES

The Trumpet

John Wallace and Alexander McGrattan

Yale University Press
New Haven and London

For information about this and other Yale University Press publications please contact:
U.S. Office: sales.press@yale.edu yalebooks.com
Europe Office: sales@yaleup.co.uk www.yalebooks.co.uk

Set in Columbus MT by IDSUK (DataConnection) Ltd
Printed in Great Britain by TJ International Ltd, Padstow, Cornwall

Library of Congress Cataloging-in-Publication Data

Wallace, John, 1949–
The trumpet / John Wallace and Alexander McGrattan.
p. cm.
ISBN 978-0-300-11230-6 (cl : alk. paper)
1. Trumpet. 2. Trumpet music—History and criticism. I. McGrattan, Alexander. II. Title.
ML960.W35 2012
788.9'2--dc23

2011053112

A catalogue record for this book is available from the British Library.

10 9 8 7 6 5 4 3 2 1

MIX
Paper from responsible sources
FSC® C013056
FSC www.fsc.org

Dedication and in memoriam

To the Tullis Russell Mills Band, our fathers, Gibby McGrattan and Kiff Wallace, and to our teachers Albert Cochrane, Willie Ross and Ernest Hall

We shall all be changed, in a moment, in the twinkling of an eye, at the last trump;
for the trumpet shall sound, and the dead shall be raised incorruptible
1 Corinthians 15:51–52

Contents

Illustrations, music examples and tables

Illustrations

Music examples

Tables

Foreword

It is a great privilege and pleasure to introduce this most necessary and inspiring book on the history of the trumpet, by two of its foremost exponents. As I shall explain, I have had a positive, but at times tortuous and chequered relationship with the trumpet world, and feel I must join John Wallace and Alexander McGrattan in encouraging stimulus, experimentation, change and transformation concerning any received ideas as to what the trumpet IS: its world is always in a state of metamorphosis, towards circumstances beyond our imaginings, as this book proves, over and over again.

Perhaps I should apologise for being so personal, but I think it important to understand that the first music I heard, along with popular music of the late nineteen-thirties, was brass band music, on long weekend walks with my parents in Peel and Buile Hill Parks, Salford. The great difference was that the brass music in the band-stand was live, and made your spine tingle, whereas the popular dance tunes were either on the wireless, or on the tiny wind-up acoustic gramophone. I always waited for the cornet tunes in the 'Zampa' and 'Poet and Peasant' overtures, and a lifelong love was firmly established.

It was my fellow student and anarchist at the Music Department of Manchester University and the Royal Manchester College of Music, Elgar Howarth, who, in the mid fifties, deepened and encouraged my love of the trumpet – so much so that in 1954–5 I wrote him a 'Sonata for Trumpet in D and Piano' – which became my opus 1. This was first performed to an audience of six, in the little university concert hall, in 1955, by Elgar Howarth and John Ogdon. I sent the score to the Society for the Promotion of New Music in London, hoping for its acceptance for performance in one of their Wigmore Hall concerts, but it was refused and returned, with elaborate explanations as to why it was technically impossible for the trumpet to play. Instead, Howarth and Ogdon played it at a London Arts Council concert, causing quite a scandal. It was next performed at the York Festival, but Ogdon had been forbidden to play it by the Manchester College, as 'that kind of stuff is not good for anyone's career' – so I had to jump in and play the piano part myself.

It is a particular pleasure to hear so many trumpet students these days practising and performing my opus 1 – in the early fifties I heard American jazz musicians on record and radio performing solos which made my Sonata sound elementary, and knew, deep down and from the start, that Elgar Howarth and I were right about its technical feasibility.

Another formative encounter came in 1964, when the London Philharmonic commissioned my 'Second Fantasia on John Taverner's In Nomine' (Taverner, the sixteenth-century English composer). I met members of the Orchestra crossing Waterloo Bridge *away* from the Royal Festival Hall, who told me the rehearsal had been abandoned, and that the scheduled first performance had been postponed for a year, or until I had revised the impossible trumpet parts. (I just doubled them, for safety, in the woodwind, and have regretted this bitterly, at every recent performance!)

Much later, as composer/conductor of the Scottish Chamber Orchestra, the BBC Philharmonic and the Royal Philharmonic, constructive, and I hope mutually beneficial relationships were established between me and the brass players. They encouraged me, with critical help, to write ever more demanding parts – particularly the trumpet sections. I remember that when the Philharmonia Orchestra commissioned my Fifth Symphony, Richard Watkins for the horns and John Wallace for the trumpets asked for the most virtuoso parts I could devise for their sections – and in recent years I have conducted this work with many orchestras, including students', with no complaints (almost!) and excellent results. How things change! I went on to write more music for John Wallace, including an 'impossible' concerto, which we performed together in many countries.

Recently I wrote an opera commissioned jointly by the Royal Academy of Music and the Juilliard School, which has trumpet parts that would have been too much for professionals only ten or fifteen years ago. The performances were absolutely brilliant.

I relate these incidents from my personal experience only to point out how much the trumpet world has changed in the last half century or so, and to encourage trumpeters and composers of all kinds of music to develop fruitful, constructive musical relationships at all stages.

Recently, as Master of the Queen's Music, I have developed a musical relationship with Kneller Hall Military School of Music, opening up a whole new world of compositional possibility and orchestral practice: I have used military trumpets in three works already, including most recently an overture for the Last Night of the Proms. You never, ever, stop learning about the trumpet!

Peter Maxwell Davies
September 2011

Preface

One of the central figures in the history of the trumpet, Louis Armstrong, was born in 1901, the same year as one of the author's grandfathers. The idea that such a universal and ancient instrument should have undergone such a fundamental transformation so recently, so tantalisingly close to within living memory at the time of writing, was the starting point for this book. The genesis of this initial idea took root in a series of BBC Radio 2 broadcasts entitled *From Jericho to Jazz*, presented by John Wallace and produced by broadcaster Bob MacDowell in 1995. This series featured interviews with jazz musicians Maynard Ferguson and Guy Barker, and freely mixed jazz and classical genres.

From a vantage point sixteen years later from initiation to completion, it remains a central thesis of this book that the advent of jazz was a fundamentally important event in the history of the trumpet. Louis Armstrong's improvised solos with the Hot Five and the Hot Seven from the end of 1925 until 1928 were the most significant evidence that a tipping point in the evolution of the playing technique of the trumpet had been reached. Over the century to follow, the idiom and technique of the trumpet flourished in all musical genres. Jazz had given players the freedom to improvise outside the parameters of instrumental orthodoxy.

Recorded sound now allows us to analyse closely the historical moment described by the advent of jazz, and Armstrong's contribution within this coincides with such a remarkable point in the history of the trumpet that it has a place to itself in the final chapter of the book. Armstrong himself is instantly recognisable through the sheer power of his sound, and the sound of the trumpet in itself is a constant idea throughout its history. The notion connecting the trumpet's tone quality with absolute power is demonstrated by the association of the sound of the trumpet with the concept of resurrection, a familiar idea in art music exemplified by Handel's famous setting of 'The Trumpet shall sound' from *Messiah* (1741/42).[1]

Past histories of the trumpet written from an earlier perspective by players, like, for example, Johann Ernst Altenburg (1734–1801) and François Georges Dauverné (1799–1874), may well have sprung initially, like the present volume, from the personal experiences of accounts of events from a living memory of family members, teachers and colleagues.[2] Both of the present authors, writing at the beginning of the twenty-first century, were inspired in their lifelong enthusiasm for the instrument by the anecdotes related to them as teenage members of the National Youth Orchestra trumpet section by the doyen of British classical trumpeters, Ernest Hall (1890–1984).

Many musicians, irrespective of nationality, irrespective of genre, are great raconteurs and carry their own aural history of music around inside their heads. Hall used to reminisce about missing the maiden and final voyage of the Titanic (one of the defining moments of the Edwardian Age) with the London Symphony Orchestra in 1912 because the boat train broke down, and freely mixed general anecdotes, now firmly fixed in the authors' collective psyche as cameos of social history, with revealing stories about the first performances of Elgar's works that he participated in. During the first performance of Elgar's Second Symphony in 1911, for example, Hall blacked out on the trumpet's climactic top C sharp in the final movement, and to his chagrin, held the note for a full bar too long. When he tracked down Elgar after the performance, he was surprised to find that the composer liked the effect so much he had already written it into the score for posterity.[3] Ernest Hall imbued his two young protégés now responsible for writing this book with a love of storytelling associated with the trumpet and its players.

In London, Ernest Hall was taught by Walter Morrow, who was taught by Thomas Harper, jun.; who was taught by Thomas Harper, sen.; who performed with John Hyde, whose career overlapped with that of John Sarjant, principal trumpeter at the 1784 Handel Commemoration. Through this sort of dynastic teacher–pupil relationship traceable patterns of continuity can be identified in any country in which the trumpet is played. To the aural history of anecdotes, add books and written records; and newer retrieval systems, with their own inbuilt obsolescence of handing down sights and sounds, like, for example, wax cylinders, shellac recordings, 78s, LPs, CDs, TV and radio broadcasts, film, video, DVDs, downloads, podcasts, you-tube and social networking. The records available to us now for the century past are more complex than those that were available to Altenburg and Dauverné, but our methodology may not be so different. This is a history of the trumpet written by two of its players.

Acknowledgements

The act of writing a book like the present one brings into question the notion of authorship. Although the final viewpoints arrived at have been chosen by the people named on the cover of this book, the knowledge contained within has been gathered from a broad community.

Our respective wives, Liz Wallace and Angela Gribben, have suffered the manifest complications of the trumpet seen through the eyes of the obsessive. Arnold Myers, Trevor Herbert, Helen Barlow and Howard Snell have read drafts and given endless advice and encouragement over the past decade and a half. Andrew Lynn, principal trumpet of Scottish Opera and an erudite scholar, has provided an ideal final sounding-board for objective balance, and for judging any opinions we may have been bold enough to express. Dr Verena Barth, post-doctoral researcher at the Royal Conservatoire of Scotland, has been a source of inspiration and ideas when the spirits began to flag as the summit of completion seemed to get further away rather than closer; and Helen Barsby, Raymond Burkhart, Maria Doehler, Nancy Gildner, Maja Helmes, Thomas Stevens and Susan Williams have given us invaluable insights along the way. Cosmo and Esme Wallace are to be thanked, not only for their stoic patience with their father, but also for dropping their own work without demur to pursue esoteric and arcane research tasks like, for example, the demise of the Cheesemakers' Guild in pre-revolutionary Calais.

Work colleagues at the Royal Conservatoire of Scotland went the extra 500 miles to assist: Carol Conway, who heroically project-managed collating the illustrations, examples, tables and permissions whilst multi-tasking in a busy office; my serene personal assistants Helen Boocock and Marie Green; Craig Quinn, the print-room supervisor for whom nothing is too much effort; Ken Dundas, the RCS's photographer, whose visual advice and input was invaluable: their enthusiasm, allied to the curiosity of our other immediate colleagues for the project, was palpable and made the loneliness of the long-distance authors easier to bear.

The patience and willingness of library staff to engage with our project, in particular at our own institution, the Royal Conservatoire of Scotland, and at Glasgow University, the National Library of Scotland and the British Library, has eased our odyssey considerably, and in this the Royal Conservatoire of Scotland music librarian, Karen McAuley, deserves her own special vote of thanks.

The UK's Arts and Humanities Research Council, the Royal Academy of Music and the Royal Conservatoire of Scotland are to be thanked for funding some of the research over the sixteen-year time span of the project. RCS research students Rui Pedro Alves and Shona Mackay are to be thanked for their advice and help, configuring and transcribing the music examples.

Bob MacDowell, an alumnus of the Royal Conservatoire of Scotland when it was still the Royal Scottish Academy of Music and Drama, is to be thanked for germinating the initial idea for the book when devising his BBC Radio 2 series *From Jericho to Jazz* at the tail-end of the last millennium. Malcolm Gerratt of Yale University Press in London grasped the concept behind this book right from the start, but even he could not have been prepared for the long wait from genesis to final production, which must have tested even his legendary kindness, tolerance and patience to its limits.

The lives of Elgar Howarth and James Watson, coming from the tradition of the cornet and trumpet in the United Kingdom – from colliery brass band through the Royal Philharmonic Orchestra and the Royal Opera House, the Philip Jones Brass Ensemble and London Sinfonietta to conducting careers – provided underlying inspiration for the overall notion behind the book. Their first-hand human experience is living proof that the trumpet is a universal and ubiquitous instrument which transcends all barriers.

John Wallace's father-in-law, the economic historian R. M. Hartwell, gave longitudinal personal lectures throughout the writing of the book until his death in March 2009 on what he described as 'the bigger picture', as has brother-in-law Roland Quinault, also a distinguished historian. Going further back to the first musical experiences of the authors, our grandfathers, mothers, aunts, uncles and other close family members are to be thanked for the intensely musical environment in which we grew up in Scotland. There, impromptu music-making was a necessary part of every family gathering; there we were encouraged passionately in our musical aspirations; there the local brass bands in the villages of Buckhaven and Markinch ran junior ensembles; there we both gained our first steps in cornet playing in a class of up to forty players.

Finally, we wish to thank our many colleagues in the music business and conservatoire sector who have tolerated our trumpet habit to beyond the bounds of human reason.

Introduction

Trumpets have been made of many different materials, in many shapes and sizes, and numerous extinct subspecies, distant cousins, and aboriginal survivors permeate its family tree. Through their ability to project a sustained sound over a wide distance, trumpets fashioned from materials at hand were adopted by most ancient societies for signalling purposes. The trumpet's identity and cultural significance often transcended its utilitarian function by serving as a marker of status and power in belief systems and their consequent ceremony. As Don Smithers remarked in his seminal study on the baroque trumpet, 'the trumpet is more than a musical instrument: it is an idea, a concept, with deeper allegorical associations'.[1] The symbolism of the trumpet was central to its introduction into art music and has remained a significant determinant of its idiom.

A distinction between trumpets and horns does not exist in many non-western cultures and was inconsistent in Europe before the early modern period. Whenever necessary therefore a broad definition of the trumpet has been applied to this study. Our intention is to explore how, where, when, why, and by whom the trumpet or trumpet-like instruments have been played, and what the trumpet meant to different societies at different moments in history.

Members of the trumpet's extended family tree continue to feature in the narrative after the instrument acquired a more discrete identity during the later Middle Ages. Attempts to extend its melodic capability by adding a slide mechanism led, in the fifteenth century, to the development of the trombone (lit. 'big trumpet' in Italian). However, slide instruments more closely related to the trumpet appeared at various times and places between the seventeenth and nineteenth centuries.

Hybridisation between horn and trumpet occurred at various times. The cornett, a conical instrument fashioned from wood with playing holes, flourished in the sixteenth and early seventeenth centuries. Although technically a horn by bore and nomenclature, the cornett's tessitura and idiom is closer to that of the trumpet. By the eighteenth century the horn itself began to accrue a discrete history with separate idioms; however, even here a common nomenclature (such as *tromba da caccia*) is sometimes encountered, and there are many occasions when the two instruments were considered interchangeable.

The identity of the trumpet began to shift with the application of valve technology in the early nineteenth century. The cornet set the pace in technological advancement and the technical capabilities of its players from its first appearance in the 1820s. Its idiom was lyrical and virtuosic. Cornet means 'little horn', and some of the earliest soloists on the valved cornet were horn players. By the 1840s, however, specialist cornet players emerged, some of whom, like Jean-Baptiste Arban, had initially trained as trumpeters. But many composers who wrote for valved trumpet in art music were conservative in instrumental terms, clinging to the ideals of the natural trumpet with its idiom of war, triumph, heroism and nobility. The cornet was not received with universal approval. Even Berlioz, who wrote prominent cornet parts in some of his orchestral works, was ambivalent about the cornet and talked of 'its tone quality with neither the nobility of the horn nor the swagger of the trumpet'.[2] The trumpet was considered an aristocrat, the cornet a proletarian.

This is the first study of the trumpet to trace systematically its development and use from prehistoric times to the present day since the publication of Edward H. Tarr's *Die Trompete* in 1977 (English trans., 1988). Tarr's monograph was preceded in 1973 by Don L. Smithers's *The Music and History of the Baroque Trumpet before 1721*, which provided a basis for future research into the baroque trumpet literature. A third researcher working during the 1970s deserves recognition for unearthing sources of baroque trumpet music from libraries and archives across Europe. During the decade before his untimely death in 1981, aged thirty-two, the amateur trumpet enthusiast Robert Minter amassed a vast collection of baroque trumpet music, in the form of facsimiles of manuscripts and early publications, as well as transcriptions in his own hand.[3]

The publications of Tarr and Smithers coincided with the emergence of professional early music performance and a widening of interest in historical brass instruments. Since its formation by Jeffrey Nussbaum in 1988, the Historic Brass Society has provided a forum for the exchange of ideas and, through its journal, a vehicle for the dissemination of research into a wide range of brass related topics. The early music movement stimulated debate and collaboration between performers, specialist instrument makers and organologists, and it encouraged the assimilation of historical performance practice into mainstream musicological discourse. Organologists and instrument makers have helped shape many of the ideas presented in this book, both in their writing and through personal communication. The instrument maker and museum curator Robert Barclay deserves special mention for his research into trumpet making in seventeenth-century Nuremberg and the way in which his findings have been disseminated. Not only have his instruments provided a benchmark for the faithful reproduction of trumpets used in the baroque period, but in workshops that have been held since the mid 1990s he has provided hands-on experience of trumpet making using tools and techniques that are essentially the same as those used by seventeenth-century Nuremberg craftsmen. Over the course of five days, participants, many of whom have no or minimal metal-working experience, produce a playable trumpet.

The Trumpet follows a broadly chronological pattern. To begin, it charts the trumpet from prehistory through the civilisations of the ancient world to the survival of primitive trumpets in contemporary societies. A chapter summarising developments in the instrument and its playing techniques follows. This provides a basis for more detailed investigations of these topics in later chapters.

Chapter 3 covers a period of more than a thousand years, from the fall of the Roman Empire in the West in the fifth century until the end of the sixteenth century. This era was long regarded as a hiatus in the history of the trumpet. Nevertheless, important articles by Don Smithers and Peter Downey from the 1980s provoked fresh interest and controversy in this relatively neglected period. Smithers challenged accepted notions that metal trumpets fell out of use in Europe after the demise of the Roman Empire. Downey opposed the majority view, as espoused by Keith Polk and others, that the single-slide trumpet as used in the fifteenth-century shawm band was the precursor of the double-slide trombone. The chapter considers cornett and trumpet playing at the Bavarian court at Munich during Lassus's tenure as maestro di cappella. The head trumpeter at Munich at this time was Cesare Bendinelli, whose manuscript method is a chief source of information on late-Renaissance trumpet playing. The chapter concludes over the Alps in Venice, where the cornett reached its zenith.

A series of four chapters explores the trumpet in the seventeenth and eighteenth centuries, the 'golden age' of the natural trumpet. The first examines the political, economic and geographical factors that underpinned the cultivation of the sophisticated performance idioms and virtuosic repertoire of the baroque period, and the organisation and working patterns of trumpeters. It also explores the quest to extend the chromatic possibilities of the trumpet towards the end of this period, a theme that is taken up in Chapter 8, where the concertos for keyed trumpet by Haydn and Hummel are analysed in detail. Chapters 5 to 7 examine the repertoire and performance traditions of important centres of trumpet playing, including detailed studies of the trumpet parts of Handel and Bach.

The nineteenth and early twentieth centuries, during which the development of valved instruments redefined the idiom of the trumpet and the ways in which it was understood by players, composers and audiences, is examined in Chapter 9. The main technical developments are charted, but the focus is on the implications of these innovations for performance. The often complex relationships between natural and valved instruments and the aesthetic tensions between the cornet (and by association the valved trumpet) and the more exalted natural, or 'true', trumpet are recurring themes in the chapter. Players of the cornet from military and amateur band backgrounds figure prominently in the discussion, as do conservatoires, since both contributed significantly to the eventual convergence of the cornet and trumpet idioms.

Chapter 10 investigates the awakening of interest in the music of the baroque era, in particular that of Bach, a nineteenth-century phenomenon in which the trumpet played a central role. The smaller, higher-pitched, instruments that were developed to negotiate this repertoire were embraced by orchestral trumpeters to perform the demanding contemporary repertoire and subsequently exploited by composers to provide an additional soprano voice to the orchestral trumpet section.

Chapter 11 traces the development of the trumpet as an orchestral and a solo instrument since the early twentieth century. The centrality of the trumpet to jazz and the rise in popularity of the concerto by Haydn brought the trumpet to prominence as a viable solo instrument in classical music. This was confirmed with the success of Maurice André, who extended the solo trumpet repertoire by commissioning new works and performing transcriptions of baroque music. From the 1960s, collaboration between trumpeters and avant-garde composers, and the involvement of trumpeters with specialist contemporary music ensembles, redefined the notion of what was possible on the trumpet and led to an expansion of its classical solo repertoire.

The role of the trumpet in jazz is the principal theme of the final chapter. Following an analysis of the early recordings of Louis Armstrong, we follow the trumpet through the various evolutionary phases of its history, focussing on the new playing styles and techniques that emerged and the players who instigated these developments. The prominence of the trumpet in jazz projected celebrated trumpeters, most notably Armstrong, into more mainstream fields of popular music and into motion pictures. Consideration of the ways in which trumpeters have been portrayed, and trumpet music conveyed, on screen leads to a discussion of the use of the trumpet in film scores. The imaging of the trumpet player is explored further by considering the role of female players in jazz and classical music. Finally, the future direction of jazz is considered through the prominence of Wynton Marsalis, and his drive to establish a canonical repertory, a move which created much public controversy and interest.

As with all historical study, the accumulation of knowledge on the history of the trumpet has provoked fresh lines of enquiry, the formulation of alternative theories and yet more unanswered questions. Not surprisingly, due to the paucity of surviving sources, our understanding of the instruments and the contexts in which they were employed is most acute before the later Middle Ages. However, lacunae also exist in our understanding of the instruments and performance practices of later periods. The portrait of the Leipzig Stadtpfeifer Gottfried Reiche holding a coiled trumpet poses questions as to the extent of its use and whether it has special relevance to the music of Bach. Another unanswered question relates to possible wider uses of the German *tromba da tirarsi* and the English slide trumpet (in its late seventeenth- and late eighteenth-century incarnations) than evidenced by the few scores in which their use is specified or suggested. The adoption of the valved trumpet and the subsequent switch from trumpets in six-foot F to shorter instruments in B flat, C or higher, by nineteenth-century orchestral players, is far from clear cut. A more recent matter of conjecture concerns Louis Armstrong's switch from cornet to trumpet in the late 1920s. Although there is a broad consensus on when this occurred, neither documentary sources nor the analysis of recordings settles the matter definitively.

As Neil MacGregor concludes in *A History of the World in 100 Objects*, which tells the story of mankind over the past two million years through the things that humans have made, 'when attempting to understand the function and significance of an historical object, after considering the historical, archaeological and anthropological evidence that may shed light on its former life, it is often necessary to add a considerable leap of imagination . . . in the hope of winning the insights it may deliver'.[4] In this exploration of the trumpet in its myriad guises, we summarise the historical evidence and arguments that have shaped our understanding of its development, and the ways and contexts in which it has been played and understood. On issues for which evidence is scant or inconclusive we assess the scholarly discourse and where necessary take the necessary 'leap of imagination'.

Chapter 1

The trumpet in the ancient and non-Western world

The trumpet is a remarkably universal instrument. Evidence from social anthropology and ethnomusicology points to religious and sacred use of trumpets by primitive social organisations stretching back enduringly into prehistory. Human beings fashioned trumpets from any suitable local elements from the earliest times. Extant primitive societies indicate what human ingenuity can achieve with materials like wood and bark, bamboo, gourds, crustacean shells, and mammal horns. The horns of wild or domesticated animals can be crafted into simple trumpets by hollowing out the core with a heated stick. Conch shells can be dried and bored with a blow-hole. Tree-branches can be hollowed out with fire or termites. Bark can be stretched around a wooden skeleton to form a cone-like trumpet or a massive horn. Even human remains have been hollowed out and lip-blown. Before the advent of written law, the celebration of ritual through music and dance served to render societies unified and coherent.[1]

Despite its eponymous appearance in most societies throughout world history, the trumpet has filled largely the same, select number of roles – perhaps a reason for its global prevalence. The many ways a lip-blown instrument can be primitively manufactured means that the trumpet often pre-dates the earliest collective memories of a society, developing into a marker of identity and of cultural pride. Even among the earliest references to trumpets, the instrument seems to hold an aura of antiquity, as a tool bequeathed to man from an ancient, unrecorded source. The Greeks, for instance, never formed a creation myth for the salpinx or conch trumpet as they had for the lyre and aulos. Other instruments required an explanation to come into being, where the trumpet had simply always existed.[2] The instrument is an example of an early man-made object that acts universally as a cultural transmitter, communicating more than a simple message between living people.

Because it is so commonly found within early societies, the little information we have for examining the origins of the trumpet stems mostly from the accumulated knowledge of ethnomusicologists, archaeologists and paleoanthropologists. It appears that in the three major stages of post-Ice Age man – sedentary agrarian societies, nomad pastoralist fringe-groups, and the development of organized military campaigning – contexts were created throughout the world in which the trumpet filled a logical niche. For farmer and nomad alike, the trumpet was an efficient hunting tool, startling prey and driving it towards prepared ground. It was an effective signalling device (so effective that it is still in – albeit ceremonial – use in mountainous regions of central Europe and the Himalayas). Between signalling and hunting, the trumpet developed an idiom that allowed it to be pushed towards an altogether more hostile role.

The first literary reference that has been interpreted as denoting a trumpet or horn stems from the world's first surviving epic, *The Battle of Gilgamesh*, detailing the adventures of a quasi-mythical king (*c.*2500 BCE) of the Sumerians. Gilgamesh's magical *pukku* and *mikka*, objects of kingship fashioned from a magical tree on the banks of the Euphrates, were interpreted by Galpin and Bate as denoting, respectively, the tube and bell of a trumpet.[3] More recently, these problematic objects have been interpreted as possibly referring to a drum and drumstick.[4] The Sumerians, under Sargon of Agade, were a prototype of the aggressive steppe descendents who would transform the face and fate of Eurasia. With their superior battle tactics, the Sumerians accumulated so much land throughout the Fertile Crescent that they formed the world's first empire, gathering together cultures, tools and techniques that had been developing for thousands of years in relative isolation. Sargon realised that drilling, intelligence, organization and communication were more important for an armed force than brute strength, providing an opportunity for the lip-blown instruments of the region to be incorporated into martial life. From the fields, the trumpet became an instrument of the battlefield. Gilgamesh's *pukku* and *mikka*, if they *are* the bell and tube of a trumpet, represent his ultimate symbols of power. The last tablet of the epic is devoted to their loss in the underworld and his attempts to retrieve them: he laments their loss as he would the loss of his greatest imperial symbol.

Whether or not the writers of the *Epic of Gilgamesh* referred to the trumpet, as an instrument of war it became so powerful and prevalent in ancient Middle-Eastern societies – from which is derived much common cultural heritage – that its legacy lives on, and not simply by the permanent presence of trumpeters in Eurasian armies. The Israelite *shofar*, a ram's horn, has survived to the present day and is played across the world in an uninterrupted tradition of almost five thousand years. The calls that a rabbi makes on the *shofar* to this day, in synagogues throughout the world, give us a greater indication of the idiom of early trumpets and horns in the ancient Eurasian world than perhaps all other ancient sources combined. A number of medieval manuscripts, the earliest dating from the thirteenth century, contain early notation linking the *shofar* calls heard today (shown in Ex. 1.1) to those described in biblical times.[5] Trumpets made from natural materials rarely conform to mathematically exact harmonic series. Because of the irregular cavity inside a ram's horn, the

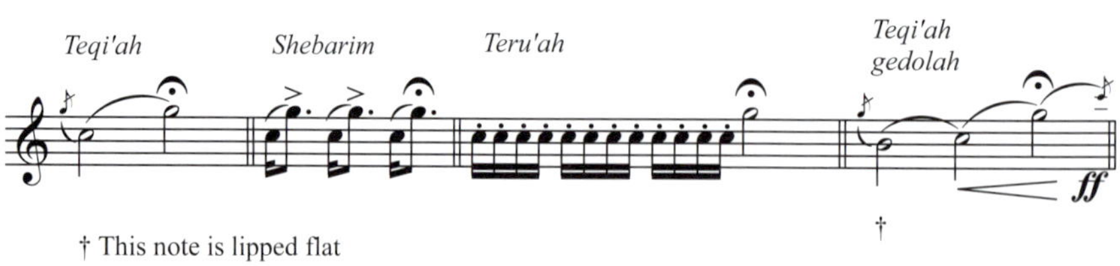

Ex. 1.1 Traditional *shofar* calls, from *Grove 2*, s.v. 'shofar' (By permission of Oxford University Press).

acoustic behaviour of the instrument is strange, with much individual variation between instruments. The intervals sounded do not always accord with those shown here. The calls also vary, depending on the extent to which the player alters the notes by 'lipping'.

The most famous use of the *shofar* was at Jericho, where, according to the biblical account (Joshua 6:20), its supernatural powers were invoked with devastating effect. On returning from forty years in the wilderness (scholarly opinion is divided as to whether this occurred *c.*1550 or *c.*1400 BCE), the Israelites besieged the city of Jericho. For six days, they marched round the outer perimeter once a day and on the seventh day circumvented the city seven times. On the seventh circuit, the priests blasted their *shofarot*, the people shouted, and the walls fell down. This account of the destruction of the walls of Jericho is one of numerous passages in the Old Testament that relate the sound of the *shofar* to the actions of God.

The Old Testament is our main source of information on the trumpets of the Israelites, the *shofar* and the silver *hassrah*. In the Book of Numbers 10:1–10 God commands Moses to make two silver trumpets, to be used for assembling the congregation and signalling the resumption of their journey out of the wilderness of Sinai: 'Make thee two trumpets of silver; of a whole piece shalt thou make them.' The instructions also stipulate that in future the silver trumpets are to be blown by priests on solemn occasions and at times of war.

During the period of the Second Temple (515 BCE–70 CE) the *hassrah* acquired an elevated status in Temple ritual, being played exclusively by priests, whilst the *shofar* was played by their assistants. Trumpet calls on the *hassrah* were sounded three times to announce the opening of the Temple gates each morning and to signal the Sabbath. Nine blasts of the *hassrah* accompanied the morning and evening sacrifices.[6] The Jewish historian Flavius Josephus (*c.*37–*c.*100 CE) reveals that the trumpet of the Israelites, in common with many short trumpets from the ancient world, was 'a little short of a cubit' in length.[7] The cubit (a measurement in common use from early times, denoting the distance from the fingertips to the elbow) is an optimum length for both ancient and modern man to hold and transport things; by curious coincidence, it is approximately the length of the modern B flat trumpet. The most often cited depiction of the *hassrah* is that on the Arch of Titus in Rome, in which two trumpets are shown among the items being brought there following the destruction of the Temple of Jerusalem in 70 CE. Several writers have cast doubt on the accuracy of this representation, however, and Smithers notes that the instruments, being almost twice the length of the forearms of the figures depicted, more closely resemble the Roman *tuba*.[8] The destruction of the Temple of Jerusalem in 70 CE marks the decline of the *hassrah* as a sacred instrument in Jewish ritual, leaving the *shofar* as the sole herald of worship.

Confusion over nomenclature between the *shofar* and the *hassrah*, and over their respective roles, originated with the use of the term *salpinx* to denote both instruments in the Septuagint, the earliest translation of the Old Testament, in Greek, which dates from before the Christian era. In the earliest versions of the New Testament, also written in Greek, *salpinx* was the sole term used to denote the trumpet.[9] Subsequent layers of translation into Latin and then into German and English in the Martin Luther and James I Authorised Versions of the Bible have confused the differentiation further.

The sacred associations of the *shofar* and *hassrah* in their military contexts are elucidated in the Dead Sea Scrolls, a collection of over eight hundred religious documents, discovered in the Qumran caves, eight miles south of Jericho, between 1947 and 1956. The scrolls also provide the most detailed descriptions of the *shofar* and the *hassrah* calls. The scrolls date from the inter-Testamental era (150 BCE–70 CE) and references to *hassrah* and *shofar* appear in the War Scroll, which has been dated between 27 BCE and the beginning of the first century CE. Although the War Scroll is religious writing, depicting a symbolic battle between the forces of light and the forces of darkness, scholarly opinion concurs that the writer of this imaginary military manual would have been acquainted with the weapons and the tactics of ancient warfare, and that the details of the war to be fought against the *Kittim* (here, the Romans) probably corresponds most closely to the art of war as practised by the Roman legions.[10] The following passage from the War Scroll stipulates 'The Rule for the trumpets of Summons and the trumpets of Alarm according to all their duties':

> the trumpets of Summons shall sound for disposal in battle formations and to summon the foot-soldiers to advance when the gates of war shall open; and the trumpets of Alarm shall sound for massacre, and for ambush, and for pursuit when the enemy shall be smitten, and for retreat from battle.[11]

The tactics of ancient warfare – harrying, signalling, corralling, with the thirteen different groups of trumpet spread around the battlefield – are listed in a way that brings back an uncanny picture of the techniques learnt on herding animals, from 'trumpets calling the congregation' to 'trumpets of return from battle against the enemy when they journey to the congregation in Jerusalem'. The trumpets, adorned with slogans such as 'The Called of God' to 'Rejoicings of God in the Peaceful Return', are detailed as being used in the same primitive way as when they had been first developed to control herds and signal to hunters:

> The priests shall sound a sustained blast on the trumpets for battle array, and the columns shall move to their (battle) array, each man to his place. And when they have taken up their stand in three arrays, the Priests shall sound a second signal, soft and sustained, for them to advance until they are close to the enemy formation. They shall seize their weapons, and the Priests shall then blow a shrill staccato blast on the six trumpets of Massacre to direct the battle, and the Levites and all the blowers of rams' horns shall sound a mighty alarm to terrify the heart of the enemy, and therewith the javelins shall fly out to bring down the slain. Then the sound of the horns shall cease, but the Priests shall continue to blow a shrill staccato blast on the trumpets to direct the battle until they have thrown seven times against the enemy formation. And then they shall sound a soft, a sustained, and a shrill sound on the trumpets of Retreat.[12]

The *hassrah* may have been similar to the Egyptian *šnb*, whose repertoire of calls and playing style is lost to us. Nevertheless, the trumpet features in many military scenes throughout ancient Egyptian iconography (Ill. 1.1). These instruments perhaps derive

1.1 The *šnb* played by an Egyptian soldier. From John Gardner Wilkinson, *The Manners and Customs of the Ancient Egyptians*, 3rd edn, 5 vols (London: John Murray, 1847, vol. 1, p. 291).

from earlier models manufactured in the Sumerian Empire, and its precursor states in Iraq. As the site of the first agrarian revolution and the first sedentary proto-modern civilizations, the Fertile Crescent was also one of the earliest centres of bronze manufacture during the period of technological advance referred to as the Bronze Age, when copper and tin were first mixed to create the hard, durable alloy that is the main building block of the first metal trumpets. Throughout the Mesopotamian city-states, trade, dialogue and diffusion in all areas of human endeavour radiated outwards into surrounding regions. The Israelites and Ancient Egyptians were both separate beneficiaries of Fertile Crescent technology. The inventory of instruments sent as an engagement gift from King Tushratta of Mitanni (a Northern Syrian state descended from part of the Sumerian Empire) to the Pharaoh Amenophis IV *c.*1400 BCE suggests the kind of craft transfer involved: the gift included forty horns, seventeen of which were described as ox horns, covered with gold, some studded with precious stones.[13] The Israelites gained this technology almost certainly from the same source, though probably not through contact with the Egyptians: the Book of Numbers, which contains the description of trumpet-making from metals, was written largely during the exile of Israel in Babylon (sixth century BCE).

The original technology would have been developed from the techniques used in making weapons, armour and jewellery. Undoubtedly, the simplest way of manufacturing metal trumpets is to roll brass, silver or gold into a sheet – as in the manufacture of body armour (although for trumpets, it needs to be rolled much more thinly, like gold jewellery). A template would then be cut into the metal with the use of shears:

the metal would be folded along its length into a tube, and then beaten with a small hammer to thin and shape the metal further. A wooden mandrel was probably used as the internal shaping agent until the meeting edges were brazed together. Cylindrical trumpets were made from a rectangular length of metal, and conical trumpets from an elliptical one. Short trumpets can be made from a single piece of metal by pouring molten metal into an already prepared mould containing a wax-coated mandrel (a metal tool shaped to the inside diameters of the trumpet). The wax coat is shaped to be the desired thickness of the trumpet's tube walls: once shaping is complete, the wax-covered mandrel is covered with clay and left to harden. Then the molten metal is poured into the wax-filled gap between mandrel and clay: the wax melts, and the molten metal takes its place. This is the so-called 'lost-wax' process. The temperatures required to melt gold, silver and bronze are very high, and this technique did not evolve until the advent of charcoal as a high-energy fuel (occurring first around 3000 BCE). This sophisticated method required tooling, pit kilns and an intensive manufacturing process. Whether separate workshops existed for musical instruments at these early times, or whether they were a sideline of other metal artefact manufacturing like armaments or jewellery, is not known. Perhaps the same procedures were followed as in the exiled Dalai Lama's metalwork workshops at Norbalinka, Himachel Pradesh, Northern India, to the present day. The main task of these particular workshops is the manufacture of Buddhist statuary, but as a sideline, when there are sufficient orders, it will fit in a day of trumpet-making, with products displaying their skill in ornamentation.

Until recently the consensus was that two trumpets found in Tutankhamun's tomb in the Valley of the Kings of Egypt in 1922 are the oldest surviving metal trumpets. In an article published in 2003, however, Bo Lawergren argued that some 'trumpet-like objects', ranging from 8 to 12 cm in length, which derive from the area of ancient eastern Iran inhabited by the Oxus civilisation of the third and second millennia BCE, were in fact trumpets.[14] Around forty of these instruments have been identified and dated between 2200 and 1750 BCE. Baines refers to three badly damaged silver and gold examples unearthed in Iran in the 1930s, but not surprisingly, given the small sampling at his disposal, merely repeats the opinion of the author of the report of the excavation that they are silver and gold 'problematic devices, perhaps signal horns'.[15] The most basic examples of the instrument consist of a simple cone, while some culminate in a slight flare. A more elaborate type has a large pommel and a widely flared bell, while the most ornate have human, or occasionally animal, faces sculpted on the pommel. The single most important feature in support of their classification as trumpets is the integral mouthpiece which, on those instruments that survive intact, is remarkably consistent in contour, though markedly different from those of other trumpets of the ancient world, or later brass instruments (Ill. 1.2). Owing to their short length, the trumpets produce a single pitch centre, approximately C6, but through experimentation Lawergren found that this can be easily altered by slight adjustment of the embouchure. He notes that with this technique they can be made to produce convincing imitations of animal sounds; since their soft dynamic level renders them unsuitable for signalling purposes, he suggests that they were sounded in this manner for hunting. Many of the surviving instruments are very ornate and made of silver or

1.2 Oxus trumpet (between 2200 and 1750 BCE). (By kind permission of Bo Lawergen)

gold, which suggests that they were highly prized possessions belonging to those from the uppermost social strata for whom the hunting of game may have been reserved. Aerophones have been used to imitate animal sounds in hunting in various parts of the world, and there is some literary evidence to support the theory that the Oxus trumpets were used in this way. According to a Zoroastrian myth, which was committed to writing *c.*200 BCE–200 CE, but has more ancient roots, Yima, the first king of mankind, was given a golden trumpet and a gold-plated whip by his god to help him bring his subjects and their animals into shelter at the onset of a severe winter.[16] Lawergren provides compelling circumstantial evidence in support of the hypothesis that the objects in question are trumpets, while acknowledging that the 'clinching argument would be a picture of a person holding a trumpet in front of his mouth playing it'.[17]

Notwithstanding the possibility that the Oxus artefacts were trumpets, the instruments from Tutankhamun's tomb, dating from the eighteenth dynasty (*c.*1324 BCE), are the earliest ancient trumpets whose function is confirmed by iconographical evidence. The instruments are conical in bore, with separately constructed flared bells and rudimentary mouthpieces attached to the outer surface of the tube. They are of different lengths, sounding almost a tone apart. The shorter of the two (50.5 cm) was manufactured from copper or bronze with gold overlay, and the other (58.2 cm) was made from silver. The tubular sections of the two instruments differ in the manner of their construction. The seams of the silver trumpet were crenollated with a series of square tabs, which were fitted together using the technique that was common in the manufacture of later brass instruments. On the other trumpet the seams were left straight, and were probably overlapped slightly for joining together.[18] The gold bell of the shorter instrument is joined to the main tube by four rivets, the joint covered with a thin leaf of gold to prevent air leaking.[19] Both trumpets survive with an accompanying wooden core, which pictorial representations reveal was held between the trumpeter's arm and body when the instrument was being played (Ill. 1.3). The rigours of military life made the trumpet vulnerable, and the core was possibly used to protect the instrument in transit and as a mandrel to facilitate repair. An alternative theory is that the object the trumpeters are shown carrying may have been a second instrument (perhaps of a slightly different length in order to produce distinct signals) and that the wooden cores were produced for the burial as a means of silencing the trumpet's sound until the resurrection of the king.[20]

Trumpeters are depicted in Egyptian military processions and occasionally participating in non-military ceremonies and sacred rituals. A religious association of the trumpet can be inferred from the engravings on the bells of the Tutankhamen instruments, which depict the young king and three gods, beneath the hieroglyphic sign for heaven. It has been suggested that the engravings may have been added to the instrument for the burial.[21] According to Eustathius of Thessalonica (d.1198), in his commentary on the works of Homer, the trumpet was used to worship Osiris, the god of the afterlife. The same commentator also attributes the invention of the trumpet to Osiris.[22] As ruler of the realm of the dead, Osiris was the supreme arbiter in the judgment of the deceased. The association of the trumpet with Osiris is relevant to the history of the trumpet, since his cult exerted a strong impact on the eschatology of Judaism and Christianity, in particular the concept of the Last Judgment, of which the trumpet was to become a potent symbol.[23]

By the Late Bronze Age (1000 BCE–300 BCE), the Celts (as a general term applied to the non-Mediterranean 'barbarian' peoples of Europe coined by the Ancient Greeks – the *keltai*), whose metallurgical skills allowed them to dominate much of Western European culture in this period, had developed their own trumpets. At least ninety bronze specimens, some incomplete, have been found in Ireland. As Peter Downey notes in his detailed study of the surviving instruments and the contexts in which they were produced and used, most have been found in hoards, deposited along with assortments of items that may have had cultic significance. The largest hoard, of

1.3 Trumpet from the tomb of Tutankhamun (c.1324 BCE) with its accompanying wooden core.

twenty-eight instruments, was discovered at Dowris, County Offaly, in 1832, and may date from the seventh century BCE.[24]

Descriptions of Celtic armies in battle dwell on the fearsome effect of the noise made by their brass instruments. The use of these instruments may have been open to cultural misinterpretation by successive commentators: it cannot be assumed that they were only used for transmitting military signals. The way that many have been found, buried along with votive objects, points also to their use in religious ritual. The Gallo-Roman treasure found in 1861 at Neuvy-en-Sullias, twenty-eight kilometres south of Orléans, in the Loire region of France, consisted of several horse, deer, wild boar, and bull sculptures, small statuettes of Roman gods, figurines of naked men and women, and of men ornamented after Gaulish custom. The horse and the great boar, because of their portability, were no doubt carried in processions. The three smaller boars are in rampant attitude with the hackles raised along the lengths of their backs. This type of stylisation is also seen on coins, and in the arc de triomphe at Orange, Provence. In Celtic civilisation, the boar was a symbol of sacerdotal status, and may account for the boar's head formation of the bell of the *carnyx*, the Celtic trumpet played like a periscope placed to the mouth instead of to the eye. It cannot be coincidental that the *carnyx* players on the Gundestrup bowl, in the National Museum of Denmark in Copenhagen (Ill. 1.4), are adjacent to a religious ceremony, possibly involving rebirth or a human sacrifice. In this depiction, the players and the instruments seem to merge: the effect is of a troupe of enormously tall bellowing boars.

No complete specimen of such an instrument has survived, but iconographical and literary sources reveal that its use was widespread. A model of a boar's head, made from sheet bronze and brass (probably recycled Roman metal) and dating from

1.4 Detail of the Gundestrup bowl showing *carnyx* players, from the first or second century BCE. (By permission of the National Museum of Denmark, Copenhagen)

*c.*80–200 CE, was discovered in Deskford in northern Scotland in the early nineteenth century, and has been identified as belonging to a *carnyx* (Ill. 1.5). Soon after its discovery, it was described as originally having had 'a wooden tongue, movable by springs'.[25] In the late twentieth century, the *carnyx* has been revived by Edinburgh trombonist John Kenny, who has transformed it into a vehicle for post-avant-garde composers. Instruments of similar shape and playing position are widely spread: carvings from the first century CE at Sanchi, India, depict instruments featuring bird-headed bells, while the Ethiopian *dinke* bears a striking resemblance.[26] The instruments were as much an expression of cultural and spiritual identity as a weapon. Polybius (*c.*203–120 BCE) described how the Romans

> were terrified by the fine order of the Celtic army and the dreadful din – for there were innumerable horn-blowers and trumpeters and, as the whole army were shouting their war cries at the same time, there was such tumult as if not only the soldiers but all the country around had got a voice and caught up the cry.[27]

Though the recent study of the genetic roots of the tribal history of Europe and current debate on this topic questions the existence of a unified Celtic people (suggesting Celtic cultures emerged as a diffusion through trade and migration across Europe rather than as one massive invasion),[28] the tribes of Scotland and Ireland had

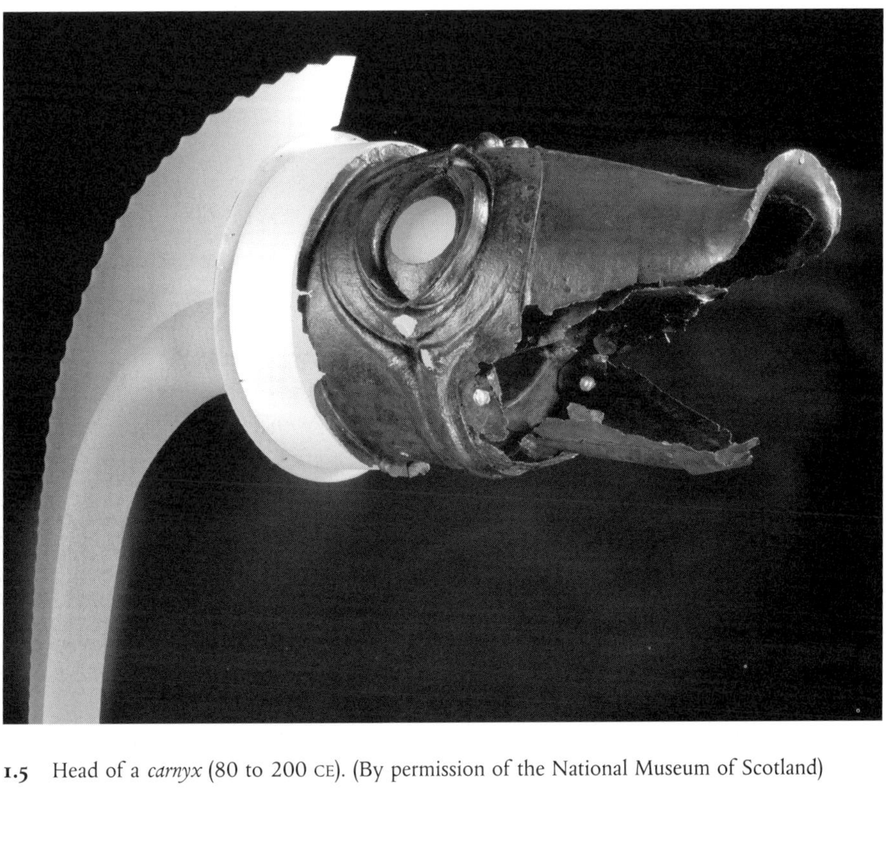

1.5 Head of a *carnyx* (80 to 200 CE). (By permission of the National Museum of Scotland)

a high level of social organisation, technological competence, and a strong identity that kept even the Roman Empire at bay. Much of Scotland and all of Ireland, like much of Celtic Europe, were never part of the Roman Empire. The Romans built two walls, Hadrian's (commenced 122 CE) and Antonine's (commenced 143 CE), to define their north-western frontier. In Ireland, the evidence from the hoards of metal lip-blown instruments unearthed in various parts of the country, the earliest in 1698 near Carrickfergus, County Antrim, points to a continuous history of trumpet- and horn-making quite discrete from Roman or Greek traditions: a separate branch of trumpet manufacture that continued for almost 2000 years, from the seventh or eighth centuries BCE until the Norman invasion of 1169–70.[29] Hoards of similar instruments have also been found in Northern Europe and Southern Scandinavia. Some remarkable instruments, ornately s-shaped, were dug from a peat bog in Brudevaelte moor, Denmark, in 1797, and were christened *lurs* at that time (their original Scandinavian name is unknown: the Irish name in early mediaeval writings is *adarc*). The Irish instruments from both the Late Bronze Age and the Iron Age, as described by Peter Downey, are remarkable for their fine craftsmanship and sophisticated technique of manufacture. The earlier instruments were cast in bronze, and in the later period sheets of metal were hammered flat and lapped into tubes held together by solder and rivets which were then bent into impressively long trumpets. The Ardbrin, County Down, instrument is 8 ft long and possesses 1094 airtight rivets. The earlier instruments were fashioned in the shape of animal horns and the later curved instruments are normally depicted as semicircular, although their component parts (and they were found in sections) can be assembled to form an s-shape. If, then, they were held and played on a vertical plane, this playing position would concur with that of the *carnyx*.

The word *carnyx* was used by Greek writers in classical times to describe types of trumpet adorned with a representation of an animal's head, usually that of a fierce wild animal – typically that of a boar.

The inheritors of the technological and cultural mantle of the Fertile Crescent empires were the Mediterranean city-states of Europe and North Africa that made up the 'classical world'. The ancient Greek trumpet, the *salpinx*, in early references is referred to specifically as an instrument of war. What was really significant about the *salpinx*, however, was not the instrument itself, but the penetrating quality of its sound. Homer describes a crack of thunder as a 'sky-trumpet', and the sky as ringing 'like a trumpet'. The power of the *salpinx* was held in great esteem by the Greeks: as well as being an instrument whose utility in war was to frighten the enemy (as with the Celts), it was valued by the Greeks for its ability to cut through the noise of battle, sounding the alarm, the advance, the retreat; it could encourage, restore order, avert panic, while evoking the reverse tendencies in the enemy. In Homeric epic, the ability to shout with clarion power was lauded as possessing equal capability to the *salpinx* and was regarded as god-like. In the following extract from the *Iliad*, Homer likens Achilles's war cry, terrifying to the Trojans, to the trumpet:

> There he stood, and shouted, and away to one side Pallas Athene raised her cry: and his shout started a mighty terror in the Trojans. As when the voice of a trumpet cries out sharp and clear, when murderous enemies are surrounding a city, so then

> Achilles's voice carried clear and loud. And when the Trojans heard the brazen shout of Achilles all their hearts were shaken in fear. . . .[30]

The classical consensus from the fifth century BCE onwards was that the *salpinx* was of Etruscan origin: Aeschylus is specific regarding the Etruscan *salpinx* in the *Eumenides*.[31] As it was a culture that did not speak an Indo-European language, that traded with both Greeks and Italians, and bordered Celtic cultures, this attribution is easy to understand and perhaps accept. Many subsequent Greek and Roman writers, from Sophocles to Virgil, attributed the provenance of the trumpets used in their societies to the Etruscans.[32] The Etruscan civilisation emerged in west-central Italy in the ninth century BCE. A period of territorial expansion up to the fifth century BCE was followed by gradual decline as it faced invasion from the Gauls to the north and the Romans to the south, and by the early years of the new millennium Etruria was under Roman control. Etruscan influences on Roman culture were far reaching and included aspects of ceremonial and military practice. In the military sphere the Etruscans adopted elements of warfare from foreign armies, which were subsequently taken up by the Romans.[33] It appears that the trumpet was part of this ceremonial and military diffusion. Three of the trumpet types used by the Romans – the *tuba, cornu* and *lituus* (described below) – were also used by the Etruscans, several examples of which survive. Much of the pictorial evidence relating to musical instruments in Etruria derives from scenes depicting funerary cult ritual, in which trumpets and horns feature.

Our knowledge of the trumpet of the ancient Greeks – the *salpinx* – derives in the main from literary sources and vase paintings. Greek writers reveal, often inadvertently, the uses to which the *salpinx* was put. They also allude to its ability to provoke an intense emotional response from the listener, but provide few pointers as to the nature of the calls that a *salpinktes* (*salpinx*-player) played. Vase paintings are equally problematic, revealing inconsistencies in the physical features of the instrument and a disparity with the surviving archaeological evidence (Ill. 1.6).

The primary use of the *salpinx* was as a military instrument. It was used to summon men to arms, sound reveille, call for silence, and signal the formation of battle lines in military encampments. On the battlefield it sounded the calls to charge and retreat, but it has been argued that it was rarely used to transmit tactical orders during battles.[34]

Non-military uses of the *salpinx* spanned the sacred and secular spheres. Players of the instrument are depicted in processions for the cult of Dionysus, and Plutarch refers to the *salpinx* being sounded in a ceremony at Argos to summon the same god.[35] In civil life its uses included summoning people to assembly and warning of impending danger, co-ordinating the launching of ships and transportation of heavy machinery, signalling the acts in theatrical performances, and announcing the start of the *Choai*, the drinking contest held at the Anthesteria festival.[36]

Both Etruscan and Greek vases and statuary depict the *salpinx* being blown: the monumental work of Beazley on Attic Black and Red vases describes several representations of the trumpet, but on the evidence of vases alone the frequency of use of the trumpet would seem to be less than that of the Greek flute, the *aulos*.[37] That evidence, however, would have to be balanced by the *salpinx*'s ubiquity in warfare, and

1.6 Amazon playing the *salpinx* – the Sappho Painter, fifth century BCE. (By permission of the Eleusis Museum, Athens)

consequent references in literature. Aristophanes even drew on trumpeters as a source of humour. In the *Frogs*, he pokes fun at 'barking old veterans' by making up a word based on *salpinx, salpingolonchypenadai*, meaning 'lancer-whiskered trumpeters'.[38]

Most Greek writers describe the *salpinx* as being made of bronze. Pollux stated that it came with a detachable mouthpiece, made of bone.[39] The only surviving instrument identified as a *salpinx*, however, in the Museum of Fine Arts, Boston, consists of thirteen lengths of ivory tubing, joined by bronze ferrules and with a bronze bell section, giving a total length of about 156 cm. Don Smithers casts doubt on the authenticity of this instrument, noting that it differs significantly from those encountered in Greek iconography and that its design would have proved problematic in performance.[40] However, Nikos Xanthoulis has pointed to the discovery of a fragment of a bronze bell and a short section of bone tubing, similar to those belonging to the instrument held in Boston and dating from *c.*350–140 BCE, as evidence supporting the existence of this form of *salpinx*.[41] The evidence from vase paintings suggests a length for the *salpinx* of between 80 and 120 cm.[42]

Representations of the *salpinx* show considerable variation in the shape of the bell, which ranges from a slight conical flare to a near-spherical bulb, similar to that of the modern *cor anglais*. Some illustrations of salpinx-players (*salpinktai*) show them wearing the *phorbeia*, the cheek brace also worn by players of the aulos. It is generally assumed that the purpose of this was to support the cheeks when the player was blowing loudly. The Romans called it the *capistrum*. Smithers has put forward the novel suggestion that it may have incorporated a mouthpiece for playing on the march and on horseback.[43]

John Hale suggests that two different sizes of *salpinx* existed: a short instrument used by the military, and a longer model for ceremonial use. He contends that the longer instrument, with its narrow bore, 'must indicate a quest on the part of both Greek instrument-makers and trumpeters alike for an instrument with melodic capabilities'.[44] An anecdote from Plutarch, which tells of a bird imitating the sound of the *salpinx*, provides additional, though tenuous, support for this theory. More significant are the indications in Aristotle's *De Audilibus* regarding the use of the breath to regulate dynamics and pitch.[45] Considering its narrow bore and length, and also the diversity of its use, it would be rash to rule out the possibility that *salpinktai* explored the higher register of their instrument.

The earliest classical fragment in Pöhlmann and West's *Documents of Ancient Greek Music* is a trumpet call transcribed from a decorated clay epinetron (a knee-guard used by seamstresses). The black figure of an Amazon plays the *salpinx* and the letters of syllables represent the sound she is making. Pöhlmann and West conclude that these are onomatopoeic syllables similar to Ennius's *taratantara*, but tantalisingly quote French scholar Annie Bélis, who transcribed the syllables behind the Amazon, Γο Γε, and those in front, Γο Γη, on the basis of a later solmization system, coming up with the solution shown in Example 1.2.[46]

Ex. 1.2 Transcription of a trumpet call from syllables on a decorated epinetron (from A. Bélis, 'Un nouveau document musical', *Bulletin de Correspondance Hellénique* 108 (1984), 99–109).

Trumpeters attained a high status at the ancient Olympics. From the 96th Olympiad in 396 BCE, a trumpet-playing competition opened the games, with an olive wreath being awarded to the contestant who could perform the loudest blast – on this occasion Timaios of Elis. The recipient sounded his *salpinx* to introduce the competitors for subsequent events, signal the start of contests, and acclaim the winners.[47] From later in the fourth century BCE the celebrated trumpeter Herodorus of Megara won ten Olympic contests between 328 and 292 BCE and was *periodonikes* (winner of the circuit of Olympian, Pythian, Nemean and Isthmian games) between seven and ten times. Herodorus's training for this event apparently included sleeping on a lion's skin and adhering to a rigorous diet. His daily allowance of food and drink was six pints of wheaten bread, twenty pounds of meat, and six quarts of wine. While Turrentine interprets this as an indication of his prodigious diet, Hale suggests that the allowance would have been intended for his retinue, which probably included his pupils.[48]

A celebrated Olympian trumpeter of the first century CE was Diogenes, son of Dionysius of Ephesus. The base of a statue erected in honour of Diogenes has survived, with an inscription stating that he won eighty trumpet-playing contests, including five Olympic honours, and was twice *periodonikes.* The female equivalent of the Olympics, the Heraia, may have had a similar event. Aglais, daughter of Megacles, was an Alexandrian trumpeter, active around 275 BCE, famous for wearing a sumptuous head dress as she performed.[49]

Trumpets and horns were a ubiquitous feature of Roman military and ceremonial activity. The status of Roman trumpet players was high, and many held special privileges. The names of around ninety *aeneatores* (brass players), classified as *tubicines, cornicines, liticines* and *bucinatores,* are known to us from inscriptions.[50] Three of the four instruments alluded to in this classification can be identified with a fair degree of certainty. The *tuba* was a straight, cylindrical brass instrument between 3 and 5 ft in length, with a flared bell. The *cornu,* also of brass, was considerably longer than the *tuba* and curved into a circular shape, with a wooden crossbar and a forward-pointing bell. Its circumference could measure up to 10 ft and the instrument was wrapped round the player's body. The *lituus* was a cylindrical brass instrument, of similar length to the tuba, with a conical bell, bent sideways in the shape of the letter 'J'. In the early Roman period these three instruments appear together in representations of processions, particularly funeral processions, betraying their common Etruscan ancestry. The *bucina* is less easily identifiable. The term originally referred to an animal horn, but eventually came to denote horns adorned with, or made entirely of, brass, and in its military use was associated in particular with the cavalry.[51] John Ziolkowski notes, however, that the historical evidence that *bucina* signified a distinct instrument is inconclusive.[52] In Roman literature *bucina* also denoted the conch trumpet.

The second-century Greek historian Arrian reveals that 38 *tubicines* and 36 *cornicines* were assigned to each Roman legion, and provides a breakdown of the numbers allocated to the various cohorts within each legion.[53] Since there were upwards of 25 legions in the Imperial army around this time, Arrian's figures suggest that there may have been as many as 2000 trumpeters in military service. Our most important source of information on the role of brass instruments in the Roman army is *Epitoma rei militaris* by Vegetius, completed between 383 and 450 CE. Vegetius reveals that in war, '*tubicines, cornicines* and *bucinatores* normally launch the battle',[54] and he describes the various roles that each of the instruments fulfilled in the military camp:

> The legion also has *tubicines, cornicines* and *bucinatores.* The *tubicines* call soldiers to battle, and again sound for a retreat. When *cornicines* sound, it is not the soldiers as such but the standards that obey their signal. So when soldiers alone are due to go out to do some work, the trumpeters sound. When the standards are to be moved, the *cornicines* sound. But when there is to be a battle, both *tubicines* and *cornicines* sound together. The *classicum* is the name for the signal sounded by

> the *bucinatores* on the *cornu.* This is considered the sign of the High Command, because the *classicum* is sounded when the Emperor is present, or when capital punishment is being inflicted on a soldier, since this must be done according to the Emperor's laws.
>
> So when soldiers go out to perform night-watch duties and outpost duties, to do some work, or hold manoeuvres in the exercise-field, they start work at the call of the *tubicine,* and stop again at the signal from the *tubicine.* But when the standards are moved or, once moved, are to be planted, the *cornicines* sound. The signals are observed in all exercises and manoeuvres, so that soldiers may obey more readily in actual battle, if ordered by the leaders to fight, stand their ground, pursue or retire. For it is obviously a sound principle that they ought always to be doing in peacetime what it is deemed necessary to do in battle.[55]

While both the *tuba* and the *cornu* were essentially signalling instruments in the military, the association of the *cornu* with the emblems of imperial power, in the form of the standards and high command, and its use for sounding the *classicum,* suggest that it fulfilled a ceremonial function. Vegetius indicates that the *classicum* was a signal associated with the high command, and other sources reveal that it was also sounded to call people to assembly. Certain writers used the term *classicum* for the instrument on which the signal was played (and occasionally as a less specific term for a trumpet or horn) and *classici* for the players of the signal.[56] Varro's definition of a *classicus* as a magistrate's attendant who plays the *classicum* on both the *cornu* and the *lituus,* and Servius's assertion that the cavalry *tubae* were called *classica,* are two of many examples that illustrate the complexity of unravelling the apparently ambiguous or contradictory references to trumpets and horns in classical literary sources.[57] Vegetius's remark that the *classicum* was performed on the *cornu* by *bucinatores* can be interpreted as an indication that players doubled on *cornu* and *bucina.* However, Ziolkowski argues that the various terms for trumpet and horn players referred more to their duties than the instruments they played, and that the duties of the *bucinator* included announcing the time, signalling the night-watches and calling an assembly, which could be performed on a *tuba, cornu, lituus* or a simple animal horn. He hypothesises that '*tubicines* and *cornicines* carried an animal horn on a cord around their necks for easy access when they had to perform certain duties of the *bucinator*'.[58]

Describing the various brass instruments used to convey military signals, Vegetius identifies the *bucina* as a bronze instrument 'curved towards itself in a circular fashion' and the *cornu* as being made of horn and bound with silver. Renato Meucci argues that the apparent misidentification of these instruments originated in the Middle Ages. Since all the surviving copies of Vegetius's military manual derive from a single sixth-century source, when the Roman *cornu* was no longer used and metal instruments were known by names deriving from the word *bucina,* he suggests that the anomaly resulted from scribes altering the text to accord with the instruments with which they were familiar.[59]

Identifying the uses to which the *lituus* was put is problematic. Meucci notes that it was mainly mentioned in poetic sources, and only in cultic or civilian settings. In the later Roman period, the terms *lituus* and *bucina* were regarded by certain writers as being interchangeable. Meucci suggests that this may have arisen through the *bucina* taking over certain functions previously fulfilled by the *lituus*.[60]

The annual Roman military campaigns traditionally started in late March, after the *Quinquatria*, the festival held in honour of Mars, which involved the symbolic purification of the accoutrements of war. On 23 March, the final day of the festival, and again on 23 May (the reason for this repeat of the ritual is unclear), the trumpets of war were purified in the ceremony known as the *Tubilustrium*. Few details of the ritual have come down to us, other than that in the early years of the common era it took place in the Hall of the Shoemakers in Rome and involved the sacrifice of a lamb.[61]

The *triumphs* awarded to victorious military leaders following a campaign in which at least 5000 of the enemy had been killed were among the most spectacular ceremonial events staged in Rome. Plutarch's account of the triumph of Aemilius Paullus, on his defeat of Perseus, King of Macedon, in 167 BCE, distinguishes between the ceremonial and military idioms of the trumpet. The third and final day of the event began with a sumptuous procession, in which trumpeters led the way, 'sounding out no marching or processional strain, but such a one as the Romans use to rouse themselves to battle'.[62]

Trumpets and horns provided an auditory backdrop to entertainments in the amphitheatre, where a longer form of *tuba* than the military model may have been used.[63] At theatrical performances *tubicines* and *cornicines* led the procession of the participants into the arena and sounded at apposite moments during the drama[64] (Ill. 1.7). But it was at the games and gladiatorial contests that brass instruments were

1.7 Detail of a Roman mosaic (*c.*200 CE) depicting a tuba player, organ player, and two *cornu* players. (By permission of the National Archaeological Museum, Tripoli)

used to greatest effect. A vivid impression of their contribution to the spectacle of these events is evoked by the account of one hundred *tubicines* and one hundred *cornicines* sounding at the games organised by Carinus in 284 CE.[65]

Roman brass instruments came with detachable mouthpieces, manufactured from cast bronze, like the two in the British Museum recovered from Hadrian's Wall, at Housesteads, Northumbria. The mouthpiece as a separate entity had become widespread by classical times. These examples possess long, tapered stems, about 7.5 inches long, and fine acorn-shaped cups, with rims carefully contoured for player comfort. Dimensions of Roman mouthpieces are large compared with modern trumpets, and large even when compared with baroque trumpet mouthpieces. This indicates a strong probability that their playing idiom was limited to the low harmonics. Ennius alludes to a style characterised by rapid articulation when he imitates the trumpet's alarum with the invented word *taratantara.*[66] A small number of *tubae* in comparatively good order have been found, including one from Saumur and another from Orléans in the Loire region of France. The Orléans *tuba* has embellished joins and a tapered mouthpipe, which seem to be influenced by Celtic ornamentation; it survives with a tiny, acorn-shaped mouthpiece, suited to the production of notes in the higher register[67] (Ill. 1.8).

Though the Roman Empire's disintegration halted a monumental level of technology transfer throughout Europe, other layers of diffusion can be traced throughout Western Eurasia before and after the Empire. The existence of an ancient Greek compound word, *lestosalpinktai*, 'robber trumpeters', has been interpreted by some classical scholars as showing that piracy and trumpeting were interchangeable professions throughout the coastal cities of ancient Greece.[68] This theory speculates that pirates roaming the Tyrrhenian Sea (which borders North Africa and Italy) brought *salpinktai* into contact with the Etruscans, Romans and Greeks from the pirates' original colonies in the heart of Lydia (whose empire spanned most of modern Turkey).

1.8 Gallo–Roman tuba, discovered at Saint-Just-sur-Dive, Maine-et-Loire, in 1823. (By permission of Château-Musée de Saumur)

1.9 Players of side-blown trumpets, Uganda, *c.*1960; photograph by Jean Jenkins. (By permission of the National Museum of Scotland)

Another example of trumpet developments diffusing in a more fragmented fashion can be traced in medieval times three hundred years after the Roman Empire's disintegration in the West, in the form of elephant-tusk trumpets. Side-blown trumpets made from horn, wood and elephant tusks are found across much of Africa and their use probably dates back several thousand years[69] (Ill. 1.9). Sable, kudu and gemsbok antelope are prized for their horns, part of the attraction of which is ornamental. Many early African trumpets of this type were richly decorated and became symbols of status and power. When metal trumpets came to be adopted by African chiefs and kings, these also tended to be of the side-blown variety.[70] From the tenth and eleventh centuries CE ornately decorated trumpets made from elephant tusks were produced by Muslim craftsmen in south Italy and Sicily.[71] This instrument, the oliphant, became greatly prized by European royalty, and many highly elaborately furnished examples survive. In the *Chanson de Roland*, the hero Roland carries the oliphant while serving in the rearguard of the army of Charlemagne (742–814). The poem was written several centuries after the events that it chronicles, and its reliability in matters of detail, including the account of the use of the oliphant, has been questioned.[72] Nevertheless, the association with such a chivalric figure as Charlemagne in this widely disseminated poem helps to account for the allure of the oliphant in the Middle Ages. The Horn of Ulphus in the Treasury of York Minster is a well-known example, as is the eleventh-century Clephane horn from Carslogie Castle in Fife, Scotland.

Don Smithers has made connections between Africa and Ireland, where side-blown trumpets made of animal horn also exist. His contention is that this concept could well have travelled along Phoenician or earlier trade routes using the Gulf Stream, up the coast of Africa to Ireland.[73] Ubiquitous in Eurasia, as in Africa, the horns of farm animals have just as regularly been turned into trumpets, and Peter Downey argues that the Irish bronze instruments were based on cow horns rather than elephant tusks.[74] Both South Asian and Saxon cultures attached great importance to cow horns. The exact type of horn played was determined by which breed of cattle was developed locally. Cow horns became common throughout South India. They were also common in Europe during Saxon times, but there is no evidence of any form of musical influence either way. The common bond was a civilisation based on agriculture. The Saxons used these horns both as drinking vessels and as end-blown trumpets.

There are many cultures, of course, where the development of the trumpet had no connection with the technologies of the Eurasian and African continents whatsoever. The fullest picture of trumpets developed free of Eurasian influence is provided to us by the great civilisations of South and Central America, most notably the Incas, the Aztecs and the Mayans. This independent process, developed at a different time in a continent with many more geographical barriers along its North–South axis (preventing easy diffusion throughout its own cultures), points towards the universality of the trumpet within 'organised' as well as 'primitive' societies.

In the Aztec area, two kinds of trumpet, conch and wooden, existed up to and throughout the colonial period among the indigenous peoples. The Spanish conquistador Bernal Díaz del Castillo described the orchestrated noise, terrifying in its effect, played by the assembled conches, horns, trumpets and drums, at the ritual sacrifice of his comrades captured after the defeat of Hernán Cortés.[75] Trumpets, almost certainly made of wood, are depicted in a series of Mayan murals discovered at the eighth-century temple of Bonampak, deep in the jungle of Chiapas (Ill. 1.10). The Mayans lacked metal at the time the murals were painted, and the same instruments were still in use when Cortés arrived.[76] Other sources describe long trumpets of black wood and shell trumpets used to instil courage for battle in Guatemala Indians, and an account by Diego de Landa from *c.*1566 mentions 'long thin trumpets of hollow wood with long twisted gourds at the ends' as principal Mayan instruments.[77]

1.10 Mayan trumpeters in a procession. (By kind permission of Mary Miller.)

In 2001 a hoard of twenty strombus-shell trumpets, many elegantly engraved, was discovered at the temple of Chavín de Huantar, high in the Andes. These instruments were found among what is believed to be a collection of Chavín ritual accoutrements, dating from between 1000 and 600 BCE.[78] A conch trumpet dated between 150 and 300 CE, discovered in Teotihuacán (the Mesoamerican city-state whose zenith occurred contemporaneously with Rome), is decorated with glyphs that have been interpreted as a religious calendar. Early accounts by Spanish colonisers suggest that the Aztecs (whose culture owed much to their Teotihuacán ancestors) regarded music as almost entirely sacred. Players' mistakes were physically punishable throughout Aztec lands as causing possible offence to the gods. No culture may have taken the trumpet more seriously as a holy instrument: in a recorded ritual for the blue, goggle-eyed fertility god Tlaloc, a priest would paint his naked body black, climb a mountain with a *tekiztli* (conch trumpet), and periodically blow the conch, chew tobacco, and mutilate himself. The link between the trumpet and mortality seems to be particularly strong with the Aztecs: in one creation myth, the serpent-deity Quetzalcoatl hollows finger holes from a conch with maggots to produce a trumpet in order to summon from the dead the skeletons of all human beings.[79]

There are separate Aztec words for conch-trumpets, *tecciztli*, which feature in late illustrations of everyday Aztec life (such as the Florentine Codex (*c.*1540–1585)), and *tepuzquiquiztli*, 'great trumpets', made from gourds, wood, clay, and later from copper. The earliest evidence from South America of the use of metal is in highland Peru *c.*1500 BCE, and in lower Central America and Colombia *c.*500–200 BCE. Metallurgy arose later in Mesoamerica, between 600 and 700 CE. The first musical application, as in China, was in the production of bells for ritual use. Small, usually about 1 to 8 cm tall, these bells were made by the lost-wax process, and are often depicted attached to wrists and ankles, and found frequently at burial sites.[80]

Dating is inexact for the first appearance of metal trumpets, but what is certain is that by the time the Spanish arrived in Peru (Francisco Pizarro, 1531), trumpets made of silver, bronze, and copper were sounded at the principal Incan shrines. The cult of the god Tantazoro, according to the first Augustine chronicle, used fourteen trumpets of copper and silver associated with its rites, and several ancient Incan copper and silver trumpets survive in museums.[81] The Incas, like the Aztecs, also gave prominence to their conch trumpet, the *pututu*. This not only was used by their *chasqui* messengers to signal throughout the Incan Empire, but also opened the solemn rites of the December solstice.

The differences in the types of trumpets, and in uses to which trumpets were applied between the Aztecs and Incas, offer interesting examples of the separate development of peoples on the same continent, separated by geographical, ecological and climatic factors.[82] Yet another group of trumpets became diffused throughout the Americas despite the divides: trumpets fashioned from the tibia, the larger of the human shin bones, were widespread. In Peru, the Huancans, a people absorbed into the Incan Empire *c.*1460 CE, gave special significance to a dog-god in their belief system, and part of their ritual entailed sounding a trumpet fashioned from a dog's skull at festivals and dances.[83]

The Tibetan Empire, whose borders stretched between Persia, India and China and which dominated the silk road between 650 and 848 CE, is the other known culture to fashion trumpets from human tibia. Like the Aztecs and Incas, the Tibetans also elevated trumpets made from metal and conches into highly significant religious objects. The Tibetan trumpet made from a human thigh-bone, the *kangling*, certainly possesses an eery, other-worldly sound, and is part of the ritual kit of the lama, used to drive away evil spirits and to communicate with the afterlife.

The famous long metal trumpet of Tibet, the *dung chen*, is over ten feet in length. It is a bronze trumpet, telescopic, and made from three or four pieces, probably to assist storage and transportation: the joins are supported by large pommels. The *dung chen* plays an important part in Buddhist worship and is a particularly interesting specimen of trumpet with its own playing traditions: like the *shofar*, the *dung chen*'s continuous use and its connection with ancient practices give trumpet scholars a thrilling, 'live' example of the instrument in religious practice before the modern era. The *dung chen* was probably introduced into Tibet by migrating Indian Buddhists as the religion declined in North India (between the seventh and eleventh centuries CE). The first European to publish an account of Tibetan music was Captain Samuel Turner, who joined the British East India Company in 1780, and was appointed chief of a mission to congratulate the Lamaist regency on the reincarnation of the Dalai Lama in the person of a child. Arriving at Tashi-lhunpo monastery in Shigatse in September 1783, he was struck by the religious ceremonies he witnessed:

> The Tibetans assemble in chapels, and unite together in prodigious numbers, to perform their religious service, which they chant in alternate recitative and chorus, accompanied by an extensive band of loud and powerful instruments. So that,

> whenever I heard these congregations, they forcibly recalled to my recollection, both the solemnity, and sound of the Roman Catholic mass.
>
> The instruments made use of were all of enormous size. Trumpets above six feet long; drums stretched over a copper cauldron ... the gong, a circular Chinese instrument of thin hammered bell-metal, capable of producing a surprising sound; cymbals, hautboys; and a double drum, shallow, but of great circumference ... these, together with the human tibia, and sea conch, a large species of the buccinum, compose, for the most part, their religious band. Harsh as these instruments, individually taken, might sound to a musical ear, yet when joined together in unison, with the voices of two or three hundred boys and men, managed with varying modulation, from the lowest and softest cadence to the loudest swell, they produced to my ear an effect extremely grand.[84]

The *dung chen* has a mouthpiece that necessitates a developed embouchure formation and can lead to a more developed musical idiom in the hands of a virtuoso exponent. Though the longer Himalayan trumpets, in the main, play only deep drones on the lower harmonics, trumpet and drum ensembles do exist in the Araku Valley of Central India in which the higher harmonics of the clarino register (to borrow a term from the European baroque period) are used.

Tibetan Buddhism, accompanied by its musical ritual, spread east into China, which had long possessed the metallurgical skills that trumpet manufacture required. A flourishing bronze industry meant that the capacity to construct metal trumpets was present by the time of the Shang dynasty (*c.*1766–*c.*1122 BCE).[85] Discoveries in burial tombs of musical instruments made of metal from this period, however, seem to have been limited to bells and drums.[86] Trumpets, both metal and animal-horn, first appear with certainty in Han dynasty (206 BCE–20 CE) stone-rubbings. On a brick carving from the fourth or fifth century CE of part of a military ensemble in procession, the trumpets are held in a near vertical plane, like the *carnyx*.[87] Thereafter, there is a wide diversity of trumpet- and horn-type instruments: the *jiao*, made of animal-horn; the *tongjiao*, known from the eighth and ninth centuries CE, made of metal; the *laba*, a telescopic brass trumpet, with a flaring bell and mouthpiece with a flattened rim, about 4–5 ft long, used by fire brigades and the military, in temple rites, and opera productions; the *hai lo*, a conch, used by boatmen and Buddhist lamas; the *hao t'ung*, similar to the *laba*, but 3 ft long; the *cha chiao*, sometimes longer than the *laba*, with the bell facing the performer, like the Roman *lituus,* used at weddings and funerals, and sometimes possessing two bells. The *kang t'ou*, or *ta wang*, virtually the same as the Tibetan *dung chen*, and probably derived from it, was about 10 ft long and used in funeral processions, the lower end being carried in a sling by an attendant. The *hao* was similar in shape and use to the *laba*, but with an oval, flattened mouthpiece, and slight conicity over half its length; the *kang tung* was a curved copper instrument with a brass rim, about 16 inches long, perhaps of Mongolian origin, and constructed in the shape of a dragon with an open mouth.[88]

Extensive trade routes between the peoples of central Asia and those from East Asia, the Mediterranean and Europe were well established by the first millennium of the common era. The Persians were influenced by the trumpets they encountered in military exchanges with the Byzantine army. The long brass trumpet of Persia, the *karnā*, and the ensemble in which it featured, the *naubat*, had widespread influence with the rapid spread of Islam in the seventh and eighth centuries CE. The *karnā* was a long brass trumpet that flourished in Persia during the Sassanid era (224–651 CE). It was conical in bore, sometimes S-shaped, and up to $6\frac{1}{2}$ ft long, producing a single pitch. Interestingly, this Arabic word originates from the same Greek root as the Celtic *carnyx*.

Though the various types of Roman trumpet fell out of use in Western Europe with the demise of the Roman Empire in the West, the tradition of using long straight trumpets survived in the Eastern Empire. Don Smithers has argued for a possible continuation of use of this type of trumpet at the court of Charlemagne, no doubt associated with Charlemagne's installation as Holy Roman Emperor in Rome in 800 CE. If this hypothesis were to be found true, however, it is more likely to have been the revival of a tradition sustained by the Eastern Empire in Constantinople, and the prelude to later developments directed through Italy, especially through city-states like Venice, given Italy's geographic role as an intermediary in the trade of ideas and goods between East and West. In this bigger picture, of which the *tuba* was, of course, only a minor cultural detail, the main catalyst for change came externally, from the East, in the form of trade and wars with Persian and Arab civilization.

Arab civilization coalesced around the unifying factor of the rise of Islam. This religious movement centred on the teachings of the prophet Mohammad and grew quickly from 622 CE. Arab civilization conceived the notion of the university as a centre of learning, and brought the idea to Western Europe, by way of Cordoba University in Spain, which by 1000 CE possessed 600,000 books. The Arab peoples possessed the advantage of direct contact with the Far East, whence came new techniques and improvements in technology. From the eighth century CE, the philosophers, mathematicians, scientists and inventors of Islam were making advances, which diffused through to Europe centuries later. Arab civilization saw a flowering of the arts, so that musical instruments –string, wind, percussion and brass – flourished and developed in this environment. The Arab peoples developed at this time a long straight trumpet, the *bûq al-nafīr*, which, as used later by Saladin's armies, had a devastating effect on the horses of the crusader knights. This points to the probability that the Arab trumpets were being used in a tactical manner similar to its most ancient martial roots: as an instrument of aggression against the enemy, as much as a signalling instrument to marshal their own troops.

The peoples of the Far East, and of the Indian subcontinent in particular, were also subject to this massive cultural shift towards Islam. In South Asia and the Indian subcontinent, the spread of Islam introduced the ceremonial *naubat* ensemble, employed at the gates of palaces and at the shrines of Muslim holy men.

Perhaps the last great example of independently produced metal trumpets throughout history can be found in West Africa. During the Sub-Saharan Bantu expansion of 3000 BCE–500 CE, smiths discovered how to produce high temperatures in their village furnaces and so to manufacture steel, many centuries before the process became commonplace in Europe. Like the Chinese, therefore, they possessed the technology for metal trumpets long before their appearance, which occurred with the

1.11 Hausa tribesmen playing the *kakaki*, northern Nigeria, *c.*1969; photograph by Jean Jenkins. (By permission of the National Museum of Scotland)

spread of Islam. Spectacularly long and elegant metal trumpets known as *kakaki*, and measuring between 6 and 13 feet in length, are still heard in certain Islamic areas of West Africa (Ill. 1.11). The instrument, which has been traced back to at least the sixteenth century, is often played in pairs and sometimes in groups of four or more, by trumpeters on horseback or along with oboes and other instruments, including wooden trumpets and drums.

Beyond metal, created in ancient and isolated communities outside the common diffusion centres of the Eurasian, African and American continents, the trumpet has developed some of its most surprising and diverse idioms. One of the most ancient and widespread of these, which we have already observed in several of the cultures discussed above, is the conch-shell trumpet. The ubiquity of molluscs along the world's coastlines and the relative ease with which they can be made into trumpets cannot hide the sheer ingenuity with which the conch trumpet has been used, or the spiritual values attached by many cultures to it.

The cleared, spiral tube inside the main shell of a conch makes a natural trumpet or horn up to 2 feet long when a hole is bored in the side of the shell, near the end of the spiral. Either the lips are placed against this, or a mouthpiece is inserted into the hole. As with some horns or tusks, another hole is sometimes bored near the end of the instrument, which doubles the number of pitches normally used from one to two. Three main varieties of conch shell have been used: the *triton* (trumpet-shaped), the *cassis* (helmet-shaped) and the *strombus* (spiral-shaped). Fishermen from Tonga to Jersey used them to relay signals over the water, and from water to shore, in sequences of long and short blasts, in the manner of Morse code, and these trumpets have also been used as foghorns throughout the Channel Islands. The large conch became, from Neolithic times, a greatly prized, expensive item used far inland in many parts of Eurasia, and as we have seen, an item married to the mysticism of many religions throughout the Pre-Columbian Americas. Called *dung* in Tibet, *faluo* in China, the conch became a part of Buddhist ritual throughout East Asia, and indeed is the only form of trumpet indigenous to Japan, where it is called the *horagai*.[89] Hindu Brahmins have used a conch trumpet, the *Sankh*, in ceremonies since at least 1000 BCE.[90]

The conch trumpet entered Greek and Roman mythology. In the early seventh century BCE, the poet Archilochus may be referring to a conch-trumpet when he calls the whirlwind, or *strombos*, a *salpinx thalassia* – a trumpet of the sea. It featured most notably, however, as the attribute of the sea-god Triton, Neptune's trumpeter, who lived in the depths of the sea as half-man, half-fish.[91] The tale of Misenus, Aeneas's helmsman, who challenged the gods to a conch-playing contest, is related by Virgil in the *Aeneid*. Misenus lost the contest and was thrown overboard to his death by Triton. Aeneas respectfully placed an oar and a *tuba* – the instruments of Misenus's trade – over his helmsman's tomb.[92]

From the sixteenth century onwards Triton became, for artists and sculptors, a symbol of Rome's illustrious past. The most famous representations of Triton appear on Bernini's *Triton* and *Trevi* fountains, which date from the early seventeenth century. Both were depicted by Otto Respighi in the tone poem *Fountains of Rome* (1916). The image of Triton blowing his conch is represented by horn calls, while trumpets announce the entrance of Neptune in a chariot drawn by sea horses, as depicted on the *Trevi* fountain. More than two centuries earlier, Alessandro Stradella composed the wedding serenata *Inventione per un Barcheggio* (1681) on the Neptune myth. The overtures to *Il Barcheggio* have secured a place in the solo baroque repertoire for trumpet, but prominent parts for trumpet, cornetto and trombone appear throughout the work and were clearly inspired by the Neptune subject. Stradella's serenata will be discussed in Chapter 5.

Trumpets made from bark and woods are also widespread, from Papua New Guinea to the Amazon in Equatorial regions, to the Alpine and Baltic areas in the Northern Hemisphere. The availability of long tree trunks means wooden trumpets are the longest of all trumpets. The *buburé* from the Amazonian rain forest is 17 ft. Yet wooden trumpets also exist in far shorter sizes: the *borija* of Slovenia, Croatia, Bosnia, and Serbia, fashioned from the bark of willow or ash, is about $1\frac{1}{2}$ ft. Such trumpets can be a hollowed-out branch: the *ndumbu* of the Angolan Mbwela and Nkangala peoples is one of these.[93] The technology used in the construction of bark wood canoes is also used for making bark wood trumpets: harder wood strips are used to provide a tightly wound skeleton to stiffen the bark. The circumference is bound with twine or yarn, which regulates the taper of the instrument's rudimentary cone shape. The Lithuanian *daudytė* (5-$7\frac{1}{2}$ ft) is made from a variety of woods and birch bark by a process involving shaping, dividing and hollowing wood; joining with putty; tarring, then wrapping with linen yarn; finally coating with soaked bark that provides an airtight seal when it dries.

Alphorns are generally made from lengths of fir, lime, poplar, or other woods split, hollowed, then bound together by bark, root, or gut binding, and vary in size from

4 ft or less, to the giant alphorns (up to 11 ft) of the Swiss, first mentioned in the fifteenth century, to those of the Slovaks (up to 17 ft).[94] Playable to the twelfth harmonic, or higher, these instruments have subsequently amassed a considerable repertoire. The pastoral and elegiac idiom of the alphorn is encapsulated by the following excerpt from a call (Ex. 1.2), quoted by Baines from Rigi in Switzerland, which must have been in Beethoven's mind when he was composing the Pastoral Symphony (Ex. 1.3).

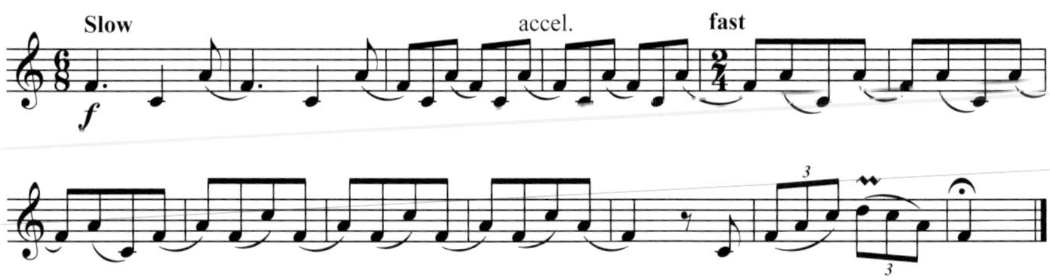

Ex. 1.3 Swiss alphorn call (first quoted by H. Szadrowsky in 'Die musik . . . der Alpenwohner', *Jahrbuch des Schweitzer Alpenclub* (1867–8)).

The alphorn can be conical, or cylindrical, like the 13 ft *trombita* of the Silesian, Zywiec Beskid region of Poland. The attachment of a modern mouthpiece transforms the alphorn into an instrument with a wide range: the original folk instrument was played from a simple hole at the narrow end. To the other end of the player is attached an upwardly curving bell, which amplifies and spreads the sound. The bell-end of giant alphorns generally rests on the ground or on a trestle, whereas the long equatorial trumpets need two people to carry them.

Highland regions, with their vast distances between habitable ground, developed long trumpets very early as a solution to the difficulties of communication over sometimes impassable terrain. Opportunely, the longer the trumpet, the more notes of the harmonic series became playable, allowing complex messages to be relayed. Upland shepherds in some areas used smaller versions to control their flocks. The last surviving example of this practice in twentieth-century Europe is the Romanian *bucinum*, which, significantly, shares the name and the profile of the ancient Roman instrument. A common assumption, that this demonstrates an unbroken tradition from ancient times, is unproven: the *bucinum* could equally be a more recent neo-classical revival.

The equatorial giant trumpets were generally played by village elders in fertility rituals and initiation ceremonies. Some, like the *molimo* of the BaMbuti of Zaire, are as much megaphone as trumpet, and indeed, the use of the voice integrated into the technique of many wooden trumpets may indicate that the trumpet evolved from megaphone-type instruments designed to enhance, alter or simply amplify the voice. Most are of such wide bore that they take a large amount of air to blow, hence they only play short notes. Trumpets are often blown alternately in pairs to sustain their one-note monody. Virtuosity, just as in the ancient Olympics, is measured by how loud the players can play. The purpose of the instruments is to communicate with the spiritual world, and the fundamental idea in primitive societies behind playing them is that they really work

– that sound governs matter, just as the sound of trumpets brought the Walls of Jericho crashing down, and that their trumpets can materialise spirits from beyond the grave.

This belief, rather than the expediency of having the materials to hand, probably gave rise to the fashioning of trumpets from human and animal bone. In more recent times brass instruments have retained associations with the supernatural. A well-known example is Mozart's use of trombones in the statue scene of *Don Giovanni.* A vernacular use is the presence of marching bands at New Orleans funerals. In a not dissimilar fashion, the spirits of ancestors are invoked or contacted by means of the trumpets used in the ceremonies that mark important rites of passage in the life-cycles of certain equatorial peoples. These trumpets are sacred, are subject to gender differentiation, and are hidden in marked pits in the jungle until the time comes, far from the eyes of women and children.[95]

Bamboo is another wood-like substance from which trumpets are easily fashioned, although flutes have been the preferred instrument made from this species of tree-plant. Trumpets made from bamboo are comparatively rare, given the wide area indigenous to this plant species. Bamboo bands playing chromatic instruments manufactured from this wood, however, exist in the Sangir Islands, to the north of Minahassa, in Indonesia. Bamboo band competitions have also been held in Lawas, Northern Sarawak, East Malaysia.

The most widespread wooden trumpet still in common use is the *didjeridu,* the Australian Aborigine instrument, which has an exceptionally developed instrumental technique. The *didjeridu's* history may take it back close to the beginnings of biologically modern man. The diverse Australasian cultures known to us collectively by the term 'Aborigine' had first migrated from the Eurasian landmass over 40,000 years ago,[96] cut off from the diffusion of later Eurasian technologies through post-Ice Age rises in sea levels and the continuing drift southwards of what we now know as Australia by the geological process of plate techtonics. The instrument has around forty aboriginal names, *Yiki yiki, yiraga* and *yiraki* being just three. *Didjeridu* was the onomatopoeic name given to the instrument by the first Europeans to come into contact with it. This word is now widespread, and is used here for easy identification. This lip-blown instrument is made from a usually straight branch of eucalyptus, or from ironwood. The normal length is from 3 to 5 ft, and the circumference flares from 3.5 cm at the lip end to 7.5 cm at the other. *Didjeridus* of up to 8 ft long exist, used in special ceremonies.

Traditionally, the *didjeridu* was hollowed out by the Aborigines in two ways – by fire, and by termites. The playing technique is complex and developed, and for us one of the few connections we may have to the music of Stone Age man, *c.*30,000 BCE. Australian Aboriginal culture elevates the sounds produced on the *didjeridu* beyond the functional world: both spiritual and rigorously intellectual, *didjeridu* music is a testament to the brilliance of all mankind's ancestors whose artistic work has been lost to prehistory. Aboriginal visual art has intrigued later societies with its insights into the animal world and the complexity of its imagery, for example the simultaneous depiction of the internal and external anatomy of an animal. The music of Aboriginal cultures is similarly complex, multi-layered and intriguing.

Little is known about the early development of the *didjeridu* in the tens of thousands of years between the arrival of the Aboriginal peoples in Australia, and the arrival of Europeans. The Australasian migrants developed the peculiar idiosyncrasies of the *didjeridu* and its technique in isolation after a rise in sea level accompanied the melting of the ice sheets after the last Pleistocene Ice Age 12,000 years ago. This isolated Australasia from New Guinea and what is now Indonesia and Malaysia from Continental Eurasia, cutting the Aborigines off from regular contact with other peoples until the modern era. The Aborigines discovered for themselves the techniques of circular breathing, multiphonics, producing simultaneous overtones, producing more than one mode of vibration, and uvular oscillation (a form of rhythmic articulation with the tongue somewhere between flutter and doodle tonguing), from which came the name *didjeridu*. These techniques were non-existent in the Europe of Tasman or Captain Cook. The complexity of this instrument's idiom and the sophistication of its playing technique are without parallel in the trumpet family. Certainly none of these techniques is yet common knowledge among today's generation of valved-trumpet players, and many of the techniques did not become widespread in the West until the adventures of 'avant-garde' music and 'free jazz' from the 1950s onwards, when new-age brass warriors like Vinko Globokar, Stuart Dempster, Albert Mangelsdorff and Bill Watrous (strangely enough, all players of the 'big trumpet' – the trombone) entered the new brass sound world of multiphonics.

The *didjeridu* has been used in contemporary art music, for example in the Requiem (2004) by Peter Sculthorpe with a *didjeridu* part written for William Barton. It is also a generic busking instrument throughout Australia and elsewhere. The British Musicians Union London directory lists seven players, most likely for film or studio work. Works by Aboriginal *didjeridu* players like David Hudson, Dr Didg, Yothu Yindi, Maningrida and Chris Adnams inhabit the world of the imagination.[97] The *didjeridu* has the longest unbroken tradition of playing of any musical instrument still in current use. And it is a trumpet. What was, in effect, a Stone Age culture was able to develop advanced techniques of transcending difficulty that few modern trumpeters can match. The authors know of no conservatoire in the Western world that has yet evolved a consistent methodology for the acquisition of equivalent skills and techniques of playing on modern instruments – a methodology, no matter how instinctive and intuitive, Australian Aboriginal culture evolved to pass on and develop without written transmission for tens of thousands of years. This should be a sobering revelation for the trumpeter, whether student, teacher or professional exponent, brought up on the notion that all histories of musical progress should end in the West and in the present.

In conclusion

For Eurasia, the world's most diverse landmass, and its immediate neighbour, North Africa, the Fertile Crescent was the originator of most 'modernising' developments in early civilisation. As Diamond notes: 'By the time of Christ, cereals of Fertile Crescent origin were growing over the 10,000-mile expanse from the Atlantic coast of Ireland to the Pacific coast of Japan'.[98] This slow spread of agriculture from the area of the Fertile Crescent, and from the other seven or eight centres on other continents where it may have arisen independently,[99] to most corners of the populated world, occurred in tandem with accompanying changes in social organisation. Statehood, widespread religious beliefs, and warfare became the defining markers of agricultural civilisation, and trumpets appeared to be useful to all three institutions. The hunting tool became a weapon, a communicator, a symbol of a priest's link with the supernatural and of a monarch's power over their people. Musical practices grew through these functions and followed these momentous shifts. Trumpets originally fashioned from local elements were developed into more powerful and dazzling instruments wherever new ideas and new technologies were introduced. Though the trumpet's original uses were overshadowed by their more developed musical successors, the genetic imprint of the original and basic functions of the trumpet can still be found embedded in the idiom of the music the contemporary trumpet plays, in the twenty-first century. A small retention of absolute and original use is still preserved in the present use of hunting horns, in the use of small trumpets used to herd animals where pastoralist traditions are maintained, and through the playing of long trumpets in remote highland regions as a form of communication.

Geography has always had a defining role in the trumpet's development. In Australia where hunter gathering was pre-determined by the environment, none of the toolmaking and spin-off technology associated with agriculture was developed. In parallel, none of the animal husbandry occurred that provided something as ubiquitous in Eurasia as the cow horn to play. As a result, musical idioms were developed through the instruments at hand. Aboriginal culture introduced developments in playing styles requiring highly advanced physical co-ordination and an acquired sophistication in technique that matches any other trumpet repertoire despite the lack of Eurasian technology diffusion. This suggests that we should strive to ignore the widespread assumption and inner voice telling us that we moderns are superior in every way to our common ancestors, and contemplate the fact that 'primitive' trumpets found in Stone Age archaeological sites throughout the world may have involved a large repertoire and highly advanced playing techniques. When compared with the huge range of world trumpets, past and present, the modern-day valved trumpet cannot be regarded as any kind of end-point, or conclusion, to trumpet history.

Chapter 2

The trumpet: definition, manufacture and technique

The trumpet is a lip-vibrated wind instrument which amplifies sounds generated by a sequence of actions in the player's body and communicates them through sound waves. At the simplest level, these sounds convey a signal and at the highest level they are organised into music. The lips of the player are central to this sound generation. They form the membrane which vibrates in the air blown from the lungs of the player to form standing waves within the instrument and sound waves without.

The twice-folded metal trumpet, which by the early sixteenth century was the standard instrument for military and ceremonial functions, changed little over the following three hundred years. During that period, however, the scope of its use widened to include participating in a variety of musical situations with other instruments and singers, becoming a regular member of the orchestra and accruing an extensive solo repertoire.

The trumpet shown in Ill. 2.1, a modern copy of an instrument manufactured in Nuremberg *c.*1700, displays the basic characteristics of trumpets produced throughout Europe during the seventeenth and eighteenth centuries. It consists of two cylindrical yards, the first of which is tapered at its end to receive the mouthpiece, and not to form a leadpipe as on the modern trumpet. The third yard, although usually made from a single sheet of metal, comprises two sections: a conical bellpipe and a flared bell. The thin outer edge of the bell is strengthened by a garland, often bearing the maker's name and date of manufacture. A hollow ball is positioned at the point where the two sections of the third yard diverge, and held in place by a tapered sleeve. The ball has no obvious function save as a more secure grip in holding the trumpet firmly to the lips, especially when in the field, and when on horseback. It may also have had an ornamental function, like the sometimes ornate garland round the bell, which also protects this exposed end of the trumpet against damage. The three yards are joined together by two u-shaped bows. The five sections of the instrument are connected by

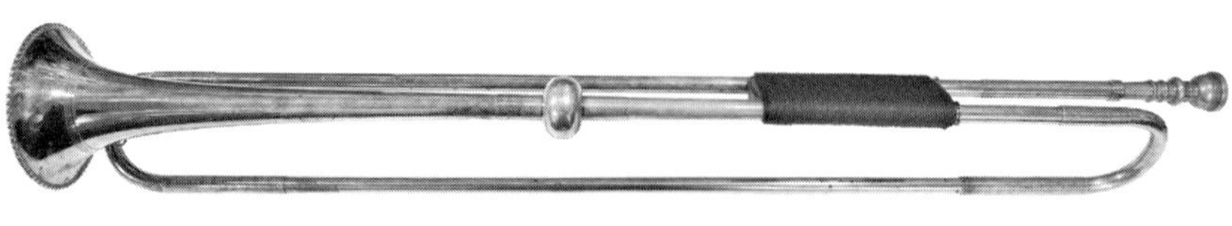

2.1 Natural trumpet by Matthew Parker (*c.*2000) based on those of J. L. Ehe II (Nuremberg, *c.*1700).

interlocking, tapered joints that are strengthened by outer sleeves (or garnishes), which, like the garland, are often decorated. The garnishes add mass to the wall of the trumpet tube, an additional factor thought by some to affect the instrument's sound. The structure is held together and made rigid by inserting a wooden block between the first yard and the bellpipe, and binding it with cord. Significantly, the constituent parts were not normally soldered together, but designed to be dismantled and reassembled as required.

It became common practice during the seventeenth century to strengthen the rim of the trumpet bell by soldering a brass wire around its edge. This allowed for thinner and more responsive bells, with a greater flare. Earlier, sixteenth-century trumpets had much less widely flared bells, as can be seen in the illustration of a facsimile of the exquisite 1585 trumpet coiled into a serpentine shape made by Anton Schnitzer of Nuremberg, and given by Cesare Bendinelli (*c.*1542–1617), chief trumpeter at the Bavarian ducal court in Munich, along with the first known trumpet method, *Tutta l'arte della trombetta*, to the Accademia Filarmonica of his home town, Verona, in 1614[1] (Ill. 2.2).

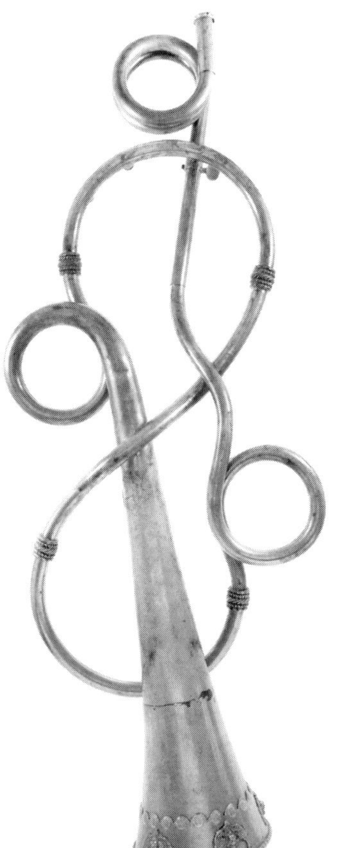

2.2 Serpentine-shaped trumpet by John Webb after the instrument by Anton Schnitzer (Nuremberg, 1585).

Acoustically, the extent of flare of the bell affects the trumpet's projection of sound waves. These waves are reflected from the tube walls on their journey down the trumpet from the lips. Finally, on reaching the bell, the greater the flare, the greater the refraction of sound into the surrounding atmosphere.

The trumpets described and depicted above have acquired the label 'natural' trumpet, an apt term for an instrument devoid of mechanical contrivances; however, since the second half of the twentieth century, this term has also come to denote trumpets configured to resemble the early trumpet but equipped with vent holes, an expediency that was alien to trumpet players until the late eighteenth century.

The natural trumpet is capable of sounding the notes of the natural harmonic series, which is shown in Ex. 2.1. The filled-in note heads in the harmonic series shown indicate those notes that are significantly out of tune on a trumpet when played using equal temperament, the system of dividing the octave into twelve equal semitones that became prominent during the eighteenth century. These notes were only slightly less problematic with the various temperaments that were prominent previously.[2] The task

Ex. 2.1 The harmonic series on C. The signs + and – indicate notes that are significantly sharp and flat respectively.

of reconciling the natural harmonic series with the desire to produce instruments suitable for performing in equal temperament has remained a primary concern of instrument makers to the present day. Skilled players were able to adjust the pitch of the problematic notes and also produce notes outside the harmonic series through the technique of 'lipping'.

The trumpet, when scored for melodically, could modulate fleetingly to the dominant and submediant keys. Classical style music modulated more freely and widely within movements than baroque music, reducing the trumpet's role in the orchestra to fanfaring at openings, endings, and returns of the home key, and to adding weight and grandeur, in conjunction with the timpani, to the orchestral sonority. In addition, instrumental forces and the places where concerts were held increased in size, especially towards the century's end. The resultant rise in dynamic levels worked against playing the trumpet in the clarino register, a subtle art enacted at subtle dynamics. Towards the end of the eighteenth century, the trumpet, like many other instruments, was subject to experiments in design to make it better suited to its role in the orchestra and extend its melodic capability in the middle register.

The earliest chromatic trumpets: the application of slides, vents and keys

The earliest attempts to extend the notes available on a trumpet involved placing a slide between the mouthpiece and the body of the instrument, allowing the player to sound the partials of multiple harmonic series. No examples of the Renaissance slide trumpet survive, although it has now been generally accepted, albeit with some dissension (discussed in Chapter 3), that it once existed The pitch-changing device on this instrument, often termed *Zugtrompete*, was cumbersome, involving the entire body of the instrument moving back and forward along a telescopic mouthpipe. The sole surviving example, by Huns Veit of Naumburg, is dated 1651.[3] Such an instrument was occasionally called for in church music, including several cantatas by J. S. Bach, who termed it *tromba da tirarsi*. In his treatise on the 'trumpeters' and kettledrummers' art' of 1795 (although believed to have been written at least two decades earlier), Johann Ernst Altenburg (1734–1801) confirmed that it was still being used by tower watchmen and by Stadtpfeifer to perform chorales during the second half of the eighteenth century[4] (Ill. 2.3).

No examples survive of the English flat trumpet, a slide trumpet described by James Talbot in a manuscript written between 1690 and 1700, now held in Christ Church Library, Oxford, and specified in several works from that period.[5] Although its

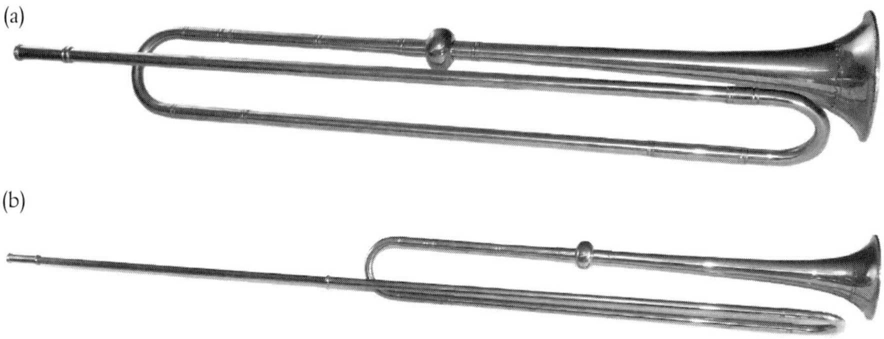

2.3 *Tromba da tirarsi* by Matthew Parker (*c*.2010) in closed (a) and extended positions (b)

appearance was brief, knowledge of its existence may well have persisted, since another slide trumpet with the slide propelled not forwards as with the trombone, but backwards past the player's right ear, appeared in England towards the end of the eighteenth century. For much of the nineteenth century this was the standard orchestral instrument in Britain. Trumpets with forward-moving slide were popular in France into the second half of the nineteenth century.

In 1959 a silver trumpet by William Shaw, dated 1787, was discovered in St James's Palace, London. The instrument had survived in pristine condition, complete with a set of four crooks and tuning bits.[6] Significantly, the second yard of the trumpet possesses four small vent holes, three of which are covered by rotating sleeves, and the fourth, by a key mechanism. The instrument was examined by Eric Halfpenny, who termed it Shaw's 'harmonic trumpet'.[7] Although this bears a superficial resemblance to the modern vented 'natural' trumpet, the holes do not conform to any of the modern venting systems and cannot in fact be used together. Instead, each vent hole functions with a particular crook to raise the pitch of the harmonic series by the interval of a fifth. Halfpenny suggested that it was an orchestral instrument, with the vent holes providing a means of quickly transposing to the dominant key, and, given that it is engraved with the royal coat of arms, intended for use in George III's private band. Whether such instruments acquired a more soloistic use, perhaps to perform Handel's obbligato trumpet parts, remains a matter of conjecture.

Shaw's practice of boring holes in the brass tubing was contemporaneous with the first attempts to mechanise the trumpet with keys. Anton Weidinger (1766–1852) is the name most closely associated with the keyed trumpet, but reports of attempts to adapt the woodwind technology of keys to brass date back as far as 1770.[8] Weidinger's keyed trumpet was successful enough for Haydn and Hummel to write concertos for him. The keyed trumpet works in a simple way. Opening a key uncovers a hole, thereby shortening the vibrating length of tube, giving a new fundamental with a new series of partials. This series of partials, however, deviates widely from a harmonic series. Owing to the cylindrical bore of the tube as far as the bell flare, only the odd-numbered partials can be made to sound, and even these behave in a strange way. Nevertheless, a fairly logical system of fingering was devised for the keyed trumpet,

2.4 Modern facsimile of the keyed trumpet by Rainer Egger

and agility and rapidity of execution presented no problem, with the keys so close together. Keys were opened singly or in combination (Ill. 2.4).

The valved trumpet

The valve was a by-product of the technology that produced the steam engine. Machine tools like lathes had existed since medieval times. As the nineteenth century unfolded, however, there was a rapid evolution in the standards of precision attainable by machine tools made of harder materials, such as steel. Already in the eighteenth century, engineers like James Watt had perfected, with great ingenuity, an airtight valve and robust piston rods capable of rapid movement without leaking pressure. The patent for the first valve was taken out in 1788 by Charles Clagget in England, which was, at that time, in the vanguard of the Industrial Revolution. The invention seems not to have found the entrepreneurs to exploit it until Heinrich Stölzel and Friedrich Blühmel, working independently, demonstrated their first valves in 1814 and 1816 respectively. Stölzel was well aware of the significance of the moment. In a letter to King Frederick William III of Prussia announcing his invention, he stated: 'I believe that I do not exaggerate in promising . . . that by means of these instruments, music may be made which will astound the world.'[9] Following independent applications for a Prussian patent, the inventors submitted a successful joint application in 1818, with the agreement that Stölzel pay Blühmel 400 thalers for sole rights to the principle of applying valves to brass instruments. Stölzel's design was adopted by many manufacturers for several decades and was used on some French cornets up to the early twentieth century, whereas Blühmel's box valve system proved less enduring. Whatever the system, the principle behind the valve was that depressing a valve opened up another length of tubing to the airway of the trumpet, producing an instrument with the possibility of rapid alternation between two harmonic series. Depressing a second valve gave a third series, and a fourth when used in combination with the first. A third valve gave a total of eight feasible harmonic series. Trumpets with three valves became the norm, with a universal standardised fingering save for some regional variation. The middle or second valve, played by the middle finger of the right hand, lowered the pitch of the instrument by a semitone. The first valve lowered the pitch by a tone, and by a tone and a half when used in combination with the second. The third was equal in length to the first and second combined, thus making two of the obtainable harmonic series identical, and reducing the total available to seven, in common with the slide trombone, though still enough to ensure a chromatic scale from the second partial of the harmonic series. A fourth valve allows for an extension of the chromatic scale at the bottom of the register, but is generally used only on some flugelhorns and shorter trumpets in E flat, G, and piccolo B flat. Ascending valves which cut off sections of tubing, thereby shortening the length of the instrument, are also possible, as are valves which divert the air through an alternative, differently shaped bell, as in the echo cornet. Five-valved trumpets have, so far, remained a rarity, championed by Merri Franquin (1848–1934) in Paris early in the twentieth century, and by Charles Geyer (b.1944) in Chicago towards its close.

Many systems of valve were in competition with one another on the early valved trumpet. After a period of great experimentation, two main systems, piston valve and rotary valve, became predominant (Ills. 2.5 and 2.6). The piston valve is ultimately traceable back to Stölzel, although its most successful type was evolved by the Parisian maker François Périnet and patented by him in 1839. Blühmel developed a

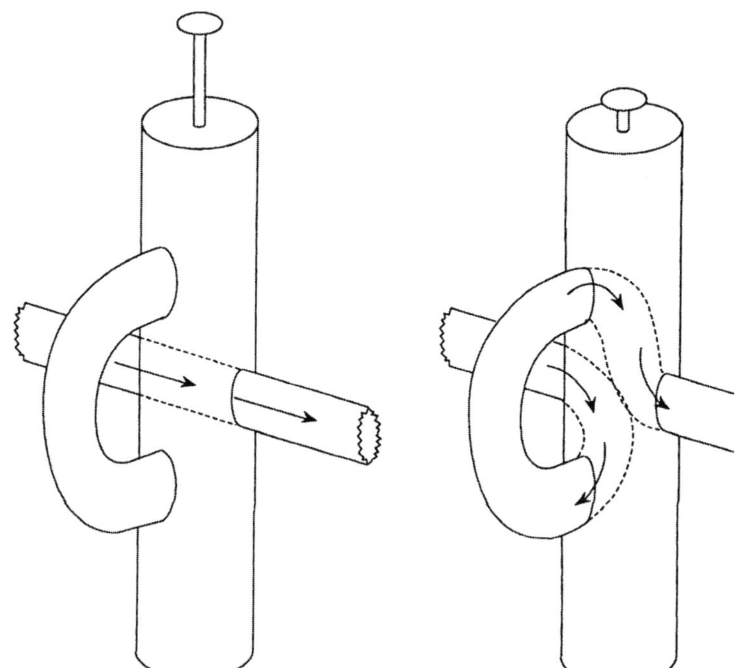

2.5 Périnet valve system. (By permission of Cambridge University Press, and with thanks to Arnold Myers)

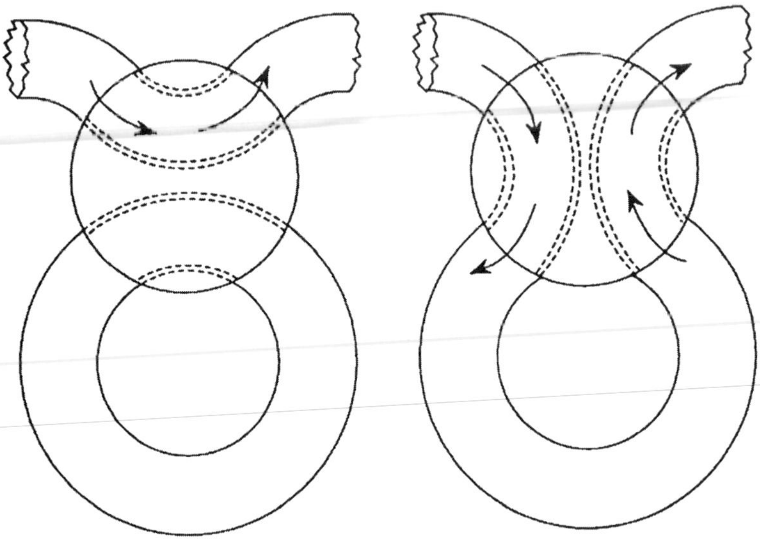

2.6 Rotary valve system. (By permission of Cambridge University Press, and with thanks to Arnold Myers)

prototype rotary valve, and after Viennese instrument maker Josef Riedl's patent of 1835, his design, with two airways in the rotor, became most common in areas influenced by the Austrian and German music industry, including, for a time, the USA. Other valve systems of these fertile decades in the first half of the nineteenth century included Christian Friedrich Sattler's double-piston valve of 1821; rotating disc valves manufactured in Paris by Halary, and in London by two makers, John Shaw and John Augustus Köhler; pistons enclosed in the windway, made by Charles Pace in London; moving vanes in the windway by Nathan Adams of Massachusetts and also the horn player Joseph Meifred in partnership with the maker Deshays; and square cross-section pistons by Blühmel and Stölzel.[10] The Berlin valve, invented in 1833 by Prussian bandmaster Wilhelm Wieprecht, remarkable for the large circumference of its valves and its less sharply curved airways, was eventually overtaken by the Périnet valve.

Valved trumpets and cornets became more common from the 1830s on, but did not supplant rival systems overnight. By the middle of the nineteenth century, valve technology had been refined and mass production of valved brass ensured an unprecedented cheapness and availability of quality instruments. The keyed trumpet was by this time virtually extinct. The keyed bugle, invented by Joseph Halliday in Dublin in 1806, an instrument of military bands and dance orchestras, became increasingly uncommon after 1860 in the USA, and disappeared from view slightly earlier in Europe. Makers of quality trumpets preferred the valve systems most common through to the present day: the rotary valve in the German lands, the Austro-Hungarian Empire, and their areas of influence; and the Périnet piston valve almost everywhere else. Rotary valve trumpets declined in orchestral use for several decades after the Second

World War before a resurgence in their popularity occurred in the closing decades of the century due to further refinements in their manufacture by specialist makers and a regional preference for their sound quality. Both systems survive, unchanged in essentials for the past 150 years, and the accompanying diagrams explain how they work. The rotary valve moves in a semicircular motion in a horizontal plane, serving the tubing of the valve slides that are placed in the same horizontal plane, giving the instrument its flat, wide look, and its characteristic holding position which makes it difficult to expedite rapid mute changes with the right hand. The piston valve moves up and down in a vertical plane, the slide tubing is arranged in the same vertical plane, and the instrument can be held easily in either one or the other or both hands, making rapid muting possible. This has been the preferred valve system in jazz and commercial music. Modifications to these valve systems have occurred infrequently. One of the most remarkable appeared in the late twentieth century, when the British maker Denis Wedgwood used ovoid valves, which removed the protrusions in the valve ports by repositioning the ports away from the axis of the valves.[11]

Most early valved trumpets were pitched in 6 ft F or G (Ill. 2.7). Around the middle of the nineteenth century the shorter valved trumpet in B flat began to find influential proponents, although it was not until the late nineteenth century (and in a few musical centres even later) that this instrument supplanted longer valved trumpets or the slide trumpet as the orchestral instrument of choice in the most prominent musical centres. The B flat trumpet gained something near its modern form in the instruments Théo Charlier (1868–1944) helped design for Mahillon towards the end of the nineteenth century. These instruments, like the cornet, had a long initial tube, the leadpipe, going into the third valve, rather than a short one going into the first valve. This gave the opportunity for a much longer, sharply tapered conical portion in this initial length of tubing, which was found to enhance certain playing characteristics.

Not only did it free the high register, it also improved flexibility, and added brilliance to the timbre. The French Besson company made similarly designed trumpets from early in the twentieth century, which stimulated makers like Vincent Bach in the United States. American instruments, like those of Conn and Martin, became prized items by European players from the jazz era onwards. Vincent Bach began production of his 'Stradivarius' trumpet in 1925, targeting the professional symphonic market. By 1994, 420,000 had been made.[12] From the 1920s, the tendency was for instruments to become larger in bore and bell size, with an emphasis on increased power and volume. American trumpets remain the most influential and innovatory in this respect, with the Rajah trumpet of David Monette the most extreme manifestation of this ongoing trend to date.

The modern valved trumpet pitched in B flat and a slightly shorter one pitched in C are now the most common trumpets used in symphony orchestras, and in jazz, popular and commercial music throughout the world. The three valves are designed to produce a sequence of seven tube lengths, producing extended harmonic series on fundamentals of B flat chromatically down to E, with a wealth of microtonal alternative fingerings thanks to the interlocking harmonic series. The range of trumpets most often used by professional and amateur musicians at the beginning of the twenty-first century corresponds to those pictured in Ill. 2.8.

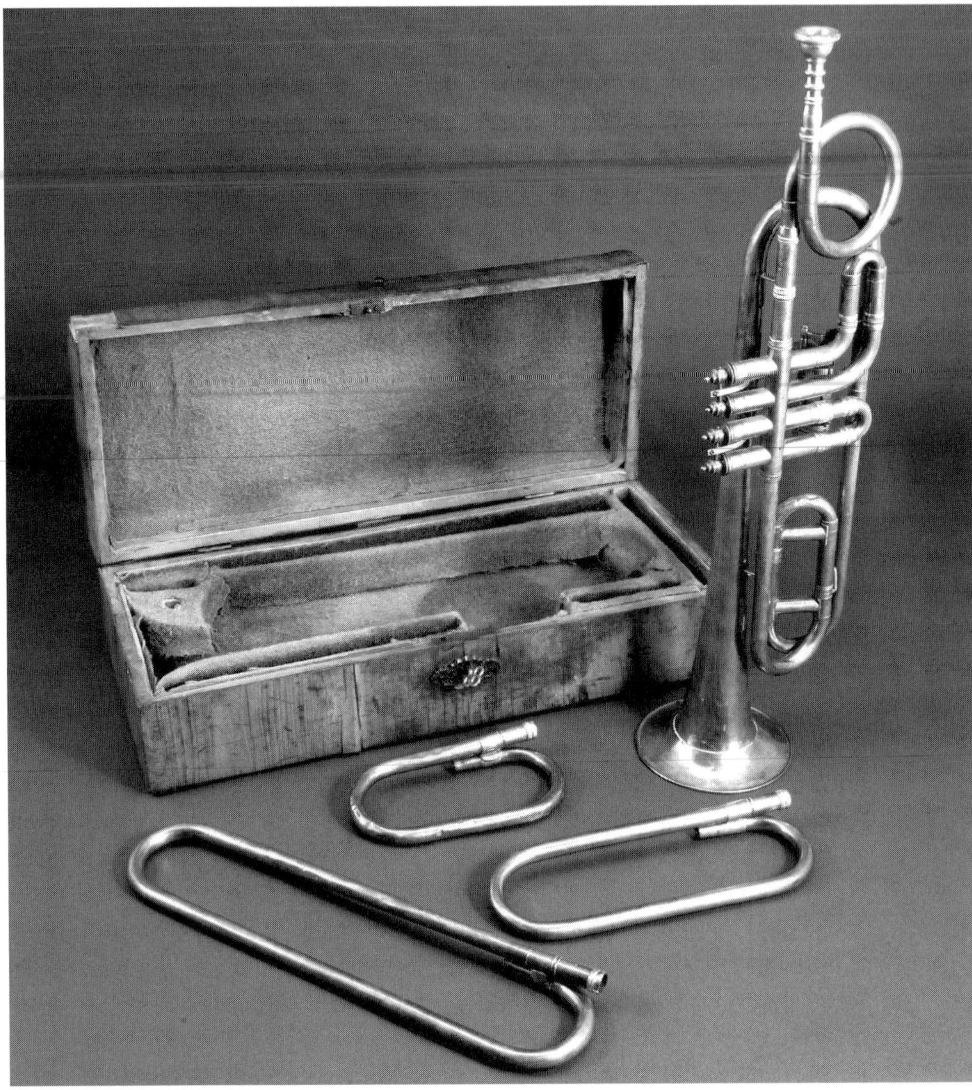

2.7 Trumpet in G with two Vienna valves (*c.*1840). The maker is not named, but the instrument is believed to have originated from the German-speaking part of Europe. The three crooks lower the fundamental pitch to E flat, D and C. With the addition of the coupler (fitted between the instrument and the mouthpiece) to the C crook, the pitch can be lowered to 9 ft B flat. A spare slot in the case suggests that it originally existed with an F crook. (By permission of the National Music Museum, The University of South Dakota, Mark Olencki, Sr., photographer)

The trumpet and the cornet

The assertion is often made that the bore of a trumpet is cylindrical, whereas that of a cornet, like the horn, is conical. That is, the tube of the trumpet is the same width throughout its length, while the cornet tubing increases in width gradually all the way from the mouthpiece to the flare of the bell. The reality, however, is not so precise. Most modern trumpets and cornets have a mixture of bore profiles. Exceptions to a

2.8 B flat trumpet, C trumpet, B flat piccolo trumpet, and cornet by Schilke. (With thanks to Gordon Rainesford)

strict definition of instrument type by bore profile exist throughout history: in fact, differently-bored members of the trumpet family were sometimes depicted together in the medieval and Renaissance periods. On closer examination, many assumptions about conical versus cylindrical bore are confusing oversimplifications. No matter how different the outside shape produced by the contrasting coiling patterns, the shape inside the tube, especially in the bore diameter at the valves and in the bell flare, is remarkably similar. During the twentieth century, trumpet and cornet mouthpiece cups and throats also converged in design. After the mouthpiece cup, throat and backbore, the bore profile follows this general pattern: a gentle expansion, followed by a cylindrical part (the length of which depends on the valves being operated), ending with the bell flare. Of this, only the gentle expansion in the leadpipe is even roughly conical. The essential difference between modern trumpets and cornets lies in the mouthpiece receiver and leadpipe, with trumpets having a minimum bore in the leadpipe of about 9 mm versus the cornet's 6 and 7 mm.[13]

The bell section also became wider on many trumpets, giving a fatter sound in the middle register, better for playing music of a lyrical nature. The trumpet, in fact, shamelessly gobbled up many of the best attributes from the cornet, and became more and more a hybrid, and it has continued to evolve in design by increments in this direction ever since.

Computer-aided design

By the 1970s, trumpet designers were using wind tunnels to help design trumpets, and computers to help them analyse the results. Micro variations in bore at certain critical points were found to bring certain modes of vibration within the trumpet tubing closer to a true harmonic series.[14] Digital analysis of wave formations increased knowledge of vital tolerances critical in trumpet construction. Many new specialist makers began making trumpets, and trumpet 'surgeons', like René Spada in Switzerland and Bob Malone in California, began customising mass-produced trumpets by rectifying design faults arising through expediencies in the industrial process. Metals created originally for use in space were even used in trumpet bells, as when the Schilke company used beryllium bronze, an alloy with the property of more efficient sound refraction than brass.

Added-mass theory

A new development in trumpet design occurred when a former Schilke employee, David Monette, began to make very heavy trumpets encased in extra brass designed to minimise energy lost through the walls of the trumpet tubing. According to this 'added-mass theory', energy not lost through the walls of the tubing would end up going through the bell converted into sound energy. This led also to a vogue for heavy mouthpieces, booster weights being added to existing mouthpieces, and all sorts of purportedly performance-enhancing aids for which wild, unsubstantiated claims were made.

Trumpet making

The most important centre of brass instrument making during the seventeenth and eighteenth centuries was Nuremberg, a city with a long metalworking tradition. Trumpets are known to have been made in Nuremberg by members of the coppersmiths' guild from the late fifteenth century. Hans Neuschel, the founder of the oldest dynasty of brass instrument makers in the city, became a master coppersmith in 1479 and is recorded as making brass instruments in 1487.[15] Four trumpets by Anton

Schnitzer, father or son, survive from the late sixteenth century. The younger Schnitzer was among ten brass instrument makers who were granted a charter by the city authorities in 1625, which limited the number of practitioners of their craft and set the period of apprenticeship at six years.[16] Like all crafts, trumpet making ran in families, and two Nuremberg families were particularly prominent during the seventeenth and eighteenth centuries, Ehe and Haas, who between them account for a significant proportion of the surviving trumpets from that city.

Our knowledge of the techniques employed by the seventeenth- and eighteenth-century Nuremberg trumpet makers, as well as the materials and tools used, owes much to the research of Robert Barclay, which is detailed in the monograph *The Art of the Trumpet-Maker* and manifest in his reproductions of trumpets from that city.[17] Barclay refutes the notion that brass instruments in Nuremberg were typically produced by a single master craftsman, arguing that 'factory-like' production methods were in place by the eighteenth century, and probably earlier, a suggestion previously mooted by Don Smithers.[18] The small number of makers named on instruments relative to the voluminous output suggests that the firms employed a number of craftsmen and journeymen with different specialisms. It is known that certain fittings were bought in and that procedures such as engraving were, on occasion, undertaken by outside craftsmen. That the name engraved on the instrument generally referred to the name of the firm of makers and not necessarily the craftsman who produced the instrument singlehandedly is highlighted by the firm of Haas, which was established by Johann Wilhelm Haas in the final quarter of the seventeenth century and spanned four generations. Both his son (Wolf Wilhelm) and grandson (Ernst Johann Conrad) signed their instruments 'J. W. Haas' and retained the trademark springing rabbit or hare on the bell garland, a representation that presumably originated as a play on the German word *Hase* (hare). No instruments by Ernst Johann's son Johann Adam, who became a master trumpet maker in 1769, survive.[19] While the most highly decorated Nuremberg trumpets, which were often made of silver and adorned with gold leaf, were clearly intended for ceremonial use, the majority were made of brass and are relatively free of decoration. Altenburg expresses his preference for instruments made of brass and notes that those made by Haas were the most highly regarded by trumpet players.[20]

Brass, silver and copper were the most common metals used in trumpet construction from around this time. Brass is an alloy of copper and zinc. Pure zinc, however, was unknown until the beginning of the sixteenth century. Early brass manufacture was a mixture of alchemy and empirical experiment. Brass was smelted by mixing copper with calamine, an ore containing zinc. When heated, the calamine released zinc as a gas. The zinc then interacted with the copper to produce the alloy brass. Molten brass was poured and flattened into thin sheets between two stones. When the brass was cool it was then 'combed', a process similar to 'puddling' in iron manufacture, which removes imperfections like air bubbles. The sheet brass was then cut, using templates, into the correct shape for folding, by tough scissors called tinsnips. Before work begins, the brass is annealed, a process involving heating followed by sudden cooling. This renders the brass soft and malleable. The shaped brass is then folded round iron mandrels, templated to the exact dimensions required in the trumpet's internal bore.

An exact meet between the edges of the tube is made by skilled tapping with a pinking hammer. This thins and spreads the metal, and is especially important at the bell. The eventual join between the meeting edges of the brass tube is sealed with solder, which is an alloy of two or more metals that have a lower melting point than the metal to be joined. Bends and bows in this hollow tube as it now stands are near impossible to achieve without cracking the brass. A technique, possibly known in classical times, evolved whereby the tube was filled with a molten substance which had a lower melting point than brass. This filler, usually pitch, or a soft metal like lead, was allowed to solidify, and then the tube was bent, or bowed, when cool. Any kinks and wrinkles were tapped out with the pinking hammer. The filler was then heated inside the tube until liquid, and then poured out for reuse.[21] From the early seventeenth century onwards, the bells on Nuremberg trumpets came to possess a more pronounced flare and narrower throat. The sharper flare was obtained through increased hammering, and fashioned to its exact shape by burnishing on a mandrel. The thinning of the metal that ensued increased the need for a wider, more protective garland.[22]

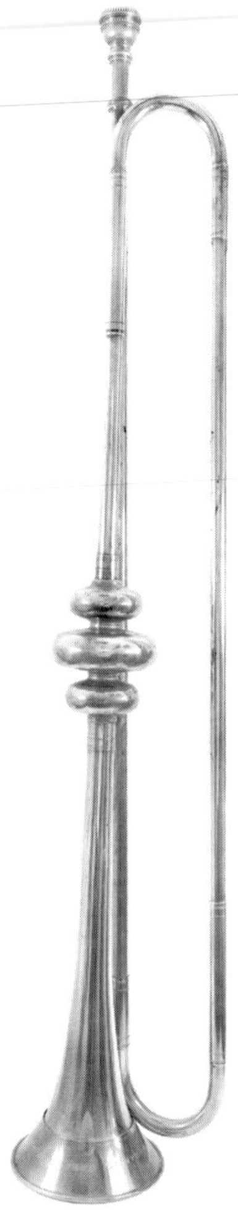

2.9 Natural trumpet by Frank Tomes after an original instrument by William Bull (1686–1700) in the Museum of London.

The output of the Nuremberg makers and the demand for their instruments were such that surviving trumpets made in that city during the seventeenth and eighteenth centuries outnumber all those produced elsewhere in Europe. Other centres of brass instrument manufacture, including London, Vienna, Prague and Lisbon, provided instruments for more localised markets. A significant number of seventeenth-century British trumpets survive, almost all of which were made by London goldsmiths, many of whom were also royal trumpeters. British trumpets differ from those made on the continent most conspicuously by their large, often tripartite, ball (Ill. 2.9)[23]. Two surviving seventeenth-century Scottish trumpets, which possess large, ornately decorated balls, and resemble contemporary English instruments, were made by Goldsmiths whose surviving work includes a wide range of silverware. Were it not for the survival of the instruments, there would be no reason to suspect that they ever made trumpets.

The mouthpiece

The mouthpiece, arguably the most crucial part of the trumpet, developed from a hole in one end or in the side of the primitive trumpet. Through time these holes became shaped to accommodate the player's lips. The trumpets from the tomb of Tutankhamun, for example, possess an outer sleeve over the narrow end of the tube, which widens the rim and cushions the player's lips. A similar mouthpiece is attached to the fourteenth-century trumpet discovered during an archaeological excavation in the Billingsgate area of London.[24] The trumpet discovered in the Dordogne region of France, stamped with the name of the maker, Guitbert, and dated 1442, survives with a mouthpiece constructed from separate parts, which includes a conical cup and a tapered backbore.[25] A similar mouthpiece survives with the instruments made by Jacob Steiger in Basle in 1578. Several mid-seventeenth-century British mouthpieces were made by combining a cast cup and a tubular shank of sheet metal, devoid of a tapered backbore, while others are of more modern design, formed from a single block of metal and with a conical backbore.[26]

Marin Mersenne confirms that mouthpieces possessing the characteristics most often associated with those of the late baroque were available around the time the trumpet entered the sphere of art music, in *Harmonie universelle* (Paris, 1636) (Ill. 2.10). In comparison with their modern counterparts, baroque mouthpieces are large. They typically possess a wide hemispherical cup, a broad, flat rim, and a sharp angle between the cup and the throat. Empirical evidence from specialist players has confirmed that these characteristics are ideally suited to the techniques required for playing the baroque repertoire on natural trumpet.

Surviving historical mouthpieces can rarely be linked to particular instruments or players. The connection between mouthpiece and player is vitally important for the consideration of performance practice, since it is safe to assume that there may have been considerable differences between the types of mouthpieces used for military and ceremonial playing, and 'musical' playing. The written sources are vague on the types of mouthpieces used for the different spheres of trumpet playing. Altenburg, for example, merely advises students that 'the teacher must have a mouthpiece carefully turned out so that it is suitable for the pupil's mouth',[27] and John Hyde (*fl.* 1780s–1820s) recommends they 'choose a proper mouthpiece, large or small proportionable to the thickness of the lips'.[28] Iconography is more helpful. The portrait of the Leipzig Stadtpfeifer Gottfried Reiche, painted when he was Bach's first trumpeter, shows him with an exceptionally large mouthpiece in his trumpet (see Ill. 6.1). The trumpeter depicted in the portrait in Fenton House, London (*c.*1753), thought to be Valentine Snow (*c.*1700–70), Handel's trumpeter in London during the 1730s and 1740s, is shown playing on a mouthpiece that may only be a little smaller. In his *Instructions for the Trumpet* (London, *c.*1835), Thomas Harper (1786–1853) provided a line drawing of a mouthpiece that he claimed was 'of the exact size and form' that he had used for twenty years, resembling the baroque mouthpiece in its dimensions and form.[29] The flat rim with a sharp

2.10 Trumpet mouthpiece from Marin Mersenne, *Harmonie universelle* (Paris, 1636). (By permission of the University of Glasgow)

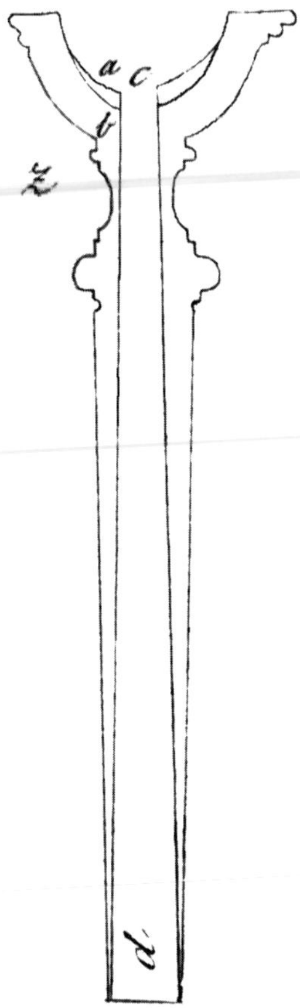

2.11 Trumpet mouthpiece from Joseph Fröhlich, *Vollständige theoretisch-pracktische Musikschule für alle beym Orchester gebräuchliche wichtigere Instrumente zum Gebrauch für Musikdirectoren-Lehrer und Liebhaber* (Bonn: N. Simrock, 1811). (By permission of the University of Glasgow)

inner edge and throat is also evident in the trumpet mouthpiece depicted by Joseph Fröhlich in his treatise on orchestral instruments of 1811 (Ill. 2.11). Fröhlich also indicates the depth of cup suitable for playing first and second trumpet parts.[30] Through the influence of cornet players, the distinction between the trumpet mouthpiece and the smaller, more conical cornet mouthpiece became blurred and it was only during the course of the twentieth century that a consensus emerged, at least in orchestral circles.

The modern trumpet mouthpiece

The main variable components of the trumpet mouthpiece are shown in Ill. 2.12. The thinner the mouthpiece rim, the more sensitive are the lips to the initial 'touch' of each note, but a thin rim tends to cut into the lip. The thicker rims spread the frontal pressure of the mouthpiece on to the lips over a wider area, and are better for player comfort, stamina, and high range, but less good for close control of articulation (in contrast to the baroque mouthpiece, for which a wide, flat rim is most suited to the style of articulation appropriate for the earlier trumpet repertoire). The lip of the mouthpiece rim can be contoured gently or steeply. This affects the edge tones set up in the mouthpiece by the passage of air over it: the sharper the lip, the more brilliant the tone; the gentler the lip, the mellower the tone.

The diameter of mouthpieces in current use on the modern trumpet varies from about 16 mm to 17.5 mm.[31] The larger the diameter, the greater the area of lip that comes into play, therefore the greater the potential richness in the sound. The training regime required, however, is more strenuous. The larger mouthpieces are generally favoured by professional symphonic players. The deeper the mouthpiece, the easier it is to produce low notes on the trumpet, and deeper mouthpieces are preferred by orchestral second trumpet players. Shallower mouthpieces are preferred by high-note players and those in jazz, pop or commercial playing situations. V-shaped mouthpieces help produce what trumpet players call a 'dark' sound, that is a sound where low to middle formants are present in the overtone series. Bowl-shaped mouthpieces help to produce what trumpet players term a 'bright' sound. This is a sound where high partials are present as formants in the overtone series.

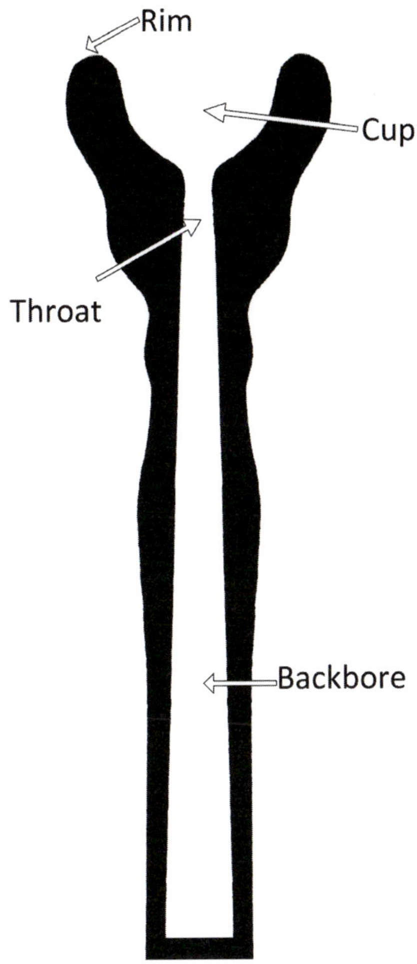

2.12 Cross-section of a modern trumpet mouthpiece.

The throat of the mouthpiece is a critical factor in the control of the player over the type of sound produced. The more closed the throat, the smaller and faster the jet of air the player can channel through it. The more open the throat, the larger and more spread the volume of air. A tight mouthpiece throat aids the production of high frequencies and brilliance of sound; an open throat aids lower frequencies and mellower sound qualities.

The backbore of the mouthpiece is also crucial to the quality of sound production. In this part the stream of air from the player's body is finally modified before entering the trumpet. The contour of the backbore affects the playing quality of the instrument in exactly the same balance between 'bright', 'dark', high and low. A good backbore for high notes is one with a steep taper, whereas a good backbore for 'dark' sound has less conicity.

The most popular contemporary mouthpieces are manufactured by the Vincent Bach company, whose range numbers from 1* to 20, with variants on each number, lettered, for example, 1X (Deep), 1B (Medium deep), to 1E (Shallow). The '1' size is set at about 17 mm cup diameter. There is a $1\frac{1}{4}$ size, and $1\frac{1}{2}$ and $1\frac{3}{4}$ sizes, before 2 (16.50 mm) is reached.[32] Other trumpet manufacturers make mouthpieces with a similar wide range of choice. Schilke, based in Chicago, are the next most universal. Some manufacturers specialise only in mouthpieces. Warburton, a company based in Geneva, Florida, makes threaded, screw-on stems so that players can pick and mix backbores and throats with different cups. Mouthpieces are a favoured topic for experimentation among trumpet players. As in woodwind reed-making, there is probably more application of instinct and intuition than scientific process at work, and there is much room for personal idiosyncrasy. There is also a big demand for mouthpieces from players looking for an answer to playing problems. This demand is answered by makers like John Stork in New Hampshire, USA, and Bruno Tilz in Neustadt A.d. Aisch, Germany, who make customised mouthpieces to order, as well as having developed their own extensive ranges.

Mutes

The application of mutes to the trumpet was probably initiated as a means of transmitting military signals covertly, a practice noted by Mersenne, who also provides the earliest detailed depiction of a trumpet mute, in *Harmonie universelle*[33] (Ill. 2.13). However, the earliest references to muted trumpets, from the early sixteenth century, relate to their use in funeral ceremonies. Daniel Speer, writing towards the end of the seventeenth century, remarked that 'If one desires to hear the trumpet sound in quiet surroundings, one needs a mute'.[34] Altenburg confirms that mutes were still used for these purposes, and, through daily use, as a means of building a strong embouchure, in the late eighteenth century. Muted trumpets are specified in a number of musical works from the seventeenth and eighteenth centuries, most of which have funerary or supernatural connotations. The endurance of the symbolism is evident from Tchaikovsky's use of a solo muted trumpet in the 'Entracte Symphonique (Le Sommeil)' from *The Sleeping Beauty* (1890).

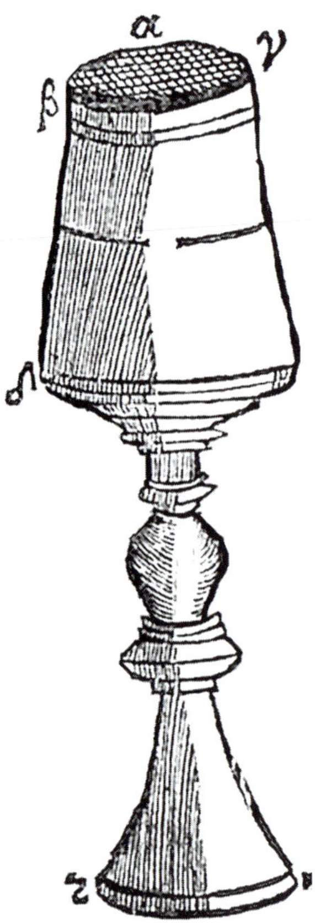

2.13 Trumpet mute from Marin Mersenne, *Harmonie universelle* (Paris, 1636). (By permission of the University of Glasgow)

The mute depicted by Mersenne closely resembles surviving examples from later in the century or the century following. When inserted into the bell of the instrument, the baroque mute provides a seal, which channels the air stream through an inner cylindrical tube.[35] Several seventeenth- and eighteenth-century writers reveal that the mute raised the pitch of the trumpet by the interval of a whole tone. Musical works from this period calling for muted trumpet, beginning with Monteverdi's introductory Toccata to his opera *Orfeo* (1607), generally concur with this transposition. Most surviving mutes, however, raise the pitch of the instrument by closer to a semitone (Ill. 2.14).

Few works from the early nineteenth century call for muted trumpets, but presumably the mute retained its function as an aid to practice and to dampening the sound in performance. During the second half of the century, composers increasingly exploited the sonority of muted brass in their orchestral writing. This period witnessed the development of a variety of innovative mute designs, like the practice mute patented in 1865 by J. F. Stratton of New York, which was essentially a prototype harmon mute. These developments had to wait until the jazz era to find influential proponents, many of whom had originally experimented with the muting effects obtained by the manipulation of

2.14 Baroque trumpet mute by Fred Holmgren (*c.*1995) after various originals. This mute raises the harmonic series by one semitone.

the hand, and objects such as beer glasses and plungers placed over the bell. The range of muting techniques and special effects fashionable in the early jazz era were described by Louis Panico, a celebrated exponent of 'wah-wah' effects, in *The Novelty Cornetist* of 1923.[36] The following year, Ferde Grofé called for the 'Wha wha' (harmon) mute in his orchestration of George Gershwin's *Rhapsody in Blue.*

The mutes most widely used in the various spheres of musical performance in the early twenty-first century are shown in Ill. 2.15. The straight mute is produced in a variety of shapes and materials, most often metal, fibre or cardboard. Some cup mutes come with an adjustable cup, allowing for variation in the levels of dampening. Both the straight and the cup mute are affixed to the bell by thin strips of cork, allowing air to be emitted from between the mute and the bell of the instrument. The harmon mute is held in position by a solid ring of cork, providing a seal between mute and bell, as with the baroque mute, and directing the air through an adjustable and removable stem. The 'wah-wah' effect is obtained by partially closing and opening the end of the stem by hand. Certain jazz soloists, notably Miles Davis (1926–1991), have exploited the timbre of the harmon mute with its stem removed. Numerous practice mute designs have been developed since Stratton's model. Like the baroque mute and the harmon mute, practice mutes typically capture the air stream within the body of the mute, but employ various means of releasing the air, balancing the requirement of providing the player with the feeling of playing an 'open' trumpet at as soft a dynamic level as possible.

Inside the trumpet – the acoustics

The trumpet looks simple, but closer observation reveals manifold complexities. A trumpet manipulates a finite volume of air by confining it in a tube. Its Roman name, 'tuba', meant literally just that – 'tube'. The player's mouth forms a seal at one end. The other end, at the bell, is open to the atmosphere. The distance from the player's lips to the end of the bell can be made to vibrate in one long pulsation, or in a pattern of shorter pulsations, subdivisions of the total tube length called 'standing waves', when the player's lips are made to vibrate by blowing air over them. The longest 'standing wave' is called the fundamental. The series of ever-shorter standing waves,

2.15 Modern trumpet mutes. Clockwise from top left: cup, harmon, straight, practice. (Wallace Collection)

mathematical subdivisions of the tube length producible by a skilled player, is referred to by trumpeters as 'the harmonic series'. A harmonic series, however, is an exact mathematical certainty, which no trumpet manufactured to date has been able to reproduce. These notes, approximating to a harmonic series, are called by acousticians 'modes of vibration' of the tube; how many are feasible – up to twenty-four in the D major Concerto of Michael Haydn (1762) – is dependent on the construction and period of the instrument, and the skill of the player. These standing waves, in whichever mode of vibration, are sustained by compressed air that comes from the lungs and is blown over the lips of the player. The air recharges the energy used in creating the 'starting transient' of the sound at the lips, the energy used in friction against the walls of the tubes; the sound energy is dissipated in the atmosphere. The 'starting transient' is the envelope of sound at the beginning of a note, and a chief determinant of the tone colour perceived by the listeners. Recordings of different instruments with these starting transients cut off have proved almost impossible to distinguish one from the other. The most important factors in sound production on the trumpet are therefore the initiating actions by the player: the starting consonant and vowel shape formed by the tongue in the mouth cavity, added to the initial vibration of the lip.

Trumpet players, perhaps mindful of a more combative past, often call the start of a note the 'attack'.

The basis of the musical idiom of the trumpet is governed by the 'modes of vibration'. Only a perfectly conical tube, however, will give modes of vibration, the frequencies of which match the harmonic series. A completely cylindrical tube, on the other hand, will only correspond to the odd-numbered harmonics. In practice, trumpets are neither perfectly cylindrical nor perfectly conical, though they work best when the pitches that can be produced by a skilled trumpeter, the modes of vibration, coincide most closely to the harmonic series. The harmonic series is a mathematically exact sequence of frequencies where each frequency is a multiple of the fundamental by its number in the series.

Whenever the harmonic series is mentioned by trumpet players, there is almost always an underlying assumption that a perfect harmonic series is attainable on any length of tube, that is 'modes of vibration' and 'harmonic series' are one and the same thing. This is far from the case, and the problems of brass manufacturers to this day stem from the difficulty of matching the modes of vibration of any tube to an exact harmonic series. Furthermore, even when the notes are in tune to a harmonic series, they may be out of tune playing with fixed pitch instruments in equal temperament like the piano. This compounds a maker's difficulties. In modern times, valved trumpets became progressively shorter, their normal range with an upward limit of the eighth or ninth harmonics, which brings 'well-tempered' intonation a closer possibility for player and maker alike.

There is another factor, however, to be added to the 'starting transient' in determining what makes a trumpet sound like a trumpet. Every frequency produced by a trumpet and its player becomes the fundamental of a new harmonic series set at the vibrating frequency of the player's lips. These harmonic series on every note produced are called 'overtones', 'formants', or 'partials'. They are the spectral components of the sound which, along with the starting transient, determine the characteristic timbre of a trumpet, and distinguish it from, say, an oboe or violin. They occur because each complete sound wave is made up of smaller wavelets reflecting against the wall of the tube. 'Formants' are areas of the overtone spectrum which are particularly strong whichever frequency is being played, and hence they are an important determinant to timbre.

None of these 'spectral sounds' known as overtones or partials is as strong as the fundamental produced by the player's lips. Some, like the 'formants', are much stronger than others, which are scarcely present. The brain mostly deciphers these overtones as timbre, picking out the fundamental frequency as the main audible pitch. These overtones are the reason why intonation in ensemble work is a matter more of relying on intuition rather than resorting to a tuning machine. Two notes played by two players may, individually, be perfectly in tune with a tuning machine, but may sound out of tune when played together, because of clashing harmonics further up the overtone series. Intonation between two trumpets is a matter of continuous readjustment through the two players listening intuitively to the 'difference tones'. When two trumpets play together, at different pitches, not only do the different series of overtones on each note intermingle and react with one another, but they produce these additional 'spectral sounds'. The frequency of these 'difference tones', plainly audible, especially to the players themselves, is the difference produced by subtracting the lower frequency from the higher. When the difference tones are in tune with the played notes, a smooth sensation of perfect harmony is felt by the players. When out of tune, a jarring 'beating' sensation between the two frequencies ensues. Trumpets in greater numbers create an ever more complex patina of spectral sounds that contribute greatly to the vibrancy and carrying power of trumpet ensembles, a major reason for their extensive ceremonial and military use in many societies, past and present.

The trumpet has a particularly rich sound spectrum when played either low or loud, or both together. The acoustic energy in high notes, however, is divided amongst only two or three partials, hence the piercing quality when played high and loud, and the smooth, flute-like tone when played high and soft.

The interaction between the modes of vibration of the column of air in the trumpet, and the overtones of each individual note, is called a 'cooperative regime'. The closer the match is between these two harmonic series systems, the better the instrument – hence the continual striving for improvements from makers. Cooperative regimes also make false pedal notes possible on a modern valved trumpet. These are the 'factitious tones', between the written bottom F sharp3, and the first true pedal note, C3. These notes can be produced on a well-built trumpet because of support to that frequency from higher multiples of that frequency higher up the chain of partials. The flexibility of the individual player is another factor.

The physiology of the player

The vibration of the lips is the most important physical action for sound production on the trumpet. This action is activated by a coordinated series of muscular processes involving the mouth, tongue, glottis, lungs, diaphragm and abdomen, and controlled by the player's senses of touch and hearing.

The lips

The lips are the first point of the player's contact with the instrument, and are the major determinant of the pitch of the sound produced. Modern trumpet players learn to alter the tensile density of their lips through contraction of the *orbicularis oris* muscle around it. The more contracted this muscle, the higher the density of the lip, the greater the resistance against the air being blown over them, and the higher the pitch achievable. The converse is also true. Another group of facial muscles forming the wall of the cheek have the anatomical name *buccinator* muscles, literally 'trumpet-playing' muscles. They control the corners of the mouth and can draw them into a smile or into a pucker. Their position also makes them pivotal in focusing the other facial muscles to the task of trumpet blowing. Many trumpeters, as a warm-up exercise, can make a passable imitation of a rudimentary trumpet by compressing the lips and blowing air over them. This practice is called, in trumpet argot, 'buzzing'.

Practising on the mouthpiece alone is now widespread, though its ultimate usefulness is still doubted by some prominent players and teachers. Its chief application, although its effects are unproven, would seem to be its isolation of specific aspects of technique as a corrective measure when a student trumpeter encounters embouchure problems. Buzzing on the lips or the mouthpiece is essentially a stamina-building and energy-saving technique which came out of the American/European school of cornet virtuosi in the closing decades of the nineteenth century and the early decades of the twentieth century. The confluence of lip and mouthpiece is the most critical area to the consequent sound quality – the personal aural fingerprint – which the player produces. Trumpeters call this characteristic a player's 'tone'. A significant determinant of this 'tone' is the amount of lip protruding into the cup of the mouthpiece, which varies from player to player, in effect reducing the volume of the cup. The angle of the bite radius as it slopes down into the cup, usually known as the 'undercut', determines the amount of lip that is allowed to protrude into the cup. Each player must therefore choose a mouthpiece where the bite radius is at an appropriate angle in terms of supporting the lips, while enabling them to vibrate freely. The mouthpiece maker Gary Radtke has defined and measured this angle, coining the term 'alpha angle' to describe this critical element of mouthpiece design.[37]

Embouchure

The word for 'mouthpiece' in French is 'embouchure'. This word, embouchure (literally, in French, 'where to put the mouth'), has also become universally adopted for the part of the face and mouth which sets on to the mouthpiece, and with which the player fine-tunes sound production. The logic of this French terminology is indisputable – there is a symbiotic relationship between the adjacent parts of body and instrument. Trumpet players are depicted blowing out their cheeks in iconography from the ancient world to the Renaissance. This is perhaps indicative of the use of only the lowest two or three modes of vibration in this period,[38] though this may represent an attempt by the artist to depict the action of blowing. Even so, some of the first expert players who wrote down their thoughts on embouchure, including Bendinelli (1614) and Altenburg (1795), regarded the habit as bad practice, and there has been near unanimity on this orthodoxy ever since, although very many of the greatest players of the twentieth century, from Louis Armstrong (1901–71) through to Dizzy Gillespie (1917–93) and even Maurice André (b.1933), blew out their cheeks when playing.

The early sources provide conflicting advice on the placement of the mouthpiece on the lips, reflecting a diversity of practice that persists to the present day. Altenburg states that 'the mouthpiece must lie on both lips, more underneath than above them', whereas both John Hyde and François Georges Dauverné (1799–1874), in his *Méthode pour la trompette* (1857), instruct the student to place more of the mouthpiece on the upper lip.[39] While Jean-Baptiste Arban (1825–89) advocates placing two-thirds of the mouthpiece on the lower lip, he also advises that 'there is no absolute rule for the position of the mouthpiece, for everything depends on the formation of the mouth and the regularity of the teeth'.[40]

Range

By the end of the fifteenth century there are reports of players possessing advanced technique. The Duke of Saxony's trumpeters were heard 'playing higher than could be imagined' by an astonished observer at a wedding in 1474.[41] A century later, trumpet music venturing into the upper register could be heard in many parts of Europe. The high range expected of the trumpet player involved in art music crept upwards during the seventeenth century. Fantini in 1638 wrote C6 regularly but sparingly. By the end of the century many composers were very free with D6. By the second decade of the eighteenth century, Fux was writing E6, by the third, Caldara wrote G6, and by the 1760s the highest written note of the virtuoso natural trumpet repertoire, A6, was reached in the D major concerto of Michael Haydn. This increase in the range is usually attributed to the genius of individual players. It is highly unlikely that any manufacturing secrets, such as changing the conical/cylindrical ratio of the bore, were used to facilitate the use of the extreme range of the natural trumpet. Surviving examples show no evidence of unusual practices.

None of the early treatises discusses the technique of 'lipping'. Fantini merely states that certain notes are 'imperfect if you want to hold them; but since they go by quickly they can be used', which accords with his use of non-harmonic pitches in the musical works in his method.[42] Altenburg confirms that it was necessary for players to adjust the pitch of the out-of-tune notes of the harmonic series, and, regarding non-harmonic notes, remarks: 'I believe that it is perhaps possible for some players with skilled embouchures to produce them – but with what effort!'[43]

Pressure

There is near unanimity in modern trumpet teaching that excessive force as an aid to sound production should be minimised. Earlier sources are less dismissive of this method. Hyde, for example, advised students that to ascend from one note to the next in the harmonic series, 'contract your ambesure [*sic*]' and 'press your Instrument harder to your lips'.[44] Dauverné was of similar opinion: 'To modulate the sound, one gradually increases or diminishes the pressure of the mouthpiece and the tightening of the lips, according to whether one wants to form a high or a low sound. It is therefore the proportional pressure of the mouthpiece on the lips which controls the pitch intervals on the Trumpet.'[45] Although this advice conflicts with modern pedagogy, theory does not always reflect practice, and a judicious use of force can still produce exciting and telling sounds from a trumpet, especially in the extreme high register. Range and endurance are a common preoccupation of trumpet players and trumpet teachers, and the science of embouchure is still relatively unformed.

Breathing

Breathing technique is equal in importance to embouchure in sustaining the sound to make music on the trumpet. The diaphragm is the crucial muscle in the act of taking in air to play, known technically as *inspiration*. Although the diaphragm is much talked about in trumpet pedagogy, the player has only indirect control of it through surrounding muscle groups, there being no 'somatic' nerve in the diaphragm. Muscles can perform two actions – contraction and relaxation. When the diaphragm contracts, the centre of this dome-shaped muscle moves powerfully downwards into the abdomen, stretching the lungs with it, and displacing the internal organs in its way. This action of the diaphragm is initiated by coordinated actions in the other surrounding muscles important to breathing technique – the scalene, and the intercostal muscles, which aid the three-dimensional expansion of the ribcage, from side to side, front to back, and top to bottom. Within the expanding ribcage, the lungs are free to fill with air, like a balloon. The volume of the lungs is increased gradually by the action of these muscles during the in-breath, the air pressure at all times inside the lungs being lower than in the surrounding atmosphere, allowing the air to rush in.[46]

During the outbreath, the act of 'blowing', some of the most powerful muscles in the body, the abdominal muscles, come into play to expel the air. The rate at which the air is expelled is controlled by the scalene and intercostal muscles braking against the push from the abdominal muscles, a physiological action commonly referred to as 'muscles in opposition'. The action of the diaphragm against the abdominal muscles ensures that the air pressure in the lungs during the outbreath is always greater than the atmospheric pressure outside the player's body. This ensures a steady stream of compressed air over the player's lips to sustain the initial vibration which stimulates the sound waves within the instrument. Breathing is an important subject which generates much interest. The most recurrent quality advocated in most writing about breathing is simplicity. Although the body is not asked to do much more in breathing and blowing to play the trumpet than it does in everyday situations, the difference is one of degree, and because a trumpeter blows out air under pressure, and sometimes has to gulp air in like a swimmer, the temptation is to interfere unnaturally with the breathing process. Most successful players think little about breathing, they do it naturally. The most complete, relaxed, refreshing breath that is taken in an everyday situation is during a yawn. The quickest, sharpest exhalation of air is caused by the kick from the abdominal muscles we call a cough. The smallest parcel of air usable in short notes is similar to that produced by the action of the diaphragm which causes a hiccup.[47]

The earliest writers allude to the importance of breath control in their discussions of phrasing and articulation, rather than encouraging students to consider the process in isolation. Daniel Speer offers practical advice, however, when he advises students to wear a wide leather belt to support the breath support.[48] The first writer on the trumpet to discuss the physiology of breathing in detail was Dauverné. He separated the inhalation and exhalation processes, which both 'deserve the total attention of the trumpeter, who must modify them as needed'. He concludes his analysis by directing students to the vocal method of the Paris Conservatoire.[49]

The tongue and throat

In its passage from the lungs to the mouth, the air has to the pass through the throat, where, situated in the larynx, are the vocal chords (also known as the glottis) that are important in trumpet playing, as they are in singing. The glottis opens or closes to start or stop the airflow. The airflow can be regulated by controlling the degree of restriction or openness in the glottis, giving more or less resistance against the air from the lungs, according to musical context. During a *diminuendo,* therefore, the glottis would gradually close, and the converse would happen during a *crescendo.*

Immediately after passing the glottis, the air is shaped by the tongue, as in speech. The tongue is a large organ, rooted far down the throat. It controls the flow of air in its passage from the glottis to the lips through forming a constantly and minutely adjustable wind tunnel in the mouth. The back of the tongue affects the shape and size of the mouth as in the production of vowel sounds. The resonating cavity within the mouth has to bear some relationship to the frequency being played, as part of a coöperative regime between player and instrument. The front of the tongue can articulate the start of a note, as in the production of consonants. The relative hardness or softness of 'attack' can be regulated by the consonant used. In former times it was often recommended to place the tongue between the lips and to imagine that a piece of paper was being spat from the tongue, to launch the initial note. Many different tongue positions are now advocated, from an anchoring behind the bottom teeth, to striking the tip behind the top teeth, and further back, on the front end of the hard palate. There is no incompatibility between these positions; all have their uses, can be learned, and used for different musical situations, in the same way as violinists use different bowings, and percussionists use harder and softer sticks.

Articulation: historical performance practices

The use of varied articulation according to recognised patterns was a fundamental aspect of musical performance from the sixteenth to the eighteenth centuries. The techniques by which this performance style was realised on wind instruments were described phonetically by Girolamo Dalla Casa, a cornettist at St Mark's in Venice, in his treatise on ornamentation, *Il vero modo di diminuir* (1584). Dalla Casa's diverse articulation patterns reflect the practice of grouping notes in pairs, with a stress on the first note of each pair, and varying the emphasis within and separation between pairs or groups of notes. On wind instruments the pairing of notes was achieved by alternating articulations based on strong and weak, or hard and soft, consonants. Single tonguing, using either *ta* or *da,* would normally be appropriate for passages incorporating long note values. For notes of shorter duration, an alternation between *ta* and *da* might be suitable, and for more florid passages, the articulations *te-re, te-re* or *da-ga, da-ga.* The last example resembles modern double tonguing; it should be emphasised, however, that this is used not merely for speeds at which single tonguing becomes impractical, but as a means of musical expression. Dalla Casa described the articulation 'Teche, teche', which also corresponds to modern double tonguing, as being appropriate 'for players who want to give an effect of terror', and, by inference, for imitating trumpet calls.[50]

Bendinelli reveals that by the late sixteenth century different articulations were used as an aid to memorising military signals. He does not provide articulations for the ensemble pieces, but notes that 'there are diverse [people] who tongue differently'.[51] That trumpet playing had reached a level of sophistication comparable with other wind instruments in the early seventeenth century is confirmed by Fantini, who provides a range of articulations broadly corresponding to those of Dalla Casa. Of particular interest in Ex. 2.2 are the articulations 'tia tia da' and 'dia dia da', which

Ex. 2.2 'Method of tonguing with a pointed tongue in different ways' from G. Fantini's *Modo per Imparare a sonare di Tromba* (1638), pp. 10–11.

are early examples of slurring. Altenburg confirms that unequal articulation, described in treatises for other instruments from the second half of the eighteenth century, remained applicable to the trumpet, advocating 'a distinction between principal and passing notes, so that the former are played somewhat louder than the others' (Ex. 2.3). Given the absence of didactic literature for the trumpet from the century and

Ex. 2.3 Example of varied articulation from J. E. Altenburg's *Versuch* (1795) (*Trumpeters' and Kettledrummers' Art*, p. 96).

a half between the treatises of Fantini and Altenburg, sources like the flute treatises by Jacques Hotteterre (1707) and Johann Joachim Quantz (1752), and the singing treatise by Pier Francesco Tosi (1723), shed light on various aspects of performance practice that are entirely relevant to the trumpet.

During the nineteenth century, the conventions governing phrasing and articulation that had evolved over generations yielded as composers provided increasingly detailed performance directions for their works. Didactic literature from the early nineteenth century reveals that unequal articulation had been replaced by the consistent use of syllables beginning with 't' or 'd', depending on the desired degree of stress for any given note or phrase, and that double- and triple-tonguing was reserved for the most rapid passages. Arban recommends using the syllable tu, 'with more or less softness, according to the amount of force you wish to give', in preference to 'du'. He notes, however, that 'when there are dots, over which there is a slur . . . the first note should be "struck" with a very soft Tu, and then substitute for it the syllable Du, because the latter syllable not only distinctly articulates each note, but also serves admirably to connect the notes'.[52]

Many nineteenth- and early twentieth-century authorities advocate placing the tongue between the lips. Harper describes the action of withdrawing the tongue to release the air as being 'similar to that of dislodging something from the lips that is offensive'.[53] Dauverné offers a similar analogy.[54] Several writers also refer to the involvement of the tongue in the formation of the embouchure, a technique that perhaps forestalls the tongue-controlled embouchure advocated by the New York teacher Jerome Callet (b.1930).[55] Altenburg states that 'the required embouchure is produced by a certain position of the tongue and a tight closing together of the teeth and lips, so that only a small opening is left between them through which, with the help of the tongue, the air is driven into the mouthpiece and further, into the trumpet', and Harper instructs the student to 'Apply the Mouthpiece to the Centre of the Lips (two thirds resting on the upper lip), at the same time introduce the tongue between the teeth (the tip just touching the upper lip), press and slide the Mouthpiece nearly one third down the upper lip, the part on the under lip remaining, and tighten the lips across the teeth'.[56]

Vibrato

Vibrato, the fluctuation of pitch or intensity of sound, is produced on a brass instrument in several ways. Pitch vibrato is the most common, and is achieved by minute fluctuations in the tensile density of the lips. Throat vibrato is produced by rapid fluctuations in the resistance to the air flow at the glottis. Hand vibrato can be subtle or produce an effect that is more lip trill than vibrato, caused by rapid fluctuations in the amount of frontal pressure of the mouthpiece on the lips. This resulted in the much-copied terminal shake that characterised Louis Armstrong's note-endings.

Vocal and string treatises from the baroque era describe vibrato as an ornament to be applied sparingly, though some writers allude to a discreet vibrato as a natural feature of performance. Although these comments are relevant to wind and brass playing, the only type of vibrato mentioned by Quantz in his flute treatise is the *flattement*, a finger vibrato involving the subtle fluctuations of timbre and pitch, obtained by opening and closing a hole beyond that required for the production of a particular pitch. Until the advent of the keyed trumpet, this had little relevance to the trumpet.

During the second half of the nineteenth century the application of vibrato to brass performance became a matter of contention. To some, it destroyed the concept of the trumpet as a noble instrument. Arban, who had studied trumpet at the Paris Conservatoire before embarking on a career as a cornet soloist, criticised players who 'abuse the use of the Tremolo by a movement of the neck which gives forth a certain ou, ou, ou; a most disagreeable sound' and advocated a judicious use of subtle vibrato, obtained by 'a light movement of the right hand'.[57] Recordings from the late nineteenth and early twentieth centuries reveal vibrato as one of the most conspicuous elements demarcating the trumpet and the cornet idioms. In British brass bands, vibrato is used as a device to collectivise the sound in the manner of an orchestral string section. The function of vibrato for the soloist is to individualise the sound. This is what gives individual soloists their sound 'fingerprint' – their 'tone' – and is a major factor in what, for example, made Maurice André sound different from Timofey Dokshizer (1921–2005).

Chapter 3

The trumpet in Europe and its environs to 1600

This chapter spans a period of more than a thousand years, from the fall of the Roman Empire in the West in the fifth century until the end of the sixteenth century. What is known about the trumpet, its players and its music during this era has to be pieced together from iconography, archival and literary references, correspondence and miscellaneous ephemera. The larger European context, historically and economically, is important to the manner in which the trumpet, as part of music-making generally, developed. The growth of Europe after 900–1000 led to increasing wealth and population, trade in manufactures, the rise of financial institutions and changes in power structures. Initially there was a great expansion in the power of the church. The Christian church became the largest landowner in Europe, and embarked upon a great programme of cathedral building. Later, during the period now known as the Renaissance, national states in the modern sense, with enduring boundaries, began to emerge. Much of the history of the period hinges on the power struggles consequent to the debate about whether ultimate power was vested in state or church. This question was of primary importance to the patronage of music and the consequent use of musical instruments like the trumpet. For example, it was official church policy to ban musical instruments from worship for much of this period. This ban relaxed gradually to include soft instruments, but it was really only in the last century and a half of the period in question that further liberalisation took place and trumpet-like instruments came into the ecclesiastical frame. When national states began to emerge, on the other hand, organised music making, both instrumental and vocal, became an essential trapping of courtly civilisation. Competence in musical performance became a necessary social accomplishment, and so part of the core education of Renaissance nobility. Courts vied with one another in ostentatious display, and music became an integral part of court status and entertainment. The trumpet, in particular, became a symbol of regality. These musical developments at court and in the chapels attached to them led to rivalry between courts, and an international trade in musicians. They were also the impetus for a competitive surge in the use of instruments in religious music sponsored by the Church. Centres of musical excellence arose in the latter part of this period, with Burgundy, Munich and Venice being prominent in the story of the trumpet. The first 'star' players emerge at this time, with Augustein Schubinger (*c.*1460–1532) the first internationally recognised virtuoso of the cornett.

Throughout this long period, the trumpet had a slowly changing role within music and society. This evolution becomes evident in three interdependent areas: changes in instrument design; the contexts in which it was utilised; and the playing techniques that evolved. But, which came first in this evolution – design, usage, or playing technique? An interesting pattern emerges during this period and it recurs later: a style of music arises in which the trumpet of the time cannot take part; an adaptation in trumpet design follows so that some form of the instrument can participate. This pattern is found again in the following centuries, notably with the adoption of the valve in the nineteenth century.

Following the demise of the Roman Empire, there was a decline in the use of metal trumpets in Western Europe, and in the early Middle Ages the trumpet most commonly depicted in pictorial sources was short and made of natural substances such as wood or horn. Metal trumpets survived in the Eastern Roman Empire and in Asia, and, as discussed in Chapter 1, some Celtic areas in northern and western Europe that had remained outside the dominion of Rome.

After 1100, longer trumpets come into the frame and the instrument begins to assume its role in the service of noble and civic establishments as a symbol of high status. During the thirteenth century a shorter instrument appears and writers differentiate between the two forms of trumpet. By the late fourteenth century, developments in metal working techniques were allowing makers to produce trumpets in an 's' shape and, by the early fifteenth century, in the folded form that it was to retain for the three centuries that followed. As the fifteenth century progresses, reports emerge of trumpeters exploring the upper register of the instrument and performing for entertainment, particularly dancing. An important development occurred in the early fifteenth century with the development of the slide mechanism and the incorporation of the single-slide trumpet into the shawm band. Towards the end of the fifteenth century the double-slide trombone emerged, creating an offshoot of the trumpet's family tree, and ultimately, a new sub-species. During the sixteenth century, cornetts often played in consort with trombones, making inroads into musical territories that were as yet outside the trumpet's technical and expressive capabilities. The natural trumpet was not rendered obsolete by these advances in design, but kept its symbolic and heraldic functions. By the early sixteenth century, the Holy Roman Emperor included a band of twelve trumpeters in his retinue.[1]

Few examples of medieval and Renaissance trumpets survive. Important as these are, they only provide a limited impression of the types of instruments most widely used during this period. There is circumstantial evidence about what trumpeters played, particularly towards the end of the period covered in this chapter, but since time immemorial players had performed an unwritten repertory, learnt and transmitted by rote, and there is not much hard evidence until around 1600, when the trumpet began to be specifically designated in musical manuscripts. Since much of what we know about the development of the trumpet during this period derives from a wide range of disparate sources that are open to different interpretations, the subject is not devoid of controversy. When facts are scarce, informed and intuitive reconstruction fills the gaps, and several of the accepted views mentioned above have been, and continue to be, challenged, generating intense and passionate debate amongst scholars and performers alike.

The Early Middle Ages, 476–1000

Despite the fact that Roman literature was read throughout the medieval period, the 'pagan' musical practices of Ancient Rome were suppressed by the Early Christian Church. The disappearance of this music was complete by the Middle Ages, although by this time inspiration was being sought from the example of Ancient Greece and Rome in many areas, including, paradoxically, the theory of music. The theory (evolving from Pythagoras *c.*500 BCE to Aristides Quintilianus in the fourth century CE), and not the practice of music, was the area in which classical Greek thought was more influential.

Roman civilisation did not die out overnight in Europe with the fall of the Empire in the west. In the conflicts over territory which ensued, following the continuing migrations of peoples like Angles, Jutes, Saxons, and Vikings, warfare was a constant, and the technology of warfare owed much to the legacy from Roman times. Don Smithers has argued that the Roman trumpet tradition was maintained by the various peoples who vied for control of the former Imperial dominions and that there has been an unbroken tradition of the manufacture and use of metal trumpets since Roman times. Moreover, he contends that there was diffusion of this tradition to the Muslim world via the Eastern Roman Empire.[2] This interpretation contradicts the widely held view that metal trumpets all but disappeared from Europe following the demise of the Roman Empire and were reintroduced through contact with the Muslim world several centuries later. Smithers's hypothesis is predicated on the premise that the overwhelming evidence for the survival of the Roman technological accomplishments and the sustained interest in Roman military strategy renders it inconceivable that the manufacture and use of metal trumpets were excluded from this. While Smithers provides a compelling case for the survival of at least a vestige of the Roman trumpet tradition, his conclusions have not been universally accepted, and the fact remains that many of the representations of trumpets from the Middle Ages depict instruments that appear to have been constructed from non-metallic material. In the opinion of Keith Polk, 'following the waning of Roman influence, trumpets seem to have almost (but not quite) vanished from view'. He attributes this to the demise of large-scale central authorities and centrally controlled military organisation, which resulted in a reduction in ritualistic ceremonies that called for trumpeters and changes to the structure of the military. He also points to Smithers's failure to consider the numerous eyewitness accounts of the Crusades, which describe the profound effect that the musical instruments of the Muslim armies had on the Christian soldiers.[3]

As has been discussed in Chapter 1, the Celts possessed metal trumpets during the Late Bronze Age. Following the demise of the Roman Empire, the Celts were increasingly forced to make way in the face of the territorial aspirations of peoples from the north and east. These peoples were eventually absorbed, and several varieties of Celtic culture survived in the western extremities of Europe. Cultural and technological exchange between Celts and these new adversaries for European territory is evident from the hoards of Irish trumpets and horns that survive from this early medieval period.[4] In addition, illuminated manuscripts from the Early Middle Ages, like the Lindisfarne Gospels, show a long, slender, curved instrument, most probably of wood or animal horn, being played. These particular Gospels are a product of a fusion of Celtic and Saxon cultures. The miniatures of St Mark and St Matthew, which contain the depictions of the trumpets, were composed *c.*698 CE by Eadfrith, Bishop of Lindisfarne (Ill. 3.1). Straight instruments of the time, such as those portrayed as part of a hunting scene on the Pictish stone at Hilton of Cadboll (*c.*800 CE), were quite possibly made of barkwood in the manner of the Lithuanian *daudytė* referred to in Chapter 1.[5]

By the reign of Charlemagne, there is little evidence for a continuing use of a metal instrument shaped like a Roman *tuba* at his court in Aix-la-Chapelle, although Edmund Bowles quotes tantalisingly from a German source that 'crude metal horns' were used to sound the beginning of Mass in Carolingian times.[6] Charlemagne was installed as Holy Roman Emperor in 800 CE, in a ceremony that was based on Byzantine ritual.[7] Several near-contemporary accounts of the event have come down to us, but none of them is particularly detailed and they mention only the sounding of musical instruments. Nor is there evidence of trumpets being used in the Frankish army, even though it adopted military technology from the Byzantines and the Arabs. Carolingian court ceremony also contained elements that derived from Rome and Byzantium, but again there is no evidence of the use of trumpets. Following the surrender of Pavia in 774, for example, Charlemagne entered the city, to the sound of 'hymns and *laudes*'.[8] The conquest of Barcelona by Frankish forces in 801 was celebrated with a similar procession in which Charlemagne's son, Louis, King of Aquitaine, 'passed through the city gate with solemn pomp and *laudes hymnidicae*, preceded by the priests and clergy'.[9]

Charlemagne looked west, to Northumbrian England, an area of influence of the Celtic Christians, for scholastic advice. England, in the eighth century, had experienced a resurgence of Latin culture, which gave rise to scholars with a European reputation, a succession of whom helped Charlemagne and his line revive education in the Frankish empire. The Hiberno–Saxon kingdom of Northumbria was custodian to some of the traditions of literature, philosophy, fine arts, and music from the ancient world, and one of its leading scholars, Alcuin of York, became head of Charlemagne's palace school, and his adviser on doctrinal issues and education from 782.[10] Slightly earlier, from the sixth to eighth centuries, missionaries from Scottish and Irish monasteries had founded schools both at home and in mainland Europe, especially in Germany and Switzerland. One result of this Carolingian renaissance was the rise of important musical centres like the Monastery of St Gall in Switzerland. The type of trumpet Alcuin would have been most familiar with was probably of the Saxon/late Celtic oxhorn type as depicted in Illustration 3.1. Alcuin was widely travelled, however, and the origins of English learning came from far-flung sources, so other influences are a distinct possibility. For example, the foundations of knowledge for his scholarship and teaching, and for that of his predecessor, Bede, were largely established by two scholars sent to England by Pope Vitalian in 668 – the new archbishop of Canterbury, Theodore, from Tarsus in Asia Minor, and his companion, from Byzantine Africa, Abbot Hadrian.[11]

The Roman tradition of using long straight trumpets survived in the Eastern Empire, which flourished until 1453, when Constantinople fell to the Seljuk Turks.

3.1 Miniature of St Matthew with an angel playing a trumpet fashioned from animal horn (Lindisfarne Gospels, 698 CE; *GB-Lbl* Cotton MS Nero D. iv, f. 25b). (By permission of the British Library)

The historian Procopius, however, reveals that the trumpet's signalling function had fallen out of use in the Byzantine army by the sixth century, when he claimed credit for the reinstatement of clear trumpet signals for advance and retreat. His advice to the Byzantine commander Belisarius to use the cavalry *salpinges* for the signal to advance and those of the infantry for retreat, being made from leather and thin wood, and metal, respectively, occurred during a siege of a town near Ancona in 539 CE as an initiative to cut losses in battle.[12] An anonymous Byzantine military treatise of the mid-sixth century reveals that 'In each unit four men should be assigned to transmit order, two by voice, one by trumpet, and one by signals'.[13]

During the reign of Emperor Maurice (582–602) the Byzantine army was reformed. Details of the organisation and tactics to be adopted were set out in the *Strategikon,* a military handbook attributed to the Emperor himself. The *Strategikon* reveals that trumpets and horns (the latter termed 'bugles' in the translation cited below) fulfilled distinct signalling functions, but appears to lack consistency on this. For military drills it states that the signals to march and halt were to be given by the horn and trumpet respectively, but for the infantry on the march 'the blast of the bugle is the signal to halt and the blast of the trumpet the signal to march'.[14] It advises against using many trumpets in battle as this could cause confusion; however, when attacking at night, 'if the attacking army is large, one or two trumpets should be blown; if it is small more should be blown to make them think it is larger'.[15] A tenth-century military manual attributed to Emperor Nikephoros Phokas adds to the trumpeters' duties sounding the signal for calling soldiers to prayer before battle.[16] The historian Leo the Deacon alludes to an Eastern influence of the military instruments used in the Byzantine army during the reign of Nikophoros Phokas in his account of the preparations in 963 to capture Tarsos:

> While his forces were gathering, he trained the men with him in the conduct of war; he sharpened their mettle and toughened them with daily exercises, he drilled them in their combat maneuvers, constantly giving the command to sound the trumpets, beat the drums, and clash the cymbals, to leap upon their horses, shoot with their bows at the target, and hurl their spears straight at the mark.[17]

Representations of Byzantine trumpets and horns appear in illuminated manuscripts from the ninth to the fourteenth centuries. Most of the illustrations accompany biblical texts, in which the *salpinx* is rendered as either a trumpet or a horn, apparently indiscriminately. Short cavalry trumpets and long, straight instruments of similar length to the Roman tuba are sometimes shown as comprising a cylindrical length of tubing, with an adjoining conical bell section. An eleventh-century illustration shows a trumpet of this type with what appear to be supportive rings, a detail that appears in Arab images of trumpets from the thirteenth century. This prompted Alfred Büchler to speculate, in agreement with Smithers, that 'early Arab military trumpets were based on Byzantine models'.[18]

There is no evidence of trumpeters taking part in Christian ritual up to this time, and for several centuries to come, though from the illustrations of trumpet-like instruments which survive from the eighth to the tenth centuries and later, they retained their association with the Day of Judgement and the Apocalypse (Ill. 3.2).

3.2 Long trumpets playing at the Last Judgement on the twelfth-century Romanesque tympanum from L'église Saint-Maur in Martel, France.

The High Middle Ages, 1000–1375

The period 1000–1200 in Western Europe was one of economic and population growth. Embryonic universities appeared in Paris, Oxford and Bologna, and a class of wandering scholars emerged, who peregrinated from university to university in search of expert knowledge. Travel and trade between different parts of Europe became more widespread. The rapid growth of towns, and of city states with courts in Italy, led to an upsurge in trade which led in turn to the development of merchant and middle classes. Rapid population growth in cities, and a massive programme of cathedral building by an aggressive and acquisitive Church hierarchy determined to win the hearts and minds of the new masses, was the background setting for major cultural change, most obvious to us now in the legacy of surviving European art and architecture. Literature and music achieved new prominence, as artistic pursuits became an aspiration of the educated society which arose in this context of growth.

A class of itinerant musicians and entertainers appeared in the tenth century. By the twelfth century, in line with trends among artisans in urban areas, these *jongleurs* or *ménestrels* were beginning to band together into brotherhoods or confraternities with the professed aim of providing social benefits for their members. Professional affiliations were sometimes confirmed in legal contracts. An early example of this type of partnership occurred in Lucca in 1310 when five trumpeters signed a contract to share profits and only to teach the 'arte tubarie et trombette' with the full agreement of the others.[19] A further development occurred in the late thirteenth and early fourteenth centuries with the formation of minstrels' guilds in some of the larger towns and cities. Like the trade and craft guilds that emerged around the same time, the minstrels' guilds strove to protect members' interests by standardising levels of payment, restricting entry by establishing set periods of training followed by examination, thereby ensuring appropriate levels of competency, and instituting codes of conduct. This form of embryonic union organisation endured into the nineteenth century, with increasing demarcation. In an age in which multi-tasking musicians were the norm, many of the brotherhoods would have undoubtedly numbered trumpet players among their members, although normally listed under less specific terms such as 'minstrel' or 'piper'. Trumpeters are mentioned in the statutes of a brotherhood formed in Stuttgart in 1458, which comprised 'trumpeters, pipers and lute-players'.[20] The following year the trumpeters of Barcelona organised themselves into a confraternity. The surviving charter records the rights and duties pertaining to membership, but the institution appears to have been short-lived, as there is no further trace of this or any other musical guild in Barcelona until the 1590s.[21]

The Crusades and the re-emergence of the trumpet in Europe

This rise of urban societies and courts coincided with a re-emergence of the trumpet, which by the fourteenth century was enjoying a return to prominence in Western Europe. Contact with the Arab world in part stimulated this growth, first through trade, and then through an increasingly chaotic and futile series of Crusades, from the First (1096–99), until the Ninth (1271–72), which ended in a truce negotiated by the future Edward I of England.

Many of the eyewitness accounts of the Crusades that were disseminated throughout Europe attest to the use of trumpets and horns in both the Christian and the Muslim armies. In his chronicle of the First Crusade, Fulcher of Chartres reports the sinking of one of the ships in the fleet soon after its departure from Brindisi on Easter Day 1097, with the loss of 400 lives. Upon discovering that crosses were imprinted on the flesh of some of the survivors, 'reason made it plain to those reflecting on it, that it was appropriate that, by such a miracle, those dead had already by God's mercy obtained the peace of everlasting life'. Fulcher relates how the crusaders resumed their journey:

> placing our hope on almighty God deep within us, with topsails raised again, and with a great trumpet sound (*tubaque sonate*), we thrust ourselves upon the sea.[22]

Like many of the chroniclers of the Crusades, Fulcher imbued his narrative with religious imagery. The reference to 'a great trumpet sound' as the fleet set sail can be regarded as more than an incidental detail: it suggests that the Crusaders were invoking the protection of God for their journey.

After almost three years travelling across Europe and the Near East, the crusaders arrived at Jerusalem, the epicentre of Christianity, on 7 June 1099. They immediately laid siege to the city and seven days later made their first, unsuccessful, attempt to penetrate its imposing walls. Given the crusaders' conviction of the divine guidance for their expedition, it is tempting to interpret Fulcher's assertion that they arrived at Jerusalem as 'June was now warmed by the heat of its seventh sun' and that 'the leaders gave the signal and the trumpets sounded (*sonantibus bucinis*) in morning's bright light of the seventh day following' as coded references to the biblical account of the destruction of the walls of Jericho.[23] Religious rituals were a perennial feature of the crusaders' campaigns, and often included the singing of hymns. Raymond of Aguilers attests to the involvement of trumpeters in one such ceremony: a procession around the walls of Jerusalem prior to the final assault on the city. A council of princes and clergy ordained that 'the clergy should lead the procession with crosses and relics of the saints, while the knights and all able-bodied men, with trumpets, standards, and arms, should follow them, barefooted. All this we did according to the commands of God and the princes.'[24]

Numerous references to musical instruments employed in both the Christian and the Muslim armies during the Third Crusade (1189–1192) are contained in the *Itinerarium Peregrinorum*, a contemporary chronicle compiled from the writings of various eyewitnesses. In the account of the arrival of King Richard I of England at Messina, Sicily, in 1190, the writer provides what is perhaps the most elaborate description of trumpet playing from this period. As crowds gathered by the shore,

> Far away they saw the sea covered with innumerable galleys, and from afar the sound of war-trumpets (*tubarum*) echoed in their ears, with clarions (*lituorum clarius*) resounding clear and shrill. . . . The ears of the onlookers rang with the thundering of war-trumpets – known as *trompes* (*tubarum intonationibus, quas trumpas*).[25]

When the King disembarked,

> Trumpets (*trompis*) resounded together, harmoniously blending alternate notes, so that they made a sort of jarring harmony of tones. They produced a prolonged tuneful even sound in which each somehow cancelled out the others' variations, thus creating a constant tone.[26]

The *Itinerarium* provides a vivid description of the role of military instruments in the Saracen army at the battle of Arsüf in September 1191, echoing the sentiments of numerous contemporary commentators:

> Certain people were assigned to go before the emirs sounding trumpets and clarions (*tubis clangentes et lituis*); others held horns (*buccinas*), others flutes, tamborines, rattles or cymbals, others had other instruments for making a noise. They were assigned the single task of raising shouts and horrible yells. The land all around resounded with the echo of their harsh cries and roaring noise. Even a thunder crash would not have been heard above the great uproar of trumpets and sounding horns. They had introduced this practice to arouse their courage and boldness: the louder the noise, the braver they became for the fight.[27]

The importance of military music in the Saracen army is evident from the bands maintained by senior officers, the size of which was determined by rank. At the upper end of the scale, the Sultan Baibars (d.1277) had a band of 68 performers: 20 trumpets, 4 reed-pipes or shawms, 4 drums and 40 kettledrums. Henry Farmer argues that the combination of trumpets, shawms and drums was the most enduring legacy of the European exposure to the Saracen martial instruments.[28] In Europe the combination of trumpets and *nakers* (small kettle-drums) is mentioned in literary sources from the early twelfth century; by the mid-thirteenth century this grouping was widespread and evidence emerges of trumpets performing in ensembles with shawms. Both of these uses suggest affinities with contemporaneous Near Eastern practice. The use of drums and cymbals in the Byzantine army before the time of the Crusades was mentioned above. The incorporation of percussive instruments into the Christian army during the crusades is attested by Jean de Joinville, who recounts that as Louis IX of France arrived at Damietta in Egypt on the ill-fated Seventh Crusade (1249–50) the decks of his galley resounded with the sound of *nacaires, tabours* and *cors sarrazinnois*.[29]

The Latin terms for trumpets and horns that were used in Classical times – *tuba, cornu, bucina* and *lituus* – were used by the chroniclers of the Crusades alongside the more modern term *trompe* to refer to the instruments employed in the Christian armies. Given the lack of iconographical evidence, it is difficult to determine the exact nature of the instruments denoted by these terms and it would be rash to equate the older words with their Roman equivalents. The terms may occasionally have been applied indiscriminately, but it still seems remotely plausible that metal trumpets deriving from the Roman *tuba* were among the instruments used by the Christians. On balance, however, it is more likely from the evidence available to us that Byzantine influence outweighed the continuation of Roman traditions in the former dominions of the Western Empire.

From about 1100, long cylindrical trumpets with small flaring bells, similar to those depicted as belonging to the Muslim armies, begin to appear in contemporary European illustrations, and by 1200 many aristocratic households of high aspiration employed a pair of trumpeters.[30] The religious symbolism that underpinned the trumpet's adoption in the Christian army may well have played a part in this resurgence of the trumpet in Europe at this time. To the crusaders, the trumpet was an aural and visual manifestation of the divine guidance afforded to their cause, and its association with the Day of Judgment and the Resurrection represented the promise of eternal life for those who died in defence of the Christian faith. In an age in which every aspect of earthly existence was viewed in terms of its relationship to the spiritual world, and temporal authority as ultimately deriving from God, the religious symbolism of the trumpet naturally resonated beyond the military spheres.

Cities were, if anything, often more ostentatious than royal and aristocratic courts in their ceremonial provision, possibly in a conscious effort to assert their sense of identity and importance. Eight trumpeters were employed in Bologna from 1286 onwards; in addition to signalling from towers, singly and in pairs, their duties may have included performing as an ensemble.[31] By the early thirteenth century Venice was prospering through its strategic position as a trading hub linking Western Europe, Byzantium and the East, and the scene was set for the spectacular civic processions and ceremonies that were to impress visitors for centuries to follow. In response to a papal proclamation for a crusade in 1198, a group of French noblemen entered into an agreement with the Venetian authorities for the provision of a fleet of ships. When the crusaders failed to pay the sum demanded for their transportation to the Holy Land, via Egypt, the Doge offered a moratorium on the debt in return for help in capturing the port of Zara in Dalmatia, which happened to be ruled by the King of Hungary, a fellow crusader. Robert of Clari described the scene as the fleet for the Fourth Crusade prepared to depart from Venice in October 1202. When the Doge appeared in his galley, 'there were four silver trumpets trumpeting before him and drums making a great noise', and as the fleet left the harbour, 'there were fully a hundred pairs of trumpets, of silver and of brass, all sounding at the departure, and so many drums and tabors and other instruments that it was a fair marvel'.[32] In 1229 the Doge agreed to pay for the manufacture of three silver trumpets for St Mark's, and during the second half of the thirteenth century there are reports that six silver trumpets featured in religious processions in the city.

Trumpeters were just as prominent in northern Europe cities. In Bruges, for example, wind instrumentalists were employed from the early fourteenth century onwards; their principal duty was to provide signals on the trumpet or horn from the city belfry, but from this early date they also fulfilled a wider musical and civic function. From 1315 they took part in the annual procession of the Holy Blood, and in 1331/2, along with four other musicians, they performed on trumpets, organs and fiddles at a banquet in the castle of Male.[33]

Big trumpets and small trumpets: **buisine** *and* **clarion***;* **trompe** *and* **trompette**

Illustrations from the thirteenth century depict straight metal trumpets of different sizes. Although many of these instruments do not readily lend themselves to a strict classification, two distinct forms of trumpet are discernible. One is the long straight instrument, the other a shorter, less ornate instrument, with a more pronounced bell flare.[34] Scribes began to differentiate between the two types of trumpet, which they often referred to side by side, and a range of terminology, some of which was geographically specific, was used to denote these pairings: *buisine* and *clarion*; *trompe* and *trompette*; *tubae* and *tubecta*; *trumpet* and *clarion*; and *trompa* and *anafil*. The etymology of these words suggests that in each of the couplings the second was the shorter of the two instruments, a hypothesis supported by the evolution of *buisine* and *clarion* into *posaune* and *clarino*. The records of the Goldsmiths' Company of London reveal that in 1391 (and up to the early sixteenth century) the clarions in their possession were a little over two-thirds the weight of their trumpets.[35] The sources provide few clues as to the contexts in which the different types of trumpets were utilised and whether the instruments of different length performed together. Although the terminology during this period is often ambiguous, one discernible tendency was for players of the longer instrument to outnumber those of the shorter variety. For example, in 1293 the King of Castile employed four *tromperos* and one *anafil*. The difficulty of reaching firm conclusions on such matters is exemplified by the reference to Edward III of England having five *trompettes* and two *clarions* in his service in 1348.

Both of these terms imply short trumpets, but Baines interprets the reference as denoting instruments of different length.[36] The following passage from a ballad telling of the defeat of the Scots at the battle of Halidon Hill by the English forces of Edward III in 1333 is typical of the manner in which different types of trumpets are referred to in literary works:

> This was done with merrie sowne
> With pipis, trompes and tabers thereto
> And loude clarionis thei blew also.[37]

The Late Middle Ages, 1375–1500

The fourteenth century saw the appearance of great literary works: Dante's *Divine Comedy* (*c.*1310), Boccaccio's *Decameron* (1353), and Chaucer's *Canterbury Tales* (1386). Music struck out in new directions. Details of the notational techniques that underpinned the increased expressive range of art music were explained by the poet-composer Philippe de Vitry in his treatise *Ars Nova* of 1322–23. The term *Ars Nova* came to represent the new music of the fourteenth century. A principal exponent of this new style of music in France was Guillaume de Machaut, who played a decisive role in the development of many of the principal secular and sacred forms.

A long-held view that instruments routinely participated in the performance of vocal polyphonic music during the fourteenth century, either doubling the vocal lines or performing the textless tenor and contratenor parts that exist in much of the repertory, now holds less currency. The prevailing view is that, with the possible exception of the organ, instruments were not used in liturgical performances until the fifteenth century, and then only on special occasions, and that the tenor and contratenor parts were conceived as untexted vocal lines.[38] The fourteenth century witnessed the emergence of the shawm band, or *alta cappella*. The tenor shawm, or bombard, appeared early in the century and was prominent by *c.*1375. By providing a tenor voice to the shawms, the bombard enabled the ensemble to mirror the development of vocal polyphony – the earlier wind repertory is believed to have been essentially monophonic. This process continued with the addition of a third instrumental part, the contratenor, to the shawm band from the final quarter of the fourteenth century onwards.[39] Contemporary reports of performances by shawm bands have led Polk to conclude that by about 1430 the repertoire of the most accomplished ensembles included 'sophisticated polyphony'.[40] There is evidence that by the latter part of the fifteenth century wind instrumentalists were drawing on the vocal repertory, both sacred and secular, for performing material. Whether this practice originated in the fourteenth century, however, remains a matter of conjecture.

Developments in trumpet design

Advances in metal-working techniques during the fourteenth century provided trumpet makers with the skills to bend narrow tubes and thereby construct instruments in a more compact form. By the final quarter of the century, long metal trumpets were being fashioned into an 's' shape, and by the early fifteenth century this design was refined to produce instruments in the twice-folded form which has endured to the present day. The recently discovered mid-fifteenth-century Guitbert trumpet (mentioned in Chapter 2) demonstrates these developments in trumpet design. Comprising seven detachable sections, it can be assembled either as an s-shaped or a folded instrument, with the first bow and bell section crossing each other diagonally.[41] Illustrations from this period sometimes depict straight, s-shaped and twice-folded trumpets side by side.

These developments coincided with a widening of the spheres in which trumpeters performed and a broadening of the instrument's musical and social functions. As the trumpet became increasingly prominent in courtly and civic settings, the trumpeter's role extended beyond providing ceremonial and military signals, and came to include performing for entertainment and for dancing. This provided the stimulus for players to explore the melodic potential of the instrument and laid the foundations for the cultivation of the trumpet ensemble as a musical entity. A separate development occurred with the integration of the trumpet into the shawm band.

The slide trumpet and the alta cappella

Details of the inclusion of a brass instrument in ensembles with shawms before the fifteenth century are sketchy. Polk suggests that the tradition originated in Germany during the second half of the fourteenth century and that the earliest brass instrument to be included with the shawm band may have been a straight trumpet, which perhaps possessed a simple slide mechanism. He suggests that the slide mechanism may have been a feature of the s-shaped and folded trumpets from their inception[42] (Ill. 3.3). It was in Germany, where the specific word for the form of trumpet that performed with shawms was *posaune*, that the earliest appearances of trumpets in wind ensembles are traceable. Payments to two shawmists and a *posaune* date from 1368 in Augsburg and 1363 in Dortmund.[43] In Italy the word *trombone* (literally 'big trumpet') was used from around 1439, and in England and France the term *sackbut* or *saquebote* appeared towards the end of the fifteenth century. The term for the brass player (and brass instrument) in the wind band at the Burgundian court was 'trompette des menestrel'. A 'menestrel de trompette' in the service of a German bishop is recorded in the Burgundian accounts for 1386,[44] and between 1411 and 1420 Hennequin Vander Pict is mentioned in the court records as both 'trompette des menestrel' and 'trompette de guerre'.[45] It is possible that John the Fearless employed a band of minstrels that included a trumpeter before his accession to the duchy in 1404. In 1398, as the Count of Nevers, he made a triumphal entry into Lille, preceded by 'three minstrels and a trumpet', and the Burgundian accounts for 1394 record a livery payment to '3 des menestreils ... et la trompette de mons. le conte de Nevers'.[46] Throughout the fifteenth century the 'trompettes des menestrel' were listed in court records alongside the members of the shawm band, and separate from the 'trompettes de guerre' or military trumpeters. By *c.*1430 archival records for courts and cities across Europe reveal a distinction between 'minstrel' trumpeters and ceremonial or military trumpeters.[47]

3.3 Slide trumpet performing with two shawms. Franco–Flemish miniature *c.*1460 (*B-Br* Ms 8, f. 33v). (By permission of the Bibliothèque Royale, Brussels)

Burgundy at this time became one of the most cosmopolitan and musically active courts in Europe. From the closing decades of the fourteenth century, and for most of the fifteenth, Burgundy also comprised Belgium, Lorraine, Luxembourg, the Netherlands and northeastern France. From the nominal capital, Dijon, the main centres of Burgundian court life peregrinated from Bruges to Brussels, Ghent and Lille. Secular use of the trumpet for court entertainments is certain: it is recorded that Burgundian courtiers in Ypres danced to 'chansons' played by trumpets in 1393, and in 1454 a Burgundian delegation to Stuttgart was entertained by a trumpeter who performed 'chansons a sa trompette'.[48] These comments are usually taken as evidence that players of the natural trumpet were exploring the higher harmonics of their instruments, the pitch area which became known later as the 'clarino' register, from the eighth to the twelfth harmonics and beyond.

The most influential composer associated with the Burgundian court was Guillaume Dufay. Dufay's celebrated Motet, *Nuper rosarum flores*, was first performed in 1436 for the consecration of Brunelleschi's new Duomo in Florence, while he was in the Pope's service. Reports exist of the presence of trumpeters at this ceremony. Whether they were there to supply the usual heraldry of such an important state occasion, or whether they participated more fully in the artistic side of the occasion, is uncertain.

Specific instrumental use in the fifteenth century must remain partly conjectural. Manuscripts almost never indicate a particular instrument, and only rarely whether a part is vocal or instrumental. Sometimes a part will have a player's name attached, but often the named musician was expert on more than one instrument. Pictorial and literary sources, however, point to trumpets participating in concerted music. Owing to the complexity of the treble vocal parts, and their limited range below the melodic area of the natural trumpet, there seems no alternative but to attach these pictured trumpets to the lower parts, and for this they must have been furnished with some device to raise and lower the pitch, most likely a single slide along the length of the mouthpipe.

That the slide trumpet became identified at an early date with instrumental tenor and contratenor parts is confirmed by the extraordinary manuscript collection of Zorzi Trombetta da Modon, dating from *c.*1445. As well as indicating the likelihood that trumpeters of the time were musically literate, it is the earliest written musical evidence we have for the participation of the trumpet in art music. Trombetta became leader of the civic wind ensemble in Venice, but earlier in his career he had been a trumpeter employed on a Venetian galley, which plied its trade between Italy, England and the Low Countries. Ships' trumpeters no doubt signalled more efficiently than the human voice in different weather conditions, including mist and fog, and perhaps provided music as light relief into the bargain. Zorzi Trombetta notated music he heard on his travels, and added his own contratenors, which show that, if he was notating them for his own use, which seems likely, he was capable of eliciting a full diatonic compass from his slide trumpet, as is shown by two of his contratenors to the tenor of *Puisque m'amour* by John Dunstable.[49]

The consensus that the brass instrument in the shawm band during this period was a single-slide trumpet was challenged in 1984 by Peter Downey, who suggested that the double-slide trombone was invented without any interim evolutionary, single-slide instrument.[50] Iconography has been crucial to this debate, with most commentators interpreting the downward playing position posture adopted by trumpeters in shawm bands as compatible with the manipulation of a single-slide instrument. Baines suggests that the 'claret-piece' referred to in several fifteenth- and sixteenth-century sources may have been a movable mouthpipe, the critical component of the slide trumpet.[51] However, alternative theories as to the nature of 'claret-piece' have been proposed. One is that it was a fixed length of tubing that lowered the pitch of the claret trumpet (described by Bendinelli as 'trombetta antiqua') for the performance of ensemble music down to that of the new Italian trumpet, which was introduced around the same time as the advent of the 'Italian style' of trumpet music (see below). Another explanation is that it may have been a mute.[52] While acknowledging that no single source proves the existence of the fifteenth-century single-slide trumpet, most scholars maintain that the various strands of evidence – iconographical, musical and archival – when considered together, overwhelmingly support the hypothesis that the instrument did exist.

Downey provides an example of how natural trumpets without slides could have provided a rudimentary bass to dance music. However, the evidence suggests that, by the mid-fifteenth century, wind instrumentalists were performing polyphonic music and, as noted above, that a brass instrument was identified with the contratenor part, which would have been unsuited to a natural trumpet. As Herbert Myers notes, 'the free mixture of trumpet with shawms makes sense only if its melodic capabilities were roughly equivalent to theirs. Such a trumpet must, therefore, have been equipped with some form of slide mechanism in order to fill in the larger intervals in the harmonic series.'[53] Downey's hypothesis implies a shift in the function of the brass instrument at some point from providing a drone bass to performing polyphony with the invention of the double slide. However, the consistency of the terminology used to denote the brass instrument in the shawm band from the late fourteenth century onwards suggests a continuity of its musical function. Several illustrations from the second and third quarters of the fifteenth century, which show a brass instrument with a trombone-like configuration in the company of shawms but lacking the necessary stays between the yards for a double-slide mechanism to function, provide a further pointer towards this evolutionary process and perhaps represent poorly illustrated depictions of early double-slide instruments.[54]

The fifteenth century was a period of transition in the evolution of brass instruments with slides. The terms *posaune* and *trombone* evolved by the century's last decades to mean the instruments with double slide, which concurs with modern usage. Confusingly, the use of different terms for slide trumpet in various languages lingered on, but almost certainly by the later fifteenth century, most descriptions refer to the instrument with double slide. The slide trumpet – illustrated as *Thurner Horn* by Sebastian Virdung in his *Musica getutscht* of 1511 – continued to exist as a functional instrument of tower watchmen throughout Europe, and of Stadtpfeifer in German lands. Whether use of a slide trumpet was continuous, or whether it was an obvious idea that kept being reinvented in various centres at different times, remains open to conjecture. Intermittent evidence of slide-trumpet use appears, notably in Leipzig (*tromba da tirarsi*) and London (*flat* trumpet), in the seventeenth and eighteenth centuries.

Demarcation between 'soft' (*bas*) and 'loud' (*haut*), quite clear in 1400, relaxed during the course of the fifteenth century. As the distinctions between 'soft' and 'loud' instruments became blurred, contrasting groupings became more common, and by the end of the century, loud and soft instrumentalists interacted freely in both ecclesiastical and secular contexts. By this time, the double-slide had clearly evolved, and the trombone was established within the family of brass instruments. The increasing freedom brought by the relaxation of 'soft'–'loud' demarcations prepared European music for greater sophistication in dynamic contrast and in variety of timbre and texture. These elements were exploited more fully in instrumental music as the sixteenth century proceeded. In the sixteenth century there existed a critical mass of players of instruments of the trumpet family in relatively secure positions at court who transcended their time-honoured association with war. Composers had jumped from anonymity to recognition and the names of trumpeters now become known to us. Don Smithers lists thirty-one (four of whom are styled 'Claretter'), who served at the Imperial court at Innsbruck between 1490 and 1519.[55] From among these players and others like them, throughout the courts and cities of Europe, there occurred a quantum leap in the playing style and technical capacity of the natural trumpet. A schooled technique of playing the trumpet melodically in the high register, which could be taught and learnt, came into being.

The number of trumpets required to put on a dignified show remained stable at two for most of the fourteenth century. By around 1400, however, the elected Holy Roman Emperor, Ruprecht von Wittelsbach, employed six, and throughout the fifteenth century numbers escalated, until in 1500 the Emperor Maximilian I employed an imposing twelve trumpets with timpani. Württemberg and Ferrara followed suit with twelve, Brandenburg and Mantua with ten, Bavaria and Count Palatine with nine. The city of Florence had possessed six trumpets and six *trombadori* since 1400. By 1500, the bishopric of Cologne employed eight trumpets, and that of Utrecht four trumpets and four 'claroenen'.[56] For most of the fifteenth century the sole instrumentalist employed in Barcelona was a trumpeter (*trompeta*), whose responsibilities included hiring additional trumpeters and drummers for important ceremonial occasions. For the Corpus Christi processions, which were organised by the civic and religious authorities (as in many European cities), ten trumpeters were normally employed, but for other events up to twenty were occasionally recruited. The charter of 1459 relating to the brotherhood formed by the trumpeters of Barcelona provides a valuable insight into their role in the Corpus Christi celebrations: on the day before the feast they were to meet at the city trumpeter's house 'at 12 noon or earlier . . . to temper, tune and put their trumpets and other instruments in order'.[57] In Bruges, where a maximum of four trumpeters were employed by the civic authorities, eighty trumpeters and six *claroenen* are recorded by the city chronicler as taking part in the procession for the entry of Philip the Good in 1440.[58]

The developments in trumpet manufacture that led to the advent of s-shaped and folded trumpets did not mark the instant demise of straight trumpets. Throughout much of Europe during the fifteenth century, and in certain places for even longer, straight trumpets of various sizes retained their ceremonial function. Illustrations of Venetian processions up to the seventeenth century show medium-length straight trumpets alongside instruments of the folded variety. A notable feature of the straight Venetian instrument, which also appears in military and naval contexts, is the unusually wide bell section, which appears to have comprised a separate conical segment. It has been suggested that this was the *tromba squarciata*, referred to in various Venetian sources of the sixteenth and seventeenth centuries, and mentioned by a contemporary chronicler in association with the performance of Claudio Monteverdi's 'Mass of Thanksgiving' in 1631.[59] Venetian illustrations of civic processions also depict long straight trumpets, often termed *trombe lunghe* or *trombe d'argento*. These instruments vary in length, but are usually considerably longer than the standard instruments of

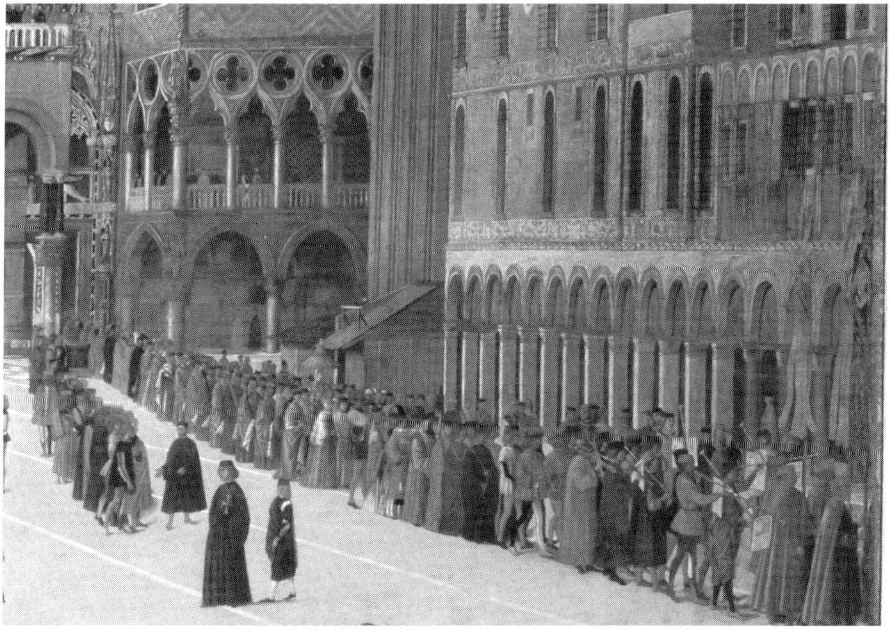

3.4 Venetian trumpeters in *Procession in St Mark's Square* by Gentile Bellini, 1496. (By permission of the Ministero per I Beni e le Attività Culturali, Venice)

approximately eight feet and required the assistance of boys, on whose shoulders they rested as the procession progressed (Ill. 3.4).

During the fifteenth century, trumpeters routinely participated in religious processions, particularly those associated with the Corpus Christi celebration, and there is evidence that in certain places instrumentalists, including trumpeters, were occasionally called upon to perform in church. The inclusion of trumpeters in an annual religious procession in Bruges from the early fourteenth century onwards was noted above. In the following century the trumpeters of Bruges also took part in processions organised by the principal churches in the city.[60] Many of the contemporary accounts that appear to allude to the sounding of trumpets in church are problematic, since it is often impossible to determine whether or not the trumpeters were performing during the service and, when other wind instruments are also mentioned, whether the reference is to the natural trumpet or a brass instrument of the shawm band. Several references are sufficiently explicit, however, to confirm that on occasions trumpeters did sound in church. One such occasion was the Mass performed in April 1475 to celebrate the league of mutual defence between Burgundy and Milan. A contemporary writer described how Charles the Bold 'came to church dressed in a rich, long robe of gold cloth. . . . After Mass was said . . . the trumpets, which were eight, started to play, then the pipers, of which there were many. Having heard two more Masses, he went to his pavilion.'[61] When trumpets sounded during Mass, it was normally at the elevation of the host. Philippe de Mézières, in a text advising Charles VI of France which instruments might be used in church, sanctioned the sounding of trumpets ('grosses trompes sacrées') at this point in the service.[62] At the wedding of Giangaleazzo

Sforza and Isabella d'Aragona in Milan in 1489, the procession to the Duomo included 'all of the trumpets and wind players of the duke, as well as of other potentates, who went playing all the way to the platform, under which there was a stand where they went to play their instruments during the Mass and the wedding'. After the raising of the host, 'with the greatest sound of all the trumpets and a most beautiful melody from the singers, the Mass proceeded to the end, after which they sang *Te Deum laudamus*'.[63]

Musical instruments featured prominently in the sacred dramas that were a feature of civic life throughout much of Europe during the late Middle Ages. Trumpets sounded to announce the start of the presentation, and performed along with other loud instruments in the processions that preceded the drama. During the performance they were used for representations of royal entries and battles, and in scenes depicting the Last Judgment or the Apocalypse.[64]

If the music that trumpeters played before the second half of the sixteenth century was written down, it has disappeared. A descriptive chanson by Clément Janequin, *La Guerre*, believed to have been composed to celebrate the Battle of Marignano in 1515, includes imitations of trumpet music (Ex. 3.1). Our encounter with Zorzi Trombetta earlier in the chapter shows that it is not safe to assume that trumpet players were illiterate, but it is probable that they committed their repertory to memory and transmitted it aurally to their pupils, given the mobility of their performing context, often on horseback, and the itinerant nature of the courts which employed them. Maximilian I travelled constantly in pursuit of imperial policy and his twelve trumpets served as a constant reminder of his ultimate authority over lesser authorities. The contemporary series of engravings, *The Triumph of Maximilian I*, dramatises this function of the ceremonial use of trumpets and kettledrums to inspire awe. The trumpet troop portrayed numbers twenty-five with five drums, probably an exaggeration of normal practice, but not beyond Maximilian's purse.[65] The livery of such musicians was of the finest quality, and no aristocrat aspiring to the status of a Renaissance prince or princess could afford to be without such a symbol of prestige. Many composed and performed: musical accomplishment was evidence of a highly cultured disposition. Henry VIII, the archetypal Renaissance prince, was a talented composer who played many instruments, and at his accession in 1509 sixteen trumpeters performed in the service.[66] Between 1521 and 1525 he supplemented his contingent of loud instrumentalists with 'six new sackbuts' (players of shawms and sackbuts) from Italy.[67] The retinue of his father, Henry VII, interestingly included a black trumpeter, pictured here in the middle of a trio of s-shaped trumpets at a tournament held at Westminster in 1511 to celebrate the birth of Prince Henry (Ill. 3.5).[68] In Scotland, several groups of Italian minstrels were recruited from Bologna for the wedding of James IV to Margaret Tudor, daughter of Henry VII, in 1503. One of these, a shawm band that included a 'draucht' (lit: drawn) trumpet, was retained as the sole instrumental ensemble in Scots royal service throughout the sixteenth century. Its members also served as trumpeters, individually and in pairs, and occasionally fulfilled non-musical duties at court.[69] This may have been a necessary expediency at small courts, but a tradition of multi-tasking instrumentalists, many of whom were Italian, doubling on a variety of wind instruments and fulfilling trumpeting duties, prevailed at many of the larger German courts and at the Danish royal court during the sixteenth century.[70]

Ex. 3.1 Imitation of trumpet music in Clément Janequin's chanson *La Guerre* (Paris, 1529).

Written evidence of trumpet music has come down to us from the last decades of the sixteenth century, both in keyboard music, and in the form of handwritten aide-mémoires. This is discussed later. For the moment, another soprano instrument with the capability of meeting the demands of the emerging styles of art music in the Renaissance was in the ascendancy – the cornett.

The cornett

The cornett rose to prominence by the second half of the fifteenth century. It evolved from simple instruments made from hollowed animal horn with added finger holes, an idea common to many parts of the world. It had two final forms: straight, used

3.5 The English royal trumpet corps, from the Great Tournament Roll of Westminster. (By permission of the College of Arms)

mainly in German lands, and curved. It was conical, narrow-bore, its outer profile normally octagonal, and it was made of ivory, or more commonly and later, from wood covered with leather, with six finger holes above, and a thumbhole below. The fingering was similar to that of the recorder, and the detachable mouthpiece so tiny, like an acorn cup, that it is normally depicted played from the side of the mouth, where the lips are thinner. A variant of the straight form became common in the sixteenth century – the mute cornett, which had an integral mouthpiece turned directly into the playing end of the instrument, an idea which resurfaced in David Monette's innovatory trumpet design towards the end of the twentieth century. The cornett was renowned for its soft, sweet quality of sound, as modern-day players such as Bruce Dickey, Jeremy West and Jean Tubery have confirmed. The cornett owes its acceptance into sacred art music to the biblical imagery of King David's psalms. King David was invariably accompanied by four Levite musicians, one of whom, Ethan, played the *shofar*.[71]

The cornett emerged as the most important and most widely used wind instrument in the soprano range by around 1500, when virtuosos such as Augustein Schubinger travelled far and wide playing the instrument. He performed, not in the outdoor 'loud music' contexts of wind instruments, which had been usual until then, but in a liturgical setting playing sacred art music, as a soloist on an equal footing with singers.[72] The rise of the cornett was contemporaneous with reports testifying to developments in trumpet technique which led to greater control of the *clarino* register. The prevalent style of composition in art music at this time was not yet suitable, however, for the strong primary colour of the trumpet, which continued nevertheless to flourish in its role as an instrument of state and of international diplomacy. In addition, the polyphony of the period demanded equality in part writing, an equality that the natural trumpet could not achieve owing to the restrictions of its melodic idiom, based as it was on the gapped nature of the harmonic series. The trumpet therefore could only take part in concerted music where other members of the ensemble imitated it, and there do exist examples of vocal and instrumental music from this and earlier periods where trumpet calls are imitated. These are alluded to elsewhere in these pages, although it must be repeated that there is no conclusive evidence that trumpets took part in music of this type until they were specifically called for in the seventeenth century.

Cornetts and trombones

The development of cornett technique, and the high levels of satisfaction with its musical qualities among composers and performers, meant that there was no need at this time for subtle refinement of trumpet technique in order to allow the trumpet to participate in art music. After all, the early trombone, which came to partner the cornett, had only recently diverged from the trumpet, and in many contemporary minds, as can be seen from the confused terminology of the period, it was still some form of slide trumpet. The trombone, as a form of trumpet, lent importance and dignity through association. To ensembles in which it took part, its sonority added a foundation of weight and majesty, which befitted occasions requiring solemnity. Owing to its low tessitura and narrow bore, with tubing and a bell no wider than that of a trumpet, the trombone, in resonant acoustics which favoured the projection of higher frequencies, managed to invoke profundity without overbalancing other voices. The double-slide trombone possessed a modal agility impossible on the natural trumpet. The trumpet's natural habitat in the sixteenth century remained the trumpet band.

The fact that the tone of the cornett was sometimes indistinguishable from the human voice in the vocal style prevalent in the Renaissance was regarded as an asset, and it was lauded for its vocal qualities from its beginnings until its obsolescence. In his description of the musical practices at Durham Cathedral in the 1670s, Roger North singled out the cornett for praise, even though he attributed its endurance there to the lack of upper parts in the choir: 'the cornet (being well sounded) . . . one might mistake for a choice eunuch'.[73] The demarcation line between vocal and instrumental music remained blurred during the sixteenth century, and there was no perceived need to specify whether a part, or even a whole piece, was to be sung or played. In this ambivalent context, the cornett was ideal. In the right hands, it possessed the flexibility to merge and blend in the low to middle register, while projecting brightly in the upper range.

The Renaissance

In the Renaissance it was the cornett, and not the trumpet, that participated most fully with other instruments and singers. The trumpet, in sometimes impressively large numbers, was active in courtly and military circles. Allusions in keyboard music, and actual written-down trumpet music towards the end of the period, point to a splendid and stirring repertory of fanfares of varying levels of sophistication. In addition, there is evidence of a steady development in the use of the 'clarino' register, which was to gather momentum and reach maturity in the baroque period.

The Renaissance, literally 'rebirth' in French, used in the sense we understand it now, was first defined by the French historian Jules Michelet in 1855, and popularised in the nineteenth century by the Swiss historian Jacob Burckhardt in his publication *The Civilization of the Renaissance in Italy* (1860), a description of the remarkable flowering of the arts which began in Italy and spread throughout Europe in the period from approximately 1400 to 1600.[74] Music underwent rapid change, though at different rates in different countries. New styles of music brought new instruments like the cornett and trombone into fashion, though, as has been stated earlier, developments in instrument manufacture and playing technique came as a consequence of changing compositional trends. The Renaissance, however, in so far as it concerned music, was more a way of thinking, and a set of attitudes and tendencies rather than a drastic new way of composing. The spirit of the Renaissance, first signalled as early as the eleventh century, involved the growth of humanism, a movement accompanying widespread revival of the learning of ancient Greek and Roman culture. Contemporary commentators like Giorgio Vasari spoke of the arts moving towards 'perfection'.[75] Although it was a commonly held view of the time, most eloquently expressed by the religious leader Bernardo Cirillo (though with no knowledge of ancient music with which to make any sort of informed judgement), that current musical composition was inferior to that of the ancients, musical practitioners, including Gioseffo Zarlino, pointed to the achievements of composers such as Adrian Willaert as heralding a new golden age worthy of comparison. Willaert became the maestro di cappella at St Mark's in Venice and was the teacher of Andrea Gabrieli. St Mark's was perceived as the most prestigious, if not the most prominent musical centre in Italy. During Willaert's tenure that reputation was enhanced and then perpetuated by his successors Cipriano di Rore and Zarlino. That such distinguished composers as Andrea Gabrieli and his nephew Giovanni held in succession the position of organist, and were only part of a stable of prominent performer/composers, demonstrates the high quality of work at St Mark's.

In the previous century, however, from 1450 to 1550,The dominant force in music was provided by the northern composers from France, Flanders and the Netherlands such as Johannes Ockeghem, Jacob Obrecht, Heinrich Isaac and Josquin des Prez. These composers, Willaert included, travelled widely, creating a north–south flow of ideas. An international style of composition, though with regional and individual variation, evolved through this exchange. The cornett saw a corresponding north–south interflow through the widely travelled careers of musicians like Augustein Schubinger, who journeyed between Germany and Italy, and the Low Countries and Spain, in the service of Maximilian I.

This intercourse of ideas coincided in the common currency of *musica reservata*, an expressive style that coalesced in the middle of the sixteenth century, but was already evident much earlier, though without any label attached to it, in the work of Josquin. 'Reserved' initially for the select circles of literati who first appreciated it, the style was more emotionally extrovert than what had gone before in the setting of words to music, and came to pervade most forms of composition. Features of the style were 'chromaticism, modal variety, ornaments, and extreme contrasts of rhythm and texture'.[76]

The cornett excelled and flourished in this extended musical language. Although it seldom took part in *musica secreta*, the most exclusive form of courtly chamber music, it was an indispensable component of civic, court and ecclesiastical public ceremonies.[77] Part of the required competences of the cornett virtuoso included the ability to improvise. The earliest solo instrumental compositions, such as the prelude, preambulum, fantasia and ricercare, resemble extemporisations. In ensemble music, the terms *ricercare, sonata, canzona* initially denoted loosely organised material with an improvisatory feel. Improvisation was integral to music making in the sixteenth century; melodic lines were ornamented, or subjected to the technique of 'division'. Performers would have needed to be able to embellish one or more contrapuntal lines to a given melody. Playing for dancing would have been one of the functions of every court musician. Dance music, like the *basse dance*, the courtly dance of the late fifteenth and early sixteenth centuries, was performed by improvising over a fixed tenor. The extent to which musical occasions were enlivened by sparkling displays of cornett virtuosity can be gauged by the examples of divisions from the treatise of Dalla Casa.[78] It is significant that the first salaried musicians had only been employed at St Mark's from the previous year, perhaps prompted by Andrea Gabrieli's experience of the standards achieved at the Bavarian court, which by that time was at its zenith, with sixty musicians in regular employment.[79]

The Bavarian court of Dukes Albrecht V and Wilhelm V at Munich

Though international styles of music were highly important in the sixteenth century, national and regional variety ensured the proliferation of diversity throughout Europe. Orlande de Lassus became one of the most celebrated composers internationally. He settled at the Munich court of the lavish musical patron, Duke Albrecht V of Bavaria, in 1556, became Hofkapellmeister in 1563, and continued under his successor Wilhelm V from 1579 until his death. Lassus was a polyglot who had spent much of his youth in Italy, spoke Italian by preference, and oversaw a gradual metamorphosis of the music at court from a Netherlands base to a pronounced Italianate character. Quite a few musicians and composers who were later active in Venice came under Lassus's influence in Munich: Andrea Gabrieli went to work at the Bavarian court in the early 1560s; his nephew Giovanni from the mid-1570s to the early 80s; others included composer Gioseffo Guami, his trombonist brother Francesco, and cornettist Francesco Laudis.[80] Bendinelli, who has left us most of what we know about the practice of late-Renaissance trumpet playing, became chief court trumpeter during the latter part of his tenure, probably coincidental with part of Giovanni Gabrieli's period of residence. The orchestra at this establishment was large, and had been important since the time of Albrecht IV at the turn of the century. Successive Dukes of Bavaria commissioned musical manuscripts, which were also lavish works of art. These provide evidence of some of the musical practices at court. In an illustration by Hans Mielich of the Bavarian Court Chapel, contained in a manuscript (1563–70) of Lassus's two-volume choir book of the Penitential Psalms, three choirboys, about twenty singers, and fifteen instrumentalists, including two cornetts (one of which was straight – perhaps a mute cornett), and a bass trombone, are directed by Lassus at the keyboard, with Albrecht V himself standing attentively to one side. Another folio, containing Lassus's setting of 'Domine, labia' from Psalm 50, is adorned with images of a choral service in the Chapel of St George, in which at least twenty trumpets are shown raised to the sky (Ill. 3.6). What could they be playing? Is it too much of a coincidence that the setting of the words 'Domine, labia mea aperies' ('O Lord, thou wilt open my lips') in the Discantus, on the same page, alternates between notes a fifth apart, entirely playable on a natural trumpet pitched in A, rising to a minor third (the seventh harmonic) above the upper of these two notes on the final word 'aperies'?[81]

Accounts of the wedding of Albrecht's son, later Wilhelm V, to Renata of Lorraine, in 1568, chronicled by the Neapolitan singer and composer, Massimo Troiano, give us a good indication of the constant presence of the sound of trumpets, trombones and cornetts in the daily ceremonials of court.[82] The wedding festivities, which lasted two weeks, saw the combined forces of town musicians, ducal trumpeters, and wind players in the service of important guests playing together in a band of over one hundred strong. When Renata entered the city, trumpets, horns and drums played for half an hour. Trumpets and cymbals welcomed her outside church before Mass, mixed groups of wind announced arrivals, departures, punctuated proceedings during hunting parties, tournaments, and proffered 'good-night' and 'good morning' to the bride and groom on their wedding night. *Tromboni* – cornetts and trombones – directed by Lassus, accompanied eating at banquets, and we know some of the music they played on 22 February 1568 – a *Battaglia a 8* of Annibale Padovano (sometime organist at St Mark's), a seven-part motet of Lassus, and a madrigal by Alessandro Striggio. Later in the banquet, they joined forces with strings to play some twelve-part music by Padovano. In between times, trumpets and drums announced the arrival of each new course. For the dance that inevitably followed, the Duke's *tromboni* played, and probably trumpets too – mention is made of a *ballo alla tedesca* with twelve *trombette et taballi*. Humour was not absent. To great after-dinner hilarity, trumpets accompanied slapstick on the jousting field, playing, 'in highly discordant style a bumbling *aria alla tedesca* as a joking reference to the two fallen horsemen'. Later, 'in jest ... two trumpeters gave a clumsy rendition of *La bella franceschina*'.[83] Lassus himself was not averse to participating in satirical entertainment and probably encouraged this early manifestation of the capabilities of brass to elicit hilarity.

Although Cesare Bendinelli reportedly did not come to Munich as chief court trumpeter until 1580, in the year that Wilhelm, the bridegroom of 1568, succeeded his father, these events and the music played must have still been fresh in the memory of those at the court. When, towards the end of his life, Bendinelli wrote *Tutta l'arte della trombetta* (1614), he included the same *La bella franceschina* in an adaptation for

3.6 Trumpeters in the orchestra of the Bavarian Court of Albrecht V directed by Orlande de Lassus, from the Mielen Codex. (By permission of the Bayerische Staatsbibliothek, Munich)

trumpets. Bendinelli continued the tradition of brass-playing horseplay at the wedding festivities of Ludwig, Count of Leuchtenberg, in 1584, composing a sonata exploiting not uncommon musicianly behavioural patterns:

> The player of the clarino part is required to hold a large glass of wine in his hand, and every time he stops playing he has to drink a little, until the sonata is over; then the other trumpeters also drink, to imitate the text of the song.[84]

Notwithstanding the above, trumpets were becoming more prominent in serious musical contexts, a fact which may have had much to do with Bendinelli. In 1587, Duke Wilhelm asked Bendinelli to arrange for trumpets *Fit porta Christi* from Lassus's *Hymnarium* (1580–1), usually sung on Christmas Day after Vespers.[85] This acceptance of the trumpet to herald such an important moment in the Christian calendar had widespread influence. In addition to Bendinelli's *Tutta l'arte,* only two further manuscripts of trumpeters survive from this period – that of Magnus Thomsen (notated 1596–1609), and that of Hendrich Lübeck (1598), German trumpeters active at the Danish court. Both notebooks contain, significantly, their own versions of *Fit porta Christi.*[86]

These three manuscripts, which comprise military signals and ensemble repertory, provide the only substantive written evidence we have of late-Renaissance trumpet music, but it is widely accepted that they represent the summation of practices which had been evolving in civic and courtly trumpet bands since the period of their great expansion in numbers 150 years earlier. The ensemble pieces in these manuscripts are mostly notated as a single melodic line (*Principal*), from which the players improvised additional parts according to recognised formulae. Bendinelli provides examples of how these pieces were constructed and performed. Girolamo Fantini provides additional information relating to their performance in his printed trumpet method of 1638, as does Michael Praetorius in volume three of his *Syntagma Musicum* of 1619.[87]

Bendinelli's trumpet ensemble consisted of five players, or multiples thereof. The melody, *sonata* (also termed *principal* or *quinta*), was in the second voice, with a range of C4 to C5. Above that, the *clarino* improvised a descant, between C5 and A5. Below it, the third voice, the *alto e basso*, followed the *sonata* in parallel, one harmonic down the chain. The fourth, the *vulgano*, and the fifth part, the *basso* or *grob*, played a rhythmic drone of a perfect fifth on G3 and C3. An optional sixth part, the *fladdergrob*, sounded the fundamental, C2. This heroically simple formula provided the foundation for the major trumpet composition of Bendinelli's period, the *sonata*, which shared this nomenclature with the principal voice of the ensemble. Downey explains the manner of performance as follows. Before playing the *sonata* proper, an *intrada* was sounded. The *sonata* itself fell into eight-bar sections, or 'posts', which gathered rhythmic momentum as the piece unfolded. An energetic *rotta*, a piece mainly of rhythmic interest with simple triadic melody, during which the *clarino* rested, followed this, and the *intrada* was repeated to round off the performance.[88] The manuscripts by Thomsen and Bendinelli also include two new military signals, set one harmonic higher than the others. Downey identifies the ensemble pieces and the new military signals contained in these sources as trumpet music in the 'Italian style'. The Italian style was cultivated at northern Italian courts during the late fifteenth century and disseminated throughout much of the German-speaking world during the course of the sixteenth century by Italian trumpeters working there.[89]

The *toccata*, as in the exuberant example sounded before Monteverdi's opera *Orfeo* (1607), was a shorter form of trumpet flourish. The keyboard *toccatas* of another St Mark's organist, Claudio Merulo, are similarly improvisatory in nature. The English variant, 'tucket', was used in stage directions of the Shakespearean period to denote a trumpet flourish,[90] and the line from *Henry V*, Act IV, Scene ii gives some idea of the ubiquitous use of trumpets: 'Then let The Trumpets sound The Tucket Sonuance, and the Note to mount'. In 1591, William Byrd wrote down the closest we will probably ever get to realising what a Shakespearean 'Tucket Sonuance' sounded like in 'The Trumpitts' from his descriptive piece *The Battle*, which is contained in his keyboard manuscript, *My Ladye Nevells Booke*. It seems that the innovations of Bendinelli had not yet reached London from Munich, as this imitation of trumpets does not venture into the 'clarino' register, the upper limit of the tessitura being the eighth-harmonic C5.[91]

The *Aufzüg* was a processional fanfare originating in the last quarter of the sixteenth century.[92] It was a more modern conception, with the melody in the first voice, the *clarino*, and was to endure as a form of trumpet composition until the middle of the nineteenth century. Bendinelli's deployment of the trumpet band in a sacred context was to have profound consequences in the baroque period which followed. As early as 1618, Michael Praetorius set *In dulci jubilo*, interestingly for the same Christmas context as Bendinelli's arrangement of *Fit porta Christi* in 1581. He added a sixth part, referring to the parts, from the top down, as two *Clarien, Prinzipal, Alter Bass, Volgan,* and *Grob*, representing a development close to Bendinell's usage.[93] When J. S. Bach came to use trumpets, these names for the upper three voices of the trumpet ensemble were still in use, and he took this nomenclature for his customary three trumpets.

The politics of the Church and developments in the liturgy had profound effects on the acceptance of trumpet playing in Christian worship. The Reformation in the sixteenth century had led to a drastic simplification of musical patterns of worship in certain Protestant churches. The Lutheran chorale first appeared in 1524, and the French (1562), English (1562), Scottish (1564), and Dutch (1566) Psalters slightly later. This simple, chordal, diatonic style was to favour the use of trumpets, which are ideal for the clear and penetrating delineation of simple phrases, in later church music. Samuel Scheidt, an early devotee of the chorale, gave a foretaste of the running trumpet part-writing to come in his 1620 setting of *In Dulci Jubilo* (see Ex. 6.1, page 140). Scheidt also composed the scintillating four-part *Canzon cornetto* in the following year, showing that in some musical centres the cornett was still thriving.

St Mark's in Venice

The example of the musical forces employed by the opulent Bavarian court must have influenced all those who experienced it. After both Andrea and Giovanni Gabrieli returned to Venice, there was a movement towards the assembly of similar instrumental forces to which they had had access in Munich. The ascent of Venice to even greater glories coincided with the relative decline of Munich. Music at the Bavarian court declined owing to several factors, not least the death of Lassus. Perhaps the most important reason, however, was economic austerity in Munich during the later Counter-Reformation, which led to redundancies and pay cuts among the salaried court musicians. In addition, less musical ostentation became normal for establishments affected strongly by the Counter-Reformation. A more sober, severe, yet serene type of music became the norm – the *stile antico* or *stile grave* in which Palestrina and his Spanish contemporary, Victoria, were pre-eminent. Venice benefited directly from Munich's decline, as many Italian musicians, referred to earlier in the chapter, found their way to employment in Venice after service in Munich. In the meantime, Venice became the mecca for composers, with Giovanni Gabrieli supplanting Lassus as the most sought-after teacher in Europe.

The trumpet, however, probably benefited from this decline in musical forces in Munich. Indications of the trumpet beginning to invade musical territory previously inhabited by the cornett are evident in Munich possibly earlier than anywhere else. Perhaps this shift in use was partly fuelled by economic necessity. Bendinelli was a talented multi-instrumentalist whose expertise stretched to trombone as well as trumpet. As is evident from his treatise, during his tenure in Munich he had developed a system of acquiring the skills necessary for the subtle art of *clarino* playing. This gave the trumpet access to a greater diversity of playing contexts and presaged its widespread acceptance into art music in the following century. It is fair to assume that

Bendinelli's didactic inclination manifested itself during his long tenure in Munich and that his colleagues' skills benefited from his example and erudition. Given the influential status of the Bavarian court under both Dukes Albrecht V and Wilhelm V, Bendinelli's innovations would have come under close scrutiny in other cultural centres.

The posthumous legacy of Gabrieli in instrumental music: Germany

The instrumental music of Giovanni Gabrieli marks a high point in the use of brass instruments. It represents a peak of technical and expressive accomplishment. Stylistically, the music bridges two centuries, demonstrating in microcosm that changes in musical style are gradual and complex. In this body of works, late-Renaissance practices coexist side by side with facets of early baroque style. The posthumous collection of *Canzone e Sonate* (1615) is an experiment in sound and instrumental colour poured into a genre Gabrieli inherited from a previous century. When Gabrieli died, he had no successor in purely instrumental music in Italy. He was quickly forgotten as a composer, and his music became old-fashioned and neglected as the new baroque style took hold. Only north of the Alps did Gabrieli's seed – his vision of concerted instrumental music as high art – take root, with further development in the works of composers such as Johann Hermann Schein, Heinrich Schütz and Christoph Strauss.

In the first half of the seventeenth century the cornett and trumpet coexisted as distinct instrumental entities, before becoming practically interchangeable after the middle of the century. Thereafter, they exchanged positions of relative importance, before use of the cornett declined to a residual and marginal fringe, before it became virtually extinct or existed only as a rare curiosity in most musical centres by the eighteenth century.

It is interesting to speculate whether the development of the natural trumpet in art music had been arrested in the sixteenth century by the superior capabilities of the cornett. Use of the trumpet came into its own in a new period of much sharper definition and contrast between voices and instruments, and between instruments themselves, which began to unfold as the seventeenth century progressed. The style of music, with a strong harmonic structure grounded in the bass, below a clear melody line, came to be classified as belonging to a period of music termed 'baroque' by later commentators. It was during the rise of this baroque period that strong instrumental flavours came into vogue, parallel to a liberated solo vocal repertory. The more dominant characteristics of instruments like the trumpet and the violin came to be preferred to the more intimate voice of the cornett or viol. The trumpet by temperament was more suited to the concept of taking an instrumental solo, or being a foil to voices; the cornett to playing in ensemble or merging with voices. Although either instrument was actually capable of both in the right hands, the roles became sharply defined with time. At the dawn of the seventeenth century the capabilities of the trumpet, as developed in the courts of Europe in the sixteenth century, were ripe for exploitation by composers. The baroque era was to become a golden age for the trumpet.

Chapter 4

The art of the trumpet player in the seventeenth and eighteenth centuries

The development of the trumpet in the seventeenth through to the early nineteenth century was affected by many interlinked factors of which three are prominent: societal change, evolutions in musical style, and developing technology. These changes, evolutions and developments happened on different, though overlapping time scales. Changes in fashion are constant, but superficial – deeper societal change is slower moving and often happens within a longer time frame than centuries. The daily culture of ordinary people – their behaviour and habits – is deeply ingrained and impervious to passing trends. The new ideas and philosophies of the Renaissance and the Reformation – essentially the idea of individuality and the inviolable right of that individual to autonomy of thought and action – did not really work through to political systems capable of delivering some of those ideals until after the Enlightenment of the eighteenth century, and to varying forms of universal suffrage during the following two or more centuries.

The chapter starts with an overview discussion of the period. Some of the argument challenges previously held opinions concerning the position of the trumpet during this period. The notion that the trumpet experienced a serious decline after the 'golden age' of the baroque is discussed and found not to reflect actuality. The presumption that the imperial privileges dictated the behaviour of trumpet players in this period is also shown to be a generalisation that did not always reflect local experience. The development of the trumpet had much to do with differing national and regional situations within a common European experience. The pace of change in the development and evolution of the trumpet matches only coincidentally what have become known as the baroque and classical periods; essentially, for the purposes of this history, 'baroque' and 'classical' have to be seen as terms of convenience used to describe a historical overview of what was in fact a wide diversity of musical composition.

'Baroque', as a term applied to music, came into general use from the 1920s onwards, and was borrowed from the terminology of nineteenth-century art historians. Originally a pejorative term, meaning 'bizarre' or 'outrageously ostentatious', when applied to music it came to encapsulate the shared values of a period extending from around 1600 to 1750. At both ends of this time scale there is an overlap. Some authorities tend to place the starting date of the baroque later, *c.*1620, while others place the beginnings of the classical, and end of the baroque earlier, *c.*1730. Half-century subdivisions into early, middle and late baroque are commonplace,[1] though various authorities adjust these to suit varying historical perspectives. 'Classical', the term usually applied to music of the period extending from around 1750 to 1825, came into general use around the same time as 'baroque' to describe the era when abstract music took on new forms and the musical structures of sonata, concerto and symphony developed to become a source of powerful and individual expression.

Handel, considered a quintessentially baroque composer, was still active in the 1750s, died in 1759, and was still alive in the spirit of his English imitators for half a century after. Weber, considered an early romantic, was active in the early 1800s, and fitted his career into what has been traditionally considered the classical period before dying in 1826, ahead of Beethoven. In fact, there is a strong case for considering Beethoven the first great romantic. If the form was classical, the content, inspiration and motivation were certainly not.

The first specific deployment of the trumpet in printed musical sources was in the early seventeenth century. The toccata for five trumpets which preceded Claudio Monteverdi's opera *Orfeo* in 1607 (Ex. 4.1) can be regarded as an elaborate version of the type of introductory flourish that would have been customarily played at any important occasion by the court trumpeters of the Duke of Mantua. Trumpets were almost certainly used previous to this in different forms of dramatic presentation involving music. However, the act of writing it down and publishing it made this short flourish something of a milestone, and ensured wider dissemination. *Orfeo* signified current use and signalled future usage of the trumpet as a melody instrument of heroic character in secular music. In contemporary sacred music, works like the *Gaudium Christianum* (1617) of Michael Altenburg showed the function of the trumpet to underline the imperial association with God's power.[2] This sacred use had probably originated in the court of Albrecht V at Munich during the time of Lassus and his court trumpeter, Cesare Bendinelli, as discussed in the previous chapter.

Ex. 4.1 Claudio Monteverdi, *Orfeo* (1607), opening of the introductory Toccata.

Within a very few years, Monteverdi's practice regarding the use of trumpets spread widely north of the Alps. Several factors explain why Venice was influential: geographic location at one of the major trading crossroads of Europe; a respectable record as an originating centre of new styles; and a critical mass of master composers. Heinrich Schütz, a favoured pupil of Giovanni Gabrieli, kept close links to Venice and was in the vanguard of composers who had influence in Northern Europe.

Later in the century, after the widespread interruptions to cultural life of the Thirty Years War (1618–48), which engulfed much of the European continent, trumpet playing as an artistic pursuit (as distinct from its ongoing functional and practical use in military organisation) became more widespread. The upper, or *clarino*, register came to be used more freely, and with greater variety of musical nuance. By the close of the seventeenth century this transformation of trumpet usage had diffused across much of Europe, the instrument was established as a solo and obbligato voice in opera and concerted church music, and celebrated performers had emerged. During the course of the century following, the trumpet reached the summit of its significance in art music. The works of Bach and Handel, two defining composers of the period, contain a great wealth of repertoire for the trumpet player.

Less well known is the trumpet writing of Bach and Handel's contemporaries Johann Joseph Fux and Antonio Caldara, and that of the later Bohemian composer Johann Samuel Endler. Well into the second half of the eighteenth century, composers such as Franz Xaver Richter, Michael Haydn and Georg von Reutter II wrote trumpet concertos transcending previous difficulty. These works are so difficult to perform successfully in modern concert hall conditions that few modern players take the risk of playing them live.

European national diversity in the seventeenth century

The development of trumpet playing in Europe in the seventeenth century happened at different speeds, in different ways, and with a different national emphasis from country to country, not only because of differences in language, culture and geography. Political and economic organisation was of paramount importance. Who the patrons were – whether solely the King, as in France, or multiple, as in the cities, courts and churches of the German-speaking lands – determined how widespread and diverse was the use of the trumpet. After the international, religious and civil wars of the seventeenth century, the map of Europe was a patchwork of different political systems, varying from republican in Switzerland and the towns of the Hanseatic League, through the elective monarchy of the Holy Roman Empire, and the constitutionally-limited monarchy of England and Scotland, to the absolutist monarchy of France, and the autocratic monarchies of Russia and the Papal States. Two main strands of economic organisation are to be observed within these political entities – *command* and *market.* Though there was a direct correlation between the two extremes of governmental systems – the republican favouring the *market,* and the absolute/autocratic favouring the *command* – every national system seemed to have its own idiosyncratic bias, or mix between the two extremes. Towns that were politically independent, that competed and traded with each other, as in the towns of the Hanseatic

League and the free cities of the Holy Roman Empire, had for some time possessed a proportion of merchants who had accumulated enough wealth to support artistic pursuits collectively. When combined with the decentralised form of government encouraged by the system of an elected monarchy in the German regions, which resulted in its many small courts that also provided patronage, it begins to become more obvious why the German-speaking regions were to become so influential in art music in the two succeeding centuries. When the plurality of religious denominations (Roman Catholic, Calvinist, Lutheran) that came to be tolerated is added to this already favourable diversity of circumstance, many more ecclesiastical potential patrons of music, and of the trumpet, emerge.

In France and England, patronage was not nearly so widespread, and was concentrated in the royal courts and the two capital cities. Musical activity in France was concentrated in the activities of the absolutist monarch. French politics were centralised, the economy dirigiste, and the state religiously intolerant (the Huguenots were expelled in 1685). There were fewer musical opportunities. In England no native written-down trumpet-specific music exists before *c.*1685. Royal patronage was augmented by the activities of the commercial theatre, whose popularity greatly increased with the restoration of the Stuart monarchy in 1660, following the Civil War and the Cromwellian Commonwealth. The music was often elaborate. Masques and entertainments, half way between opera and plays, like Purcell's *The Fairy Queen*, enjoyed a vogue. Trumpet overtures, influenced initially by Italian models, abounded, perhaps partially to refocus the audience's attention back to the stage in a period when often the happenings on stage were only one among many reasons for attendance. Curtis Price alludes to the fact that there were no reserved seats beyond the royal box in the Restoration playhouse; many courtiers attended to pay court, not to see the play, and got their money back if they left before curtain up. There was often a last-minute rush for gentlemen to finalise bargaining arrangements with courtesans so that they could leave before the 'last Musick', the second tune of the second music, after which there was a spoken prologue, before finally the overture was played. The practical point of all of this preliminary music was to let the audience know when the play was to begin – the equivalent of the first, second and final bells in the modern theatre.[3]

New forms of public entertainment accompanied societal change. The growth of the public concert for a new class of middle-class patron – those benefiting from a burgeoning market economy – started to gain in importance, from modest beginnings, in entrepreneurial centres of commerce like London. Public concerts were initiated in London in 1672 by John Banister, who was a royal musician-in-ordinary, a freelance composer and entrepreneur. At first he used his own home, then the concerts spread to larger venues. Thomas Britton, 'the musical small-coal man' of Clerkenwell, whose portrait hangs in the Handel House Museum in London, followed suit in 1678 and became famous for his early demonstration that art music was open to anyone – signalling a future where it was no longer exclusive to those born into it:

> Tho'doom'd to small-coal, yet to arts ally'd,
> Rich without wealth, and famous without pride,
> Musick's best patron, judge of books and men. . . .[4]

Social inclusion did not diminish the excellence of the musical product. The standard of Britton's concerts was famously high: the composers Pepusch and Handel were numbered among the performers at the concerts in their existence of nigh on forty years.

Italy in the early seventeenth century: the innovations of Fantini

Italy held a special place in the music of the seventeenth and eighteenth centuries, and was a font of ideas for the rest of Europe. Its multiplicity of small city-states and aristocratic courts with a cultured tradition supported a rich and varied musical environment. The 'Academies' of cultured citizens with a keen interest in the arts and sciences made for an atmosphere in which innovation flourished. The Accademia di Santa Cecilia, which survives as a national institution to this day, was founded in Rome in 1585. The new music of the baroque germinated in the philosophical coteries of the *literati*, and spread from Italy throughout Europe. In the continuity of Italian instrumental music, Gabrieli, the composer with whom our previous chapter finished, became a dead end, forgotten in his native country, which was more concerned with the new and the fashionable. The fresh and direct communication of baroque music, which eventually came to favour the trumpet, supplanted the previous contrapuntal and polychoral instrumental traditions of the Venetian school, which, reaching its apotheosis in Gabrieli, had favoured the cornetto. These polychoral and contrapuntal traditions, however, were exported, notably to the German-speaking lands, and particularly through the court composers of the Austro-Hungarian Empire at Vienna, Prague, Salzburg and Kroměříž – Antonio Bertali, Johann Heinrich Schmelzer, Alessandro Poglietti, Heinrich Ignaz Biber, Pavel Josef Vejvanovský, culminating in Caldara, Fux, and their pupils. Caldara and Fux carried on the tradition of writing for cornetto well into the eighteenth century. Polychoral music has continued to fascinate composers, performers and audiences to the present day, when the performance resources are available. Gabrieli's legacy survives.

Italy was the crucible of the new style of music, which came to be labelled baroque. The change of style occurring at the beginning of the seventeenth century was radical and rapid, and it was reinforced later by generational waves of new composers that radiated out of Italy, bringing yet more new trends and ideas in the 1660s and the 1690s.

The old style of composition did not disappear, however. It remained as an element of composerly technique and expression. This old style, linear rather than vertical, was labelled *prima pratica* by Claudio Monteverdi in 1605. The new style, vertical rather than linear, he called *seconda pratica*. This new simplicity with the emphasis on the top and bottom parts can be seen at its starkest in the trumpet sonatas of Fantini. These sonatas are passed over by many modern trumpet players because of their very simplicity. Paradoxically, however, herein lies their strength. They are the epitome of simplicity and directness of expression, and few more elementary examples of *seconda pratica* exist. These first solo trumpet sonatas may be rudimentary in structure and harmony, yet there is nothing like them before this date, and in them can be perceived the seeds from which grew the later developments in trumpet writing. The sonatas are short – literally living up to their original meaning of 'a sounding together' – and multi-sectional. They are discursive rather than developmental. They have a declamatory introduction and coda. Forward momentum is provided by the use of dance rhythms in the middle sections. They are sonatas in microcosm.

Fantini's playing technique is already far advanced and not limited to the harmonic series. Non-harmonic notes are common: C sharps abound in passing; and he uses D's, F's and A's in between the fourth, fifth, sixth and seventh harmonics, quite freely (Ex. 4.2). Fantini was a revelation to his contemporaries. A group of French trumpeters who heard him perform with Girolamo Frescobaldi on the organ of Cardinal Borghese in Rome in 1634 found his new concept of the trumpet disconcerting and bewildering.[5] Fantini had also developed the technique of unlocking the high register of the trumpet. He saw no obstacle to ascending to the eighteenth harmonic, D6, in 'Seconda Ricercata detta l'Acciaioli' (Ex. 4.3). That playing to this level was not just the province of one inspired individual is shown by the previous existence of a methodology for acquiring the set of skills to play sonatas like Fantini's. Cesar Bendinelli's *Tutta l'arte della trombetta* (1614) had already appeared in manuscript by 1611, and Fantini's sonatas themselves were collectively published as part of a much larger treatise, containing all sorts of musical examples. This treatise, *Modo per imparare a sonare di tromba*, appeared in 1638. There has been speculation over its place of publication. Although Frankfurt is specified on the title page, the paper watermarks and details of the typography point to it having been published in Florence, where Fantini had resided since 1630 or 1631.[6]

Germany in the seventeenth century

Though Heinrich Schütz, after his studies with Gabrieli, wrote extensively for cornett and trombone, his *Danket dem Herrn*, performed in Dresden in 1617, but possibly composed several years earlier, may also be the earliest example of the trumpet participating in concerted music-making in Germany.[7] Michael Praetorius's scoring for a six-part trumpet ensemble in his polychoral setting of *In dulci jubilo* from *Polyhymnia*

Ex. 4.2 G. Fantini, Sonata No. 5, detta dell'Adimari, bars 10–18.

Ex. 4.3 G. Fantini, 'Seconda Ricercata detta l'Acciaioli', opening.

caduceatrix et panegyrica (1619) and his comments on the use of trumpets in concerted compositions in the third volume of his *Syntagma Musicum* from the same year show the contemporary German absorption of Italian influence.

Schütz's trumpet writing developed further in the first set of *Symphoniae Sacrae* (1629), where the trumpet appears in *Buccinate* and *Iubilate Deo.* His second set of *Symphoniae Sacrae* (1647) is indicative of a growing mid-century interchangeability between trumpet and cornett, providing two parts, 'cornetto o trombetta I and II', in *Meine Seele erhebt den Herren.* Towards the end of his long career, in 1660, he gave modern trumpeters one of the earliest pieces in the repertoire to contain trumpets that is still regularly played – *Historia von der Geburt . . . Jesu Christi* (*Christmas Story*). The trumpet writing in the *Christmas Story* also has close affinities to cornetto style. It was highly unusual for C trumpets to play in the pastoral key of F major, and it is reminiscent of the trumpet writing of Moravian composer Pavel Josef Vejvanovský (*c.*1633 or *c.*1639–1693) in the same decade.

Schütz was Kapellmeister in Dresden, the principal city of the electorate of Saxony, and a city with a rich musical tradition. One hundred kilometres away was Leipzig, another Saxon city famous for its music. The succession of Kantors at the Thomaskirche, Leipzig, before Bach succeeded to the post in 1723 is worth examining. Johann Hermann Schein, incumbent between 1616 and 1630, is known to have composed for trumpets from the occasion on which the Leipzig City Council had to account to the Elector of Saxony in Dresden for his use of trumpets in the service at the Thomaskirche, resulting in an instruction that in future he must use cornetts.[8] Unfortunately, nothing survives of Schein's trumpet writing. We know that his successor, Tobias Michael, *Kantor* from 1631 to 1657, published in 1637 a vocal collection, *Musikalische Seelenlust,* containing one work with two trumpets, *Lass dich ihre Lebe.* The writing is simple in the manner of Michael Altenburg, the influential composer of *Gaudium Christianum,* already alluded to, who was active in Tröchtelborn, near Erfurt in Thuringia, nearly 100 kilometres to the south west of Leipzig. Michael's output of music was curtailed by the Thirty Years War.

With Tobias Michael's successor, Sebastian Knüpfer, St Thomas post-holder between 1657 and 1676, the two trumpet parts become much more complex with independent lines. The C trumpet is used imaginatively in the minor mode, and the unusual non-harmonic notes E flat5 and A flat5 figure prominently. The more usual B4 features to an extent rare in the Germany of the times, and is again reminiscent of contemporaneous Moravian practice as exemplified by Vejvanovský.

Trumpet writing developed quickly in Leipzig. The virtuosity of Leipzig trumpet players was certainly in evidence before the birth of Bach. One of the most important trumpeters active in Leipzig during this period was the Stadtpfeifer Johann Christoph Pezel (1639–94), who was a published composer in addition to being a violinist. He shows that by the second half of the seventeenth century trumpet players' musical literacy had increased compared with the time of Michael Altenburg, when trumpeters seem to have been given a written-down musical text only as an optional extra. The voluminous collections of Pezel's instrumental ensemble music which survive are an indicator of the sort of music that Stadtpfeifer played as part of their daily routines. His *Hora Decima* (Leipzig, 1670) comprises forty sonatas for two cornetts and three

Ex. 4.4 J. C. Pezel, *Bicinium* No. 69 for two trumpets and continuo, opening.

trombones. Meals were eaten earlier when urban populations were more closely attuned to agrarian rhythms and markets opened eye-wateringly early. This charming, cheerful and robust music was probably played to signal the midday meal taken by a population of early-risers at the early hour of 10 am, from the Pfeiferstuhl outside the Leipzig Rathaus. Five out of the 76 Intradas, Allemandes, Ballets, Courents, Sarabandes and Gigues in his *Fünff-stimmigte blasende Music* (Frankfurt, 1685) can be played on natural trumpet. Pezel also wrote *Bicinia* (published in Leipzig in 1675) for pairs of instrument – violins, cornettos, and trumpets. Their title probably implies that, like Lassus's *Bicinia* of the previous century, their intent was didactic. Nevertheless, the six *Bicinia* from the collection for two trumpets, nos 69–74, transcend didactic functionality, and their very simplicity leads to moments of great beauty in performance. Like Fantini's earlier sonatas for one trumpet and keyboard, they are open to underestimation and are often overlooked by contemporary players. Pezel's *Bicinia* are among the handful of works from this period for trumpets and keyboard. The lively opening of Bicinium No. 69 (Ex. 4.4) is the earliest published instance of a theme later used by Paganini and developed by Rachmaninov in his *Rhapsody on a Theme by Paganini* Op. 43.

Pezel was active in Leipzig during the tenure of the successor to Knüpfer, Johann Schelle (1648–1710). Schelle was a radical and, against much local opposition, was the first to insist on composing sacred cantatas to exclusively German text. He was the first composer to use a solo trumpet in what was to become the common context of an obbligato to voices and large instrumental ensemble in the German Church music of the time. Three cantatas of this sort by Schelle survive: *Gott sei mir gnädig, Schaffe in mir Gott* and *Salve solis orientis*. The trumpet designated in this last work is a *clarino piccolo*, explained in a note as 'a small Italian trumpet which sounds a tone higher'.[9] In other works Schelle scored for two, three or four trumpets with various combinations of wind and string instruments, including cornetts, cornettini and trombones. An example of his virtuosic trumpet parts that were presumably written for Pezel, and perhaps Reiche, appears in the cantata *Nun danket alle Gott*, in which the first trumpet enters, following several bars rest, on C6.

The flowering of trumpet writing and playing in Leipzig in the seventeenth century happened, however, in spite of the earlier instruction to Schein in the 1620s to cease the use of trumpets forthwith in the Thomaskirche. This increase in the use of trumpets in Leipzig churches during the second half of the seventeenth century illustrates how imperial edicts aimed at the preservation of trumpet playing as a mark of princely status, and the reinforcement of the privileges of court trumpeters, were ineffective when the musical demands for trumpets (and kettledrums) were strong enough.

The organisation and working patterns of trumpet players

The imperial privileges regarding trumpeters and kettledrummers, which appeared first in 1623, are an important starting point towards an understanding of the social significance and the employment opportunities for trumpet players in this two-century-long period. The imperial privileges were out of the ordinary. No other trade or profession seems to have been regulated centrally by the imperial rulers. In all other trades and professions, organisation was devolved to localised authorities. Succeeding imperial edicts periodically reinforced the rights of the trumpeters, whereas in edicts concerning other trades and professions the imperial authorities were more concerned with limiting the power of guilds and trying to prevent abuses of their privileges.

The genesis of the imperial privileges, according to Altenburg, lay in such an attempt to reward field trumpeters returning from active service. Only those who had 'served with the cavalry in time of war and . . . participated in at least one campaign with expeditions and guard duty (and still better, has been despatched to the enemy)' were allowed to take apprentices.[10] They earned this right through 'offering up life and limb, upon which the imperial privileges are actually based'.[11]

The apprentice system was also common to municipal musicians, who, in the area of their most systematically organised, and best-documented activity, the German-speaking lands, were called Stadtpfeifer. The Stadtpfeifer were well placed to provide the occasional musical needs of the peoples of the towns and their hinterlands: weddings, funerals, baptisms, fairs, church processions and festivals. This 'freelance' activity contributed greatly to a musician's income and the opportunity to supplement income was one of the attractions of a musical career. In addition, church services of all denominations became more elaborate in their use of musical forces after the Thirty Years War. By the time of the Treaty of Westphalia in 1648, which ended the war, much of the German Lands lay devastated, the population was decimated, the central authority of the Habsburgs was undermined in favour of the German princes, and the ascendant European power was France. The 'imperial privileges', such as they were, were conceived at a time of maximum instability. It was only when stability started to return, and the Spanish and Swedish garrisons had gone home in the 1650s, that the art of trumpet-playing revived in the 1660s with tangible results which have come down to us, both in Leipzig, and notably in the Moravian Prince-Bishopric of Olomouc, with the trumpet music of Vejvanovský and Biber.

Leipzig was typical of the organisation of municipal musicians throughout Germany, where Stadtpfeifer were members of town bands in municipalities that had kept musicians in regular employment to fulfil civic functions from the fourteenth century onwards. These organisations were to persist into the future as the basic principle underlying Germany's enviable network of civic orchestras in the nineteenth and twentieth centuries. The Stadtpfeifer were the jobbing musicians of the day, and had expanded into playing concerted and notated music from the formerly utilitarian functions of what were known in Great Britain and Ireland as the city waits: tower watchmen (Türmer), fire watchmen (Feuerwächter), and in general, the audible arm of a system of law and order ensuring civic security. They were skilled multi-tasking musicians. Like theatre musicians of the twentieth and twenty-first centuries, they were expected to play to a high standard on several instruments, sometimes of different species: for example, a musician adept on violin, oboe, flute, trumpet, horn, and various bass instruments would not have been in any way unusual.[12] Local organisations seeking to foster and protect the livelihood of musicians came into being, formed from within the body of musicians themselves. Most developed systems of apprenticeship training. The favoured title for these was brotherhood (Bruderschaft), or society of friends (Kameradschaft).

Stadtpfeifer became in great demand, at first for special festivals, then, in some centres of musical excellence, every week in church for cycles of cantatas, often composed by the civic director of music. Court musicians also benefited from an increased demand for instrumental music. Inevitably, however, they came into conflict with the Stadtpfeifer over how the local market for musical performers should be organised. The imperial privileges were an attempt to regulate the work opportunities to the advantage of the court trumpeters, designed to elevate them to an exclusive professional class. As specialist high-class musicians in the service of aristocrats, they felt they had precedence over the multi-instrumentalist Stadtpfeifer. And yet the municipalities within the jurisdiction of the Holy Roman Empire were always fiercely antagonistic to any Imperial interference in their internal affairs and were always indulging in complicated politics – playing off their local Elector and his aspirations against the distant Emperor. Their instinctive course of action would have been to pay lip service to the privileges whilst favouring their own men – the Stadtpfeifer. The informally organised Stadtpfeifer, and the spontaneous nature of their freelance work, were impossible to regulate, and if notice was taken of the privileges, it was generally to circumvent them. The excitement, travel and employment opportunities of a Stadtpfeifer's life are alluded to in three autobiographical novels by Daniel Speer, published anonymously in 1683 and 1684.[13] The situation of the musician was more clear-cut in Russia. Most members of eighteenth-century Russian orchestras were serfs, members of the legion of highly skilled serfs who were fundamental to the cultivation of European art forms in Russian noble houses.[14]

It would be a mistake to conclude that a direct consequence of the 'privileges' was to cause an Olympic cadre of trumpet players who could play the virtuoso parts of the baroque period, whilst the Stadtpfeifer were the journeymen. Although this may have been true close to the centre of power in the imperial capital Vienna, making possible the emergence of players like Johann Heinisch (*fl.*1727–50), described by Edward Tarr (b.1936) as 'probably the greatest player of the natural trumpet and one of the greatest players of all time',[15] the Stadtpfeifer and similar civic organisations elsewhere in Europe endured, and were, on balance, probably more important ultimately to the development of trumpet playing and trumpet music than the 'imperial privileges'. The 'privileges' were in effect a statute of limitation, which proved unenforceable in the long run. They were an attempt to limit the number of players in order to increase the status, remuneration and working conditions of military and court trumpet players. But there can be no effective legislation without an effective bureaucracy of control and inspection. Exclusivity was impossible to police and the reality across Europe was much more complex. This held true for the decay of the guild system as a whole during this period, not only for the trumpet 'privileges'. Don Smithers quotes the historian Nicholas Bessaraboff to indicate 'the social significance of the baroque trumpet' and its players:

> The real trumpet is the haughty aristocrat of musical instruments. In Western Europe only emperors, kings, great nobles and prominent municipalities enjoyed the privilege of having trumpets. Trumpeters were of 'knightly kind' and their calling was considered not a trade but a free and knightly art.[16]

Statements like this can tend to mislead. They fuse instrument and player, and assume that importance of function led to elevation of rank. Granted, the instrument was a symbol of power and high authority, and attempts were made to limit its use to keep its symbolism pure. But the fact remained that trumpet players themselves belonged mostly to the servant class, some rising to the highly responsible position of 'court, chamber or travelling quartermaster'. In the army, the rank usually attained was the equivalent of sergeant major.[17] Their fine liveries, wigs and banners were symbolic, not of their own status and wealth, but of that of their masters.

Much of the greatest trumpet music, however, was written outside the jurisdiction of the privileges. Altenburg, in his treatise of 1795, lists courts in European capitals outside the area of the imperial privileges that employed trumpeters:

> St Petersburg, Constantinople, Lisbon, Madrid, Versailles, London, Copenhagen, Stockholm, Warsaw, Naples, Turin, as well as the princely courts of Italy.[18]

Some of the most sumptuously-scored trumpet ensemble music from the eighteenth century is contained in a set of partbooks that formed the repertoire of the royal court corps (Charamela real) in Lisbon. Dating from about 1770, the fifty-four sonatas in the collection are scored for between one and four choirs of six trumpets. Some of the sonatas, including the single work in twenty-four parts, call for trumpets pitched in two different keys (E flat and B flat), a technique that was more often exploited in the nineteenth century.

In capital cities which lay outside the Holy Roman Empire, like London, and in prominent centres of culture, learning and commerce, like Leipzig, the standard and status of trumpet players do not seem to have been affected by lack of 'guild' coverage. In London, trumpet players like John Shore (*c.*1662–1752) were part of a self-regulating local mixed economy, picking up a living from performing in theatres and concert venues, alongside periodic and discretionary royal and aristocratic patronage. In Leipzig and London, famed trumpet players like Gottfried Reiche and Shore gained a high level of local celebrity, status, and hence higher pay, not by automatic right, but, very much as in modern times, because of their own personal accomplishment.

Most trumpet players in Europe were town musicians like Pezel and Reiche in Leipzig, who earned money from civic performance, teaching and freelancing, very much like their modern counterparts. Once the difficulty of the music is taken into account, the standards these town musicians achieved seem to be as high as those achieved anywhere else. Granted the difficulties of the music Bach composed for his Stadtpfeifer to play, it is surprising that they were deemed to be *ungelernten* (untutored) by implication of the very same imperial privileges that were reinforced by successive mandates of the Elector of Saxony. This is the contradiction inherent in the 'privileges'. Their regulatory thrust was all about ceremony and ostentation, and nothing to do with creating great music. Their very restrictions meant that it was more likely that art music would flourish outside than within their jurisdiction. In practice, the unforeseen consequence of these mandates was, to all intents and purposes, to put music in cities of creative innovation like Leipzig, outside the jurisdiction of Imperial or Electoral control. And, in fact, it could be argued that any hindrance that the Imperial Privileges of the Trumpet Guild had to the development of trumpet playing was countered by a stimulus that this gave to the relatively freehand status already enjoyed by the Stadtpfeifer. The obsession of the authorities with the ceremonial and military aspects of the trumpeters' art is evident from the following 16th article of the 1653 privileges, which arguably would have hindered the development of trumpet playing *within* courtly circles:

> If a sovereign, prince or lord allows a boy to learn the art of the trumpet or the drum, and does not let him go into the field after his term of apprenticeship and his release, but he has to serve as a court instrumentalist, then this trumpeter could be passed as regards his skill in the art, but would not be permitted to teach an apprentice.[19]

It was a necessity, however, to provide military trumpet players, as part of a standing army, with peacetime employment. Although the peace after the Thirty Years War coincided with an expansion of opportunities for trumpet players in concerted music-making, the spontaneous nature of much civic and church musical activity was such that the well-established organisations of Stadtpfeifer, with their flexible multi-instrumentalists, were better placed to take advantage of the new opportunities. The Privileges could be seen as an attempt to extend to court trumpeters the earning opportunities which had been created and fostered over preceding generations by Stadtpfeifer.

Understandably, conflict between court trumpeters and Stadtpfeifer was inevitable once the 'Privileges' were used to attempt to usurp the areas of work that had traditionally given the Stadtpfeifer their living. Unenforceable legislation breeds civil disobedience and according to Altenburg,

> things must have later proceeded so much out of control that it became necessary, at the request of the Electoral Saxon brethren-in-art, to publish successively three reinforced mandates Against the Unauthorised Playing of Trumpets and Military Kettledrums in the years 1661, 1711, and 1736.

Altenburg adds that the third mandate of 1736 was necessary because 'the misuse of these instruments gained ground anew'.[20]

These mandates reinforcing the power of the Trumpet Guild contradict the tenor of the times, which was to encourage deregulation. Most of those charged with governing the economies of the countries of Europe appear to have favoured the dismantling of the old guild system. The late date of this 1736 mandate is interesting when seen in the context of other proclamations made with the intent of suppressing the powers of the guilds, such as the *Imperial Law Concerning the Abuses of the Guilds*, enacted at Regensburg in 1731, which concludes, in threatening tone:

> In view of the above ordinances, as well as those proscribing irresponsible journeymen from leaving, striking against, or ridiculing and defaming their masters – the true sources of the deplorable state into which the guilds have fallen – it is hoped that in their own true interest, masters and journeymen will henceforth be more sedate in their ways, showing due obedience to their appointed authorities. Nonetheless, it has proven absolutely necessary to abandon our former patience and to point out in all seriousness to masters and journeymen that, if they continue in their irresponsible, evil, and stubborn ways, the Emperor and the Diet might easily be moved, following the examples of other countries, and in the interest of the public, which is hurt by such criminal, private quarrels, to suppress and abolish the guilds altogether.[21]

The Holy Roman Empire was, by this time, a concept in decay. It had always constituted a loose organisation of states riven by internal strife and threatened by external pressures. Although at the heart of Europe, it did not constitute the major portion of it. The Imperial Privileges were introduced during the Thirty Years War, in 1623, as part of a concerted measure to keep centralised control of an empire that was never far from falling apart. Such attempted legislation probably served only to underline the authorities' impotence. As revellers in the tavern of Goethe's *Faust* sang:

> The dear old Holy Roman Empire,
> How does it hang together?

Furthermore, when granted these privileges, cities did not always take up the opportunity to employ specialised trumpeters – even such a quintessential centre of brass manufacture as Nuremberg seemed satisfied with the Stadtpfeifer it already employed.[22]

The end of the eighteenth century was a time of shattering social change in Europe. Though Altenburg's *Trumpeters' and Kettledrummers' Art* appeared at this time, in 1795, and is an invaluable source of information on the activities of trumpet players over the previous two centuries, the contrast between its antiquarian content and the contemporary context could not be starker. It appeared at a time of European revolutionary ferment when the Imperial Privileges had become an anachronism. The guild system itself had become increasingly irrelevant to the increasing prosperity within the contemporary economic situation of the eighteenth century. An example of the abuses perpetrated by the guilds that led to their demise appeared in *Cahiers des Doléances* (Grievances) presented to the Guild Assembly of Rouen on 21 March 1789 by the Hatmakers, Fur-skin dealers and Furriers.[23] The restrictive practices and 'luddite' attitudes outlined, barely three months before the onset of the French Revolution, contributed to the economic stagnation that kept much of France poorer than it ought to have been during the eighteenth century.

In France itself, attempts at reform had been made by Anne-Robert-Jacques Turgot (1727–81), appointed finance minister by Louis XVI fifteen years before the Hatmakers made their presentation at Rouen. One of the foremost economists of his time, friend and confidant of Adam Smith, author of *An Inquiry into the Nature and Causes of the Wealth of Nations* (1776), which was influenced by his own *Reflections on the Formation and Distribution of Riches* (1766), Turgot was brought in to halt the economic decline of France, and solve the crisis in the public finances. After freeing the grain trade, he presented his famous *Six Edicts* to the *conseil du roi* in January 1776, the fifth of which dissolved the Guild system in France:

> Your majesty has known my views on guilds for some time. I dare say that this way of thinking is shared by all those who have any notion about the nature of commerce. I believe that it is impossible to maintain seriously and in good faith that these corporations, their exclusive privileges, the barriers they erect against work, competition, and the progress of industry are of any usefulness whatsoever.

The forces of reaction against Turgot were too great and he was forced to resign on 12 May 1776. It was not only writers of treatises on the trumpet like Altenburg who were nostalgic for the old ways and their privileges. A fair proportion of the population and the bulk of public opinion were with him and fiercely against change.

When European economies had begun to expand in the eighteenth century, the guild system, which had been strengthened in the seventeenth century, had done little to lead the economic recovery. The guilds seemed 'restrictive, hostile to change, impeding commerce with endless demarcation disputes'.[24] Towns where the guilds remained strong were usually not those that led the urban revival. In the boom towns of the eighteenth century, involved in new trades such as shipbuilding, and those connected to trade with European colonies, where trade guilds existed they tended to be bypassed. Glasgow, one such boom city, saw its population rise from 13,000 in 1708 to 84,000 in 1801.[25] An interesting example of restrictive practices being bypassed occurred in 1660s Glasgow. Thomas McCuir, the maker of one of the two surviving trumpets made in seventeenth-century Scotland, was admitted as a goldsmith burgess of Aberdeen in 1643 and was elected Deacon of the Hammermen there six years later. Around 1660 he moved to Edinburgh, where he served as a journeyman, presumably with the intention of gaining entry to the guild of Edinburgh goldsmiths. In 1664 he successfully petitioned Glasgow Burgh Council to set up shop there and was immediately granted entry to the Glasgow Hammermen's Guild.[26] The Edinburgh goldsmiths were amongst the most prosperous craftsmen in Scotland, had the authority to inspect the quality of all gold and silverware produced in other burghs, and many were involved in banking and speculative ventures. As a newcomer to Edinburgh, McCuir was unable to penetrate the closed guild network, but he was welcomed in Glasgow, where the economy was beginning to expand rapidly. McCuir's Edinburgh experience echoes the complaint expressed regarding closed shops in the *Imperial Law Concerning the Abuses of the Guilds*, already referred to above, issued in Regensburg in 1731:

> In certain places a young master, even though he has travelled for many years as a journeyman, may not exercise his trade unless he has lived in that place for a certain number of years, having visited the so-called fraternity for some years, or unless he has paid a certain sum in order to become a member of the guild.[27]

The locally proliferating machinations of the guild system make the Imperial Privileges, with their centrally reinforced rights, even more remarkable.

Nevertheless, despite this evidence as to their patchy coverage and limited effectiveness, the Privileges are worthy of their prominence because they were a largely successful attempt to confer a mark of high status on a class of musician who had previously enjoyed a lowly status. Court trumpet players in 1623 were given a document to advance their vocation, addressing their calling as 'the noble, knightly art of trumpet playing'.[28] By the last part of the eighteenth century, however, the document had lost any power it may once have had to make a difference to the trumpet player's lot. Altenburg refers to 'the poor salary', the need for German trumpet players to seek their fortune outside Germany, because of being held in higher esteem abroad, and being given higher pay there, and finally, the lack of perquisites and gratuities at courts and in military service which ultimately undermines motivation.[29]

Developments in the later eighteenth century

During the seventeenth and eighteenth centuries and the subsequent period, a preponderance of major composers tended to be keyboard or string players. As the period developed, keyboard and strings had the most advanced technologies, techniques, the widest range of expression and thus, in the final analysis, the most interesting solo repertory. Notwithstanding this, the solo repertory of the trumpet from the baroque period is rich and abundant. The playing technique of the natural trumpet developed astonishingly and continuously throughout the period 1600–1750, and an underlying reason must be the succession of performers who composed and understood the trumpet like Bendinelli, Fantini, Pezel, Reiche, and the fair number of prominent composers like Vejvanovský and J. J. Quantz (the latter more famous as a flautist) who played trumpet themselves. However, just as the slide was developed during the first quarter of the fifteenth century to play the tenor and contratenor parts in the polyphonic repertoire of the shawm band, keys appeared towards the end of the eighteenth century in an attempt to make the trumpet a more prominent participant in a style of music which had been evolving since the 1730s. The effect of the application of advancing technology to other instruments had not been entirely positive for the trumpet. During the last fifty years of the period in question, refinements in woodwind instrument technology had given the clarinet an undoubted superiority over the trumpet as an expressive instrument in the musical language of the classical period. The clarinet appeared around the same time as the chalumeau in the early eighteenth century. According to the musical treatise *Musicus Autodidaktos* by J. P. Eisel, which appeared in Erfurt in 1738, the usual clef for the clarinet was the treble, where it was treated like a trumpet, and when written for in soprano or alto clef it was treated like a chalumeau. In England the early form of chalumeau was

(a)

(b)

Exx. 4.5a & b. J. M. Molter, Clarinet Concerto in D, first movement, bars 23–5 (a); J. M. Molter, Trumpet Concerto No. 2 in D, first movement, bars 15–17 (b).

known as the 'mock' trumpet, the earliest surviving music for which, *The Fourth Compleat Book for the Mock Trumpet* (London: Walsh and Hare, *c.*1706–8), comprises a collection of trumpet tunes described on the title page as suitable for the 'brazen' (i.e. brass) trumpet.[30]

Caldara was one of the few composers who wrote for both instruments, and extensively for trumpet, and left us with the earliest use of clarinets and trumpets used together (with timpani) in *Iphigenia in Aulide* of 1718. By the time of the concertos of Johann Melchior Molter from the 1740s, the writing fits the 'clarino' register of the clarinet and the trumpet of the period equally well, so that the two instruments are virtually interchangeable (Exx. 4.5a and b).

By the time of the mature Mozart it is a different story. Mozart's Clarinet Quintet K581 and Concerto K622, both in A major and dating from his final years, between 1789 and 1791, and his inventive orchestral writing for this instrument, had developed clarinet idiom far beyond the trumpet-imitations of the 'clarino' register. By this time, the clarinet, which had started off with a weak bottom register, had, in the hands of virtuosos like the original player of Mozart's concerto, Anton Stadler, developed a rich low register, known as the 'chalumeau' register, in memory of the sweet pastoral instrument it had helped on its way to extinction. The trumpet in Mozart's orchestra was not used in a soloistic way, although two trumpets and timpani were a common feature of works composed for important occasions. The trumpet was as much a colouristic as a melodic device. Its presence lent a context of importance to the *tutti* sound by adding apposite sonority and rhythmic drive. It was a building brick of the melodic structure. That Mozart was aware of the capabilities and the limitations of the natural trumpet is shown by the delightfully inventive writing in his Divertimento K240b, written for 2 flutes, 5 trumpets and timpani in 1773. This work was modelled on Joseph Starzer's *Musica da Camera molto particulare fatta e presentata alla Regina di Muscovia*, for 2 chalumeaux, 5 trumpets and timpani, composed for the Russian Imperial court; this was copied by Leopold Mozart and a version with additional movements originally composed by Gluck was attributed to Wolfgang Mozart as K187. Mozart composed his own trumpet concerto, K47C, now lost, which was performed at the dedication of the new church of the orphanage in the Rennweg at Vienna in December 1768, and 'composed on purpose for a boy and in honour of the orphanage'.[31] The trumpet as a solo instrument did not hold his attention for long, with the clarinet able to do what both the trumpet and the chalumeau could do, and latent potential to do yet more besides.

Mozart's writing for the other orchestral brass of the period was progressive. The trombone writing of the Masses is a major test for any trombonist and the five solo works for horn form the core of its solo repertoire. He was not averse to novelty, as the inclusion of post horn solos in two works, the *Post horn* Serenade K320 and *Schlittenfahrt* K605 No. 3, shows.

Other brass instruments were advancing. The horn became a regular member of the classical orchestra, as its idiom grew wider than that of an allegory for the hunt. For horn players too had instituted innovations in their playing techniques. Hampel and others from the 1730s onwards had devised an ingenious hand-stopping system, which widened the scope of the horn in serious music making. Meanwhile, performance trends were working against the uncomplicated participation of the trumpet. The increasingly uniform adoption of a scientific method of tuning, equal temperament, in all centres of musical performance, boxed the seventeenth- and eighteenth-century trumpet, with its 'natural' intonation, into an increasingly tight corner as a melody instrument in mixed ensembles. In addition, in comparison with the woodwinds, it possessed limited ability to modulate freely into all but the most closely related keys.

From around 1770, trumpeters strove to extend the chromatic possibilities of the instrument. The German trumpeter Michael Wöggel (1748–1811) is credited with applying the technique of hand-stopping to the trumpet, for which the instrument had to be slightly curved to allow the hand access to the bell, and also with developing the invention-trumpet. The latter was based on the invention-horn developed by Anton Joseph Hampel: crooks were fitted to the body of the instrument instead of the mouthpipe, creating a more compact instrument which also lent itself to hand-stopping. It may also have been around this time that a Weimar court trumpeter by the name of Schwanitz took the first steps towards the development of the keyed trumpet. Altenburg attests to having heard Schwanitz perform on a trumpet with a single hole bored into the tubing, which he opened by moving 'a little leather slider', by which '*a′* and *b′* could be sounded perfectly in tune'. Details of the development of the instrument during the following two decades are scant, but in the 1790s Anton Weidinger, trumpeter at the Royal Imperial Theatre in Vienna and acquaintance of Haydn (who was a witness at the trumpeter's wedding in 1797), developed a more fully-chromatic keyed trumpet.[32]

In 1796, Haydn's imagination revelled in the new capabilities of Weidinger's keyed trumpet in his Trumpet Concerto in E flat. He exercised some of the new freedoms it afforded the adventurous composer by modulating from the already exotic tonic A flat major of the second movement to the outlandish new world as far as the trumpet was concerned of C flat minor. Perhaps this was one of the reasons it took Weidinger four years to bring the concerto to the public.

The timbre of the natural trumpet was still used to add weight and majesty to the orchestra, especially in music of a ceremonial flavour, but, in the main, composers of the new classical style, with notable exceptions, became more careful when scoring orchestrally for trumpets, generally allowing the range above the twelfth harmonic to fall into disuse, and only letting the trumpets inhabit the foreground at beginnings, ends, and moments of high drama. Though Haydn in his Trumpet Concerto still labelled his solo trumpet line 'clarino', it ascended only to the fourteenth harmonic, or B flat on the E flat trumpet, and he had second thoughts about a later adventure to the thirteenth-harmonic A (3rd movement, bar 216), rubbing it out and replacing it with A the octave below.

Idiomatic writing for the natural trumpet in the clarino register does not occur only in the baroque period, however. In fact the examples of the most extreme, most virtuoso-sounding, high-register writing occur well outside the latest dates conventionally put on the baroque period. Players who trained during an earlier period of high expectations in the upper register survived and remained active well into the latter part of the eighteenth century. Certainly, prominent composers of the transitional period between late baroque and early classical, sometimes referred to as 'rococo' or 'style galant' (dates roughly coinciding to 1730–80), were adventurous with the natural trumpet, writing concertos which took the trumpet to a tessitura that was not to be explored again fully until the jazz soloists of the twentieth century. Much of the most complicated and difficult music for the natural trumpet appeared in the third quarter of the eighteenth century and, conceptually, is typical of the classical period. These works were written in Salzburg by Joseph's younger brother, Michael Haydn (Ex. 4.6), probably for the Salzburg court trumpeter J. B. Resenberger (who was praised by Leopold Mozart for his purity of sound and ability to play in the high register), in Mannheim by Franz Xaver Richter (Ex. 4.7),[33] in Vienna by Georg von Reutter II, presumably for Heinisch or his successor, Ernst Bayer,[34] and in Darmstadt by Johann Samuel Endler.

Notwithstanding this repertoire, there was a shift in the idiom of the natural trumpet during the second half of the eighteenth century with a vogue for low register use of the instrument – perhaps as an echo of ominous gathering clouds of war (Ex. 4.8). The trumpet's association with armed conflict and triumph ensured its survival, indeed its growth, as an instrumental voice in art music. Hand in hand with

Ex. 4.6 Michael Haydn, Trumpet Concerto No. 1 in D, first movement, bars 35–43.

Ex. 4.7 F. X. Richter, Trumpet Concerto, first movement, bars 50–6.

Ex. 4.8 Joseph Haydn, Symphony No 100 ('Military'), second movement, bars 152–9.

the growth of military activity, if not militarism, which accompanied first the American Wars of Independence (1775–1783) and then the French Revolution (1789), along with the conscript armies and the European Wars which this latter event engendered, the trumpet's role became ubiquitous. It expanded to encompass not only the authority of kings, queens, emperors and empresses, but also any higher authority, whether that was dictator, republic or the will of the people.

New opportunities in the Age of Enlightenment

As has been discussed at length, an attempt to legislate against just such an outcome had been made as early as 1623 by the Holy Roman Empire, when the Imperial Privileges granted to trumpeters and timpanists sought to limit this aural emblem of status, authority and glory to be the sole province of the Emperor and his Electors. This was the supreme point of the Privileges – to underline the absolutist authority of the Emperor. This time was now past. Civil society had travelled quite a way in the intervening 150 years since 1623. The closure of many European courts around the time of the French Revolution adversely affected trumpeters' traditional employment opportunities. But new opportunities arose, and it is unlikely that the actual numbers of trumpet players, or those that played trumpet-like instruments, declined. Revolutionary fervour needed stirring music to express *La Gloire*. Small wind bands of around eight to a dozen players, each containing at least one and sometimes two of trumpets, were organised to serve the musical needs of every Paris arondissement. Songs like *La Marseillaise*, scored by Gossec for such a band, with its trumpet-call imitations, show the importance of the trumpet in a new context – as a symbol of republican heroism, rather than absolute rule.

Emancipating the trumpet from its imperial and aristocratic connections and putting it to the service of the greater glory of the population at large was one factor which led to an increase in the numbers of brass players in the following century, especially by its second quarter. Until the later eighteenth century, European wars were, in the main, fought by small standing armies. The outcomes were often decided by diplomatic manoeuvring. There was a balance of power in Europe which ensured a modicum of stability, and which shifted only gradually to satisfy Prussian and Russian expansionism. Military might, inflated by the conscription of huge armies in the Napoleonic wars which engulfed Europe at the turn of the nineteenth century, ensured not only the survival, but a growth in use of the natural trumpet both in the field, and in the music accompanying military ceremony. This endured into the period of general European peace following Waterloo and the Congress of Vienna in 1815. It was not only military organisations like the Prussian cavalry and the Royal Bavarian Rifles that used natural trumpets on parade. Civic and ecclesiastical ceremonies continued traditions steeped in many generations of practice, the roots of which went back to the Middle Ages.

The 'processional' (*Aufzug*) for groups of three or more natural trumpets was a genre which lived on well past the invention of the valve. The published output for natural trumpets actually grew, rather than disappeared, in the nineteenth century. It would be an easy assumption to make that writing for the natural trumpet died out with the invention of the valve. In fact, more natural trumpet ensemble music survives from the nineteenth than from any other century.[35]

The ideals of the Enlightenment preceded the tumultuous social upheavals which spread from France at the end of the eighteenth century. The Enlightenment spread the idea that the world, and along with it, the lot of man, could be understood and improved. It was a catalyst to social change and by the end of the century most of the serfs of Europe (with Russia a notable exception) had been given their freedom, if not the vote. One of the more benign and enduring legacies that the Enlightenment catalysed was the spread of the ideal of education for all, an idea that met stern opposition, as it was widely seen as the most serious threat to the status quo.[36] Educational reform affected music profoundly and led to a more systematic method of nurturing musical talent in most countries. By one of the strange coincidences of history, Altenburg's swansong lament to the old world of the natural trumpet was published in the same year, 1795, as the foundation of the Paris Conservatoire. The conservatoire was a revolutionary concept in the education of musical performers, and spawned imitators throughout the Western world. It effectively provided the master–apprentice tuition of the old guild system, described, lauded and lamented by Altenburg, but now within a broader-based education, and available to a much wider franchise of the population.

Technological change accompanying the Industrial Revolution

The inventions and changing technology accompanying the Industrial Revolution, which gathered pace, initially in the British Isles, then elsewhere, during the course of the eighteenth century, were to affect the design of brass instruments profoundly in the century to follow. The keyed trumpet enters the frame towards the end of the eighteenth century and Charles Clagget's valve system was submitted for patent in London in 1788. But it was not until the growth of mass production of brass instruments and the rise of amateur music making, towards the middle of the century following, that valved brass became ubiquitous. It took many years from the first experiments with keys and valves to work through into universally available and accepted keyed and valved brass.

Localised experimentation in brass mechanisation was widespread in a period that saw increasingly rapid uptake of the advances in science and technology accompanying the Industrial Revolution. Clagget, who had a presence in London and owned a musical instrument shop in Dublin, corresponded with James Watt, the Scottish inventor and musical instrument maker. At this time of the Enlightenment when scholars, scientists and philosophers were part of a European network, in close and constant touch with one another, his work gained widespread attention. An account of it appeared in the journal of the *Königliche Böhmische Gesellschaft der Wissenschaften* in Prague in 1789. Even so, no one invention aimed at increasing the musical capabilities of the trumpet in the eighteenth and early nineteenth centuries could achieve more than localised and temporary success.

By the second quarter of the nineteenth century, the adaptation of steam-age technology to trumpet design resulted eventually in a radically different instrument, with more complex capabilities, albeit still based on the same lip-blown principles. This progress, however, was not all perceived as gain, and there was considerable nostalgia for the sound of the 'true' trumpet – the natural trumpet – which continued to be played in different contexts, mainly military. Although the trumpet gained increasing chromatic capability as valves gained currency, the new instruments took some time to bed down to common, universal use.

These mechanical developments seem to have been of little concern to the major intellects composing at this time, save for the flurry of works composed in Vienna at the turn of the nineteenth century for Weidinger and his keyed trumpet. In addition to the concertos by Haydn and Hummel, these include a *Sinfonia Concertante* in E flat by Leopold Kozeluch, performed in 1798, and a concerto by Joseph Weigl, dated 1799.[37] Why this outburst of invention towards the close of the eighteenth century? Could it have only happened in Vienna? Was it due to a combination of factors: *fin-de-siècle* adventure, the availability of a critical mass of adventurous composers competing with one another in Vienna, and a contemporaneous taste for exoticism?

The success of Weidinger was short-lived, however – musical capitals like Vienna are characterised throughout history by the rapidity of changing tastes and fashions, and he had no rivals or successors who left any discernible trace. The advent of key and valve, however, did lead to a complicated evolution of identity throughout the entire course of the nineteenth century and beyond for the trumpet and the related treble brass instruments which became popular. Although keyed and valved brass were accepted rapidly in popular, vernacular and military music, the composers of art music, with exceptions like Spontini and Berlioz, had little use initially for new-fangled novelty per se and were concerned more with abstract matters of form and content. There was a long time lag before the developing idiom of the valved brasses in popular music brought about important changes in the evolution of musical style and taste. This occurred at a later stage of the nineteenth century and migrated notably from the stage works of Verdi and Wagner to the concert platform in the work of composers such as Strauss and Mahler.

The significance of the trumpet in the baroque period and its legacy

At certain times the trumpet and its players have influenced the development of musical styles. This is most obvious when other instrumentalists and musicians imitate the idiom of the trumpet. This occurred at points both earlier and later than the period of the present chapter, in the Renaissance motets of Dufay and others around 1450 and during the Jazz Age. It also occurred towards the final third of the seventeenth century, stemming from the early innovations in use of the trumpet by Monteverdi and

Fantini in Italy. Further development of the characteristic idiom of the trumpet associated with the baroque period continued with a school of composers active in Bologna and Modena of whom Giuseppe Torelli was the most prolific.

Throughout the seventeenth century, because of the spread of more demanding music, more trumpeters seem to have come to grips with the increasingly advanced playing techniques of the late Renaissance and early baroque. The diatonic simplicity of the trumpet's limited range, its directness of utterance, its capacity for transmitting catchy and memorable musical phrases of an optimistic demeanour, were qualities ideally suited to a rational and scientific age which explained the laws of nature as mechanical formulas, as in Newton's theories of motion and gravity, and was able to postulate reconciliation between science and 'God's will'. The century that ended with Newton had begun with Galileo being put under house arrest by the Vatican for saying that the earth moved. The modern world was in the process of being born. A list of the great minds of the period is salutary. The sciences and mathematics flowered – Hooke, Boyle, Wren, Huygens, Wallis, Descartes, Kepler, Napier, Fermat, Pascal, Leibnitz – as did philosophy – Hobbes, Spinoza, Locke – and literature – Shakespeare, Cervantes, Donne, Corneille, Racine, Molière, La Fontaine, Marvel, Milton – art – Poussin, Claude, Caravaggio, Bernini, Rembrandt, Hals, Vermeer, Rubens, Velasquez.[38] What part did music, and more particular to this book, the trumpet and its players, have to play within this vast canvas? The trumpet, in the music of the period, seemed to be expressive of an emerging confidence, presaging the Enlightenment. Protagoras' humanist dictum, 'Man the measure of all things', which had come to vogue in the previous century, now seemed to come further within grasp in the seventeenth century and there was no more confident expression of the ethos contained within that dictum than the heroic trumpet music of the mature baroque. Towards the end of the seventeenth century, composers of various European nationalities came to reflect the increasing confidence of an age of economic and colonial expansion, using the trumpet as an emotional and patriotic tool to stir the blood. The incidental music composed for the London theatres in the 1690s and early 1700s is a good example. In the operas of mercantile Venice, the goddess of fame, reputation and rumour, Fama, appeared regularly to elevate the hero of the plot, accompanied by her own laudatory obbligato trumpets (Ill. 4.1).

A simpler example of this transference of use, namely putting the martial trumpet in a civilian context, is in the French operas of Lully. Perhaps, initially influenced by the French example, this transposition of idiom – from the military and utilitarian to the symbolic and psychological – also occurred in London's Restoration theatre, resulting in the great number of late seventeenth- and early eighteenth-century trumpet tunes composed by the composers of the world's most assertive colonialist nation of the period, England. The English of this period, with a Whig parliament, and a constitutional monarchy, believed that they had evolved the most perfect form of government the world had known, and their music reflected this. That is perhaps one of the reasons – the psychological environment – why Handel, the naturalised Englishman from a German background, came to write such different trumpet music from Bach.

The trumpet's capacity to grab an audience's attention with brief musical motifs also influenced the way composers came to organise the material of their larger-scale instrumental works. The simple method of works like Torelli's monumental Sinfonia

4.1 Queen Elizabeth of England, attended by Fame and a herald of arms, from a manuscript by Sir William Teshe, dated 1570, dedicated to the Queen (*GB-Lbl* Sloane MS 1832, f. 7v).

à 4 trombe in C, G.33, with a repeated-note block-chord trumpet fanfare used as the cornerstone of its musical construction, came, as the following century unfolded, to be an oft-imitated and favoured way to make a composer's most public compositions memorable (Ex. 4.9).

As will be seen in Chapter 5, Fux and Caldara took this device a stage further in their double trumpet choir *Introduzione* to operas written for the Viennese Court. The capacity for such a motif to lodge in the audience member's memory made it a useful device for later classical period composers. Such devices were still being used as building blocks, with increasing subtlety, as long as there was life in sonata form. Beethoven's Fifth Symphony (1808), a work of quintessential public appeal, uses a

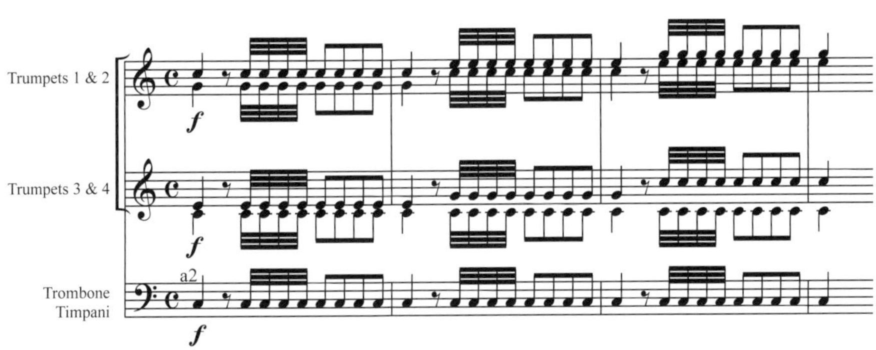

Ex. 4.9 Giuseppe Torelli, Sinfonia à 4 (G.33), opening.

Ex. 4.10 Ludwig van Beethoven, Symphony No. 5, Op. 67, fourth movement, opening.

Ex. 4.11 Ludwig van Beethoven, Symphony No. 3, Op. 55, first movement, bars 37–40.

trumpet and drum rhythmic motif throughout the first movement, and a triumphal trumpet tune as the first and main subject of the last movement (Ex. 4.10) The Third Symphony (the 'Eroica', 1804) also begins with, and is held together by, a motif with its roots in a simple military trumpet call (Ex. 4.11).

For the trumpet, the long period covered in this chapter began in flux and ended in ferment. The trumpet's attainment of a prominent position in art music could not have been predicted at the beginning of the seventeenth century. At the end of the eighteenth century, an interested observer could have been forgiven for thinking that the best days of the trumpet were over. Traditional sources of employment were disappearing, and those that survived were under threat. All over Europe the shock waves of the French Revolution reverberated, and, measured against this, the fate of the trumpet and its players would have provoked very little conscious thought, when, as it seemed to many, the whole of European civilisation was under threat. The rapid growth of population in eighteenth-century Europe was to stimulate Thomas Malthus to publish his influential, but pessimistic, *An Essay on the Principle of Population* in 1798. Contemporaneously there appeared the most important treatise to appear on the trumpet since Fantini's of 1638. Altenburg's *Trumpeters' and Kettledrummers' Art* is interesting for the light it sheds on a trumpet player's perception of the end of an era. This raises important social, political and economic questions about the function and status of trumpet players, in dramatic contrast to issues relating to the nineteenth century. The nineteenth century is the subject of Chapter 9, when the revolution in manufacturing of the Industrial Revolution, which had been gathering pace in the last half of the eighteenth century, impacted on societies, economies and political systems, changing the face of music-making, and with it trumpet playing, for ever.

Chapter 5

Italy and the imperial court at Vienna in the seventeenth and eighteenth centuries

Italy

Whereas the trumpet was introduced into concerted music in Germany through the insertion of short, essentially self-contained, ensemble pieces in the Italian style, it was the instrument's solo idiom, as demonstrated by Fantini, that influenced its introduction into art music in Italy. The Toccata from Monteverdi's *Orfeo* may be representative of the type of instrumental piece performed to announce the commencement of the most lavish dramatic performances, but most early seventeenth-century operas were more intimate affairs, for which a small ensemble of strings augmented the continuo group for introductory sinfonias and ritornelli. From early in the seventeenth century, military or ceremonial scenes, or references to war in opera libretti, were routinely marked by imitations of trumpets in the string writing, often in the key of D. With the development of the opera aria, references to war or battle initiated movements in a trumpet style.[1] The popularity of such arias with string figuration imitating trumpets provided the impetus for the introduction of the trumpet itself into the opera orchestra.

The first opera staged for a fee-paying public in Venice in 1637, *Andromeda* by Francesco Manelli, was performed by a troupe from Rome that included twelve instrumentalists, including two trumpeters.[2] Since the score for this opera has not survived, it is not known whether the trumpeters played in consort with the other instrumentalists or served a more utilitarian role. Antonio Cesti may have provided the stimulus for composers in Venice to incorporate the trumpet into opera scores by including two sinfonias for two trumpets and strings in *Il pomo d'oro*, which was performed at the imperial court in Vienna in 1668 (see Ex. 5.3 below). The sinfonias announce the arrival of Pallas in Act II. Trumpets feature prominently in later works based on the story of Pallas and the golden apple, notably the settings of *The Judgment of Paris* composed for London in 1701. In 1669 Gian Partenio included a 'sinfonia con trombe' (for two trumpets and strings) in his opera *Genserico* and another in his music for Act I of the composite opera *Iphide Greca* in 1671.[3] Antonio Sartorio scored for two trumpets in the opening Sinfonia to *L'Adelaide* (Venice, 1672). In the aria 'Vittrici schieri' from this opera, however, he reverted to the practice of imitating trumpet idiom with strings.[4] The following year, in the opera *Massenzio*, Sartorio included what Edward Tarr considers to be the earliest trumpet obbligato to the Goddess *Fama*.[5] In *Giulio Cesare in Egitto* (Venice, 1676), Sartorio included two sinfonias for trumpet and strings,

Ex. 5.1 Antonio Sartorio, 'Su trombe guerriere' from *Giulio Cesare in Egitto* (1676).

a trumpet flourish within a recitative, and four arias with trumpet obbligato, in which the trumpet and soprano engage in a manner that was soon to be emulated by composers throughout Italy and beyond (Ex. 5.1). Equally prominent trumpet writing features in the operas of other Venetian composers of this period, including Giovanni Legrenzi, Marc'Antonio Ziani and Domenico Freschi,[6] and in many of the operas composed by Alessandro Scarlatti for Naples and Rome. Scarlatti was important to the development of the three-movement opera *sinfonia* (fast–slow–fast), some instances of which include solo parts for trumpets.

From early in the seventeenth century, librettists began to apply the same terminology relating to war to other dramatic situations and as a metaphor for emotional conflict. This broadened the emotional range of trumpet arias and trumpet-style writing, both in opera and the genres into which operatic forms and styles were adopted. Alessandro Scarlatti used the trumpet to highlight the textual imagery of war as a metaphor for the sorts of conflict associated with love in the cantata *Su le Sponde del Tebro* and in several of his 7 *Arie con Tromba Solo*. The opening aria to Alessandro Melani's cantata *All'armi Pensieri*, for soprano, trumpet and continuo, is typical of those that combine the themes of love and war:

> To arms, my thoughts,
> Courage, my heart,
> In fighting let us hope
> For victory in love.

The use of the trumpet to symbolise both love and war travelled and endured. One of the most spectacular and virtuosic 'victory in love' arias is 'Pace una volta' from *Zenobia* by the Bolognese composer Luca Antonio Predieri, first performed in Vienna in 1740. In this aria Zenobia wishes for inner peace in place of 'war and tempest' in her heart.

In Chapter 3 we met the Venetian ship's trumpeter Zorzi Trombetta. In Italy, trumpets and the sea was another enduring theme. The serenata *Inventione per un Barcheggio* by Alessandro Stradella was composed for a Genoese wedding in 1681 and performed on barges positioned in Genoa Bay. The work is scored for three solo singers, 'Tromba o. Cornetto', two violins and continuo; in part two a trombone is added. Each of the two parts of the drama begins with a sinfonia for trumpet or cornett, two violins and continuo; a third sinfonia (to which a trombone is added) is introduced during the second part. Stradella was one of the earliest exponents of concerto grosso techniques and the sinfonias in *Inventione per un Barcheggio* are possibly the first such works to include wind instruments.[7] Parts for trumpet or cornett ('Tromba o cornetto') are included in many arias and ritornelli in the keys of C, F, G and B flat major, and A minor. While several of these movements are idiomatic of trumpet writing, many others appear to have been intended for cornett: even some of those in common trumpet keys and in a trumpet style venture freely outside the notes of the harmonic series and possess a melodic contour that would be extremely difficult to execute on trumpet. The prominence of brass instruments was clearly fitting for a work based on the Neptune theme, and the cornett, as a representation of the conch, the instrument of Neptune's son, Triton, would have been particularly appropriate.[8]

In the opera house, *da capo* arias with obbligato accompaniment in the manner of 'Pace una volta' occasionally turned into a contest between singer and instrumentalist, who vied for the adulation of the audience through displays of melodic embellishment and stamina. Charles Burney described one such competition that arose during the run of an opera in Rome in the early 1720s between the celebrated castrato Farinelli and a trumpeter, as related by the singer when they met in Bologna in 1771:

> There was a struggle every night between him [Farinelli] and a famous player on the trumpet, in a song accompanied by that instrument: this, at first, seemed amicable and merely sportive, till the audience began to interest themselves in the contest, and to take different sides: after severally swelling out a note, in which each manifested the power of his lungs, and tried to rival the other in brilliancy and force, they had both a swell and a shake together, by thirds, which was continued so long, while the audience eagerly waited the event, that both seemed to be exhausted; and, in fact, the trumpeter, wholly spent gave it up, thinking, however, his antagonist as much tired as himself, and that it would be a drawn battle; when Farinelli with a smile on his countenance, shewing he had only been sporting with him all this time, broke out all at once in the same breath, with fresh vigour, and not only swelled and shook the note, but ran the most rapid and difficult divisions, and was at last silenced only by the acclamations of the audience.[9]

Concurrent with the introduction of the trumpet into the opera orchestra, the trumpet began to feature in ecclesiastical contexts. This tradition may have originated in Bologna, where sonatas for one, two or occasionally four trumpets came to be performed before the celebration of Mass in the basilica of San Petronio on important days in the church calendar.[10] The legacy of this is the substantial repertory of trumpet music and church music with prominent trumpet parts that survives in the basilica's archives. The great majority of the pieces for trumpets and strings, labelled sinfonia, sonata or concerto, were written by composers active in the city between 1680 and 1695, many of whom were employed at San Petronio.

During the sixteenth century, instrumentalists, including the wind players of the Concerto Palatino, were employed at San Petronio for important days in the church calendar. By 1595 four trombonists, one player of the cornett and one violinist were in receipt of regular salaries from the basilica; a decade later three additional trombonists were recruited from Germany.[11] Thereafter, string instruments began to gain prominence in the ensemble. During the tenure of Maurizio Cazzati as maestro di cappella (1657–71), the musical establishment was augmented for the principal dates in the church calendar, in particular for the patronal feast on 4 October. For these occasions, Cazzati composed Vespers psalms for two choirs, solo voices and an orchestra that included two trumpets.[12] Cazzati may also have been responsible for establishing the tradition of performing trumpet sonatas in San Petronio since he included three in his Op. 35 collection of string sonatas (Bologna, 1665). These are the earliest published solo works for trumpet and strings. In his preface to the collection, Cazzati indicates that the trumpet sonatas can be performed on violin when no trumpeter is available, an expediency that was probably directed at the music-buying market, rather than an indication of performance practice in Bologna. Like Fantini, Cazzati provided colourful titles for his trumpet sonatas: 'La Caprara', 'La Bianchina' and 'La Zâbeccari'. In comparison with Fantini's sonatas, however, Cazzati's are conservative, with the solo part covering a narrower range, C4 to A5. The first of the three is in D major, with the trumpet part played on a muted trumpet ('tromba serrata, che vuol dire sordina'), and Cazzati notes that if it is to be performed on an 'open' trumpet, it should be played a tone lower. The other two sonatas are in C, with an instruction that they can be performed in D if the trumpeter uses a mute and the other instrumentalists transpose their parts one step higher.

During the tenure of Giovanni Paolo Colonna as *maestro di cappella* (1674–95), the musical establishment of San Petronio was increased further. Trumpeters were never included in the regular musical establishment of the basilica, but were among the many extra musicians imported for special occasions, in particular for the patronal feast. From 1679 until 1699 the trumpeter Giovanni Pellegrino Brandi was listed as performing at the patronal feast each year. It seems safe to assume that he performed many of the solo works in the collection. Colonna's output of instrumental music is small, though he composed one sonata for two trumpets,[13] and included trumpets in some of his Masses and Vespers psalms. These developments were influential, and Colonna's sacred works were represented in Emperor Leopold's chapel in Vienna.

The earliest dated solo work in the collection, the sonata in D for 2 trumpets and strings by Petronio Franceschini, of 1680, is also one of the most interesting. It is in the four-movement *sonata da chiesa* form, and unlike many of the later Bolognese trumpet works, the trumpets play in each movement. Harmonic and melodic interest is maintained through repeated excursions into A minor in trumpet passages. This is achieved primarily by using the trumpet's seventh harmonic C5. Franceschini's trumpet writing is technically demanding, with both trumpet parts ascending to D6, and like Fantini, he employs the non-harmonic pitch C sharp5 as a short lower-auxiliary note to D5. From this time on, virtually all the surviving solo works for trumpet(s) in the archives of San Petronio were written in D major.

Among the composers that contributed to the Bolognese trumpet repertory between 1680 and the dissolution of the cappella in 1696 were the San Petronio cellist-composers Domenico Gabrielli and Giuseppe Maria Jacchini, both of whom introduced obbligato passages for cello in several of their solo trumpet works. Other composers represented in the repertory include Giuseppe Aldrovandini, Francesco Manfredini and Guiseppe Matteo Alberti. It is tempting to conjecture that Jacchini's 'Da morto sonata con trombe sordine' for two trumpets, obbligato cello and strings, which is dated 1695, was composed for the funeral of Colonna that year.

The four *sinfonie* for trumpet(s) and strings (two for one trumpet and two for two trumpets) in Giovanni Bononcini's *Sinfonie à 5. 6. 7. e 8. Istromenti, con alcune à una e due Tromb.* Op. 3 (Bologna, 1685) are among the most virtuosic trumpet pieces composed in Bologna. The collection was published after Bononcini had studied with Colonna for five years, and the trumpet works reveal that the fifteen-year-old composer had a close affinity with the city's solo trumpet tradition. Although Bononcini included trumpets in some of his later works, he never again wrote for the instrument with such exuberance. Given the thriving music publishing industry that existed in Bologna, it is significant that the bulk of the solo trumpet pieces in the San Petronio archives survive only in manuscript. Besides the *Sinfonie* by Bononcini, the only solo works for trumpet published in Bologna around this time were the three sonatas for trumpet and strings from Andrea Grossi's *Sonate . . .* Op. 3 (Bologna, 1682). Grossi served at the court of Mantua from 1678 to 1685 (or later) and all his surviving music, which is solely instrumental, was published in Bologna. The custom of including trumpet pieces in collections of string music, which appears to have originated in Bologna with Cazzati's Op. 35 collection, was adopted elsewhere in Italy – the two sonatas for trumpet and continuo by Giovanni Buonaventura Viviani were included in his *Sonata a Violino Solo* Op. 4 (Venice and Rome, 1678) and in other parts of Europe during the eighteenth century.

Giuseppe Torelli, the composer with the largest number of trumpet sonatas in the San Petronio archives, is an important figure in the development of the baroque concerto. The majority of the 36 trumpet sonatas attributed to Torelli were composed before his departure from the city in 1695 at the disbandment of the San Petronio musical establishment.[14] Those with oboes were presumably written after his return in 1701, following the re-establishment of the *cappella*, since oboes appear to have been introduced to the ensemble at that time.

A feature of many of the Bolognese trumpet pieces that was to have an impact on instrumental writing elsewhere was the construction of movements using short, contrasting melodic fragments. In many of the trumpet pieces entire movements are created through the juxtaposition of separate thematic ideas for trumpet and strings. Smithers identifies an evolution in Torelli's trumpet sonatas from 'a simple imitative-antiphonal style' to one in which the thematic material is more fully developed and inter-related.[15]

Colonna was succeeded as *maestro di cappella* by Giacomo Antonio Perti, who held the position for nearly sixty years. Perti's arrival in 1696 came shortly after the disbandment of the *cappella*. Singers and instrumentalists continued to be hired for important feast days, but several of the most prominent members of the group, including Torelli, left to find employment elsewhere. The San Petronio archives contain several sonatas for one, two and four trumpets by Perti, as well as a vast corpus of his sacred vocal works, some with trumpets. Surviving sets of parts for several of Perti's vocal works indicate that the orchestration, as represented in the score, was enlarged with the addition of trumpets and/or oboes.[16]

There is evidence that some of the Bolognese trumpet repertory became widely disseminated. Manuscript sources of pieces from the repertory are found in various parts of Europe and a letter to Perti, dated 1699, confirms the popularity of a trumpet sonata by Jacchini in Florence.[17] Three of Torelli's sonatas were published by Roger of Amsterdam in the early eighteenth century and it is possible that Torelli presented some of his trumpet music in Ansbach and Vienna when he was residing in those cities between 1696 and 1700. Several of the Bolognese composers of trumpet music composed operas in Bologna and elsewhere, for which the instrumental sinfonias for Bolognese operas were on occasion borrowed from the San Petronio repertory.[18]

After the death of Torelli in 1709 few solo works for trumpet were composed in Bologna. Some of this earlier repertoire may have continued to be performed, if not in the basilica then in the theatre or in concert performances. The legacy of the Bolognese trumpet tradition is evident with the inclusion of two or four trumpets in ten of the twenty-four symphonies that the renowned teacher and theorist Padre Martini composed for performance in Bologna between 1736 and 1777. However, Martini's symphonies demonstrate the change that had occurred in the role of the trumpet in concerted music around the middle of the eighteenth century from a soloistic function to providing a harmonic and rhythmic reinforcement to ensembles in which strings and woodwind carried the melodic argument.

Trumpeters were included in instrumental ensembles in church in other Italian cities during the second half of the seventeenth century. For the feast of St Louis at the church of San Luigi dei Francesi in Rome, for example, an instrumental ensemble was employed, which included one trumpeter in 1670 and two trumpeters in 1675.[19] From the 1680s on, trumpets were regularly added to the large string ensembles that were employed in Rome for festive occasions in church, celebratory events outdoors, and oratorio performances. For approximately three decades, up to his retirement in 1709, almost all of these ensembles were organized and directed by Arcangelo Corelli.[20] Many of these occasions, including performances of oratorios by other composers, featured *sinfonie* by Corelli, some of which included trumpets. In 1689, for example, Queen Christina of Sweden's recovery from illness was celebrated at the church of Santa Casa di Loreto with a Mass for four choirs, along with a sinfonia with trumpets by Corelli.[21] Also in 1689, the oratorio *Il colosso della costanza* by Bernardo Pasquini was performed with four sinfonias by 'Il Bolognese' (as Corelli was often labelled), one of which was described as 'Sinfonia da guerra con tromba'.[22] Three sinfonias by Corelli were also included in performances of the serenata *Applauso musicale* by Giovanni Lorenzo Lulier in Rome in 1693, one of which, a 'Sinfonia strepitosa con quattro trombe', introduced the Goddess Fama.[23]

Corelli's only surviving work for solo trumpet, the Sonata in D for trumpet, two violins and continuo, enjoyed wide circulation during the late seventeenth century, with manuscript copies surviving in Naples, Vienna, London (where it was published in 1704) and Segovia.[24] Although the attribution has been questioned, current scholarly opinion confirms that the sonata was in fact composed by Corelli, although its date of composition is unknown. Corelli studied in Bologna during the tenure of Cazzati and the sonata may date from this period. Given that he is known to have composed trumpet music in Rome, however, it is perhaps just as likely that it was composed there.

Since many concertos and *sinfonie* by Corelli are known only through contemporary accounts of performances, it seems certain that a large part of his oeuvre is lost. His surviving instrumental music is largely accounted for by four sets of trio sonatas and the Concerti Grossi Op. 6, and it has been argued that Corelli adapted orchestral works, or individual movements from them, for inclusion in his published works. Several of the concertos from his Op. 6 include movements with trumpet-like features and it is possible that some of these were originally performed in versions for trumpets and strings.[25] Interestingly, trumpet and kettledrum parts were added to Corelli's Op. 6 No. 4 by Nicolo Pasquali in Edinburgh around the middle of the eighteenth century, but there is no evidence that this was based on an earlier version of the work.

Antonio Vivaldi regularly featured trumpet style writing for strings and woodwind. The concerto in C for two trumpets and strings RV 537, his only instrumental work with trumpets (the Concerto in D RV 563, although playable on trumpets, is for two oboes), incorporates a wide variety of melodic and rhythmic motifs in an exuberant interplay between the two solo parts. When, or for whom, the concerto was written is unknown. Many of Vivaldi's concertos were composed for performances at the Ospedale della Pietà, the girls' orphanage where he worked between 1703 and 1740 and which was famous for its concerts. The trumpet was not taught at the Pietà during Vivaldi's tenure (the horn and timpani were introduced in 1747 and 1750 respectively), but trumpeters were evidently brought in for occasional performances, like that of Vivaldi's oratorio *Juditha triumphans* in 1716. It seems likely that he composed the concerto for another venue or occasion, perhaps as interval entertainment in the theatre.

Although the trumpet featured prominently in Vivaldi's operas, his most imaginative writing for the instrument appears in his sacred music. In the *Gloria* RV 589 Vivaldi follows the Venetian tradition in church music of scoring for one trumpet and one oboe as a single unit. His most original trumpet writing appears in his three settings of Psalm 110, *Dixit Dominus*. The two earliest, RV 594 and RV 595, date from the mid 1710s. The third, RV 807, from the 1730s, was discovered in Dresden in 2005, having previously been attributed to Baldasarre Galuppi. In each of these settings Vivaldi announces the Day of Judgement ('Judicabit in nationibus') with a trumpet call that eschews the instrument's conventional melodic and rhythmic figuration in favour of sudden dynamic contrasts and an unusually wide tessitura, emphasising the instrument's symbolic association with the biblical narrative (Exx. 5.2a and b). The most dramatic of the three passages is that in RV 594. The rising scale and downward arpeggio can be interpreted as a reference to the ascent to heaven and descent to hell. The dramatic effect of Vivaldi's representations of the Day of Judgement was scarcely matched in sacred vocal music until the nineteenth century, when Berlioz and Verdi employed massed brass forces for the Dies Irae in their settings of the Requiem Mass.

Exx. 5.2a & b Antonio Vivaldi, *Dixit Dominus* RV 594 (a); and RV 595, opening of the 'Judicabit in nationibus' section (b).

The imperial court at Vienna

For geographic and political reasons, Vienna was the first beneficiary of successive migratory waves of innovating Italian composers during the seventeenth century. Vienna was the first great capital city on the other side of the Alps for them to reach and they were attracted there by the ruling Habsburgs who governed large tracts of Italy. The most influential Italian composers at court during the first two-thirds of the century were Giovanni Valentini, Giovanni Priuli, Antonio Bertali, Antonio Cesti and Alessandro Poglietti. The earlier of these composers brought the Venetian polychoral style associated with Gabrieli and his contemporaries to Vienna. This influence is seen first in Vienna in the sacred and instrumental music of Priuli and Valentini. Both composers worked for the Archduke Ferdinand of Inner Austria in Graz prior to his election as the Holy Roman Emperor Ferdinand II in 1619.

Ferdinand was an ambitious ruler who sought to end instability and bring political greatness to the Habsburg realms. He laid the foundations for his successors to provide music and ceremony commensurate with that greatness. He invested heavily in music at court, even during the early years of the Thirty Years War, diverting finance from the Duchy of Inner Austria for this purpose.[26]

Gabrieli's pupil Priuli became Hofkapellmeister to Ferdinand at Graz in the second decade of the seventeenth century, and accompanied him in the same capacity to Vienna when he became Ferdinand II in 1619. The direct influence of Gabrieli can be seen in his twelve-part Canzon in echo of 1619, in which the echoes have dynamic markings, and sixteen such works exist in two volumes from the years 1618 and 1619.

Composer, keyboard virtuoso and poet, Valentini became chamber organist to Ferdinand in Graz in 1614 and, like Priuli, followed his employer to Vienna, where Ferdinand deposed the incumbent Kapellmeister, Christoph Strauss, in favour of the Italians, who proceeded to lead his music jointly. Although he had more tenuous links to Venice than Priuli, Valentini was considered a 'Venetian of the famous school of Gabrieli' by his contemporaries, and he consolidated the hold that the Venetian school had gained in the Viennese Court through Priuli.[27]

Valentini succeeded Priuli officially as Kapellmeister around 1626, but was the more prolific of the two composers from about 1622. The era of Italian influence on Viennese court music had begun. Furthermore, the Italian influence coincided with a new style of trumpet writing emerging in the second and third decades of the seventeenth century. This change is referred to in Fantini's treatise of 1638. The trumpet metamorphosed from an instrument expressive of war that plays only with other trumpets and drums, to a musical instrument with a new status and role enabling it to take a full part in musical dialogue with string and wind instruments in concerted music.

Several composers came to this new use of the trumpet around the same time – Reimundo Ballestra, Michael Praetorius, Heinrich Schütz, Christoph Strauss and others – but Valentini composed some of the most prominent pieces to use the trumpet in this new way. Composed in 1618, for Ferdinand's coronation as King of Hungary, Valentini's *Magnificat* was innovatory in its use of seven choirs of instruments including trumpets, which, in effect, established a taste for trumpets sounding alongside voices that proved enduringly popular in Austria. Valentini himself wrote about the difficulties he encountered trying to write for trumpets alongside voices and other instruments.[28] Steven Saunders, in his study of music at Ferdinand's Viennese court, makes a convincing case that the Mass which Valentini wrote for the same forces as the *Magnificat* was written for Ferdinand's imperial coronation in Frankfurt the following year, but was not actually performed on that occasion, and the similarly scored *Jubilate Deo* for his first major victory of the Thirty Years War at the Battle of White Mountain.[29] Thus a thirst for instrumental performance on a massive scale was created: music in which the brilliance of trumpet timbre was a necessary accessory. Priuli and Valentini were both instrumentalists of distinction and Stewart Carter points out that their appointment to prominent Kapellmeister positions was a break from tradition and was a portent of the future: henceforth instrumentalists would hold the highest positions at court, and instrumental colour and timbre as well as virtuosity would be important in the music at court. Carter calls it 'the era of the instrumentalists'.[30] Along with Biagio Marini and G. B. Buonamente, Priuli and Valentini were first to introduce the new Italianate style of violin writing north of the Alps, and Priuli's *Missa concertata in festivitatibus B.M.V.* (1624), with its florid violin and cornett obbligatos, is a fine example of their instrumental innovations.

Antonio Bertali arrived in Vienna in 1624, shortly after Priuli and Valentini, and came with an excellent reputation as a violinist. After Valentini's death in 1649, he succeeded into the Kapellmeister post. He became known as a composer of operas and was the first Kapellmeister to establish regular performances of operas beginning from the 1660s. His dramatic works model Cavalli and Cesti. The theorist Christoph Bernhard, in *Tractatus compositionis augmentatus* (1657), included him with Monteverdi, Cavalli and Rovetta as a model of 'luxuriant style'.[31] Venetian influence is shown in his *canzone* for brass instruments and he produced many festive polychoral pieces with large instrumental forces in the manner established by Priuli and Valentini. His liturgical music includes thirty-three Masses, covering a wide spectrum of styles. He continued to develop the use of the trumpet in a musical and artistic way in concerted works, and notable works to include trumpets are the eleven sonatas 'con trombe solenni' in thirteen to eighteen parts. The instrumentation of these remarkable pieces mixes strings and brass, and within this grouping, trumpets, trombones, cornetts and mute cornetts, on an equal basis. The desire for contrasting instrumental colour and timbre is most evident in the first sonata in eighteen parts. This sonata is divided into three choirs, the first comprising 5 trumpets, the second, 2 cornetts and 4 trombones, and the third, 2 violins, 2 *violette,* trombone or bassoon, and timpani.

During the final years of Bertali's tenure, in 1666, Antonio Cesti moved to Vienna as Vize-Kapellmeister and began work on an opera designed to a new 'colossal' imperial scale for the wedding celebrations of Leopold I and Margarita Teresa of Spain. This was *Il pomo d'oro,* which was first produced on 13/14 July 1668 in Vienna.[32] Cesti, a renowned singer as well as a composer, and by that time the most celebrated Italian musician of his generation, delivered opera on a conceptual scale transcending Viennese practice hitherto, setting the bar for all later operatic production in Vienna. Opera was at the centre of Cesti's professional life and his development as a composer can be traced more to the Roman lineage of Carissimi and Luigi Rossi than to the Venetian influence of Cavalli and Monteverdi. Cesti's style tended towards the simple and monumental, and he created grand effect through economical means. His use of brass in opera was influential. He used the solemn idiom of cornetts and trombones to describe the supernatural at the gates of hell, and he used trumpets to energise scenes with chorus (Ex. 5.3).

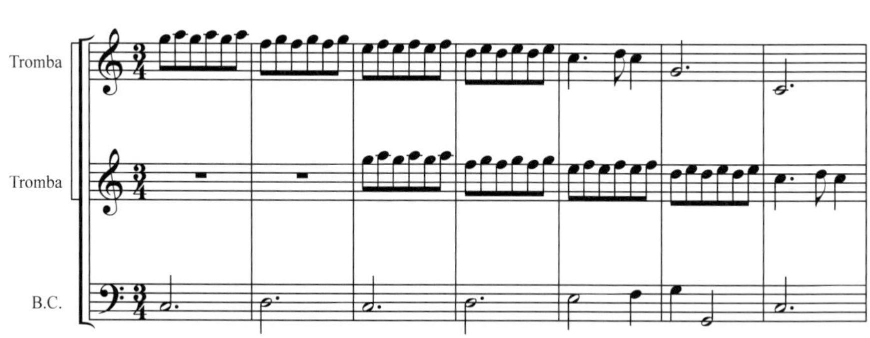

Ex. 5.3 Antonio Cesti, *Il pomo d'oro,* Sonatina 2, Act II, Scene 14.

Alessandro Poglietti's only known opera, *Endimione festeggiante*, was produced in 1677. Appointed as court organist in July 1661, and eventually elevated by the Pope to the rank of a Knight of the Golden Spur, he played an important part in the evolution of Viennese trumpet style as evidenced by his *Balletti* in C for four trumpets and strings and the *Sonata a tre* for flute, trumpet, bassoon and basso continuo. He was a significant keyboard composer, renowned as a teacher, and is chiefly known today for his *Il Rossignolo*, a programmatic cycle of organ music which entered an experimental realm more familiar to us through the works of his younger Bohemian contemporary, Heinrich Ignaz Biber.

Bohemia and Moravia

By the 1660s, the musical life of the courts of Austria, Bohemia and Moravia was flourishing and artistic use of the trumpet was widespread. One of the most prominent, with the best-preserved archives containing music of interest to the development of the trumpet, was at the Bishop's Palace of Kroměříž in Moravia, now the Czech Republic. Among the most influential composers was gamekeeper's son Heinrich Biber, born in Stráž pod Ralskem on the estate of Count Christoph Paul von Liechtenstein-Kastelkorn in Northern Bohemia. After working initially in Graz in Styria, Biber entered the service of Count Christoph Paul's brother, the Prince-Bishop Karl, Count Liechtenstein-Kastelkorn of Olomouc at Kroměříž, as a violinist in 1668 before moving to the Kapelle of the Salzburg Court in 1670–1. Biber was an influential composer of violin music, the composer of a remarkable virtuoso set of solo sonatas for violin – the *Mystery* (also known as *Rosary*) *Sonatas* – and he was part of a vibrant and innovative court at Salzburg, which included Georg Muffat, organist from 1678 to 1690. Biber's music has a wild, improvisatory quality based deeply in the folk music of his region, and indeed this has been an enduring characteristic of many Czech composers up to and beyond Janáček and Martinů in the twentieth century. Biber's earlier writing for violin, with its scordatura, folk borrowings, programmatic effects, virtuoso passage work, and the adventurousness of its range up to the sixth and seventh positions, was in contrast to the Italian School, which by comparison was more restrained in its technical demands. The early Biber violin style was the epitome of the exuberant *stylus phantasticus*. Biber also wrote prominently for trumpet, and his first trumpet ensemble music was composed during his employ at Kroměříž – the Sonata for six trumpets, timpani and continuo (1668), similar in style to the flamboyant *Sonata Sancti Polycarpi*, for eight trumpets and timpani, composed at Salzburg in 1673.

The Kapellmeister at Kroměříž during Biber's period of employment there was the chief trumpeter and composer Pavel Josef Vejvanovský, who was putting his own 'Czech' stamp on trumpet idiom, stretching the limits of the instrument's capabilities to new levels, in contrast to the Italian models, which were by now beginning to seem simple and austere in comparison, like the violin music. Vejvanovský and Biber formed part of a cadre of Jesuit-trained musicians which would endure for generations in the Courts of Greater Austria. Although it is thought that Biber studied with both Bertali and Vejvanovský, he is also believed to have been a pupil of Austrian violinist-composer Johann Heinrich Schmelzer, who wrote a considerable body of instrumental and dance music, much of which used trumpets. During the first decade of Schmelzer's employment at the imperial court, in which he rose from the position of violinist in the court chapel to Vize-Kapellmeister in 1671 and Kapellmeister a few months before his death in 1680, he also served as a cornettist at St Stephan's Cathedral, Vienna. Between 1665 and 1685 Schmelzer composed ballet music for almost all theatrical productions at the imperial court. Much of the repertory survives at Kroměříž, with many works including prominent parts for wind and brass instruments. Ensembles of up to five trumpets and timpani were used in the music that Schmelzer composed for lavish equestrian ballets and outdoor spectacles, such as *La contessa dell'aria e dell'aqua festa a cavallo,* performed in 1667 for the marriage of Leopold and Margarita (which included music by Bertali). Trumpets also played their part in chamber music by Schmelzer: two trumpets are included in the *Sonata prima à 8* and *Sonata duodecima à 7* from his *Sacro-Profanus Concentus Musicus* (Nuremberg, 1662).[33]

It was Vejvanovský who was the most likely inspiration, however, for Biber and the other Kroměříž composers to write for the trumpet. He was first appointed to the court as a trumpeter in 1661, working additionally as a copyist. Many of the works of Viennese composers such as Bertali and Poglietti survive in his hand in the Kroměříž archives. In 1664 he became Kapellmeister, a position which he held until his death.[34] Vejvanovský's writing for trumpet was notable for its use of the minor key, non-harmonic notes (Ex. 5.4), and an independence of part writing between the first and second trumpets. His writing for trumpets was the most adventurous of the seventeenth century before Purcell, and it is an interesting supposition that some influence of Vejvanovský's Moravian trumpet style transferred to London in the 1680s when composer Gottfried Finger emigrated to there from Olomouc. Although in many of Vejvanovský's works trumpets appear alongside cornetts, in some, like the *Sonata Vespertina,* the trumpets seem to have supplanted the cornett, appearing alongside three trombones with two violins and organ. Typical of Vejvanovský's larger-scale writing for the instrument is the *Sonata Ittalica a 12,* while his more virtuosic solo trumpet style is displayed in *Sonata Tribus Quadrantibus* (*c.*1667).

Biber's son, Karl Heinrich Biber, became Kapellmeister in Salzburg, like his father before him, and left several exciting short works for solo trumpet and orchestra, notable among which are the *Sonata Paschalis* (1729), and the sonatas of 1729 and 1744 for up to nine trumpets and orchestra.

Ex. 5.4 Pavel Josef Vejvanovský, *Sonata a 4 Be mollis,* bars 1–4 (a); and 53–4 (b)

Fux and Caldara

The seventeenth and eighteenth centuries provided many coincidences of the right conditions for the trumpet, its music, players and composers, to flourish to a hitherto unprecedented degree. Vienna of the second, third and fourth decades of the eighteenth century was a particular highpoint. There had been a long period of enlightened support for music since Ferdinand II's accession in 1619, and now an imperial aspiration to take staged arts on to an altogether higher plane brought together a critical mass of collective genius. The collaborative yet competitive environment allied to an intense performance schedule of the cluster of players and composers around Johann Joseph Fux and Antonio Caldara ensured that the extended idiom of the virtuoso 'baroque' trumpet rapidly developed to its final peak of virtuosity and expressiveness during these decades in Vienna.

In Vienna, the trumpet was a symbol of *Imperium*: the authority of absolute imperial power. It had been so since the first Imperial Privileges concerning trumpet playing were announced in 1623. By 1721 there were sixteen *Musikalische Trompeter* and two *Paucker* (balanced by thirty violinists) answerable to the Hofkapelle plus twenty-four *Hof-* and *Feldtrompeter* and two *Paucker* organised through the court's stables and kitchens department. Six trumpeters also dressed in chain mail to form part of the imperial bodyguard. The dowager Empress, Wilhelmine Amalie, was also entitled to trumpeters in her bodyguard.[35] With so many trumpets and so many bespoke occasions for different dispositions of trumpet players with differing skills, the trumpets needed their own organization. For many years this was provided by the *Ober-Trompeter*, Franz Anton Küffel, under whom the *Musikalische Trompeter und Hör-Paucker* and, indeed, the entire body of trumpet players at court, became privileged with a certain amount of administrative autonomy.

The sound of the trumpet was essential to the *Bekanntmachungsschall* – the music to herald the arrival of the Emperor or Empress in any city. With the accession of the new Emperor, Charles VI, in 1712, trumpets became yet more important as the musical manifestation of his own imperial motto. This motto was *Costanza e Fortezza* (constancy and fortitude), which became the subject of Fux's most substantial work, the 1723 opera of the same name. Peter Brown makes a compelling case, in 'Caldara's trumpet music', as to why two (and no more than two) choirs of trumpets were used with such frequency and such exclusivity for the imperial *Galatage* associated with the Emperor: they were symbolic of the two pillars of Hercules either side of the Straits of Gibraltar – Mount Abyla on the African side, and Mount Calpe on the European side. Charles had developed this unwavering personal creed over the first decade of the eighteenth century, holding an ambitious court in Barcelona as Charles III, pretender to the throne of Spain. Strength, stability, war and peace: this is what the double group of trumpets and timpani, which preface the festive operas produced at court for grand occasions, represent.[36] Despite the great number of trumpet players at court, there is evidence that they were used with great discretion. The large numbers very rarely played together in consort – they were spaced out in groups of usually no more than four, whereas double choirs were reserved for the Emperor himself.

The operas produced at court that featured the trumpet were designed to impress, and the overtures with eight trumpets were part of that impression. Many of the operas were thinly disguised autobiographical allegories about the current rulers and events. Operas were spectacular, abounding in war and battle scenes, and the sound of the trumpet was equated with the emperor or ruler, who was often the hero of the plot. Caldara was first exposed to opera of this sort in his home city of Venice. One of the influential composers working there was Carlo Francesco Pollarolo. In his opera *L'Irene* (1694) the tyrant role of Memete, played by a castrato contralto, is portrayed as a tragic character forced into a hopeless situation by love and war from which only his magnanimity of character can save him. One of Pollarolo's specialities was the 'rage and revenge' aria, and in Act I Scene 3, 'Guerra, guerra, voglio guerra', the ideal instrument to set off and complement Memete's vehemence and his agitato, presto-style *coloratura* is the trumpet. These operas contained elaborate stage effects and pantomimes. *L'Irene* featured a ballet-intermezzo at the conclusion of Act IV – a Janissaries and Moors war-game, danced to the sound of trumpet and drum. Battle scenes and choruses like the Act III Scene 1 'Su, di metalli, e di feroci trombe' were enhanced by prominent trumpet writing.[37] The Viennese imported these operatic ideas along with the composers, librettists, choreographers and stage designers from Italy, notably from Bologna and Venice. Virtuoso use of the trumpet was an incidental consequence.

Music and the staged arts held a special place in the political and religious context of Vienna. Music was revered as a vehicle for religious faith. The court radiated a deeply embedded Catholicism reinforced by the Counter-Reformation. Vienna was a stronghold of Catholic Church music rooted in a centuries-old tradition, and its church music had been continually refreshed by innovative Venetians like Caldara, who were equally adept in liturgical and non-liturgical styles. This ambition to be the standard bearers of a religious music tradition more glorious than any other gave Fux and Caldara a highly respected place in the hierarchy at court.

Furthermore, stability and encouragement were provided by three extraordinarily musical emperors in succession: Leopold I and his sons, Joseph I and Charles VI, were excellent composers and performers who often directed performances. A long period of musical growth and stability lasted from 1680 to 1740, which has been described as a *Blütezeit* (Golden Age).[38] By the time of Charles VI this was in full flower, with ceremonies representing the Emperor's exceptional musical and religious ambitions in much the same way as in Rome, where they symbolised the majesty of the pope.[39]

A third reason for the pre-eminence of Vienna in music was that its geographic position just north of the Alps combined with its ability to pay made it a place where musical happenings could occur on a scale and of a quality unattainable anywhere else. Vienna had been the first destination for the waves of Italian innovators from the early and middle baroque and, at the cusp of the eighteenth century, was an early beneficiary of another wave of composers bringing late baroque style to the rest of Europe from Bologna, Venice and Florence.

From Bologna in 1697 came Giovanni Bononcini, joined in 1703 by Attilio Ariosti, and in 1705 by his brother Antonio Maria Bononcini and Pier Francesco Tosi; from Venice, Carlo Agostino Badia in 1694 and Marc'Antonio Ziani in 1700; and from Florence, Francesco Bartolomeo Conti in 1701. Successive emperors were prepared to allocate the resources necessary to bring together, not only the best composers, but also all of the best and most cutting-edge talents across the performing arts. Lady Montagu Worsley, coming from London to attend the opera in Vienna, reported an expenditure of £30,000 sterling for the 'decorations and habits' alone for Fux's *Angelica* in 1716.[40]

The innovative savoir-faire that the Viennese court mustered in the staged arts was a coming together of all the talents. The demand for performance, both secular and religious, led to an intense production calendar. Music existed on varying levels of intimacy and privacy alongside the public and diplomatic entertainments. Ecclesiastical works were produced every Sunday, and special works composed for the additional forty Church Festival days – the *Festtage der Heiligen* – which existed during Charles VI's reign. In addition, secular works for special name days and Court feasts were produced. Choirs of four trumpets and timpani formed part of such celebrations. The four trumpets were usually split into two *clarini* and two *trombe.* The *clarini* played florid runs in the upper tessitura, and one of the *trombe* doubled the timpani at the octave, while the other provided the equivalent of a simple viola part on the natural harmonics available to it. Kilian Reinhardt, Konzertmeister, in his *Rubriche Generali* of 1727, which laid out the musical requirements of the performance schedule, called this a *pleni chor.*[41] Reinhardt seems to have fulfilled this function of Konzertmeister from around 1698, when orchestral music began to increase in importance at court, and the number of players and performances began to grow. The term Konzertmeister did not have its modern meaning, but meant a combination of responsibilities including orchestral librarian, copyist and general orchestral manager. A *pleni chor* seems to have performed either within the ensemble of instruments during Mass and Vespers, or played fanfares (*Intraden*) on its own before, during and after the service, and during the processions to and from the service. The *Intraden* seem to have been improvised, or memorised from a courtly canon that would have been built up over time and retained by what was a stable group of players.[42] Two *pleni chor* playing together, as has been discussed above, symbolised the Emperor and his motto, 'Constancy and Fortitude'. They also symbolised special Imperial occasions, like the birth of an heir to the throne or the wedding celebrations of Maria Theresa in 1736. Three and four choirs were very occasionally used, and then notably only for processionals involving the Festival of the Holy Name of Mary.[43]

Although Fux's main remit was ecclesiastical music, he composed *serenate* for the imperial family's name days, and three full-blown operas. Caldara, whose main remit was secular music, composed 100 masses in ordinary for court. This intermingling had extraordinary results and must have been one of the reasons Charles VI commissioned Fux, and not Caldara, to compose *Costanza e Fortezza.* How complete the symbiotic relationship was between the two composers is shown by the fact that Caldara conducted the work's first performance in Prague. This display of the highest standards of performance achievable to accompany his and his wife's enthronement as King and Queen of Bohemia was important to the Emperor's foreign diplomacy. *Costanza e Fortezza* was designed to be the most memorable event of the year in 1723. The flautist Johann Joachim Quantz, who was a guest performer, speaks of one hundred singers and two hundred instrumentalists who were assembled from all over Europe to join the orchestra.[44] Apostolo Zeno, librettist and literary scholar, reported that the

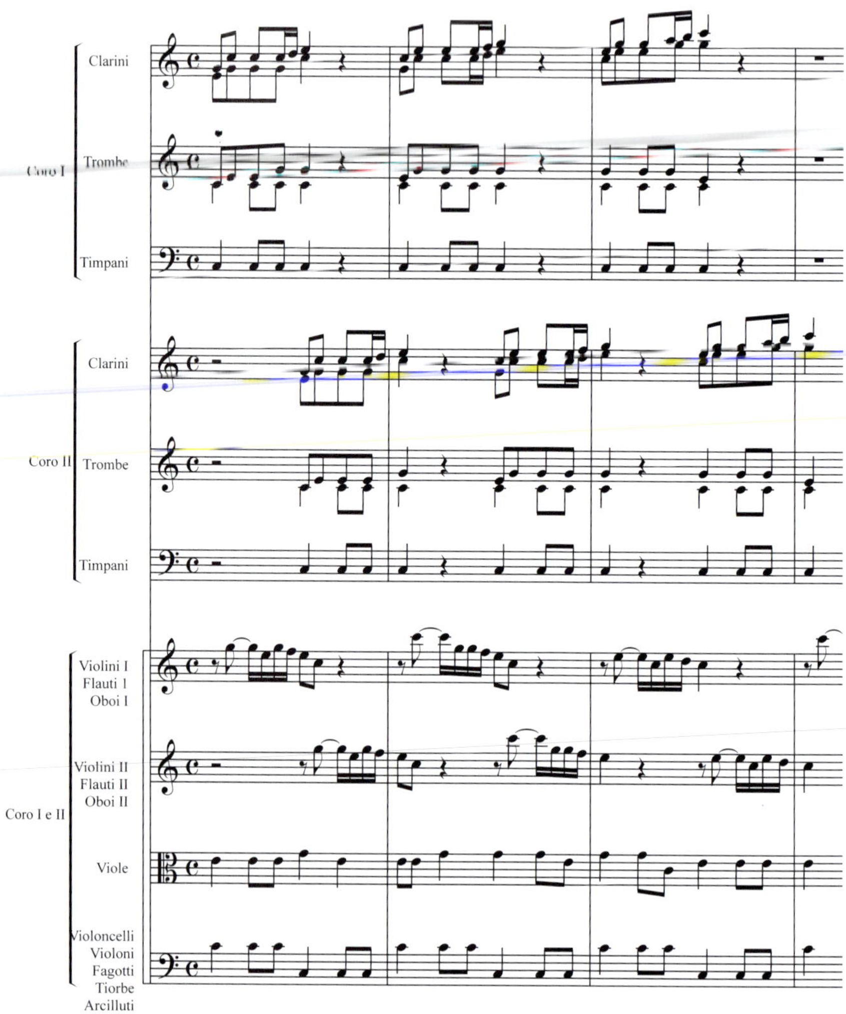

Ex. 5.5 J. J. Fux, *Costanza e Fortezza* (1723), opening Sinfonia.

amphitheatre could hold 4,000 people. Quantz also commented on the 'church style' of the opera.[45] Fux's monumental style and counterpoint were ideal for a piece meant to reflect and communicate to the assembled diplomatic élite of Europe, Charles VI's own belief system, reinforced by the symbolism of his motto and the twin pillars of Hercules – the double choirs of trumpets – which open the work (Ex. 5.5).

These productions were an astonishing stage spectacle and the Emperor demanded the highest production values. Caldara's association with the architect and stage designer Ferdinando Galli Bibiena began in Venice, continued in Barcelona, and culminated in Vienna, where Caldara worked closely with Francesco and Antonio Galli Bibiena as well as Ferdinando.

Fux and Caldara assembled an extraordinary collection of players to perform their works. Franz Küffel filled the position of Ober-Trompeter from 1711 to 1754. Franz

Josef Holland (1687–1747) was as highly paid as Küffel, and established a family trust for his descendants.[46] The player who gained most contemporary plaudits for his playing, however, was Johann Heinisch, who came to court as a Scholar Hof- und Feldtrompeter in 1726, subsequently serving in the Hofkapelle as a Musikalische Trompeter from 1730 to 1750. The following account appears in the diary of a Kremsmünster monk named Beda Planck. It concerns a performance Heinisch gave in 1746 of an obbligato to an aria from Bernasconi's *Artaserse*:

> Mr Heinisch, the famous trumpeter, performed a solo in this aria so artfully and high that it seemed almost beyond human capability, for the trumpet was more like a piccolo. At the end of the aria, this female sang such a long and lovely trill that I really believed she would run out of breath; she then performed a longer and still longer trill accompanied by Mr Heinisch on his trumpet.[47]

The orchestra was full of talent: André Wittman was, according to Fux's own audition report of 21 April 1721, 'an oboe and chalumeau virtuoso, such as I have never before heard'.[48] Two Bohemian horn players, Wenzel Rossi and Friedrich Otto, were part of the Hofkapelle from 1712. The horn began to join the orchestra from around that time to add authenticity to scenes like the *Ballo di Cacciatori e Cacciatrice* in Caldara's *Sirita* of 1719.[49] Large dispositions of forces lent spatial depth and width to action scenes – as in Fux's *Elisa* of the same year, where the hunt scene requires eight trumpets, two sets of timpani, four horns and oboes in addition to strings. Horn-playing reinforcements must have been brought in from Bohemia or provided from within the corps of trumpet players at a time when there were few specialist horn players.

The most striking change regarding the number of trumpets at the Viennese Court in the eighteenth century was the doubling of their number from seven to fourteen on the accession of Charles VI in 1711 and the immediate halving at his death from twelve to six on Maria Theresa's succession in 1740. These timings coincided with either end of Fux's tenure. The numbers never dropped below twelve during Charles VI's reign.[50]

When Fux became Kapellmeister on the death of Ziani in 1715, and Caldara stepped into his Vize-Kapellmeister shoes in 1716, oversight of instrumental music became part of Caldara's duties. The principal violinist he inherited, English-born Nicholas (Nicola) Matteis, was Direttore della musicale instrumentale in charge of operational matters. Matteis had been in the employ of the imperial court since 1700. His responsibilities included the musical directorship of the court balls and the writing of a major part of the ballet music performed at court. This included 426 instrumental dances for 33 of the operas Caldara had a hand in composing. Trumpets were prominent in Matteis's scoring.

During Caldara's tenure (1716–36) the contours of the court orchestra came to resemble that of the late classical orchestra. The violin section increased in size by fifty per cent between 1716 and 1727. In 1721, the orchestra gained its maximum complement of eighty-four. This broke down to 9 oboes, 4 bassoons, horn, 2 cornetts, 4 trombones, 18 trumpets, 2 timpani, 30 violins, 7 cellos, 3 violone, gamba, lute and theorbo.[51] Caldara's years of residence in Venice and Vienna were remarkable in that they coincided with the peak decades of orchestral activity in both centres.

Despite widespread obsolescence of the cornett elsewhere, it played a vital role in the music of Fux and Caldara. The cornett, according to contemporary observer Johann Mattheson, had all but disappeared, along with the trombone, in Germany and elsewhere. Both instruments, however, were regarded as an essential feature of the instrumentation for the *ordinari* music written in the *stylus mediocris* of the Viennese chapel. One hundred and seven of Fux's 290 church compositions call for *ripieno* cornett. The cornett does not appear in Fux's operas, although it does in Caldara's. Two cornett players were permanently on the staff between 1721 and 1740.

Caldara's output was huge. He composed some 34 operas and 25 oratorios for Vienna during the last twenty years of his life. But the staggering amount of music and staged works produced was due to carefully managed collaboration and collective authorship of larger works. The three main collaborators were Fux, Caldara and Matteis. Their music had great diversity and they composed in all sorts of different genres for different contexts and purposes, private and public. They provided the cornerstones of the contemporary Viennese style in close teamwork over four decades: Fux started as a court composer in 1698, Nicholas Matteis joined the employ of the imperial court in 1700, and Caldara became Vize-Kapellmeister in 1716.

Nevertheless, these were by no means the only composers working in court at this time. The production calendar was so intense that many major operatic events became necessarily multi-authored. Matteis wrote a major part of the ballet music associated with Caldara's operas for the dancing masters Alexandre Phillebois and Levarossi della Motta. The ballet was aimed at scenographic rather than dramatic effect. There was a wide gamut of spectacle achieved by Matteis, including the supernatural, arcadian and pastoral, through the martial and maritime to the hunt and the four seasons.

The martial allegory led particularly to the use of trumpets, for example 'Ballet of young Romans in military exercise' in Act II of Caldara's *Lucio Papirio* (1719); 'Ballet of the Egyptian Knights' in Act III of *Nitocri* (1722); 'Ballet of the Polish and Lithuanian Knights' in Act V of *Il Venceslao* (1725); and the 'Ballet of the Knights' in Act V of *Don Chisciotte* (1727). The ballets added to the spectacle of the Vienna Opera and were designed to set off the superb scenic architecture, stage designing and costuming presided over by the Galli Bibiena family.

Trumpets took part mainly in *intradas, entrées* and *marcias* which Matteis wrote for the ballet. With *trombe* and timpani instrumentation, they are festive in character, and some acted as a *retirada*, an opportunity for the entire ballet company to present themselves to take applause in sequence and then together before leaving the stage. Trumpets are generally grouped in threes and fours in the *marcia, entrée* and *retirada* movements. Fux's *Enea negli Elisi* ballet music (1731) is exceptional, in that it requires two choirs of trumpets.

Matteis had a long and fruitful career as a dance composer for the Vienna court. Some of his dances, especially those of a pastoral, arcadian or maritime hue, showed a folk music influence. He used English, Scottish and Austrian melodies, introduced the hornpipe to Austria, and invented the *aria grotesca*, a type of novelty slapstick dance, one of which graced Act I of Caldara's *Sirita*: the *Aria Burlesca Scozzese.* His court career spanned the era of Fux and Caldara, and his music endured after his death. His ballet music was used for Predieri's *Zenobia,* notable for the stunning trumpet obbligato, 'Pace una volta'.

The production of Antonio Cesti's *Il pomo d'oro* in 1668 had had a lasting impact on the scale of aspiration relating to opera in Vienna, where the legacy was such that full-scale operatic composition was considered Italian territory. Fux wrote three full-blown operas compared with Caldara's thirty-four. Fux's main contribution to the genre was on the smaller scale of the *serenata.*

Fux wrote his first full-scale drama in three acts, *Angelica vincitrice di Alcina,* to celebrate the birth of Crown Prince Archduke Leopold in the busy year of 1716. Like many of the celebratory works of the period, it was composed for the open air. As in all of his open-air compositions, Fux avoids soft-toned instruments. He uses two orchestras as in the earlier *Gli ossequi* of 1709. There are eight trumpets in the *Intrada* and in the final chorus. As well as this use in *Angelica,* trumpets add imperial splendour to *Elisa* (1719) and *Costanza e Fortezza* (1723). The use of trumpets in choral movements can be broken into three categories: warlike mode, praise and worship, and rejoicing. In warlike mode, the trumpets interject stylised signals; in choruses of praise and worship, trumpet scoring is applied more unusually and sensitively; and the rejoicing manner, as in the final choruses of *Angelica* and *Le Nozze di Aurora* (1722), is often intended to accompany dance.

From his 67th year Fux was hampered periodically by illness and, after composing another *festa teatrale, La Corona d'Arianna* in 1726, there was a five-year gap before his last work, *Enea negli Elisi* (1731). This was the first libretto by the new court poet Pietro Metastasio. The only solo instrument used is obbligato trumpet. In Fux and Caldara's writing for trumpet of this period, the trumpet's idiom has changed subtly since the initial influence of the 'revenge and rage' style of Pollarolo's operas forty years earlier. Bacco's proclamation, 'Più non empia mie trombe famose', from *La Corona,* is accompanied by a virtuoso trumpet part. In the words of Detlef Altenburg:

> Bacco is not here the brave warrior or the glorious victor – the loss of the trumpet idiom in both vocal and clarino sections makes this clear. Instead, the splendid military victor speaks as a lover.[52]

Caldara's operas with prominent trumpet obbligatos include *La Contessa de'numi* (1723); *Gianguir* (1724); *I due dittatori* (1726); and *Il Temistocle* (1736). Artists like the great castrato alto Gaetano Orsini were in residence, and the ability to pay determined that most of the great singers of the period performed in Vienna. The trumpet imitated the brilliant virtuosity of these singers.

In Fux's ecclesiastical works the scale and impact of the choral movements in particular distinguish his treatment of the Roman Catholic oratorio from its cultivation elsewhere. Instrumentally, Fux's ecclesiastical works are remarkable for their use of the chalumeau and trombone as well as trumpet. The trombone had deeply affective connotations for composers working in Vienna and was closely identified with death and suffering.[53]

Trumpets were more rejoicing in character, and Fux used trumpets mixed with cornetts in his works set to liturgical texts for the offertory composed in *stile mediocre* and *stile solenne*. In the motet K168 *Reges Tharsis et Insulae*, he uses two trumpets with one cornett, in the *Missa pro defunctis Domine Jesu Christe* (K53), two trumpets with two cornetts, and in the *Solenner Besetzung* of the *Missa pro Defunctis Domine Jesu Christe* (E16), two clarinos, two cornetts and two trumpets. And set to non-liturgical texts, in *Mediocrer Besetzung*, he uses cornett and two trumpets in the *Motetta della Madonna SS* (K173) and two trumpets each in the motets *Ponis nubem ascensum tuum* (K169) and *Celebremus cum gaudio* (K181). In the non-liturgical *Solenner Besetzung* genre, many works use trumpets, including *Motetto de Resurrectione Domini*, and *Plaudite, sonat tuba* (K165).[54]

Caldara's early Venetian training had rendered him equally effective in church and staged music. He made 100 settings of the ordinary of the Mass, and twice as many Psalm settings, providing the bulk of the Hofkapelle's staple repertoire. In the liturgical texts of Caldara, the four-part (SATB) choruses are generally reinforced by cornett, alto/tenor trombones, and bassoon. When brass obbligatos are employed, the trombone is generally used to generate a mood of introspection. The trumpet, on the other hand, is used for bravura display, usually as a foil to a soprano or bass solo voice. Oratorios by Caldara which include trumpet obbligatos are *Assalone* (1720), which uses two *clarini*, and *Ester* (1723), which uses one *tromba*. The 'Quoniam' from Caldara's *Missa S. Bernardi* is typical, and bears testament to the impressive technique attained by the Viennese stable of trumpeters (Ex. 5.6).

Fux's Masses carry on the Viennese tradition of *Missa solemnis* with trumpets and timpani begun with Priuli and Valentini: in K2, K5, K26, K38 and K44 he scores for trumpets in five parts. The *Te Deum*, K270, calls for a *Toccata di Trombe* between verses 19 and 20 without providing music.[55] This was probably customary, the trumpet corps being expected to provide music from its repertoire committed to memory.

As well as the three major operas of his later career, Fux wrote nineteen Italian secular-dramatic compositions on a smaller scale, and he was particularly prolific in this genre in the first decade of the eighteenth century. These works were generally termed *serenate*, and Fux wrote one for each name day of the imperial family. Trumpets are used as a celebratory ingredient of these works, either solo or in pairs, as in *Julo Ascanio Re d'Alba*, a serenata for the name day of the Emperor Joseph I, on 19 March 1708. *Pulcheria*, written for the name day of the Empress on 21 June 1708, has an *Intrada* for solo trumpet and strings and a martial aria for trumpet and orchestra. The trumpet was often used to ornament a heroic aria, as in *Il Mese di Marzo* of 1709.

Ex. 5.6 Antonio Caldara, 'Quoniam' from the *Missa S. Bernardi*.

Gli Ossequi della Notte, written in honour of Empress Amalie Wilhelmine and first performed in the open air on 15 July 1709, used a large orchestra of forty-eight players. In the six-movement *Sinfonia* Fux uses two orchestral groups. For the first time, two pairs of obbligato trumpets participate in one aria, anticipating *Rinaldo* (1711), Handel's first London opera, by two years. *La Decima Fatica d'Ercole* uses two trumpets with timpani and Fux deploys these instruments in a warriors' chorus and an aria for Hercules. The Habsburgs, especially those with a Spanish connection, were associated with the Hercules myth, and the trumpet, a symbol of strength, often accompanied Hercules. The castrato Orsini was often cast as Hercules, although on this occasion the title role was sung by a tenor, Silvio Garghetti, Orsini undertaking another role.[56]

Fux is also remarkable for early non-dramatic use of the trumpet in the Serenade à 8 for two trumpets, two oboes and bassoon, two violins, viola, and continuo from his *Concentus musico-instrumentalis* (1701). He also shows progressive use of horns, being one of the first composers to use horns in F in his 1706 orchestra.[57] A taste for novelty is also shown in his use of the *tuba pastoricia*, possibly a form of alphorn used by shepherds, in a *Pastorella* for SATB, strings, organ and tuba pastoricia from the same decade.[58]

The influence of Fux and Caldara as teachers and trendsetters was wide throughout Europe and was not confined to their own pupils. The libretti of all their operas were published internationally and much of the music was widely disseminated. Some works were deemed important enough for the scores to be published in full, like *Elisa*, mentioned above, published by Jeanne Roger in Amsterdam, complete with its eight-trumpet *Introduzione* and four-horn hunting scene.

Performances of Fux's and Caldara's works were widespread, notably in courts throughout Moravia and in Dresden. Some courts were scarcely less active than the imperial court. In the Jaroměřice nad Rokytnou court, ten operas and eighteen *commedias* were produced in 1738 alone. The Chapel of Count Franz Anton Rottal in Holešov was another renowned for its music, and, interestingly, in this situation, tower musicians provided the brass parts.

The Dresden connection to Viennese music-making is highlighted by reference to the *Inventarium* of the Dresden repertory compiled in 1726 by Fux's pupil Jan Dismas Zelenka. The establishment of Catholicism at the court of Protestant Saxony in 1697 had been a political move which stabilised after 1720 owing to the connection of the houses of Wettin and Habsburg through marriage in 1719. The musical connections by virtue of the requirements of the Catholic liturgy had become very strong. In Zelenka's *Inventarium* dating from 1726, compositions by Caldara are prominent, confirming his importance in the current performance practice of the royal chapel. Strong links also existed between Prague and Dresden. In the 1728 Inventory from the Loreto Church in Prague are found many of the same composers as encountered in Dresden, including Fux and Caldara.

Both composers had many influential pupils. Among Fux's were Zelenka, Gottlieb Muffat, Franz Tuma, and Christoph Wagenseil. Caldara collaborated on joint compositions, *La Forza dell'amicizia* (1728) and *La pazienza di Socrate* (1731), with his pupil, Georg Reutter II. Reutter, later to become Kapellmeister in succession to Predieri, continued to write demanding trumpet parts until his death in 1772.

Fux's legacy extended beyond his musical compositioins. His treatise on composition – the *Gradus ad Parnassum* – was the most influential of its time. The work's importance was not founded on Fux's reputation as a theorist, but on his reputation as a composer. After its publication in Latin in 1725, it sold out within a year. J. S. Bach's copy of *Gradus* still survives, and Bach's pupil Lorenz Mizler, a lecturer at Leipzig University, was responsible for the first German translation in 1742.

Haydn, who had spent the previous decade from 1739/40 as a chorister at St Stephan's Cathedral while living in Reutter's house, entered into an intensive period of self-instruction from around 1750 based on the *Gradus*. It was Haydn who initiated the classical legacy for the treatise, recognising that the work of Fux was based on timeless principles, not arbitrary rules. Haydn's personal copy was used with all his pupils, including Mozart and Beethoven. Beethoven designed a course of instruction based on Fux's *Gradus* for his patron and friend Archduke Rudolph. Mozart used *Gradus* extensively with his English pupil, Thomas Attwood, in 1785. Haydn had also been instructed as a choirboy from the vocal instruction manual Fux had compiled some twenty years before *Gradus*: the *Singfundament*. This method, circulated in manuscript copies, remained in use until Schubert, who possessed a version for violin duet.

This continuity in compositional technique through and beyond Haydn from Fux is noteworthy. Perhaps a penchant for instrumental adventure was also handed on. Haydn went on to extend the technique of the trumpet at the close of the century, mirroring Fux at its opening.

Chapter 6

Germany in the seventeenth and eighteenth centuries, and the trumpet writing of Handel, Telemann and Bach

The importance of Germany and Austria to the development of trumpet playing in the seventeenth and eighteenth centuries was highlighted in Chapters 4 and 5, with the discussion of the Imperial Guild of Trumpeters and Kettledrummers and the use of the trumpet by composers in Leipzig and at the Imperial court at Vienna. In this chapter we will consider the traditions of trumpet playing and the styles of writing for the trumpet at other musical centres within the network of more than 300 principalities, ecclesiastical states and municipalities in the German-speaking realm, before assessing the music of Handel, Bach and Telemann, who were born in east-central Germany within five years of each other.

Twenty-five miles northwest of Leipzig lies the city of Halle, which in the early seventeenth century was the seat of the Margrave Christian Wilhelm of Brandenburg. In 1609 Samuel Scheidt was appointed court organist at Halle. Scheidt's promotion to Kapellmeister coincided with the publication in 1620 of his collection of polychoral motets, *Cantiones sacrae*, which includes his setting of *In dulci jubilo*, his only surviving work with trumpets. Whereas Praetorius (who as holder of an honorary court position occasionally visited Halle) incorporated a six-part trumpet ensemble into his setting of the same text, which was published in 1618, Scheidt used two trumpets to embellish the treble lines (Ex. 6.1). During the Thirty Years War, while court life was suspended, Scheidt was appointed director of music at the Marktkirche in Halle. It seems likely that Scheidt composed large-scale vocal works with instruments both for the court and for the Marktkirche, since the second volume of his *Geistliche Concerte* (1634) includes an appeal for a publisher to print the works in the six proposed volumes in the series (of which four actually appeared) in their full versions, 'namely with eight and twelve voices . . . with symphonies and all sorts of instruments'.[1] That this did not transpire is unfortunate, since it is possible that some of these works included brass instruments. The dislocating factor was the Thirty Years War.

Court life did not return to Halle until after the war, in 1648, with the arrival of Duke August, the younger brother of the Duke of Saxony. On the accession of Johann Adolph I in 1680, the court moved to Weissenfels. The municipal authorities in Halle retained a choir and the Stadtpfeifer, and music continued to flourish at the Marktkirche. In 1684 Friedrich Wilhelm Zachow was appointed organist at the Marktkirche, with responsibility for the musical performances that took place there every third Sunday. Much of Zachow's church music is lost, but several of his more than thirty surviving cantatas are available in modern editions. As he was the son and grandson of a Leipzig

Ex. 6.1 Samuel Scheidt, *In dulci jubilo*, closing flourish.

Stadtpfeifer, it is perhaps not surprising that some of these include prominent parts for wind and brass instruments. Several include sinfonias and obbligato movements for horns. The opening chorus of *Ich will mich mit dir verloben* includes passages of imitation between the two trumpet parts, involving difficult leaps in the upper register, and serves as an indication of the virtuosity of the municipal players in Halle (Ex. 6.2). Few of Zachow's surviving cantatas are dated, but there is evidence to suggest that works with instruments may have been performed at the Marienkirche during Handel's period of study with the organist.[2] The cantata *Siehe, ich bin bei euch alle Tage*, which is scored for two trumpets in one chorus, concludes with a chorale in A minor. In the edition by Max Seiffert, this is given as four vocal lines with indications of the instrumental doublings.[3] The melody in the first treble is marked 'Clarini I. II. Violin I. Canta'. This suggests that the doubling of chorale melodies by slide trumpet, as manifest in the numerous chorale settings by J. S. Bach in Leipzig, also prevailed in Halle.

Ex. 6.2 Friedrich Wilhelm Zachow, *Ich will mich mit dir verloben* (1693 or earlier), opening chorus, bars 43–6.

At the establishment of the court at Weissenfels, the court organist Johann Philipp Krieger was appointed Kapellmeister. Between 1684 and 1725 Krieger recorded details of the vocal music performed at the court. His inventory lists over two thousand of his own cantatas, of which only seventy-six survive. The instrumentation of the works listed is rarely recorded, but the inclusion of trumpets appears to have been routinely noted: more than three hundred works are recorded as having trumpet parts. Several sonatas with trumpets by Krieger are also listed. Three of Krieger's seven surviving works with one or more trumpets, along with a transcript of his inventory, are included in *Denkmäler deutscher Tonkunst* 53 (1916). The first trumpet ascends to the eighteenth-harmonic D6 in the *Magnificat* in C for New Year 1685 (one of Krieger's many *Magnificat* settings). In his cantata *Preise, Jerusalem, den Herren,* for New Year 1698, which calls for two cornetts and three trombones in addition to two trumpets and timpani, typically exuberant brass writing is contrasted with more intimate passages for trumpet, cornett and violin. The list of works performed at Weissenfels provides a tantalizing insight into the music performed at a German court over a period of forty years. One of the most intriguing entries records a performance of Krieger's *In dulci jubilo* at Christmas 1712 'Mit 12 Trompetten 2 Tymp. auf 2 Chor'.

The Weissenfels trumpet corps during the tenure of Krieger included Bach's father-in-law, Johann Caspar Wilcke (served 1718–31), and Johann Caspar Altenburg (served 1711–46), father of Johann Ernst Altenburg. Johann Ernst was born there in 1734 and reveals in his treatise that his father was particularly noted for his clarino playing.[4] It was in Weissenfels that Gottfried Reiche, Bach's principal trumpeter in Leipzig, was born (in 1667) and trained with the local Stadtmusikus, before moving to Leipzig in 1688 as a journeyman Stadtpfeifer. Reiche may already have begun his apprenticeship when the court arrived in 1680 and it is interesting to consider the effect that exposure to the court trumpet ensemble might have had on the trainee Stadtpfeifer.[5]

Krieger's inventory lists works by numerous composers unconnected to the Weissenfels court and attests to the dissemination of music between courts and cities. This practice, frequently overlooked in discussions of the trumpet that focus on conflicts between court and municipal players, was a consequence of the mobility of many composers between the two spheres of employment. One such composer was Johann Pachelbel. A native of Nuremberg, he took up his first post as deputy organist of St Stephan's Cathedral in Vienna in 1673. Positions as court organist at Eisenach and town organist in Erfurt (where he became acquainted with Ambrosius Bach and his family) were followed by similar positions at the Württemberg court at Stuttgart and in the town of Gotha. In 1695 Pachelbel returned to Nuremberg, where he served as organist of St Sebaldus for the last decade of his life. Pachelbel's earliest datable works are two arias composed in Erfurt in 1679, one of which is scored for solo voice, four-part chorus, four trumpets and timpani, and strings. A Mass in C, for four voices, two violins, two trumpets and continuo, however, may predate these arias. Pachelbel scored for either four or five trumpets in several of his cantatas and Vespers settings. None of these is dated, but the Vespers music is believed to have been composed in Nuremberg after 1695. Pachelbel's scoring in his church music reflects the influence of Vienna and illustrates the dissemination of this style of concerted church music across Germany. Surprisingly, his music has escaped the attention of brass scholars.

Given Nuremberg's pre-eminence in the manufacture of brass instruments, it is satisfying to consider that the sound of trumpets from the church of St Sebaldus provided a melodious counterpoint to the clangour of the brass instrument makers' workshops, which must have formed an integral part of the city soundscape.

Pachelbel was appointed organist at St Sebaldus on the death of Georg Caspar Wecker. One of the few surviving works by Wecker is the cantata *Allein Gott in der Höh sei Ehr*, which includes parts for two trumpets. The work is in F major, but the trumpet parts are not playable on a natural trumpet in F and are most suited to slide trumpets in C.[6] Wecker was preceded as organist at St Sebaldus by Paul Hainlein, the son of Sebastian Hainlein the younger, a member of the prominent family of brass instrument makers. Paul Hainlein evidently practised the family craft, since two trumpets and a trombone of his making survive.[7] None of the few extant vocal works by Hainlein calls for brass instruments; a Sonata 'Battallia' in C, held in the University of Uppsala Library, however, is scored for two violins, two violas (the second marked 'viola è trombett'), violon and continuo. The sonata juxtaposes contrapuntal sections, which are clearly for strings, with trumpet-style passages that are playable on four natural trumpets. Were it not for the indication in the second viola part, this could be regarded as an example of trumpet-style string music. If, however, we interpret the rubric 'viola è trombett' literally, we may surmise that Hainlein composed the sonata for trumpets and strings.

Peter Downey has identified the funeral motet *Trauer- und Begräbnüslied* by Adam Drese as the earliest concerted work calling for slide trumpets.[8] Drese composed the motet in 1648, at the end of the Thirty Years War, soon after taking up the post of Kapellmeister at the court at Weimar, where it was performed that year. No trumpet parts are included in the published version of the motet, although the title-page states that it was composed 'as the result of *Invention* having given advantage to *Music* and to the *Trumpet*', and an instruction to sound a trumpet *Intrada* appears at the final cadence. Downey provides a convincing case for the inclusion of slide trumpets in the first and last sections of the work, which are characterised by short homophonic phrases in the key of C minor, in contrast to the predominantly polyphonic texture of the inner sections. These declamatory statements are punctuated by rests, over which the indication *Tr* appears in each of the parts. The reconstructed trumpet parts offered by Downey, in adhering to the sequential contour of the melodic line and the implied harmonic progressions, include numerous non-harmonic notes in contexts that exceed the possibility of lipping. Downey argues that the Weimar court trumpeters developed the single-slide trumpet around this time and that it was subsequently adopted by municipal players. Tarr disagrees with this hypothesis, citing references from late sixteenth- and early seventeenth-century inventories to what he interprets as being slide trumpets. He suggests that the slide trumpet that appeared in seventeenth-century compositions was descended from the single-slide trumpet of the Renaissance,[9] a notion that Downey rejected in an earlier article (see Chapter 3). Arguments over when the single-slide trumpet first appeared obscure the importance of Drese's funeral music as possibly the first piece of concerted church music to include slide trumpets and as evidence that the slide trumpet, which we have come to associate with town players, was also used by the Weimar court trumpeters around the middle of the seventeenth century.

Of the twenty-one surviving works for organ and obbligato wind instrument by Johann Ludwig Krebs, seven are scored for organ and trumpet. Six of these are chorale preludes with the chorale melody assigned to the trumpet; the other is a Fantasia on the chorale 'Wachet auf', in which the trumpet engages in contrapuntal dialogue with the organ. Four of these pieces, including the Fantasia, are evidently for slide trumpet, since the obbligato part makes full use of the diatonic scale in the instrument's triadic octave. The trumpet part to the other three pieces is labelled 'Clarino', with the melody set an octave higher. Two of the pieces with slide trumpet are dated 1743, when Krebs was organist at the cathedral of St Marien in Zwickau, and one of those labelled 'Clarino' dates from 1745, the year after he took up the position of organist at the court at Zeitz. Although these dates do not signify when they were composed, it is tempting, considering the evidence linking the slide trumpet to municipal players at this time, to conjecture that Krebs composed the pieces with obbligato slide trumpet for town players, and those for clarino for court trumpeters.

Trumpet playing flourished in the cities and at the courts of northern Germany. In Hamburg, the commercial capital and principal port of north Germany, the municipal authorities retained the largest instrumental establishment in Germany. The Hamburg Ratsmusikanten were specialist string players, but the city also employed trumpeters and, from the late seventeenth century, a band of oboes.[10] Evidence of the use of trumpets in church music in Hamburg before the arrival of Telemann is scant. Of the thirty-one surviving church cantatas by Joachim Gerstenbüttel, Telemann's predecessor as Kantor of the Johanneum Lateinschule and director of music in the city's five main churches, only one, *Lobet den Herrn, ihr seine Engel,* calls for trumpets (or oboes). However, trumpets were evidently included in six of the forty cantatas by Gerstenbüttel listed in the inventory of vocal music formerly owned by the monastery of St Michael in Lüneburg, all of which are lost but probably date from his time in Hamburg.[11] The Lüneburg inventory, which was drawn up in the 1690s, provides an insight into the music performed in the monastery shortly before Bach was admitted to the Michaelisschule in 1700. It records numerous works that have not survived, including twenty-four vocal works by August Braun, the Lüneburg Kantor during the period of Bach's study in the town, eight of which called for trumpet(s) and timpani.

Matthias Weckmann, organist of the Jacobikirche in Hamburg from 1655 until his death in 1674, wrote sonatas for cornettino and trombone, but none of his surviving works include trumpet parts. Don Smithers states that the cantata *Es erhub sich ein Streit im Himmel* includes parts for two violins and three trumpets; however, the edition by Max Seiffert calls for two violins and three trombones.[12] One of the five surviving vocal works by Vincent Lübeck, organist at the Nikolaikirche in Hamburg from 1702 until his death in 1740, the cantata *Gott wie dein Nahme,* is scored for the unusual combination of three voices, three trumpets and continuo. It appears, however, that this was composed before Lübeck's arrival in Hamburg, when he was organist in the nearby town of Stade.[13]

In 1768 Carl Philipp Emanuel Bach succeeded Telemann as director of music of the five principal churches in Hamburg and Kantor of the Johanneum. As well as composing for the Hamburg churches, Bach made use of cantata cycles and other works by Telemann as well as some by his father. In 1772 Handel's *Messiah* received its first

German performance in Hamburg, and it was performed by C. P. E. Bach on several further occasions during the 1770s. Following the success of his oratorio *Die Israeliten in der Wüste* in 1769, Bach composed *Die Auferstehung und Himmelfahrt Jesu* ('The Resurrection and Ascension of Jesus') in 1774. This includes the aria 'Ich folge dir, verklärter Held' ('I follow Thee, transfigured Hero'), with a trumpet obbligato that ascends to the sixteenth-harmonic D6. Given that Bach performed *Messiah* around this time, it is tempting to infer that he was as inspired by 'The Trumpet Shall Sound' in writing this aria as by his own father's music; however, it is possible Telemann's trumpet writing was also influential in this regard. The popularity of *Die Auferstehung* in Hamburg extended to other parts of Germany and it was published in Leipzig in 1787. The following year Mozart directed three performances of the oratorio at the home of the Count of Esterházy in Vienna, with an orchestra of 86 members.[14] For these he adapted the trumpet aria in a manner similar to that in which he altered 'The Trumpet Shall Sound' for performances of *Messiah* in Vienna between 1786 and 1790. Whether Mozart simplified these trumpet parts because they were problematic for the players in Vienna or for aesthetic reasons remains a matter of conjecture. However, it is difficult to imagine that trumpet playing in Vienna, a city with such an exalted tradition of trumpet playing where the clarino register was in extended use only two decades earlier, had plummeted in such a short period. It seems plausible that Mozart may have been dissatisfied with the intonation of the natural trumpet as a solo instrument and that this spurred him to rescore the trumpet movements in a more contemporary style.

The Baltic port of Lübeck, like Hamburg, maintained both Ratsmusikanten and trumpeters throughout the seventeenth century. Between 1668 and 1707 Dieterich Buxtehude was organist at the Marienkirche in Lübeck and played a leading role in the musical life of the city. Although provision of church music was not a requirement of his post, it represents a significant part of his output. Twelve of his more than 120 surviving sacred vocal works and three wedding arias include trumpets. Buxtehude's scoring practices in his vocal works are of interest: several are scored for two trumpets and strings, while others include cornetts and trombones. His most sumptuously scored work, *Benedicam Dominum*, is set for two vocal and four instrumental choirs, one of which (choir 4) comprises four trumpets, trombone and bombard or bass trombone. This motet contains some of his most demanding trumpet writing, with the first trumpet frequently ascending to C6. Buxtehude alternates between imitative writing for two pairs of trumpets and treating the four trumpets as a single unit. In this work, he takes the trumpets into unusual harmonic territory by modulating to B flat major, using the seventh-harmonic B flat5 as the root of the chord.

Beginning in 1673 or earlier, Buxtehude revived the tradition of presenting a series of free concerts at the Marienkirche each winter. For each series of concerts, known as *Abendmusiken*, Buxtehude normally composed a new oratorio. None of this music has survived, although three librettos are extant and other works are known by their title. In his account book for November 1673, Buxtehude noted the purchase of

> two trumpets for the embellishment of the Abendmusik, made in a special way, the likes of which have not been heard in the orchestra of any prince, where otherwise everything in noble music is advanced.[15]

What Buxtehude meant by describing the trumpets as having been 'made in a special way' is a matter for conjecture. The fact that he distinguishes this type of instrument from that used at court suggests that they may have been slide trumpets. It seems likely that slide trumpets were used in Lübeck, since the town trumpeter, Christoffer Knölcke, whose main duty was that of guard and signaller, and who Snyder suggests may have performed in Buxtehude's church music, performed four-part chorales on feast days, with his colleagues, from the tower of the Marienkirche.[16]

Three years after the purchase of these trumpets, a local turner made mutes for six trumpets belonging to the church.[17] Buxtehude called for muted trumpets in two of his surviving works, the cantata *Ihr lieben Christen*, which includes a section for bass with two muted trumpets, and the wedding aria *Auf! stimmet die Saiten*, which also calls for two muted trombones. Both of these works are in D major, whereas all of his other works with trumpets are in C major. It should be noted, however, that the organ in the Marienkirche was tuned to Chorton (i.e., high pitch). As was customary in northern Germany, Buxtehude applied the terms *tromba, trombetta* and *clarino* without apparent discrimination. In the final chorus of *Ihr lieben Christen* the switch from 'Clarino' to 'Trombetta' may be significant, however, since it coincides with a change from trumpet parts that employ only natural trumpet notes to those that include many non-harmonic notes. Don Smithers postulates that an error in the copying from the manuscript organ tablature score led to the parts being notated an octave lower than intended.[18] The other possibility is that Buxtehude composed these parts for slide trumpets. On 2 and 3 December 1705 Buxtehude presented two 'extraordinary' Abendmusiken to commemorate the death of Leopold I and the accession of his successor, Joseph I. The libretto for *Castrum doloris* (Temple of Sorrow), performed in the first concert, instructs that 'the two musical choruses [situated] by the organ are dressed in black; the trombones and trumpets are muted, and all the other instruments are also muted'. For the following evening's performance of *Templum honoris* (Temple of Honour), which called for two choirs of trumpets and timpani, the church purchased two new kettledrums.[19]

The practice of instrumental church music followed in German-speaking courts extended to cities in the Baltic and in Scandinavian kingdoms that embraced Lutheranism in which the ruling dynasties maintained connections with their German counterparts. The larger settings included trumpets, cornetts and trombones. A more intimate work is the *Jubilate Deo* by Johann Valentin Meder, for solo voice, trumpet, violin, violone and continuo. The composition is undated and its place of composition is not known, since Meder worked at various courts and cities in northern Germany, Scandinavia and the Baltic region, after studying theology in Leipzig. The German composer Christian Geist spent his entire working life in Scandinavia. During the 1670s he was employed at the Swedish royal court, where he composed the motet *Quis hostis in coelis*, one of his several surviving works with trumpets, for the accession of Charles XI in 1672.[20] The opening sinfonia to *Quis hostis*, for two trumpets in C, two violins, violone and continuo, is exceptional with regard to the wide tessitura of the trumpet writing and the inclusion of the non-harmonic note D4 in the opening fanfare (Ex. 6.3).

The transformation of the German court instrumental Kapellen from ensembles that typically performed with one player to a part into the classical orchestra began towards

Ex. 6.3 Christian Geist, *Quis hostis in coelis* (1672).

the end of the seventeenth century with the introduction of additional string players and new French woodwind instruments, in emulation of the musical practices at the court of Louis XIV. The origins of these developments at the court of Landgrave Ernst Ludwig of Hesse-Darmstadt can be traced to 1685, when the Landgrave visited Paris and returned with several French violinists and wind players to supplement his court ensemble. Under Ernst Ludwig and his son Louis VIII (Landgrave from 1739) music flourished at Darmstadt. In 1709 Christoph Graupner was appointed Vice-Kapellmeister, being promoted to Kapellmeister in 1712. While in Leipzig auditioning for the post of Thomaskantor in 1723, Graupner recruited Johann Samuel Endler for the Darmstadt Kapelle. Both Graupner and Endler were innovative in writing for trumpets and horns. At Darmstadt, Graupner was highly prolific, composing over 1,400 cantatas, as well as operas and instrumental music, including 113 symphonies. His major contribution to the development of brass writing was his scoring for horns, and horns and trumpets, in different keys simultaneously. Thomas Hiebert has identified twelve vocal and three orchestral works composed by Graupner between 1728 and 1753 that call for trumpet(s) and horn(s) in this way.[21] This technique became common in late eighteenth-century orchestral brass writing, but, as Hiebert notes, while various composers employed the technique during the first half of the century, none did so as routinely, over such an extended period, as Graupner. The cantata *Das Ende kommt, der Tod* (1732) exemplifies this scoring practice: the opening chorus calls for one trumpet and two horns, the former pitched in C and the latter in G and F, as well as timpani tuned to four different pitches.[22] Almost all of the surviving works by Endler are orchestral. Many of his sinfonias and suites were composed for festive occasions between 1748 and 1761, and they include prominent parts for trumpets and horns. In treating the stringed, wind and brass instruments as clearly defined groups, Endler was embracing the most up-to-date scoring practices; however, he also exploited the melodic capability of the trumpet and horn in the clarino register. Although other composers wrote for the horn in the clarino register around the middle of the eighteenth century, for example Haydn in his early symphonies, Endler was exceptional in scoring for trumpets in this manner, and his trumpet parts bear testimony to the virtuosity of the players at Darmstadt.[23]

A similar expansion of the Kapelle occurred at the court of Zerbst, under the direction of Graupner's pupil and fellow Thomasschule alumnus Johann Friedrich Fasch. Fasch was appointed Kapellmeister at Zerbst in 1722 and remained in this post for the rest of his life. At Zerbst he composed much church music, including nine yearly cycles of cantatas, almost all of which has perished. His reputation rests with his instrumental music, which includes several concertos and overtures for between one and three trumpets and strings (most of which have additional solo parts for wind instruments and violin).[24] Although none of his music appeared in print, it was widely circulated within Germany: Telemann performed a cycle of his cantatas in Hamburg in 1733 and copies of his instrumental works survive at Dresden and Darmstadt. None of his concertos and overtures with trumpets are dated, but Reine Dahlqvist suggests the Concerto à 8 was written after 1743, and the others might also date from the latter part of his career.[25] While certain characteristics of his music, such as the colouristic use of wind instruments in his concertos, point forward to the classical era, other aspects of his style, including his writing for trumpets and horns in group concertos, reveal a style that was essentially baroque.[26]

Handel, Telemann and Bach

George Frideric Handel and Johann Sebastian Bach, the two composers whose music has come to epitomize the late baroque trumpet style, were born a mere twenty-eight days and eighty miles apart – on 23 February and 21 March 1685, in Halle and Eisenach respectively. Four years earlier, Georg Philipp Telemann, whose music may be less well known today, but was as highly regarded as Bach and Handel during his lifetime, was born in Magdeburg, fifty miles north of Halle.

That Bach should have embarked upon a career in music is not surprising given his lineage. His father, Johann Ambrosius Bach, who died shortly before his son's tenth birthday, was a musician at the court of the Duke of Eisenach and leader of the Eisenach town band. Handel and Telemann, by contrast, appear to have been directed towards other careers, but abandoned their academic studies in favour of music. Both Telemann and Bach were based in Germany throughout their working lives and held a variety of musical posts before settling into municipal positions in Hamburg and Leipzig that combined teaching with the composition and administration of church music. Handel's attraction to opera led him to Hamburg, where he played violin, then harpsichord, in the opera orchestra and had his first operas performed. From there he ventured to Italy, where he travelled between Rome, Naples and Florence, before settling in London in 1711. Telemann and Handel became lifelong friends after meeting in Halle or Leipzig around 1701, and Telemann and Bach evidently formed a close relationship while Telemann was employed at Eisenach between 1707 and 1712, since Telemann became godfather to Carl Philipp Emanuel Bach (b.1714). Bach and Handel never met: planned meetings on at least two occasions failed to materialize. As products of the central German church music tradition, the three composers shared a common musical heritage that provides an interesting backdrop for a comparison of their trumpet writing and the extent to which this was influenced by the musical and cultural environments in which they worked.

Handel

None of the music that Handel is known to have composed while studying with Zachow in Halle survives. This is unfortunate, since there is evidence that this repertory included cantatas with orchestra.[27] Trumpets appear fleetingly in his first opera for Hamburg, *Almira* (1705), but feature more prominently in the music he composed during his four years in Italy (1706–10). The prohibition of opera in Rome at this time exposed Handel to unstaged dramatic genres, such as oratorios, cantatas and serenatas, which, *force majeure*, adopted the musical forms and styles of opera. Handel's most substantial work for Rome, the oratorio *La Resurrezione*, was performed at the palace of his principal patron, the Marquis Ruspoli, on Easter Sunday 1708, as the culmination of a series of musical performances that included oratorios by Alessandro Scarlatti and Antonio Caldara. Handel included one trumpet in two cantatas that he composed in Rome: *Alla caccia* (1707) and *O come chiare e belle* (1708), both of which include *da capo* trumpet arias. *Alla caccia*, which is scored for solo soprano, tutti sopranos, two violins, trumpet and continuo, is perhaps Handel's least known work with trumpet.[28] The opening D-major March includes the only example of the non-harmonic leading-note C sharp5 in Handel's trumpet writing. The aria 'Foriera la tromba' forms the central section of the work, which is rounded off with a chorus in which each short phrase is first presented by tutti sopranos and repeated by solo soprano, then trumpet ('Tromba in eco') (Ex. 6.4).

Following the success of his opera *Agrippina* in Venice in December 1709, Handel returned to Germany and was appointed Kapellmeister at the court of Hanover the following June. The commencement of his duties was deferred, however, to enable him to visit London. He was presumably enticed to London by the moves that were under way to establish Italian opera there. The first opera sung entirely in Italian, *L'Idaspe fedele* by Francesco Mancini (which includes a trumpet overture), was performed at the Queen's Theatre in the Haymarket in March 1710. On 24 February 1711, *Rinaldo*, Handel's first opera for London, and the first Italian opera composed specifically for that city, received its first performance, to great acclaim. Less than three weeks before the premier of *Rinaldo*, Handel performed one of his Italian vocal compositions, with singers from the opera, at the royal court for the birthday celebrations of Queen Anne. The work performed on this occasion is not recorded, but according to a Russian diplomat, Handel's writing for trumpets made a strong impression on those present.[29] It is tempting to conjecture that Handel's offering included Rinaldo's aria 'Or la tromba in suon festante', with its four obbligato trumpet parts, in an attempt to muster support from court circles for the Italian opera company. Handel's return to Hanover after eight months in London was brief, for the following year he was granted permission to return to London, where he resided until his death in 1759.

During his first two decades in London, Handel was primarily occupied with composing Italian operas. Two of his operas from the period of the Haymarket company (which went out of business in 1717), *Silla* (possibly performed in 1713) and *Amadigi di Gaula* (1715), and his first opera for the Royal Academy of Music (the association formed in London in 1719 for the promotion of opera), *Radamisto* (1720), include some of his most virtuosic trumpet arias. Although the Royal Academy of Music enjoyed the patronage of royalty and members of the nobility, the financial viability of this and subsequent ventures to promote Italian opera in London remained precarious owing to the exorbitant cost of recruiting and retaining the principal singers, and competition from theatres offering plays and musical entertainments in

Ex. 6.4 George Frideric Handel, *Alla caccia* HWV 79 (1707), opening of the final chorus.

English. Following the success of his oratorio *Esther* at the King's Theatre in 1732 (the work was originally composed in 1718 for a private performance at the residence of his patron the Duke of Chandos), Handel turned increasingly to composing oratorios in English for performances in the theatre. While Handel scored for a single trumpet in the chorus 'The Lord our enemy has slain' in the 1718 version of *Esther*, the later version calls for an additional two trumpets in the same movement. Following the overture, the 1732 version opens with a rendition of the Coronation anthem *My Heart is Inditing*, and in Act II the music of *Zadok the Priest* is used for the anthem 'Blessed,

blessed are all they'. This fusion of the Italian operatic forms of aria and recitative with choral styles deriving from English church music defined the highly distinctive genre that Handel created in his oratorios.

In *La Resurrezione*, composed in Rome, Handel had enhanced the dramatic narrative by featuring trumpets in movements that alluded to the instrument's biblical associations. The instrument was used to similar effect in many of Handel's English oratorios, most notably in the trumpet arias from *Messiah* (1742), *Samson* (1743) and *Judas Maccabaeus* (1747), each of which appears at a dramatic and musical highpoint of the third and final part of the oratorio. The build-up of tension in the sequence of choruses beginning with 'As by man came death' and culminating in the recitative 'Behold, I tell you a mystery' in *Messiah*, through the alternation between major and minor tonalities and sudden shifts in pace and mood, for example, heightens the dramatic impact of the resolution to forthright D major at 'The trumpet shall sound'. The aria 'With honour let desert be crown'd' from *Judas Maccabaeus*, in A minor, and playable on a trumpet in D, is Handel's only trumpet movement in a minor key. By highlighting the trumpet's funerary associations, the aria adds solemnity to a work composed to celebrate the victory over the Jacobite forces under 'Bonnie Prince Charlie' (Charles Edward Stuart) at Culloden the previous year.

Throughout his career in London, Handel enjoyed the patronage of the royal court. His performance at the Queen's birthday celebrations in 1711 was followed by an invitation to compose the Birthday ode in 1713, *Eternal Source of Light Divine*. The opening duet of the ode, for alto and trumpet, displays a delicacy of trumpet writing unsurpassed in his later works. Owing to the Queen's poor health, the birthday celebrations may have been cancelled that year; whether the ode was performed on another occasion is not known. With the accession of Georg Ludwig, Elector of Hanover, to the throne of Great Britain as George I in 1714, Handel was reunited with the patron he had left abruptly only a few years earlier. Most of Handel's music for the court was written for the Chapel Royal. Works with trumpets were composed for occasions of national rejoicing, when additional instrumentalists were engaged to supplement the Royal Musicians. For the thanksgiving service in St Paul's Cathedral in July 1713 to mark the signing of the treaty of Utrecht, which ended Britain's involvement in the War of the Spanish Succession, Handel composed the 'Utrecht' *Te Deum and Jubilate*. The opening movement of the *Jubilate*, like the Birthday Ode, features a duet for alto and trumpet, which Donald Burrows suggests reflects the influence of Purcell. Purcell's *Te Deum* and *Jubilate* of 1694 had been performed between 1702 and 1708 to mark military victories.[30] Purcell's influence is also evident in Handel's scoring of the 'Caroline' *Te Deum* of 1714 for an orchestra of two trumpets and strings. The Dettingen *Te Deum*, composed in response to the victory over France in 1743, was conceived on an altogether grander scale, presumably in anticipation of an elaborate celebration in St Paul's; in fact, it was performed in the more intimate setting of St James's Palace to mark the King's safe return. Amid the representation of military pomp, highlighted by some of his most rousing writing for three trumpets and timpani, Handel invokes the image of the 'last trumpet' by quoting the rising arpeggio figure from 'The trumpet shall sound' in a passage for two trumpets, before the words 'We believe that Thou shalt come to be our judge'. The Dettingen *Te Deum* became Handel's most popular church composition after *Zadok the Priest*, one of the three anthems with trumpets that Handel composed for the coronation of George II in 1727. *Zadok the Priest* has been performed at every subsequent coronation of a British monarch.

Two of Handel's most popular instrumental works with trumpets, the *Water Music* (1717) and *Music for the Royal Fireworks* (1749), were composed for less formal al fresco royal occasions. The *Water Music* was composed (or possibly assembled) for a water party on the Thames in July 1717 at which the King and a gathering of the nobility processed from Whitehall to Chelsea and back in a fleet of barges. A newspaper account of the event reveals that one of the barges 'was employ'd for the Musick, wherein were 50 Instruments of all sorts, who play'd all the Way from Lambeth . . . the finest Symphonies, compos'd express for this Occasion by Mr Hendel [*sic*]; which his Majesty liked so well, that he caus'd it to be plaid over three times in going and returning'.[31] None of the manuscript or printed musical sources reveals the order in which the pieces were performed; it cannot be assumed therefore that they were grouped according to instrumentation and key in a manner corresponding to the three suites (in F, D and G) in which they are customarily now presented.

The *Fireworks Music* was composed for the public celebration in London in 1749 for the Peace of Aix-la-Chapelle. The Duke of Montagu, Master General of the Ordnance, revealed Handel's plans for the work in a letter to the Comptroller of His Majesty's Fireworks:

> I think Hendel [*sic*] now proposes to have but 12 trumpets and 12 French horns; at first there was to have been sixteen of each, and I remember I told the King so, who, at that time, objected to their being any musick; but, when I told him the quantity and number of martial musick there was to be, he was better satisfied, and said he hoped there would be no fidles. Now Hendel proposes to lessen the nomber [*sic*] of trumpets, &c. and to have violeens.[32]

In the end, Handel's score specified nine horns, nine trumpets and three sets of timpani, as well as twenty-four oboes, twelve bassoons, contrabassoon and serpent, with strings doubling the wind parts. We can only imagine the effect that the massed forces of brass and wind must have had on the 12,000 who reportedly caused traffic gridlock on London Bridge travelling to hear the rehearsal in Vauxhall Gardens or the performance in Green Park a week later. Handel made few concessions to the many players assigned to the various trumpet and horn parts – the overture and *La Réjouissance* include some of his most florid writing, with the first trumpet regularly ascending to D6.

Details of the membership of the opera orchestra in London during the early eighteenth century are scant. The few surviving documents that list the regular members of the orchestra suggest that only one trumpeter was employed for each season; additional players were presumably employed on an ad hoc basis. Several opera orchestra rosters from between 1708 and 1711 include the royal trumpeter Henrick Davant, while others from around the time of Handel's arrival mention John Baptist Grano (after 1692–before 1748). Grano, who was equally proficient as a flautist, is also listed in the orchestra roster for the first season of the Royal Academy of Music. Burrows suggests that Grano may also have performed the trumpet parts in Handel's Chapel Royal compositions from his first decade in London: although he did not obtain a position in the royal trumpet corps on account of his Catholicism, he may have been hired as an 'extra' player.[33] By the late 1720s Grano's career had plummeted and he found himself incarcerated in the Marshalsea Prison for debt. While in the Marshalsea (May 1728–September 1729), he kept a diary in which he chronicled prison life and his comings and goings around London (for much of his sentence he was allowed out to pursue his professional and social business) as he attempted to revive his freelance career.[34]

Handel's principal trumpeter throughout most of the 1730s and 40s was Valentine Snow, for whom he composed the trumpet overture to *Atalanta* (1736) and the obbligato parts to arias in *Samson* and *Judas Maccabaeus*. Handel may have had Snow in mind when composing *Messiah* in 1741; however, the orchestra for the first performance in Dublin was recruited locally and the trumpeters at the first performance have not been identified.[35] Snow was appointed Sergeant-Trumpeter in 1753, in succession to John Shore, after which he appears to have been less active as a trumpeter. On the basis of Handel's trumpet writing, it has been deduced that 'Snow was more gifted for his endurance than for sheer range'.[36] The most fitting testimony to Snow's skill, however, is Burney's recollection that his 'exquisite tone and fine shake must still be remembered by many persons living, who have heard him at Vauxhall, and in Mr. Handel's oratorios'.[37]

In most of his operas and oratorios, Handel scored for a pair of trumpets and timpani. A single trumpet was called for in some of the early operas, and three trumpets and timpani were included in the more festive works. Handel almost exclusively wrote for trumpets in D. The only works for trumpets in C are the oratorios *Saul* and *Israel in Egypt*, both of which include trombones in the movements with trumpets. With the exception of the cantata *Alla caccia*, Handel avoids non-harmonic notes in his trumpet writing, but occasionally makes use of the seventh-harmonic C natural in D major; as well as in the aria 'With honour let desert be crown'd' (see above), this note appears fleetingly in the second trumpet part of the chorus 'I will sing unto the Lord' from *Israel in Egypt*. Handel uses the sixteenth harmonic D6, the upper limit of his trumpet range, sparingly. It would be wrong to regard this as a reluctance to exploit the upper register of the instrument, however, since examples of his use of this pitch appear in music throughout his career, and it seems that he reserved the sixteenth harmonic for the most apposite moments. Handel scored for horns in many of his operas and oratorios, but he rarely called for trumpets and horns in the same movement. Many of the principal brass players in London doubled on other instruments, but trumpeters do not appear to have routinely doubled on horn; this expediency was more common in other British cities. In the D-major movements from the *Water Music* and in the *Fireworks Music*, Handel scored for both trumpets and horns, presenting essentially the same material in octaves and in alternation. For performances of *Messiah* under the composer's direction during the 1750s, horns and serpent augmented the orchestra.

Telemann

Telemann, like Bach, held various court and municipal positions before accepting in 1721 the position of Kantor of the Johanneum Lateinschule and director of music in Hamburg's five main churches. Telemann's duties in Hamburg were remarkably similar to those expected of Bach in Leipzig, and like Bach, Telemann remained in this post until his death in 1767. Whereas Bach was normally obliged to prepare one cantata each Sunday, Telemann was expected to provide two. Moreover, Telemann continued to supply complete cycles of cantatas to Eisenach and Frankfurt for many years after taking up his post in Hamburg. Telemann's prolific output includes at least 1,700 church cantatas, of which about 1,400 have survived. This level of productivity is all the more remarkable considering that throughout his time in Hamburg, Telemann was actively involved in public concerts, opera and the publication of his music.

As only a small portion of Telemann's church music is available in modern editions, most of it remains comparatively unknown. The most comprehensive guide to his works with brass instruments is the catalogue compiled by Matthew Cron and Don Smithers.[38] Telemann regularly scored for two or three trumpets with timpani, but he occasionally called for a single trumpet and also combined trumpets with horns. He used the designated Tromba or Clarino with near equal regularity, often designating the third part Principale. Whether these terms were applied with discrimination is unclear. Cron and Smithers suggest tentatively that clarino may have referred to the coiled trumpet. Telemann occasionally called for muted trumpets or horns, for example in *Der Geduldige Socrates* (1721), the first of twenty operas he composed for Hamburg.[39] Several of his works in F major call for a small trumpet, labelled 'Clarino piccolo', 'Kürze Trompete' or 'Trompetta ex [in] F'.

Telemann's popularity today rests with his instrumental works. Several of the concertos for one, two or three trumpets with various combinations of strings and oboes, and the *Musique de table* (Hamburg, 1733) have gained a place in the canonical repertoire. The Concerto in D for trumpet, two violins and continuo predates his arrival in Hamburg in 1721. This work points forward to the concertos from later in the century in its exploitation of the upper register in the opening adagio, and contrasts tellingly in its tessitura with Handel's equally ravishing and similarly plangent *Eternal Source of Light Divine.* The inventory by Cron and Smithers provides a valuable insight into the extent to which Telemann incorporated brass instruments into all of the genres in which he composed; however, a more comprehensive appraisal of his scoring for brass instruments will only be possible through the study and performance of a larger portion of his monumental output.

Bach

Bach's earliest work with trumpets, Cantata No. 71 (his only work with trumpets that was published during his lifetime), was composed in 1708 for the annual inauguration of the Mühlhausen city council, during his brief tenure as organist there. Bach's appointment as court organist at Weimar later that year prompted a hiatus in his writing for trumpet, but his promotion to Konzertmeister at Weimar resulted in the composition of a further four cantatas with trumpets. Bach's tenure as Kapellmeister at Cöthen from 1717 to 1723 marked a further lull in his trumpet writing. However, it was during this period that Bach assembled his 'Six Concerts avec plusieurs Instruments' – the Brandenburg Concertos BWV 1046–1051 – which he dedicated and sent to the Margrave of Brandenburg. The autograph manuscript of the set, a carefully prepared 'presentation' copy, is dated 1721. It has been suggested that the Brandenburg Concertos were composed for the Cöthen Kapelle. If this was the case, the trumpet part of Concerto No. 2 was presumably written for one of the two court trumpeters, Johann Ludwig Schreiber or Johann Christoff Krahl.[40] Christoph Wolff, however, suggests that the concertos may pre-date Bach's Cöthen period.[41] The virtuosity of the trumpet parts of the Weimar cantatas certainly suggests that Bach had trumpeters at his disposal who were capable of negotiating Concerto No. 2. No contemporary performances of the Brandenburg Concertos have been identified, but they may have been heard at meetings of the collegium musicum that Bach directed in Leipzig between 1729 and 1741, since a manuscript copy of the set was made in Leipzig during his residency in the city.[42] The designation 'Tromba ô vero Corno da Caccia' in the trumpet part (but not the score) of this set has given rise to the hypothesis that it was intended for the horn, sounding an octave lower than the high trumpet pitch. Smithers rejects this suggestion, arguing that the designation 'Corno da Caccia' denoted the coiled trumpet with which Reiche is depicted in the portrait by E. G. Haussmann that was commissioned by the Leipzig city council[43] (Ill. 6.1). While this is credible, the possibility that in Leipzig, on occasions, the part was played on either horn or trumpet, depending on the players available, and that this was endorsed by Bach, cannot be ruled out.

The Brandenburg Concerto No. 2, scored for a concertino group comprising trumpet, violin, oboe and recorder, is one of the most demanding works for trumpet. Although this is the only work in which Bach scored for a trumpet in F, trumpet music in this key was produced by other composers of this period, including Telemann (see above). It is now widely accepted that the pitch standard at both the Berlin and Cöthen courts was *tief-Cammerton*, which, at A4 = 390 Hz, was approximately one tone lower than the modern pitch standard of A4 = 440 Hz. This would have had significant implications for the trumpet part, since the instrument required would have been a trumpet in D at the high choir-pitch (Chorton), approximately equivalent to modern E flat.

In May 1723 Bach moved to Leipzig, on his appointment as Kantor at the Thomasschule, a post that he was to retain for the rest of his life. In addition to his teaching duties at the school, which mainly involved training the choir, Bach's position included responsibility for the music in the city's two main churches, the Thomaskirche and the Nikolaikirche. For this he had at his disposal the services of the civic wind and string players, and, on occasion, students from the city's collegia musica. Bach's first undertaking in his new post was to compose the first of his five cycles of cantatas for the church calendar.

The first two cantatas in the first cycle, nos 75 and 76 (performed on 30 May and 6 June 1723), are typical of many of those from Bach's early years in Leipzig: they include a single trumpet, which provides obbligato accompaniments to arias and choruses in the clarino register and doubles the melody in chorales, functioning as a fully chromatic instrument in its triadic octave. The most widely known work in this

6.1 Portrait of Gottfried Reiche by E. G. Haussmann, *c.*1727, held in the Altes Rathaus, Leipzig.

category is Cantata No. 147, in which the trumpet doubles the melody of the chorale 'Wohl mir, dass ich Jesum habe' (widely known in English by the title of the 1926 piano transcription by Myra Hess: 'Jesu, Joy of Man's Desiring'). Bach does not specify a slide trumpet in any of these works, but in certain other cantatas he designates parts that double chorale melodies or provide obbligatos to arias or choruses and include non-harmonic notes as being for a *tromba da tirarsi*. Smithers argues that the *tromba da tirarsi* was used in the manner of a trombone only when doubling the soprano part in chorales, and that in arias and choruses in which the trumpet part ventures freely outside the notes of the harmonic series, the slide was used to transpose the trumpet into a more suitable key from which the non-harmonic pitches could be obtained by

Exx. 6.5a & b Johann Sebastian Bach, Cantata No. 126 (*Erhalt uns Herr, bei deinem Wort*), opening chorus, bars 36–39.

lipping.[44] A more recent theory, based on the evidence from surviving instruments that display markings which have been interpreted as deriving from the movement of slides, is that some baroque trumpeters, including those in Leipzig, used short slides to finely-tune certain notes in the harmonic series and facilitate the production of non-harmonic notes.[45]

In Cantata No. 126 the use of the slide to transpose the harmonic series for an entire phrase in the manner suggested by Smithers seems plausible. Transposing bars 36–39 by extending the slide not only eliminates the non-harmonic E flat, but also improves the intonation, by substituting harmonics seven and eleven with the more secure harmonics eight and twelve (Exx. 6.5a and b). The vast majority of the non-harmonic notes in these movements lie one semitone below a pitch from the natural harmonic series, and while their execution by lipping is possible, it seems likely that Bach wrote these movements with the slide trumpet in mind.

Cantata No. 46 is particularly interesting in relation to its scoring for a slide trumpet in B flat. The trumpet part for the opening chorus and the final chorale is labelled 'Tromba ô corno da tirarsi', and the aria with trumpet obbligato, which clearly was also written for a slide instrument, is marked 'Tromba'. The designation 'corno da tirarsi' is perplexing: various explanations as to the instruments that it denoted have been proposed, none of which is entirely convincing.[46] Bach scored for the slide trumpet in one pre-Leipzig cantata, No. 12, performed in Weimar in 1714. Since the slide trumpet was identified with civic wind instrumentalists, this poses a question as to the identity of the player. Five field trumpeters and a timpanist were employed at the Weimar court at this time, but town musicians were regularly imported for important performances.[47] Should we infer from this that it was the local Stadtpfeifer and not the court trumpeters who performed Bach's trumpet parts in Weimar?

Table 1 lists the cantatas in Bach's first cycle chronologically, revealing that the services of one or more of the Leipzig brass players were called upon almost on a weekly basis. Two-thirds of the cantatas with brass call for a single trumpet or horn, both of which were presumably played by the senior Stadtpfeifer, Gottfried Reiche. None of the cantatas in this cycle is scored for both trumpets and horns. On the few occasions when Bach scored for trumpets and horns together in his later works, he avoided writing for both instruments in the same movement. In Cantata No. 128, from the second cantata cycle, for example, a solo trumpet provides an obbligato to one aria, while two horns accompany the opening chorus. For the third Sunday in the first cycle, Bach revived Cantata No. 21, which he had composed in Weimar in 1714 and performed in Hamburg when he visited the city in 1720, adding parts for four trombones (including soprano) to the penultimate chorus. Three trumpets are included in the final chorus, but not in the movement with trombones.

The majority of the trumpet parts in the first cantata cycle were written for the instrument pitched in C. Most of the others are for trumpet in D, but in Cantata No. 90 Bach wrote one of his most florid trumpet obbligatos for a natural trumpet in B flat.

For Christmas 1723 Bach composed the Magnificat in E flat BWV 243a, a work that he revised sometime between 1732 and 1735, transposing it into D major and altering the text to render it suitable for performance on any festive occasion. The performance schedule for the Leipzig trumpeters on Christmas Day 1723 seems daunting: services at the Thomaskirche at 7 a.m. and at the Paulinerkirche (Universitätskirche) at 9 a.m.

Table 1.

BWV	Date	Trumpet	Horn	Cornett	Trombone	Notes
75	30 May 1723	1*				
76	6 June	1*				
21	13 June	3 + timp			4	Composed 1714; performed in Hamburg 1720; 4 trombones added 1723
24	20 June	1*				
185	20 June	1*				Composed 1715 (original version with oboe instead of trumpet)
167	24 June	1*				
147	2 July	1*				Original version composed 1716 (music lost)
186	11 July					Original version composed 1716 (music lost)
136	18 July		1			
105	25 July		1			
46	1 Aug	1 (tirarsi)				
179	8 Aug					
199	8 Aug					Composed 1714
69a	15 Aug	3 + timp				
77	22 Aug	1 (tirarsi)				
25	29 Aug			1	3	
119	*30 Aug*	*4 + timp*				*Composed for the election of the city council (not part of the annual cycle)*

(*Continued Overleaf*)

BWV	Date	Trumpet	Horn	Cornett	Trombone	Notes
138	5 Sept					
95	12 Sept		1			
148	19 Sept	1				
48	3 Oct	1*				
162	10 Oct		1 (tirarsi)			Composed 1715
109	17 Oct		1			
89	24 Oct		1			
163	31 Oct					Composed 1715
60	7 Nov		1			
90	14 Nov	1				
70	21 Nov	1*				Original version composed 1716 (music lost)
61	28 Nov					Composed 1714
63	25 Dec	4 + timp				Composed *c.*1714–15
40	26 Dec		2			
64	27 Dec			1	3	
190	1 Jan 1724	3 + timp				
153	2 Jan					
65	6 Jan		2			
154	9 Jan					
155	16 Jan					Composed 1716
73	23 Jan		1			
81	30 Jan					
83	2 Feb		2			
144	6 Feb					
181	13 Feb	1				
18	13 Feb					Composed 1713–14 or 1715
22	20 Feb					Composed 7 Feb 1723
23	20 Feb			1	3	Composed 7 Feb 1723; cornett and 3 trbn added 1724
182	25 Mar					Composed 1714
31	9 Apr					Composed 1715
4	9 Apr			1		Composed c. 1708; 3 trbn added 1725
66	10 Apr	1				
134	11 Apr					

BWV	Date	Trumpet	Horn	Cornett	Trombone	Notes
67	16 Apr		1 (tirarsi)			
104	23 Apr					
12	30 Apr	1*				Composed 1714
166	7 May					
86	14 May					
37	18 May					
44	21 May					
172	28 May	3 + timp				Composed 1714
59	28 May	2 + timp				
173	29 May					
184	30 May					
194	4 June					Composed 1723
165	4 June					Composed 1715

Table 1. Brass instruments in Bach's first cycle of church cantatas for Leipzig, 1723–24 (* = cantatas with unspecified *tirarsi* parts)

included Cantata No. 63, the largest of his Weimar cantatas, and the Vespers service in St Nicholas's at 1.30 p.m. included the Magnificat and the same cantata.[48]

Bach's second cantata cycle, compiled between June 1724 and May 1725, featured a greater variety of combinations of brass instruments, as summarised in Table 2.

As with the first cycle, brass instruments are included in over half of the cantatas. Half of those with brass from this cycle feature a single trumpet or horn, with twice as many calling for one horn as for one trumpet. Although only two of the cantatas specify the *tromba da tirarsi*, four of the five cantatas scored for one trumpet include idiomatic slide-trumpet doubling of chorale melodies as well as trumpet arias in which the trumpet part ventures outside the notes of the harmonic series.

Trumpets and horns also feature prominently in Bach's third cycle of cantatas, compiled between December 1725 and November 1726, and in the surviving cantatas from the 1730s, which belong to his two further cycles. By 1730 Bach was involved in the collegium musicum that had been founded by Telemann in 1702, for which he both revived earlier works and composed new vocal and instrumental music (much of it believed lost). There is evidence that the orchestral suites BWV 1066–9 were performed at the collegium musicum concerts; the two D-major suites with three trumpets and timpani (nos 3 and 4) are believed to have been written in Leipzig, but their dates of composition are uncertain.

In addition to performing Bach's trumpet and horn parts, Reiche would have performed on cornett, and possibly soprano trombone, in performances of his church music. As if that were not already daunting by the standards of today's one-discipline specialists, when not required to play a brass instrument, Reiche may well have played

Brass instrumentation	Number of cantatas featuring this combination	BWV
1 Trumpet (* = unspecified, but assumed, *tirarsi* parts)	6	10*, 103*, 126*, 127, 20 (*tirarsi*), 5 (*tirarsi*)
2 Trumpets	1	175
3 Trumpets, timpani	3	41, 74, 130
1 Trumpet, 2 horns	1	128
1 Horn	12	8, 26, 62, 78, 99, 107, 114, 115, 116, 124, 125, 178
2 Horns	1	1
2 Horns, timpani	1	91
1 Horn, trombone	2	3, 96
1 Horn, cornett, 3 trombones	1	68
1 cornett	1	133
1 cornett, 1 trombone	1	135
1 cornett, 3 trombones	3	4, 101, 121
4 Trombones	2	2, 38
No brass instruments	27	

Table 2. Summary of Bach's scoring for brass instruments in his second cycle of cantatas for Leipzig, 1724–25.

violin, since he served as a *Kunstgeiger* in Leipzig before attaining the more lucrative position as a wind instrumentalist. Edward Tarr has warned against overemphasising the importance of Reiche to Bach in connection with his trumpet writing, noting that Bach composed many demanding trumpet parts both before his arrival in Leipzig and after Reiche's death in October 1734 (Brandenburg Concerto No. 2 and Cantata No. 172 are prime examples).[49] While this is a valid point, the church music that Bach composed during his first two years in Leipzig represents a flowering of his brass writing which bears a glowing testimony to the abilities of the players at his disposal. Considering the number of cantatas calling for a single trumpet or horn, the virtuosity of Gottfried Reiche must have inspired Bach, and it is significant that Bach's portraitist, Haussmann, also painted Reiche.

Reiche's successor was Ulrich Heinrich Ruhe (d.1787), who presumably played in the first performance of the *Christmas Oratorio* BWV 248 two months after Reiche's death. The *Christmas Oratorio* comprises six cantatas, which were first performed in separate services between Christmas Day and Epiphany (6 January) 1734–35. Although each cantata is scored for different forces, the work as a whole was evidently conceived as a unified cycle, even though Bach probably never envisaged it being performed in its entirety. Many of the arias and choruses from the *Christmas Oratorio* derive from the celebratory birthday cantatas Nos 213 and 214, composed the previous year. For example, Bach recycled the music for the chorus 'Tönet, ihr Pauken!

Erschallet, Trompeten!' ('Sound, ye drums! Ring out, trumpets!') from the *dramma per musica* BWV 214 for the opening chorus of the oratorio, 'Jauchzet, frohlocket, auf, preiset die Tage' ('Rejoice, exult! Up, glorify the days'). The transference of music conceived for the celebration of a royal birthday was thus deemed appropriate for the glorification of the nativity of Christ.

In 1733 Bach presented a Lutheran Mass, comprising the Kyrie and Gloria of the Mass in B minor BWV 232, to the Elector of Saxony; this was performed in Dresden in July that year and possibly also in Leipzig around the same time.[50] Between 1748 and 1749 he expanded this into a full setting of the Mass, borrowing extensively from his existing corpus of church music, a process that he had used for at least two movements of his Mass of 1733. There is no evidence that the B minor Mass was performed during Bach's lifetime or that it was composed with a particular performance in mind. A widely held view is that Bach was attracted to the immutability of the Latin Mass and that by drawing on the best of the music that he had composed for the Lutheran church, he assembled a summation of his life's work for posterity. Much of the trumpet writing in the B minor Mass derives from his earlier church music for Leipzig. Bach's technical facility was such that he was able to adapt music that had been conceived for settings of liturgical texts in German to the Latin Mass, with few alterations. The music for the chorus 'Wir danken dir, Gott' from Cantata No. 29 (1731) – one of Bach's most remarkable trumpet movements, in which all three parts ascend into the clarino register – was used for both the 'Gratias agimus tibi' and the 'Dona nobis pacem' sections of the Mass, with the trumpet and timpani parts intact. The 'Dona nobis pacem', the concluding movement of Bach's final work with trumpets, serves as a fitting culmination to his remarkable contribution to the baroque trumpet repertoire.

Chapter 7

France and Britain in the seventeenth and eighteenth centuries

France

The reputation of French trumpet music of the seventeenth and eighteenth centuries has fared poorly in comparison with other European national styles. Don Smithers's assertion that there was 'almost no tradition of "clarino" playing' in France and that French trumpet writing was 'in a simpler style than elsewhere in Europe' was for many years widely accepted.[1] Peter Downey has challenged this view, arguing that the survival of an 'unprecedented and rich trumpet ensemble repertory' points to a flourishing tradition of trumpet playing at the French royal court and that the high tessitura and technical demands of much of this repertory, which includes frequent use of non-harmonic notes, reveals that seventeenth-century French trumpeters possessed a 'true *clarino* technique' and were adept at lipping.[2]

During the reign of Louis XIV (1643–1715) the staging of lavish entertainments, for which the French royal court had long been renowned, reached its zenith. The trumpeters and wind instrumentalists of the Grande Écurie provided music for outdoor *divertissements*, such as carousels and boating parties on the canals of Versailles, and added splendour to banquets and balls. As noted in Chapter 3, Italian-style trumpet ensemble music failed to gain a foothold in France during the sixteenth century. The type of ensemble music performed in France can be surmised from a fragment of trumpet music cited by Marin Mersenne in *Harmonicorum libri* (1635) and *Harmonie universelle* (1636). This excerpt comprises two high-sounding (*dessus*) parts and one low (*bourdon*) part, restricted to the notes C3, G3 and C4. The grouping of one or more *dessus* parts with a single *basse de trompette* part (corresponding to the range of Mersenne's *bourdon*) and timpani is a key feature of French trumpet ensemble music of the late seventeenth century. Most of the surviving repertoire from the reign of Louis XIV, which includes music by composers prominent at the royal court, was collected and copied by the royal music librarian and oboist André Danican Philidor l'Ainé. Much of this repertoire is identified as having been performed at specific events or as deriving from particular stage works.

Unlike trumpet ensemble music performed elsewhere on the Continent, which remained idiomatically separate from mainstream instrumental genres, the French repertoire conformed to the baroque aesthetic of a melodic line supported by a harmonically-functioning bass and encompassed many of the forms associated with wind bands of the period. Binary dance movements are prominent, as are marches and warlike pieces, some of which were intended for functional military use, while others appear to have been composed for the theatre. The textural transparency of the French trumpet ensemble style, along with a harmonic rhythm that corresponded to that of mainstream instrumental music (in contrast to the more sonorous, harmonically static, drone-based ensemble music deriving from the Italian style), facilitated the assimilation of the trumpet into the orchestra. This may have evolved through the combination of the trumpets and oboes of the Grande Écurie, in the manner of Lully's *Carousel Music* of 1686. The earliest known deployment of trumpets with strings and woodwind in France, however, is in Lully's ballet music for a Paris production of Cavalli's opera *Xerse* in 1660. Lully subsequently scored for various groupings of trumpets, in either C or D, in many of his works for the stage.

Although Lully typically deployed trumpets and drums in military or ceremonial scenes, such as in the 'Premier Air des Combattants' that opens the battle scene from Act I of *Amadis* (1684), one or two trumpets sometimes double the violins or oboes in dance movements in which the melody is based on the notes of the harmonic series. The 'Second Air' minuet from the same scene in *Amadis* is one such movement. The 'Air des Combattants' highlights a problem of establishing the intended instrumentation of Lully's works with trumpets.[3] The movement is scored for four instrumental parts, with the rubric 'Trompettes' above the uppermost staff. The upper three parts are suitable for trumpets, however, the lowest part includes arpeggiated passages incorporating the pitch E3, which lies between the second and third partials of the harmonic series for the instrument pitched in C. This note would belong to the harmonic series of an instrument twice the length of the standard trumpet, but there is no evidence that such an instrument existed and the *basse de trompette* parts in both the ensemble and the orchestral repertoire generally contain only the notes C3, G3 and C4. Most authorities agree that the term *basse de trompette* denoted the standard 8-foot instrument, with perhaps a large bore, as alluded to by earlier writers. Although we cannot be certain that the lowest instrumental line in the 'Air des Combattants' is a trumpet part, the factitious note between harmonics 2 and 3 is easily obtained by a skilled player by lipping.

Identifying which lines of music should be assigned to trumpets is a recurring problem with French scores well into the eighteenth century. The problem is most acute with respect to passages that include non-harmonic notes. Ex. 7.1, from the Prologue to *Alceste* (1674), includes the non-harmonic passing notes A4 and B4 between the natural pitches G4 and C5; the passage is also noteworthy on account of the sixteenth harmonic C6. Despite the appearance of these notes in the trumpet writing of Fantini and Mersenne several decades earlier, and given that there is no evidence that slide trumpets were used in France at this time, scholars have been reluctant to accept that such passages in Lully's scores represent genuine trumpet parts. French scores of this period rarely give precise indications of instrumentation and

Ex. 7.1 Jean-Baptiste Lully, Prologue to *Alceste* (1674).

often have more than one instrument assigned to each staff. Evidence from slightly later English sources indicates that in passages labelled as being for trumpet, but which were clearly intended to be doubled by violin and oboe, the trumpeters would either replace the non-harmonic notes with the nearest note from the harmonic series, or omit the problematic passages. While many second *dessus* orchestral parts that accompany melodic lines labelled 'Trompettes' but stray outside the natural notes of the harmonic notes can be discounted as trumpet parts, passages such as that from *Alceste* are more equivocal. As Downey illustrates, non-harmonic notes appear in sources of French trumpet ensemble music that were evidently assembled with care and cannot be readily dismissed as scribal errors.[4]

Lully rarely provided trumpets with wholly independent melodic material. Most often they doubled the violin and oboe lines, and for contrast, sounded in alternation with those instruments. While this enabled trumpets to participate in movements in a wide variety of styles, it proved detrimental to the development of a distinct trumpet idiom once Italian influences and more complex contrapuntal textures took hold towards the end of the century. For example, composers in France did not construct movements using short trumpet-style motifs in the manner of their counterparts in Bologna, and it was only with Purcell in England that the trumpet came to feature in idiomatic French Overtures.

During the reigns of Louis XIV and Louis XV military victories and important royal events were often celebrated with the performance of a Te Deum with orchestral accompaniment. The inclusion of trumpets by Lully in his Te Deum of 1677 was emulated by Michel-Richard de Lalande (1684), Marc-Antoine Charpentier (*c.*1692) and André Campra (1729). Lalande's Te Deum received repeat performances at the royal court for several decades and in the Concert Spirituel from the inaugural season in 1725 up to 1755; there is also evidence that it was performed in Lille in the early 1780s.[5] Charpentier's D-major Te Deum (H146), from the early 1690s, with parts for one *trompette dessus, basse de trompette* and timpani, is the only one of his four surviving settings to call for a full orchestra of oboes, trumpets, timpani and strings. Trumpets are prominent throughout this work, and the rondo Prelude, with its rousing trumpet theme, has become one of the most recognisable melodies of the baroque trumpet repertoire. Charpentier featured the same combination of trumpets and timpani in the 'Rondeau pour les Corinthiens' from his opera *Médée* (1693), and two *trompettes dessus, trompette de basse* and timpani in two orchestral *rondeaux* from the early 1690s: *Marche de triomphe* and *Second air de trompettes.*

Following the death of Lully, a vogue for Italian music gained momentum in France. Italian arias were occasionally included in operas otherwise sung in French; more often *da capo* arias in French (*airs* or *ariettes*) were included. Campra included *da capo ariettes* with obbligato parts for trumpet and violin in his music for a revival of the tragédie *Thétis et Pélée* (1708) and the tragédie-lyrique *Télèphe* (1713),[6] and Jean-Joseph Mouret included *da capo* airs with trumpet obbligato in *divertissements* composed for plays performed at the Nouveau Théâtre Italien between 1717 and 1737.[7]

The independence of the trumpet in these movements did not mark the end of the practice of doubling trumpet parts with violins (and oboes). This was retained by Louis-Nicolas Clérambault, for example, in the *da capo* air 'Au son des trompettes' from his cantata *La Muse de l'Opéra*, published (and possibly performed at the Opéra) in 1716, and Mouret in his *Fanfares pour des Trompettes, Timbales, Violons et Hautbois* (1729). The survival of this practice can be attributed to the continued popularity of earlier repertoire, such as Lalande's *Symphonies pour les soupers du Roy.* This includes a *Concert de Trompettes,* comprising movements from the ballet *Saint Louis* of 1691 and pieces that were originally performed outdoors at Versailles, possibly for trumpet ensemble alone. Lalande's *Symphonies* remained popular at the royal court throughout the reigns of Louis XIV and XV and survive in various manuscript sources from the first half of the eighteenth century.[8]

Jean-Philippe Rameau, the leading opera composer in France during the second quarter of the eighteenth century, is noted for his innovative use of the orchestra. Although his trumpet writing has been adjudged conservative in some quarters in comparison with his use of the horn, many of his trumpet parts bear his idiosyncratic stamp and demand considerable technical dexterity.[9] One of his most important developments was the use of trumpets in E. Several of his operas feature trumpet tunes in the Lullian tradition and airs with trumpet obbligato that retain the pairing of trumpets and timpani. The 'First Air' from the 'Second Entry' of *Les Fêtes d'Hébé* (1739), a binary-form gavotte, is perhaps the most daring piece of the entire trumpet-tune genre. The melody begins with a descending arpeggio starting on the sixteenth-harmonic D6; development of this motif takes the trumpet part outside the notes of the harmonic series and culminates with an entry on E6. (Ex. 7.2a and b)

The trumpet in France did not acquire a solo repertory comparable to that which emerged in other countries during the seventeenth and eighteenth centuries. However, the highly distinctive trumpet ensemble repertoire from the reign of Louis XIV highlights a tradition of trumpet playing at Versailles that matched, and arguably surpassed, in its sheer *joie de vivre,* that from anywhere else in Europe of that time. The airs with trumpet obbligato that were composed for the theatre may be few in number, but they constitute an important branch of the repertory, reflecting an Italian influence on eighteenth-century French music and a solo trumpet tradition that is seldom recognised.

Ex. 7.2 Jean-Philippe Rameau, *Les Fêtes d'Hébé* (1739), opening (a) and bars 35–40 (b) of the 'Danse des Lacédémoniens'.

Britain

The restoration of the Stuart monarchy in 1660 heralded the reopening of the London theatres. After having lain dark for almost two decades, the burst of cultural energy emanating from the Restoration theatre served as a magnet for musicians from across Europe. Many found additional employment at court and played a key role in the city's burgeoning concert scene. Throughout the interregnum a vestige of the royal trumpet corps had been retained. At the Restoration this was bolstered with the addition of 'Four Dutchmen', who formed the first of the four groups (described as the 'king's group') into which the corps was divided. No ensemble music that can be linked to the English royal trumpet corps from this period survives; however, the sudden appearance of technically demanding trumpet parts in works from the 1680s suggests that such a repertoire may well have existed. A collection of 'Arie e Passaggi ad imitatione della Trombetta' was included in a volume of solo violin music by Nicola Matteis in 1685. The same pieces reappeared two years later as 'Concerto di Trombe a Tre Trombette con violini e Flauti'. Whether the work was intended for three trumpets, strings and recorders or a trio of trumpets, perhaps with timpani, in the manner of the French ensemble style, with the 'violini e Flauti' representing an alternative scoring, remains a matter of debate. It is possible that the pieces originally existed for trumpet ensemble, to which additional parts were added sometime before 1687.[10]

The earliest surviving work with trumpets by a composer based in England is a setting by Giovanni Battista Draghi of John Dryden's ode *From Harmony, From Heav'nly Harmony* for the St Cecilia's Day celebrations in 1687.[11] Trumpets, however, may have been included in earlier concerted compositions. A note in the libretto of Matthew Locke's *Psyche* of 1675 states that the D major chorus 'He turns all the horrors of war to delight' should be accompanied by trumpets and drums. However, both the veracity of this instruction and the suitability of trumpets in this chorus have been questioned.[12] Nicholas Staggins, Master of the King's Musick, received payment for copying the parts for various instruments, including trumpets, of a composition for the coronation of James II in 1685. Whether the work referred to was an anthem he composed for that occasion or, as Peter Holman suggests, a lost instrumental piece, is not clear.[13]

Peter Downey has speculated that trumpet parts existed for Purcell's Welcome Song of 1684, *From those serene and rapturous joys*,[14] although the earliest works by Purcell that unquestionably call for trumpets appeared in 1690: the Yorkshire Feast Song *Of old, when heroes thought it base*, for the annual meeting of Yorkshire gentlemen in London; the court ode *Arise, my muse*, for the birthday of Queen Mary; and the semi-opera *The Prophetess, or The History of Dioclesian*. During the last six years of his life, Purcell scored for the trumpet in music for the royal court, the theatre, and, on demand, for certain special occasions. Trumpet overtures and trumpet songs are prominent in his theatre works and odes from his active period of writing for the instrument. The overture to the Yorkshire Feast Song, modelled stylistically on the French overture, may be the earliest solo piece for trumpet and strings by an English composer. Like much of Purcell's music up to 1693, this overture includes two trumpets, democratically spanning the same range. (Purcell's later music more commonly called for one trumpet.) The opening statement of this overture demonstrates the equality of part writing in Purcell's scoring for two trumpets. The C sharp5 in the second trumpet part is typical of his free use of this non-harmonic pitch (Ex. 7.3). Other non-harmonic notes occasionally appear in Purcell's scores as passing or auxiliary notes. His most striking use of a non-harmonic trumpet pitch occurs in the closing bars of the alto solo 'The Fife and all the

Ex. 7.3 Henry Purcell, Yorkshire Feast Song (1690), overture.

Harmony of War' from the St Cecilia's Day ode *Hail, bright Cecilia* (1692), in which the first trumpet sounds a sustained F natural5, approached from D5, and marked 'loud' in Purcell's manuscript.[15] The wide tessitura that characterises much of Purcell's trumpet writing is a feature of the overture to *Hail, bright Cecilia*, in which the first trumpet spans the two and a half octaves from A3 to D6. By scoring for one trumpet in the later overtures, such as the introduction to Act III of *The Indian Queen* (1695), Purcell was able to incorporate the instrument more fully into contrapuntal textures. The well-known Sonata in D for trumpet and strings, discovered in the Library of York Minster in 1950, is his only solo work for trumpet in the three-movement Italian *sinfonia* form. The alto solo 'Sound Fame' from *The History of Dioclesian* (1690) shows how in touch Purcell, in London, was with current Italian innovations. In this aria he freely borrows from Venetian opera the idea of invoking the Goddess Fame with a trumpet obbligato.

A similar style of trumpet writing to Purcell's was immediately adopted by the older composer John Blow, who first scored for trumpets in his ode for St Cecilia's Day, 1691, the earliest English work to explicitly call for kettledrums. Four of Blow's surviving court odes include trumpet, as do his odes for St Cecilia's Day in 1695 and 1700. For the 1695 celebration, which was held the day after Purcell's death, Blow provided the ode and a *Te Deum and Jubilate*, in which trumpets feature prominently. Blow emulated Purcell in his adventurous writing for two trumpets, which are often treated independently. The obbligato to 'To Triumph, sound that story' from the birthday ode for Princess Anne, *Come, bring the song* (1700), is as demanding as any of Purcell's trumpet obbligatos (Ex. 7.4).

According to a report in the *Gentleman's Journal* of January 1692, at the St Cecilia's Day celebrations at Stationers' Hall the previous November, 'Mr. Showers' played 'some flat Tunes, made by Mr. Finger'. 'Mr. Showers' was presumably John Shore, who performed many of Purcell's difficult trumpet parts. The reference to 'flat Tunes' has been interpreted as alluding to the flat trumpet,[16] an instrument described by James

Ex. 7.4 John Blow, trumpet obbligato to 'To Triumph', from *Come, bring the song* (1700).

Talbot as a trumpet with a backward-moving double slide.[17] As Peter Holman has noted, however, it is just as likely that the writer was referring to a performance of trumpet tunes in the minor tonality on natural trumpet.[18] This is plausible given that trumpet music in minor keys was composed by Finger's Moravian contemporaries Biber and Vejvanovský.

Three surviving works, which are thematically related, specify parts for flat trumpet: a Prelude for 4 flat trumpets by Purcell from the incidental music to *The Libertine* (1695); a *March* and *Canzona* for 4 flat trumpets by Purcell for the funeral of Queen Mary (1695); and a three-part 'Symphony of Flat Trumpets' by Daniel Purcell from the semi-opera *The Island Princess* (1699). A fourth work, Jeremiah Clarke's ode on the death of Purcell, *Come, Come Along for a Dance and a Song* (1696), includes passages that were almost certainly intended for flat trumpets. These pieces point to a distinct slide-trumpet idiom: they are all in a minor key, slow moving and solemn, and the theatre pieces derive from scenes that evoke the supernatural.

Through the writing of Roger North, we know that John Shore added a 'turne screw' or 'worme' to his trumpet to help produce the 'exotic notes' that appear in the music of Purcell and his contemporaries and as a means of fine-tuning notes within the harmonic series. It is not clear from North's descriptions how the device functioned, but it apparently manipulated a slide mechanism, which North clearly regarded as being different from that of the sackbut. In a manuscript written around the turn of the eighteenth century, North explained that

> to cure these defects [in tuning] trumpetters have found some expedients, as the sackbut, which prolongs the tube ad libitum. But a more ingenious devise is that which Mr. Shoar [Shore], a most exquisite trumpetter, used to adapt his trumpet to consort. It was by an imperceptible lengthning or shortning the tube, by the help of a screw or worme, so as by turning the trumpet round he gained, or remitted of the length, by which his exotick notes fall all into use.[19]

North also referred to the device in a manuscript written *c.*1710, but is no more explicit in describing how it functioned:

> As for those devices of a turne skrew to lengthen or shorten ye tube to aid ye tuning some notes, or the protracting ye tube by sliding one into another, which is the sackbutt, I medle not here becaus [*sic*] they are shifts built upon ye simple proposition of a plain trumpet wch here onely I intend to speak off.[20]

Crispian Steele-Perkins has suggested that the *turne skrew* was 'a subtle device on the mouthpipe' that enabled the length of tubing to be adjusted.[21] Significantly, it seems that Shore used this type of trumpet routinely for the standard trumpet repertoire.

Two odes by Jeremiah Clarke, neither of which can be dated, contain passages that were clearly intended for slide trumpets. *Hark, she's called, the parting hour is come*, subtitled 'A Song on the Glorious Assumption of the Blessed Virgin', opens with a symphony for two trumpets and strings (Ex. 7.5). Although the ode is undated, it was clearly written for the Feast of the Assumption of the Blessed Virgin Mary (15 August).

Ex. 7.5 Jeremiah Clarke, *Hark, she's called*, overture.

Clarke is not known to have had links to Catholicism, and the circumstances surrounding the composition and performances of the ode are unknown. The second Clarke ode, *No more, great rulers of the sky*, which was dedicated to 'ye Gentlemen of ye Island of Barbadoes', includes a passage for trumpet that incorporates non-harmonic notes and is idiomatic of flat-trumpet writing. Of the two contemporary manuscript sources, only one (*GB-Ob* Tenbury MS 1232) indicates that this melodic line was intended for trumpet: the designation 'Trump', which was often used by scribes in England at this time as an abbreviation for trumpet, appears below the first treble line. Other English works of this period with parts for slide trumpet include 'A Song for St Cecilia's Day' by Vaughan Richardson, performed at Winchester in 1700,[22] and the Second English Partita by James Paisible, in the unusual trumpet key of B flat major.[23] Intriguingly, by the time Handel arrived in England in 1710, the slide trumpet appears to have fallen into disuse. Roger North's remarks in the later of the two manuscripts mentioned above probably refer to the late seventeenth century, when he was actively involved in the musical life of London.

During the period between the death of Purcell and the arrival of Handel, a wealth of trumpet music was composed for London theatre productions, and the trumpet came to prominence in other performance contexts. Newspaper advertisements and reports attest to the popularity of celebrated players such as John Shore, both in London and the spa towns frequented by London's upper classes in summer.[24] In Scotland, Daniel Thomson was performing much the same solo repertoire as his London counterparts from 1695 onwards.[25] Many suites of incidental music for the London stage were published by John Walsh during the first decade of the eighteenth century, and a wealth of trumpet music for the theatre survives in manuscript. One such collection, a set of partbooks held in Magdalene College, Cambridge, comprises 656 pieces, of which 43 include trumpet. Another, in the British Library (Add. MSS 30839 and 39565–7), includes the well-known Suite in D by Jeremiah Clarke.[26]

In 1701 'several persons of quality' organised a competition for the setting of William Congreve's masque *The Judgment of Paris* in an attempt to encourage all-sung music drama on the London stage. It is not known how many composers took up the challenge, but the settings by the four finalists – John Eccles, Gottfried Finger, Daniel Purcell and John Weldon – were performed at the Dorset Garden Theatre on 3 June 1701, each having been previously performed separately. Finger's score is the only one of the four not to have survived. Although the veteran theatre composer John Eccles was favourite to scoop the first prize of 100 guineas, the relative novice John Weldon won. Each of the three surviving settings includes trumpet sonatas and trumpet arias. Trumpet obbligatos accompanied Pallas Athena, goddess of war, as she competed against Juno and Venus for the golden apple to be awarded by Paris. The most dramatic use of the trumpet was in Eccles's setting, which included four trumpets and timpani in the scene featuring Athena. After Athena's introductory statement, the trumpets and drums enter with a ritornello, which opens with each of the four trumpets ascending in turn from C4 to G5 (Ex. 7.6). They accompany the aria 'Hark, hark, the glorious voice of war' that follows and are incorporated into the chorus with which the scene ends. The impact of trumpets and drums was heightened by the positioning of the orchestra inside a tin dome which amplified the sound.[27]

Ex. 7.6 John Eccles, *The Judgment of Paris* (f.p. 1701; published 1702), introductory flourish to the chorus 'Hark, hark, the glorious voice of war'.

Many English trumpet sonatas of this period were composed as overtures or instrumental interludes to theatrical works, or to extended vocal compositions.[28] A collection of instrumental music by several of the leading composers active in London is contained in a manuscript held in the British Library (Add. MS 49599). Of the seventeen pieces in the collection, ten are trumpet sonatas, five of which have been identified as deriving from the theatre: three sonatas by Daniel Purcell and one by John Eccles from their settings of *The Judgment of Paris*, and a sonata by John Barrett from the play *Tunbridge-Walks* (1703). It is possible that one or more of the four sonatas in this collection by Finger, for one or two trumpets, derived from his setting of *The Judgment of Paris*.[29] The care with which the collection was assembled and the high quality of the gilt-edged paper has led Smithers to conjecture that it may have been intended for royal performances.[30]

Sonatas for trumpet that may have been composed for concert performances include the three by the German-born harpsichordist and composer Gottfried Keller (Amsterdam, *c.*1700), and William Corbett's *Six Sonatas with an overture* Op. 3 (London, *c.*1708; Amsterdam, *c.*1708) and Sonata No. 12 from his *XII Sonate a tre* Op. 1 (Amsterdam, *c.*1700). Corbett's Op. 3, which includes four sonatas for trumpet and strings in D major and two in E major, only survives complete in its Amsterdam edition. The trumpet part for the E major sonatas is written in D major and may have been intended to be performed on a muted D trumpet; if so, they are the only known English works calling for the use of a transposing mute.[31] The suite in D, for two trumpets, oboes and strings, which concludes the set, if it was not composed for the theatre, certainly inhabits the same genre.

From his arrival in London in 1710 until his death in 1759, Handel was the dominant figure in music in Britain. Handel's early successes in London were tempered by the precarious footing on which Italian opera operated. Competition between rival companies led to a resurgence of operatic works in English, particularly after the success of John Gay's *The Beggar's Opera* in 1728, which ran for 62 successive performances and remained in the repertoire until the end of the century. A work that enjoyed success on a par with *The Beggar's Opera* was a parody of Italian opera, *The Dragon of Wantley* by John Frederick Lampe. First performed in 1737, this satirical opera received 76 performances in the twelve months after its first performance and then enjoyed revivals in most seasons for the following forty years. The high trumpet writing in the overture appears to parody the august trumpet style of Handel, while the florid writing of the First Tune, with trumpets and horns supporting the violin lines, is a pastiche of the virtuosic style associated with Italian opera. Whether the opera retained its original scoring up to the 1780s is uncertain. Prominent trumpet parts also appear in the theatre music of Thomas Arne, such as the masque *Alfred* (1740) – which includes 'Rule, Britannia!' – and *Eliza* (1754). The trumpet song 'Rise glory rise' from the opera *Rosamond* (1733) became popular as interval entertainment in London theatres and was performed at a benefit concert in Edinburgh in 1769.[32]

Several published collections containing trumpet concertos appeared around the middle of the century, including those by Richard Mudge (London, 1749) and Capel Bond (London, 1766). These works failed, however, to gain a foothold in the concert repertoire.[33] In 1752 the Italian violinist and composer Niccolo Pasquali moved from

London to Edinburgh, where he remained until his death in 1757. In 1755 he received payment from the Edinburgh Musical Society for adding trumpet and kettledrum parts to the '4th Concerto of Corelli', presumably the Concerto No. 4 in D from Corelli's *Concerti Grossi* Op. 6.[34] These parts have not survived; however, the arrangement was still in the Edinburgh concert repertoire in 1767 and Corelli's *Concerto Grosso* No. 4 was performed at Marylebone Gardens in London during the 1770s, with 'additional parts for Trumpets, French Horns, and Kettle Drums . . . by the late ingenious Sg. Pasquali'.[35]

The emergence of a canon of 'ancient' music during the second half of the eighteenth century ensured the survival of a tradition of solo trumpet playing in London and the main provincial musical centres in Britain. Performances of Handel's oratorios and concerts comprising mixed programmes based on his choral music formed the mainstay of the music festivals that first began to be organized in English provincial cities around the middle of the century. In these, as well as concerts incorporating a wider miscellany of music, 'The Trumpet Shall Sound' from *Messiah* and 'Let the Bright Seraphim' from *Samson* became popular showpieces for singers and trumpeters.

To mark the twenty-fifth anniversary of Handel's death and what was believed at that time to be the centenary of his birth, a commemorative festival was organised in London in 1784. The commemoration consisted of four concerts in Westminster Abbey: two concerts of his sacred music, which included the coronation anthem *Zadok the Priest* and the Dettingen *Te Deum*, and two performances of *Messiah*, as well as a concert of secular music at the Pantheon. The prospect of performances by mammoth forces, including 'a band far superior to any thing [*sic*] of the kind ever attempted before in England', fuelled the feverish anticipation.[36] For the performances in the Abbey, the choir and orchestra numbered more than 500 performers. Interest in the commemoration prompted the music historian Charles Burney to publish an account of the event, which in turn established this as the model for subsequent provincial festivals (Ills. 7.1a and b).

In his account of the first of the two performances of *Messiah*, on 29 May, Burney paid particular attention to James Sarjant's rendition of 'The Trumpet Shall Sound' and in doing so addressed wider issues relating to trumpet performance:

> The favourite Base song, '*The Trumpet shall sound*,' (I Cor. XV. 52) was very well performed by Signor Tasca and Mr. Sarjant, who accompanied him on the trumpet admirably. There are, however, some passages in the trumpet-part to this Air, which have always a bad effect, from the natural imperfection of the instrument. In HANDEL'S time, composers were not so delicate in writing for Trumpets and French-horns, as at present; it being now laid down as a rule, that the fourth and sixth of a key on both these instruments, being *naturally* so much out of tune that no player can make them perfect, should never be used but in short passing notes, to which no base is given that can discover their false intonation. Mr. Sarjeant's tone is extremely sweet and clear, but every time that he was obliged to dwell upon G, the fourth of D, displeasure appeared in every countenance; for which I was extremely concerned, knowing how inevitable such an effect must be from such a cause (*a*).

7.1(a) 'View of the Orchestra and Performers in Westminster Abbey during the Commemoration of Handel' (1784), in Charles Burney, *An Account of the Musical Performances*, plate 7. (By permission of the University of Glasgow)

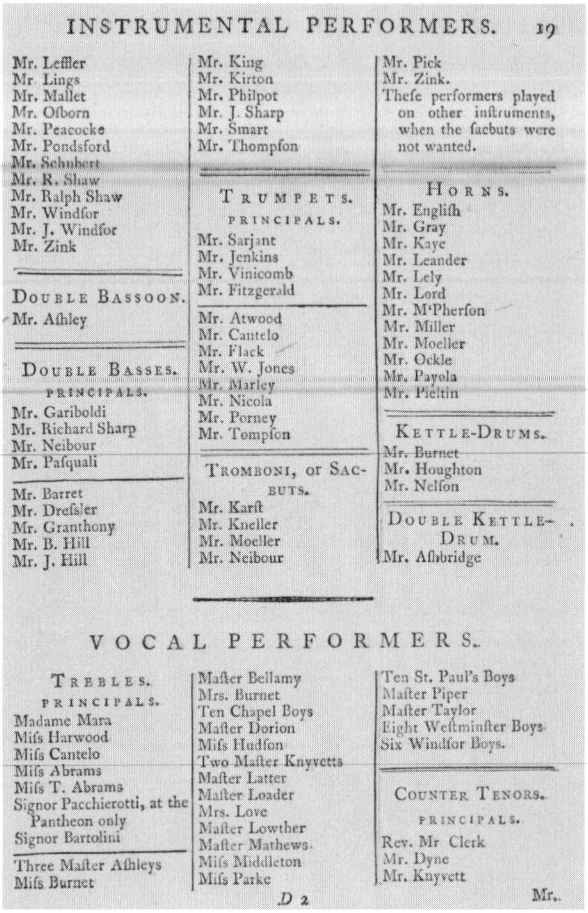

INSTRUMENTAL PERFORMERS. 19

Mr. Leffler
Mr. Lings
Mr. Mallet
Mr. Oſborn
Mr. Peacocke
Mr. Pondsford
Mr. Schubert
Mr. R. Shaw
Mr. Ralph Shaw
Mr. Windſor
Mr. J. Windſor
Mr. Zink

DOUBLE BASSOON.
Mr. Aſhley

DOUBLE BASSES.
PRINCIPALS.
Mr. Gariboldi
Mr. Richard Sharp
Mr. Neibour
Mr. Paſquali

Mr. Barret
Mr. Dreſsler
Mr. Granthony
Mr. B. Hill
Mr. J. Hill

Mr. King
Mr. Kirton
Mr. Philpot
Mr. J. Sharp
Mr. Smart
Mr. Thompſon

TRUMPETS.
PRINCIPALS.
Mr. Sarjant
Mr. Jenkins
Mr. Vinicomb
Mr. Fitzgerald

Mr. Atwood
Mr. Cantelo
Mr. Flack
Mr. W. Jones
Mr. Marley
Mr. Nicola
Mr. Porney
Mr. Tompſon

TROMBONI, or SACBUTS.
Mr. Karſt
Mr. Kneller
Mr. Moeller
Mr. Neibour

Mr. Pick
Mr. Zink.
Theſe performers played on other inſtruments, when the sacbuts were not wanted.

HORNS.
Mr. Engliſh
Mr. Gray
Mr. Kaye
Mr. Leander
Mr. Lely
Mr. Lord
Mr. M'Pherſon
Mr. Miller
Mr. Moeller
Mr. Ockle
Mr. Payola
Mr. Pieltin

KETTLE-DRUMS.
Mr. Burnet
Mr. Houghton
Mr. Nelſon

DOUBLE KETTLE-DRUM.
Mr. Aſhbridge

VOCAL PERFORMERS.

TREBLES.
PRINCIPALS.
Madame Mara
Miſs Harwood
Miſs Cantelo
Miſs Abrams
Miſs T. Abrams
Signor Pacchierotti, at the Pantheon only
Signor Bartolini

Three Maſter Aſhleys
Miſs Burnet

Maſter Bellamy
Mrs. Burnet
Ten Chapel Boys
Maſter Dorion
Miſs Hudſon
Two Maſter Knyvetts
Maſter Latter
Maſter Loader
Mrs. Love
Maſter Lowther
Maſter Mathews
Miſs Middleton
Miſs Parke

Ten St. Paul's Boys
Maſter Piper
Maſter Taylor
Eight Weſtminſter Boys
Six Windſor Boys.

COUNTER TENORS.
PRINCIPALS.
Rev. Mr Clerk
Mr. Dyne
Mr. Knyvett

D 2 Mr.

7.1(b) Detail of the list of performers for the Handel Commemoration of 1784, in Charles Burney, *An Account of the Musical Performances*, p. 19. (By permission of the University of Glasgow)

(*a*) In the Allelujah, p. 150, of the printed score, G, the fourth of the key, is sounded and sustained during two entire bars. In the Dettingen *Te Deum*, p. 30, and in many other places, this *false concord*, or interval, perpetually deforms the fair face of harmony, and indeed the face of almost every one that hears it, with an expression of pain. It is very much to be wished that this animating and brilliant instrument could have its defects removed by some ingenious mechanical contrivance, as those of the German flute are, by keys.[37]

Significantly, Burney's criticism was directed less at the playing of James Sarjant (d.1798) and more at what he perceived to be the trumpet's inherently faulty intonation. The Handel commemoration, taking Burney's criticism, which gained widespread currency, into consideration, has been regarded as the catalyst for the re-emergence of the slide trumpet. However, the earliest evidence of the slide trumpet in late eighteenth-century London comes in William Shield's opera afterpiece *The Magic Cavern*, first performed in December 1784, a few months after the festival, but before the publication of Burney's account of the event. Slide trumpets may also have been used in Shield's opera *Robin Hood*, which was first performed in April 1784.[38]

An arrangement of Handel's aria 'Se l'arco' from the opera *Admeto* and the March in *Scipione*, as a single item, was performed by James Sarjant on the slide trumpet at Vauxhall Gardens on numerous occasions between 1787 and 1791.[39] Whether a concerto by James Hook, the resident composer at the Gardens, that Sarjant performed there in August 1786 was also for slide trumpet cannot be ascertained. Two overtures by Thomas Attwood, from opera afterpieces composed for the Theatre Royal in the Haymarket, *Caernarvon Castle* (1793) and *The Castle of Sorrento* (1799), include prominent solo passages for slide trumpet.[40] As was customary with English theatre music of this period, these operas were published in short score with instrumental cues. The reconstruction of Attwood's scoring is therefore partly conjectural. However, several passages that include prominent non-harmonic notes are designated for trumpet, and it seems certain that these were performed on slide trumpet (Ex. 7.7). There are no surviving orchestra rosters for the Theatre Royal in the Haymarket, where Attwood's two operas were performed, for this period. It seems likely that James Sarjant, the most prominent trumpeter in London at this time, performed the solo part in *Caernarvon Castle*; however, *The Castle of Sorrento* was first performed the year after Sarjant's death. John Hyde, who published a trumpet tutor in the same year, 1799, in which he claimed to have invented the slide trumpet, may have performed that particular solo trumpet part in Attwood's opera.

The slide trumpet is also prominent in the introductory fanfare to the overture to Johann Peter Salomon's opera *Windsor Castle* (1795). In the audience for the second

Ex. 7.7 Thomas Attwood, overture to *The Castle of Sorrento*, bars 17–25.

performance of this opera was Joseph Haydn. Haydn attended a performance of William Shield's opera *The Woodman,* which includes one song with an obbligato for two slide trumpets, in 1792, on his first visit to London.[41] Given his apparent familiarity with the development of the slide trumpet in London and the fact that he was to compose his concerto for Anton Weidinger's keyed trumpet after returning to Vienna, it is unfortunate that Haydn did not compose any solo pieces for John Sarjant, with whom he was evidently acquainted.

Chapter 8

The concertos of Haydn and Hummel

Chapter 7 ended with the reappearance of the slide trumpet in England. Another manifestation of the quest to chromaticise the trumpet was the application of keys. The Enlightenment and the Romantic era which followed was an age of inspired individual genius, and it was the Viennese Court trumpeter Anton Weidinger who became the first to explore more fully the chromatic potential of the trumpet. In one short decade he provided the inspiration for the concertos of Haydn and Hummel, and further repertoire by Kozeluch, Weigl and Neukomm.

In these works, the technique of the chromatic trumpet advanced such a long way in so few years that it remains an enigma that these concertos were not more influential in their own time, and only became popular a century and a half later. Haydn's concerto, though written in 1796, was not performed until 28 March 1800. It was followed in 1803 by the Hummel Concerto in E major. One of the readiest solutions to the enigma is that the chromatic trumpet was listened to more as an exotic curiosity rather than a viable solo instrument at this time, and the contemporary notices in the newspapers confirm this perception.[1] The works written for Weidinger had to wait until the second half of the century following for full public recognition. Weidinger lived on until 1852, but there is no trace of a legacy of pupils or imitators. In the trumpet concertos of Haydn and Hummel, the solo trumpet took a leap forward conceptually, but this concept was ahead of its time. Though the trumpet played an increasingly important role in orchestral music, its profile as a solo instrument remained insignificant during the nineteenth century.

The Haydn Trumpet Concerto in E flat

Haydn wrote the trumpet concerto in his full maturity. It was his final orchestral work, after more than a hundred symphonies. After this he wrote solely choral works. The concerto is scored for a large classical orchestra – double wind without clarinets, but with horns, trumpets and timpani, which lend gravitas to the orchestral tuttis. The autograph manuscript, held in the Gesellschaft der Musikfreunde in Vienna, is clear but shows signs of having been written at speed. The thematic shaping of the concerto seems to revolve around the simple notion that this new *Inventionstrompete* was capable of playing the hitherto impossible – a complete scale in its low register. The first subject of the first movement begins with a three-note motif E flat, F, G. The second movement weaves around the statically grounded pedal point of the

Exx. 8.1a–c Joseph Haydn, Trumpet Concerto, first movement, bars 37–8(a); second movement, bars 9–12(b); third movement, bars 45–8(c).

subdominant A flat. The third movement completes the scale with a rondo tune based on the last four steps – B flat, C, D, E flat – repeated over and over with changing emphasis (Ex. 8.1a–c). The rondo melody injects a playful mood and the summit of the scale is reached with a measure of triumph.

In the first movement, the opening three-note motif is soon extended in the opening phrase to the entire scale, ending with a classical arch to the dominant. Typically for Haydn, the phrase-length is asymmetric. Before the exposition proper, in the orchestral *ritornello* that opens the concerto, the solo trumpet surprises by blundering in after seven bars on a single low E flat, and then joins in the tutti. Haydn loved a joke.

The exposition proper under way, the trumpet plays in short, pithy phrases, with thematic material being bandied between orchestra and soloist. Therein is one of the difficulties of the work for the performer, as the phrases have to be played as though having a conversation with the orchestra. The first group of material closes with a humorously-placed military trumpet cliché in the bottom, *principale*, register, as if Haydn were saying – here we have an instrument melodious enough to be able to converse on equal terms with an entire orchestra, but lest you forget, it really is a trumpet! (Ex. 8.2)

The second subject group of materials begins with the opening theme in reverse – a palindromic G, F, E flat – and immediately modulates to the relative minor, where it indulges in simple chromatic motion between C and B. Haydn relishes this and impresses the extraordinariness of this on the audience by repeating it no fewer than four times before releasing the melody on to the dominant of the dominant (Ex. 8.3).

Ex. 8.2 Haydn, Concerto, first movement, bars 49–50.

Ex. 8.3 Haydn, Concerto, first movement, bars 52–9

At this point, the trumpet, as if buoyed by its newfound capabilities, ascends stepwise from the dominant, throwing in a couple of triumphant trills for good measure, something it could never have negotiated hitherto with such aplomb. But this trumpet is a subtle show-off, and after exchanging pleasantries with the orchestra, proceeds chromatically with a series of descending accented passing notes and appoggiaturas of surpassing wistfulness. The exposition ends positively, with the trumpet solo reasserting itself with a heroic scale ascending to high B flat and a flourish of descending semiquavers leading to an affirmative cadence.

The development section is infused with a strange ambivalence. It inhabits the *clarino* register, but rather than show off the *allelujah* side of the trumpet in an uncomplicated fashion, it spends its few fleeting moments (this is not a long concerto) improvising around areas of risk and danger for the natural trumpet. It is thus a *development* section in more ways than one – it is also developmental for the idiom of the instrument. The entire movement is monothematic, and the three-note motif provides the basis for the development, this time in the relative minor. C minor was an inversion of normality for the trumpet, outside the normal certainty of C major. And the development section moves yet further into areas formerly thought precarious for the natural trumpet by dwelling repeatedly on the eleventh partial, an ambivalent note sounding somewhere between A flat and A natural on the E flat trumpet, which usually needed lipping up or down into diatonic conformity. A flat major was, as such, an exotic destination for the trumpet prior to the development section of this concerto, and, as if to underline the rarity of the atmosphere, Haydn repeats the sequence three times, the third time with flamboyant decoration. It is almost as if Haydn is rising to Charles Burney's challenge of 1784, referred to in Chapter 7. Haydn knew Burney well. It is not beyond the realms of the possible that this was one of the stimuli to invention lurking at the back of Haydn's mind.

Whatever the inspiration, the passage soon becomes more playful. Throughout the development section, the soloist is constantly interlocking in a display of dexterity with first and second violins, and the whole passage has the feel of a game of 'catch as catch can' with three equal protagonists. After further upwardly moving chromaticism from the trumpet, the trumpet breaks free into neo-baroque passage-work which leads to the highest note of the piece, D flat6, after an extravagant sequence of semiquavers. This highest note signals a sidestep into the remote key of D flat, which delays the home certainty of E flat until the trumpet brings the recapitulation home with the reaffirmation of the three-note motif. The recapitulation shows just how effectively suited to the trumpet is the simplicity of the material. The second group of material this time round makes way for a sequence of display passages where the trumpet shows off its ability to leap, skip and jump. There is a build-up to a cadenza, and a further opportunity for the soloist to shine. At all times in this movement,

Haydn seems to have been careful about leaving rests, not overtaxing the soloist, and phrasing in the trumpet part always allows for breathing. Haydn presumably took advice from Weidinger. The work is intimately crafted to the capabilities of the keyed trumpet and the likeliest conclusion is that the melodic and harmonic design of the concerto is intelligently built around these capabilities.

The second movement is grounded on A flat major, the fourth measure of the scale of E flat. As if to underline the obsessive eleventh partial in the middle of the first movement development, Haydn anchors the entire movement on the A flat an octave lower, and during the course of the melody, touches this A flat no fewer than ten times. Subtly played, this gives the entire melody an air of tranquillity, and Haydn has ingeniously crafted a syncopated middle strand within this melody, with the main beat falling on the third quaver of the three-note group to deflect the tendency of stresses on main beats to sound pedestrian. Add to this subtle syncopation a slow tactus in two, a lilting staccato accompanying string figure and a prominent flute in the orchestral blend, and we have a perfect setting for a languid pastorale. In the middle section, however, this pastoale has a hint of romance, and the fact that romance can be poignant is demonstrated by the *rinforzandi* in the violins, stressing, again, the syncopated sixth and third quavers in the bar. Though short-lived – this is the most chromatic and turbulent part of the work as far as the trumpet is concerned – it modulates through key after key until it arrives in the outlandish key for any instrument, far less the trumpet at that time, of C flat major. It is one of those Haydnesque 'Let there be light' moments. The effect is as if the sun had just come out from behind a cloud. Strangely enough, there is a similar moment in the second movement of the Hummel concerto. The opening theme of Haydn's short ternary movement returns, and is ornamented by the addition of more demisemiquavers, which at this tempo look faster than they are. On the manuscript, there is no slur over these quick notes, although a modern playing tradition seems to have built up of slurring over the complete group. This probably grew from the first widely available edition of the work, the 1945 Boosey & Hawkes edition, which adds this slur and other expression marks without providing any editorial rationale.[2] Admittedly, there are many inconsistencies to reconcile in the original, and the speed with which the manuscript was set down leaves room for ambiguity. The second movement ends simply, with the trumpet joining the strings to fade away together on their staccato accompanying motif. The second movement is left up in the air, an anacrusis to the last movement. It is as if this movement were designed to follow straight into the third.

All three movements of the concerto begin quietly. The first movement begins in a hush, opening, as has already been described, with an elliptical seven-bar phrase typical of Haydn. The 'false' entry of the solo trumpet on the downbeat of bar 8 triggers the first big tutti. The third movement grows out of the quiet at the end of the second, and quickly builds momentum. It is one of the catchiest rondo themes in classical music, and its memorability is one of the reasons for the work's popularity. It completes the ascent of the E flat scale begun in the first movement. Haydn's playfulness with varied repetition gives the movement a cheeky character. Although this movement is also monothematic, Haydn introduces such a microcosm of ideas into the episodes that the whole movement bubbles with felicitous invention.

Weidinger, as any subsequent interpreter of this concerto can vouch, must have been capable of subtle and rapid articulation. Interestingly, the trumpet part in the exposition of the rondo theme has no slurs or legatos, although the violins have bowing marks. There is a rationale for matching bowing and articulation, as in the development section of the first movement, although this type of symmetry between wind and strings always looks better to the eye than it sounds to the ear. Following the manuscript and tonguing these passages throughout does have the advantage of sounding nimble and virtuosic on the trumpet. The A flat major version of the Rondo theme, in duet with the first bassoon, does have added slurs, however, and they are worth adhering to, to give a gentler feel. The movement is peppered with acrobatic moments, when the trumpet player is made to jump through some virtuoso hoops – E flat broken arpeggios, A flat broken arpeggios, B flat broken arpeggios, then octave leaps tracing the path from E flat to A flat that has been such an *idée fixe* throughout. It is at this point that Haydn is in two minds as to how heroic to make this high point of the work, with still a little way to go before the end, and a few more surprises in store. Or perhaps it was at this point that Weidinger, the first champion of the work, ran out of stamina. The high A flat, at the top of the octave leaps, ascends on its repetition to a B flat. Originally, Haydn topped the B flat with a triumphant C, a tone higher, but his second thought was to rub it out and place the high C down the octave. There is a case for both approaches. From this point on, the orchestra takes over. There is a series of trills for the soloist to interject brilliance, but the orchestra build-up leads to a dramatic piece of theatre when the orchestra drops for five bars to a measured *pianissimo* tremolo before surprise *fortissimo* orchestra chords signal a grand entrance. But grand entrance is there none. Haydn quite clearly marks two bars *general pause* and the trumpet enters quietly, repeating the final steps of the scale, B flat to E flat, gradually melting back into the texture of the orchestra. It is a brilliant orchestral effect. In the final eight bars the trumpet reverses roles, from soloist to accompanist, pumping out tonic and dominant in the *principale* register, while the orchestra makes triumphant noises above. At the end of what is arguably the most revolutionary work in the trumpet repertoire, it is almost as if Haydn were saying – it was an illusion, here it is, in the end, just an ordinary trumpet after all.

This route map through the Haydn concerto from behind the trumpet gives an inside, player's view of the work. Although the concerto is, partially, a test piece for a new instrument, the elements of discovery, risk and danger are difficult to recreate with a modern audience. That is, unless the concerto is played on a keyed trumpet, which is a completely different listening experience. In comparison with the modern instrument, the keyed trumpet cannot compete with the modern trumpet's evenness of tone. But there lies one of its attractions – its variety of colours. The fact that Anton Weidinger took four years from the point of composition to first performance speaks for its relative difficulty at the time – both technical and conceptual.

By the time the concerto became well known, in the second half of the twentieth century, before the period instrument revival, the limitations of the natural trumpet were a distant folk memory, and most of the work's technical difficulties could be negotiated by a promising student. The reason for the work's present popularity is its quality of invention, the attractiveness of the melodic material, and the ability of the sound of the trumpet to enliven the spirit.

The Hummel Trumpet Concerto in E major

The Hummel Concerto is a simpler construct than the Haydn. A more straightforwardly tuneful composer than Haydn, Hummel seems to have grasped immediately the lyrical side of the keyed trumpet. The impact of this lyricism is heightened through contrast. The first movement, especially, inhabits an area delicately poised between operatic aria and military call. Hummel's Concerto is pitched a semitone higher than Haydn's, in E major, which is a rich-sounding key on strings. Weidinger may have had a new trumpet built for this work, although it is possible to play the same keyed trumpet crooked into E flat and E natural without creating insurmountable intonation problems. Clarinets replace the *clarini* of the Haydn concerto. There are tympani despite the lack of trumpets. The clarinets fulfil the orchestral trumpets' function. There is a lightness and transparency about the scoring, with many deft touches of orchestral colour, the horns and oboe (especially in the second movement) being used as a foil to the trumpet.

After a long and imposing orchestral exposition, reminiscent in places of Mozart's Haffner Symphony, the trumpet enters affirmatively with a typical fanfare – a rising arpeggio and a dotted rhythm (Ex. 8.4). Immediately after this opening flourish, Hummel continues by following a contrary melodic profile to Haydn. The Haydn concerto opens with upwards-rising stepwise motion; the Hummel concerto is initially in downward stepwise motion, interspersed with energetic, upward leaps of a sixth and an octave. This exploitation of the low register right from the beginning creates an immediate impression of mellowness, and Hummel wastes no time in showing how lyrical this new trumpet can be by continuing the first group of ideas with an arioso over a quaver accompaniment in the strings. The first group of ideas ends heroically with a virtuosic extension of the opening triplets.

Neither Haydn nor Hummel eschews the simple effectiveness of a single long note – the immemorial device of the trumpet – to sound well in their concertos, and Hummel opens his second group of material in this sonata form movement with two bell tones against simple quaver accompaniment – in the relative minor, the same key as Haydn's second subject. Hummel extends the phrase with an octave leap upwards, then follows that with a falling phrase to an appoggiatura, resolving, as Haydn does at the very same point, on to the dominant of the dominant. Here Haydn injects muscle into the trumpet part through a sequence of trills. Hummel, instead, uses the military side of the trumpet as contrast. A trumpet call acrobatically descends to a low B before leaping a tenth and resolving once more on to the dominant of the dominant. Another military reminiscence follows, in the major key, and is followed in its turn by a contrary-motion minor version that whips the orchestra into a

Ex. 8.4 Hummel, Trumpet Concerto, first movement, bars 66–8.

dramatic response, reminding one that *Sturm und Drang* still has life left in it by 1803. It has to be remembered that this is also the period when the Peace of Lunéville, agreed between Napoleon and Austria in 1801, and the Peace of Amiens, agreed with England, ended, and Napoleon re-embarked on his expansionist adventures. This gives added significance to the distant trumpet effects and then the more urgent rising motifs. Napoleon was to declare himself Emperor in the following year, which resulted in the rededication of Beethoven's Third Symphony in E flat (the *Eroica*) Op. 55, which is contemporaneous with Hummel's work. The *Eroica* begins with a triadic military call, of the sort that pervades the first movement of Hummel's concerto.

Europe was in political and military turmoil. The Napoleonic Wars that had followed the French Revolution had mobilised most of Europe's armies, so it should not be surprising to find echoes of this throughout Hummel's trumpet concerto. The manuscript, held in the British Library, includes corrections in different coloured pencils and offers two versions of the second movement. The Universal Edition publication of the concerto, edited by Edward Tarr, in the original key of E, in contrast to the E flat version of most other editions, is an excellent introduction to the various readings that can be made of the concerto based on the original manuscript.[3] The first published edition of the concerto, by Fritz Stein (Leipzig, 1957), was transposed down a semitone to E flat to render it more suitable for the B flat trumpet. Armando Ghitalla of the Boston Symphony Orchestra made the first recording of the work in 1964, in the original key of E, on a C trumpet. However, his edition of the work, which had appeared in 1959, is in E flat.

Spurred on by these trumpet calls, the orchestra does battle in a long development section balancing the opening tutti of the exposition. This sets the scene for the entrance of the trumpet in the triumphant key of C major, quite a distance from the opening E major. The trumpet grasps the opening fanfare and takes the opportunity for lyrical melody at this point. And then, with the stress of syncopation, the melody takes an ardent, passionate turn, before, as in the Haydn concerto, the development section peters out. Hummel devises an intricate interlocking passage between solo trumpet and woodwinds to wend back into the recapitulation. The recapitulation is remarkable for having a written-out accompanied cadenza, like the Mozart Clarinet Concerto.

Throughout the first movement, Hummel uses the trumpet in a highly athletic way – wide leaps abound, and the writing does seem to owe a debt to Mozart's writing for clarinet (Ex. 8.5). The *tessitura* of Hummel's concerto is not quite as high-lying as Haydn's. Nevertheless, he does make more of the low register and goes some way towards inventing an equivalent of the clarinet's 'chalumeau' register for the trumpet. He uses the low D (sounding F sharp), and the 'pedal' E, with stentorian effect to herald the final dramatic trumpet call of the first movement (Ex. 8.6).

The second movement opens in the unrelated key of the subdominant minor (the Haydn second movement is in the subdominant major). A buoyant triplet accompaniment is set up in the strings, over a pizzicato bass that propels the rhythmic motion of the movement forward. This could be an operatic aria accompaniment. On the other hand, it does share a passing similarity to the second movement of Mozart's

Ex. 8.5a & b Hummel, Concerto, first movement, bars 138–43(a); Mozart, Clarinet Concerto in A, K622, first movement, bars 216–21(b).

Ex. 8.6 Hummel, Concerto, first movement, bars 245–7.

Piano Concerto in C major K565. However, Hummel brings his own original ideas to the movement – the ornamentation of the solo line is special, and the atmosphere of romantic sentiment is compelling. Hummel's piano music, unlike this trumpet concerto, did become popular during the first half of the nineteenth century. He was one of the great piano virtuoso composers of the age, and an influence on later composers like Chopin, who is said to have modelled his two piano concertos, E minor (1830) and F minor (1829), on those of Hummel.

This movement has a disguised rhythmic complexity that keeps it buoyant and interesting. The triplet accompaniment gives the feel of 12/8, but the *alla breve* marking implies a tactus of two slow beats to a bar, which keeps the rhythmic movement light, minimising the tendency to 'sit down' on every beat of the bar. Then, though much of the melody could be thought of as 12/8 because of the triplet rhythms, many bars are in 4/4, which gives the passing duplets in the solo part an expressive *trattenuto* feel over the accompanying triplets. A scene of romantic melancholy is quickly set and the trumpet appears in bar three holding a long note. Playing one note and making it beautiful is the ultimate test of any performer. This one note, however, is of improbable length – twelve beats – and is a test of the soloist's ability to hold the audience. The first bar semibreve is tied to another two bars worth of semibreves which have a wavy line over them – clearly an indication *to do something*. The wavy lines occur in three places later in this movement and in one place in the last movement. One possibility is that it signified a tremolo through trilling with a key rendering minimal pitch alteration, similar to that described by Charles Nicholson in his flute tutor of 1816.[4] Another is that it invited the performer to improvise. A signpost of how to go about inflecting long notes in this piece has already been given

Ex. 8.7a & b Hummel, Concerto, second movement, bars 3–5 (a); ornamented version by John Wallace (b).

by Hummel at the end of the first movement. An echo of the closing trill of the first movement can sound highly effective here (Ex. 8.7).

Hummel's harmony is richly romantic and forward looking. This first cadence point is preceded by a Neapolitan/German sixth pivot chord – of the sort that Schubert was especially fond over the following two decades. The sustained D flats and A flats in the solo part, notes to be nursed on many valved trumpets, sound sonorous and characterful on the keyed trumpet. They also fall on stress points in the melody where their special colour helps to add poignancy to the shape of the phrase, for example in bars 8–10 (Ex. 8.8).

The Neapolitan/German sixth chord into this first cadence presages a modulation into the relative major of C for the most extended melody of the movement, which is remarkable for its sustained long melodic line. The slow movements of Mozart's Horn Concertos (notably K495) foreshadow this, but, in general, composers were slow to grasp the ability of brass instruments to sustain a cantabile melody. In the nineteenth century, Schumann was the first to introduce a 'long line' into his horn parts, both orchestral and solo, but this was getting on for a half-century later. This passage is a test to any trumpet player's breath control, then or now. It is also a test of maintaining a beautiful sound at a gentle dynamic. If Schumann transferred the cantabile idiom from cello to horn to achieve his 'long line', Hummel borrowed his trumpet 'long line' from his own piano writing (Ex. 8.9). A near contemporaneous solo work for horn by Beethoven, the Sonata Op. 17 (1800), demonstrates how motivic and short-breathed Beethoven's concept of solo brass writing was by comparison at this time – although by the time of the *Adagio* of the Ninth Symphony (1822–4), his concept had expanded to embrace a wide-ranging extended orchestral solo for fourth horn.

Ex. 8.8 Hummel, Concerto, second movement, bars 8–12.

Ex. 8.9 Hummel, Concerto, second movement, bars 13–28.

A long, dark passage follows the 'long line' melody in Hummel's second movement, orchestral *rinforzandi* heighten the effect of yet more Neapolitan/German sixth pivot chord progressions, until the trumpet modulates into the central section of the movement, and suddenly there is a magical transformation as the oboe wrests the melodic initiative from the trumpet, and 'the sun comes out' in the tonic major. A similar moment in the second movement of the Haydn concerto has been mentioned above. Hummel's effect is enhanced by the use of oboe timbre shining through the orchestral texture. The trumpet takes over from oboe and leads via D major to the climax of the movement in a decorated and ornamented version of the 'long line' now modulated into a glorious A major. More wavy lines invite the performer to improvise.

After this, follows a reflective coda. Hummel pays homage to Haydn, quoting the opening three notes of the older composer's concerto, and then ruminating on it. The passagework is very pianistic before closing in A major. This movement covers a broad emotional spectrum in its short span, an opening atmosphere of melancholy transforming into an eventual mood of optimism.

We have travelled a long way from the eighteenth century where the natural trumpet could not take part in music which modulated so freely, and key centres had to be quite static. The concerto for seven trumpets and timpani in Altenburg's treatise, published less than a decade earlier, in 1795, never modulates further than the dominant and even then only sparingly. It is antiquarian by comparison. The keyed trumpet, as used by Haydn and Hummel, could take a leading part in advanced music in the mainstream of contemporary developments, during a period of turbulent change.

An orchestral interlude now prepares the scene for the final movement modulating towards the dominant of E major. This bridge contrasts swirling broken scales in the strings against portentous dotted-rhythm chords in the wind. Though not strictly necessary from a harmonic point of view, this transition is, at this point, an imaginative solution to the mood swings which accompany the wide-ranging modulations in this Hummel concerto. These are more extreme than in previous solo trumpet repertoire, and such a distance has been travelled during the course of the second movement that this bridge is necessary to build expectation for the exuberance of the Finale.

The final movement begins with the solo trumpet emerging out of the expectant last chord of the slow movement with the type of repeated-note galloping figure that fits so well, as in the fanfare which opens the *Allegro* section of Rossini's *Guillaume Tell* overture (1829). As in the first movement, Hummel opens with the converse of Haydn, with descending instead of ascending phrases. The contour of the melodic line is in contrary motion to the rondo theme of Haydn's concerto. Hummel's rondo theme bubbles with effervescence – and like Haydn, he makes ample use of repetition, giving the soloist opportunities for shading, nuance and echo. The following orchestral *tutti* is notable for a very tricky 'Scotch snap' dotted rhythm in the strings. The 'Scotch snap' is in fact ubiquitous in the folk music of Europe, and this passage, with its heavily syncopated displaced accent on the second quaver of the bar, would not be out of place in a Dvořák Slavonic Dance. Hummel was born in Bratislava, now in Slovakia, but at that time in Hungary. Bratislava was part of the ancient kingdom of Bohemia before assimilation into the Austro-Hungarian Empire. Hummel's Bohemian origins are visible in this movement. Bohemia, of course, had been a main source for developments in horn playing over the previous century. Jan Václav Stich (1746–1803), who internationalised his name to Giovanni Punto, was a Bohemian horn player active in a period when the technique of hand-stopping chromaticised the horn. Hummel, through his close friendship with Beethoven, is likely to have been acquainted with innovations to the horn. Beethoven wrote his Horn Sonata Op. 17 for Stich in 1800 (in such a rush that he is purported to have improvised the piano part at the first performance).

Hand-stopping on the trumpet, although widespread, never led to the same outpouring of solo and chamber music as on the horn. Edward Tarr refers to seven lost concertos by J. A. Schmittbaur written in the 1770s for Michael Wöggel, the Karlsruhe trumpeter associated with the half-moon or *demi-lune* trumpet that became widespread in the first part of the nineteenth century.[5] Stopping on the trumpet persisted throughout the nineteenth century. Later in the century, it was used for a particular effect, to make a passage either sound grotesque when overblown, or poignant when used in *sforzato* at the lower end of the dynamic scale. There are passages marked with a cross (+) as in horn parts, for example, in Rimsky-Korsakov's orchestration of Moussorgsky's *Night on a Bare Mountain*, and the first versions of Mahler's first five symphonies use the term *gestopft* (stopped) liberally. Later versions change the *gestopft* to *gedämpft* (muted). There are few passages in the first and third movements of the Hummel Trumpet Concerto that could not have been played an octave lower on a hand horn in E using stopping technique. These outer movements are probably influenced by contemporary developments on the horn just as much as the second movement demonstrates the effect of a partial transference of idiom from piano to trumpet.

Coming out of the Bohemian orchestral interjection, the solo trumpet shows its capacity for fast semiquaver runs from the lowest register upwards, indulging in showy successions of semiquaver scales and chromatic sequences that eclipse even the technical demands of Cherubini's Sonata No. 2 for horn and string orchestra, composed a few months later, in 1804. Did Cherubini, then resident in Paris, have the opportunity of hearing Weidinger play his keyed trumpet when he visited that city in the same year on tour? Was Cherubini challenging the dedicatee, Frédéric Duvernoy,

Ex. 8.10 Luigi Cherubini, Sonata No. 2 for horn and strings, bars 99–103.

to the same feats of agility and acrobatics as were possible on the keyed trumpet of Weidinger? (Ex. 8.10)

Keyed instruments are capable of great rapidity of execution. The short travel of the key gives an advantage of agility over the long travel of the valve, and over the technique of hand-stopping.

After more Bohemian rhythms from the orchestra, and a rapid throwing of melodic fragments backwards and forwards from orchestra to soloist, the solo line emerges again out of the repeated-note figure into the rondo theme – but this time with even more notes. After the reprise of the rondo theme, and more Bohemian rhythms, the movement changes tack, embarking into a tonic minor episode, reminiscent of Smetana's 'Dance of the Comedians' from *The Bartered Bride* (first performed 1866). Hummel's rhythmically urgent accompaniment, a quaver rest followed by three quavers, drives his melody forward in similar Slavonic fashion.

There is a one-in-the-bar feel at this point. Trumpet and orchestra make a virtuoso exchange in G major, before returning to a broad melodic sweep in E minor that rises to a climax on a high B5. After dramatic swooping arpeggios, the trumpet and the strings exchange triplets in competitive fashion. The violins imitate triple tonguing with dexterity before settling on the dominant and entering a *Maggiore* (major key), the eccentric coda section of this unusual work. Cherubini comes into the frame once more. The new theme which Hummel introduces to begin the coda is a direct quote from Cherubini's 'Rescue' opera, *Les deux journées,* premiered in 1800 in Paris and subsequently transferred to Vienna.[6] The solo trumpet interjects fragmented fanfares and melodic tags. The effect is of a distant marching band. The fragmented trumpet commentary draws the listener's attention to the band coming closer, and the imminent 'rescue'. Attention successfully drawn, the solo trumpet celebrates virtuosically, borrowing the flamboyant flourish reminiscent of bagpipe grace notes, from the first episode of Haydn's rondo, and building on it (Ex. 8.11).

At this point, the written trumpet part begins to resemble a sketch, and the momentum of the movement has a tendency to stall unless Hummel's wavy line over the long B that follows in bars 218 to 221 is interpreted as meaning *do something.* The descending minims over the previous six bars also invite treatment as a skeleton, in the manner of many Mozart piano concertos. Like Beethoven, with whom he had become a fellow pupil of Haydn in 1791, Hummel was a prodigious improviser, and, following Beethoven's wishes, was asked to improvise at Beethoven's memorial concert shortly after his death in Vienna. The text of this unpublished work cannot

Ex. 8.11a & b Haydn, Concerto, third movement, bars 86–93 (a); Hummel, Concerto, third movement, bars 194–202 (b).

be said to have achieved its final form, frozen in time, in its manuscript. Just as the opening of the second movement is an invitation to the trumpeter to use some imagination, here is another opportunity to improvise. The following musical example shows only one solution, taking elements from the entire concerto – based on the opening arpeggio of the work, mixed with the diminished harmonies of the last movement, before joining the strings in unison (Ex. 8.12). The movement concludes with a dancing, Bohemian 'scotch snap'.

Hummel's concerto was played first at the New Year's Day Concert in 1804 at the Viennese court.[7] Of the composers for keyed trumpet, Leopold Kozeluch wrote his Symphonie Concertante in E flat (1798) probably for an occasion when there was a special group of visitors to Esterházy, given its solo *concertante* of mandolin, keyed trumpet, double bass and pianoforte with orchestra. In 1799, Joseph Weigl, whose father, also Joseph Weigl, had been a cellist in the orchestra at Esterházy (and for whom Haydn almost certainly wrote his Cello Concerto in C, Hob. VIIb:1), wrote the most exotic of the pieces associated with the keyed trumpet. The Concerto in E flat

Ex. 8.12 Hummel, Concerto, third movement, bars 210–21 (a); ornamented version by John Wallace (b).

was scored luxuriantly for cor anglais, flauto d'amore, keyed trumpet, viola d'amore, cembalo, cello, euphon, and an echo group of instruments including a second keyed trumpet.[8]

Outside these Esterházy works, there is a scattering of other works for keyed trumpet. Notable among these are the Josef Fiala Divertimento in D (1816),[9] and the keyed trumpet obbligatos which are included in the Requiem of Sigismund von Neukomm written for the Congress of Vienna in 1815.[10] This Congress followed the Battle of Waterloo and set the scene for a significant period of peace in Europe.

The use of solo keyed trumpet in the brass ensemble interludes which punctuate this Requiem Mass is a noteworthy innovation in the funereal use of the trumpet. The trumpet, like the trombone, has had a long association with death and mourning. However, the main thrust of trumpet idiom, to this point in art music, had been to symbolise war, heroism and military victory. The trumpet's usual idiom presented war as idealised and glorious rather than terrible and catastrophic, and its use in this Requiem Mass is a departure from previous norms. Here, the solo interludes reflect on the fallen and those who have given their lives.

Through Weidinger's tours and grand occasions like this, composers would have become aware of the new melancholic capabilities of the trumpet in specialised hands, although its use in a context of sadness remained exceptional to the norm. It is part of the enigma of the Haydn and Hummel concertos that we have to wait until 1843 for Donizetti's Introduction to Act II of *Don Pasquale* to find another truly doleful trumpet solo. Sigismund von Neukomm, however, went on to contribute further to trumpet repertoire in the medium of mixed chamber music. For the Philharmonic Society Subscription Concerts in London, he composed a *Fantaisie Concertante for Trumpet, Horn, Flute, Clarionette, Oboe, Bassoon and Double Bass* (1832), a Nonet (1836), and a *Divertimento for Trumpet Solo, 2 Horns, and 3 Trombones* (1834). Thomas Harper, sen., performed the trumpet parts. Neukomm also wrote marches for military band with keyed bugle parts during stays in Derbyshire (*March*, 1832) and Birmingham (*March and Gallop*, 1834).[11]

Why did the classical trumpet concertos that Weidinger championed, however, not become more widely known and successful within the nineteenth century? Players and composers were obviously slow or unwilling to grasp new technologies. Neukomm seems to have been an exception. The following excerpt from a letter by Neukomm to an unspecified Englishman in Paris in 1829 demonstrates his enthusiasm for the trumpet, the possibilities being opened up by its contemporary mechanisation, and his wish to find a 'star' player to champion it:

> It is possible that he [Cherubini] will forget to have you listen to the *trompette à pistons*, the one which is able to play all the tones, therefore I will urge you to become acquainted with this beautiful instrument that I would love to see in the hands of Mr. Harper. Please write to Mr. Dauverné. . . . I implore you to simply ask him to show you for the first time this trumpet, he will do it with the greatest of pleasures.[12]

Presumably, Harper remained unpersuaded, because the subsequent repertoire written for him was all tailored to his favoured slide trumpet.

The trumpet concertos of Haydn and Hummel remain enigmas of the classical repertory. They were composed at a particular time in the early nineteenth century when there was much freshly created novelty around competing for the audience's attention span. It could be argued that the sequence of concertos for Weidinger was the end of a tradition of the classical trumpet as a solo instrument and not the beginning, in the context of a forty-year history since the concertos of Leopold Mozart and Michael Haydn of 1762–64.

However, the concertos of Haydn and Hummel were also composed with a view to exploiting the large middle-class concert-going public springing up in the capital cities of Europe at this time. These concertos were up against fierce competition for public favour. Concertos composed around this time that did gain a permanent place in the repertory were by Beethoven – the Violin Concerto (first performed 1806) and the five piano concertos (1795–1809). It took a long time for these and other works now considered core repertory to become established, and the process by which this happened was through repeated performance in the philharmonic society concerts that were to spring up in every major city throughout the western world. But this proliferation was to occur from the third decade of the nineteenth century, and was too late for the keyed trumpet. The first Philharmonic Society commenced in London in 1813, following on from a tradition of subscription concerts that had forerunners back in the seventeenth century.[13]

In 1803 Weidinger embarked on a concert tour to Paris and London. Notices in *The Times* announcing his arrival and forthcoming concerts at the King's Theatre revealed that he was to perform 'on the organized Trumpet, (which he has invented), of which Mr. Haydn himself speaks with enthusiasm'.[14] Despite the tantalising reference to Haydn, the programme for these concerts is not known. Assuming that he guarded his hard-won repertoire with the zeal he applied to keeping his newly-developed trumpet to himself, this was another factor which hampered the dissemination of these concertos.[15] There is nothing like well-publicised rivalry to foment interest. However, this did not come to pass, and interest waned in the keyed trumpet as a solo instrument. Newspaper reviews of Weidinger's playing appeared occasionally in the early years of the century, but little by little the contemporary media went silent about the keyed trumpet. Even a work like the Beethoven Violin Concerto did not become fully established as part of the canonical repertoire until it received sustained advocacy from Joseph Joachim, whose career only began to flourish in the 1840s. Previously, violinist virtuosi like Viotti, Paganini and Spohr toured their own specially composed repertoire. So, with Weidinger's solo career over by the 1820s, no successor keyed trumpet soloist waiting in the wings, no real Philharmonic concert circuit established yet, and the valved trumpet still in its infancy, it is not surprising that Weidinger's keyed trumpet repertoire vanished from sight. It could also be that the changing tastes of this new, larger audience would have deemed this repertoire from an earlier age too exuberant to constitute legitimate trumpet idiom, given the widespread nineteenth-century perception of the trumpet as a 'noble' instrument.

Ebenezer Prout, one of the barometers of musical opinion in Victorian Britain, and an arbiter of popular taste, would definitely not have approved of an exuberant solo trumpet. His book on the orchestra, from 1878, differentiates between the 'coarse and vulgar' cornet on which 'rapid passages can be executed with great ease' and the trumpet. The cornet is 'more fit for performance of dance-music' or 'of solos in operatic selections at promenade concerts', and the trumpet is more at home in 'classical compositions' and 'dignified and serious' music.[16]

Certainly, when Hummel ventured to London, twenty-six years after the composition of his concerto, and composed a soloistic part for Thomas Harper, sen., in the *Military Septet* (1829), its idiom was restrained to the natural harmonics of the trumpet, and the main focus of the work was the piano, despite the title. The one brass solo work contemporaneous with the Hummel trumpet concerto with an afterlife beyond the first decade of the century was Carl Maria von Weber's Concertino for horn and orchestra (1806). It was revised for further performances in 1815, and was subsequently arranged for the celebrated Leipzig trombone virtuoso Carl Queisser, who played it with the Gewandhaus orchestra in 1836.[17] This has one of the few cadenzas for brass by a major composer from the period – and it is interesting to note how adventurous it is, replete with multiphonics (Ex. 8.13).

After the composition of Hummel's concerto, the trumpet had to wait a further ninety-six years for another concerto of similar dimensions – the Oskar Böhme Concerto of 1899. Although this and the following chapters explore the reasons for the slow evolution of trumpet idiom in the nineteenth century, and the reluctance of the musical public to accept the trumpet as a solo instrument, this distance between Hummel writing in 1803 and Böhme in 1899 is an enigmatic historical discontinuity. Despite this long lapse of time, traces of continuity do exist and can be found by burrowing deep down into interrelationships between successions of performers, teachers and pupils. In the Weimar/Leipzig/Dresden area in Germany, in the mid-nineteenth century, a particular continuity of individuals kept the flame of brass innovation alight.

Hummel was Kapellmeister and conductor in Weimar from 1818 until his death in 1837, during which time he developed performance standards and enhanced Weimar's reputation as a musical capital by inviting the best musicians of the day to visit. Ernst Sachse (1813–70), hailed as a 'superb' player of valved trumpet by Hector Berlioz in his memoirs, was principal trumpet. Sachse also played trombone, and

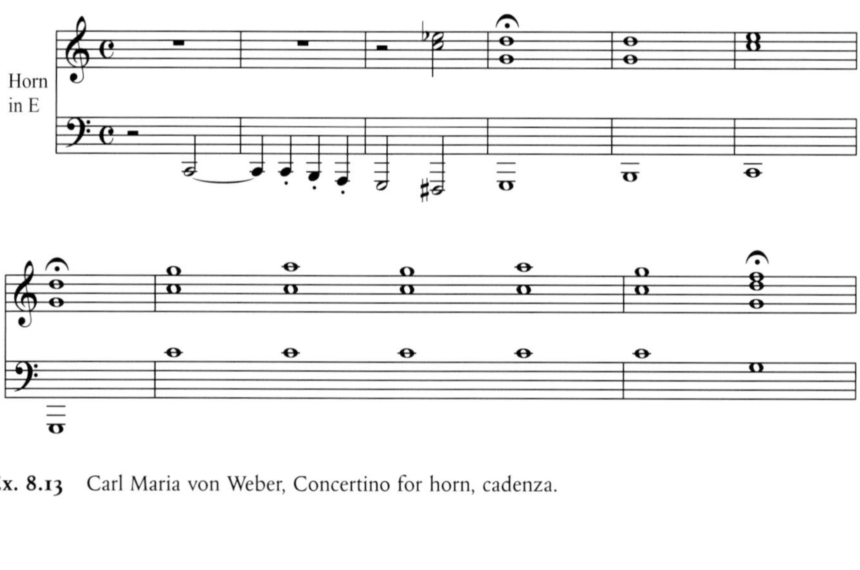

Ex. 8.13 Carl Maria von Weber, Concertino for horn, cadenza.

played a performance of one of his own trombone concertos in Leipzig conducted by Franz Liszt, Hummel's successor, in the 1840s.[18]

Mendelssohn, a former piano student of Hummel (other influential students of Hummel included Czerny and Thalberg), had become conductor of the Leipzig Gewandhaus orchestra in 1835, and went on to found the Leipzig Conservatory in 1843. The most obvious model for Böhme's concerto was Mendelssohn's violin concerto (premiered in 1845), which became one of the most influential concertos of the nineteenth century. The clearest link that Böhme's concerto shares with Mendelssohn's is its key of E minor (Böhme's work was originally written for valved trumpet in A). Böhme's first movement leans more towards minor than major, bringing out the darker hues of the trumpet's personality, which was a common romantic affect used by Mendelssohn, possibly following the example of the violin concertos of Louis Spohr. Behind Mendelssohn's work, however, was another model – an influence of an influence, perhaps – and this was the trombone concerto by Ferdinand David, leader of Mendelssohn's Leipzig Gewandhaus Orchestra.

Eight years before he gave the first performance of the Mendelssohn violin concerto, Ferdinand David wrote, in 1837, a trombone concerto in B flat for Carl Queisser, who proceeded to play it no fewer than thirty-seven times until his death in 1846.[19] This concerto shares common features, such as linking passages between movements, with both Mendelssohn's and Böhme's concertos (Hummel's trumpet concerto, also in E, interestingly, also has a very early example of a link passage between its second and third movements). In fact, David's trombone concerto was first conceived as a violin concerto, and it is likely that Mendelssohn and David, who were close confidants, discussed mutual problems and solutions during the writing of their respective concertos. David, one of the most influential violinists of the age, and teacher of Joseph Joachim, provides the seminal impetus for this equation of cross-influence. His concerto, which provided both stimulus and model for Mendelssohn, is hence the disguised forerunner of the Böhme Concerto. And Böhme, born in the Dresden area, composition student at the Leipzig Conservatoire, was probably also a student of Ferdinand Weinschenk (1831–1910), to whom he dedicated his concerto. Weinschenk was the first teacher of trumpet at the Leipzig conservatory, and had studied with the 'superb' Ernst Sachse in Weimar. So, underneath the surface impression of profound historical discontinuity, there does lie a complex tracery of influence and transmission of ideas running from Hummel in 1803 to Böhme in 1899.

What the success of the David concerto (which was performed frequently through to the 1860s) and the performances of Sachse's concertos do show, however, is that by the mid-nineteenth century there was a place for brass soloists playing with one of the finest orchestras in a prestigious musical centre in Europe. But the novelty in the second third of the nineteenth century in Leipzig was trombone, not trumpet.

Chapter 9

The trumpet and its players in the nineteenth and early twentieth centuries

The nineteenth century was a century of reform, politically, socially and economically. The Industrial Revolution that drove western economies during this century gave rise to the idea that the environment could be understood, manipulated, and shackled to progress. The period that began with the high ideals and certainties of the American and French revolutions and ended with the First World War featured long periods of stability punctuated by periodic volatility. The growth of democracy, the migration from countryside to town, the revolution in the methods of production and finance which instigated a vast increase in trade and a new era of colonisation: all of these factors were reflected in the performing arts and created a mass market for music of all sorts. Many new instruments were invented through the new technologies springing from the Industrial Revolution. The trumpet family tree spread new branches and new popularity in the mass musical market. Social evils were identified and legislated against. It became a charitable century. Some of the charities crusaded against poverty and ignorance. The Salvation Army was one of these, and, like most armies of old, used brass instruments in their battle plan. But these brass instruments were radically different from those of preceding centuries. Whole new species of mechanised brass instruments came into being and were taken up by the fastest-growing sector within the population – the industrial working class.

The old co-habited with the new. Although the application of radical new design concepts at the beginning of the period revolutionised the trumpet's capabilities, for many, the idea of the trumpet remained rooted in direct simple utterance – whether a symbol of nobility itself, or of nobility of the spirit. The rising arpeggio, whether triadic, or bare fifths and fourths, remained part of the idiom of the trumpet throughout the nineteenth into the early twentieth century, from Beethoven's Fifth Symphony (1807) through Schumann's Spring Symphony (1841) and Wagner's *Götterdämmerung* (1874) to Richard Strauss's *Ein Heldenleben* (1898) and Mahler's Sixth and Seventh Symphonies (1903/4; 1904/5) (Exx. 9.1a–e). In the trumpet solo that opens the first movement, 'Trauermarsch', of his Fifth Symphony (first petrformed 1904), Mahler evoked the trumpet's funereal associations with the rising arpeggio in a minor key (Ex. 9.2).

And so, although, by the start of the period, the application of keys and valves to trumpet design meant that it was capable of playing melodically and lyrically, as well as in a virtuoso fashion in all registers, and although that technology became widely available as the century wore on, its role for much of the century was to continue to

Ex. 9.1 Robert Schumann, Symphony No. 2, Op. 61, first movement, opening (a); Richard Wagner, *Götterdämmerung*, Act III, Scene 2 (Funeral March), 3 bars before Reh. No. 42 (b); Richard Strauss, *Ein Heldenleben*, Op. 40, closing bars (c); Gustav Mahler, Sixth Symphony, Finale, 5 bars after Reh. No. 110 (d); Gustav Mahler, Seventh Symphony, Rondo-Finale, 3 bars after Reh. No. 228 (e).

Ex. 9.2 Gustav Mahler, Fifth Symphony, opening.

Ex. 9.3 Jules Levy, *The Whirlwind Polka* (1862), beginning of the opening cadenza.

do what it had done best for composers and performers since its introduction into art music – to say simple things simply.

Meanwhile, in the arenas of mass entertainment new inventions like the cornet and keyed bugle became popular solo instruments and played passages like the example above (Ex. 9.3).

One of the unexpected side effects of the social changes that followed the French Revolution was the birth of the music conservatoire and a more systematic method of musical education for all. The long general peace after the Congress of Vienna in 1815 brought prosperity, and the majority of the population in Western Europe and the New World became wealthier and better educated throughout the course of the century.

Many of the landowning aristocracy had made intelligent use of their resources during the Industrial Revolution, and had retained and expanded their wealth and continued musical patronage of one sort or another. Some newly rich industrialists became musical patrons; in Britain particularly, many encouraged the formation of works brass bands that led to a national movement with, according to some commentators, close on one million players towards the end of the century.[1] Robert Thompson Crawshay, whose family founded the Cyfarthfa Ironworks at Merthyr Tydfil in South Wales, was one of the first, and his band, founded in 1838 with professional players, set from the beginning an ethos of virtuosity which has characterised the British brass band scene ever since.

Though brass playing became a working-class pursuit in Britain, it was not the same throughout the world. In Russia, Tsar Alexander III, like one of his predecessors, Peter the Great, loved innovation, and while the tsarevich was taught to play cornet by Wilhelm Wurm (1826–1904), the Tsar himself invited the English cornetist Jules Levy to spend periods as his house guest, and received a dedicated copy of Arban's cornet *Méthode* during one of the cornet virtuoso's annual visits to St Petersburg with his French orchestra in the summers of 1873 to 1876.[2] The Tsar created a vogue for brass chamber music in the salons of St Petersburg that has left us with a small but telling repertoire including the brass quintets by Victor Ewald.

In the USA, industrialists like Andrew Carnegie and John D. Rockefeller began a trend of philanthropy where the new rich, who had benefited from being at the helm of a massive expansion in production, used their enormous wealth to buy a form of immortality by endowing universities and libraries, as well as by supporting the formation of civic orchestras, and the building of concert halls and opera houses.

For the professional class, the Industrial Revolution brought ever greater prosperity, and an ever-widening interest in music as a form of social and aesthetic accomplishment. This class was important in the formation of opinion; it was also a large and important consumer of the latest music, and it spread the idea that works of art were important in themselves as statements of the human condition. The concept of originality, and the notion of the pre-eminence of great individuals – the romantic geniuses – fanned the aesthetic fancies of these professional classes, and gave them exemplars of lives lived beyond the normal parameters of life that they themselves, mere mortals, did not have licence to aspire to. The pianists Liszt and Chopin and the violinist Paganini were templates for the god-like composer virtuosos who energised the musical world of the nineteenth century. The trumpet produced no truly comparable figure. In central Europe, Weidinger came too early to benefit from the full power of nineteenth-century celebrity cults. In England, Thomas Harper, sen., did not generate sufficiently colourful performing material, either from his own pen or from other sources, to benefit fully from opportunities like appearing on the same bill as Paganini in London in 1832. Nevertheless, Harper came the closest. With his good looks, lithographs of him abounded in England, and sopranos queued to sing 'Let the Bright Seraphim' to his famed obbligato (Ill. 9.1).

The cornet had a large number of colourful composer-virtuosi who enlivened the world of popular musical entertainment, including Jean-Baptiste Arban, Louis St Jacome, Jules Levy, Herman Bellstedt and Alessandro Liberati. A tradition of cornet virtuosi survived well into the twentieth century, with figures like Herbert Clarke, Paris Chambers and Frank Simon. By the time of Del Staigers in the 1930s, it could have been thought that the genre of each great cornet player having to have their own variant of the *Carnival of Venice* had reached a natural final cadence. However, the genre continues to the present day, mutated to trumpet, with Donald Hunsberger's version for Wynton Marsalis (b.1961) in the 1990s following versions like those of Harry James (1916–83) from the 1940s.

Musicians aspiring to make a comfortable living from music and wishing to settle down to something other than the nomadic life of a travelling virtuoso had a great upwardly mobile desire to join the professional classes. They formed their own professional associations, such as the Incorporated Society of Musicians in London, to enable ascent of the social ladder. Like the Trumpet Guilds of the previous chapter before them, however, these societies had only limited success, although some survive to the present in various forms. They found it impossible over the decades to limit entry and forge a true 'music profession'. Although musicians themselves refer to their collective selves as the 'music profession', this idea, at least in Britain, is a chimera. In many European countries, orchestral musicians have the somewhat different, though enviably secure status of civil servants. American musicians aspire to this status, although their employment prospects seem permanently in flux. The 'music

9.1 Thomas Harper and the soprano Clara Novello. Frontispiece to *The Musical World* 2 (17 June–9 September 1836). This volume includes a biographical sketch of the trumpeter, which states that 'Some two or three seasons ago, Mr. Harper announced a benefit concert, when he received upwards of a dozen offers from young ladies, to sing "Let the bright Seraphim" to his trumpet accompaniment; and at the first Exeter Hall Festival, *thirty-six* applications were sent in to the same effect.'

profession' has never existed in the same way as a medical or legal profession, because entry qualification levels were never placed high enough, there was no clear demarcation line between performer and teacher (and why should there be?), and there was no control of supply. Since the demand for music teachers always outstripped supply, unqualified teachers had free access. The professional classes themselves, with their keen amateur interest in music, popularised the perception that music, although a vital part of the social graces, was perhaps less essential to the fabric of society and its wellbeing than the law or medicine, so that it never attained the status of a true profession. Nevertheless, remarkable individuals like the Harpers in London and their counterparts in metropolitan centres like Paris, New York, Berlin and Vienna, and musicians in demand at the Philharmonic concerts in all of these cities, were able to build up their own prestigious practices almost like members of a true profession, largely by word of mouth.

Status, however, remained elusive. Towards the end of the period, John Solomon (1856–1953), principal trumpet of the London Symphony Orchestra, would leave his home in Brixton for a morning rehearsal at the Queen's Hall, or lessons at the Royal Academy of Music, with bowler hat, morning coat, and hands garbed in white gloves grasping a doctor's bag – the epitome of an Edwardian professional. The doctor's bag, however, contained a trumpet.[3] Apparently it was still *infra dignitatem* in the England of the first few decades of the twentieth century to admit, in a middle-class district, to a career as a musician.

New patterns of concert-giving emerged to cater for new levels of consumption among the middle and working classes, and an entertainments industry arose, which, although tracing its roots to past innovations such as public concerts, subscription concerts, vaudeville and variety theatre, now grew rapidly into an international mass popular cultural movement. If in previous centuries there had been a division between art music and folk music, with varying amounts of free traffic periodically between genres, there was now a cultural demarcation between high-, middle-, and lowbrow music. The trumpet was a 'highbrow' instrument. It was thought to be 'hard to play'. It was made in small numbers, it was largely handcrafted, and it had a small number of specialist players. In his book *The Last Trumpet: A History of the English Slide Trumpet*, Art Brownlow lists 52 professional trumpeters who were active in England, Scotland and Ireland from 1780 to 1900 – a tiny number when compared with the number of cornet players, whose numbers must have run into the tens of thousands.[4] The cornet was 'lowbrow'. It was thought to be 'easy to play'. It was mass-produced in huge numbers, and was played by everyone from the harmonious blacksmith of Merthyr to the future Tsar of Russia. Berlioz captures the highbrow/lowbrow divide aptly:

> The cornet is highly fashionable in France today, especially in circles where pure elevated styles are held in low esteem. It has thus become the indispensable solo instrument for *contredanses, galops, airs variés* and other such inferior compositions.[5]

Domestic music remained an in-between category where the boundaries between different genres were obscured. There was a special form of art music – mainly with keyboard involvement – aimed at domestic consumption, and composers were prolific in this area. The piano became the beneficiary of new ways of working in iron and steel. The iron frame became normal, steel-clad strings held pitch for much longer periods, could exist in greater temperature fluctuations, more compact designs came on stream, and soon the upright piano became a status symbol desired by every middle class, and, in many instances, respectable working-class homes. An instrument that belonged exclusively to the middlebrow brass slot in this cultural demarcation was the soft-toned ballad horn – a tenor instrument, circular in shape, which played in the parlours of lower to higher middle-class households which possessed a piano. It had no repertoire of its own. It existed to play the popular vocal repertoire of the time or to support the family voices singing this repertoire. It was constructed in C concert pitch, so that it could play the vocal part of songbooks at sight. Instruments of this type were produced by the various members of the Distin family in England and the USA, and by Couesnon and Courtois in France. The keyed bugle in the USA was more socially mobile. This was perhaps indicative of less rigid social demarcations within a more democratic society. As well as being a popular band instrument, it also became popular as an instrument, pitched in C like the ballad horn, played in the parlours of polite and middle-class society, perhaps because of its ability to play soft, mellow sounds.

In 1857, Dauverne wrote that the valved trumpet

> has only the advantage of being easier and faster in rapid passages, be they diatonic or chromatic; but the excessively rapid oscillation of the pistons produces a confusion of sounds. The breaking up of the continuity of the inner wall of the resonant tube weakens the sound and at the same time makes the piston trumpet lose that clear and silvery sound which is possessed by all natural and slide trumpets to various degrees.[6]

Although successful experiments in applying the valve to the trumpet had existed for several years before the invention of the valved cornet, and instruments had become available, and an early repertoire was springing up (notably in Prague), there was a strangely conservative resistance against universal adoption – strange in a century that was otherwise so progressive. After a first flash of experiment with valves, a reaction seemed to set in against acceptance of the valved trumpet, perhaps because it was un-'natural' to hear the trumpet play anything other than its heroic triads and broken arpeggios. The English composer Frederick Corder, in his treatise on orchestration (1894), confirms that this was a common nineteenth-century perception when he expresses the opinion that melodies on trumpet are 'dangerous' and, in addition,

> most musical hearers are sorely offended at hearing on this instrument a melody which departs very markedly from the natural scale.[7]

When the trumpet was used lyrically and outside its normal context, however, as by Donizetti in the Introduction to Act II of *Don Pasquale* (1843), it was capable of extraordinary melancholy, as Haydn had demonstrated in the second movement of his trumpet concerto. Of course, this concerto was forgotten, and was unknown for all but the first few years of the nineteenth century. It had no influence.

This reluctance to extend the trumpet's idiom persisted in art music until the later decades of the century when composer/conductors like Richard Strauss and Gustav Mahler began to probe the new powers of expressiveness that the valves on the trumpet had opened up. Richard Wagner's genius at drawing an unprecedented range of emotion from his use of the orchestra led him to discover new capabilities in the trumpet. His second and third trumpet parts in *Der Ring des Nibelungen* (composed 1853–74; first complete performance, 1876) opened up a new expressive use of the lower and middle registers respectively. The second trumpet seems to inhabit a land of foreboding, whereas the third trumpet, perhaps because it is often used in the same register as the first horn to reinforce its line (and Wagner followed Schumann in being among the first to recognise the usefulness of the third trumpet in this respect in the orchestra), is invariably the bringer of more positive messages. Passages like the

Ex. 9.4 Richard Wagner, *Parsifal*, Prelude, bars 28–33.

trumpet solo in the Prologue to *Parsifal* (first performed 1882) demonstrate Wagner's insight into the capabilities of instruments beyond their normal range (Ex. 9.4). Played softly, in the high register, the trumpet gains a mystic quality, and Wagner was perhaps the first composer to recognise this.

Playing outside the normal parameters, however, creates difficulties for performers. It involves taking risks with trying new things. Players during this period, and perhaps of any period, were often reluctant to confront the greater technical demands being asked of them. There were, however, notable exceptions. There are hungry young players in any period. Ernest Hall related to his students how Tchaikovsky's symphonies first reaching London early in his career caused great consternation among the players of the day because of the outlandish demands they made on contemporary technique, stamina and range. Hall took advantage of the expertise gap by following John Solomon's example and by being an early advocate of the B flat trumpet in London. By the end of the nineteenth century, composers like Tchaikovsky were generating music that required mastery of a more complex idiom and recognised the usefulness of the smaller trumpets in this regard. The Fifth and Sixth (*Pathétique*) Symphonies of Tchaikovsky ask for trumpets in B flat and A. The disapproval of elder statesmen notwithstanding, Hall took lessons from Walter Morrow (1850–1937) on the F trumpet by day, and performed on the B flat trumpet by night.

Around the time when the valve was introduced, certain instrumentally adventurous composers used the new instruments enthusiastically. Berlioz's first version of *Symphonie fantastique* (1830) was scored for one valved and two natural trumpets, whereas the published version of 1845 was scored for two natural trumpets and two valved cornets. Wagner's *Rienzi* (first performed 1842) is written for two chromatic trumpets and two cornets. It is Wagner's *Lohengrin*, however, first performed at Weimar in 1850, with Liszt cionducting, and written for some fifteen trumpets, that provides the tipping point in the transition to valves among the players themselves. Wagner, consummate alchemist of the theatre, developed the theatrical use of the trumpet, its power to depict struggle, battle and warfare, albeit in an idealised fashion, and took to new heights the *natural* idiom of the imperial trumpet of former times, reinventing it spectacularly for the Romantic period. In the 'Morgenröte' from *Lohengrin* (Act III, Scene 3), he uses the power of rapid modulation between the different primary colours of groups of natural trumpets in different keys to depict the transformation from darkness to light at dawn (Ex. 9.5). But although the effect of Wagner's trumpet writing is revolutionary in many respects, he uses evolutionary methods towards his goal. He continues to write for the instrument, in the same manner as he writes for the horn, as if the instrument's valves were crooks in need of constant change. This results in the frequent transposition changes within Wagner's trumpet parts, which happen sometimes systematically and multiply over measure after measure. If composers

Ex. 9.5 Richard Wagner, *Lohengrin*, Act III, Scene 3, 3 bars before Reh. No. 47.

thought *naturally*, however, as in this excerpt, performers thought *pragmatically*. It cannot be a coincidence that the transposition studies of Ernst Sachse occur at the same time and in the same place as the first performance of *Lohengrin*, and that from the 1850s onwards the B flat trumpet championed in Sachse's studies took root in Dresden and Leipzig and among many other major German orchestras in addition to Weimar. With the three-valve B flat trumpet, the player had seven natural trumpets within one instrument, and skilled players like Ernst Sachse would have undoubtedly believed, by their adoption and championing of the instrument, that they were producing a sound of sufficient quality, consistency and accuracy, and that the results spoke for themselves. Berlioz was a hard person to please, but his verdict on Sachse when he visited Weimar in January 1843 was an unequivocal 'superb', a verdict that he also bestowed on the Hanover valved trumpet exponent F. Sachse, who has been identified as Ernst's brother.[8] Though Wagner's later writing, in *Der Ring des Nibelungen*, seems to epitomise the heroic symbolism of the trumpet, he was, in many ways, highly aware of its latent potential, as has been alluded to above, with its extraordinary use in the Prologue to *Parsifal*.

The trumpet has always seemed to possess a mystique, partly genetic, partly cultivated by its practitioners. This is nowhere better illustrated than in the famous battle that occurred in Niblo's Pleasure Gardens in New York City in 1834 between the English slide trumpeter John Norton (d.1868) and the Italian valved trumpet player Alessandro Gambati. Since arriving in the United States in 1827, Norton, the first trumpet professor at the Royal Academy of Music in London, had earned a reputation for his renditions of Handel's obbligato parts to 'The Trumpet Shall Sound' and 'Let the Bright Seraphim'. Gambati, in contrast, had recently arrived in America

– apparently recruited by the Italian Opera in New York in 1833 – having previously appeared as soloist and in the orchestra, along with his brother, playing keyed trumpets in the opera houses in Florence, Paris and London. By the time of his arrival in New York, his main instrument appears to have been the valved trumpet.

After much deliberation, it was agreed that both players should perform two pieces of their own choice using the same duelling instruments – the natural trumpet, with the allowance of handstopping. On the face of it, this would appear to favour the slide trumpeter Norton. However, both players chose to perform sets of variations on popular melodies, a genre in which Gambati excelled. When the judges declared the contest to be drawn it was decided to hold a rematch several days later at which the players could perform on the instrument of their choice. On this occasion, Norton was the victor, an indication that it was taken for granted that popular opinion of the period was unusually discerning in the finer matters of taste, tone production and technique in relation to the natural trumpet and its mechanical competitors.[9]

In general, there did seem to be a preference for the sound of the natural trumpet that persisted long into the nineteenth century – Dauverné's 'clear and silvery sound'. Perhaps this long-lasting preference for the retention of anything approaching the sound of the natural trumpet was really rooted in something inherently of primary importance to the basic concept of the trumpet – the nobility and sanctity of its quality of sound. At any rate, the common perception persisted tenaciously throughout the century that manufacturers and players of valved instruments were unable to replicate this 'true' quality on mechanical instruments. However, the astonishing diversity in brass manufacture of the nineteenth century, coupled with cross-breeding by manufacturers of different instrument types, led to a growing convergence of solutions to 'the trumpet problem' by the end of the century. It was then a short step from specialist trumpet players in leading orchestras adopting the instrument that best coped with the demands of great composers, to the universal adoption of shorter trumpets in B flat and C. And from there it was only another short step to the new complex trumpet of the twentieth century with a multi-layered personality played not only by scions of the jazz age like Louis Armstrong but also by players active in the western classical orchestral and solo repertoire.

Paris

Although the Paris Conservatoire was founded in 1795, it was not until 1833, with the appointment of François Georges Auguste Dauverné, that the trumpet became fully established in the curriculum. The initial staff roster, which comprised personnel from its precursor institutions, the École de Musique de la Garde Nationale and the École Royale de Chant, included three teachers who taught trumpet along with other instruments and solfège. François Guthmann was described as 'violoniste du théatre Italien' and taught 'trompette, solfège [and] opéra'. Financial pressures led to the abandonment of trumpet teaching at the Conservatoire in 1800,[10] and the military remained the main provider of trumpet tuition in France. An École de trompette pour la Cavalerie was formed in 1805 under the direction of the trumpeter David Buhl. During the following two decades Buhl's career diversified, as indicated in the title of his *Method for trumpet adopted for instruction in the School for Trumpet established in Saumur . . . By David Buhl, conductor of the Life Guards Band, performer of the King's Music and of the Royal Academy of Music* (Paris, 1825; The Royal Academy of Music referred to the Paris Opéra). He was one of three trumpeters appointed to the Société des Concerts du Conservatoire on its formation, the others being his nephew Dauverné and a player named Legros.[11] Buhl's method contains the trumpet signals used by the French cavalry as well as exercises and studies for the *trompette de cavalerie* (military trumpet) in E flat and the *trompette d'harmonie* (orchestral trumpet), which was supplied with crooks. He provides instructions on hand-stopping for the *trompette d'harmonie*, noting that the technique results in a loss of the heroic quality of the trumpet's sound and is most suited to lyrical passages. The quartets he includes for both types of trumpet display this idiomatic distinction.

A key element of the performance curriculum at the Paris Conservatoire, which endures to the present day, is the Concours de Prix, an annual solo competition for each instrument, using specially composed test-pieces (*morceaux*). The first concours took place in 1797 and the concours pour trompette was established in 1835. Throughout his tenure, Dauverné provided the trumpet *morceaux*, some of which were used on more than one occasion.

Dauverné submitted his trumpet method to the directors of the Conservatoire for approval after having taught there for over twenty years. His stated aim was to provide a systematic course of instruction for the trumpet equivalent to that produced for other instruments by his colleagues at the Conservatoire. Dauverné was an advocate of the valved trumpet from the time of its first appearance in Paris in 1826,, encouraging composers to write for the instrument and makers to copy instruments in his possession. He produced tutors for the two- and three-valved instruments *c.*1827–8 and *c.*1834–5 respectively. Significantly, however, around three-quarters of the exercises and studies in his Method are for natural trumpet. This emphasis reflects the conservatism of the Conservatoire towards the introduction of new instruments and the transitional nature of the new instruments, as well as Dauverné's conviction that 'it is impossible to become a skillful trumpeter, in any style, if one does not begin with a complete study of the natural Trumpet'.[12]

In his historical overview of the development of the trumpet, Dauverné describes the arrival of valved instruments in Paris and the introduction of the valved trumpet into the Opéra orchestra. He dates the abandonment of circular natural trumpets, which allowed for hand-stopping, and the reintroduction of instruments built in traditional straight form, which he insisted was better for retaining the 'essential character' of the instrument, to 1826. This move was clearly related to the arrival of valved trumpets that year, since players were then able to alternate between the natural trumpet and the valved trumpet.[13] It seems likely that Dauverné incorporated the valved trumpet into his trumpet class at an early date, although it is not clear when it was first used in the concours. A review of the concours in 1836 mentions the players using hand-stopping,[14] even though Dauverné implies in his tutor that, with the advent of valves, this technique was on the wane. In Dauverné's opinion the most successful chromatic trumpet was the slide trumpet. He credits the invention of the slide trumpet to John Hyde, whose design he modified by applying a forward-moving slide, which provided a shift of one and a half tones – an illustration of this instrument is included in his Method – and reveals that the slide trumpet was incorporated into his teaching at the Conservatoire.[15] There is evidence that the slide trumpet featured in the 1845 concours, at which the first prize was awarded to Arban.

The slide trumpet had been introduced into France around 1821, when a musician in the Royal Guards, named Legram, applied for a patent for the instrument he had developed with the maker François Riedloker. A *Tablature* (slide chart) for the slide trumpet was produced by Legram that year. Reports from 1833 attest to Buhl performing on this instrument, although with little success. Interestingly, however, Buhl does not mention this instrument in his tutor.[16] The slide trumpet's use in professional circles in France appears to have been brief, with players preferring to choose between valved trumpet and natural trumpet, as the musical situation demanded.

The extent to which the cornet was incorporated into the trumpet class at the Conservatoire is more conjectural. Arban is known to have played cornet throughout his time at the Conservatoire, since he was granted leave to travel to London to perform as a cornet soloist on several occasions. His arrival in London in May 1845 – the month before he won first prize in the trumpet concours – was heralded in one newspaper by the announcement: 'Mr Arban, the celebrated cornet-à-piston player, from the Académie Royale, has arrived from Paris, and will appear this evening at Vauxhall, and with Laurent will play Bellini's duet of "Deh Conte".'[17] A trumpeter named Messemer, who in 1836 was the second player to win a first prize for trumpet, was playing cornet, if not while at the Conservatoire, then soon after, since by 1841 he was enjoying success as a cornet soloist in New York.[18]

Dauverné's solos continued to be used for the concours during most of his successor Jules-Henri-Louis Cerclier's twenty-five-year tenure as professor. Cerclier provided three *morceaux* of his own composition. Cerclier's successor at the Conservatoire in 1894 was Merri Franquin, a former cornet student (during Arban's six-year absence) and winner of a first prize for cornet in 1877.[19] His principal achievements during his twenty-five years at the Conservatoire were the introduction of the C trumpet as the standard instrument for solo and orchestral playing, against initial opposition, and the commissioning of a wealth of solo material for the trumpet concours, some of which has entered the staple solo trumpet repertoire. Another former cornet student at the Conservatoire, George Mager (1885–1950), was influential in establishing the C trumpet as an orchestral instrument in America. He was winner of a first prize in 1906, a vintage year for the trumpet in Paris – the year that Georges Enesco wrote *Légende*, which he dedicated to Franquin, and composed his poem for four trumpets, *Au soir*.

The introduction of the C trumpet into the orchestra in France began around two decades before Franquin's appointment at the Conservatoire, when Xavier-Napoléon Teste (1833–1905 or 1906), first trumpet with the Société des Concerts, procured a set of slides for the D trumpet that he used for performances of Handel to lower the pitch of the instrument to C.[20] In his entry on the trumpet in the *Encyclopédie de la Musique et Dictionnaire du Conservatoire*, Franquin revealed that up to 1891 the trumpeters of the Opéra each had a natural trumpet and a valved trumpet at their disposal, and a set of crooks that fitted either instrument.[21] The first performance of Wagner's *Lohengrin* in Paris was a decisive event for the trumpeters of the Opéra. Although much of the trumpet writing in *Lohengrin* is rooted in the idiom of the natural trumpet, the rapidity of the key changes and consequent intonation problems rendered both natural trumpets and valved trumpets in G or F problematic for a truly effective performance. The conductor Charles Lamoureux's insistence after the *Lohengrin* experience that henceforth only valved trumpets were to be used in the Opéra orchestra was followed by the appointment of Teste as first trumpet and the subsequent adoption of the C trumpet.[22]

In 1912 Franquin developed a four-valve C trumpet with the maker Thibouville-Lamy – the fourth valve, which was activated by a finger of the left-hand, raised the pitch by a tone – and in 1916 he designed a five-valve instrument, the additional valve lowering the pitch by the interval of a third.[23] Franquin revealed that the five-valve instrument was used by Conservatoire students with great success for the concours between 1917 and 1920, and attributed its failure to gain acceptance in professional circles to resistance from older players. The four-valve trumpet enjoyed a renaissance when it was adopted by Roger Voisin (1918–2008) of the Boston Symphony Orchestra in 1956. Voisin was introduced to the instrument by his father, René Louis Voisin (1893–1952), who played in the orchestra for twenty years, beginning in 1927, and had studied trumpet at the Paris conservatoire with Eugène Foveau (1886–1957), winning a first prize around the time that Franquin developed the four-valve trumpet.[24]

Belgium

Conservatoires of music, modelled on that in Paris, were founded in Liège and Brussels in 1826 and 1832 respectively. A professor of horn was employed from the outset in Liège, whose register of pupils for the inaugural year included trumpet, cornet and trombone players. An independent class for trumpet, cornet and flugelhorn was established in both Liège and Brussels in 1838. The teachers for this class were typically from a military band background and were specialist cornet or flugelhorn players. In 1878 Dieudonné Gérardy (1848–1900), a former Paris Conservatoire first prize winner on cornet, was appointed professor of trumpet, flugelhorn and cornet at Liège, following a period in Arban's orchestra, with which he visited St Petersburg. Among the graduates of Gérardy's class was Théo Charlier, composer of *Thirty-Six Transcendent Studies* (1926) and pioneer of the performance of Bach's trumpet parts on the piccolo trumpet. Charlier succeeded Gérardy as professor of cornet and trumpet at the Conservatoire in 1901, and within a few months had established a class exclusively for trumpet. An advocate of the B flat trumpet in preference to the instrument in C that was favoured in France, Charlier developed a piston-valve B flat trumpet in collaboration with Mahillon of Brussels, which had the bore profile of a German rotary-valve instrument. The Charlier-Mahillon trumpet was adopted by Belgian trumpeters, many of whom gained employment elsewhere in Europe, and also by some of the most prominent orchestral players in England during the first half of the twentieth century.[25] Alphonse Goeyens (1867–1950), the professor at Brussels, was responsible for reviving early interest in the Haydn Trumpet Concerto, which students at the Conservatoire were performing from around 1907.[26]

Prague

An early example of extensive championing of the newly valved brass trumpet was in the conservatoire in Prague, which was founded in the first wave of enthusiasm for this type of institution in 1811. Bedřich Diviš (Friedrich Dionysus) Weber, its director, wrote one of the first works for valved trumpet and orchestra, *Variations in F* (*c.*1827). This work is scored for a large orchestra, has a grand opening introduction, and has elegance and poise. The work sounds at its best on a low F trumpet because of its deep *tessitura.* The orchestral interludes are sprightly and upbeat and there are some deft touches of orchestration (solo trumpet trios with a pair of bassoons playing mellifluously in Variation II).

Josef Kail (1795–1871), the first professor of valved trumpet (and valve trombone) at the Prague Conservatoire, composed another set of *Variations for the Trumpet in F* in 1827, the first surviving piece for trumpet with piano accompaniment. A review of the first performance of this work, which was given by a second-study trumpet student (a first-study double-bass player), is enthusiastic about the newly-invented valved trumpet, noting that it 'has the advantage over the keyed one in that all the chromatic intervals sound perfectly on it, like the natural tones of the normal trumpet' and credits its invention to Kail.[27]

Kail was among the first intake of students of the Prague Conservatoire in its inaugural year, as a horn player, graduating in 1817. Two years later he performed *Variations for the Newly Invented Keyed Horn* by F. D. Weber in a conservatoire concert. In 1826 Kail was appointed teacher of both trumpet and trombone at the Conservatoire, remaining in that post for over forty years, retiring in 1867. A manuscript tutor for valved trumpet in F and E flat by Kail (segments of which are located in the Prague Conservatoire and Museum of Czech Music) provides a valuable insight into his teaching method: after a series of progressive technical and scalic exercises, the work focuses on melodic studies, many of which are based on operatic themes.

Other works from this prolific period in Prague include Conradin Kreutzer's *Variations on God Save the King* (1826) for two trumpets or horns and orchestra; the same composer's *Variations Concertante* (1823) – originally for bassoon, horn and piano (1823), later adapted for valve trumpet, valved trombone and piano; his *Variations in G for Chromatic Trumpet and Orchestra*, first performed in Prague in 1837; and Kalliwoda's *Potpourri for Two Valved Trumpets and Orchestra* (1832) – in G major, with the trumpets crooked in low D.[28]

Spain

In 1830 the Real Conservatorio de Música María Cristina opened in Madrid. From the outset, trumpet teaching was included in the curriculum, with José de Juan Martínez appointed teacher of *clarín* and keyed trumpet, a post he retained for over fifty years. A trumpet method (*Método de Clarin*) by José de Juan, dated 1830 and written for use at the conservatoire, survives in manuscript.[29] Much of the text and many of the musical exercises in this tutor derive from the method by Buhl, but it includes the military calls of the Spanish cavalry. It also deals with hand stopping on circular trumpets (equivalent to the French *trompette d'harmonie*) that were used in orchestras in Spain. José de Juan played both trumpet and cornet and, like Buhl, was involved in military bands. The teaching of the keyed trumpet was eventually replaced by a cornet class, reflecting the popularity of the latter instrument in Spanish orchestras from around the middle of the century.

Italy

Italian orchestras were among the first in Europe to embrace keyed and valved trumpets. The Milan Conservatoire was founded in 1808, with the purpose of training singers and instrumentalists for La Scala theatre. The founder members of staff included the horn virtuoso Luigi Belloli, who was also required to teach trumpet and trombone. It was not until 1882 that a trumpet teacher was employed, with the additional role of teaching trombone.[30] A short manual for keyed trumpet, appended to an elementary book on the rudiments of music by Bonifazio Asioli, the founding director of the Milan Conservatoire, was published in Milan in 1825. Although Asioli left Milan in 1814, the publisher Bertuzzi continued to issue the generic text with brief methods for different instruments. A more substantial tutor was issued a decade later when Giuseppe Araldi, first trumpet at La Scala, produced his method for keyed and valved trumpet (Milan, *c.*1835). Like several later Italian methods, and that by Dauverné, this work also includes a section for natural trumpet. The keyed trumpet survived longer as an orchestral instrument in Italy than elsewhere. Tracking the transition from keyed to valved instruments in Italian orchestras is made difficult, however, by the use of the term *chiavi* (keys) to denote both types of trumpet.[31]

A substantial corpus of solo music for valved trumpet was composed in northern Italy around the middle of the nineteenth century, much of it written by trumpet players and teachers. Raniero Cacciamani, first trumpet of the Royal Opera of Parma, published a method for valved trumpet (Milan, 1853), and between 1853 and 1855 a collection of solos for trumpet and piano. Shortly after, in 1859, he was appointed professor of trumpet at the Parma Conservatoire. His solos are typically sets of airs and variations on popular opera melodies by Bellini, Donizetti and Verdi. Similar works were published in Milan around this time by, among others, Domizio Zanichelli, who also wrote a method for valved trumpet (Milan, 1855). Both Cacciamani and Zanichelli devote considerable space to exercises and studies using only the notes of the natural harmonic series, some of which, particularly in the method by Cacciamani, are technically very demanding. A tutor for trumpet in E flat was produced by Gustavo Rossari, the last horn teacher at the Milan Conservatoire also to teach trumpet (between 1849 and 1881). This work was published (or re-issued) in Milan in 1904, with a note that it was used at the Conservatoire. Substantial solo works, two concertos, one in F, and another in E flat, Op. 198, were written by Amilcare Ponchielli, composer of *La Gioconda*, when a bandmaster in the 1860s, first in Piacenza, then in Cremona. The Concerto in F, in a one-movement, quasi fantasia style, flowing freely from an opening introduction, through an aria to a theme and variations, was first performed in a similar context to Arban's solos in St Petersburg, in the open air Piazza Garibaldi in Cremona, on 14 April 1866.[32]

During the early nineteenth century the Gambati brothers were prominent exponents of the keyed trumpet outside their home country. Alessandro Gambati, who emigrated to America in 1833 to perform with the Italian Opera Company in New York, was encountered above as a contestant in the trumpet 'battle' at Niblo's Gardens in 1834. In 1826 the brothers played with Harper and Norton (Alessandro's future adversary) in a concert at the Royal Academy of Music, in London's Hanover Square, and in 1829 they were hired to perform at the King's Theatre, with the departure of many of the leading players, including the trumpeters Harper and John Irwin, following a dispute with the management.[33] The newspaper critics were disparaging of the makeshift orchestra that was assembled for this season, and the trumpeters were singled out for criticism: 'we never before heard so many blunders and so much bad playing in this theatre; and as to the Signori Gambati, they are a perpetual source of distraction and head-ache'.[34] They were subject to further derision in an English press review of music in Florence in 1831: 'The brothers Gambati have been astonishing the galleries here by their performances upon the keyed trumpet. In concerto pieces their trumpeting may be allowed to pass free, but when they undertake to drown the whole orchestra for the edification of the gods, it may be too much.'[35] Significantly, however, this opinion was not shared by Dauverné, who presumably encountered them when they performed at the Paris Opéra and Opéra Italien in 1827 and 1829, and describes them as 'artists of merit', perhaps out of gratitude to one of the brothers for petitioning the directors of the Conservatoire to appoint a professor of trumpet.[36]

By the beginning of the nineteenth century the orchestra of La Scala numbered around eighty players. When Louis Spohr visited the theatre in 1816 he was impressed by the high standard of orchestral playing, but, like Berlioz, was distracted by the noise emanating from the audience. The orchestra at the San Carlo Theatre in Naples was of a similar size to that in Milan, but opinions as to its standard of performance were divided; most commentators agreed, however, that orchestras in Rome were the worst in Italy.[37] Mendelssohn's assessment of the orchestras that he heard during a visit to Rome in 1830–31 included the comment that 'The trumpeters play all the time on the accursed keyed trumpets' and that 'there is one here who plays variations on it!'[38]

Following Rossini's example in *Ricciardo e Zoraide* (Naples, 1818), composers began routinely to include stage bands in operas, and many of the larger Italian theatres retained a group of instrumentalists for this purpose. A French critic noted disparagingly: 'you have the noise of the great drum, of cymbals, octave flutes, and, above all, of trumpets, the performers on which appear to make a merit of drowning the whole orchestra'.[39] Before long, a stage band was to become an integral part of the Paris Opéra.

Germany and Austria

It was not until late in the nineteenth century that wind and brass instruments were taught at German music conservatoires. At the Leipzig Conservatoire (founded in 1843), for example, wind and brass instruments only entered the curriculum in 1882. Ferdinand Weinschenk, the first teacher of trumpet at the Leipzig Conservatoire, was typical of many orchestral players of his generation in receiving his formative musical education with a 'city music director'. Weinschenk also studied with the seminal valved trumpet virtuoso Ernst Sachse in Weimar, and after ten years of military service, during which he continued his musical training, joined the Leipzig Gewandhaus Orchestra in 1861.[40] Small, private music schools run by a 'city music director' existed in many German towns and cities. As Tarr explains, they served a 'municipal function' but were not supported financially by civic authorities. Pupils typically entered this type of school around the age of fourteen and remained there for up to six years, residing with the director, in the master and apprentice tradition. Students received tuition on several instruments and were organised into various ensembles, which the director hired out for private engagements, providing the students with valuable performance experience and himself with a steady stream of income.[41]

Although there is scant information on instructional material used in the private music schools, method books for trumpet in German appeared early in the century. The *General Trumpet Method* by Andreas Nemetz, 'trombonist in the Imperial Royal Court Opera House in Vienna' (Vienna, 1828), includes sections for natural, keyed and valved trumpet, and is one of the earliest methods for the valved instrument. Karl Bargans, 'First trumpeter to the King of Prussia', writing sometime before 1830, however, stated that keyed and valved trumpets were rarely used in the orchestra and that their primary purpose was 'to carry the melody' in military trumpet bands. Orchestral players, he declared, favoured 'the common, or proper trumpet', on which additional tones could be produced through hand-stopping.[42]

As alluded to above, German trumpeters were among the first to make the transition from the low F to the B flat trumpet. Tarr identifies the Dresden trumpeter Albert Kuhnert (d.1889) as one of the first players to adopt the B flat trumpet in the orchestra, during the 1850s, and notes that by the 1870s first trumpet players in many German orchestras had followed suit.[43] During the 1880s the Berlin firm Adolph Fürstner published a series of popular works for cornet and piano, arranged by Kuhnert and the virtuoso cornet and trumpet player Julius Kosleck (1825–1905). This suggests that Kuhnert may also have been a cornet soloist. The prevalence of players who doubled on trumpet and cornet was probably a significant factor in the adoption of the B flat trumpet. Interestingly, however, the portion of Kosleck's *Grosse Schule für Cornet à Piston und Trompete* (Leipzig, 1872) devoted to trumpet was written for the instrument in low F.

As has been discussed in the previous chapter, the German cities of Leipzig, Weimar and Dresden, as in Bach's day a century earlier, were pivotal in the idiomatic development of composition for brass. Hummel had been Kapellmeister in Weimar, not far from Leipzig, from 1818 until his death in 1837, but none of his Weimar writing for trumpet, although it strays occasionally from the harmonic series, approaches the adventurousness of his earlier work.[44] During his successor Liszt's tenure, in the 1840s, the Weimar orchestra, already significant, broke further new ground in orchestration as a consequence of its locus in the development of the tone poem. The career of Ernst Sachse, principal trumpet during this time, is worthy of further exploration. Sachse was composer of numerous works, including a Concertino for bass trombone, a Concerto for tenor trombone, a Concerto for trumpet *simple*, and 100 celebrated transposition studies for trumpet. He may also have been the composer of the Concerto in E flat for trumpet and band published in Boston in 1871, although this is open to conjecture.[45] His transposition studies are a model of musical taste as applied to the concept of the étude. They were to be used for generations to come, indeed throughout the twentieth century, in conservatoires throughout the world. Championed by teachers as diverse as the New York Philharmonic's William Vacchiano (1912–2005) and the London Symphony Orchestra's George Eskdale (1897–1960) at the Juilliard School and the Royal Academy of Music respectively, Sachse's studies provided a thread of continuity for many twentieth-century trumpet players back to the beginnings of the first virtuosos of the valved trumpet.

German conservatoires, like those in Paris and Prague, placed emphasis on the importance of solo performance. Details of student performances regularly appeared in the press and reveal that students in Leipzig performed on trumpet or cornet with near equal regularity. They performed much of the same repertoire, which was rooted to the cornet idiom. At the Sondershausen Conservatoire the students played similar repertoire to their counterparts in Leipzig, but, it appears, always on trumpet; for example, on 21 January 1895 a trumpeter named Schmidt performed Jules Levy's *Carnival of Venice* on trumpet.[46] In 1899 the Trumpet Concerto in E minor by Oskar Böhme (1870–1938), which was dedicated to Weinschenk, received its first performance at a Leipzig Conservatoire student concert. A piano score of the concerto was published that year and a full score followed in 1903. Böhme attended the Conservatoire between 1896 and 1897, but Tarr has cast doubt on the assumption that he was there as a trumpet student, even though he had previously worked as a trumpet and cornet player and went on to become a successful player in Russia.[47] It is plausible that in composing a three-movement concerto for trumpet Böhme was striving to raise the quality of the instrument's solo repertoire: the title page of the concerto states that it was for trumpet in A and gives the alternative 'Cornet à pistons' in parentheses.[48]

From newspaper reports of student concerts it is evident that a steady stream of cornet and trumpet players passed through the Leipzig Conservatoire during Weinschenk's twenty-five year tenure; these included Eduard Seifert (1870–1965), principal trumpeter of the Dresden Staatskapelle from 1895 to 1935. Seifert attended the Conservatoire from 1888 to 1894, after which he toured Hungary and Russia as a cornet soloist, an activity that he maintained throughout his career.[49] Like many players of his generation, Seifert used a rotary-valve B flat trumpet by the Dresden firm Heckel as his standard orchestral instrument and a French-made cornet. For his performance of the Haydn concerto in Dresden in 1914 – six years after the work's first performance since the time of Weidinger, by Franz Rossbach (1864-1941), principal trumpet of the Vienna Philharmonic[50] – he used a high F trumpet, presumably the high G trumpet made for him by Heckel in 1908 with a shank to lower the pitch of the instrument to F.[51] Seifert used the high G trumpet for certain orchestral passages. This choice of instrument is significant given the repertoire he encountered around this time: in 1905 he would have played first trumpet in Richard Strauss's opera *Salome*, and in 1909 and 1911, respectively, Strauss's *Elektra* and *Der Rosenkavalier*. According to Tarr, this was one of the contributing factors to Seifert's nickname, 'Never-Miss'.[52]

Britain

The enduring popularity of the music of Handel in Britain during the nineteenth century, together with the dominance of Thomas Harper, father and son, in the oratorio and orchestral spheres of trumpet playing, ensured the survival of the slide trumpet for a half century or more after valved trumpets had ousted the natural trumpet from the orchestra elsewhere in Europe. By the time that valved trumpets appeared in Britain in the 1830s, the slide trumpet had been around for over four decades and Thomas Harper had been using it professionally for at least fifteen years. While the advent of the valved trumpet led to the demise of hand-stopping on the natural trumpet in orchestral playing on the Continent by the early 1830s, in Britain it failed to supplant the slide trumpet, which players and commentators agreed offered superior intonation and more consistency of timbre. Few trumpet parts written for valved instruments during the first half of the century would have posed insurmountable difficulties for players of the slide trumpet, since parts requiring dextrous valve technique were invariably given to the cornet.

As composers on the Continent began to embrace more fully the chromatic possibilities of the valved trumpet during the second half of the century, the slide trumpet became less suited to its generic function in the orchestra and players began to reach increasingly for the cornet when performing trumpet parts. This practice was criticised by Thomas Harper, jun., (1816–98) in his trumpet method of *c.*1875,[53] even though he, like most of the other leading slide-trumpet players of his generation, played cornet early in his career.

Although Thomas Harper, sen., rejected the valved trumpet in his professional performances, he included an illustration of, and finger chart for, the 'Russian' valved trumpet in his trumpet method, *Instructions for the Trumpet, With the Use of the Chromatic Slide, Also the Russian Valve Trumpet, the Cornet à Pistons or Small Stop Trumpet, and the Keyed Bugle* (London: 1st ed. 1835; 2nd ed. 1837). The use of the prefix 'Russian' was suspected as being a misprint for 'Prussian' until Clifford Bevan uncovered evidence that the valved trumpet arrived in Britain by way of Russia. A report in a military journal in 1831 referred to the 'Russian chromatic trumpet-band of the 2nd Life Guards, (the only one in England)'. Anecdotal evidence suggests that Earl Cathcart, Colonel of the regiment, was gifted a set of valved trumpets by the Tsar, following a visit by the Earl to St Petersburg around 1830, during which he expressed his admiration for the band of the Imperial Guards and their valved trumpets.[54] Harper did, however, play keyed bugle professionally, having presumably been introduced to the instrument during his twenty-year association with the Royal East India Volunteers Band, which he joined around the age of twelve. The title-page of a collection of solos, duets and trios for keyed bugle ('Royal Kent Bugle') arranged by Harper describes him as 'First trumpet and Bugle to the King's Theatre, the Ancient and Philharmonic Concerts, &c.'.[55]

A commentary on the orchestra of the King's Theatre for the 1825–6 season in *The Harmonicon* described Harper as

> the best performer in Europe. He may, perhaps, not be inclined to play so many tricks on his instrument as those who have wit enough to address their efforts to

> such a love of quackery, but his tone – almost as soft as a flute, when necessary – is perfection itself, and his certainty both as an orchestral and solo player, has never been . . . called in question.[56]

Fétis too praised Harper in his report on the state of music in London in 1829, comparing him favourably with the trumpeters working in Paris.[57] But critics were cognisant of the limitations of the slide trumpet. Regarding a performance in 1834, the critic for *The Athenaeum* remarked: 'Mr Harper (played) a trumpet concerto wonderfully, but his instrument is not, and cannot be made one for *solo* performance.'[58]

The Harpers' prominence as performers was reinforced by their holding the most prestigious teaching posts in London: Harper, sen., was appointed professor of trumpet at the Royal Academy of Music following the departure of John Norton for America in 1827 and was succeeded on his retirement in 1845 by his son, who in 1884 also became the first professor of trumpet of the Royal College of Music and Sergeant Trumpeter to the Queen.

At the time of his admission to the Royal Society of Musicians in 1838, two years after completing his studies at the Royal Academy of Music, Thomas Harper, jun., was 'engaged at Her Majesty's Theatre for the Violin and Cornet, [and] at the Opera Buffa for the Trumpet'.[59] At a season of popular orchestral promenade concerts at the Lyceum Theatre between December 1838 and January 1839, in imitation of those presented in Paris by Musard, Harper played a cornet duet from *Norma* with French virtuoso Charles Emile Laurent.[60] The collection of concert programmes featuring performances by Thomas Harper held in the Royal College of Music testify to him performing regularly as soloist on the valved trumpet and the cornet in provincial concerts. Brownlow cites one such concert, in the town of Coalbrookdale in 1876, in which Harper played a solo and an obbligato to a song on slide trumpet, an arrangement of *Ave Maria* on the valved trumpet, and a posthorn galop of his own composition.[61] Tapping into the lucrative market for solo and instructional material for valved instruments, Harper arranged a collection of dances for cornet *c.*1859 and a cornet method *c.*1865 (a decade before his trumpet method).[62] F. McGrath, who, after Harper, was the foremost exponent of Handel's trumpet parts in London during the 1880s, and who performed Saint-Saëns's Septet with the composer on piano in London in 1885,[63] appeared as cornet soloist in a Season of promenade concerts at Her Majesty's Theatre in 1865.[64]

One of the leading trumpet players outside London was John Ellwood, principal trumpet of the Hallé Orchestra from its formation in 1858 until 1872. Ellwood came to prominence during the 1840s as a cornet soloist and an exponent of Handel's obbligato trumpet parts in the north of England. He also directed the Earl of Ellesmere's military band and adjudicated brass band contests.[65] A review of a performance of *Messiah* at the Free Trade Hall, Manchester, on 11 September 1843, judged that in the 'The Trumpet Shall Sound'

> Mr Ellwood's trumpet obligato was a delicious performance, and surprising to all who know the proverbial uncertainty of the trumpet, which too often brays when it should sing. Indeed, it is beginning to be the practice in some societies to

> substitute a keyed [valved] trumpet for the common one, as more sure and safe; but Mr. Elwood's [*sic*] was the ordinary old form of trumpet and the tone was very clear and fine, and every note well and distinctly given.[66]

It appears that in this performance Ellwood performed on the natural trumpet, even though he had been presented with a slide trumpet 'by a few musical friends' in Leeds three years earlier.[67] Ellwood presumably played slide trumpet in the Hallé Orchestra, which from its inaugural season until 1910 employed two trumpet and two cornet players. The extent to which trumpeters in provincial British orchestras reverted to cornet for certain areas of repertoire and the question of when the transition to valved trumpets occurred, however, warrant further investigation.

When Michael Costa, conductor of the Italian opera at Her Majesty's Theatre, resigned to take charge of a new, rival company at the Covent Garden Theatre in 1847, he was joined by many of the principal singers and a majority of the orchestra, including Thomas Harper. The replacement orchestra for Her Majesty's comprised players from various European countries, including Carl Zeiss, professor of cornet and trumpet at the Brussels Conservatoire, as first trumpet.[68] A review of that season singled out several of the new members of the orchestra for comment and noted that 'the first trumpet player is clever, but we object to the military, dragoon, short trumpet superseding the silvery toned long trumpet, which produces every shade of sound, from the most subdued *sostenuto* to the most penetrating *sforzando*'.[69] In 1854 Zeiss replaced Harper as first trumpet of the Philharmonic Society, following a dispute between Harper and the directors.[70] It is not known whether Zeiss adopted the slide trumpet for this engagement. In 1857 he was appointed teacher of cornet and trumpet at the Royal Military School of Music at its formation, a post he held until his death in 1869.[71] It seems likely that in this capacity he would have trained many more players than the Harpers, whose position at the Royal Academy of Music, although prestigious, was a nominal one. The student registers for the Royal Academy of Music list five trumpeters (including the young Harper) between 1823 and 1873.[72] A similar situation prevailed at the Royal Manchester College of Music, which opened in 1893. After securing the services of Franz Paersch, his principal horn, Sir Charles Hallé suggested appointing a second brass teacher, Thomas Reynolds, the third horn in the orchestra, to teach horn or trumpet. The choice of Reynolds instead of the principal trumpet, Jaeger, seems curious, but was inconsequential since no brass students appear on the register for the first two decades of the college's existence.[73]

Most of the prominent orchestral trumpet players in London after the retirement of Thomas Harper in 1885 and into the twentieth century began their careers as cornet players. Walter Morrow and John Solomon, the leading trumpeters of the generation after Harper, played cornet and occasionally slide trumpet in their theatre and concert work into the 1890s, after studying slide trumpet at the Royal Academy of Music in the early 1870s. The documents recording Morrow's admission to the Royal Society of Musicians in 1887 relate that he was 'Professor of Cornet & Trumpet' at the Guildhall School of Music.[74] By the time of his appointment as professor of trumpet at the Royal College of Music in 1894, he had rejected the use of the cornet as a substitute for the trumpet in orchestral music. In an address to the Musical Association in June 1895, he argued passionately for the use of the slide trumpet or the valved trumpet in F and expressed his disapproval of the B flat trumpet, which he termed the 'Trumpetina' (after Boosey & Co., who first offered this instrument in 1868)[75] and regarded as a 'deception', since it was 'in reality only a cornet'.[76] Morrow's promotion of the F trumpet was short-lived, however, since, through the influence of John Solomon, who had played cornet before studying with Harper at the Royal Academy of Music, the B flat trumpet began to gain currency among orchestral players in London. As discussed above, the consolidation of the B flat trumpet in London orchestras was continued by Ernest Hall, who had begun his professional life in his early teens playing cornet in a theatre orchestra in Liverpool, before studying with Morrow at the Royal College of Music from 1910. Another influential B flat trumpet player was Herbert 'Bertie' Barr, who was recruited by Thomas Beecham as first trumpet in his orchestra around 1913, before becoming first trumpet with the Philharmonic Society and subsequently co-principal trumpet of the BBC Symphony Orchestra at its formation in 1930.

In his reviews and articles on music, the writer and critic George Bernard Shaw was as scathing of the slide trumpet ('an impracticable nuisance') as he was of the use of the cornet for orchestral trumpet parts ('an imposture and an outrage'). He acknowledged that slide trumpets, 'if it were worth anyone's while to learn to play them, would doubtless give the peculiar close, ringing, penetrating sound that the cornet so completely misses; but then they would probably fail in the soft cornet effects in which Wagner's and Gounod's scores abound'. Hence, 'Herr Richter and other first-rate conductors connive at the substitution of the more manageable cornet'.[77] In Shaw's opinion, the instrument that yielded the ideal timbre for the orchestra was the straight, two-valved trumpet in A, used by Julius Kosleck of Berlin at the 1885 Albert Hall performance of Bach's B minor Mass and which Walter Morrow had since adopted for the baroque repertoire (see Chapter 10). The fact that this instrument was not fully chromatic in its middle and lower register was overlooked by Shaw. Of more significance was its 'silvery, carillon-like clangor' in the upper register, a quality that was lost when trumpet parts were played on cornet, and rarely heard on the slide trumpet. The way to achieve this, he believed, was for contemporary composers to write for the instrument. A composer who did just that was Ethel Smyth in her Mass in D, which was performed at the Albert Hall in 1893. The work was enthusiastically received, with both the composer and Walter Morrow earning individual applause from the audience.[78]

Later, around the time that Ernest Hall was his pupil, Morrow edited Otto Langey's tutor (for trumpet and cornet), which was issued around 1911 by Hawkes & Son through their London and New York branches. Morrow was evidently resigned to the fact that cornet players would end up playing trumpet parts, for he includes a section on transposition with the following advice to cornet players:

> A Cornet player is not of much use in an orchestra unless he can transpose at sight, from one key to another. So many Trumpet parts in all manner of keys will be placed before him, that it is impossible to have several instruments to avoid transposing, and do justice to music. Some people try, and fail miserably. I advise the

> study of transposition at once; learn to play Trumpet as well as Cornet by all means but do not imagine that if you play the Trumpet you will avoid transposition. If the student has committed all the scales and chords well to memory, a little application will enable him to transpose easily. Studies which have been well learned, should be practised a note, minor third, fourth and fifth higher.[79]

Ernest Hall, at the Royal College of Music, and, from the late 1930s, George Eskdale, at the Royal Academy of Music, taught generations of players, including influential teachers like David Mason (1926–2011) and Howard Snell (b.1936) who were instrumental in establishing the twin strands of a distinctive British orchestral sound, reflecting the different orthodoxies of the conservatoire and amateur brass-band traditions, which survived throughout the twentieth century. It is notable that both Hall and Eskdale came from the industrial North of Britain, Liverpool and Greenock respectively, with their strong brass-band roots.

Instruments

Mentor players like those described in this chapter were intimately involved in the detail of the evolution of their instrument's technology. Many surviving slide-trumpets from the first half of the nineteenth century are conversions of eighteenth-century natural trumpets. For example, two instruments that belonged formerly to Thomas Harper, jun., in the Bate Collection at Oxford and the Royal College of Music in London, were made by John Harris in the early eighteenth century (the Oxford instrument was later owned by Walter Morrow) (Ill. 9.2). The earliest known conversion was made by the watchmaker Richard Woodham some time before 1797 on a natural trumpet by G. H. Rodenbostel of London from the 1760s. Woodham fitted this instrument with a clock-spring mechanism that was adopted by subsequent makers. Clementi and Co. began making clock-spring slide trumpets during the second decade of the nineteenth century in partnership with Thomas Harper. After the death of Clementi in 1832, Harper collaborated with John Köhler, and then Köhler's son, receiving commission on each instrument sold. The instruments made by Clementi and Köhler were typically marked 'Harper's Improved', even though Harper made only minor modifications to the instrument. By the middle of the century the clock-spring mechanism (and a later spiral-spring system) was being replaced by a simpler expansion spring or elastic cord positioned inside the tube between the two main yards of the slide.

9.2 Slide trumpet, converted from a natural trumpet by John Harris. (By permission of the University of Oxford)

Although the era of the slide trumpet was coming to a close by the last decade of the nineteenth century, a few instruments continued to be made, and Hawkes & Son published a tutor for the valved and slide trumpet in 1906.[80] In 1890 the trumpeter William Wyatt patented the first fully chromatic English slide trumpet, which, by incorporating two double slides, allowed for shifts of a major third. (Hitherto, slide extension only allowed for shifts of a major second, creating gaps in chromatic scale in the low register.) At around the same time, Boosey and Co. patented a forward-moving slide trumpet, advertised in their 1892 catalogue as an 'Orthochromatic Trumpet'. It has been estimated that only around ten of Wyatt's instruments were made by William Brown and it is known that Boosey and Co. (who had only produced eight slide trumpets between 1868 and 1913) manufactured as few as two of these 'orthochromatic' instruments (both in 1891).[81]

Algernon Rose reported that Higham of Manchester produced what they described as a 'Cornet and Trumpet, combined', an instrument with the appearance of a trumpet, but which accepted a cornet mouthpiece.[82] During the 1920s Rudall Carte made B flat trumpets with a shank that received a cornet mouthpiece: the mouthpiece supplied with the instrument had the cup profile of that for a trumpet.[83] The Mahillon B flat and A trumpet used by Ernest Hall until the 1940s (dating from the 1890s), now in the Royal College of Music collection, survives with a cornet mouthpiece and a brass adaptor made from another mouthpiece[84] (Ill. 9.3). This instrument was formerly owned by Hall's father, who presumably used it with the associated mouthpiece. Boosey & Co were offering a B flat trumpet, which they termed 'trumpettina' (later termed 'soprano trumpet'), from 1868, but fewer than ten of these were produced up to 1899.[85] The advent of the dance band era generated a huge demand for B flat trumpets, and by 1929 this was one of the best-selling instruments in Boosey & Co's catalogue.[86]

Russia

By the beginning of the nineteenth century a thriving musical and theatrical environment existed in St Petersburg and Moscow, supported by the Russian imperial court and a prosperous aristocracy eager to embrace many facets of European culture. Since the 1730s, Italian opera had flourished in the orbit of the court, alongside French, German and eventually Russian theatre and dance troupes. During the reign of Catherine the Great (reigned 1762–96), a German cultural influence began to dominate the imperial court, and by the reign of Alexander I (reigned 1801–25) the members of the imperial orchestras were predominantly German. Our knowledge of trumpet-playing in Russia up to the early twentieth century has been greatly enhanced by the publication of Edward Tarr's monograph *East Meets West*, from which most of this discussion derives. Tarr identifies numerous foreign (mostly German) trumpet and cornet players who settled in Russia from the early nineteenth century onwards and established a distinctive Russian school of trumpet playing. The individuality of the Russian trumpet style was also cultivated through the demanding trumpet writing of many Russian composers in the second half of the nineteenth and early twentieth centuries. Russian émigrés also exerted a strong influence on trumpet playing in America in the early twentieth century.

9.3 Ernest Hall, *c.*1940, with his Mahillon trumpet. (By permission of the Royal College of Music, London)

In 1847 the German cornet player Wilhelm Wurm moved to St Petersburg and for more than thirty years was cornet soloist of the ballet orchestra of the Mariinsky Theatre. Wurm toured extensively as a cornet soloist within Russia, and in 1862 he was honoured by Tsar Alexander II with the title of 'Soloist to His Imperial Majesty'; he also taught Alexander III to play the cornet and conducted his amateur brass band. In 1867, Wurm began teaching cornet at the St Petersburg Conservatoire, where he remained until 1904, and for which he wrote his *Method for Playing the Cornet* (1879).[87] Interestingly, Wurm was teaching cornet two years before Arban's cornet class was instituted at the Paris Conservatoire. The St Petersburg Conservatoire was founded in 1862, and a comparable institution opened in Moscow four years later. Brass instruments were taught at both institutions from the outset, by the German trumpeters Gustav Johann Metzdorff (1822–68 or later) and Theodor Richter (1826–1901) at St Petersburg and Moscow respectively.[88]

Richter was succeeded in 1899 by another German, Willy (Vasily Georgiyevich) Brandt (1869–1923), whom Tarr describes as 'a founder of the Russian trumpet school' and whose thirty-four études on orchestral excerpts are still used.[89] Brandt moved to Moscow in 1890 to join the Bolshoi Theatre Orchestra, and throughout his career he also performed as a cornet soloist. In 1908 he moved from first trumpet to first cornet at the Bolshoi Orchestra, before retiring from the orchestra the following year. According to his pupil Pyotr Yakovlevich Lyamin (1884–1968), Brandt used a B flat rotary-valve trumpet by Heckel and a French model cornet by a St Petersburg maker. In 1912 he moved to Saratov to teach at the newly-opened Conservatoire. Besides Lyamin, Brandt's pupils included Mikhail I. Tabakov (1877–1956) and Vladimir Drucker (1897–1974).[90]

By the middle of the nineteenth century, the imperial theatres in St Petersburg and Moscow maintained separate orchestras for opera and ballet. The relative status of the trumpet and the cornet in the opera and ballet orchestras in Russian ballet music, composers routinely assigned important solo parts to the cornet, while in operas it tended to assume a subordinate role to the trumpet – was reflected in the status of the players. Tarr notes that in the opera orchestra the trumpeters generally sat in front of the cornet players, while in the ballet orchestra this arrangement was reversed. In 1897 Oskar Böhme, composer of the Trumpet Concerto in E minor, moved to St Petersburg and joined the Mariinsky Theatre Orchestra as principal cornet, a position he held until 1921. He was known principally as a cornet player, and not as a trumpeter.

Tabakov joined the Bolshoi Theatre Orchestra in early 1898 and, in succeeding Brandt at the Moscow Conservatoire, became the most influential teacher of the next generation. Lyamin and Drucker in contrast made their mark outside Russia. After completing his studies with Brandt, Lyamin travelled to Paris to play trumpet and cornet in the orchestra of Diaghilev's Ballet Russe, and, according to Tarr, played the cornet solo in the original production of Stravinsky's ballet *Petrushka* (1911). On completing his studies at the Conservatoire in 1913, aged sixteen, Drucker played alongside Tabakov in Serge Koussevitzky's orchestra, before emigrating to the USA in 1919 and becoming one of the most influential players and teachers on the West Coast.

USA

The rivalry between John Norton and Alessandro Gambati that enthralled audiences at Niblo's Gardens in New York in August 1834 resumed the following year when the two players were engaged at rival theatres in New Orleans. Norton left New Orleans after a few months, before a mooted rematch could take place, but Gambati appeared regularly as a soloist in the city for several years. The popularity of solos for wind and brass instruments in the theatres of New Orleans, which began with players such as Gambati and the trombonist Felippe Cioffi (who had been in the band at Niblo's Gardens the previous year and later moved to London), gave rise to a lasting tradition of wind and brass playing in the city that produced, in the early years of the next century, musicians like the cornetists Buddy Bolden, Joe 'King' Oliver and Louis Armstrong, and the clarinettist Sidney Bechet. These pioneers of a new style of music that would become known as jazz drew on popular European art music forms, including instrumental airs and variations, in their improvisations.[91]

Gambati was a regular visitor to New York during the 1830s and 40s and retained a loyal following at Niblo's Gardens, where he was featured as a soloist on valved trumpet and, occasionally, on cornet. Norton occasionally appeared in New York during the same period, most often as soloist for Handel's obbligato parts. A trumpeter by the name of Rives, the regular trumpeter with the Sacred Music Society, also specialised in the Handel repertoire, as did J. F. Woler and Mason, the trumpet players of the New York Philharmonic at its formation in 1842. Both Woler and Mason also appeared as soloist on the valved trumpet and on cornet. Any lingering animosity between Gambati and Norton appears to have been vanquished as the two players performed a duet together at a benefit concert in Niblo's Gardens in 1835, and in 1838 Gambati performed at a benefit concert for Norton. At a concert in the City Hotel the following November, Norton performed a solo on the cornet. It is not known if he adopted the valved trumpet, but given his reputation as the foremost exponent of Handel's obbligato trumpet parts, it seems likely that he continued to perform this repertoire on the slide trumpet.[92]

By the second half of the century in America, Handel's obbligato trumpet parts were often performed on cornet, and celebrity players such as Matthew Arbuckle (1828–83) set a standard of performance for 'Let the Bright Seraphim' that must have been difficult for trumpet players to match.[93] When Friderick Dietz (first trumpet in the New York Philharmonic, 1865–99) performed 'Let the Bright Seraphim' in 1868, he was criticised for playing some of the solo part an octave lower than written. (Gambati was criticised in 1835 for adapting 'The Trumpet Shall Sound' in this manner.) Dietz's rendition of 'Let the Bright Seraphim' the previous year, however, had been more favourably reviewed.[94]

Until the second quarter of the twentieth century most of the players who occupied trumpet positions in symphony and opera orchestras – both the immigrants from Europe and American-born players – began their careers as cornet players. While some of these players adopted the trumpet for orchestral playing, this was by no means universal. As André M. Smith observes, the trumpet section of the New York Philharmonic before World War I was essentially a section of cornet players.[95] Max Schlossberg (1873–1936), who studied trumpet in Moscow and with Julius Kosleck in Berlin before settling in New York in 1902, was one of many Jewish musicians from central and eastern Europe who emigrated to America in the late nineteenth and early twentieth centuries. Although his teachers were noted cornet players, Schlossberg appears to have primarily played trumpet. Schlossberg joined the New York Philharmonic in 1910, and played second or fourth trumpet with the orchestra until his death in 1936, but his greatest influence was as a teacher, both as a private practitioner and from 1923 at the Institute of Musical Art. Tarr describes Schlossberg as the 'founder of the American school of playing'.[96] Among his many influential pupils was William Vacchiano, who joined the New York Philharmonic in 1935 and began his 31-year tenure as principal trumpet in 1942, following the departure of Harry Glantz.[97]

On the West Coast, another influential former trumpet student of the Moscow Conservatoire was Vladimir Drucker, who was appointed principal trumpet of the newly-formed Los Angeles Philharmonic soon after arriving in America in 1919. Drucker remained in this post (with gaps) until his retirement in 1945 and earned a reputation as one of the leading teachers in America. His teaching philosophy focused on sound quality in all registers and at all dynamic levels, which, in Tarr's view, reflected the influence of his two main teachers, Brandt and Tabikov, and defines him as 'an important mediator between the Russian and the American schools of playing'.[98]

Although celebrated players provided private instruction John Norton, for example, advertised lessons for ladies on the pianoforte and in singing, and offered to teach gentlemen the trumpet and Kent bugle, as well as the flute and flageolet[99] – most trumpeters in the USA received their musical education through military or amateur bands, and methods like *Distin's tutor* (Boston: O. Ditson, *c.*1853) and *Arbuckle's Complete Cornet Method* (Boston: O. Ditson, 1866) clearly found a ready market. Arban's method was issued in Boston in 1872, and in Philadelphia several years later, with the seductive title *Arban's world renowned method for the cornet.*

Music conservatories were founded in several American cities during the second half of the nineteenth century. The New England Conservatory of Music opened in Boston in 1867, followed in 1877 by the Philadelphia Conservatory. The first teacher of cornet and trumpet at the New England Conservatory was J. E. Eichler. He was succeeded by the cornet players Richard Shuebruk, *c.*1889, and Pierre Mueller (1891 until 1900).

It was not until 1905 that a comparable institution was founded in New York – the Institute of Musical Art (which became the Juilliard School of Music in 1926). The first trumpet teacher at the Institute was Adolphe Dubois, formerly of the Théâtre de la Monnaie, Brussels. Dubois had been invited to New York by the director of the Institute, Frank Damrosch, to play first trumpet in the New York Symphony Orchestra.[100] The initial intake of students included the twelve-year-old cornet prodigy Edna White (1892–1992). Dubois changed White's instrument from cornet to trumpet and provided her with a glowing endorsement at the culmination of her period of study, although she did not obtain a degree on account of her age. As a female trumpet player in the early twentieth century, a career as an orchestral musician was not open to White. Over the following two decades she formed several all-female brass quartets, with which she toured extensively across the USA.[101] In 1908, aged sixteen, she formed the Trunette Quartet (which also performed as the Aida Quartet), comprising four trumpets or various combinations of trumpets and cornets. In 1914 she formed the Edna White Trumpet Quartet, and in 1919 a quartet of two trumpets and two trombones, known as the Gloria Trumpeters. During the 1920s she made solo recordings for Thomas Edison and Columbia. One of her first recordings for Edison, Herbert L. Clarke's *The Debutante,* demonstrates a command of the instrument and level of musicianship that would have enhanced the brass section of any symphony orchestra (Ill. 9.4). She maintained an interest in the classical solo trumpet repertoire and in 1949 gave a highly acclaimed solo trumpet recital in New York's Carnegie Hall that included the first performance of Virgil Thomson's 'concert waltz' *At the Beach* and Georges Enesco's *Légende,* composed and published during Edna White's period of study with Dubois, and which she may have played at that time.[102]

9.4 Edna White, with the baritone Torcum Bezazian, and Carlo Peroni conducting, at the Edison Studio, New York, 1920s.

Until the outbreak of World War I the membership of the Boston Symphony Orchestra was predominantly German. The first and second trumpeters for the orchestra's first three seasons, beginning in 1881, Ezra Bagley (1853–86) and Benjamin Bowron, were American-born cornet players, as was Richard Shuebruk, who succeeded Bagley as first trumpet for one season in 1886. Thereafter the trumpet section comprised a mix of German, Austrian, Czech, Italian and French players. Between 1888 and 1898 the principal trumpet player was the Belgian, Pierre Mueller, who had previously worked in Paris and, according to Keith Clark, was the first player to play trumpet as opposed to cornet in the Boston Symphony Orchestra.[103] In 1914 Vincent Bach (originally Vincenz Schrottenbach; 1890–1976) was appointed associate principal trumpet of the Boston Symphony Orchestra, having fled England at the outbreak of the War, but left the following year while on tour in San Francisco, to resume his career as a cornet soloist. On returning to New York, Bach performed for the Diaghilev Ballet during the winter of 1915–16, after which he again reverted to working as a cornet soloist, in which capacity he had enjoyed success in Germany. In a letter to Alick Maclean, conductor of the Scarborough Spa Orchestra, dated 23 June 1913, Bach explained that he had declined the invitation to spend that summer in the English resort, where he had appeared the previous year and was to return the following season, in order to realise his ambitions on the German music-hall circuit, noting that the physical demands of the job were detrimental to his solo performances.[104] Bach made his first mouthpiece for the commercial market in 1919 and five years later began making instruments. Thereafter he gradually retired from playing. Bach's successful instrument-making business was founded on his desire to cater for professional performers at a time when competitors were targeting the amateur band market (Ill. 9.5).

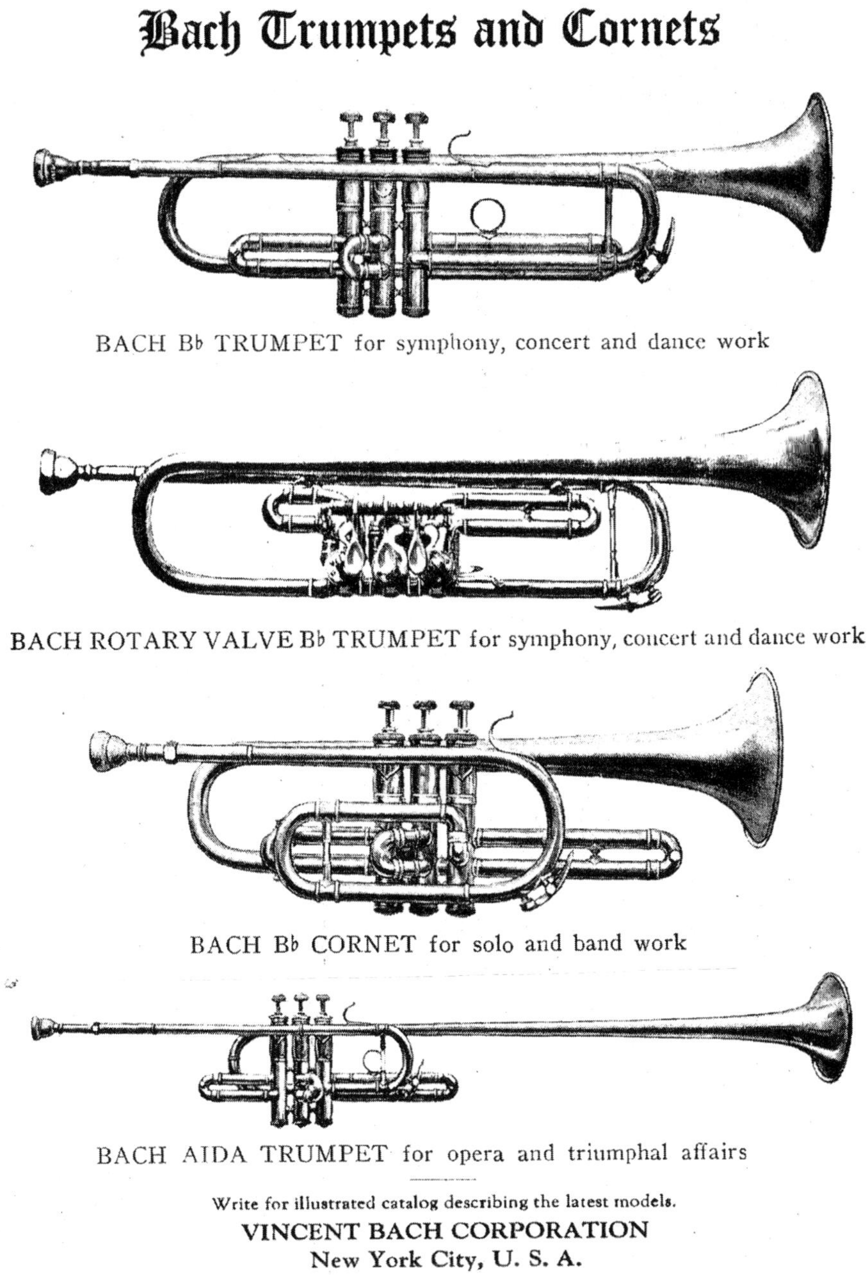

9.5 Advertisement for Bach trumpets and cornet, from Vincent Bach, *The Art of Trumpet Playing* (New York: V. Bach Corporation, 1925).

The transformation of the Boston Symphony Orchestra from a predominantly German orchestra to a French ensemble immediately after World War I had profound consequences for the development of the distinctive American orchestral trumpet style that was to evolve during the twentieth century. George Mager, one of several members of a French military band that was touring America in 1918 who auditioned for the orchestra, had studied cornet with Jean Joseph Mellet at the Paris Conservatoire, receiving a first prize in 1906. Since there was no vacancy in the trumpet section of the orchestra, Mager was hired to play viola; the following year he was appointed third trumpet, and in 1920 principal trumpet, a position that he held for thirty years. In 1927 Mager was joined in the trumpet section by his fellow Paris Conservatoire alumnus René Louis Voisin, whose son, Roger, he taught at the New England Conservatory. Roger Voisin joined the Boston Symphony Orchestra in 1935, aged seventeen, and succeeded Mager as principal trumpet following his former teacher's death in 1950. Mager was one of the most influential teachers in America during the first half of the twentieth century and the most influential advocate of the C trumpet as an orchestral instrument. Besides Roger Voisin, Mager's pupils included Adolph Herseth (b.1921), principal trumpet of the Chicago Symphony Orchestra from 1948 to 2001.[105]

The European identity of many American orchestras in the early twentieth century, exemplified by the Boston Symphony Orchestra, and the eventual fusion of distinctive musical traditions that came to characterise American orchestras, reflects the wider current of cultural synthesis shaping the USA at that time. Nowhere did the cultural fusion have a more profound impact on musical developments than in New Orleans, where the blend of musical traditions emanating from the diverse ethnic groups that inhabited the city led to the emergence of ragtime, then jazz, 'the most original, distinctive, and influential musical style' to emerge in the twentieth century.[106] Jazz was to provide a fertile environment for a fresh approach to the solo trumpet. Both the playing technique and the idiom of the trumpet were now set to develop rapidly in the century to come.

Chapter 10

The 'Bach revival', 'Bach' trumpets, and the advent of the piccolo trumpet

The revival of the music of J. S. Bach, which gathered pace during the second quarter of the nineteenth century and coincided with the advent of the valve trumpet, had profound consequences for the development of the trumpet and trumpet playing. For the generation of trumpeters schooled in the orchestral repertoire of the late eighteenth and early nineteenth centuries, Bach's trumpet parts presented a seemingly insurmountable challenge. As players strove to negotiate a repertoire that appeared to many to represent a 'lost art', the higher pitched instruments that emerged influenced the trumpet writing of contemporary composers and initiated the trend towards using shorter trumpets for the wider orchestral repertoire.

The performance of Bach's St Matthew Passion by Mendelssohn and the Berlin Singakademie in 1829 was a seminal event in the 'Bach revival'. Previous to this, several of Bach's choral works with trumpets had been performed in Germany. This happened first at private gatherings, and then, notably, in public performances of excerpts from the B minor Mass in Frankfurt and Berlin in 1828.[1] After Mendelssohn's appointment as municipal music director for the city of Leipzig and conductor of the Gewandhaus orchestra in 1835, he presented his first series of 'historical' concerts in 1838, which included a performance of Bach's Orchestral Suite No. 3 in D.[2] Later that year he directed performances of Bach's *Ascension Oratorio* at the Lower Rhine Music Festival in Cologne.[3] It was probably for the Leipzig performance of the orchestral suite that Mendelssohn altered Bach's orchestration, assigning the first trumpet part to clarinets whilst relegating the three trumpets to a supportive role in keeping with their contemporary orchestral function. This arrangement was published after Mendelssohn's death in an edition by Ferdinand David (Leipzig, 1866)[4] (Ex. 10.1). The first concert in Mendelssohn's second series of 'historical' concerts in Leipzig, in January 1841, included the 'Crucifixus', 'Et resurrexit' and Sanctus from Bach's B minor Mass. The manuscript score that Mendelssohn owned and used for this performance, held in the Bodleian Library, Oxford, includes emendations to the trumpet parts of the latter two movements, involving downward octave transpositions of some of the highest passages and a reworking of all three trumpet parts in others[5] (Ill. 10.1).

For the first performance of the B minor Mass in Dresden, on 28 October 1850, the three trumpeters from the court orchestra used natural trumpets, correcting the problematic notes of the scale by hand-stopping.[6] When the work received its first performance in Leipzig by the Riedel-Verein in 1859, a reviewer singled out the first trumpeter, T. E. Reichelt of the Gewandhaus Orchestra, for special praise, but does

(a)

(b)

Exx. 10.1a & b J. S. Bach, Orchestral Suite No. 3 in D BWV 1068, Gigue, opening (a); the same passage in the arrangement by Mendelssohn, ed. David (Leipzig, 1866) (b).

not reveal the type of instrument he used; Tarr suggests that it may have been a valved trumpet in D, half the length of the natural instrument for which it was written. That valved trumpets were not universally perceived as resolving the intractable problem of Bach's trumpet parts is revealed by one critic who suggested that the trumpeters who performed on valved instruments for a performance of the Christmas Oratorio by the Berlin Singakademie in 1859 should have used natural trumpets, which he asserted were easier to play.[7]

As performances of Bach's choral works became more frequent from the middle of the century onwards, it became accepted that the original trumpet parts were unplayable on the instruments in current use. The publication of arrangements of Bach's Magnificat and Christmas Oratorio (parts 1 and 2) by the composer Robert Franz, with the high

10.1 J. S. Bach, B minor Mass, opening of the Sanctus, with reworked trumpet parts by Mendelssohn inserted in pencil (*GB-Ob* MS. M.D.M. c.67). (By permission of the University of Oxford)

trumpet parts assigned to clarinet, circulated widely throughout Europe and by the mid 1870s were being performed in America.[8] Franz's arrangement of the Magnificat was performed at the Cincinnati Festival in 1875 and in Theodore Thomas's series of concerts in Boston in 1876, and his version of Bach's Christmas Oratorio was used at the Fourth Triennial Festival of the Handel and Haydn Society of Boston in 1877.[9] Instead of transferring the entire first trumpet part to clarinet, as with Mendelssohn's adaptation of Bach's Suite in D, Franz only substituted the clarinets for the highest trumpet passages, thereby maintaining melodic interest in the trumpet parts. This technique is illustrated in his adaptation of the trumpet obbligato to the bass aria, 'Mighty Lord, and King all glorious' from the Christmas Oratorio (Ex. 10.2). For a performance of the B minor Mass at the Cincinnati Festival in 1902, for which a chorus of 500 voices and an orchestra of 129 (including six trumpets and six clarinets) were deployed, Theodore Thomas altered the trumpet parts in a manner similar to that of Franz.[10]

The leading exponent of the baroque trumpet repertoire in Leipzig during the final quarter of the nineteenth century was Ferdinand Weinschenk, first trumpet of the Leipzig Gewandhaus Orchestra from 1867. Weinschenk is known to have performed the B minor Mass on a D trumpet in 1890. He may well have used this instrument for performances of the work in 1881 and the Christmas Oratorio in 1884, at which he was praised for his playing in the high register, even though the version used was that by Robert Franz.[11]

The use of high-pitched trumpets for performances of the baroque repertoire was embraced early by players in Belgium and France. In 1861, the cornet player and Brussels Conservatoire professor Hippolyte Duhem (1828–1911) commissioned Courtois of Paris to make a trumpet in D. Charles Mahillon of Brussels followed suit around 1870,[12] and the maker's son Victor-Charles Mahillon referred to the use of D trumpets for the music of Bach and Handel in his treatise on acoustics of 1874.[13] The Brussels Conservatoire was influential in promoting the use of the D trumpet for the music of Bach and Handel, particularly after the appointment of Alphonse Goeyens as professor of trumpet in 1890, when students had to perform excerpts from those composers' works on the D trumpet at their final examination.[14]

(a)

(b)

Exx. 10.2a & b J. S. Bach, 'Mighty Lord, and King all-glorious' from the Christmas Oratorio BWV 248; opening of the aria in its original version (a), and the same passage arranged by Robert Franz (b).

In February 1874, Xavier-Napoléon Teste performed Handel's Messiah in Paris on a D trumpet by Besson.[15] Apparently dissatisfied with this instrument for playing Bach's trumpet parts, Besson provided Teste with an instrument in high G for a performance of the Magnificat in 1885.[16] He presumably used this instrument in a performance of the B minor Mass by the Société des Concerts in 1891 – the first complete performance of the work in France – at which his playing was described by the secretary of the Society as 'fearless and error-free'.[17]

A trumpet in high F, which was used in early performances of the Brandenburg Concerto No. 2 (see below), was produced by Alexander of Mainz in the mid-1890s, and around 1905 Mahillon produced their first piccolo trumpet in B flat for Alphonse Goeyens.[18] An instrument of the same pitch as the B flat piccolo trumpet, but with a slightly more conical bore, had in fact been developed by Adolph Sax half a century earlier. Sax's piccolo saxhorn in B flat was designed primarily for use in military bands; however, Berlioz scored for the instrument in the 'Marche pour la Présentation des Drapeaux' that he appended to his Te Deum before its first performance in 1855 (when the part was played by Arban) and in the off-stage band in *Les Troyens* (1856–8).[19]

It is perhaps surprising that Sax's piccolo saxhorn was not adopted for Bach's trumpet parts; it was not until Adolf Scherbaum (1909–2000) adopted the piccolo trumpet in B flat in the early 1950s that an instrument of this size began to be widely accepted for the music of Bach and Handel. Before Scherbaum's championing of the instrument, players were reluctant to compromise the timbre of the D trumpet, the instrument that had come to epitomise the ideal trumpet sound for baroque music. The self-interest of trumpeters who were beginning to specialise in performing the music of Bach and Handel may have obstructed the introduction of smaller instruments. To them the substitution of the clarinet for the high trumpet parts would have been preferable to admitting interlopers from military bands to this élite sector of the profession.

One of the few players known to have adopted a high-pitch, conical-bore instrument for Bach's trumpet parts was Adolf Scholz (1823–84) of Breslau, who used a 'Flügelhorn in high F' for performances with the Breslauer Singakademie, a society which had played a seminal role in the Bach revival.[20] It seems that conical bore instruments may also have provided the inspiration for the straight, two-valved trumpet in A and B flat that Julius Kosleck developed around 1880 to perform the music of Bach. In 1871 Kosleck gave a demonstration of Bach's trumpet parts to the Musical Artists' Association of Berlin using a straight 'buisine' with a conical bore. The instrument was pitched in 4 ft B flat, but lowered to D by an additional length of cylindrical tubing. According to the music critic Otto Lessmann, writing in the *Neue Berliner Musikzeitung*:

> Mr. Kosleck played a complete diatonic scale with perfect intonation, both in cantilena and florid passages; even the trill, that unknown ornament of past times, was mastered.[21]

Lessmann also asserted that the instrument demonstrated by Kosleck was the type used by Bach and Handel's trumpeters, laying the foundation of a myth that was to be propagated, particularly in Britain, where the straight, 4 ft trumpet with two valves became known as the 'Bach' trumpet. Kosleck used his newly-developed instrument for a performance of the B minor Mass in Berlin on 21 November 1881. In September 1884, he performed the same work at a festival at Eisenach, Bach's home town, at the unveiling of a statue of the composer. According to one review of this performance, the oboe d'amore 'with its sweet tone . . . found more general applause than the long trumpet, built after an old model for a Berlin performance and entrusted to his colleague Mr. Kosleck; its sound was almost too soft', a criticism that Tarr interprets as an unintended compliment[22] (Ill. 10.2).

10.2 Julius Kosleck (*Neue Zeitschrift für Musik* 93/48, 1 December 1897, 525). (By permission of the University of Oxford)

The popularity of the music of Handel in Britain during the nineteenth century ensured the survival of a tradition of solo trumpet playing, but did little to equip the players for the trumpet parts of Bach. Whereas by the last quarter of the century trumpeters on the Continent were beginning to adopt short D trumpets for this repertoire, their counterparts in London, whose reputations owed much to their performances of Handel's obbligato trumpet parts on the slide trumpet, were reluctant to abandon their favoured instrument for the music of Bach. Movements from Bach's Magnificat and the B minor Mass were included in the series of Ancient Concerts held in London in April and May 1838.[23] A review of the performance of the B minor Mass in the *Musical World* alluded to the difficulty of the first trumpet part and the unsuitability of the instruments in current use for this purpose: 'This part of course Mr. Harper could not play, nor indeed could anybody, with the instrument now in use in our orchestras'.[24] In June 1844 the Philharmonic Society included Bach's Suite in D in a concert conducted by Mendelssohn, presumably in the arrangement he made for Leipzig.[25] The Bach Society (of London) was formed in 1849 and until its dissolution in 1870 presented several of Bach's large-scale choral works. The first London performance of the St Matthew Passion (using Mendelssohn's manuscript parts) in 1854 was followed by movements from the B minor Mass in 1860 and the Christmas Oratorio the following year.[26]

According to a review in *The London Telegraph* of a performance of the Christmas Oratorio by the Royal Albert Hall Choral Society on 15 December 1873, 'the orchestra was precisely that ordained by Bach . . . [and] was neither numerous nor noisy', and 'Dr. [John] Stainer rendered good service at the organ, especially in the performance of those trumpet passages which the trumpeters of our day decline to attempt'.[27] In another review of the concert Ebenezer Prout asserted that 'the quality of the trumpet stop on the organ' on the Royal Albert Hall organ, which had been installed two years earlier, 'was so close an imitation of the original instrument as to render it sometimes difficult to detect the difference'.[28]

The first complete performance of the B minor Mass in London was given on 26 April 1876 at St James's Hall, by a choir specially formed for the occasion and an orchestra of seventy players, directed by Otto Goldschmidt.[29] The review of the performance from *The Musical Times* is worth quoting at length:

> To all conversant with Bach's score it was a matter of great disappointment to hear the important passages for three trumpets in the "Gloria" performed by clarinets; but as on the modern trumpets, we are told the parts are unplayable, we may fairly presume that the best authorities have been consulted on the matter. Seeing, however, that the horn *obbligato* to the "Quoniam" (so finely played by Mr. Wendland), although written for the *Corno da Caccia*, was executed on the valve horn, it becomes a question whether some near approach to the tone of the trumpets could not have been thought of in the "Gloria;" for certainly the clear, ringing soprano passages intended by the composer were but poorly represented by the comparatively dull notes of the clarinets.[30]

The same issue of *The Musical Times* included an article on the B minor Mass by Prout, in which he espouses the prevailing view that 'Bach's first trumpet parts are almost invariably written so high as to be absolutely impracticable now-a-days'. However, he referred to a conversation with Thomas Harper, jun., in which the trumpeter revealed his conviction that 'by the use of a suitable mouth-piece such passages could undoubtedly be played with practice, but that modern composers write for the instrument in such a different fashion that a performer who played Bach's passages would lose the command of lip necessary for the music of the present day'.[31] A reply to this article by an anonymous correspondent insisted that the supposedly unplayable trumpet parts could be performed successfully on saxhorns, in particular the 'Little high Saxhorn in B♭', the 'Saxhorn Soprano in E♭' and the 'Saxhorn Contralto in B♭'. Moreover, he asserted, no doubt to the annoyance of the professional élite, that cornet players could play Bach's trumpet parts on those instruments 'without difficulty'.[32]

The success of the 1876 London performance of the B minor Mass led to the choir being established on a permanent basis, as the Bach Choir. In April 1878 the choir performed the first three parts of the Christmas Oratorio in St James's Hall, with additional instrumental parts by Prout.[33] Although this arrangement has not survived, we can assume that the trumpet parts were assigned to either clarinets or the organ. The second of the Bach Choir's two concerts the following year, on 14 May 1879, included Bach's Cantata No. 50 'Now shall the grace' (the first concert consisted of the B minor Mass). A short score of Bach's Cantata No. 50, in the Bad Säckingen Trumpet Museum, dated 'April 79', can be linked to this performance. The score comprises the three trumpet parts arranged for two clarinets and two trumpets and bears a note in a different hand, dated April 1906, stating that the arrangement was 'used only at the performances up to March 1885 at the R. Albert Hall'.[34]

The correspondent for *The Musical Times* at the Eisenach performance of the B minor Mass considered the absence of additional accompaniments and the restoration of the trumpet to the place traditionally occupied by the clarinet as being particularly significant. Kosleck was singled out both for his virtuosity and his integrity as 'an artist whose aim it is to restore his instrument to the high position which it held a century and a half ago. His own instrument is an exact copy of one three hundred years old, which he found in a shop at Heidelberg.'[35] He concluded by noting that Kosleck had been invited to 'introduce his remarkable re-discovery to the London public' at the forthcoming performance of the work by the Bach Choir the following year.

In his address to the Royal Musical Association in 1895 Walter Morrow reflected on the excitement that both he and John Solomon felt in anticipation of Kosleck's arrival, believing that the visitor was to perform the work on a natural trumpet. (Morrow and Solomon played the second and third parts respectively on valved trumpets in F.) Their disappointment on discovering that Kosleck was using a valved trumpet was eclipsed by their admiration for his playing and fascination with his instrument, which Morrow considered to possess a tone that was 'beautiful in the higher register, but, being only the same length as the cornet . . . poor in the lower register'.[36] Kosleck's playing was widely praised by newspaper critics, who were also intrigued by his instrument. George Bernard Shaw's report in *The Dramatic Review* captures the prevailing sentiment:

> Herr Julius Kosleck, of Berlin, shewed us on Saturday that the old trumpet parts are as feasible as ever. He brings out the high D with ease, executes shakes, rivals our finest flautists in the purity of the tone he produces in the upper register, and seems able to do, with his prodigiously long, straight instrument, all the feats that the first-cornet heroes of our military bands accomplish in the '*staccato* polkas,' and the like double-tonguing atrocities.[37]

Morrow revealed that Kosleck allowed him to try his instrument but was secretive of his mouthpiece, which he observed was noticeably different from his own. A line drawing of a mouthpiece belonging to Kosleck, possessing a deep, conical cup, similar to that of a horn, is reproduced in Werner Menke's *History of the Trumpet of Bach and Handel* (1934).[38] If Kosleck did in fact use such a mouthpiece with his straight trumpet in A, this would account for his soft, mellow tone attested to by commentators. Having argued passionately against the use of the cornet and the B flat trumpet in orchestras, Morrow justified his endorsement of this 'cornet in A', which by this time he had fully embraced, by insisting that 'it is not intended to supplant the real trumpet', but to perform the high parts of Bach with 'equal intonation, good tone, and some certainty'.[39]

Kosleck's trumpet was not widely adopted in Germany; the few instruments of this type that were produced appear to have been used for ceremonial purposes.[40] The trumpeter Hermann Pietzsch, writing in 1900, stated that the trumpet in A was suitable for Bach (and preferable to the cornet in A, with its 'characterless timbre'), but that the short D trumpet, which facilitated the execution of the high passages, was the preferred instrument for players in Germany.[41] To players in Britain who were averse to deviating from the instrument that they used for Handel, Kosleck's instrument offered an acceptable compromise.

Morrow subsequently provided the makers Silvani & Smith, who had recently opened a branch in London, with a line drawing of Kosleck's trumpet in order for them to produce a copy.[42] John Solomon evidently also ordered a copy at or around the same time, since the Silvani & Smith instrument that he owned, stamped as being made in Paris, survives in the Bate Collection, Oxford[43] (Ill. 10.3). Morrow presumably acquired his instrument later that year, since at the New Year's Day performance of Messiah by the Royal Albert Hall Choral Society in 1886 it was noted that 'the obbligato in "The Trumpet shall sound" was played upon the long trumpet re-manufactured for the Bach commemoration performance last March'.[44] Not surprisingly, the enthusiasm of the London critics for this instrument diminished when it was adopted for the music of Handel. As the reviewer noted, 'On this instrument the high notes can be obtained with greater ease, but the tone will not compare with our modern slide trumpet'. The instrument was received more enthusiastically later that year when it was adopted by Morrow (and according to one reviewer, his two colleagues) for a performance of the B minor Mass at the Leeds Festival, under the direction of Sir Arthur Sullivan:

> That the original trumpet parts might be played as written, the trumpets were expressly made on the old German model and placed in the capable hands of Messrs. Morrow, McGrath, and

10.3 'Bach' trumpet in A by Silvani & Smith. (By permission of the University of Oxford)

> Ellis. . . . Mr Mann undertook the difficult solo for *corno da caccia* which is usually played on a clarinet.[45]

Even for the music of Bach, however, the new instrument did not meet with universal approval. A review of a performance by the Bach Choir in February 1891 in the theatrical newspaper *The Era* commented that 'The principal trumpet was played by Mr Morrow on an unwieldy instrument in appearance like an elongated posthorn with keys'. This prompted a stern rebuke from Silvani & Smith, who, claiming to be the inventor and sole maker of the 'Bach trumpet', considered the remarks to be 'both incorrect and misleading'. The letter's author proceeded to explain that 'the object in having the instrument in the straight is so that the column of air remains unbroken, and, owing to the very gradual bore, it is possible to obtain an extra compass five notes more than any other trumpet extant', and that 'the instrument is made in three parts, which act as slides; the object is to tune equally'.[46] An article in favour of the addition of other instruments to Bach's orchestra appeared in *The Musical Times* in 1895, in which the author expressed his preference for assigning the high trumpet parts to clarinets:

> . . . now it is thought to be displaying a spirit of reverence towards Bach to re-manufacture the coarse-toned instruments used in his day – the long trumpet, the harsh tones of which simply split the ear. Formerly the high trumpet parts were allotted to clarinets, with effect surely more in consonance with the composer "as he meant it to be".[47]

The Bach trumpet in A remained popular in England throughout the 1890s but was eventually superseded by the shorter, straight 'sopranino' trumpet in D, which was developed by Victor-Charles Mahillon around 1894. British makers continued to produce 'Bach' trumpets in A in small numbers during the first decade of the twentieth century, but they too began to produce straight D trumpets, which also became known as 'Bach' trumpets.[48] Walter F. H. Blandford, writing in 1935, asserted that the most experienced players in Britain considered the straight trumpet to be 'more brilliant in tone and surer in the extreme register' than the short, folded D trumpet but that the convenience of the latter instrument in the orchestra had resulted, since around 1920, in the demise of the straight trumpet.[49]

To commemorate the fiftieth anniversary of their first performance of the B minor Mass, in 1926 the Bach Choir organized a Jubilee Festival, in which they were joined by the London Symphony Orchestra and conducted by Ralph Vaughan Williams. The final concert of the festival consisted of the B minor Mass, on which the critic for *The Musical Times* commented:

> it is at least common-sense to give to Bach's orchestrally accompanied choral works the scoring that, according to the best judgment, best suits the music. This is what Dr. Vaughan Williams has done, and we may have no fear in deferring to his judgment. . . . The boldest, or rather the most easily noticed, of the doctorings was the introduction of clarinets. It was not done at haphazard. As a rule the clarinets piped

> or trilled with the high Bach trumpets, or they hid themselves in the middle of chords and were helpful without being obtrusive.[50]

The same writer also approved of Vaughan Williams's re-orchestration of the Quoniam section of the Mass:

> Probably no one will quarrel with the alteration in the 'Quoniam.' The *corno da caccia* and bassoon music was divided round the orchestra, especially among the strings, and clear, articulate, part-playing took the place of the usual gurglings.[51]

Bach's Brandenburg Concerto No. 2

As popular interest in Bach's music extended to his instrumental works, the Brandenburg concertos most easily adaptable for modern orchestral performance entered the canonic repertoire. By the close of the nineteenth century it was becoming customary for the trumpet parts in Bach's choral works to be performed in the tessitura intended by the composer. The exceptional technical demands of Bach's Brandenburg Concerto No. 2, however, presented a seemingly insurmountable obstacle to its revival. Blandford reveals that Kosleck demonstrated the trumpet part of the concerto during his visit to London, apparently with difficulty, and Tarr identifies several trumpeters who tackled the work in the late nineteenth century, with the highest passages transposed down an octave. The first trumpeter documented as performing the concerto with the trumpet part in its original tessitura is Théo Charlier, in Antwerp, in 1898. For a performance of the work in Liège in 1901, Charlier used a G trumpet by Mahillon, which he probably also used in 1898 and for highly acclaimed performances in Marseille, Paris and Brussels over the next few years.[52] In 1902 Alphonse Goeyens from Brussels performed the work in a public concert on an F trumpet by Mahillon and from 1905 on a piccolo B flat trumpet by the same maker.[53]

The catalyst for introduction of the Brandenburg Concerto No. 2 into the wider concert repertoire was the publication in 1901 of an arrangement of the work by the Austrian conductor and composer Felix Mottl. As well as adding extra instruments to the score, Mottl divided the trumpet part between two players and transposed the high trumpet passages down an octave. Concert notices, programmes and reviews of performances of the concerto after 1901 often refer to Mottl's arrangement being used, and it seems safe to infer that the sudden entry of the work into the orchestral repertoire during the first decade of the twentieth century reflects the wide dissemination of this publication.

The first documented performance of the Brandenburg Concerto No. 2 in America was given by the Boston Symphony Orchestra in December 1901, in the version by Mottl.[54] Significantly, the principal trumpet of the Boston Symphony Orchestra at this time was Louis Kloepfel, who studied with Weinschenk in Leipzig before emigrating to America. Further performances of Mottl's arrangement were given in Philadelphia, New York and Chicago during the following two decades.[55] It appears that the work may have been performed in New York in 1904 with the trumpet part in its original tessitura. A newspaper announcement for a forthcoming series of concerts of 'old music' by Sam Franko and his American Symphony Orchestra noted that for their performance of the Brandenburg Concerto No. 2, 'The soprano trumpet, which Mr Franko had made to order in Brussels, will make it possible to hear this work exactly as the composer wrote it'.[56] Unfortunately, the newspaper did not print a review of this concert, but it seems likely that the trumpeter alluded to was Adolphe Dubois, who had recently arrived from Belgium and was presumably aware of the pioneering work of Charlier and Goeyens.

In 1921 Leopold Stokowski presented his own arrangement of the Brandenburg Concerto No. 2 in concerts with the Philadelphia Orchestra. After performing the work in Philadelphia in February 1921, and again in December, he presented it in New York. The review in *The New York Times* reveals that Stokowski treated the trumpet part similarly to Mottl:

> Mr. Stokowski . . . divides the trumpet between two players, and transposes some of it an octave lower. Mr. Stokowski has superb trumpeters . . . and they sent up no signals of distress.[57]

In 1928 Stokowski recorded the concerto with the Philadelphia Orchestra, in which the orchestra's principal trumpeter Sol Caston (1901–70) performed many of the high passages an octave lower than written.[58]

In London, the concerto was included by Henry Wood at the Promenade concerts in 1898, the same year as Théo Charlier's landmark performance, with Walter Morrow on trumpet. Morrow probably used his 'Bach' trumpet in B flat (equivalent in length to the modern B flat trumpet) and presumably performed a simplified version of the trumpet part. Henry Wood included the concerto in every season of Promenade concerts between 1906 and 1929 except three (1922, 1924 and 1927), with Francis Gyp (*fl.*1915-35) as trumpet soloist.[59]

The concerto was performed in Manchester in November 1915 by the Hallé Orchestra, conducted by Thomas Beecham, with the orchestra's principal trumpeter Johannes Valk as soloist.[60] At the Leeds Festival in October 1922 Herbert Barr (1882–after 1958) performed the trumpet part of the Brandenburg Concerto No. 2 at its original pitch for the first time in Britain, using a high F trumpet by Besson.[61] The review in *The Musical Times* noted:

> The performance of the trumpet part was an amazing tour de force. Mr. Barr used one of the revived instruments of Bach's time, a 'clarino' of high compass, over which he exercised a superb control, playing all the brilliant passages as they were written, and never an octave lower, as has been necessary with the modern trumpet. It is doubtful whether this had ever been done, at any rate in this country, since Bach's time. The perfect balance that was observed between his instrument and those of the other soloists was remarkable, and though something of the thrilling quality which we associate with trumpet-tone was necessarily sacrificed, the effect was admirable.[62]

Like the earlier commentators on the instrument introduced by Kosleck, this writer confused the modern valved trumpet with the instrument of Bach's era. Ironically, however, Herbert Barr did perform on a natural trumpet earlier that year: on 26 January he played the solo part for natural trumpet in E flat in the first performance of Ralph Vaughan Williams's Pastoral Symphony (No. 3).[63] Performances of the Brandenburg Concerto with both Herbert Barr and Ernest Hall on trumpet were broadcast by the BBC in 1925, and in 1929 Hall recorded the concerto with the London Chamber Orchestra conducted by Anthony Bernard, performing many of the high passages an octave lower than written.[64] At the formation of the BBC Symphony Orchestra in 1930 Hall was appointed first trumpet and player of the 'piccolo D trumpet', and Herbert Barr, third trumpet. Ernest Hall was soloist in several broadcast performances of Brandenburg Concerto No. 2 during the early 1930s and Barr performed as soloist in broadcasts of several other works by Bach during the same decade.

During the 1930s the first recordings of the Brandenburg Concerto No. 2 were issued with the trumpet part restored to its original tessitura. Two of these appeared in 1932: one by the Berlin Philharmonic Orchestra, under Alois Melichar, featured Paul Spörri, principal trumpeter with the orchestra, using a high F trumpet,[65] the other by the Orchestre de Chambre de l'École Normale de Musique de Paris, conducted by Alfred Cortot, with an unidentified trumpeter, who, according to Tarr, is playing on a piccolo B flat trumpet. In both of these recordings the trumpet part is performed with only fleeting octave transposition.[66] In 1935 Adolf Busch recorded the six Brandenburg Concertos in London with the Busch Chamber Players, and George Eskdale on trumpet (Ill. 10.4). With the exception of the downward transpositions of the high G6 and a short high passage in the first movement which is given to the flute, Eskdale performs the work as written, using a specially constructed F trumpet by Besson.[67] Given that in these recordings each movement had to be recorded in a single take, with no possibility of editing, it is hardly surprising that the trumpeters transposed the most perilous passages down an octave.

The availability of trumpeters capable of performing Bach's Brandenburg Concerto No. 2 and the familiarity of audiences hearing the work with its original instrumentation did not end the practice of replacing the trumpet with a woodwind instrument. When Arturo Toscanini conducted the concerto with the BBC Symphony Orchestra in May 1938, for example, he replaced the trumpet with an E flat clarinet, prompting the critic from *The Musical Times* to remark that 'the gain in fluency was no compensation for the tiring sound and the loss of trumpet character'.[68] Otto Klemperer adopted a similar stance in his 1946 recording with the ensemble Pro Musica of New York, for which he divided the part between saxophone and clarinet.[69]

An alternative to the short valved trumpet for the early trumpet repertoire came in the early 1930s with the development of a two-valved trumpet in 7 ft D (and a higher-pitched model in F) by the choral director Werner Menke and the instrument maker Alexander of Mainz. In his *History of the Trumpet of Bach and Handel*, written to promote the new instrument, Menke argued that the most appropriate trumpet for the music of Bach and Handel was one with the same length of tubing as that for which the music was conceived, and to capture further the tonal characteristics of the earlier

10.4 George Eskdale, by Norman Parkinson (1953). (Courtesy of Norman Parkinson Archive)

trumpet his instrument was made with thinner metal and fitted with a smaller bell than was customary at that time. Menke reported that the trumpet had been used successfully in performances under his direction in Leipzig, citing a press report that compared its 'clear, flexible and easily controlled tone' in the high register to that of a flute. However, the instrument failed to gain any influential champions outside Leipzig and it was not until the awakening of interest in the use of period instruments around the middle of the twentieth century that trumpeters turned to instruments of equivalent length to those of the seventeenth and eighteenth centuries.[70]

The early music revival

Finding a suitable instrument for the demanding baroque trumpet parts was as problematic for the early music movement as it had been for the pioneers of the Bach revival more than a century earlier. The short valved trumpets, which by the middle of the twentieth century had been universally adopted for this repertoire, were further removed from the instrument for which the music was written than the modern equivalent of any other instrument in the baroque orchestra. For increased accuracy in the upper register of the natural trumpet and to 'correct' the intonation of problematic notes of the harmonic series – particularly the eleventh and thirteenth partials – players began to experiment with instruments furnished with vent holes, an expediency that had been tentatively explored towards the end of the eighteenth century.

In 1960 Otto Steinkopf and Helmut Finke developed a trumpet with the same length of tubing as its baroque predecessor, but with three vent holes. The largest of these effectively transposed the harmonic series upwards by a fourth, allowing the problematic eleventh and thirteenth partials of the series to be replaced by the eighth and ninth partials, providing F5 and A5 (for the instrument in C); two smaller holes theoretically provided upward transpositions of an octave and a major seventh, the former affording the player more security in the high register and the latter providing B natural4 and F sharp5[71] (Ill. 10.5). To accommodate this venting system, the Steinkopf-Finke trumpet was coiled in the manner of the instrument held by Gottfried Reiche in the portrait by E. G. Haussmann (p. 155, above). This instrument was used by Walter Holy in performances and recordings of many of Bach's most demanding trumpet parts with the Cappella Coloniensis (the period instrument ensemble of the Cologne broadcasting station) between 1960 and 1981. Experiments in instrument design, notably by Edward Tarr and Michael Laird, led to the development of a trumpet employing the same three-hole system on an instrument that more closely resembled the shape of most surviving instruments of the period. The most prominent maker of instruments of this type has been Rainer Egger in Basel. Laird then developed a four-holed system that enabled the vented trumpet to be constructed in its traditional twice-folded form; this became the preferred instrument for players in Britain.[72] These instruments were popularised by a new generation of specialist players active internationally in the early music scene, with Friedemann Immer a prominent pioneer in Germany, Crispian Steele-Perkins and Michael Laird in England. A new generation of students of Laird, like Robert Farley (b.1963) and Mark Bennett

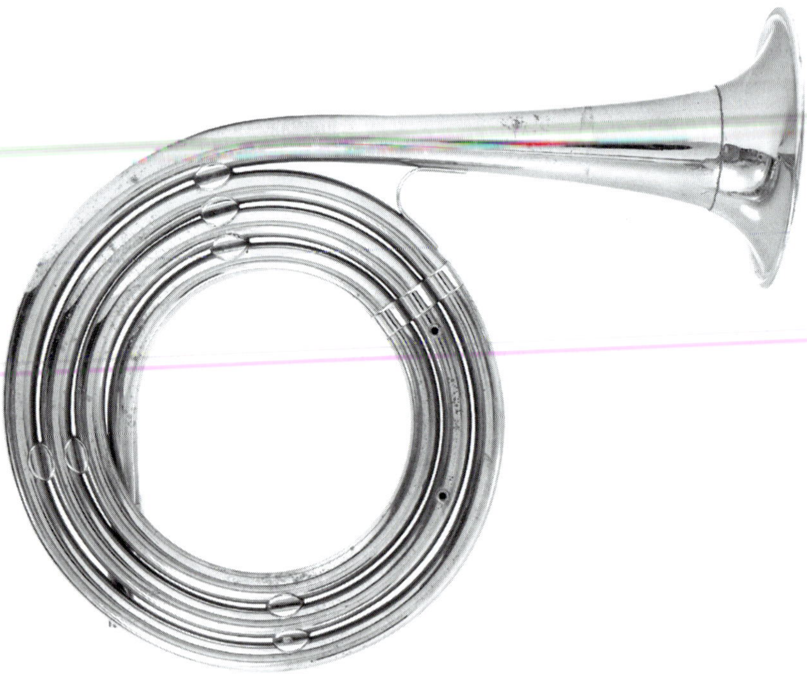

10.5 Modern replica of a coiled trumpet by Finke, showing nodal vents.

(b.1962) in England, and of Tarr, like Niklas Eklund (b.1969) from Sweden and Gabriele Cassone (b.1959) from Italy, came to prominence from the mid 1980s onwards.

The vented trumpet was readily embraced by the early music movement and trumpet players alike; its visual resemblance to the earlier instrument, together with its capacity to blend with the other instruments of the baroque orchestra and match the homogeneous intonation of the ensemble, outweighed the loss of the instrument's true timbral characteristics resulting from the use of vents. Since only a tiny minority of trumpeters active in the field of period performance are able to earn their living entirely from this sphere, the vented trumpet offers performers an instrument that can be adopted with minimum disruption to playing technique on the valved trumpet, particularly when played with a modern mouthpiece. Its acceptance has been further enhanced through its integration into the curriculum of conservatoires, almost invariably as a subsidiary option for students of the modern trumpet, and its more recent adoption in modern instrument orchestras, primarily for Classical period repertoire, following the example of the Chamber Orchestra of Europe under Nikolaus Harnoncourt.

Some of the most prominent exponents of the vented trumpet, including Crispian Steele-Perkins and David Staff in London, have also been committed advocates of the true natural trumpet. The most vociferous opponent of the vented instrument has been the trumpet player and scholar Don Smithers, who made several pioneering recordings on the natural trumpet in the 1970s. The beacon that Smithers has shone over the early brass community in his unremitting insistence on the use of uncompromised instruments – in which he has been supported by instrument makers such as Robert Barclay and Graham Nicholson by providing faithful copies of early instruments – has, in recent years, stimulated a small band of players, the most prominent being Jean-François Madeuf, to take the bold step of adopting the natural trumpet without vents for Bach's most demanding trumpet parts. At the Schola Cantorum Basiliensis, Madeuf directs a class devoted exclusively to the unvented trumpet, enabling students to cultivate a technique specific to that instrument, using larger mouthpieces than those normally adopted by players who double on modern trumpet.[73] While the near ubiquity of the vented trumpet presents a formidable obstacle to the revival of the natural trumpet and to employment opportunities sufficient to sustain specialist players on the latter instrument, the success of Madeuf and his colleagues makes it entirely plausible that in the foreseeable future the term 'Bach trumpet' will be applied to an instrument that the composer himself would have recognised.

Chapter 11

Repertoire, technique and performance idioms since 1900

Three clear trends are apparent in the trumpet in the twentieth century: experimentation with the use of trumpets as sound colours in orchestral writing; its re-introduction as a solo instrument; and the emergence of new idioms deriving from popular music, especially jazz. The jazz idiom is a main theme of Chapter 12. In Chapter 11 we shall consider the twin influences of jazz and modernism on composers writing for trumpet in 'classical' or 'art' music, and the consequent rapid evolution of trumpet technique and idiom for players schooled in that tradition.

Musical modernism and the emergence of jazz coincided with a rapid growth of those devices that facilitated the global dissemination of music. The twentieth century was the century of the radio, recorded music and film. These developments widened access to music-making generally, and through the popularity of jazz the trumpet captured the public imagination perhaps more than any other instrument. The rapid evolution of the idiom of the trumpet in classical music, caused by the general mood of change and experimentation generated by musical modernism, created a viable solo idiom for the trumpet through the integration by the classical tradition of ways of playing that had their origins in popular music. This was realised by the re-emergence, after a hiatus of more than a century, of the trumpet virtuoso. Throughout Europe and the USA, players of remarkable brilliance stimulated new ways of writing for and playing the trumpet. An interesting point about this group of players is that they were widely dispersed and their style of playing was often idiosyncratic.

The widening franchise of brass playing during the second half of the nineteenth century had provided a cadre of players ready to rise to the challenges posed by composers at the vanguard of developments in instrumental writing. Many of these players were products of military bands, or amateur brass bands, which appeared in varying forms in different countries. Both groupings had been quick to embrace the valve and they provided a ready-made network for the production and distribution of instruments, music and the other paraphernalia that players needed. Crucially, they also redefined virtuosity and brass playing in the public consciousness. As discussed in Chapter 9, the new chromatic brass idioms were often at odds with the accepted concept of the trumpet as an élite instrument appropriate to high art music. By the late nineteenth century, however, trumpeters had developed sufficient technique to provide composers with the means to overcome these aesthetic restrictions and exploit the instrument's capacity to enrich the orchestral palette.

The trumpet as a solo voice in the orchestra

From the last decade of the nineteenth century, composers of orchestral music, with Mahler and Strauss in the foreground, had been writing increasingly colourful, expressive and soloistic trumpet parts which stretched the range and technique of the trumpet. From around 1900 a high level of virtuosity became the normal expectation of all players in the trumpet section, which sometimes contained two principal parts, as in Strauss's *Ein Heldenleben* (1898), or difficult solo offstage parts, as in Mahler's Second (first performed 1895) and Third Symphonies (first complete performance 1902). Vienna's wealth of excellent players is demonstrated by the inventive use of ten trumpets in Mahler's Second Symphony ('Resurrection'). The principal players that Mahler and Strauss wrote for were extraordinary individuals who reintroduced the trumpet concerto of Haydn after a century of neglect. The Haydn concerto received its first twentieth-century performance in Vienna in 1908 by Mahler's first trumpet Franz Rossbach, at that time the principal trumpet of the Vienna Philharmonic Orchestra. Strauss's favourite trumpeter, Eduard Seifert, of the Dresden Staatskapelle, then took it up and played it in Dresden in 1914 on a small F trumpet.[1]

The trumpet's milieu was still the orchestra, and new repertoire, mainly by minor composers, was slight in impact. This lack of interest may have been due to the general perception of that period that the cornet was the credible solo instrument, and that the context for cornet solos was popular and vernacular music. This was reinforced by the ragtime and jazz waves breaking over Europe in the period before, during and after the First World War. Ragtime and early jazz bands almost invariably used cornets.

The composers of the Second Viennese School, Arnold Schoenberg, Alban Berg and Anton Webern, built on the orchestral trumpet idiom developed by Mahler and Strauss and were influential in discovering a new range of trumpet colours. Webern rarely wrote for trumpet without mute, and his fastidious ear demanded sensitive technical control and delicacy at extremely soft dynamics from the player in works like the Six Orchestral Pieces Op. 6 (1909/10) (Ex. 11.1) and Concerto for 9

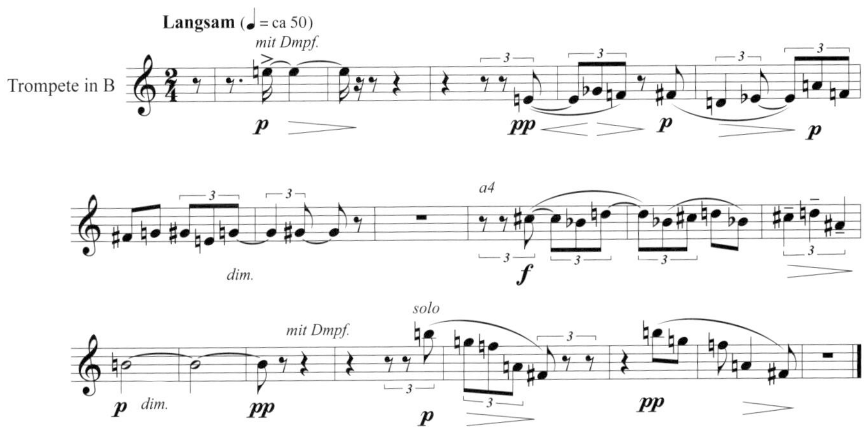

Ex. 11.1 Anton Webern, Six Orchestral Pieces Op. 6, first movement.

Instruments Op. 24 (1934). Schoenberg could write heroically for orchestral trumpet, as in works like *Pelleas und Melisande* Op. 5 (1902/3) and *Gurre-Lieder* (1901/11), but his writing for trumpet is more extreme than anything that went before in the range of dynamics and sudden shifts in nuance demanded. Interlocking trumpet parts, often muted, peppered with a restless mix of *sforzati* and *crescendo/diminuendo*, often with the added edge of flutter tongue, bring a dark, anxious, and sometimes menacing colouration to his orchestral timbre. This can be heard in *Fünf Orchesterstücke* Op. 16 of 1909 (Ex. 11.2a and b).

Berg, especially in his operas *Wozzeck* (1917–22) and *Lulu* (1929–35), stretched the trumpet's technical limits further even than Schoenberg in the search for new modes of expression. Like Mahler, he did not eschew the potency of the vulgar and the vernacular as a source of nostalgia. The opening act of *Wozzeck* contains an offstage

(a)

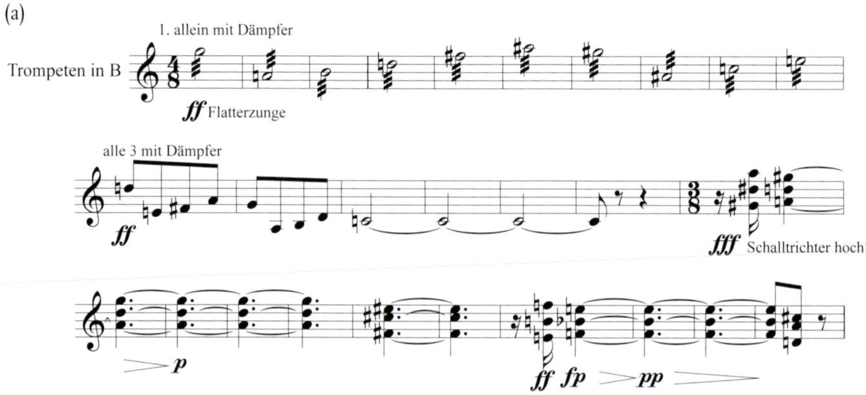

(b)

Exx. 11.2a & b Arnold Schoenberg, *Fünf Orchesterstücke* Op. 16, first movement, Reh. No. 10 (a); second movement, one bar after Reh. No. 1 (b).

military band with two prominent F trumpets playing the sweeping melody, and, in the orchestra, from curtain up, four prominent orchestral trumpets underscoring the moral dilemmas of the plot with a refined sensitivity which is strikingly new (Ex. 11.3).

Lulu has a jazz band on stage with two florid 'jazz' trumpet parts (in addition to 'jazz' trombones and 'jazz' drum kit) taking the bulk of the melodic lead, playing in 'rag-time' (Ex. 11.4).

Ex. 11.3 Alban Berg, *Wozzeck*, Act I, Scene 1, bar 115.

Ex. 11.4 Alban Berg, *Lulu*, Act I, Scene 3, bar 1007.

Berg, like Mahler, wrote trumpet parts that are intrinsically satisfying to play, because they encourage interpretive input from the player. Both Berg and Mahler wrote trumpet parts which possessed moments of exposed isolation and loneliness appearing out of dense orchestral textures. The trumpet solo in Mahler's Ninth Symphony ia a good example (Ex. 11.5).

The lung-bursting climb down from the 'primal scream' trumpet moment in Mahler's Tenth (Ex. 11.6) is another.

Although rewarding to play, if they come off well in performance, such moments, as in the 'Zarathustra leap' of Richard Strauss's *Also Sprach Zarathustra* (1896), need a well-developed control of stage fright in even the most hardened professional player (Ex. 11.7).

Ex. 11.5 Gustav Mahler, Symphony No. 9, third movement ('Rondo Burlesque'), after Reh. No. 36.

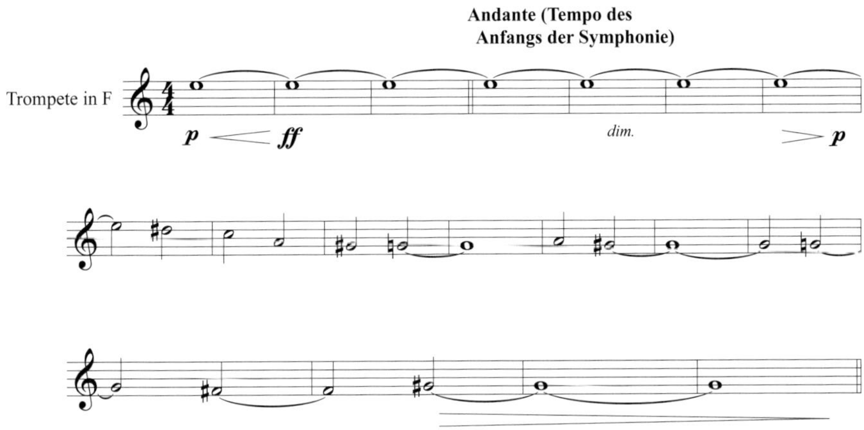

Ex. 11.6 Gustav Mahler, Symphony No. 10, fifth movement (Finale), bar 281.

Ex. 11.7 Strauss, *Also sprach Zarathustra*, one bar after Reh. No. 18.

The muted trumpet solo strands in the final scene of *Wozzeck* help capture the complex duality of the moment: mourning death whilst underscoring the innocence of Marie's orphaned son (Ex. 11.8a and b).

Berg understood the expressive capabilities of the trumpet, and it is a pity he never wrote a trumpet concerto. This Bergian vein of expressionist lyricism is exploited fully

Exx. 11.8a & b Alban Berg, *Wozzeck*, Act III, Scene 5, bar 382 (a); bar 387 (b).

in the Trumpet Concerto written by a Schoenberg pupil, Adolph Weiss, in Los Angeles in 1952.

American composers like Charles Ives wrote majestically for trumpet. In *The Unanswered Question* (1906), Ives, like Berg and Mahler, seems to use the trumpet to embody the notion of the human spirit as a lone voice picking its way through a universe of uncertainty. Elsewhere, as in his orchestral work *Three Places in New England* (1910–14), Ives's uninhibited brass idiom was imported directly from the American military band. Carl Ruggles's exquisitely voiced *Angels* (1921), for six muted trumpets, shows the broad palette of colour opened up by 1920s musical modernity to the trumpet. Elliott Carter, American doyen of modernity, though writing much later, in 1976, developed further this notion of the trumpet signifying freedom of spirit in *A Symphony of Three Orchestras.* The opening solo trumpet soliloquy depicts the freedom of a lone seagull high above Brooklyn Bridge.

The trumpet spreads its wings

Parallel to the Second Viennese School, Stravinsky's writing for trumpet in his ballets for Diaghilev's Ballets Russes, especially *Le sacre du printemps* (*The Rite of Spring*) (1913), had comparable impact. Stravinsky built on his teacher Rimsky-Korsakov's innovative use of the trumpet, from bass to piccolo, creating an arresting, primary-colour, five-part block harmony for the trumpet grouping. The anguished screaming sound produced by muted trumpets when overblown *fortissimo* he used eerily in the final bars of *Petrushka* (1911). Here Stravinsky uses two muted piccolo trumpets in D in major seconds to signify the tortured ghost of the puppet Petrushka. Stravinsky's trumpet writing embraced extremes of mood from exuberant dominance to haunting reticence. His understanding of the instrument's latent potential in orchestral music must have been influenced by the presence in Paris of players like Merri Franquin and Eugène Foveau, and in St Petersburg, by such as Oskar Böhme. The *Petrushka* cornet solo was written for Pyotr Lyamin, who also played in the first performance of *The Rite of Spring* and fulfilled a distinguished career in the Bolshoi Theatre.[2] The following excerpts from *The Rite of Spring* demonstrate that by 1913 the demands on range and technique were now approaching levels not required of trumpet players since the baroque period (Exx. 11.9a–e):

(a)

(b)

Tr. picc.
in Re.
con sord.
Tr. in Do
1.2.3.4
1.2.3.4
2.3.4

(c)

Tr. picc.
in Re
Tr. in Do
1.2.3.4

(d)

Tr. picc.
in Re
Tr. in Do 1
Tr. in Do 2
Tr in Do 3
(non legato)
Tr. in Do 4
sempre

(e)

Exx. 11.9a–e Igor Stravinsky, *Le sacre du printemps (The Rite of Spring)* one bar before Reh. No. 11 (a); four bars before Reh. No. 17 (b); Reh. No. 34 (c); Reh. No. 70 (d); Reh. No. 132 (e).

By the first three decades of the twentieth century, colourful and complex writing for trumpets and cornets abounded in the remarkable series of ballets commissioned by Diaghilev for his Ballets Russes by Maurice Ravel, Claude Debussy, Erik Satie, Manuel De Falla, Sergey Prokofiev, Francis Poulenc and Ottorino Respighi, as well as Stravinsky. Instrumental practice for dance in the theatre rapidly influenced instrumental practice in concert music. By the 1920s composers like Edgard Varèse and Ravel, influenced by *The Rite*, were topping off large trumpet sections with a piccolo trumpet in D, as in *Intégrales* and *Boléro*.[3] The extended high range and the growing exuberance of the trumpet's vocabulary were welcomed by composers. Two examples from as diverse locations as Mexico and Czechoslovakia – Silvestre Revueltas's *Sensemayá* (1938) and Leoš Janáček's *Sinfonietta* (1926) – show the enthusiasm internationally for adventurous trumpet writing.

The cornet was prominent in American popular music, for which there was a fascination in Europe which predated Sousa's introduction of ragtime at the Paris Expo in 1900. American troops, active in France by 1917, marched on duty and danced on leave to syncopated music played by the band of the 369th Infantry Regiment (the 'Harlem Hellfighters'), led by the New York bandleader James Reese Europe. The exuberance of this new imported music, which captivated European audiences, proved seductive to some of the most progressive composers, including Erik Satie, who incorporated ragtime episodes (with a prominent cornet part) into his music for the Diaghilev ballet *Parade*, premiered in Paris, with costumes and sets by Picasso, in 1917. The Swiss conductor Ernest Ansermet heard the clarinetist Sidney Bechet on tour in London in 1919, after a first introduction to jazz in America in 1916.[4] He wrote an insightful report on the new music, and kept his colleague Stravinsky well informed.[5] These developments and the easy access to the new dance styles provided by the gramophone and sheet music influenced composers, especially the avant-garde, who had their finger on the popular pulse of the times.[6] The eleven-piece band of Stravinsky's *Ragtime* (1918) contains a cornet, as does the smaller six-piece group of *Histoire du soldat* (*Soldier's Tale*) (1918), in which the princess of the story dances ragtime and tango.

In *Façade* (1921/22), full of early jazz inflection and dance band influence, William Walton replaces cornet with a wide-ranging and flexible C trumpet, as does Darius Milhaud's jazz parody *La création du monde* of 1923, in which two trumpets are used. Milhaud's band is bigger than Walton's, in the emerging style of dance orchestra typified by Paul Whiteman. The 1927 ballet *Kuchyňská revue* (*La revue de cuisine*) by Bohuslav Martinů, by then resident in Paris, was again for a smaller band, sporting a Charleston and a prominent jazzy B flat trumpet part (Ex. 11.10). It was this liberated idiom of the trumpet which made most impact on the progressive composers of the 1920s.

The slow growth of solo repertoire

The revival of the Haydn concerto by influential trumpeters such as Rossbach in Vienna, Seifert in Dresden, and Goeyens in Brussels only began to take root after a gap of some twenty years, and was seminal to the rediscovery of a largely forgotten earlier solo repertoire for the trumpet. It was not until 1929 that the Haydn concerto appeared in print, in an edition by Goeyens with piano reduction; a full score appeared in Berlin in 1931.[7] The dislocation and discontinuity of the period around World War I is, of course, a major reason for the slow dissemination of Haydn's concerto and the lack of growth of the trumpet as a solo instrument in classical music.

During the first decade of the twentieth century, the trumpet accrued only a small cachet of solo repertoire around some of the leading players of the day. Charles Bordes wrote a *Divertissement for Solo Trumpet and Strings* for Théo Charlier in 1902, and Georges Enesco wrote his *Légende* for Merri Franquin as a Paris Conservatoire *morceau de concours* in 1906. Seifert was in considerable demand as a soloist, but his repertory did not consist, in the main, of original compositions for trumpet. As a solo instrument, the cornet was still popular. Seifert also played cornet, and a flavour of his large repertory is given by the following sample: his own *Variationen über Der alte Dessauer*, Oskar Böhme's shorter pieces, Hartmann's *Facilita*, Arban's *Fantasie brillante*, Levy's *Levy–Athen* Polka, Paul Wiggert's *Klänge aus Schottland*, fantasies, romances, and operatic transcriptions.[8] The trumpet concertos in his repertoire included Oskar Böhme's

Ex. 11.10 Bohuslav Martinů, *La revue de cuisine*, third movement, 'Charleston', three bars after Reh. No. 4.

E minor of 1899, plus another four by the composers Oskar Geier, Paul Pfitzner, Richard Stöhr and S. Stapf. Although the re-emergence of the Haydn concerto demonstrated the desire of leading players to create solo art music repertory early in the century, the first solo sonatas of substance for trumpet and piano only appeared in the thirties after the trumpet came to prominence in jazz.

When Paul Hindemith wrote his Trumpet Sonata in 1939, in American exile, his intention was simple: to expand the instrument's repertory. This is a work steeped in the mainstream idiom of the trumpet, contrasting by turns the heroic and funereal, the bucolic and melancholic. It is a true duo sonata with a sweeping lyricism and a haunting final chorale, apt for the time it was written, *Alle menschen müssen sterben* ('All people must die'). Large-scale works for solo trumpet had already been contemplated elsewhere: in Vienna, Karl Pilss had written his Sonata (1935) for a successor of Rossbach, Helmut Wobisch (1912–80). A year earlier, he had composed a concerto for another Vienna Philharmonic principal trumpet, Franz Dengler (1890–1963). Pilss directed the Vienna Trompetenchor, for which, in 1943, Richard Strauss wrote his most extended, quasi-concertante trumpet solo in *Festmusik der Stadt Wien*.[9] In the same year, Rutland Boughton wrote a nostalgic Elgarian concerto for performance by William Overton (*c.*1911–76) of the BBC Symphony Orchestra. Because of the upheaval of total war in Europe, however, it was not until the 1950s that the creation of new solo repertory started to gather real momentum.[10]

As an unforeseen consequence, players active in classical music benefited from the rapid ascendance of the solo voice of the trumpet in jazz. It became less unusual to hear a trumpet soloist in a classical concert, and the Haydn concerto came to rapid prominence in the immediate postwar period through the medium of gramophone recordings by George Eskdale (2nd and 3rd movements; Columbia, 1939), Harry Mortimer (Columbia, 1946) and Helmut Wobisch (Haydn Society, 1951). At the same time, there began a steady stream of new compositions for solo trumpet. Berndt Alois Zimmerman wrote the one-movement concerto, *Nobody knows de trouble I see*, in 1954, and Iain Hamilton wrote *Concerto for Jazz Trumpet* in 1958. The trumpet writing in both was heavily influenced by the jazz trumpet idiom. Although George Swift (1911–86), Britain's answer to Harry James, played the first performance of Hamilton's concerto at the Royal Festival Hall in the 1958 BBC Light Music Festival, the soloist for Zimmerman's concerto was the classical specialist Adolf Scherbaum, who played the first performance in 1955 with the North German Radio Orchestra in Hamburg. National and state radio orchestras could afford to be more adventurous in their programming policy and were significant patrons of new music from the postwar period. Scherbaum's solo career blossomed from his first orchestral position in Brno in 1930, through the Berlin Philharmonic with Furtwängler in wartime, to Hans Schmidt-Isserstedt's North German Radio Orchestra, from which he retired to concentrate on his solo career in 1964.

Adolf Scherbaum was the first classical trumpet soloist in the mid-twentieth-century postwar period to make a sustained impact in Europe, and this was largely due to his astonishing facility in the upper register of the instrument. The re-emergence of a general perception that the trumpet could play in the extreme high register was facilitated by the example of players like Dizzy Gillespie in bebop and Cat Anderson

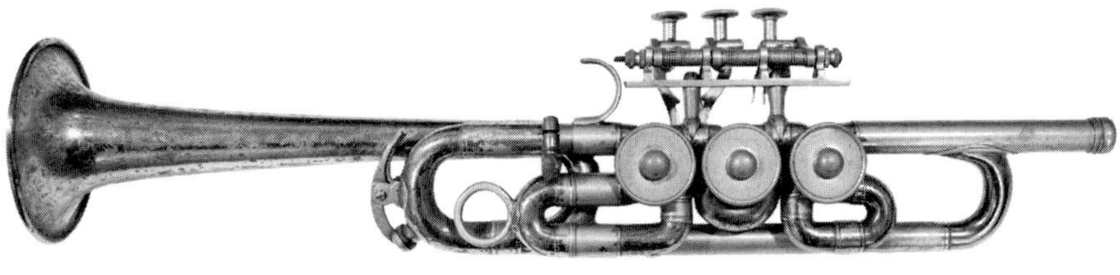

11.1 Piccolo trumpet in B flat by Scherzer (c.1950). (Photograph by Kenneth Dundas)

(1916–81) in Duke Ellington's Band. Scherbaum's solo career was founded on his ability to play the trumpet part of Bach's Brandenburg Concerto No. 2 with accuracy and flair in the original octave on a piccolo B flat trumpet made by Scherzer of Augsburg. Scherzer manufactured these trumpets with redundant, 'blind' tubing, perhaps to disguise their small size, in order to make them look more dignified and substantial in keeping with the seriousness of the repertoire they were designed to play (Ill. 11.1). During his career, Scherbaum made fourteen recordings of this concerto, playing it over 400 times in concert.[11] The care he took in preparation, surely one of the secrets behind his sustained success, is shown by his own handwritten manuscript of the Zimmerman concerto, complete with Zimmerman's painstakingly annotated jazz inflections[12] (Ill. 11.2).

Some additions to trumpet technique beyond shakes and trills could not be communicated through conventional notation. The need grew for composers to devise special markings and invent special dictions to communicate to the player how

11.2 Closing pages of Adolf Scherbaum's manuscript copy of the solo part of B. A. Zimmerman's 'Nobody knows de trouble I see'. (By permission of MDS, on behalf of Schott Music Limited, and courtesy of Elfriede Scherbaum)

they wanted a passage to be played. In *Nobody knows de trouble I see*, shakes, trills and arrows pointing glissandos upwards and falls downwards, with footnoted instructions, signpost the characteristics of trumpet players in the Armstrong tradition.

Maurice André, doyen of classical soloists

As trailblazer, Adolf Scherbaum studied at the Military Music School in Prague in the 1920s, finishing his studies with Franz Dengler in Vienna in 1929. Few trumpet players up to and after this time graduated to orchestras solely through a formal conservatory route. A band background, whether military, brass or Salvation Army, was more usual. In these different band environments, some of which were overtly competitive, many players developed an extraordinary facility, and, as we have seen, composers were inspired to write for them.

Maurice André, the most successful classical trumpet soloist of the twentieth century, received his first cornet and early training from his father, a miner and gifted amateur trumpet player. At the age of fourteen he followed his father into the mine, but continued his trumpet studies and four years later, in 1951, entered the class of Raymond Sabarich (1909–66) at the Paris Conservatoire. By the end of his second year of study at the Conservatoire, André had won a *premier prix* for both cornet and trumpet. He entered into an orchestral career in 1953, but success in international competitions paved the way for the glittering solo career that was to follow.

There was a postwar boom of excellent trumpet players in every genre by the 1950s. Maurice André had to face very stiff competition to win the Geneva International Competition in 1955 and the ARD Wettbewerb in Munich in 1963. André was to go on to become a celebrity among trumpet players and the musical world more generally. He became an icon of taste because of his supreme artistry. He achieved the level of refinement that the constituency of professional players aspired to. Above all, he expressed himself effectively through lyricism. Although André played and recorded an enormously wide-ranging and diverse repertoire in all styles of music, including many twentieth-century works (some of which he commissioned), the public demand, stimulated through the medium of long-playing records, was for his performances of transcribed oboe, violin and flute sonatas, concertos and suites by baroque composers.[13] André played these transcriptions with unparalleled ease and fluidity on Selmer piccolo trumpets in B flat, A and G. Within a few years, these small Selmer piccolo trumpets had become accepted as an indispensable part of every professional trumpeter's equipment for the repertoire of the baroque trumpet. Having a mouthpiece with a smaller cup, tighter backbore and sharper rim than in normal orchestral use, these small trumpets brought most of the baroque repertoire within the expected capability of the professional player. André went on to enjoy a stellar international career, commanding some of the highest fees for a soloist of his era.

André was one of the first solo classical artists to use microphone technique, the recording studio, and post-production processes in the quest for perfection. One of the present authors played in recording sessions with the Philharmonia Orchestra conducted by Riccardo Muti in Abbey Road Studios, accompanying André in the

Haydn Concerto.[14] André sat throughout, bell close to the microphone. He faced the orchestra, but some distance from it, to stop the sound 'bleeding' from the orchestra into his microphone. He played rarely above an unforced *mp*. In the studio, the musical result was unbalanced; yet in the control room the musical result was revelatory: the balance was perfect, and the bloom on the trumpet sound radiant. André was a true *recording artist*. Herbert von Karajan was one of the first conductors to use close editing to chase the elusive goal of 'perfection' in his recorded interpretations through choosing the best takes and inserting ever smaller corrective 'tags'. André's recording of Hummel's concerto with von Karajan and the Berlin Philharmonic became a best seller.[15] With recordings like this, André's playing defined for many across the world the way that the solo classical trumpet idiom was understood.

The less positive part of André's legacy was the creation of a general orthodoxy which grew out of his personal playing style. He attained, virtually, the status of a cult figure. It became difficult to give trumpet players first prize in international competitions, because they fell short of André and the ideal of 'perfection' as registered on his many long-playing records. After André, there was a forty-year gap before a first prize was again awarded to a trumpeter at the ARD Wettbewerb in Munich. David Guerrier (b.1984) was the winner in 2003.[16] The policy of the long-serving ARD competition director (he had retired by 2003) not to give first prizes contributed to the mystique and aura surrounding those exceptional few selected, like Maurice André, as first-prize winners in the 1960s: they included the oboists Heinz Holliger and Maurice Bourgue, and the sopranos Ileana Cotrubas and Jessye Norman.

Despite the dominant position André came to assume, the 1950s and the 1960s saw a proliferation of trumpet soloists, many of whom branched out from their base in an orchestra, where the growth of co-principal systems gave players licence to mix their orchestral responsibilities with solo tours and projects.[17] The growth of chamber orchestras playing baroque and classical repertoire also meant that a good living could be made in freelance work for trumpeters. Roger Delmotte (b.1925) and Pierre Thibaud (1929–2004) were slightly older contemporaries of André, with prominent solo careers. Though André became the most visible, the work of Delmotte and Thibaud, through their teaching at the Paris Conservatoire, laid the foundations for the techniques of the soloists of the latter part of the twentieth century. About 900 trumpet students went through Delmotte and Thibaud's hands over four decades, and they placed hundreds of students in different positions throughout the music world.

The avant-garde

One of the successor generation to André, Markus Stockhausen, was born into an environment charged with creativity in 1957. His father, Karlheinz Stockhausen, though not the first composer of the avant-garde to exploit the trumpet, had a consolidating effect on the instrument's future use in extreme modernism. Through the works Karlheinz wrote for his performer/composer son, Markus became an important influence on the idiom of the trumpet in the second half of the twentieth century. Among brass players, trombonists had been the first to attract the attention of avant-garde composers, with Stuart Dempster inspiring Luciano Berio to write his groundbreaking *Sequenza V* in 1966. Karlheinz Stockhausen's presence in Darmstadt and Cologne provided a focus for a Europe-wide avant-garde movement for a period in the 1950s which radiated new techniques and new practice. One of the new avant-garde composers, Vinko Globokar, was also an astounding trombonist, and his *Discours II* (1967–8) for five trombones broke further new ground for brass players. Yet more complex demands on virtuosity and stamina were made by Iannis Xenakis in his extraordinary setting for piano, two trumpets and three trombones, *Eonta* (1962–4). The first trumpet part at one point has 150 consecutive high C6's, the last six of which are flutter tongued.

Extreme complexity was typical of the 1960s and 70s. Stockhausen's music became simpler and more monumental as his career progressed and his influence on the avant-garde waned in the final decades of the twentieth century. After an initial allegiance to the concept of total serialism, Stockhausen went on to embrace the influence of John Cage's aleatory techniques and the ensemble performance methods of Mauricio Kagel. At around the same time, the free improvisation championed by jazz saxophonist Ornette Coleman, heard to brilliant effect in his *Free Jazz* album of 1960, was a big influence on Stockhausen and the avant-garde. Markus grew into a precociously mature improvising artist in his teens. He made his jazz début in 1974, aged seventeen, at the Newcomer Jazz Festival in Frankfurt, and his classical début in 1976 in his father's musical drama *Sirius* at the Bicentennial celebrations in Washington DC. His father wrote *Aries*, which came out of *Sirius*, for his son's twentieth birthday in 1977 and, from that point, Markus, with the trumpet as his voice, became one of the main characters – Michael – in the largest operatic project since Wagner, *Die Sieben Tage der Woche*, with an opera composed for each day of the week. *Donnerstag* (1978–81) was the first day to be performed in its entirety at La Scala, Milan, on 3 April 1981. In 1981 Markus also became the winner of the Deutscher Musikwettbewerb, a coveted and prestigious competition open to every young instrumentalist in Germany under the age of thirty. *Licht* came to be composed in modular fashion, and parts of *Donnerstag* featuring Markus had already been given as separate works in concert performance, and in several different configurations: *Michaels Reise um die Erde* (1978), *Eingang und Formel* (1978), *Mission und Himmelfahrt* (1978), *Michaels Jugend* (1978–9), and *Michaels Heimkehr* (1979).

The complete seven days of the opera were not finished until 2003. It remains unperformed in its entirety because of its horizon-stretching demands. Whether this enormous work, with a solo trumpeter, representing the character Michael, at its heart, will overcome the practical obstacles of performance to become a vehicle for twenty-first century trumpet soloists remains to be seen at the time of writing.

The new trumpet player and the specialist modern chamber ensemble

Avant-garde composers created the need for a new type of flexible ensemble for the performance of their emerging repertory. At one level it can be seen as a virtuoso chamber orchestra, but in fact it was a small ensemble of a type that had specialisms in terms of technique and knowledge of notations that had not been previously necessary. It was this type of ensemble that was the focus for much of the idiomatic developments that led to the creation of some of the most original solo writing for trumpet.

Various forms of state sponsorship backed the formation of these ensembles in Europe because of their seminal link to the development of musical creativity. Many, perhaps most, of the players attracted to play in these groups were not just adept and fit for the very particular purposes that were required of them; they also had qualities and personalities that attracted them to musical experimentation. They were curious, broadly educated players with marked qualities of leadership. The subsequent careers of many of these players provide some evidence for this.

Kagel and Stockhausen were among the first to build up their own ensembles. Stockhausen formed his first small group in 1964, initially to perform *Mikrophonie I*. Increasingly thereafter he wrote for a small group of musicians, and from around 1975 the clarinettist Suzanne Stephens and his own children Markus (trumpet), Majella (piano) and Simon (keyboards) became prominent. This close-knit 'family of musicians' approach became influential, and, similar to the practice cultivated by Duke Ellington on the road and in the recording studio over the previous four decades, Kagel and Stockhausen began to develop their new music through intensive immersion and interaction with performers in rehearsal. Both wrote for groupings of instruments in a new way, often with live electronic interaction, with musicians increasingly used as interdisciplinary artists in non-traditional settings. Concurrently, the new beat groups of popular music began to make their rock albums in a similar collective and immersive way, and it is telling that Stockhausen was one of the hero images on the cover of the Beatles 1967 album, *Sgt. Pepper's Lonely Hearts Club Band.* Stockhausen called this flexible approach to instrumentation, mixing synthesizers and amplified instruments, a 'modern orchestra'. The trumpet's focused timbre excelled in the sound envelope of electronic and amplified instruments diffused through a powerful sound system. One of Kagel's trumpet collaborators in his Cologne-based Ensemble for New Music was Edward H. Tarr. Kagel dedicated the solo pieces *Atem* (1970) and *Morceau de concours* (1972) to Tarr. Tarr's centrality to the construction of a coherent historic repertory for the trumpet has already been discussed. Less well known is his early involvement with the avant-garde.

The London Sinfonietta was founded in 1968 by conductor David Atherton and musical entrepreneur Nicholas Snowman to play the music of the twentieth century, based on a small and flexible fourteen-player instrumentation of string quintet, woodwind quartet, brass trio, percussion and keyboards. Similar groups, with their own concert series, soon proliferated in other cities: the Schoenberg Ensemble founded in Amsterdam in 1974, the Ensemble Intercontemporaine in Paris in 1976, and the Ensemble Modern in Frankfurt in 1980. The organic growth of opportunities like this were part of the developments in a growing musical marketplace. For example, leading principal trumpet players in London like Elgar Howarth (b.1935) and Howard Snell left the relative security and predictability of their symphony orchestras – the Royal Philharmonic and London Symphony respectively – to play with small groups like the London Sinfonietta, in an exciting and new open market during the late 1960s and mid 1970s. Both went on to become conductors, arrangers, and important initiators of change in the British and European brass scene. This pattern of players establishing a reputation first in a symphony orchestra, then branching out to assemble a portfolio career, was replicated in other centres throughout the world.

Trumpet players at the heart of these new developments turned the trickle of new works for trumpet from the early 1970s into a strong current by the end of the decade. Principal trumpet chairs in the late 1960s and early 1970s began to be occupied by highly individualistic players with a spirit of adventure. Gordon Webb (b.1937) of the London Philharmonic and Howard Snell of the London Symphony commissioned Iain Hamilton, who had written his concerto for George Swift a decade earlier, to write an exuberant work for two trumpets and orchestra entitled *Circus* (1969). Gerard Schwarz (b.1947), renowned for his florid technique at the Juilliard School, before becoming first trumpet of the New York Philharmonic, commissioned and recorded Lucy Dlugoszewski's *Space is a Diamond* (1970), notable for its four and a half octave range, multiphonics, and new muting and tonguing techniques. Gunther Schuller wrote his virtuosic, Ellington-influenced Concerto for Trumpet and Chamber Orchestra for Schwarz in 1979. By that time, Schwarz was embarking on a conducting career and Schuller's concerto remained unperformed until John Wallace played it with the composer and the BBC Symphony Orchestra in 1982. The concert was never broadcast and the concerto sank from view, although its quality and appeal is such that it deserves revival. On the other hand, Stanley Friedman's strikingly influential *Solus* (1975), the first written-down piece to make a feature of deconstructing the trumpet, became a classic, winning over young players to the new trumpet. Deconstruction involved removing parts of the trumpet and playing it while incomplete, in this case removing selected valve slides and using special fingering to redirect the air through the valve slide openings to achieve distorted timbral effects. Friedman came into contact with many of the USA's finest young trumpeting talents from his teaching position at the Interlochen Academy of Arts, one of America's most prominent specialist schools. Interlochen prepared the way to conservatoire for many music students and Friedman was an important factor in opening hearts and minds to the trumpet's new capabilities in North America. Robert Erickson's *Kryl*, written in 1977, was a work deemed impossible to play when it was written, and owing to the enlightened attitudes of composer/performer/teachers like Friedman is now demystified to the point that there is a clear learning journey to play such repertoire for a young player. A small but influential group of trumpet players migrated from playing into management and administrative positions in orchestras and arts organisations which commissioned new works. This may have had some bearing on the intellectual credibility and the growth in esteem of the trumpet as a solo instrument internationally. Conradin Groth (b.1947) became chairman as well as principal trumpet of the Berlin Philharmonic; Howard Snell was first trumpet and chairman of the London Symphony Orchestra when Hans Werner Henze wrote his *Sonatina* (1974) for solo trumpet for him; Gordon Webb was chairman of the London Philharmonic Orchestra at the same time as ex-principal trumpet, Eric Bravington, was its managing director.

Increasing dialogue between composers and trumpet players led to more solo works being written. The trumpet, as one of the loudest voices in the orchestra, is an important factor in shaping the sound of any orchestra. In an era of global competitiveness between orchestras, the 'string sound' or the 'brass sound' became a reason for choosing one recording over another. Many principal trumpets, with Adolph Herseth, principal trumpet of the Chicago Symphony Orchestra for more than fifty years, the most notable, came to be celebrated as part of the unique sound and distinctiveness through which the orchestra was sold to recording companies and international tour promoters. Thomas Stevens (b.1938) of the Los Angeles Philharmonic was another, lauded for his refinement, superlative technique and taste. Luciano Berio was commissioned by Ernest Fleischman, the Los Angeles Philharmonic Chief Executive, to write his *Sequenza X* for trumpet and piano resonance (1984) for Stevens. Works like those by Henze, Erickson and Berio pushed the boundaries of what was achievable by a solo trumpet.

By the mid 1980s a new generation of players had come to prominence and one in particular gained rapid international recognition, Håkan Hardenberger (b.1961), a student first of Bo Nilsson (b.1940) in Malmö and then Pierre Thibaud at the Paris Conservatoire. Hardenberger formulated a clear idea of developing his own career, advised by Elgar Howarth in London and Thomas Stevens in Los Angeles. In establishing his solo career, Hardenberger differentiated himself from other soloists through creating his own repertoire. The trajectory of his career was based on his advocacy of new compositions for trumpet to the musical public, and he set about commissioning works to challenge audiences to listen to the trumpet afresh. In 1986/87 Harrison Birtwistle wrote *Endless Parade* for Hardenberger and, after the première with Paul Sacher and the Lucerne Festival Orchestra, Hardenberger proceeded to play this groundbreaking work with orchestras all over the world, his high-voltage performing style making an indelible impression on the concert-going public. Subsequently, he commissioned many composers to write for him, and the most played of these later concertos is perhaps *Aeriel* by H. K. Gruber, premiered with Neeme Järvi and the BBC Symphony Orchestra at the BBC Proms in 1999.

In Europe, from the late 1980s, given a proliferation of solo opportunities and the emergence of a new generation of exciting young players, there was a greater willingness among audiences to listen to new works for trumpet and for composers to devote serious time to creating major works for the instrument. After the success of Birtwistle's *Endless Parade*, Sir Peter Maxwell Davies (1988) and James MacMillan (1993) wrote two of the most substantial trumpet concertos for one of the present authors, John Wallace. The Maxwell Davies concerto was first performed in Hiroshima in 1988 with the Philharmonia Orchestra and Giuseppe Sinopoli, and MacMillan's work, *Epiclesis*, was first performed at the Edinburgh International Festival with the Philharmonia conducted by Leonard Slatkin in 1993. The MacMillan and Maxwell Davies concertos are significant milestones. The MacMillan has a striking opening, beginning before the applause has died down as the soloist and conductor walk on stage, and continues with a long accompanied cadenza which sets a mystical, transcendental atmosphere.

In 1994–5, Mark Antony Turnage wrote a double trumpet concerto for Hardenberger, Wallace and the Philharmonia, *Dispelling the Fears*, conducted by Daniel Harding (formerly a trumpet student before taking up conducting), which forms the closing part of *Blood on the Floor*, a substantial nine-movement piece which includes three jazz soloists and large ensemble.[18] Gruber, in *Aeriel*, pushed the boundaries further in projecting advanced contemporary playing techniques to a mainstream art music audience. *Aeriel* featured multiphonics (in this instance singing and playing simultaneously to get three-part chords), deconstructing the trumpet, as in the Friedman, to give a counterpoint of tone colours, and playing the cowhorn and piccolo trumpet in addition to the standard trumpet. *Aerial* was also uninhibited in its technical demands and use of a wide range (Exx. 11.11a and b).

The use of two staves by Gruber to notate his multilayered trumpet parts highlights the fact that was brought to our attention earlier in Zimmerman's *Nobody knows de trouble I see.* Avant-garde and jazz use of the trumpet had broken through the boundaries of what could be conventionally notated and new dictions were necessary to notate elements of the new trumpet vocabulary. Thomas Adès, in *Living Toys* for fourteen instruments Op. 9 (1993), included phonetics under each note of his plunger-muted 'talking trumpet' part. Graphic and proportional notation, as used by Tim Souster in *The Transistor Radio of St Narcissus* (1983) for flugelhorn and live electronics, became a common method of communicating to the performer the intention of the composer in aleatory and improvisatory music[19] (Ex. 11.12).

Contemporaneous with Hardenberger, there was a proliferation of individualistic and idiosyncratic young players who could play with a new extended technical facility: Reinhold Friedrich (b.1958) from Germany and Ole Edvard Antonsen (b.1962) from Norway became prominent internationally.[20] In Finland, Jouko Harjanne (b.1962) commissioned much new Finnish repertoire and Italy's Gabriele Cassone (b.1959), a fervent advocate of Berio's *Sequenza X*, inspired Berio to realise an orchestral version of this *Sequenza: Kol-Od (Chains VI)* (1996). A tipping point had been reached, leading to a shift in perception of what was achievable by a solo trumpet. The American

(a)

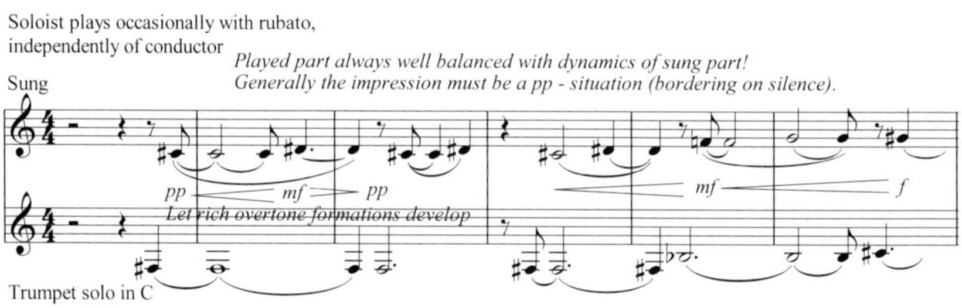

(b)

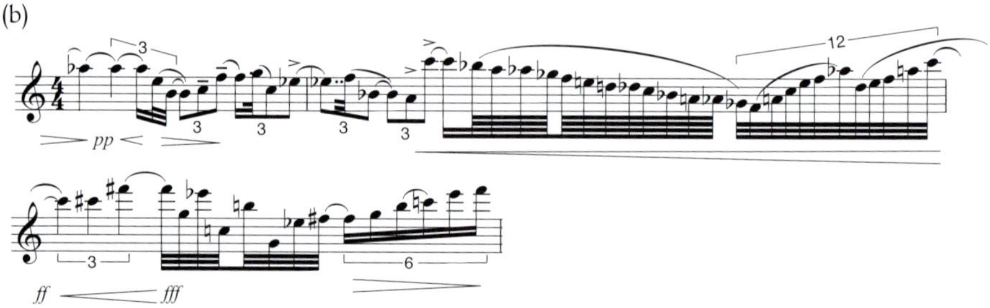

Exx. 11.11a & b H. K. Gruber, *Aeriel*, first movement, bars 3–8(a); first movement, bars 12–14(b).

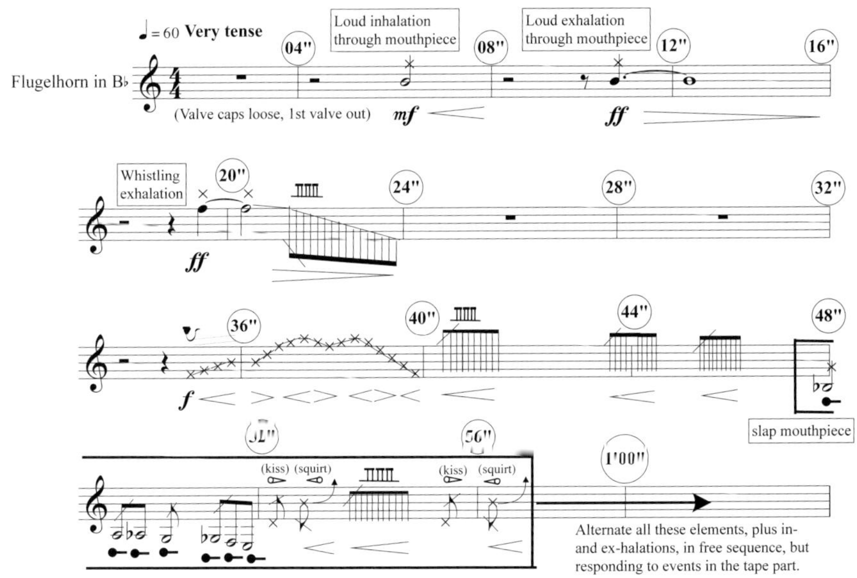

Ex. 11.12 Tim Souster, *The Transistor Radio of St Narcissus.*

virtuoso Stephen Burns (b.1959), who won the Maurice André competition in 1988, arranged his own solo version of Mussorgsky's *Pictures at an Exhibition,* for trumpet, cornet, flugelhorn, piccolo trumpet, bass trumpet, and piano. He also wrote and commissioned music for a wide range of instrumental ensembles up to and including multimedia.[21] The career pattern of the trumpet player had been transformed in the thirty-three years since André's Geneva competition win of 1955. Many players developed a portfolio career of solo and ensemble opportunities mixed with a teaching post, or an orchestral position with flexible working patterns.

The brass ensemble

Brass chamber music provided another opportunity for trumpet players ambitious to exploit the mobility of their instrument across genres. The Philip Jones Brass Ensemble (PJBE) in the UK and the American Brass Quintet in the USA became pioneers of a new vogue for brass chamber music which had its origins in the 1950s.[22] An international market for brass ensembles became viable largely through the crossover nature of their programming. This flourished in the work of Canadian Brass. Fred Mills (1935–2009) contrasted lightness of touch on piccolo trumpet with the red-blooded flair of Ronnie Romm (b.1946) on the B flat trumpet. The American Brass Quintet commissioned the classic of the genre, Malcolm Arnold's *Quintet for Brass* Op. 73 (1961), and along with the PJBE and Canadian Brass, they built such a vogue for brass quintet that most student brass players at conservatoire belonged to one. It became possible to leave the symphony orchestra for an international circuit, where the personal rewards – financial, musical and reputational – could prove greater than being buried in the collective of an orchestra. Rolf Smedvig (b.1952) left the Boston Symphony Orchestra to form Empire Brass, with which he toured extensively, setting a gold standard in quintet performance. Brass chamber music gave trumpet players the opportunity to develop idiosyncratic careers in line with their own characteristic talent. The remarkable Läubin brothers, Hannes (b.1958), Bernhard (b.1959) and Wolfgang (b.1965), as well as pursuing their separate orchestral and solo careers, were members of German Brass, which took a ten-piece brass ensemble format developed initially by Philip Jones to new levels of virtuosity in a competitive environment in Europe which included groups like London Brass, the Wallace Collection and World Brass.

Many of the composers discussed in this chapter had been drawn into writing for solo trumpet after writing for brass more generally. The vogue for brass ensembles depended on their staple repertoire of light popular music played normally in the second half of the programme. However, brass ensembles craved artistic recognition and the challenge of credible repertoire by established composers. Elliott Carter wrote for the American Brass Quintet in 1974, and Maxwell Davies was commissioned in 1981 by Rolf Smedvig and the Harvard Musical Association to write his Brass Quintet for Empire Brass. For the first public performance in the Town Hall, New York, Maxwell Davies wrote:

> It attempts to provide the repertory with a work of real chamber music, in so far as the players are involved in the intimate kind of music-making associated with a string quartet, requiring exactly the same kind of responsibility and musical intelligence. This goes beyond the obvious extreme virtuosity of playing – all of which makes this perhaps the most demanding brass quintet to date, bearing in mind that it requires about half-an-hour's extreme concentration on the part of players and listeners alike.[23]

Stockhausen's former assistant, Tim Souster, wrote prolifically for brass: *Equalisation* for Equale Brass and live electronics in 1980, *Rabbit Heaven* for English Brass in 1986, *Echos* for Besses o' th' Barn Band and live electronics in 1990, and *La Marche* for Fine Arts Brass in 1993. This last piece personifies the first trumpet in the quintet as Margaret Thatcher, the second as Josef Stalin, the horn as Che Guevara, the trombone as Adolf Hitler, and the tuba as Chairman Mao. In constructing a successful brass quintet concert, the theatrical and entertainment element was eventually to become as important as the music.

Orthodoxy and the limits of technique

In a century which saw the development of new techniques and the creation of new musical languages (in both the popular and art music spheres) and the emergence of virtuosos who changed the paradigm of what is possible, a question arises about what the idiom of the trumpet actually is. Is there an orthodox idiom and is there something beyond that which can only be entered by players of exceptional ability? We have seen in previous chapters that the composers of the baroque wrote for a very small select group of trumpet players. The virtuoso clarino register was something that was often assigned to players in a highly personalised way and composers knew the capabilities of the players assigned to their parts. Many of the new pieces from the second half of the twentieth century were deemed similarly rarefied – impossible to play except only by a few very specially gifted players endowed with an exceptional technique. Many players, through adopting trumpet training methods and regimes, like those of Carmine Caruso (1904–87), Jerome Callet (b.1930), Rolf Quinque (b.1927) or Vladimir Pushkarev (b.1954),[24] aspired to play almost the entire range of the piano keyboard on the trumpet. Conventional wisdom, however, still held that this extended range was abnormal even in professional circles and well beyond the limits of the amateur player and younger student. The orthodox 'safe' range was later mirrored in electronic notation software like Sibelius when notes below 'bottom' C4 on trumpet and notes above G5 were coloured red to denote they were to be used sparingly. The guidance of most teachers which fed the progression of learners was that the extremes of range were harmful to the young player. Indeed, the expectation was that, if the young player was stretched too far too soon, the consequences could be ruinous for long-term success on the trumpet. In fact, as many young players not yet in their teens showed, as evidenced by both Giuliano Sommerhalder (b.1985) from Switzerland and David Guerrier from France, with excellent teaching and careful guidance, and some thousands of hours of practice condensed into the early years, much as on any other instrument, trumpet players were capable of aspiring to a far wider range than that of orthodox expectation. Giuliano was taught initially by his father Max Sommerhalder (b.1947), and Guerrier by Pierre Dutout (b.1946), both of whom were trumpet teachers and performers of considerable standing. By the 2010 version of the Sibelius software, Sibelius 6, the range warning had been refined to an amber colour, and began at E3 at the lower end and F sharp6 at the high end, reflecting changing expectations.

Stamina was allied to range and was generally predicated on the number of thoughtful hours spent daily in a training regime. This involved breaking down the components of technique into simple elements like buzzing, deep breathing, practising long notes, lip flexibilities, pedal notes, extended range scales and arpeggios, in order to develop the necessary muscle strength, the focus, and the mental resilience to be able to attempt the new repertoire of the trumpet. Many of the unaccompanied pieces from the 1960s and 70s in the Appendix, by composers like Wolpe, Rautavaara, Pousseur, Lang, Scelsi, Arnold and Sommerfeldt, were no more than four or five minutes long. New standards of physicality, however, were continuing to be set by the virtuosos of jazz. The capacity for the trumpet to play for longer and to break through the orthodox barriers of range and stamina was highly visible and audible in the freer world of jazz. That was a primary reason for the greater weight of expectation on a trumpeter's range and stamina.

Despite the rapid evolution in technique described above, didactic literature for children remained traditionally melodic, based on popular classical and folk melodies. In the USA, the growth of the high school band movement during the 1920s, with the support of the musical instrument firm Conn, led to the publication of a wealth of didactic material. Some of the American teaching methods, notably Paul Herfurth's *A Tune a Day* series of tutors, were adopted elsewhere, including the UK, when formal school instrumental lessons provided by local authority music services supplemented the organic systems of teaching offered by brass bands. The present authors, growing up in the British brass band tradition in the 1950s and 60s, played marches, hymn tunes and folk melodies in a junior band, which formed a rudimentary group lesson.

In parts of Europe with highly developed networks of music schools and local conservatoires, tutors such as Arban's remained the bedrock of initial training. Attempts at innovation, like Jean-Pierre Mathez's three-volume trumpet method for Universal Edition, piloted in 1976, did not gain widespread acceptance.[25] Mathez's tutor was ahead of its time, beginning with improvisation and graphic notation. Children, however, seemingly had to be protected from contemporary developments.

Conservatoires too were slow to grasp change, despite the potential of the proximity of performers to composers in their environment and their subsequent important position in the development of repertoire. The *morceaux de concours* adopted at the Paris Conservatoire were still the most widely distributed pieces in the trumpet repertoire. Partially in reaction to the inhibiting effect of prescribed repertoire, well-attended new music clubs proliferated from the 1950s at conservatoires despite official disapproval, leading to interesting new repertoire. The Royal Manchester College (now the Royal Northern College of Music) spawned the Op. 1 Trumpet Sonata of Maxwell Davies for Elgar Howarth and John Ogdon in 1955. At the same time, innovative trumpet music by Cornelius Cardew and Richard Rodney Bennett emerged at the Royal Academy of Music in performance by the composers and Howard Snell.[26]

Is there a limit to the range and endurance of the trumpet player? Experience of the twentieth century and the example of jazz-based artists like Arturo Sandoval (b.1949) and James Morrison (b.1962) would suggest otherwise. The trumpet, formerly an instrument which in classical music played in stanzas with frequent rests for recovery, has to be played all night every night all over the range if a sustained professional career in jazz has to be maintained. And although, in 'straight' trumpet playing, pieces like Henze's *Sonatine* (1974), Erickson's *Kryl* (1977), Smalley's *Echo III* (1978) or Berio's *Sequenza X* (1984) were regarded as being impossibly daunting when they were first written, learning pathways were quickly plotted to make these works achievable. Thirty years after these works were first performed, at the 2009 Chosen Vale trumpet seminars in New Hampshire, USA, organised by the inspirational American performer/teacher Ed Carroll (b.1953), at which Gabriele Cassone, Håkan Hardenberger, Thomas Stevens, Mark Gould (b.1947) and John Wallace provided the teaching faculty, the starting point for many of the students was playing the Berio and Erickson works from memory. The work of Ed Carroll has been seminal to the creation of a new generation of adventurous young trumpet players since his work at the Rotterdam Conservatory, and the establishment of the Lake Placid Music Seminars in the mid-1990s in New York State.

Despite this growth in the vocabulary of the trumpet, and heightened expectations of its technical capability into the twenty-first century, the professional cadre ideal of 'what is good' in trumpet playing and its players lives on. As boundaries at the extremes of technical possibilities stretched further during the course of the century past, experiment and conservation came increasingly to cohabit inside the performance of and composition for the trumpet. Although strength, range, stamina and extended techniques became more important, the core-defining characteristics of a truly great trumpet player still embodied taste, refinement and artistry. Maurice André became the iconic classical soloist. In the final chapter we shall investigate the context of the wider audience within which the trumpet rose once more to prominence as a solo instrument. The overarching thesis which these two final chapters pursue is that it was not until the advent of jazz that the trumpet gained the liberating momentum to free it from its perceived limitations by performer and public alike. Influence, however, went both ways. New Orleans was the originating crucible. A succession of players beginning with Louis Armstrong via an explosion of jazz talent through to Wynton Marsalis gave impetus to the trumpet as a solo instrument across all genres including classical. Later in the, the absorption of the classical trumpet and its canonic repertory by Marsalis was to have a profound effect not only on the future of the trumpet but also on the history of jazz.

Chapter 12

Jazz and the image of the trumpet since 1900

In this final chapter jazz is the dominant theme. Jazz, though a highly absorbent form open to outside influences including that of classical music and its players, was, in itself, an irresistible influence. The central discussion of the chapter concerns jazz trumpet players, the integration of their music with audiences, their influence on the way the trumpet is understood and, finally, their impact on the way that the sound and image of the trumpet and the personalities who have been most strongly associated with it, have been projected since the start of the twentieth century.

Trumpets and cornets

The favoured instrument of jazz became the B flat trumpet. The cornet, however, provided the treble brass voice in the earliest Jazz bands and in the bands of the ragtime craze. On its first European tour in 1900 Sousa's Band played ragtime at the Paris Exposition Universelle. The Original Dixieland Jazz Band from New Orleans led by cornetist Nick La Rocca (1889–1961) created a sensation in London, based at the newly opened Hammersmith Palais de Danse throughout much of 1919 and 1920.[1] Louis Armstrong described the situation around 1921:

> Of course in those early days we did not know very much about trumpets. We all played cornets. Only the big orchestras in the theatres had trumpet players in their brass sections . . . at that time we all thought you had to be a music conservatory man or some kind of a big muckity-muck to play the trumpet. For years I would not even try to play the instrument.[2]

When Armstrong switched to trumpet in the late 1920s, he instinctively relinquished an instrument with a mellow blending tone colour, ideally suited to the collective ensemble jazz of the early New Orleans style, for an instrument with the capacity to dominate any ensemble, no matter how large. Distinctive cornet players, like Bix Beiderbecke (1903–31) and Rex Stewart (1907–67), were still prominent in jazz. The cornet as a vehicle for infectious exuberance is well demonstrated by recordings made by Beiderbecke in New York with Frankie Trumbauer and his Orchestra, such as *Clarinet Marmalade* (4 February 1927) or *Mississippi Mud* (9 January 1928). Cornet players, like Del Staigers (1899–1950) and Walter M. Smith (1891–1937), continued to flourish in brass and wind bands, and a distinctive voice of the cornet

– warm, rich and mellow – was fostered throughout the century by a succession of British players like, for example, Harold Jackson (1913–86), William (Willie) Lang (1919–2006), Jim Shepherd (b.1936), James Watson (1951–2011) and Phillip McCann (b.1955). In jazz, by contrast, the cornet's character tended to be chirrupy, smiley and boisterous. The virtuosoic flair of popular cornetists of the period when Armstrong was first making his mark with a very different brand of virtuosity on trumpet is well represented by the recordings of British cornetist Jack Mackintosh (1891–1979), complete with his trademark 'cowboy cadenzas'.[3] These date from 1928–33.[4] Mackintosh's playing, and that of his colleague Harry Mortimer (1902–92), is remarkable for the same quality of articulation for which Bix Beiderbecke won the following comment from Hoagy Carmichael – 'Like a mallet striking a chime'.[5]

The reception of the personalities of jazz

During the period marked by the emergence of jazz, many players migrated to and fro between cornet and trumpet, causing the playing styles of the two to converge into a new hybrid trumpet idiom in the milieu of jazz. The speed of development in the self-inventing, experimental music of jazz between 1900 and 1970 led to rapid changes in trumpet technique, style and idiom, and the cornet, by comparison, faded in importance. In classical music, there was a parallel decline. Stravinsky, a writer of prominent cornet parts in the 1910s, wrote solely for trumpet from the early 1920s, incorporating cornet lyricism into his writing for trumpet, as in the lyrical and melodic trumpet in A part of his Octet of 1922–3. The cornet gradually fell out of use in the work of orchestral composers. One of the last great extended and characteristically lyrical parts written for it was in Prokofiev's ballet score *Romeo and Juliet* (1935). When Stravinsky came to re-orchestrate *Petrushka* in 1947, he rescored the famous cornet solo for B flat trumpet.

Trumpet players, from Louis Armstrong to Wynton Marsalis, hold central positions in the evolution of jazz. The public received Louis Armstrong as the first great soloist of jazz and the excitement that he generated through his 'hot' style built an expectancy that trumpeters could and would hit high notes again and again. Armstrong would confound the audience's expectations that there was a limit to his endurance – commentators wrote that he had a 'freak lip'.[6] The physicality of 'hot' jazz built an expectation for players to compete with one another in extrovert behaviour, virtuosity, range and stamina. Players like Bubber Miley, Oren 'Hot Lips' Page, Roy Eldridge and many others fulfilled an early public demand for 'hot' trumpet.[7] In the decades that followed, in bebop and beyond, first John Birks 'Dizzy' Gillespie (1917–93) and then Maynard Ferguson (1928–2006) took the trumpet range beyond the highest notes written for natural trumpet in the 1760s. The excitement generated by the virtuoso feats of jazz trumpeters such as, for example, Harry James, the 1940s pop star of the trumpet, was similar to that generated by sports celebrities.

Jazz was not received with universal approval. Totalitarian regimes in the thirties banned it as dangerous and subversive, and conservative music critics like, for example, Alfred Einstein condemned it.[8] Condemnation often has a perverse effect with audiences – the trumpet was such a symbol of jazz that the association with forbidden fruit may have heightened its attractiveness. Post World War II, jazz became more respectable and a legitimate pursuit of intellectuals. During the reconstruction of Europe, this new musical form from America became embedded in European culture, with national and regional radio stations employing jazz musicians in big bands and various other groupings. Though the immense strength of jazz continued to reside in the fact that knowledge and expertise in it proliferated through aural transmission, formal routes for the learning and teaching of jazz gradually spread to conservatoires across the world following the example of the first jazz courses from 1945 at Berklee College, Boston.

Phases in jazz and its key players

New Orleans and Louis Armstrong

Of the cornetists who preceded Armstrong in the New Orleans phase of early jazz, Buddy Bolden and Joe 'King' Oliver were pioneers of the new emerging music. Bolden has mythical status. Little evidence remains of his work, but the rhythmic, driving force of his playing impressed all who heard him.[9] Oliver took the driving New Orleans style of early jazz to Chicago in 1918.[10] He strongly influenced Armstrong, who joined his band as second cornet in 1922. Although Armstrong became the role model for future jazz trumpet soloists, his early career was as an ensemble player in small New Orleans jazz bands, and his second playing to Oliver was a model of its kind.[11] Whereas Armstrong rarely played with a mute, preferring to personalize his sound with his trademark cocktail of half-valve glissandos, shakes, hand vibrato and terminal-fall note endings, Oliver was much imitated for his renowned plunger-muted techniques.

A vogue for 'jungle music', 'farmyard hookum', and the use of all sorts of kitchen utensils as novelty effects had grown to become part of the variety act of most dance bands by the second decade of the century. This had its roots in the minstrel shows stretching back into the nineteenth century.[12] The first cornet player to make an international hit in New Orleans style was Nick La Rocca of the Original Dixieland Jazz Band. The ODJB played 'jungle' and 'farmyard' as part of the wildness of their act during their 1919/20 London visit, and were actually sacked after the opening night of their first performance of the revue *Joy Bells* for being 'too jungle'.[13]

Louis Armstrong was the most influential trumpet player to come out of the early jazz period. Concentrated listening to his Hot Five and Hot Seven recordings on cornet and trumpet in the period from 12 November 1925 to 12 December 1928 reveals that Armstrong's burst into prominence coincided with an important point in the evolution of the trumpet. Armstrong's growing mastery of the solo jazz trumpet idiom grew directly out of his jazz cornet playing. His mature style developed from and through his cornet playing, and as a consequence realised the latent capabilities of the trumpet, rendering it for the first time a complete instrument with the full panoply of expressive and technical possibilities. The new idiom invented by Armstrong, through a fusion of the capacities of both cornet and trumpet, became identified as belonging to the trumpet, and marked the re-emergence of the trumpet as a viable solo instrument after a gap of over a century.

The cornet as played in the 12 November 1925 *Yes, I'm in the Barrel* blends beautifully with the other instrumentalists in the group: Kid Ory (trombone), Johnny Dodds (clarinet), Lil Hardin (later, Armstrong) (piano) and Johnny St. Cyr (banjo). The music created is high-level, New Orleans ensemble jazz. Armstrong's contribution is always evident through a highly individual cornet sound, but does not dominate the ensemble. The cornet's capacity for melancholy is exploited here in the menacing opening few bars and, later, in the heavy, sad opening of *Skid-Dat-De-Dat*, recorded 16 November 1926. In recordings of 26 February 1926, *Cornet Chop Suey, Muskrat Ramble, Heebie Jeebies*, the cornet sounds amiable, friendly and benign, not challenging or threatening, and is a perfect foil to Armstrong's scat singing in the last number – similar to an alternating obbligato. More surprise technical tricks like the unexpected and disorienting opening glissando of *Heebie Jeebies* start to creep in. By the 16 November recordings, Armstrong is taking his cornet playing to its limits. *Jazz Lips* is full of 'rips' and has an impromptu, exploratory feel. *Big Butter and Egg Man* again demonstrates ensemble cornet playing, but his ego is becoming uncontainable, and he bursts into a brilliant, squeezed-sound solo. Six months later, on the Hot Seven recordings of 7 May 1927, he takes wing, and begins to soar. *Wild Man Blues* demonstrates the irrepressible personality lying beneath Louis Armstrong's early shy persona. Immediately, there is a 'bigger' sound and greater use of a more powerful high register.

Lip trills and shakes in the upper register now become a permanent feature of his playing. In *Willie the Weeper*, recorded the same day, he rides the ensemble, dominating through an exuberantly high decibel level and brilliance of timbre. By *Alligator Crawl*, three days later, every time he plays, it is as leading voice, and by 11 May, *Melancholy Blues*, he seems to have crossed the threshold of a new idiom, with a solo full of tricks, slides, squeezed sudden top notes with lip trills, and surprising bursts of double-tempo. By 13 May, he demonstrates the potential of his new idiom to energise an ensemble. *S.O.L. Blues* swings right from the start. *Gully Low Blues*, recorded the following day, is uproarious.

Four months later, the numbers are reduced again, and, with the Hot Five on 2 September 1927, he reverts to a more traditional cornet style in *Ory's Creole Trombone* and *Put 'Em Down Blues.* Although writers on the subject have reached a broad consensus on the topic of Armstrong's change from cornet to trumpet, it is not totally clear-cut.[14] Later that year, from 9 to 13 December, his recordings of *Struttin' With Some Barbecue, Once in a While, I'm not Rough* and *Hotter Than That* sound like a cornet played trumpet-style. The staccato cornet sound permeates *Struttin' With Some Barbecue*, but the far-ranging line – played all over the compass, with high lip trills – is pure trumpet. But the overall effect is less dominating, and more blended. *Once in a While* is full of cornet pyrotechnics from within the ensemble. The solo is full of tricks, and invention. The timing of silences is exquisite, and the ending beautiful. By *I'm not Rough*, there is some indication that Armstrong is working much harder physically than he would have to on trumpet, although the end-tag is pure cheeky cornet, and sounds like a moment of minimalism. In the wonderful number *Hotter than that* he takes his cornet very high, into what was to become his favourite trumpet register, but with a thinner sound in comparison.

Six months later, on 27 June 1928, playing *A Monday Date*, Armstrong is generally credited as playing trumpet, although the use of a mute, unusual for him, adds a thinner, vocal quality similar to open jazz cornet. The addition of percussion to the 'Five' makes for a more driving style, and the presence of Earl Hines on piano gives unexpected twists and more direction to the harmonic movement. Yet, Armstrong must have still been feeling his way among the myriad directions opened by Hines. *Skip the Gutter* sounds experimental. All of his solos are disjointed, avant-garde sounding, unpredictable, even impressionistic. By the following day, 28 June 1928, the exuberant solo voice of the trumpet reaches an early milestone with *West End Blues*. Armstrong's restrained, crooning vocals in this give this whole miniature form, constrained by one side of a 78 rpm gramophone record, a perfectly balanced, but very wide emotional and dynamic range.

By the end of 1928, the cornet fades from view, and Armstrong wholeheartedly embraces the trumpet. He reaches a high point, indicative of his fully mature style, in the harmonically inventive, wide-ranging duo, *Weather Bird*, recorded with Hines on 5 December 1928. *Beau Koo Jack*, recorded the same day, shows that Armstrong has the stamina to play throughout a number, leading and inspiring the ensemble. One week later, on 12 December, he demonstrates that his trumpet playing has fully assimilated all the more intimate subtleties of the cornet, in the creepy, bluesy, recessed sonorities of *St. James' Infirmary*. That he has consummate control over his high-energy instrument is shown in another recording made that day, *Tight Like This*, which starts sparse but gets more and more intense, working up almost unbearable tension. With all of this power and range, he was now ready to start his fully-fledged solo career fronting big bands. And the trumpet had proved that it possessed the vocabulary to be a vehicle for virtuosos.

Duke Ellington's trumpet players

Jazz proliferated quickly from its New Orleans origins, and subsequent developments between 1925 and 1935 saw the rise of Chicago and New York as the major jazz hubs, with other cities like Kansas and St Louis also influential. Bix Beiderbecke (1903–31) teamed up with his collaborator, the saxophonist Frankie Trumbauer, in St Louis, and then migrated to Paul Whiteman's Band which toured out of New York. Unlike Armstrong, Beiderbecke did not switch cornet for trumpet. The impeccable taste of his improvisations gathered a large posthumous following for his fastidious and intimate jazz cornet style.

Duke Ellington began his career in Washington in the early twenties. Many of the changes in trumpet idiom from 1925 to 1950 and beyond can be traced in his recordings. If Stravinsky's instrumental innovations came to the fore first in music for the ballet, so then many of the developments in jazz trumpet appeared first in the dance halls played by Ellington. Ellington's bands almost invariably featured plunger-mute-specialists who had developed the technique brought out of New Orleans initially by King Oliver. By deft co-ordination of hand, mouth, tongue and air, they could make the trombone and trumpet talk, laugh and cry.[15] The first complete masters of this style were Joseph 'Tricky Sam' Nanton and James Wesley 'Bubber'

Miley (1903–32). In the early Duke Ellington Band they elevated this technique from a novelty effect into an art form. They added a dimension to Ellington which no other band of the period could match.[16] These 'talking trumpet' sounds were to influence later composers from Berndt Alois Zimmerman to Thomas Adès. From his earliest days 'jungle' was part of Ellington's instrumental resource.

Ellington's compositional technique continued to grow more advanced in the 1940s and 50s, partly as a consequence of an intense close working relationship with collaborator Billy Strayhorn. In parallel, his trumpet soloists became ever more wide-ranging in technique. The five-strong trumpet section, topped off with a lead trumpet who could 'scream' up to 'super' A6, and above to 'double high' C7, added an excitement to the big band sound that ran parallel to the extended trumpet section Stravinsky had established in the symphony orchestra.[17]

Ellington developed an intense collaborative working relationship with the players in his band. This resulted in an environment conducive to mutual experimentation in which there was the continuing possibility of composer and performer exploring new sounds. This is seen to good effect in the spontaneity of Ellington's 1927 collaborations with Bubber Miley: *Black and Tan Fantasy* and *East St. Louis Toodle-Oo*.[18] Successors to Miley in Ellington's Band, like Cootie Williams, Ray Nance, Dizzy Gillespie, Cat Anderson and Clark Terry, turned Miley's improvisational contributions to Ellington's structural framework into canonic repertory. Similar to an act of homage, they continued to play his solos of the late 1920s in the same way as he had played them originally, through to the 1950s. Meanwhile, in new original material, they continued to expand the solo language of the 'talking trumpet' of which Miley was the first great exponent.[19]

Although Miley, and his contemporaries in Ellington's Band, Arthur Whetsol and Freddie Jenkins, could make their trumpets 'wail' through manipulating a plunger in the bell, many players, like cornetist Rex Stewart and Armstrong, preferred the expressiveness of 'bending' and 'squeezing' notes. How did they develop this seemingly limitless capability to manipulate and vary the timbre of each note they produced? It was not only through 'half-valving', a way of pushing the valves half down and bringing them up lazily to making a glissando or smear between notes; it was also through altering the amount of lip in the mouthpiece, the vowel shape in the mouth cavity, and other instinctive unorthodox techniques which are not fully understood, as, for example, the relative 'puffiness' of the cheeks. Long sets playing for dancing through evenings and nights into the early hours provided an ideal laboratory for experiment. Embouchure orthodoxy was challenged in this period of the great jazz improvisers. Cootie Williams can be heard using the F2 pedal note in *I've Got To Be A Rug Cutter* (1937).

Swing and the progressives

The swing era brought to the fore the loose rhythmic feel which had always been evident in Armstrong's playing. Displacement of the beat became the rule rather than the exception. Armstrong avoided the main beats of the bar in his melodic playing by playing just before or after the beat. The new style called swing emerged initially in

Kansas City, gelling into a coherent new direction with Count Basie's Band. Roy Eldridge (1911–89) was perhaps the leading trumpeter of the swing era and was looked on by his contemporaries as a successor to Armstrong. New directions like bebop which were developing underground out of swing music during wartime broke through to the surface on the cessation of hostilities. There was a pent-up burst of creative energy in the jazz of the immediate postwar era. Internationally, the dynamism of jazz was irresistible. A whole new generation of young trumpet players made their mark, side by side with the continuing international stardom of a mature Louis Armstrong who formed his own All-Stars Band. In swing, Harry James impressed all with his mastery of the instrument.[20] In bebop, first the forays into the extreme high register of Dizzy Gillespie, and then, as this new style in jazz developed, the intellectual message of Miles Davis (1926–91) became prominent.

Although the early progressives of bebop – Dizzy Gillespie and Theodore 'Fats' Navarro (1923–50) – coexisted initially with swing music, by the late 1940s through to the late 1950s the jazz public began to become more diffuse, partially through the fragmentation of styles of the later progressives into the hard bop represented by players similar to Clifford Brown (1930–56), the soul jazz of Donald Byrd (b.1932), and the cool typified by Chet Baker (1929–88). Partially as a reaction against progressive jazz, there was a revival of New Orleans Traditional Jazz in the forties hand-in-hand with older players like Bunk Johnson (1889–1949) being rediscovered.

Ellington mapped on to most of these developments. During the swing era, Ellington continued to write features for his soloists. His first, for Cootie Williams, the dark 1936 'Echoes of Harlem' (Cootie's Concerto), contrasts with his second, the 1940 'Concerto for Cootie'. In the space of four years, the subtle contrast both between and within muted sounds and open trumpet had grown. 'Concerto for Cootie' is a masterpiece in miniature, lasting the 3 minutes 18 seconds of one side of a 78 rpm record. André Hodier, a seminal writer on jazz, understood the balance of invention between composer and performer:

> Few records do more than the *Concerto* to make possible an appreciation of how great the role is that sonority can play in the creation of jazz. The trumpet part is a true bouquet of sonorities. The phrases given to it by Ellington which have a melodic beauty which should not be overlooked, are completely taken over by Cootie. He makes them shine forth in dazzling colors, then plunges them in the shade, plays around with them, makes them glitter or delicately tones them down; and each time what he shows us is something new.[21]

Dizzy Gillespie played in Ellington's band in the early forties, and Clark Terry (b.1920) throughout most of the 1950s. Terry, with Milton 'Shorty' Rogers (1924–94), played a leading role in popularising the flugelhorn. When played gently, the flugelhorn fitted perfectly into the cool jazz milieu. Concurrently, major art music composers discovered the flugelhorn, notably Stravinsky in *Threni* (1957–8) and Vaughan Williams in his Ninth Symphony (1956–7). A cross between flugelhorn and trumpet, the flumpet, was developed by David Monette in the late 1980s for jazz trumpeter Art Farmer (1928–99).

Miles Davis

In jazz, Miles Davis's use of flugelhorn on *Miles Ahead* (1957) was a catalyst for the growth of this popularity. Further collaborations with Gil Evans on albums like *Porgy and Bess* (1958) and *Sketches of Spain* (1959–60), originally composed with the recording studio in mind, and assembled extempore, came to prominence after Miles Davis performed a selection of them at the Montreux Festival in 1991 shortly before his death. A recording of these performances was released posthumously in 1993, titled *Miles and Quincy Live at Montreux*. These arrangements became a regular feature of concert seasons of organisations like the London Sinfonietta in the 1990s, with trumpeters such as Randy Brecker (b.1945), Guy Barker (b.1957), and Lew Soloff (b.1944) playing the solo role originated by Miles Davis. Although the history of jazz is saturated with great and influential trumpet players, Miles Davis was the most influential of the generation following Armstrong. His career, spanning five decades beginning with Billy Eckstine and Charlie Parker, saw a succession of the biggest-selling and most successful jazz records of all time, from *Kind of Blue* (1959) – over 4 million sales – through *Bitches Brew* (1970), to the posthumously released *Doo-Bop* (1992). His was a transformational journey traversing most of the ground covered by jazz in the second half of the twentieth century – bebop, cool, hard bop, modal, fusion, electric, funk, jazz rap – and his was the trumpet solo idiom that most influenced art music composers of the period when writing for the instrument, as professed by such diverse figures as Gunther Schuller, Tim Souster, Sir Peter Maxwell Davies and Mark Anthony Turnage.[22]

Miles Davis held a central position in the evolution of jazz from the late 1940s into the 1980s. During its long history, the trumpet's use as a loud instrument has overshadowed its ability to be played in a gentler, introverted manner. One facet of early jazz was to exaggerate its exuberant tendencies. Miles Davis was a contrary artist who bucked this trend, and almost every other trend he encountered. This was a prime source of his creative energy. He was the first jazz player to explore fully the intimate soulfulness of the trumpet, which had been part of the art of trumpet playing since Fantini in the early seventeenth century and was used by Haydn in the Andante of his concerto. Though not the only or the first jazz artist to feature this introverted approach, he was the first to emphasise it to such a degree. By the sixth decade of the twentieth century this had grown into an alternative, 'cool' philosophy of playing the trumpet, partially as a reaction to the 'hot' tendency.

The Miles Davis Nonet's recording of *Birth of the Cool* (recorded 1949–50; released 1957) was the significant event in the public reception of this new word that defined a new style of jazz. This recording was made a decade before audiences were ready for it; it was a turning point in the history of jazz, and probably one of the most important cultural events of the century.[23] As far as the wider audience for music was concerned, the change of perception which stemmed from the genius of Miles Davis was the realisation that the trumpet was a vehicle through which to express important and relevant things about the human condition.

The trumpeter as pop star

In the world of show business, the arena of the mass audience, the trumpet became an ideal vehicle, from the 1940s through to the 1960s, for a particular type of leading man who exuded the glamour and masculinity of the matinee idol. Harry James set the mould. His breathtaking virtuosity, his ability to play higher, louder and faster than anyone else, was the musical equivalent of the swashbuckling daredevilry of romantic leading man, film star Errol Flynn. But it was in those quieter moments of tenderness that fall to romantic leading men that the trumpet became the ideal instrument for the projection of a ballad. Beginning with *You Made Me Love You*, Harry James had seventy hits between 1940 and 1953. His twenty-year marriage to the film star Betty Grable enhanced his appeal. The USA was brimful with commercial trumpet talent, from legendary film studio artist Mannie Klein (1908–94) to Al Hirt (1922–99), whose 1961 album *The Greatest Horn in the World* was among his twenty-one other hits in the Billboard Pop Charts in the 1950s and 60s. Al Hirt, denizen of New Orleans, was later to give six-year-old Wynton Marsalis his first trumpet.

The Hispanic stream in popular music and jazz surfaced in the playing of Rafael Mendez (1906–81), who brought a Latinate style – violinistic, with a fast, tight vibrato – into his recordings from the 1950s. It fell, however, to Herb Alpert (b.1935) and his Tijuana Brass in the 1960s to find a laid back, lazy Latin groove, in hits like *Peanut Vendor* and *A Taste of Honey*, which captivated a mass public to the extent of six Grammy awards, fifteen gold discs and fourteen platinum discs, with thirteen million recordings sold in 1966 alone. In April 1966, four Herb Alpert albums were in the Top 10 Billboard Pop Album Chart simultaneously. Herb Alpert showed keen business acumen, and he set up his own recording label, A&M Records, with Jerry Moss, initially to benefit fully from his own material rather than allow it to be exploited by the major recording companies. A&M then diversified into publishing, promotion, concert agency, film and TV production. After selling his interest in the company he co-founded, Herb Alpert became a major music education philanthropist, endowing the University of California, Los Angeles Herb Alpert School of Music in 2007, and a new music pavilion at the California Institute of the Arts in 2008.

In Europe, Harry James's example was emulated. In 1953, the UK's Eddie Calvert (1922–78), 'The man with the golden trumpet', had his first million-selling hit, *Oh Mein Papa*, and in 1955, his second, *Cherry Pink*. However, practically every European country produced its own 'golden trumpet' player. Germany's Horst Fischer (1930–86) had a prolific string of recordings from *Fantaisie in Silber* of 1949 to *Don't Cry for Me Argentina* in 1978. Italy's Nini Rosso (1926–94) originated perhaps the biggest hit of them all – *Il Silenzio* – a ten-million seller in its many cover versions. Switzerland's Hazy Osterwald's (b.1922) biggest hit with his sextet was *Kriminal Tango*, and Austria's Charly Tabor (1914–99) contributed the million bestseller *Wunderland bei Nacht*.

Although the trumpet ballad was a passing vogue in the ephemeral genre of pop, the popularity of a ballad played on trumpet lingers in jazz and in film. Chet Baker's treatment of ballads, as in *My Funny Valentine* (1952) and *I Fall in Love Too Easily* (1953), has accrued for him a special, much imitated, position in the lasting art of ballad playing.

Popular music underwent profound changes during the transition from postwar austerity in Western economies to consumer-driven affluence and rising living standards. In the 1960s, the rise of the electric guitar and the composition of the rock group fronted by a lead guitarist relegated the trumpet in pop music to the status of a backing instrument. Pronounced on-stage sexuality became the default position of popular music presentation. The trumpeter as pop star had become an obsolescent concept by the late 1960s, although some continuity was provided by the ingenuity of Miles Davis, whose electric period commenced in 1967. Davis's pioneering jazz-fusion trumpet led first to the album *In a Silent Way* (1969), and then to *Bitches Brew* (1970). From 1967, the 'jazz-rock' group Blood Sweat and Tears took on board a string of brilliant trumpet improvisers, beginning with Randy Brecker, then Lew Soloff (b.1944), whose stature was augmented rather than diminished by the association with rock music.

It had been Louis Armstrong, as the first trumpeter to become a household name on the international stage, who started this journey towards the iconic status that chart-topping pop stardom brings. And it was Armstrong who brought this phase to a close (Ill. 12.1). From his recording of *When the Saints Go Marching In* for Decca in 1938 to the early 1960s, he put together a stream of popular hits like *Blueberry Hill, A Kiss to Build a Dream On, La Vie en Rose, C'est Si Bon, That's for me, Dream a Little Dream of Me* (with Ella Fitzgerald) and *What's New?* (with Oscar Peterson).[24] Finally, the overwhelming popularity of *Hello, Dolly!*, which knocked the Beatles off the number-one

12.1 Louis Armstrong in the 1960s.

spot in the US and UK in 1964, and *What a Wonderful World* (1967), served to draw attention in his late career to the impact of his contribution to the evolution of jazz which had begun some four decades earlier.

The trumpet in film and on screen

Louis Armstrong proved to be an enduring image of the trumpeter on screen. He became an icon of the trumpet by appearing in more than fifty films over the course of his career, beginning with the short *Rhapsody in Black and Blue* (1930). In the early films, the exuberance of his personality catapulted him out of the live music background into minor acting roles. He transcended the racial stereotyping which was a by-product of the then current Hollywood Motion Picture Production Code, playing cameos alongside Bing Crosby in *Pennies from Heaven* (1936) and Ronald Reagan in *Goin' Places* (1939).[25] During the 1930s, Armstrong also played a major part in desegregating the movie theatres of many northern American cities through being the first black bandleader to appear in the stage shows which were performed between the film showings.[26] In later films in which he appeared, *The Glenn Miller Story* (1954), *High Society* (1956), *The Five Pennies* (1959) and *Hello Dolly* (1969), his iconic status was such that he played himself. On-screen or diegetic use of the trumpet played in a jazz club background was common in films from the 1930s to the 50s.[27] An early Duke Ellington project, *Black and Tan Fantasy* (Dudley Murphy, US 1929), however, went further, portraying trumpeter Arthur Whetsol at the heart of the creative process, putting the finishing touches to *Fantasy* with Ellington at the piano.[28]

Movies about jazz trumpet players themselves were rare. Rex Stewart played King Oliver in William Dieterle's *Syncopation* (1942). Bunny Berigan dubbed his solos on the sound track and Harry James featured in an on-screen jam session. *Young Man with a Horn* (1950) starred Kirk Douglas as Bix Beiderbecke. Harry James overdubbed Douglas's mimed trumpet playing. The film's level of aspiration can be gauged from leading lady Lauren Bacall's memorable lines: 'Put down your trumpet, jazz man – I'm in the mood for love!' The tragedy of ill-fated trumpeting genius was explored further in Bruce Weber's documentary film *Let's Get Lost* (1988), which compared the photogenic rise of Chet Baker in the 1950s with his haggard substance-induced decline of the 1980s. Tragedy and the trumpet were bedfellows also in Federico Fellini's *La Strada* (Italy, 1954), in which the circus strongman anti-hero and his peasant girl assistant both play the trumpet. Composer Nino Rota's nostalgic, quasi-operatic treatment of the trumpet contributes to one of its most effective on-screen uses.[29] Much happier, in accordance with its ebullient subject, was the 1956 TV documentary *Satchmo the Great.* Television first began to reach a mass audience in the 1950s, and Louis Armstrong was the first jazz musician to have a documentary devoted to him in the new medium. Armstrong was a television natural, ubiquitous on US television from its inception until his death, a favourite of 'The Ed Sullivan Show', a regular on 'Tonight', and a playing guest for celebrity hosts from Perry Como to Johnny Cash.

The trumpet as used on film soundtracks – its non-diegetic use – raises interesting questions about how its idiom was received by the wider public. The use of specific instruments in film music to underscore the emotional complexity of a film's narrative underlines the power of any instrument to conjure up associations within the mind of the audience for film.[30] The starting point for composers using trumpet on soundtracks was to transport its symbolism from staged music, and to this end, silent cinema most often used scores compiled from already existing sources. The *Ride of the Valkyries* became a particular favourite, and Wagner's use of *leitmotif* became one method for composers to emulate as they constructed coherent through-composed scores for talking pictures with recognisable reference points for different scenes and characters.[31] The trumpet was declamatory, triumphant and heroic in classic Hollywood film scores in romantic idiom by Korngold, Rózsa, Steiner and others. Miles Davis achieved a totally different atmosphere of cool detachment in Paris, while at the same time showing that a through-composed score was only one way to record music for film, by improvising the music to Louis Malle's *Ascenseur pour l'échafaud* (France, 1958).

From around the mid-century, new musical vocabularies and compilations of different genres from many different sources put together by a music supervisor increasingly supplanted the single composer using symphonic instrumentation. Use of the trumpet, however, persisted in big budget movies. Romantic symphonic treatment was preserved for major 'blockbusters'. John Williams gave the grand manner of the trumpet a heroic comeback in his music to George Lucas's *Star Wars* trilogy (1977–83). John Barry, in his music for *From Russia with Love* (UK, 1963) and the subsequent James Bond series, etched the scaring Bond theme in the minds of a generation of filmgoers through his use of a stratospheric trumpet section led by Derek Watkins, omnipresent in all Bond series recording sessions. Film composers often had special performers in mind, and John Williams aimed his heroic trumpet parts at Maurice Murphy of the London Symphony Orchestra, saying in a tribute to Murphy that he was a 'heraldic spirit' who articulated 'the ideal voice of a hero'.[32] Another prolific film composer, Ennio Morricone, had himself studied trumpet before becoming one of the most successful of twentieth-century film composers. His music for Sergio Leone's spaghetti westerns like *The Good, the Bad and the Ugly* (Italy, 1966) is full of wild mariachi-style trumpet effects which help set the scene for the hard-bitten action to follow.

The trumpet could also be evocative of the lone voice of humanity lost in an urban landscape, similar to its use by Charles Ives and Elliott Carter described in Chapter 11. In Aaron Copland's *Quiet City* (1940), written for a short film, muted trumpet symbolises the first light of day penetrating the tranquillity and peace of the urban nightscape.

Film scores are written to relentless deadlines. Jerry Goldsmith was given ten days to write his score for *Chinatown* (1974) after director Roman Polanski sacked the original composer. Goldsmith envisaged the main title *Love Theme from Chinatown,* a ballad featuring trumpet, instantaneously on viewing the film. This was played on the soundtrack by Uan Rasey (b.1921). A synthesis of the nostalgic idiom of Rota and the lone lost voice of Copland into a pop ballad for trumpet created one of the most tragically haunting of all movie theme tunes. The unsettling ambiguity of the trumpet as used on the soundtrack to represent lost innocence and lost love in a film noir whose subject is the taboo area of incest was indicative of the way in which composers were increasingly using the trumpet in cinema. In *Chinatown,* Goldsmith's innovative bittersweet ballad confirmed an aspect of soundtrack use of trumpet which had been developing for some time among composers. This transgressed into the traditionally saxophone territory of the darker undercurrents of urban disquiet. A lyrical trumpet melody in the cinema came to express something of a descant to the ruthless efficiency of modern city life. And pathos was never far away, as in the ironic rendition of the Last Post at the end of Francis Ford Coppola's *Apocalypse Now* (1979).

Female players

The imaging of the trumpet has been predominantly male. Throughout the twentieth into the twenty-first centuries, the perception of the trumpet as a male instrument played by males has been resistant to change. A considerable literature on instrumental gender-coding exists: why girls tend towards playing flutes and harps, and boys towards trombones and tubas.[33] Female role models on brass instruments, however, are not a recent phenomenon. American cornetist Anna Teresa Berger (1854–1925) received star billing and a gold medal during the 1889 Covent Garden Promenade concert series in London, and was one of many exceptional female players who made a lasting impression and a not inconsiderable solo career.[34] Edna White, discussed in Chapter 9, was another. She made her first Carnegie Hall, New York, appearance as a cornet soloist at the age of nine in 1901, and as the first trumpet player to give a recital at the same venue in 1949, she helped to establish the trumpet as a plausible recital instrument. In 1957, when Edna White gave her Farewell Concert at the Carnegie Hall at the age of sixty-five, Leona May Smith (1914–99),became the first female trumpeter to be hired, as an extra, by the Metropolitan Orchestra. It was not until 1964 in the US that Marie Speziale (b.1942) was the first to win a permanent position in a major orchestra, the Cincinnati Symphony, and not until 1972 that a major orchestra – the St Louis Symphony – elected a woman, Susan Slaughter (b.1945), to a principal chair.

Carole Dawn Reinhart (b.1941) was the first female trumpet player to enrol at the Wiener Akademie, where she studied with Helmut Wobisch. In the 1970s, Reinhart began to fulfil in excess of 100 solo engagements a year, and Jean Françaix wrote *Le Gay Paris* (1974), for trumpet and winds, for her. In 1984 she returned to her place of former study in Vienna as a professor of trumpet, and she ran a successful career from this teaching base in the last two decades of the twentieth century, making two solo appearances at the Salzburg Festival, one of the most prestigious engagements in the world for any concert artist.[35]

Alison Balsom's (b.1978) solo trumpet career in the first decade of the twenty-first century is a notable development in the reception of the trumpet in classical music. In 2009 she won the award of 'Female Artist of the Year' at the Classical BRIT awards in London, and continued a series of award-winning recordings with EMI classics while cultivating a worldwide audience.

In Jazz, a few female players – Valaida Snow (1904–56), Ernestine 'Tiny' Davis (1907–1994), Clora Bryant (b.1929) among them – made an impact from the vintage and swing eras. Valaida Snow played and sang with some of the all-time greats, including Earl Hines and Count Basie (Ill. 12.2), was heard and praised by Louis Armstrong in 1928,[36] toured the world, recorded her best work in London in the

12.2 Valaida Snow performing with the Count Basie Orchestra.

1930s, and was interned in occupied Denmark for three months in 1942 after the US declared war on Germany. Her remarkable life has been the subject of much speculation and has been the subject of a biography and two semi-biographical novels.[37] Canadian Ingrid Jensen (b.1966) started to make inroads into European jazz circles working out of Austria in the early 1990s. Her triumph in the 1995 Carmine Caruso International Jazz Trumpet Competition in Kalamazoo, Michigan, marked an important watershed in the acceptance of female players.

Wynton Marsalis – icon of the trumpet?

Louis Armstrong developed his wide-ranging career as a jazz soloist, celebrity entertainer, singer and bandleader, after compressing his most rapid period of musical growth into a fertile period in his late twenties. Wynton Marsalis rose to international stardom in similarly meteoric fashion, at an even earlier age. This was marked by his becoming the first artist to win Grammy awards in both jazz and classical in 1984 at the age of twenty-three. As Armstrong's career as a musical celebrity proliferated in directions dictated by the mass market for music, so did opportunities soon arise for Marsalis. However, the opportunities of the 1980s were very different from the 1920s and 30s. Whereas Armstrong's manager Joe Glaser had to have the necessary mob connections, jazz had since become legitimized, and recognized as perhaps the most significant American contribution to twentieth-century music. Through his own considerable strength of will and formidable intellect, and with the commercial strength of global giant Sony as his recording company behind him, with astonishing rapidity Marsalis became an important figure in American music. His trumpet-playing prowess soon co-existed within a portfolio of responsibilities including those of composer, administrator, educator and cultural leader.

In 1987, Wynton Marsalis became the artistic director of jazz at the Lincoln Center, New York. Here he brought his own eclectic mind to bear on making a century of musical development cohere into a jazz canon. Marsalis worked towards embedding the importance of seminal figures like Armstrong and Ellington into the canon. His work towards establishing a canonical repertory met with considerable resistance. There was a pervasive philosophical concern that the establishment of a jazz canon would inevitably lead to a restrictive and conservative orthodoxy. In some quarters, resistance erupted into hostile opposition. Accusations of bias, cronyism, and even racism were made.[38] Marsalis was undeterred by the heated criticisms. He responded:

> I thought the attack that my critics mounted was pitiful. It was poorly researched. It wasn't based on facts. It was really just emotion. Fear. Anger. Ignorance. It hasn't changed how I do my job. I am ready to confront them at any time. I was hired to do a job and I am going to do it.[39]

The ensuing controversies and stormy public debate showed that there was still much vitality left in jazz.[40] His public clash with James Lincoln Collier created intense heat in the pages of *The New York Times* and elsewhere.[41] Marsalis's radical thinking attracted controversy, and the excitement and outrage that Marsalis as a trumpeter, composer and cultural leader generated in equal measure only served to highlight the prominence of his achievements.[42] It is improbable that he paid any attention to controversial advice given by Miles Davis, that by playing classical music, Marsalis was wasting his talent playing 'that tired-ass shit'.[43] However, in the nineties, Marsalis largely gave up playing classical repertory, and began to write his own large-scale compositions. The three-hour long Oratorio, *Blood on the Fields*, an epic work about African-American slavery, premiered by him and the Lincoln Center Jazz Orchestra in 1994, won the Pulitzer Prize in 1997.

The work that followed *Blood on the Fields* – *All Rise* – was on a similar epic scale. It was commissioned and performed by the New York Philharmonic Orchestra and Kurt Masur, as the last of the NYPO millennial compositions of 1999. It was premiered by the NYPO with the Lincoln Center Jazz Orchestra and a 100-voice gospel choir at the Lincoln Centre, in the last days of the millennium, December 29 and 30, 1999. *All Rise* is a work which reaches across styles and genres, from jazz and blues to classical and world music. In Marsalis's own words: 'This piece for me was the culmination of a ten-year odyssey during which I sought to realize more complex orchestrations for long-form pieces based in American vernacular music and jazz.'[44]

All Rise made a major impact and a demand grew for Marsalis to tour it throughout the world. The performance with Esa-Pekka Salonen and the Los Angeles Philharmonic on 13 September 2001 and the recordings which followed this performance were a powerful testament to the growth of his popular appeal as a modern icon. Despite the widespread state of shock in the US following the al-Qaeda attacks on the Twin Towers of 9/11, Marsalis cemented his position in the consciousness of the American public as a national cultural leader, bolstering national morale by going ahead with the scheduled Los Angeles performance, despite calls to abandon it. In the event, CNN broke from Ground Zero coverage to broadcast excerpts of *All Rise* (Ill. 12.3).

12.3 Wynton Marsalis and Esa-Pekka Salonen.

Marsalis's roots in New Orleans come to the surface in works like *Blood on the Fields* and *All Rise*, as does his firm belief in equality. Following the hurricane which devastated New Orleans in 2005, his work became more politicized. He played a prominent part in the advocacy for the reconstruction of his home city, publicising widespread feelings of impatience and anger with the continuing plight of African Americans in New Orleans in the face of perceived federal neglect. His *Congo Square* for Jazz Band and African Ensemble was first performed on 23 April 2006 in Congo Square, New Orleans, now part of the Louis Armstrong Park, symbolically where African-American slaves were originally allowed to perform their own music in the 1700s and early 1800s. This was subsequently toured and recorded. The increasing topicality of his work to societal concerns gained added urgency with his album *From the Plantation to the Penitentiary* in 2007, a gritty work where Marsalis questions the speed of progress of equality in the United States, and the unfinished business of the civil rights movement, underlined by the slowness of effective responses by governmental agencies to the Hurricane Katrina disaster.

As a composer and trumpeter of international stature who had absorbed an eclectic range of musical influences including classical and jazz, who participated on stage in his own works, leading from the front as a performer, with the major orchestras of the world, as well as in a plethora of settings from jazz to African ensemble, Marsalis came to attain a unique position during the opening decade of the twenty-first century. He had fulfilled Louis Armstrong's prophetic pronouncement, put forward half a century earlier, for the universality of the trumpet:

> That horn, you see that horn? That horn ain't prejudiced. A note's a note in any language.[45]

The trumpet has moved on. The profound influence of Maurice André has made lyrical sensitivity an essential – perhaps the most important – priority of classical trumpet playing. The astounding technical developments and advances in range and stamina originating in jazz were emulated by Håkan Hardenberger and his contemporaries in classical music. The developments of the twentieth century in all genres of music have led to a complex instrument emancipated to a level where it can be an artistic vehicle for serious musical discourse in any context. However, the trumpet's core identity has endured the test of time. From the discoveries of our early ancestors that sounds of varying pitch could be obtained by placing the lips on one end of a tube fashioned from natural materials of bone, shell, stone, wood and gourd, and blowing air through it, to the discovery that musical signals could be transmitted over long distances through tubes manufactured from the metals of the new technologies pioneered in the Fertile Crescent; to the assembly of a wide melodic and artistic range for an instrument which became known as the 'natural' trumpet, through the invention and adoption of mechanical trumpets to the advent of jazz, the trumpet has been a ubiquitous instrument with a universal audience, lauded for its glorious, expressive sound and the power of its emotional impact.

Appendix

A selective list of twentieth-century solo works

Composer	Composition	Date	Location	Player
Charles Bordes	Divertissement for Solo Trumpet and Strings	1902	Liège	Théo Charlier
Georges Enesco	Légende	1906	Paris Conservatoire morceau de concours	Merri Franquin
Charles Ives	The Unanswered Question	1906	f.p. New York, May 11, 1946	Chamber orchestra of graduate students at the Juilliard School
Karl Pilss	Concerto	1934	Vienna	Franz Dengler
Karl Pilss	Sonata	1935	Vienna	Helmut Wobisch
Oscar Geier	Trumpet Concerto in E flat	1938	Leipzig	Eduard Seifert
Hindemith	Sonata	1939		
Richard Strauss	Fanfare der Stadt Wien	1943	Vienna	Vienna Trompetenchor
Rutland Boughton	Concerto	1943	London	written for William Overton
Jolivet	Concertino for piano, trumpet and strings	1948	Paris Conservatoire	morceau de concours
Henri Tomasi	Concerto	1948	Paris	Ludovic Vaillant
Alexander Arutiunian	Concerto	1949	Moscow	Haykaz Mesiayan
Jean Françaix	Sonatine	1950	Paris Conservatoire	morceau de concours
John Addison	Concerto for Trumpet and Strings	1951	London	David Mason
Georges Delerue	Sonate with Organ	1951	Paris	Roger Delmotte
Adolph Weiss	Concerto	1952	Los Angeles	Lester Remsen (1918–2007)

George Antheil	Sonata	1953	Saratoga Springs, NY State	Harry Herfurth (Cleveland S.O.)
Halsey Stevens	Sonata	1953–56	Hartford, Connecticut	Theodore Gresh and Geraldine Douglas
Kryukov	Poem for trumpet and orchestra	1954	Moscow	Timofei Dokschizer
Berndt Alois Zimmerman	Nobody knows de trouble I see	1954	Hamburg	Adolf Scherbaum
Jolivet	Concerto No. 2	1954	Vichy	written for Roger Delmotte but premiered by Raymond Tournesac
Florent Schmitt	Suite Op. 133 for trumpet and orchestra	1955	Paris	morceau de concours
Jean Rivier	Concerto for alto saxophone, trumpet and strings	1955	Aix-en-Provence Festival	Roger Delmotte
Martinů	Sonatine	1955		
Honegger	Intrada	1955		
Maxwell Davies	Sonata Op. 1 for trumpet in D and piano	1955	Manchester	Elgar Howarth and the pianist John Ogdon
Cornelius Cardew	Three Rhythmic Pieces	1955	RAM, London	Howard Snell
Richard Rodney Bennett	Parallels	1955	RAM, London	Howard Snell
Giacinto Scelsi	Quattro Pezzi	1956		
Kent Kennan	Sonata	1956		
Chaynes	Concerto	1956	France	Maurice André
Iain Hamilton	Concerto for Jazz Trumpet	1958	Royal Festival Hall, BBC Light Music Festival	George Swift
Grace Williams	Concerto	1963	Manchester Hallé Orchestra	Bram Gay (b.1930)
Hans Zender	Cantata Vexilla Regis (Trumpet obbligato)	1964	Munich	Rolf Quinque
Henry Barraud	Symphonie Concertante for Trumpet and Orchestra	1966	Paris Semaines Musicales Internationales de Paris	Yves Coueffé

Stefan Wolpe	Solo Piece for Trumpet	1966		Ronald Anderson (b.1934)
Weinberg	Concerto (op. 94)	1966–67		Timofei Dokschizer
William Lovelock	Concerto	1969	Sydney	John Robertson
Malcolm Arnold	Fantasy	1969	Royal College of Music, London	dedicated to Ernest Hall
Øistein Sommerfeldt	Divertimento	1970	Oslo	Harry Kvebæk (b.1925)
Boris Blacher	Concerto for Höhe trompete	1970	Nurnberg	Maurice André
Jan Koetsier	Partita for Trumpet and Organ op. 41	1971	Regensburg	
John Carmichael	Concerto	1972	Sydney	Kevin Johnson
Tamberg	Concerto No. 1	1972	Moscow	Timofei Dokschizer
Eberhard Kraus	Concerto for Trumpet and Organ, Versi contrarii	1972		Rolf Quinque
Harald Genzmer	Cantata for Soprano and trumpet			Rolf Quinque
Krzysztof Meyer	Concerto	1973		Timofei Dokschizer
Hans Werner Henze	Sonatine	1974		Written for Howard Snell
Stanley Friedman	Solus	1975	Eastman School of Music, NY	Stanley Friedman
Einojuhani Rautavaara	Tarantará	1976		written for the participants of the National Brass Competition held in Helsinki
Roger Smalley	Echo III, for solo trumpet and tape-delay	1978	Perth, Australia	Written for Gordon Webb
Henri Pousseur	Flexions II	1979	Conservatoire Royal de Musique de Liège	Pierre Cox
István Lang	poco a poco dim.,	1979	Liszt Academy, Budapest	Dedicated to Frigyes Várásdy (b. 1930)
Tim Souster	The Transistor Radio of St Narcissus for flugelhorn and live electronics	1983	The Roundhouse, London	John Wallace/Tim Souster

Verne Reynolds	Calls and Echoes	1986		Barbara Butler and Charles Geyer
Franco Donatoni	Short	1988	Cosenza, Italy, 4th Festival Musica d'Oggi	Gabriel Cassone
Tim Souster	Trumpet Concerto with orchestra and live electronics	1988	BBC National Orchestra of Wales/ Cardiff/Stephen Cleobury	John Wallace
Maxwell Davies	Strathclyde Concerto No. 3 for Horn and Trumpet	1990	City Halls, Glasgow	Robert Cook and Peter Franks
York Höller	Fanal	1991	Paris, Auditorium des Halles	Jean-Jacques Gaudon
Caspar Johannes Walter	Vier Stücke gegen den Stillstand	1993	New Japan Philharmonic Orchestra, Tokyo	Reinhold Friedrich
Jarmo Sermilä	Final Conclusions for trumpet and tape	1988	Vantaa Brass Happening	Joukko Harjanne
Ivan Fedele	High	1996	Strasbourg, Festival Musica	Gabriel Cassone
John Williams	Concerto for Trumpet	1996	The Cleveland Orchestra	Michael Sachs (b.1961)
Berio	Kol-Od (Chains VI)	1996	Luzern Festival Paul Sacher	Gabriel Cassone
Michele Tadini	Notturna	1998	Rome	Gabriel Cassone
Benedict Mason	Concerto for trumpet and orchestra in 6 groups	1997	Berlin	Reinhold Friedrich
Harrison Birtwistle	Silkhouse Antiphonies for two trumpets and percussion	1997	Queen Elizabeth Hall, London	Edward Carroll and John Wallace
Tamberg	Concerto No. 2	1997	Tampere	Matthias Hofs
Harrison Birtwistle	Placid Mobile for 36 trumpets	1998	Lake Placid, NY	Conducted by Edward Carroll
Helge Iberg	Dromo Dance	1998	Norway	Ole Edvard Antonsen
Wolfgang Rihm	Marsyas Rhapsodie für Trompete mit Schlagzeug und Orchester	1998	Karlsruhe	Reinhold Friedrich

Maxwell Davies	Quintet Op. 200 for trumpet and string quartet	1999	Aberdeen	John Wallace, Ygdrassil Quartet
Maxwell Davies	Litany for a Ruined Chapel between Sheep and Shore, Op. 202, for solo trumpet	1999	St Magnus Cathedral, Kirkwall, Orkney	John Wallace
Andrew Powell	Plasmogeny	1999	RAM, London	John Wallace
HK Gruber	Exposed Throat	2000	RAM, London	John Wallace
Mark Antony Turnage	From the Wreckage	2004	Esa-Pekka Salonen Helsinki Philharmonic	Haken Hardenberger
Mark Antony Turnage	An Aria (with Dancing) For trumpet solo	2004	RSAMD, Glasgow	John Wallace

Notes

Introduction

1. Don L. Smithers, *The Music and History of the Baroque Trumpet before 1721*, 2nd edn (Carbondale, Ill.: Southern Illinois University Press, 1988), pp. 242–3.
2. Hugh Macdonald, *Berlioz's Orchestration Treatise: A Translation and Commentary* (Cambridge: Cambridge University Press, 2002), p. 193.
3. Trevor Herbert (2008), 'The Robert Minter Collection: a handlist of seventeenth- and eighteenth-century trumpet repertoire', <http://www.open.ac.uk/Arts/minter>, accessed 20 August 2009.
4. Neil MacGregor, *A History of the World in 100 Objects* (London: Penguin, 2010), p. xvii.

Chapter 1 The trumpet in the ancient and non-Western world

1. Richard Fortey, *Life: An Unauthorised Biography, A Natural History of the First Four Thousand Million Years of Life on Earth* (London: Harper Collins, 1997), p. 358.
2. See John Ziolkowski, 'The invention of the tuba (trumpet)', *The Classical World* 92/4 (1999), 367–73.
3. Philip Bate, *The Trumpet and Trombone: An Outline of Their History, Development and Construction*, 2nd edn (London: Ernest Benn, 1978), pp. 94–5; Francis W. Galpin, *The Music of the Sumerians and their Immediate Successors the Babylonians & Assyrians* (Cambridge: Cambridge University Press, 1937), pp. 21–2.
4. Stephanie Dalley (ed.), *Myths from Mesopotamia: Creation, the Flood, Gilgamesh, and Others* (Oxford: Oxford University Press, 1991), p. 126.
5. David Wulstan, 'The sounding of the shofar', *The Galpin Society Journal* 26 (1973), 29–46.
6. Markus N. A. Bockmuehl, '"The trumpet shall sound": *shofar* symbolism and its reception in early Christianity', in *Templum Amicitiae: Essays on the Second Temple Presented to Ernst Bammel*, ed. William Horbury (Journal for the Study of the New Testament Supplement Series 48, Sheffield: JSOT Press, 1991), p. 211.
7. Flavius Josephus, *Flavius Josephus. : Translation and Commentary*, ed. Steve Mason. Vol. 3, Judean Antiquities; translation and Commentary by L. H. Feldman (Leiden: Brill, 2000), p. 320.
8. Don L. Smithers, 'A new look at the historical, linguistic and taxonomic bases for the evolution of lip-blown instruments from Classical Antiquity until the end of the Middle Ages', *Historic Brass Society Journal* 1 (1989), 18.
9. Markus N. A. Bockmuehl, '"The trumpet shall sound"', pp. 204, 216.
10. Geza Vermes, *The Complete Dead Sea Scrolls in English* (London: Penguin, 1997), pp. 162–3.
11. Vermes, *The Complete Dead Sea Scrolls*, p. 165.
12. Ibid., pp. 165–6, 171.
13. Curt Sachs, *The History of Musical Instruments* (New York: Norton, 1940), p. 73; cited in Bate, *The Trumpet and Trombone*, p.95.
14. Bo Lawergren, 'Oxus trumpets, ca. 2200–1800 BCE: material overview, usage, societal role, and catalog', *Iranica Antiqua* 38 (2003), 41–118. Lawergren uses the phrase 'trumpet-like objects' to describe these artefacts in *Grove 2*, s.v. 'Iran, §1, 2: Pre-Islamic, 3rd millennium BCE'.

15. Anthony Baines, *Brass Instruments: Their History and Development* (London: Faber and Faber, 1976; repr. London: Constable and Co., 1993), p. 54.
16. Lawergren, 'Oxus trumpets', 94–5.
17. Ibid., 88.
18. Lise Manniche, *Musical Instruments from the Tomb of Tut'ankhamên* (Oxford: Griffith Institute, 1976), pp. 7–13.
19. Jeremy Montagu, 'One of Tutankhamon's Trumpets', *The Galpin Society Journal* 29 (1976), 115.
20. Manniche, *Musical Instruments*, pp. 12–13.
21. Manniche, *Musical Instruments*, p. 11; Henry G. Fischer, 'The trumpet in ancient Egypt', in *Pyramid Studies and Other Essays Presented to I. E. S. Edwards*, ed. J. Baines [et al.] (London: The Egypt Exploration Society, 1988), pp. 103–4.
22. Curt Sachs, *The History of Musical Instruments* (New York: Norton, 1940), p. 100.
23. See J. Gwyn Griffiths, 'Osiris', in *The Oxford Encyclopedia of Ancient Egypt*, ed. Donald B. Redford, 3 vols (Oxford: Oxford University Press, 2001), vol. 2, pp. 617–19.
24. Peter Downey, 'Lip-blown instruments of Ireland before the Norman invasion', *Historic Brass Society Journal* 5 (1993), 75–91.
25. Stuart Piggott, 'The carnyx in early Iron Age Britain', *The Antiquaries Journal* 39 (1959), 24; see also Fraser Hunter, 'About the carnyx: historical background', at <http://www.carnyxscotland.co.uk>, accessed 20 July 2009; and the review of Piggott's article by Anthony Baines in *The Galpin Society Journal* 13 (1960), 108–11.
26. See Alastair Dick, 'The earlier history of the shawm in India', *The Galpin Society Journal* 37 (1984), 80–98; and Smithers, 'A new look', 34, fig. 7.
27. Polybius, *The Rise of the Roman Empire*, ed. by F. W. Wallbank, trans. by Ian Scott Kilvert (London: Penguin, 1979), referred to in Ellis, *The Celtic Empire*, p. 38.
28. See Bryan Sykes, *Blood of the Isles: Exploring the Genetic Roots of our Tribal History* (London: Bantam, 2006).
29. See Downey, 'Lip-blown instruments', 75–91.
30. Homer, *The Iliad*, trans. M. Hammond (Harmondsworth: Penguin, 1987), p. 300.
31. The *Eumenides*, third play of the *Oresteia* trilogy (*l.* 568).
32. Sophocles, *Ajax* 17: *Tyrsenikê Salpinx* (Etruscan salpinx). Virgil, *Aeneid* VIII 526: *tyrrheneus tubae* (Etruscan tuba).
33. P. F. Stary, 'Foreign elements in Etruscan arms and armour: 8th to 3rd centuries B.C.', *Proceedings of the Prehistoric Society* 45 (1979), 179, 201.
34. Peter Krentz, 'The *salpinx* in Greek warfare', in *Hoplites: The Classical Greek Battle Experience*, ed. V. D. Hanson (London: Routledge, 1991), pp. 114–17.
35. Gullög C. Nordquist, 'The *salpinx* as an instrument of Eros and Dionysus', *Imago Musicae* 8 (1991), 66; Martin L. West, *Ancient Greek Music* (Oxford: Clarendon Press, 1992), p. 119; Krentz, 'The *salpinx*', p. 113.
36. Nordquist, 'The *Salpinx*', p. 67.
37. There are several references to the portrayal of trumpeters on vases held in the Vatican, Naples, London, Rome, Florence and Berlin, in J. D. Beazley, *Attic Red-Figure Vase-Painters*, 2nd edn, 3 vols (Oxford: Clarendon Press, 1963), vol.1, pp. 55, 57, 60.
38. Aristophanes, *Frogs* (*l.*966).
39. West, *Ancient Greek Music*, p. 118.
40. Smithers, 'A new look', 16–17.
41. Nikos Xanthoulis, 'The salpinx in Greek antiquity', *International Trumpet Guild [ITG] Journal* (Oct. 2006), 44.
42. West, *Ancient Greek Music*, p. 118.
43. Smithers, 'A new look', 20.
44. John R. Hale, '*Salpinx* and *salpinktes*: trumpet and trumpeter in Ancient Greece', in *Literature, Art, History: Studies on Classical Antiquity and Tradition in Honour of W. J. Henderson*, ed. A. F. Basson and W. J. Dominik (Frankfurt and New York: Peter Lang, 2003), p. 269.
45. See Xanthoulis, 'The salpinx in Greek antiquity', 41.
46. Egert Pöhlmann and Martin L. West, *Documents of Ancient Greek Music: The Extant Melodies and Fragments* (Oxford: Clarendon Press, 2001), p. 8.

47. Edgar Turrentine, 'Notes on the ancient Olympic trumpet-blowing contests', 1969, in *Brass Anthology: A Compendium of Articles from The Instrumentalist on Playing the Brass Instruments* (Evanston, Ill.: The Instrumentalist Publishing Company, 1980), pp. 497–8.
48. Hale, '*Salpinx* and *salpinktes*', p. 272.
49. Turrentine, 'Notes', p. 497; Halle, '*Salpinx* and *salpinktes*', p. 272.
50. John Ziolkowski, 'The invention of the tuba (trumpet)', *The Classical World* 92/4 (1999), 367–73.
51. Renato Meucci, 'Roman military instruments and the lituus', *The Galpin Society Journal* 42 (1989), 89.
52. John Ziolkowski, 'The Roman *bucina*: a distinct musical instrument?', *Historic Brass Society Journal* 14 (2002), 52.
53. See Yann le Bohec, *The Imperial Roman Army*, trans. R. Bate (London: Routledge, 2000), p. 50.
54. Flavius Vegetius Renatus, *Vegetius: Epitome of Military Science*, trans. N. P. Milner (Liverpool: Liverpool University Press, 1993), pp. 38–9.
55. Ibid., pp. 55–6.
56. Ziolkowski, 'The Roman *Bucina*', 41–2.
57. Ibid.
58. Ibid., 52–3.
59. Meucci, 'Roman military instruments', 85–6.
60. Ibid., 86–8.
61. H. H. Scullard, *Festivals and Ceremonies of the Roman Republic* (London: Thames and Hudson, 1981), p. 94.
62. Plutarch, *Lives*, trans. B. Perrin, 11 vols (London: Heinemann, 1914–26), vol. 6, p. 443. See Scullard, *Festivals and Ceremonies*, p. 216.
63. Baines, *Brass Instruments*, p. 64.
64. J. E. Scott, 'Roman Music', in *Ancient and Oriental Music*, ed. E. Wellesz, New Oxford History of Music 1 (London: Oxford University Press, 1957), p. 415.
65. Ibid., p. 416.
66. West, *Ancient Greek Music*, 120; Baines, *Brass Instruments*, p. 63.
67. See Baines, *Brass Instruments*, p. 64.
68. See 'Tuba' in William Smith, William Wayte, G. E. Marindin, *A Dictionary of Greek and Roman Antiquities*, 1890.
69. Christopher Ehret, *The Civilizations of Africa: A History to 1800* (Oxford: James Currey, 2002), p. 73.
70. Ibid., p. 346.
71. *Grove 2*, s.v. 'Oliphant'.
72. Ibid.
73. Smithers, 'A new look', 31–2.
74. Downey, 'Lip-blown instruments', 89–90.
75. Robert Stevenson, *Music in Aztec & Inca Territory* (Berkeley: University of California Press, 1968), pp. 12–13.
76. Ibid., pp. 19, 20, 74; see Mary E. Miller, *The Murals of Bonampak* (Princeton, N.J.: Princeton University Press, 1986).
77. Stevenson, *Music in Aztec & Inca Territory*, pp. 74, 76.
78. Meredith Alexander, 'Discovery of shell stash sheds light on ancient society', *Stanford Report*, 24 October 2001, <http://news.stanford.edu/news/2001/october24/chavin-a.html>, accessed 12 June 2006. For a discussion of a previously discovered Chavín shell-trumpet, see Robert Stevenson, 'Ancient Peruvian instruments', *The Galpin Society Journal* 12 (1959), 25–6.
79. Karl A. Taube, *Aztec and Maya Myths* (London: British Museum Press, 1993), pp. 37–9.
80. Dorothy Hosler, *The Sounds and Colors of Power: The Sacred Metallurgical Technology of Ancient West Mexico* (Cambridge, Mass.: MIT Press, 1994), pp. 3–17, 52.
81. Karl Gustav Izikowitz, *Musical and Other Sound Instruments of the South American Indians: A Comparative Ethnographical Study*, 1934; reprint (East Ardsley: S.R. Publishers, 1970), pp. 221–2.
82. For a concise yet thorough evaluation of the development of societies in different parts of the world, see Jared M. Diamond, *Guns, Germs and Steel: A Short History of Everybody for the Last 13,000 Years* (London: Jonathan Cape, 1997).
83. Robert Stevenson, 'Ancient Peruvian instruments', *The Galpin Society Journal* 12 (1959), 34–5.
84. Samuel Turner, *An Account of an Embassy to the Court of the Teshoo Lama, in Tibet; Containing a Narrative of a Journey through Bootan, and Part of Tibet* (London: W. Bulmer, 1800).

85. Li Jun, *Chinese Civilisation in the Making, 1766–221 BC* (London, 1996).
86. Cheng Te-K'Un, *Archaeology in China: Volume Two [Shang China]* (Cambridge, 1960).
87. A drawing of this carving is given in Alan R. Thrasher, *Chinese Musical Instruments* (Oxford: Oxford University Press, 2000), pp. 41–2.
88. A. C. Moule, *A List of Musical and Other Sound-Producing Instruments of the Chinese*, 1908 (Buren: Frits Knuf, 1989).
89. Margaret Sarkissian, 'Lip-vibrated instruments of the ancient and non-western world', in *The Cambridge Companion to Brass Instruments*, ed. T. Herbert and J. Wallace (Cambridge: Cambridge University Press, 1997), pp. 12–13.
90. Alastair Dick, 'Sankh', *Instrument Grove*, vol. 3, pp. 289–90.
91. Robin Skeates, 'Triton's trumpet: a Neolithic symbol in Italy', *Oxford Journal of Archaeology* 10 (1991), 22.
92. Ibid. (Virgil, *Aeneid* 6.161–235).
93. There are two types, one megaphone-like, 10–16 ft long, the other with a mouthpiece, 3–4 ft long, played to the eighth or ninth harmonic.
94. Baines, *Brass Instruments*, pp. 51–3.
95. See Sarkissian, 'Lip-vibrated instruments', pp. 16–18.
96. Where calibrated radiocarbon dates are available, these are used in preference to uncalibrated radiocarbon dates. The dating may therefore be earlier than that with which the reader is familiar.
97. A pioneering recording of solo music for didgeridoo is David Hudson, *Woolunda: Ten Solos for Didgeridoo*, 1993. Compact disc. Fortuna/Celestial Harmonies 13071.
98. Diamond, *Guns, Germs and Steel*, p. 185.
99. Fertile Crescent (by 8500 BCE), China (by 7500 BCE), Mesoamerica (by 3500 BCE), Andes and Amazonia (by 3500 BCE), Eastern United States (by 2500 BCE), Sahara (by 5000 BCE), Tropical West Africa (by 3000 BCE); (Diamond, *Guns, Germs and Steel*, p. 100).

Chapter 2 The trumpet: definition, manufacture and technique

1. Cesare Bendinelli, *The Entire Art of Trumpet Playing, 1614*, trans. with commentary by E. H. Tarr (Nashville, Tenn.: The Brass Press, 1975).
2. On the relationship between the natural harmonic series and different temperaments, see Tim Collins, 'So, how many holes is a baroque trumpet supposed to have?', *Historic Brass Society Newsletter* 9 (1996), 11–15.
3. Berlin, Staatliches Institut für Musikforschung, Musikinstrumenten-Museum, no. 639.
4. Johann Ernst Altenburg, *Essay on an Introduction to the Heroic and Musical Trumpeters' and Kettledrummers' Art: For the Sake of a Wider Acceptance of the Same, Described Historically, Theoretically, and Practically and Illustrated with Examples*, 1795, trans. E. H. Tarr (Nashville, Tenn.: The Brass Press, 1974), p. 14.
5. See Anthony Baines, 'James Talbot's manuscript (Christ Church Library Music MS 1187). I. Wind instruments', *The Galpin Society Journal* 1 (1948), 9–26.
6. Eric Halfpenny, 'William Shaw's "Harmonic Trumpet"', *The Galpin Society Journal* 13 (1960), 7–13.
7. Ibid.
8. See Reine Dahlqvist, *The Keyed Trumpet and its Greatest Virtuoso, Anton Weidinger* (Nashville, Tenn.: The Brass Press, 1975).
9. Herbert Heyde, 'On the early history of valves and valve instruments in Germany (1814–1833)', *Brass Bulletin* 24 (1978), 11.
10. See Arnold Myers, 'Design, technology and manufacture since 1800', in *The Cambridge Companion to Brass Instruments*, ed. T. Herbert and J. Wallace (Cambridge: Cambridge University Press, 1997), pp. 115–30.
11. Denis Wedgwood, 'Ovoid' About valves', *Brass Bulletin* 102 (1998), 29–33.
12. The authors are grateful to Tedd Waggoner, Director of Bach Operations at Conn-Selmer, Inc., for confirmation of this fact.
13. David B. Sharp, Arnold Myers, and D. Murray Campbell, 'Using pulse reflectometry to compare the evolution of the cornet and the trumpet in the 19th and 20th centuries', *Proceedings of the International Symposium on Musical Acoustics, Edinburgh, 19–22 August 1997: Institute of Acoustics* 19/5 (1997), 541–8.

14. See, for example, Richard A. Smith, 'Recent developments in trumpet design', *ITG Journal* 3 (Oct. 1978), 27–9.
15. *Grove 2*, s.v. 'Neuschel' (by Edward H. Tarr).
16. Edward H. Tarr, *The Trumpet*, trans. S. E. Plank and E. H. Tarr (London: Batsford, 1988), pp. 99–102.
17. Robert Barclay, *The Art of the Trumpet-Maker: The Materials, Tools, and Techniques of the Seventeenth and Eighteenth Centuries in Nuremberg* (Oxford: Clarendon Press, 1992).
18. Ibid., p. 24; Don L. Smithers, *The Music and History of the Baroque Trumpet before 1721*, 2nd edn (Carbondale, Ill.: Southern Illinois University Press, 1988), p. 337.
19. Don L. Smithers, 'The trumpets of J. W. Haas: a survey of four generations of Nuremberg brass instrument makers', *The Galpin Society Journal* 18 (1965), 23–41.
20. Altenburg, *Trumpeters' and Kettledrummers' Art*, pp. 9–10.
21. For a more detailed description of the manufacturing process, see Richard Seraphinoff, Raymond Parks and Robert Barclay, *Making a Natural Trumpet: An Illustrated Workshop Guide* (Edinburgh: EUCHMI, 2003).
22. Barclay, *The Art of the Trumpet-Maker*, pp. 103–17.
23. See Maurice Byrne, 'The Goldsmith-trumpet-makers of the British Isles', *The Galpin Society Journal* 19 (1966), 71–83.
24. See John Webb, 'The Billingsgate trumpet', *The Galpin Society Journal* 41 (1988), 59–62.
25. Pierre-Yves Madeuf, Jean-François Madeuf, and Graham Nicholson, 'The Guitbert trumpet: a remarkable discovery', *Historic Brass Society Journal* 11 (1999), 182–3.
26. Eric Halfpenny, 'Early British Trumpet Mouthpieces', *The Galpin Society Journal* 20 (1967), 78–9; Eric Halfpenny, 'Four seventeenth-century British trumpets', *The Galpin Society Journal* 22 (1969), 53–5.
27. Altenburg, *Trumpeters' and Kettledrummers' Art*, p. 10.
28. John Hyde, *A New and Compleat Preceptor for the Trumpet and Bugle Horn, With the Whole of the Cavalry Duty as approved of and ordered by his Royal Highness the Duke of York, Commander in Chief* (London: Printed and to be had of the Author, [1799]), p. 1.
29. See Thomas Harper, *Instructions for the Trumpet*, 2nd edn, London: The Author, 1837, facsimile edn (Homer, NY: Spring Tree Enterprises, 1988).
30. Joseph Fröhlich, *Vollständige theoretisch-pracktische Musikschule für alle beym Orchester gebräuchliche wichtigere Instrumente zum Gebrauch für Musikdirectoren-Lehrer und Liebhaber* (Bonn: N. Simrock, 1811), part 3, p. 21.
31. Bruno Tilz catalogue, 1988.
32. The manual is available at <http://www.bachbrass.com>, accessed 20 November 2009.
33. Marin Mersenne, *Harmonie universelle* (Paris: Pierre Ballard, 1636), part 3, p. 259.
34. Daniel Speer, *Grund-richtiger, kurtz- leicht- und nöthiger, jetzt wol-vermehrter Unterricht der musicalischen Kunst, oder Vierfaches musicalisches Kleblatt* (Ulm: Im Verlag G. W. Kuhnen, gedruckt bey C. B. Kuhnen Seel. Erben, 1697), p. 219.
35. For examples of the various designs of baroque trumpet mutes, see Jindřich Keller, 'Antique trumpet mutes', *Historic Brass Society Journal* 2 (1990), 100.
36. Panico, Louis, *The Novelty Cornetist: A Complete, Thorough Exposition of how to Execute Every Known Trick on the Cornet Such as Baby Talk, Baby Cry, Blues, Chinese Effect, Flutter Tongue, Horse Neigh, Laugh, Sneeze, Improvisation and Other Effects*, 2nd edn (Chicago: Forster Music Publisher Inc., 1927).
37. The authors are indebted to Andrew Lynn, principal trumpet, Scottish Opera, for this information. Gary Radtke produces a range of mouthpieces where the alpha angle is varied in a systematic way. See <http://grmouthpieces.com/tutorialalphaangle.htm>.
38. In fact an observation of many present-day trombone and tuba players will demonstrate partial but habitual puffing out of the cheeks, particularly in the lower register. This aids sound production in this register by providing a sympathetic resonating cavity in the mouth.
39. John Hyde, *A New and Compleat Preceptor for the Trumpet and Bugle Horn, With the Whole of the Cavalry Duty as Approved of and Ordered by His Royal Highness the Duke of York, Commander in Chief* (London: The Author, [1799]), p. 1; François Georges Auguste Dauverné, 'Method for trumpet', trans. Gaetan Chenier, Ruby Miller Orval, Rebecca Pike and Jeffrey Snedeker, *Historic Brass Society Journal* 3 (1991), 230.
40. Jean-Baptiste Arban, *Cornet Method*, 1864, trans. E. Ruch, ed. J. Fitz-Gerald (London: Boosey & Hawkes, 1907), p. 3.

41. Anthony Baines, *Brass Instruments: Their History and Development*, 1976 (London: Constable and Co., 1993), p. 91.
42. Girolamo Fantini, *Modo Per Imparare a Sonare di Tromba Tanto di Guerra Quanto Musicalmente*, 1638; facsimile reprint with English translation and critical commentary by Edward H. Tarr (Nashville, Tenn.: The Brass Press, 1978), p. 6.
43. Altenburg, *Trumpeters' and Kettledrummers' Art*, pp. 69–74.
44. Hyde, *A New and Compleat Preceptor*, p. 2.
45. Dauverné, 'Method for trumpet', 230.
46. See John Ridgeon, *The Physiology of Brass Playing* (Manton: Brass Wind, 1986).
47. See Ralph T. Dudgeon, Phillip Eastop, Trevor Herbert and John Wallace, 'Playing, learning and teaching brass', in *The Cambridge Companion to Brass Instruments*, ed. T. Herbert and J. Wallace (Cambridge: Cambridge University Press, 1997), pp. 193–206.
48. Speer, *Grund-richtiger*, p. 219.
49. Dauverné, 'Method for trumpet', 223–4.
50. Jesse Rosenberg (trans.), '*Il vero modo di diminuir* [by Girolamo dalla Casa]: a translation', *Historic Brass Society Journal* 1 (1989), 112.
51. Bendinelli, *The Entire Art of Trumpet Playing*, p. 4.
52. Arban, *Cornet Method*, p. 4.
53. Harper, *Instructions for the Trumpet*, p. 13.
54. Dauverné, 'Method for trumpet', 230.
55. Jerome Callet and his former student, Robert (Bahb) Civiletti, have collaborated on a book, *Trumpet Secrets* (2002), which purports to have rediscovered the 'lost art' of clarino playing, and introduces techniques they claim were lost with the demise of the Guilds. Callet's method, Tongue-Controlled Embouchure (TCE), permanently places the tip of the tongue on the top underside of the bottom lip (while articulating off the top lip with the top of the tongue) to create and regulate the air pressure and control the whole system. Callet and Civiletti claim that evidence exists in the iconography and some written texts of the time of the Guilds to support the idea that some sort of similar technique would (and must) have been used at the time of the great virtuosi of the clarino register.
56. Altenburg, *Trumpeters' and Kettledrummers' Art*, p. 116; Harper, *Instructions for the Trumpet*, p. 12.
57. Arban, *Cornet Method*, p. 8.

Chapter 3 The trumpet in Europe and its environs to 1600

1. Keith Polk, *German Instrumental Music of the Late Middle Ages: Players, Patrons, and Performance Practice* (Cambridge: Cambridge University Press, 1992), p. 47.
2. Don L. Smithers, 'A new look at the historical, linguistic and taxonomic bases for the evolution of lip-blown instruments from Classical Antiquity until the end of the Middle Ages', *Historic Brass Society Journal* 1 (1989), 3–64.
3. Keith Polk, 'Brass instruments in art music in the Middle Ages', in *The Cambridge Companion to Brass Instruments*, ed. T. Herbert and J. Wallace (Cambridge: Cambridge University Press, 1997), pp. 38–40.
4. See Peter Downey, 'Lip-blown instruments of Ireland before the Norman invasion', *Historic Brass Society Journal* 5 (1993), 75–91.
5. Held by the National Museum of Scotland; see http://www.nms.ac.uk/our_collections/collection_highlights/hilton_of_cadboll_stone.aspx>, accessed 8 March 2010.
6. Edmund A. Bowles, 'Were musical instruments used in the liturgical service during the Middle Ages?', *The Galpin Society Journal* 10 (1957), 51.
7. Janet L. Nelson, 'The Lord's anointed and the people's choice: Carolingian royal ritual', in *Rituals of Royalty: Power and Ceremonial in Traditional Societies*, ed. D. Cannadine and S. Price (Cambridge: Cambridge University Press, 1987), p. 142.
8. Michael McCormick, *Eternal Victory: Triumphal Rulership in Late Antiquity, Byzantium, and the Early Medieval West* (Cambridge: Cambridge University Press, 1986), p. 374.
9. Ibid., pp. 374–5.
10. For an appraisal of Alcuin's importance, and his Northumbrian successors in the Frankish empire, see Frank M. Stenton, *Anglo-Saxon England*, 3rd edn (Oxford: Clarendon Press, 1971).
11. Stenton, *Anglo-Saxon England*, pp. 180–3.

12. Alfred Büchler, 'Horns and trumpets in Byzantium: images and texts', *Historic Brass Society Journal* 12 (2000), 27. (Procopius, *History of the Wars*, VI, 23.)
13. George T. Dennis, *Three Byzantine Military Treatises* (Washington, DC: Dumbarton Oaks Research Library and Collection, 1985), p. 93.
14. Dennis, George T. (trans.), *Maurice's Strategikon: Handbook of Byzantine Military Strategy* (Philadelphia: University of Pennsylvania Press, 1984), pp. 38, 155.
15. Ibid., pp. 33, 96.
16. Eric McGeer, *Sowing the Dragon's Teeth: Byzantine Warfare in the Tenth Century* (Washington, DC: Dumbarton Oaks Research Library and Collection, 1995), p. 45.
17. Ibid., p. 197.
18. Büchler, 'Horns and trumpets', 25.
19. Gretchen Peters, 'Urban musical culture in late Medieval Southern France: evidence from private notarial contracts', *Early Music* 25 (1997), 405.
20. Edward H. Tarr, *The Trumpet*, trans. S. E. Plank and E. H. Tarr (London: Batsford, 1988), p. 63.
21. Kenneth Kreitner, 'Music in the Corpus Christi procession of fifteenth-century Barcelona', *Early Music History* 14 (1995), 168.
22. Edward Peters (ed.), *The First Crusade: The Chronicle of Fulcher of Chartres and Other Source Materials*, 2nd edn (Philadelphia: University of Pennsylvania Press, 1998), pp. 60–1.
23. Ibid., pp. 87–9. Seven was an important symbolic number of the church: 'Wisdom hath builded her house, she hath hewn out her seven pillars' (Prov. 9:1). Solomon's Temple took seven years to complete, was dedicated in the seventh month of the year, and the service of dedication took two times seven days (1 Kings 8:65).
24. August C. Krey, *The First Crusade: The Accounts of Eye-Witnesses and Participants* (Princeton: Princeton University Press, 1921), p. 255.
25. Helen J. Nicholson (trans.), *Chronicle of the Third Crusade: A Translation of the Itinerarium Peregrinorum et Gesta Regis Ricardi* (Aldershot: Ashgate, 1997), p. 157. The Latin citations are from William Stubbs (ed.), *Chronicles and Memorials of the Reign of Richard I. Vol. 1: Itinerarium Peregrinorum et Gesta Regis Ricardi* (London: Longman, 1864), p. 156.
26. Nicholson (trans.), *Chronicle of the Third Crusade*, p. 158; Stubbs (ed.), *Chronicles and Memorials*, p. 157.
27. Nicholson (trans.), *Chronicle of the Third Crusade*, p. 248; Stubbs (ed.), *Chronicles and Memorials*, pp. 262–3.
28. Henry G. Farmer, 'Crusading martial music', *Music and Letters* 30 (1949), 248.
29. Ibid., p. 246–7.
30. Polk, 'Brass instruments in art music', p. 41.
31. Osvaldo Gambassi, *Il Concerto Palatino della Signoria di Bologna* (Florence: L. S. Olschki, 1989), pp. 589–92; Polk 'Brass instruments in art music', p. 290, n. 6.
32. Robert de Clari, trans. E. H. McNeal, *The Conquest of Constantinople* (New York: Columbia University Press, 1936), p. 42.
33. Reinhard Strohm, *Music in Late Medieval Bruges* (Oxford: Clarendon Press, 1985), pp. 75–6.
34. Keith Polk, *German Instrumental Music*, p. 46; Polk, 'Brass instruments in art music', p. 42.
35. Maurice Byrne, 'Instruments for the Goldsmiths Company', *The Galpin Society Journal* 24 (1971), 63–4.
36. Anthony Baines, 'The evolution of trumpet music up to Fantini', *Proceedings of the Royal Musical Association* 101 (1974–75), 8.
37. Gustave Reese, *Music in the Middle Ages* (New York: Norton, 1940), p. 409. Reese defines 'clarion' as 'a shorter form of the *buisine*'.
38. See Andrew Parrott, 'Performing Machaut's Mass on record', *Early Music* 5 (1977), 492–5; and Daniel Leech-Wilkinson, *Machaut's Mass: An Introduction* (Oxford: Clarendon Press, 1990), pp. 114–15.
39. Polk, *German Instrumental Music*, pp. 52–3.
40. Ibid., p. 83.
41. See Pierre-Yves Madeuf, Jean-François Madeuf, and Graham Nicholson, 'The Guitbert trumpet: a remarkable discovery', *Historic Brass Society Journal* 11 (1999), 181–6.
42. Keith Polk, 'The trombone, the slide trumpet and the ensemble tradition of the early Renaissance', *Early Music* 17 (1989), 393, 395.
43. Polk, *German Instrumental Music*, p. 63.

44. Craig M. Wright, *Music at the Court of Burgundy, 1364–1419: A Documentary History* (Henryville, Pa.: Institute of Mediaeval Music, 1979), p. 41; Polk, *German Instrumental Music*, p. 61
45. Wright, *Music at the Court of Burgundy*, pp. 47–8. See also Ross W. Duffin, 'The *trompette des menestrels* in the 15th-century *alta capella*', *Early Music* 17 (1989), 400; and Keith Polk, 'The invention of the slide principle and the earliest trombone or, the birth of a notion', in *Perspectives in Brass Scholarship*, ed. Stewart Carter (Stuyvesant, NY: Pendragon Press, 1997), p. 26.
46. Polk, *German Instrumental Music*, pp. 60–1.
47. See Polk, 'The invention of the slide principle', for a chronology of the introduction of a brass instrument to wind bands in various parts of Europe.
48. Polk, 'Brass instruments in art music', p. 44.
49. Polk, *German Instrumental Music*, p. 158.
50. Peter Downey, 'The Renaissance slide trumpet: fact or fiction?', *Early Music* 12 (1984), 26–33.
51. Anthony Baines, *Brass Instruments: Their History and Development*, 1976 (London: Constable and Co., 1993), pp. 103–6.
52. Downey, 'The Renaissance slide trumpet', 31; Peter Downey, 'From the rim to the hub: Fortuna's wheel and instrumental music at the German-speaking Renaissance courts', in *Perspectives in Brass Scholarship*, ed. Stewart Carter (Stuyvesant, NY: Pendragon Press, 1997), p. 10.
53. Herbert W. Myers, 'Slide trumpet madness: fact or fiction?', *Early Music* 17 (1989), 384.
54. See Herbert W. Myers, 'Evidence of the emerging trombone in the late fifteenth century: what iconography may be trying to tell us', *Historic Brass Society Journal* 17 (2005), 7–35.
55. Don L. Smithers, *The Music and History of the Baroque Trumpet before 1721* (London: Dent, 1973), pp. 165–6.
56. Keith Polk, 'Patronage and innovation in instrumental music in the 15th century', *Historic Brass Society Journal* 3 (1991), 163–5.
57. Kreitner, 'Music in the Corpus Christi Procession', 170.
58. Strohm, *Music in Late Medieval Bruges*, pp. 80–1.
59. Jeffrey Kurtzman, and Linda Maria Koldau, '*Trombe, trombe d'argento, trombe squarciate, tromboni, and pifferi* in Venetian processions and ceremonies of the sixteenth and seventeenth centuries', *Journal of Seventeenth-Century Music* 8 (2002) <http://www.sscm-jscm.org/jscm/v8/no1/kurtzman.html>, accessed 20 April 2009.
60. Strohm, *Music in Late Medieval Bruges*, pp. 45, 53.
61. Paul A. Merkley and Lora L. M. Merkley, *Music and Patronage in the Sforza Court* (Turnhout: Brepols, 1999), p. 120.
62. Edmund A. Bowles, 'Were musical instruments used in the liturgical service during the Middle Ages?', *The Galpin Society Journal* 10 (1957), 52; Richard Rastall, 'Minstrelsy, church and clergy in Medieval England', *Journal of the Royal Musical Association* 97 (1970), 92.
63. Merkley and Merkley, *Music and Patronage*, pp. 317–18.
64. See Edmund A. Bowles, 'The role of musical instruments in medieval sacred drama', *The Musical Quarterly* 45 (1959), 79–82.
65. Hans Burgkmair, *The Triumph of Maximilian I: 137 Woodcuts by Hans Burgkmair and Others. With a Translation of Descriptive Text, Introduction and Notes by Stanley Appelbaum* (New York: Dover 1964).
66. Andrew Ashbee (ed.), *Records of English Court Music*, 9 vols; vols 1–4 (Snodland, 1986–91); vols 5–9 (Aldershot, 1991–96), vol. 7, p. 29.
67. David Lasocki, with Roger Prior, *The Bassanos: Venetian Musicians and Instrument Makers in England, 1531–1665* (Aldershot: Scolar Press, 1995), p. 174.
68. See Sydney Anglo, *The Great Tournament Roll of Westminster: A Collotype Reproduction of the Manuscript* (Oxford: Clarendon Press, 1968).
69. See Alexander McGrattan, 'Italian wind instrumentalists at the Scottish royal court during the 16th century', *Early Music* 24 (2001), 534–51.
70. See Downey, 'From the rim to the hub'.
71. See Bruce Dickey, 'The cornett', in *The Cambridge Companion to Brass Instruments*, ed. T. Herbert and J. Wallace (Cambridge: Cambridge University Press, 1997), p. 52.
72. See Keith Polk, 'Augustein Schubinger and the zinck: innovation in performance practice', *Historic Brass Society Journal* 1 (1989), 83–93.
73. John Wilson (ed.), *Roger North on Music: Being a Selection from his Essays Written During the Years c.1695-1728* (London: Novello, 1959), p. 40.
74. Nicholas Mann (ed.), *Atlas of the Renaissance* (London: Cassell, 1993), p. 14.

75. Ibid.
76. Donald Jay Grout and Claude V. Palisca, *A History of Western Music*, 6th edn (New York and London: Norton, 2000), p. 177.
77. Dickey, 'The cornett', p. 57.
78. Ibid., p. 64.
79. Denis Arnold, *Giovanni Gabrieli and the Music of the Venetian High Renaissance* (Oxford: Oxford University Press, 1979), p. 10.
80. Ibid., pp. 1–10.
81. See James Haar, 'Munich at the time of Orlande de Lassus', in *The Renaissance, From the 1470s to the end of the 16th century*, Man and Music 2, ed. I. Fenlon (London: Macmillan, 1989), pp. 246–51,
82. Ibid., pp. 252–4.
83. Ibid.
84. Tarr, *The Trumpet*, p. 72. Cesare Bendinelli, *The Entire Art of Trumpet Playing, 1614*, trans. with commentary by E. H. Tarr (Nashville, Tenn.: The Brass Press, 1975), p. 7.
85. Peter Downey, 'The Trumpet and its Role in Music of the Renaissance and Early Baroque' (Ph.D. thesis, The Queen's University of Belfast, 1983), vol. 1, p. 115. Cited in Edward H. Tarr, 'The trumpet before 1800', in *The Cambridge Companion to Brass Instruments*, ed. T. Herbert and J. Wallace (Cambridge: Cambridge University Press, 1997), p. 85.
86. Downey, 'The Trumpet and its Role', vol. 2, pp. 295–310; cited in Tarr, 'The trumpet before 1800', p. 86.
87. Girolamo Fantini, *Modo Per Imparare a Sonare di Tromba Tanto di Guerra Quanto Musicalmente*, 1638; facsimile reprint with English translation and critical commentary by Edward H. Tarr (Nashville, Tenn.: The Brass Press, 1978). See Smithers, *The Music and History*, pp. 135–9, for a discussion of Praetorius's remarks on the use of trumpets.
88. Downey, 'The Trumpet and its Role', vol. 1, pp. 84–7.
89. For a description of the Italian style and its introduction to the Danish court around the middle of the sixteenth century, see Downey, 'A Renaissance correspondence'.
90. For example, William Shakespeare, *Richard II*, I. iii. 26 (1593): 'Tucket. Enter Hereford, and Harold'.
91. Downey states that Italian-style military music was adopted in England and France towards the end of the sixteenth century, but that an earlier style of treble-dominated trumpet ensemble music prevailed in those countries (Downey, 'The Trumpet and its Role', vol. 1, p. 88).
92. Ibid., vol. 1, p. 105.
93. Edward H. Tarr, 'The trumpet before 1800', p. 87.

Chapter 4 The art of the trumpet player in the seventeenth and eighteenth centuries

1. Manfred F. Bukofzer, in *Music in the Baroque Era from Monteverdi to Bach* (New York: Norton, 1947), for example, distinguishes between Early (1580–1630), Middle (1630–80) and Late (1680–1730) Baroque, while acknowledging that these classifications varied in different geographical areas.
2. An edition of this work is included in Peter Downey, 'The Trumpet and its Role in Music of the Renaissance and Early Baroque', 3 vols (Ph.D. thesis, The Queen's University of Belfast, 1983), vol. 3, pp. 1–63.
3. Curtis A. Price, *Music in the Restoration Theatre* (Ann Arbor, Mich.: UMI Research Press, 1979), pp. 54–5.
4. John Hawkins, *A General History of the Science and Practice of Music*, 1776, ed. O. Wessely, 2 vols (Graz: Akademische Druck- u. Verlagsanstalt, 1969), vol. 2, p. 790.
5. See Igino Conforzi, 'Girolamo Fantini, "monarch of the trumpet": recent additions to his biography', trans. Jesse Rosenberg and Henry Meredith, *Historic Brass Society Journal* 5 (1993), 159–73.
6. See Conforzi, 'Girolamo Fantini', 167.
7. The 1617 performance is referred to in *Grove 2*, s.v. 'Schütz'. See also Don L. Smithers, *The Music and History of the Baroque Trumpet before 1721* (London: Dent, 1973), pp. 140–1.
8. Timothy A. Collins, '"Of the differences between trumpeters and city tower musicians": the relationship of stadtpfeifer and kammeradschaft trumpeters', *The Galpin Society Journal* 53 (2000), 58.
9. Smithers, *The Music and History*, p. 150.

10. Altenburg, *Trumpeters' and Kettledrummers' Art*, p. 29.
11. Ibid., p. 30.
12. See, for example, Bach's adjudication report of 24 July 1745 concerning *Stadtpfeifer* apprentice Carl Friedrich Pfaffe, quoted in Smithers, *The Music and History*, p. 125.
13. See Henry Howey, 'The lives of *hoftrompeter* and *stadtpfeiffer* as portrayed in three novels of Daniel Speer', *Historic Brass Society Journal* 3 (1991), 65–78.
14. Orlando Figes, *Natasha's Dance: A Cultural History of Russia* (London: Penguin, 2003), p. 39. Figes notes that there were serf orchestras on 300 estates during the late eighteenth and early nineteenth centuries.
15. Edward H. Tarr, *The Trumpet*, trans. S. E. Plank and E. H. Tarr (London: Batsford, 1988), p. 119.
16. Smithers, *The Music and History*, p. 22.
17. Johann Ernst Altenburg, *Essay on an Introduction to the Heroic and Musical Trumpeters' and Kettledrummers' Art: For the Sake of a Wider Acceptance of the Same, Described Historically, Theoretically, and Practically and Illustrated with Examples*, 1795, trans. E. H. Tarr (Nashville, Tenn.: The Brass Press, 1974), pp. 27, 56.
18. Altenburg, *Trumpeters' and Kettledrummers' Art*, p. 28.
19. Don L. Smithers, 'The Hapsburg Imperial *Trompeter* and *Heerpauker* Privileges of 1653', *The Galpin Society Journal* 24 (1971), 91.
20. Ibid., pp. 48, 51.
21. Imperial Law Concerning the Abuses of the Guilds, Regensburg, 16 August 1731, translated from Jacob Gottlieb Sieber: *Ubhandlung von den Schwierig keiten in den Reichstadten das Reichgesetz von 16 Aug. 1731* ... (Goslar und Leipzig: Hechtel, 1771) pp. 229–42, 257–8, 260–6, 269–70.
22. Keith Polk, *German Instrumental Music of the Late Middle Ages: Players, Patrons, and Performance Practice* (Cambridge: Cambridge University Press, 1992), p. 48.
23. '*Cahiers des Doléances* of the Hatmakers, Fur-skin Dealers, and Furriers of Rouen, presented on the 21 March 1789', in Selected Sources on the Organisation of Work and the Guilds, <www.ucl.ac.uk/history/courses/europe1/weeks/guilds.htm.>.
24. William Doyle, *The Old European Order, 1660–1800*, 2nd edn (Oxford: Oxford University Press, 1992), p. 31.
25. Ibid., p. 32.
26. The instruments are described in Eric Halfpenny, 'Four seventeenth-century British trumpets', *The Galpin Society Journal* 22 (1969), 51–7.
27. Imperial Law Concerning the Abuses of the Guilds, Regensburg, 16 August 1731 in paragraph XIII, part 7, translated from Jacob Gottlieb Sieber: *Ubhandlung von den Schwierig keiten in den Reichstadten das Reichgesetz von 16 Aug. 1731* ... (Goslar und Leipzig: Hechtel, 1771), pp. 229–42, 257–8, 260–6, 269–70.
28. Altenburg, *Trumpeters' and Kettledrummers' Art*, p. 36.
29. Ibid., pp. 45, 39, 53.
30. See Thurston Dart, 'The mock trumpet', *The Galpin Society Journal* 6 (1953), 35–40. The earlier volumes were evidently published in 1698, 1699 and 1706.
31. Don L. Smithers, 'Mozart's orchestral brass', *Early Music* 20 (1992), 264 (n.12). The performance is referred to in a letter from Leopold Mozart to his son, Wolfgang, dated 12 November 1768.
32. Altenburg, *Trumpeters' and Kettledrummers' Art*, p. 112; cited in Reine Dahlqvist, *The Keyed Trumpet and its Greatest Virtuoso, Anton Weidinger* (Nashville, Tenn.: The Brass Press, 1975), pp. 6–12.
33. Kevin Eisensmith suggests that Richter's concerto and the other three trumpet concertos from the music collection of the Hofkapelle at Fulda, now held in the Library of Congress, Washington, may have been composed for the Munich court trumpeter Joseph Arnold Gross (Kevin Eisensmith, 'Joseph Riepel's Concerto in D à Clarino Principale', *ITG Journal* 27/4 (June 2003), 8–16). The other trumpet concertos in the collection are by Gross, Joseph Riepel, and an anonymous concerto that has been attributed variously to Johann Stamitz and Johann Georg Holzbogen.
34. See Tarr, *The Trumpet*, p. 143.
35. See Albert Hiller, *Trompetenmusiken aus drei Jahrhunderten (ca. 1600-nach 1900)* (Cologne: Haas, 1993).
36. Nowhere was the principal of education-for-all embraced more universally than in Scotland, where the provision of a national system of parish schools had been a prime objective of the Presbyterian authorities since the Reformation. A series of statutes from the early seventeenth century onwards culminated in an act of Parliament in 1696 which decreed that a school be

maintained in every parish and paid for by local taxation (see T. M. Devine, *The Scottish Nation, 1700–2000* (London: Allen Lane, 1999)).
37. See Dahlqvist, *The Keyed Trumpet*, pp. 12–14.
38. Observation borrowed from A. C. Grayling, *What is Good?: The Search for the Best Way to Live* (London: Weidenfeld & Nicolson, 2003), pp. 110–13.

Chapter 5 Italy and the imperial court at Vienna

1. Ellen Rosand, *Opera in Seventeenth-Century Venice: The Creation of a Genre* (Berkeley: University of California Press, 1991), pp. 330–2.
2. Donald Jay Grout and Claude V. Palisca, *A History of Western Music*, 6th edn (New York and London: Norton, 2000), p. 276.
3. Simon Towneley Worsthorne, *Venetian Opera in the Seventeenth Century* (Oxford: Clarendon Press, 1954), pp. 100, 104.
4. See Grout and Palisca, *A History of Western Music*, p. 310.
5. Edward H. Tarr, liner note to *The Art of the Baroque Trumpet, Vol. 5: An Italian Concert.* Niklas Eklund and Jeffrey Segal, trumpet. Wasa Baroque Ensemble. 2000. Compact disc. Naxos 8.555099, p. 6. See the musical example from this aria in *Grove 2*, s.v. 'Sartorio'.
6. Edward H. Tarr, 'The trumpet before 1800', in *The Cambridge Companion to Brass Instruments*, ed. T. Herbert and J. Wallace (Cambridge: Cambridge University Press, 1997), p. 89. A facsimile of a ritornello for two trumpet and strings from *Totila* by Giovanni Legrenzi (Venice, 1677), in which the first trumpet ascends to C6, is reproduced in Worsthorne, *Venetian Opera*, p. 105.
7. Carolyn Gianturco, 'Music for a Genoese wedding of 1681', *Music & Letters* 63 (1982), 39.
8. Gianturco, 'Music for a Genoese wedding', 40.
9. Charles Burney, *An Eighteenth-Century Musical Tour in France and Italy*, ed. Percy A. Scholes, Dr. Burney's Musical Tours in Europe 1 (London: Oxford University Press, 1959), p. 153.
10. Don Smithers's suggestion that the sonatas served as antiphon substitutes during the Mass (Don L. Smithers, *The Music and History of the Baroque Trumpet before 1721* (London: Dent, 1973), p. 95) has been rejected by Edward Tarr in the preface to his edition of Giuseppe Aldrovandini's *Tre Concerti per due Trombe* (Edinburgh: McNaughtan, 1992).
11. Anne Schnoebelen, 'Performance practices at San Petronio in the Baroque', *Acta Musicologica* 41 (1969), 44.
12. Anne Schnoebelen, 'Bologna, 1580–1700', in *The Early Baroque Era: From the Late 16th Century to the 1660s*, Man and Music 3, ed. C. Price (Basingstoke: Macmillan, 1993), p. 113.
13. This is not listed in the worklist for Colonna in *Grove 2*, but it is included in the list of instrumental works for trumpet(s) in the San Petronio archives in Tarr's preface to Aldrovandini, *Tre Concerti.*
14. Tarr, preface to Aldrovandini, *Tre Concerti.*
15. Smithers, *The Music and History*, pp. 103–5.
16. Jean Berger, 'The sacred works of Giacomo Antonio Perti', *Journal of the American Musicological Society* 17 (1964), 377.
17. Smithers, *The Music and History*, p. 105.
18. Schnoebelen, 'Bologna', p. 116.
19. John Spitzer and Neal Zaslaw, *The Birth of the Orchestra: History of an Institution, 1650-1815* (Oxford: Oxford University Press, 2004), pp. 106–8.
20. See Spitzer and Zaslaw, *The Birth of the Orchestra*, pp. 115–32.
21. Peter Allsop, *Arcangelo Corelli: New Orpheus of our Times* (Oxford: Oxford University Press, 1999), p. 45.
22. Ibid., pp. 41–2.
23. Ibid., p. 52.
24. Pablo-L. Rodríguez, 'Corelli's Music in Spanish Royal Chapel'; paper presented at the 9th Biennial Conference on Baroque Music, Trinity College, Dublin, July 2000.
25. Spitzer and Zaslaw, *The Birth of the Orchestra*, pp. 133–6.
26. For a detailed survey of music at the court of Ferdinand II, see Steven Saunders, *Cross, Sword, and Lyre: Sacred Music at the Imperial Court of Ferdinand II of Habsburg (1619–1637)* (Oxford: Clarendon Press, 1995).

27. Saunders, *Cross, Sword, and Lyre*, pp. 64–5. Although Liberati penned this remark in the 1680s, he may well have known Valentini personally, since both lived in Vienna during the 1640s.
28. Ibid., p. 99.
29. Ibid., pp. 99–118.
30. Stewart Carter, review of Saunders, *Cross, Sword, and Lyre*, in *Journal of Seventeenth-Century Music* 3/1 (1997) <http://www.sscm-jscm.org/v3/no1/carter.html>, par. 3.2, accessed 17 July 2009.
31. *Grove 2*, s.v. 'Bertali, Antonio'.
32. On the background to this production, see Carl B. Schmidt, 'Antonio Cesti's *Il pomo d'oro*: a reexamination of a famous Hapsburg court spectacle', *Journal of the American Musicological Society* 29 (1976), 381–412.
33. For a more detailed discussion of Schmelzer's works with trumpets and trumpet music for Viennese equestrian spectacles, see Smithers, *The Music and History*, pp. 172–8.
34. The Kroměříž archive is discussed by Don L. Smithers in 'Music for the Prince-Bishop', *Music and Musicians* 18 (1970), 24–7; and Smithers, *The Music and History*, pp. 182–90.
35. A. Peter Brown, 'Caldara's trumpet music for the imperial celebrations of Charles VI and Elisabeth Christine', in *Antonio Caldara: Essays on his Life and Times*, ed. B. W. Pritchard (Aldershot: Scolar Press, 1987), pp. 5–9.
36. Ibid., pp. 43–4.
37. Olga Termini, '*L'Irene* in Venice and Naples: tyrant and victim, or the *rifacimento* process examined', in *Antonio Caldara: Essays on his Life and Times*, ed. B. W. Pritchard (Aldershot: Scolar Press, 1987), pp. 372, 378, 394, 398 n42. In Pollarolo's setting for Venice, trumpets and oboes double the top two vocal lines. For a revival in Naples nine years later, Domenico Scarlatti set the same text with an accompaniment of trumpets and strings (ibid., p. 394).
38. For example, by Pritchard in his introduction to *Antonio Caldara* (p. xiii), and by Brown, in 'Caldara's trumpet music', p. 3.
39. Wolfgang Suppan, 'The use of wind instruments (excluding chalumeau) in Fux's music', in *Johann Joseph Fux and the Music of the Austro-Italian Baroque*, ed. H White (Aldershot: Scolar Press, 1992), p. 96.
40. Herbert Seifert, 'The secular-dramatic compositions of Fux: a general survey', in *Johann Joseph Fux and the Music of the Austro-Italian Baroque*, ed. H. White (Aldershot: Scolar Press, 1992), p. 144.
41. Brown, 'Caldara's trumpet music', pp. 4–5.
42. Ibid., pp. 6–9, for tables of players active at court during this period.
43. Ibid., p. 5.
44. These numbers seem exaggerated for the opera itself. The engraving published with the libretto shows around 100 musicians.
45. Seiffert, 'The secular-dramatic compositions of Fux', p. 148.
46. Brown, 'Caldara's trumpet music', p. 7.
47. A. Peter Brown, 'The trumpet overture and sinfonia in Vienna (1715–1822)', in *Music in Eighteenth-Century Austria*, ed. David Wyn Jones (Cambridge: Cambridge University Press, 1996), p. 39. See also 'Caldara's trumpet music', p. 7; and Tarr, *The Trumpet*, trans. S. E. Plank and E. H. Tarr (London: Batsford, 1988), pp. 119–20.
48. Suppan, 'Wind instruments', p. 98.
49. Andrew D. McCredie, 'Nicola Matteis the younger: Caldara's collaborator and ballet composer in the service of the Emperor, Charles VI', in *Antonio Caldara: Essays on his Life and Times*, ed. B. W. Pritchard (Aldershot: Scolar Press, 1987), pp. 176–7.
50. See the tables of trumpeters and drummers active at court during Caldara's years in Vienna in Brown, 'Caldara's trumpet music', pp. 6, 8–9.
51. Eleanor Selfride-Field, 'The Viennese court orchestra in the time of Caldara', in *Antonio Caldara: Essays on his Life and Times*, ed. B. W. Pritchard (Aldershot: Scolar Press, 1987) pp. 125, 128.
52. As quoted in Suppan, 'Wind instruments', p. 101. (Detlef Altenburg, 'Instrumentation im Zeichen des Hofzeremoniells. Bemerkungen zur Verwendung der Trompete im Schaffen von Johann Joseph Fux', *Alta Musica* 9 (1987), 157–68, (163).)
53. See Stewart Carter, 'Trombone obbligatos in Viennese oratorios of the Baroque', *Historic Brass Society Journal* 2 (1990), 52–77; and Suppan, 'Wind instruments', p. 104.
54. See the list of liturgical settings by Fux in Rudolf Walter, 'Bemerkungen zu den Kompositionen von Johann Joseph Fux zum *Offertorium*', in *Johann Joseph Fux and the Music of the Austro-Italian Baroque*, ed. H. M. White (Aldershot: Scolar Press, 1992), pp. 256–60.

55. Suppan, 'Wind instruments', p. 103.
56. Seiffert, 'The secular-dramatic compositions of Fux', pp. 138–52.
57. Horace Fitzpatrick, *The Horn and Horn Playing and the Austro-Bohemian Tradition from 1680 to 1830* (London: Oxford University Press, 1970), p. 60.
58. Suppan, 'Wind instruments', p. 105.

Chapter 6 Germany in the seventeenth and eighteenth centuries

1. *Grove 2*, s.v. 'Scheidt, Samuel'.
2. See Donald Burrows, *Handel* (Oxford: Oxford University Press, 1994), pp. 6–7.
3. In *Denkmäler deutscher Tonkunst* (*DDT*) 21–2 (1905), pp. 129–44.
4. Johann Ernst Altenburg, *Essay on an Introduction to the Heroic and Musical Trumpeters' and Kettledrummers' Art: For the Sake of a Wider Acceptance of the Same, Described Historically, Theoretically, and Practically and Illustrated with Examples*, 1795, trans. E. H. Tarr (Nashville, Tenn.: The Brass Press, 1974), p. 62.
5. Timothy Collins argues that since Reiche and the court trumpeters belonged to entirely different social and professional classes, it is unlikely that they would have come into contact in the course of their professional activities (Timothy A. Collins, 'Gottfried Reiche: a more complete biography', *ITG Journal* 15/3 (1991), 8).
6. A modern edition of the cantata is included in *Denkmäler der Tonkunst in Bayern* (*DTB*) 10 (1905), pp. 46–68.
7. *Grove 2*, s.v. 'Hainlein'.
8. Peter Downey, 'Adam Drese's 1648 funeral music and the invention of the slide trumpet', in *Irish Musical Studies 1: Musicology in Ireland*, ed. G. Gillen and H. White (Dublin: Irish Academic Press, 1990), pp. 200–17.
9. *Grove 2*, s.v. 'Slide trumpet'.
10. John Spitzer and Neal Zaslaw, *The Birth of the Orchestra: History of an Institution, 1650–1815* (Oxford: Oxford University Press, 2004), p. 239.
11. Max Seiffert, 'Die chorbibliothek der St. Michaelisschule in Lüneburg', *Sammelbände der Internationalen Musikgesellschaft* 9 (1908), 605–6.
12. Don L. Smithers, *The Music and History of the Baroque Trumpet before 1721* (London: Dent, 1973), p. 160. See *DDT* 6 (1901/57).
13. Smithers (*The Music and History*, p. 160) and *Grove 2*, s.v. 'Vincent Lübeck'.
14. For an account of these performances, see Hans-Günter Ottenberg, trans., P. J. Whitmore, *C.P.E. Bach* (Oxford: Oxford University Press, 1987), p. 192.
15. Kerala J. Snyder, *Dieterich Buxtehude: Organist in Lübeck* (New York: Schirmer, 1987), p. 60.
16. Ibid., pp. 91–2.
17. Ibid., p. 375.
18. Smithers, *The Music and History*, pp. 162–3.
19. Snyder, *Dieterich Buxtehude*, p. 69.
20. Geoffrey Webber, *North German Church Music in the Age of Buxtehude* (Oxford: Clarendon Press, 1996), p. 170.
21. See Thomas Hiebert, 'Early examples of mixed-keyed horns and trumpets in works of C. Graupner', *Historic Brass Society Journal* 6 (1994), 231–43.
22. In *DDT* 51–52 (1926), pp. 151–72.
23. See, for example, J. S. Endler, Symphony in D (for New Year's Day 1751), ed. J. C. Biermann in *The symphony, 1720–1840*, series C, vol. 2 (New York: Garland, 1984), pp. 141–77.
24. For a list of the extant concertos by Fasch with trumpet(s), see E. H. Tarr, Preface to Johann Friedrich Fasch, *Concerto à 8* ([Coburg]: McNaughtan, 1993).
25. Tarr, Preface to Fasch, *Concerto à 8*, citing Reine Dahlqvist.
26. See David A. Sheldon, 'Johann Friedrich Fasch: problems in style classification', *The Musical Quarterly* 58 (1972), 92–116.
27. Burrows, *Handel*, p. 42.
28. This cantata is not included in *G. F. Handel: Complete Trumpet Repertoire*, ed. Robert Minter, 4 vols (Monteux: Musica Rara, [1974]).
29. Winton Dean, *The New Grove Handel* (London: Macmillan, 1982), p. 14.
30. Burrows, *Handel*, pp. 91–2.
31. Burrows, *Handel*, p. 78.

32. Otto Erich Deutsch, *Handel: A Documentary Biography* (London: A. and C. Black, 1955), p. 661; cited in Burrows, *Handel*, p. 297.
33. Donald Burrows, 'Of Handel, London trumpeters, and trumpet music', *Historic Brass Society Journal* 11 (1999), 3–4.
34. See John Grano, *Handel's Trumpeter: The Diary of John Grano*, ed. John Ginger, with a foreword by Crispian Steele-Perkins (Stuyvesant, NY: Pendragon Press, 1997).
35. David Hunter identifies the royal musicians in Dublin, including the royal trumpeters who may have taken part in the first performance of Messiah in 'The Irish state music from 1716 to 1742 and Handel's band in Dublin', *Göttinger Händel-Beiträge* 11 (2006), 171–98.
36. *Grove 2*, s.v. 'Valentine Snow' (W. H. Husk and E. H. Tarr).
37. Charles Burney, *A General History of Music: From the Earliest Ages to the Present Period (1789)*, ed. F. Mercer, 2 vols (London: G. T. Foulis, 1935), vol. 2, p. 397; quoted in Scott P. Sorenson, 'Valentine Snow, Handel's trumpeter', *ITG Journal* 4 (1979), 8.
38. Matthew Cron and Don Smithers, *A Calendar and Comprehensive Source Catalogue of Georg Philipp Telemann's Vocal and Instrumental Music with Brass* (Tallahassee, FL: International Trumpet Guild, 1995).
39. George J. Buelow, 'Opera in Hamburg 300 years ago', *The Musical Times* 119 (1978), 28.
40. See Malcolm Boyd, *Bach: The Brandenburg Concertos* (Cambridge: Cambridge University Press, 1993), p. 4; and Heinrich Besseler, preface to *Sechs Brandenburgische Konzerte* (Kassel: Bärenreiter, 1956).
41. Christoph Wolff, *Johann Sebastian Bach: The Learned Musician* (Oxford: Oxford University Press, 2001), pp. 232–3.
42. Don Smithers suggests that it may also have been performed at nearby courts such as Weissenfels, where Bach's father-in-law, Johann Caspar Wilcke, was one of the trumpeters (Don L. Smithers, 'The Baroque trumpet after 1721: some preliminary observations. Part two: function and use', *Early Music* 6 (1978), 357).
43. Don L. Smithers, 'Bach, Reiche and the Leipzig *Collegia Musica*', *Historic Brass Society Journal* 2 (1990), 29–30.
44. Smithers, 'The Baroque trumpet after 1721 . . . Part two', 359–60.
45. This hypothesis was postulated by Gisela Csiba and Jozsef Csiba in *Die Blechblasinstrumente in J.S. Bachs Werken* (Kassel: Merserburger, 1994). For an overview in English, see the review by E. H. Tarr in *Historic Brass Society Journal* 6 (1994), 380–1.
46. Suggestions as to its meaning include a trumpet with a horn mouthpiece (Charles Sanford Terry, *Bach's Orchestra* (London: Oxford University Press, 1932), pp. 34–6), a coiled trumpet with the slide mechanism from an alto trombone attached (Smithers, 'The Baroque trumpet after 1721 . . . Part two', 361n), and a type of trombone (Reginald Morley-Pegge, *The French Horn: Some Notes on the Evolution of the Instrument and of its Technique*, 2nd edn (London: Ernest Benn, 1973), p. 143).
47. Wolff, *Johann Sebastian Bach*, pp. 157–8.
48. Ibid., pp. 264–5.
49. *Grove 2*, s.v. 'Reiche, Gottfried'.
50. See Wolff, *Johann Sebastian Bach*, pp. 367–8.

Chapter 7 France and Britain in the seventeenth and eighteenth centuries

1. Don L. Smithers, *The Music and History of the Baroque Trumpet before 1721* (London: Dent, 1973), p. 241.
2. See Peter Downey, 'Trumpet style in 17th-century France and the music of *Les Trompettes du Roy*', *Historic Brass Society Journal* 7 (1995), 67–99.
3. This air is described as calling for 'trumpets in five parts plus timpani' in John Spitzer and Neal Zaslaw, *The Birth of the Orchestra: History of an Institution, 1650–1815* (Oxford: Oxford University Press, 2004), p. 462.
4. Downey, 'Trumpet style in 17th-century France', 79.
5. Lionel Sawkins, *A Thematic Catalogue of the Works of Michel-Richard de Lalande (1657–1726); with the Assistance of John Nightingale* (Oxford: Oxford University Press, 2005), p. 213.
6. James R. Anthony, 'Air and aria added to French Opera from the death of Lully to 1720', *Revue de Musicologie* 77 (1991), 215–18.

7. 'Terribile e fiera' from *La Naissance de Jupiter* (*c.*1720) and 'Genereux atletes le son des Trompettes' from *Les Jeux Olimpiques* (1729).
8. Sawkins, *A Thematic Catalogue*, pp. 427–33, 442–4.
9. See Graham Sadler, 'Rameau and the orchestra', *Proceedings of the Royal Musical Association* 108 (1981–2), 61.
10. See Peter Downey, 'What Samuel Pepys heard on 3 February 1661: English trumpet style under the later Stuart monarchs', *Early Music* 18 (1990), 417–28. Responses to this article by J. Montagu, P. Holman, and A. Pinnock and B. Wood in *Early Music* 19 (1991) challenge Downey's view on the reconstruction of the Matteis concerto and some of the wider issues addressed in the article.
11. See Roger Bray, 'Dryden and Draghi in harmony in the 1687 "Song for St Cecilia's Day"', *Music & Letters* 78 (1997), 319–36.
12. Peter Downey, 'On sounding the trumpet and beating the drum in 17th-century England', *Early Music* 24 (1996), 272.
13. Peter Holman, *Four and Twenty Fiddlers: The Violin at the English Court, 1540–1690* (Oxford: Oxford University Press, 1993), pp. 328–30.
14. Downey, 'What Samuel Pepys heard', 424–7.
15. For a more detailed survey of Purcell's trumpet writing, see Smithers, *The Music and History*, pp. 205–27.
16. See, for example, Andrew Pinnock and Bruce Wood, 'A counterblast on English trumpets', *Early Music* 19 (1991), 437.
17. Anthony Baines, 'James Talbot's manuscript (Christ Church Library Music MS 1187). I. Wind instruments', *The Galpin Society Journal* 1 (1948), 21–2.
18. Holman, *Four and Twenty Fiddlers*, pp. 433–4.
19. Mary Chan and Jamie C. Kassler, *Roger North's Cursory Notes of Musicke (c. 1698–c. 1703): A Physical, Psychological and Critical Theory* (Kensington, N.S.W.: Unisearch, University of New South Wales, 1986), p. 119.
20. *GB-Lbl* Add. MS 32,537, f. 85v. An abridged version of this passage is quoted in John Wilson (ed.), *Roger North on Music: Being a Selection from his Essays Written During the Years c.1695–1728* (London: Novello, 1959), p. 229.
21. Crispian Steele-Perkins, 'Practical observations on natural, slide and flat trumpets', *The Galpin Society Journal* 42 (1989), 124.
22. Ibid., 123–4.
23. See Alexander McGrattan, 'The trumpet in Restoration theatre suites', *Historic Brass Society Journal* 14 (2002), 136–8.
24. See Michael Tilmouth, 'A calendar of references to music in newspapers published in London and the provinces (1660–1719)', *Royal Musical Association Research Chronicle* 1 (1961); and Michael Tilmouth, 'The beginnings of provincial concert life in England', in *Music in Eighteenth-Century England: Essays in Memory of Charles Cudworth*, ed. C. Hogwood and R. Luckett (Cambridge: Cambridge University Press, 1983), pp. 1–17.
25. Alexander McGrattan, 'The solo trumpet in Scotland, 1695–1800', in *Perspectives in Brass Scholarship*, ed. S. Carter (Stuyvesant, NY: Pendragon Press, 1997), pp. 79–90.
26. See McGrattan, 'The trumpet in Restoration theatre suites', 1–28.
27. See Spitzer and Zaslaw, *The Birth of the Orchestra*, p. 274.
28. See Peter Holman, 'The trumpet sonata in England', *Early Music* 4 (1976), 424–9, in particular the table of trumpet sonatas from the period 1685–1714.
29. This manuscript is discussed in Don L. Smithers, 'Seventeenth-century English trumpet music', *Music & Letters* 48 (1967), 358–65; and Smithers, *The Music and History*, pp. 194–204. See also, Holman, 'The trumpet sonata', 428.
30. Smithers, *The Music and History*, pp. 197–8.
31. Robert Minter made this suggestion in an annotation to his copy of the publication. The Minter Collection is held by the Royal Conservatoire of Scotland; see Trevor Herbert (2008), 'The Robert Minter Collection: a handlist of seventeenth- and eighteenth-century trumpet repertoire', <http://www.open.ac.uk/Arts/minter>, accessed 20 August 2009.
32. *The Caledonian Mercury*, 15 February 1769.
33. See Mary Rasmussen, 'English trumpet concertos in some eighteenth-century printed collections', *Brass Quarterly* 5 (1961), 51–7.
34. *GB-Edinburgh, National Archives of Scotland* GD 113/5/208/199.

35. Roger Fiske, *English Theatre Music in the Eighteenth Century*, 2nd edn (Oxford: Oxford University Press, 1986), p. 260.
36. H. Diack Johnstone, 'A ringside seat at the Handel Commemoration', *The Musical Times* 125 (Nov. 1984), 633; quoting John Marsh, who attended the event.
37. Charles Burney, *An Account of the Musical Performances in Westminster Abbey and the Pantheon, May 26th, 27th, 29th; and June the 3d, and 5th, 1784 in Commemoration of Handel* (London: Payne, 1785), pp. 86–7.
38. Art Brownlow, *The Last Trumpet: A History of the English Slide Trumpet* (Stuyvesant, NY: Pendragon Press, 1996), pp. 56–8.
39. Pamela McGairl, 'The Vauxhall Jubilee, 1786', *The Musical Times* 127 (1986), 613; and Charles Cudworth, 'The Vauxhall "Lists"', *The Galpin Society Journal* 20 (1967), 24–42.
40. *Caernarvon Castle* received 8 performances in August 1793. *The Castle of Sorrento* received 23 performances between July and September 1799 and 8 the following year. These are documented in *The London Stage, 1660–1800. A Calendar of Plays, Entertainments & Afterpieces … Compiled from the Playbills, Newspapers and Theatrical Diaries of the Period*, 5 pts (Carbondale: Southern Illinois University Press, 1960–68).
41. H. C. Robbins Landon, *The Collected Correspondence and London Notebooks of Joseph Haydn* (London: Barrie and Rockliff, 1959), pp. 274, 299.

Chapter 8 The concertos of Haydn and Hummel

1. See Reine Dahlqvist, *The Keyed Trumpet and its Greatest Virtuoso, Anton Weidinger* (Nashville, Tenn.: The Brass Press, 1975), pp. 14–15.
2. Joseph Haydn, *Trumpet Concerto*, ed. Ernest Hall, piano reduction by Harold Perry (London: Boosey & Hawkes, 1945).
3. J. N. Hummel, *Concerto a Tromba Principale*, ed. E. H. Tarr (Mainz: Universal, 1972).
4. Edward Tarr makes this suggestion in the Preface to the Universal edition of the concerto.
5. Edward H. Tarr, 'The romantic trumpet', *Historic Brass Society Journal* 5 (1993), 220.
6. John A. Rice, 'The musical bee: references to Mozart and Cherubini in Hummel's "New Year" concerto', *Music & Letters* 77 (1996), 421.
7. Rice, 'The musical bee', 404.
8. Dahlqrist, *The Keyed Trumpet*, pp. 13–14. The euphon was a recently invented instrument which produced sound by rubbing wet fingers over hollow glass rods.
9. See the modern edition by John Wallace and Trevor Herbert (London: Faber, 1989).
10. An excerpt from Neukomm's Requiem is quoted in Anthony Baines, *Brass Instruments: Their History and Development*, 1976 (London: Constable and Co., 1993), p. 193.
11. See Brownlow, *The Last Trumpet*, pp. 153–9.
12. Ibid., p. 155.
13. See Cyril Ehrlich, *First Philharmonic: A History of the Royal Philharmonic Society* (Oxford: Clarendon Press, 1995).
14. *The Times*, 2 February 1803. See also the announcement on 7 March 1803.
15. Dahlqvist cites a review of a concert at Leipzig in December 1802 which states that Weidinger was 'retaining closer knowledge of the instrument to himself for the moment' (Dahlqvist, *The Keyed Trumpet*, p. 15).
16. Ebenezer Prout, *Instrumentation* (London: Novello, Ewer and Co., 1878), p. 105.
17. Sebastian Krause, 'God of the trombone', *Brass Bulletin* 117 (2002), 74.
18. David Cairns (trans. and ed.), *The Memoirs of Hector Berlioz*, 1870, 2nd revised edn (London: Everyman's Library, 2002), p. 352. For more on Sachse, see Christian Ahrens, *Valved Brass: The History of an Invention*, trans. Steven Plank (Hillsdale, NY: Pendragon Press, 2008).
19. Michael Lewis, 'Solo Trombone Performances at the Gewandhaus in the Nineteenth Century', *International Trombone Association Journal* 20, No. 3 (Summer 1992), 27–32.

Chapter 9 The trumpet in the nineteenth and early twentieth centuries

1. Wright and Round's *Amateur Brass Band Teachers' Guide* of 1889 claims that there were 40,000 brass bands in Britain at that time (Trevor Herbert, 'Victorian brass bands: the establishment of a "working class musical tradition"', *Historic Brass Society Journal* 4 (1992), 1).

2. André M. Smith, 'Arban in Russia: a memento in the Library of Congress', *ITG Journal* 17/3 (Feb. 1993), 4–11, 34.
3. This anecdote was related to John Wallace by his teacher Denis Clift, who, as a boy, lived next door to Solomon.
4. J. Art Brownlow, *The Last Trumpet: A History of the English Slide Trumpet* (Stuyvesant, NY: Pendragon Press, 1996), pp. 226–34.
5. Hugh Macdonald, *Berlioz's Orchestration Treatise: A Translation and Commentary* (Cambridge: Cambridge University Press, 2002), p. 193.
6. François Georges Auguste Dauverné, 'Method for trumpet', trans. Gaetan Chenier, Ruby Miller Orval, Rebecca Pike and Jeffrey Snedeker, *Historic Brass Society Journal* 3 (1991), 243.
7. Frederick Corder, *The Orchestra and How to Write for it: A Practical Guide to Every Branch and Detail of Modern Orchestration*, 5th edn (London: J. Curwen [1896]), p. 55.
8. David Cairns (trans. and ed.), *The Memoirs of Hector Berlioz*, 1870, 2nd revised edn (London: Everyman's Library, 2002), p. 292. See Adam Carse, *The Orchestra from Beethoven to Berlioz: A History of the Orchestra in the First Half of the 19th Century, and of the Development of Orchestral Baton-Conducting* (Cambridge: Heffer, 1948), p. 152, and Edward H. Tarr, *The Trumpet*, trans. S. E. Plank and E. H. Tarr (London: Batsford, 1988), p. 167.
9. See Cynthia A. Hoover, 'A trumpet battle at Niblo's Pleasure Garden', *The Musical Quarterly* 55 (1969), 384–95.
10. Frank Edward Romero, '*Morceaux de concours pour trompette et cornet*, contest pieces of the Paris Conservatory 1835–1999' (DMA thesis, University of Oklahoma, 2001), pp. 10, 24.
11. D. Kern Holoman, 'The Société des Concerts du Conservatoire (1828–1967)', <http://hector.ucdavis.edu/SdC/default.html>, accessed 21 July 2008.
12. Dauverné, 'Method for trumpet', 219.
13. Ibid., 218.
14. Daniel Kelly, 'The competition solos of J. B. Arban', *ITG Journal* 30/3 (March, 2006), 18.
15. Dauverné, 'Method for trumpet', 207, 214, 243.
16. See Friedrich Anzenberger, 'The earliest French tutor for slide trumpet', *Historic Brass Society Journal* 4 (1992), 106–11.
17. *The Morning Chronicle*, 19 May 1845.
18. Lee J. Weimer, 'The trumpet as a solo instrument in New York City from 1835 to 1845' (DMA thesis, University of Memphis, 1999), pp. 42–5.
19. Constant Pierre, *Le Conservatoire National de Musique et de Déclamation: Documents Historiques et Administraitifs, Recueillis ou Reconstitués par Constant Pierre; Sous-Chef du Secrétariat* (Paris: Imprimerie nationale, 1900), p. 647.
20. Merri Franquin, 'La Trompette et le Cornet' in *Encyclopédie de la Musique et Dictionnaire du Conservatoire*, pt. 2, vol. 3 (Paris: Delagrave, 1927), p. 1611. There is confusion in the brass literature over Teste's full name. Both Franquin and Constant Pierre (*La Facture Instrumentale à l'Exposition Universelle de 1889. Notes d'un Musicien sur les Instruments à Souffle Humain Nouveaux & Perfectionnés* (Paris: Librairie de l'Art Indépendant, 1890), p. 116) merely give his family name; however, Birkemeier and Tarr identify him as André-Joseph Leclerc (Richard P. Birkemeier, 'The history and music of the orchestral trumpet of the nineteenth century, part 2', *ITG Journal* 9/4 (May 1985), 19; and Edward H. Tarr, 'The "Bach trumpet" in the nineteenth and twentieth centuries', in *Musique Ancienne – Instruments et Imagination: Actes des Rencontres Internationales Harmoniques, Lausanne 2004* (*Music of the Past – Instruments and Imagination: Proceedings of the Harmoniques International Congress, Lausanne 2004*), ed. M. Latcham (Bern: Peter Lang, 2006), p. 21). Through his research in the archives of the Société des Concerts, Kern Holoman has established that his full name was Xavier-Napoléon Teste.
21. Franquin, 'La Trompette et le Cornet', pp. 1606–7.
22. Ibid., pp. 1611–12; see also Birkemeier, 'The history and music', 20–1.
23. *New Grove 2*, s.v. 'Franquin, Merri' (by E. H. Tarr).
24. Franquin, 'La Trompette et le Cornet', pp. 1612–13; H. M. Lewis, 'Roger Voisin: an orchestral legend', *ITG Newsletter* 6/2 (Feb. 1980), 6.
25. See Rosario Macaluso, 'Brass playing in Belgium: school of trumpet in Liège', *Brass Bulletin* 88 (1994), 38–42; 89 (1995), 74–81; 90 (1995), 8–21; 91 (1995), 60–72. See the photograph of Ernest Hall playing a Mahillon B flat trumpet in Martin Hurrell, 'The BBC Symphony Orchestra trumpet section', *ITG Journal* (Sept. 1995), 5. This instrument is now in the Royal College of Music Museum of Instruments.

26. Reine Dahlqvist, *The Keyed Trumpet and its Greatest Virtuoso, Anton Weidinger* (Nashville, Tenn.: The Brass Press, 1975), p. 20.
27. Edward H. Tarr, 'The romantic trumpet: part two', *Historic Brass Society Journal* 6 (1994), 114.
28. For a detailed discussion of this repertoire, see Tarr, 'The Romantic trumpet: part two'.
29. Beryl Kenyon de Pascual, trans. with introduction, 'José de Juan Martínez' *Método de Clarín* (1830)', *Historic Brass Society Journal* 5 (1993), 92–106.
30. Jean-Pierre Mathez, and G. Bonino, 'The Milan Conservatory (1808–1999)', *Brass Bulletin* 106 (1999), 64–5.
31. Edward H. Tarr, 'The romantic trumpet', *Historic Brass Society Journal* 5 (1993), 225.
32. Preface to A. Ponchielli, *Concerto per tromba e banda*, ed. E. Hermann (Bulle: Editions Bim, 1985).
33. Carse, *The Orchestra*, pp. 166–7, 180.
34. Ibid., p. 167, citing *The Harmonicon*, May 1829, 122.
35. *The Harmonicon*, Feb. 1831, 48–9.
36. Dauverné, 'Method for trumpet', 208. On Gambati's petitions to the inspectors of the Conservatoire, see Romero, '*Morceaux de concours*', p. 25, citing Mary Gillian MacKay, 'Trumpet and cornet concours music at the Paris Conservatoire, 1835–1925: the development of styles and roles' (DMA thesis, Northwestern University, 1996), p. 16.
37. Carse, *The Orchestra*, pp. 270–3.
38. Tarr, 'The romantic trumpet', 225, 248n.
39. *The Harmonicon*, March 1829, 53; quoted in Carse, *The Orchestra*, p. 275.
40. Edward H. Tarr, 'Ferdinand Weinschenk (1831–1910), pivotal figure in German trumpet history', *Historic Brass Society Journal* 11 (1999), 10–11.
41. See Edward H. Tarr, 'Oskar Böhme revisited: young musicians' training, instruments, and repertoire in the late nineteenth and early twentieth centuries', in *Brass Scholarship in Review*, ed. S. Carter (Hillsdale, NY: Pendragon Press, 2006), pp. 193–9.
42. Karl Bargans, 'On the trumpet, as at present employed in the orchestra', *The Harmonicon* (Jan. 1830), 23–5.
43. Tarr, *The Trumpet*, p. 170.
44. Fragments of orchestral music composed by Hummel for theatre productions at Weimar during the 1830s, held in the British Library, contain trumpet parts of this nature (*GB-Lbl* Add. MSS 32188, 32196 and 32211).
45. The composer in this publication is identified merely as Sachse; see the edition of the concerto by Stephen L. Glover and H. M. Lewis (Nashville: The Brass Press, 1980).
46. Tarr, 'Oskar Böhme revisited', p. 214.
47. Edward H. Tarr, *East Meets West: The Russian Trumpet Tradition from the Time of Peter the Great to the October Revolution* (Hillsdale, NY: Pendragon Press, 2003), pp. 203–7. It could be that, like one of the present authors, John Wallace, he was a first-study composition student, and second-study trumpet student.
48. Tarr, 'Oskar Böhme revisited', pp. 203–4.
49. Seifert's music library, which was given to the Bad Säckingen Trumpet Museum after his death, includes many cornet solos (see Tarr, *East Meets West*, pp. 153–63).
50. Verena Jakobsen Barth, *Die Trompete als Soloinstrument in der Kunstmusik Europas seit 1900: mit besonderer Berücksichtigung der Entwicklung ab 1980 am Beispiel der Solisten Håkan Hardenberger, Ole Edward Antonsen und Reinhold Friedrich* (Gothenburg: University of Gothenburg, 2007), p. 45.
51. Hans-Joachim Krumpfer, '1797–1908: the long sleep of the Haydn trumpet concerto', *Brass Bulletin* 75 (1991), 37–9. A photograph of Seifert holding his Thibouville-Lamy (Paris) cornet, dating from 23 June 1929, is reproduced in this article, and in Edward H. Tarr, 'Two great trumpet virtuosos and their instruments' *ITG Journal* 16/3 (Feb. 1992), 17.
52. Tarr, *East Meets West*, p. 153.
53. *Harper's School for the Trumpet* (London: Rudall, Carte & Co., 1875).
54. Clifford Bevan, 'The (P)Russian trumpet', *The Galpin Society Journal* 41 (1988), 112–14. Edward Tarr has identified a trumpet in the State Museum of Musical Culture 'M. I. Glinka' in Moscow, dated 1825, which closely resembles the instrument illustrated in Harper's tutor, confirming Bevan's theory (Tarr, 'The romantic trumpet', 239).
55. Thomas Harper, *A Selection of Favourite Airs, Adapted and Arranged as Solos, Duets, and Trios, for the Royal Kent Bugle* (London: Clementi & Co., *c.*1830). See Scott Sorenson and John Webb, 'The Harpers and the trumpet', *The Galpin Society Journal* 39 (1986), 40–1. The title page of this publication refers to Harper as Inspector of Trumpets and Bugles to the East India Company.

56. Sorenson and Webb, 'The Harpers and the trumpet', 38–9.
57. François-Joseph Fétis, *Curiositiés historiques de la musique, complément nécessaire de La musique mise à la portée de tout le monde* (Paris: Janet et Cotelle, 1830), p. 194; cited in Carse, *The Orchestra*, p. 218.
58. Sorenson and Webb, 'The Harpers and the trumpet', 38.
59. This is recorded at his admission to the Royal Society of Musicians (Sorenson and Webb, 'The Harpers and the trumpet', 45).
60. Adam Carse, *The Life of Jullien: Adventurer, Showman-Conductor and Establisher of the Promenade Concerts in England, Together with a History of Those Concerts up to 1895* (Cambridge: Heffer, 1951), p. 9.
61. J. Art Brownlow, *The Last Trumpet: A History of the English Slide Trumpet* (Stuyvesant, NY: Pendragon Press, 1996), pp. 166–9.
62. *Boosey's One hundred dances for the Cornet à pistons, arranged by T. Harper* (London, *c.*1859); *Harper's School for the Cornet à pistons* (London, *c.*1865).
63. *The Pall Mall Gazette*, 7 Dec. 1885.
64. Carse, *The Life of Jullien*, p. 13.
65. Roy Newsome, 'Belle Vue and brass bands', *Manchester Sounds* 2 (2001), 8.
66. *The Manchester Times and Gazette*, Sat. 16 Sept. 1843.
67. 'The First by "Buckland"', in *The Centenary 100th Anniversary of the Great September Open Championship Brass Band Contest. Held in the Kings [sic] Hall, Belle Vue / Manchester, England[,] on Saturday, 6th September, 1952* (Souvenir Programme), pp. 4–5.
68. Carse, *The Orchestra*, p. 186; Rosario Macaluso, 'Brass playing in Belgium', *Brass Bulletin* 88, (1994), 41.
69. *The Morning Chronicle*, 22 Feb. 1847.
70. *GB-Lbl* RPS MS 330, ff. 58, 79v, 88.
71. Gordon Turner and Alwyn W. Turner, *The Trumpets Will Sound: The Story of the Royal Military School of Music, Kneller Hall* (Tunbridge Wells: Parapress, 1996), pp. 36, 153.
72. *A list of pupils received into the Academy since its foundation in 1822–3* (London: Royal Academy of Music, *c.*1838). The authors are grateful to Bridget Palmer for this information, which derives from a database compiled from the student register of the Royal Academy of Music for 1837–1873.
73. Geoffrey Thomason, 'Hess, huffs and Hallé facts: staff appointments in the early years of the Royal Manchester College of Music', *Manchester Sounds* 3 (2002), 55–7.
74. Richard P. Birkemeier states that Morrow taught at the Guildhall School of Music from 1882, in 'The F trumpet and its last virtuoso, Walter Morrow', *Brass Bulletin* 65 (1989), 37.
75. Arnold Myers, 'Brasswind innovation and output of Boosey & Co. in the Blaikley era', *Historic Brass Society Journal* 14 (2002), 401.
76. Walter Morrow, 'The trumpet as an orchestral instrument', *Proceedings of the Musical Association* 21 (1895), 133–47.
77. G. Bernard Shaw, ed. Dan H. Laurence, *Shaw's Music: The Complete Musical Criticism in Three Volumes* (London: Bodley Head, 1981), vol. 1, pp. 222, 323; vol. 3, pp. 149–50.
78. Ibid., vol. 2, pp. 588, 790.
79. *Otto Langey's Tutor for the Cornet. Revised, re-arranged & many studies added, selected from works of the great masters, also some exercises & melodious studies with marks of phrasing & expression carefully marked, composed for this tutor by Walter Morrow, Professor of the cornet & trumpet at the Guildhall School of Music & member of the orchestras:- Philharmonic Society, Royal Choral Society, Richter Concerts, London Symphony Concerts etc.* (London: Hawkes & Son; New York: Jos. W. Stern & Co., *c.*1911).
80. Brownlow, *The Last Trumpet*, pp. 81–9.
81. John Webb, 'The English slide trumpet', *Historic Brass Society Journal* 5 (1993), 270–3; Myers, 'Brasswind innovation', 406.
82. Algernon, S. Rose, *Talks with Bandsmen: A Popular Handbook for Brass Instrumentalists*, 1895; facsimile edn with introduction by Arnold Myers (London: Tony Bingham, 1996), p. 179.
83. Arnold Myers and Frank Tomes, 'PCB cornets and Webster trumpets: Rudall Carte's patent conical bore brasswind', *Historic Brass Society Journal* 7 (1995), 109–10. The cornet virtuoso Jack Mackintosh who was a founder member of the BBC Symphony Orchestra appears to be playing a Rudall Carte instrument of this design in the photograph from 1939, shown in Hurrell, 'The BBC Symphony Orchestra trumpet section', 10.
84. See <http://www.cph.rcm.ac.uk/Catalogues/Wind%20Catalogue/Trumpets4valve&pisttpts.htm> accessed 30 July 2008. See also Myers and Tomes, 'PCB cornets', 107–22.

85. Myers, 'Brasswind innovation', 401.
86. Ibid.
87. See Tarr, *East Meets West*, chapter 2.
88. Ibid., p. 63.
89. Ibid., p. 150.
90. Ibid., chapters 3 and 4.
91. Henry A. Kmen, *Music in New Orleans: The Formative Years, 1791–1841* (Baton Rouge: Louisiana State University Press, 1966), pp. 138–9, 210. On the influence of popular European art music on the early jazz style and the music of Louis Armstrong in particular, see Peter Ecklund, '"Louis Licks" and nineteenth-century cornet etudes: the roots of melodic improvisation as seen in the jazz style of Louis Armstrong', *Historic Brass Society Journal* 13 (2001), 90–101.
92. Lee J. Weimer, 'The trumpet as a solo instrument in New York City from 1835 to 1845' (DMA thesis, University of Memphis, 1999).
93. In a biographical sketch of Arbuckle published in *Jacobs' Band Monthly* in 1931, the author, Herbert L. Clarke, mentions a performance of 'Let the Bright Seraphim' for cornet and voice by Arbuckle and the soprano Parepa Rosa at the National Peace Jubilee in Boston in 1869 (David Baldwin, '*Arbuckle's Complete Cornet Method* (1866)', *ITG Journal* 14/3 (Feb. 1990), 32). See the report of Arbuckle performing the same aria on cornet at the Boston Music Festival in *The New York Times*, 12 June 1870; and in the benefit concert for the soprano Anna Bishop in 1882, in *The New York Times*, 28 May 1882.
94. Keith C. Clark, 'Trumpet sections of American symphony orchestras: The Chicago Symphony Orchestra', *ITG Journal* 8/2 (Dec. 1983), 17; *The New York Times*, 11 March 1867 and 20 May 1868.
95. André M. Smith, 'Max Schlossberg: founder of the American school of trumpet playing in the twentieth century', *ITG Journal* (May 1997), 48n.
96. Tarr, *East Meets West*, pp. 226–7.
97. See Brian Shook, 'William Vacchiano (1912–2005): a tribute to his life, career, and pedagogical method', *ITG Journal* 30/3 (March 2006), 6.
98. Tarr, *East Meets West*, pp. 248–53.
99. Cynthia A. Hoover, 'A trumpet battle at Niblo's Pleasure Garden', *The Musical Quarterly* 55 (1969), 387.
100. Andrea Olmstead, *Juilliard: A History* (Urbana and Chicago: University of Illinois Press, 1999), p. 25. See also *The New York Times*, 11 June, 1905, 8 Oct., 1905, and 8 Dec., 1907.
101. The most extensive study of brass chamber music in the USA during the late nineteenth and early twentieth centuries is Raymond David Burkhart, 'Brass chamber music in Lyceum and Chautauqua' (PhD dissertation, Claremont Graduate University, 2010). Burkhart identifies sixty-one professional brass ensembles that performed on the Lyceum and Chautauqua circuits between 1877 and 1939 and many others that were active during the same period. Several of the most prominent ensembles were all-female.
102. See Michel Laplace, 'A woman and a life in the service of the trumpet: Edna White', *Brass Bulletin* 48 (1984), 10–16; and the biography of Edna White by Susan Fleet at <http://www.susanfleet.com> (2008), accessed August 2010.
103. Keith C. Clark, 'Trumpet sections of American symphony orchestras: The Boston Symphony Orchestra', *ITG Newsletter* 5/3 (May 1979), 7.
104. *GB-Lbl* MS Mus. 200, ff. 95–6.
105. Clark, 'Trumpet sections ... Boston', 7; H. M. Lewis, Jr., 'Roger Voisin: an orchestral legend', *ITG Newsletter* 6/2 (Feb., 1980), 6. See also Harry Herforth, Adolph Herseth and Martin Lessen, 'A tribute to George Mager (1885–1950)', *ITG Journal* 10/2 (Dec. 1985), 14–16.
106. Trevor Herbert, 'Brass playing in the early twentieth century: idioms and cultures of performance'. Introduction to *Early Twentieth-Century Brass Idioms: Art, Jazz, and Other Popular Traditions*, Studies in Jazz 58, ed. Howard T. Weiner (Lanham, MD: Scarecrow Press, 2009), p. xi.

Chapter 10 The 'Bach revival'

1. John Butt, *Bach: Mass in B Minor* (Cambridge: Cambridge University Press, 1991), p. 28.
2. Susanna Grossmann-Vendrey, *Felix Mendelssohn Bartholdy und die Musik der Vergangenheit* (Regensburg: Gustav Bosse, 1969), p. 161.

3. Peter Mercer-Taylor, 'Mendelssohn and the institution(s) of German art music', in *The Cambridge Companion to Mendelssohn*, ed. Peter Mercer-Taylor (Cambridge: Cambridge University Press, 2004), p. 17.
4. Adam Carse, *The Orchestra from Beethoven to Berlioz: A History of the Orchestra in the First Half of the 19th Century, and of the Development of Orchestral Baton-Conducting* (Cambridge: Heffer, 1948), pp. 461–2. Although in the score the clarinet parts are only printed in the Gigue, the trumpet parts are simplified throughout, suggesting that clarinets also substituted for trumpets in the other movements.
5. See Anselm Hartinger, 'A "fairly correct copy of the mass"? – Mendelssohn's score of the B-minor Mass as a document of the Romantic's view on matters of performance practice and source criticism', in *International Symposium: Understanding Bach's B-minor Mass* (Discussion Books 1 and 2), ed. Yo Tomita, E. Crean, I. Mills and T. Kovačević (Belfast: Queen's University, 2007), pp. 290–1.
6. Edward H. Tarr, 'The "Bach trumpet" in the nineteenth and twentieth centuries', in *Musique Ancienne – Instruments et Imagination: Actes des Rencontres Internationales Harmoniques, Lausanne 2004* (*Music of the Past – Instruments and Imagination: Proceedings of the Harmoniques International Congress, Lausanne 2004*), ed. M. Latcham (Bern: Peter Lang, 2006), pp. 19–20.
7. Ibid., p. 20.
8. Neither of these gives a date of publication, but the Preface to the Magnificat is dated 1864, and the edition of the Christmas Oratorio appears to be near contemporaneous.
9. *Dwight's Journal*, 29 May 1875, 25–8; 18 March 1876, 198–9; 26 May 1877, 31.
10. The score that Thomas used for this performance, with copious markings and the alterations to the trumpet parts pasted in the manuscript, is held in the Newberry Library in Chicago; see Paul Luongo, 'Theodore Thomas's 1902 performance of Bach's Mass in B minor: working within the Grand American Festival', in *International Symposium: Understanding Bach's B-minor Mass.* Discussion Book 1 and 2, ed. Yo Tomita, E. Crean, I. Mills and T. Kovačević (Belfast: School of Music and Sonic Arts, 2007), pp. 322–43.
11. Edward H. Tarr, 'Ferdinand Weinschenk (1831–1910), pivotal figure in German trumpet history', *Historic Brass Society Journal* 11 (1999), 12–14.
12. Tarr, 'The "Bach trumpet"', p. 21.
13. Victor Charles Mahillon, *Éléments D'Acoustique Musicale et Instrumentale: Comprenant L'Examen de la Construction Théorique de Tous les Instruments de Musique en Usage Dans L'Orchestration Moderne* (Brussels: C. Mahillon, 1874), p. 144.
14. Tarr, 'The "Bach trumpet"', pp. 24–5.
15. Merri Franquin, 'La Trompette et le Cornet', in *Encyclopédie de la Musique et Dictionnaire du Conservatoire*, pt 2, vol. 3 (Paris: Delagrave, 1927), p. 1611.
16. Constant Pierre, *La Facture Instrumentale à L'Exposition Universelle de 1889. Notes d'un Musicien sur les Instruments à Souffle Humain Nouveaux & Perfectionnés* (Paris: Librairie de L'Art Indépendant, 1890), p. 116; see also Katharine Ellis, *Interpreting the Musical Past: Early Music in Nineteenth-Century France* (New York; Oxford: Oxford University Press, 2005), p. 98.
17. D. Kern Holoman, *The Société des Concerts du Conservatoire, 1828–1967* (Berkeley: University of California Press, 2004), p. 64.
18. Anthony Baines, *Brass Instruments: Their History and Development*, 1976 (London: Constable and Co., 1993), p. 239. Verena Jakobsen Barth, *Die Trompete als Soloinstrument in der Kunstmusik Europas seit 1900: mit besonderer Berücksichtigung der Entwicklung ab 1980 am Beispiel der Solisten Håkan Hardenberger, Ole Edward Antonsen und Reinhold Friedrich* (Gothenburg: University of Gothenburg, 2007), p. 136.
19. Denis McCaldin, Preface to Hector Berlioz, *Te Deum*. New Edition of the Complete Works 10 (Kassel: Bärenreiter, 1973), pp. x–xi.
20. Werner Menke, *History of the Trumpet of Bach and Handel*, trans. G. Abraham, London, 1934, repr. (Nashville,Tenn.: The Brass Press, 1985), p. 62.
21. Translated in W. F. H. Blandford, 'The "Bach trumpet"', *Monthly Musical Record* 65 (1935), 50; quoted in Tarr, 'The "Bach trumpet"', p. 27.
22. Tarr, 'The "Bach trumpet"', p. 29.
23. F. G. Edwards, 'Bach's Music in England', *The Musical Times* [*MT*] 37 (Nov. 1896), 725.
24. Ibid.
25. *MT*, 1 Dec 1896, 797.
26. *MT*, 1 Dec. 1896, 798-9.

27. *Dwight's Journal*, 26 Jan. 1874, 161–2 (from *The London Telegraph*, 18 Dec. 1873).
28. *Dwight's Journal*, 25 July 1874, 268 (from *The Academy*, 3 Jan. 1874).
29. Edwards, 'Bach's Music in England', *The Musical Times* 37 (Dec. 1896), 800; see also *Dwight's Journal*, 27 May 1876, 237 (from *The Musical Standard*, 29 April 1876).
30. *MT*, 1 June 1876, 499–500.
31. Ibid., 487–90.
32. *MT*, 1 Aug. 1876, 568.
33. *MT*, 1 May 1878, 274–81.
34. Tarr, 'The "Bach trumpet"', pp. 32–3.
35. *MT*, 1 Nov. 1884, 644.
36. Walter Morrow, 'The trumpet as an orchestral instrument', *Proceedings of the Musical Association* 21 (1895), 141.
37. G. Bernard Shaw, ed. Dan H. Laurence, *Shaw's Music: The Complete Musical Criticism in Three Volumes* (London: Bodley Head, 1981), vol. 1, pp. 222–3; cited in Tarr, 'The "Bach trumpet"', p. 30.
38. Menke, *History of the Trumpet*, p. 121.
39. Morrow, 'The trumpet as an orchestral instrument', 141.
40. Tarr, 'The "Bach trumpet"', pp. 30–1.
41. Hermann Pietzsch, 'The natural trumpet and the valve-trumpet and their use in the orchestra', in *The Trumpet as an Orchestral Instrument and its Treatment During the Different Periods of Musical Culture*, trans. J. Bernhoff, rev. edn by C. P. Lillya and R. Schilke (Ann Arbor, Mich.: University Music Press, n.d.), pp. 17–18.
42. Morrow, 'The trumpet as an orchestral instrument', 142. Silvani & Smith began business in London in 1884 (*New Grove 2*, s.v. 'Bach Trumpet', and Philip Bate, *The Trumpet and Trombone: An Outline of Their History, Development and Construction*, 2nd edn (London: Ernest Benn, 1978), p. 190).
43. Baines, *Brass Instruments*, p. 190.
44. *MT*, Feb. 1886, p. 81. It should be noted that none of the newspaper reports of this performance consulted mentions Morrow as the trumpet soloist. F. McGrath, who played second to Morrow in the performance of Bach's B minor Mass in Leeds later that year, was also prominent in *Messiah* performances throughout Britain around this time.
45. *MT*, 1 Nov. 1886, 655.
46. *The Era*, Sat. 7 March 1891.
47. *MT*, 1 Feb. 1895, 81–2.
48. The Edinburgh University Collection of Historic Musical Instruments possesses a 'Bach trumpet' by Boosey & Co. dated 1909, as well as two 'Bach trumpets' in D: one in E flat/D from *c.*1916 by Hawkes & Son, the other in D from 1926 by Boosey & Co. The archives of Boosey & Co. record the production of twelve Bach trumpets in A between 1896 and 1910. The authors are grateful to Arnold Myers for providing this information.
49. Blandford, 'The "Bach trumpet"', 76; see Tarr, 'The "Bach trumpet"', p. 32.
50. *MT*, 1 July 1926, 648.
51. Ibid.
52. Rosario Macaluso, 'A grand master: Théo Charlier', *ITG Journal* 25/4 (June 2001), 31–2. Charlier continued to use a D trumpet for other works by Bach. For example, he played the first trumpet part of the B-minor Mass on a D trumpet in 1931 (ibid., 32).
53. Edward H. Tarr, *The Trumpet*, trans. S. E. Plank and E. H. Tarr (London: Batsford, 1988), p. 190; and Tarr, 'The "Bach trumpet"', p. 36.
54. See Keith C. Clark, 'Performances of the Brandenburg Concerto No. 2 in the United States', *ITG Journal* 3/3 (1978), 24.
55. Ibid., 25.
56. *The New York Times*, 8 Nov. 1903. In his autobiography Franko stated: 'I had Mahillon of Brussels construct for me high trumpets, especially to be used in Bach's works' (Sam Franko, *Chords and Discords: Memoirs and Musings of an American Musician* (New York: Viking Press, 1938), p. 102). Franko's declared intention for this series was 'to present [the music] in the spirit of the composers and in the character of the time; in a small hall with a small orchestra' (Ibid., pp. 97–8).
57. *The New York Times*, 21 Dec. 1921.
58. Tarr, 'The "Bach trumpet"', p. 37.
59. BBC Proms Archive, at <http://www.bbc.co.uk/proms/archive>, accessed 5 September 2010.

60. Johannes Valk was principal trumpet of the Hallé Orchestra between 1901 and 1917. The authors are grateful to Eleanor Roberts, archivist of the Hallé Orchestra, for identifying Valk as soloist. Although there is no evidence that Mottl's arrangement was used on this occasion, a copy of this publication, annotated with the conductor's customary blue pencil markings, is included in the Beecham Collection in the University of Sheffield Library.
61. Edward Tarr notes that he had been informed by one of his trumpet teachers in the USA, who attended the concert, that Barr in fact transposed several passages down an octave (Tarr, 'The "Bach trumpet"', p. 36).
62. *MT*, 1 Nov. 1922, 797.
63. The performance was given by the Orchestra of the Royal Philharmonic Society in the Queen's Hall, London. In an article for the Royal College of Music Magazine, Ernest Hall revealed that the composer purchased a natural trumpet which he intended to lend to trumpeters who did not have access to such an instrument (Michael Kennedy, *A Catalogue of the Works of Ralph Vaughan Williams*, 2nd edn (Oxford: Oxford University Press, 1996), p. 90). January 1922 was a significant month for Barr: on 24 January he took part in the first (private) performance of William Walton's *Façade*.
64. Robert Philip, 'Brass playing before globalization', in *Brass Scholarship in Review*, ed. S. Carter (Hillsdale, NY: Pendragon Press, 2006), pp. 278–9. Tarr dates this recording 1928 and does not identify Hall as the trumpet soloist ('The "Bach trumpet"', p. 37).
65. See Philip, 'Brass playing', p. 279. The third movement of this recording of the Brandenburg Concerto No. 2 is included in *European Cornet and Trumpet Soloists 1899–1950*. Compact disc. International Trumpet Guild Supplement, 2005. Liner notes by Edward H. Tarr.
66. See Tarr, 'The "Bach trumpet"', p. 38.
67. Philip, 'Brass playing', pp. 277–8; see Tarr, 'The "Bach trumpet"', p. 38, for details of the performances leading up to this recording.
68. *MT*, June 1938, 462.
69. Malcolm Boyd, *Bach: The Brandenburg Concertos* (Cambridge: Cambridge University Press, 1993), p. 30.
70. See Menke, *History of the Trumpet*, pp. 117–18.
71. See Crispian Steele-Perkins, *The Trumpet* (London: Kahn & Averill, 2001), pp. 88–9, and Tarr, 'The "Bach trumpet"', p. 42.
72. On the development of the two systems, see Steele-Perkins, *The Trumpet*, pp. 86–92.
73. See Mike Diprose, 'Partial success: natural trumpet – the march forward', *Early Music Review* 105 (Feb. 2005), 9–10; and Mike Diprose, 'Return to the natural trumpet', *Early Music Review* 110 (Dec. 2005), 6–7.

Chapter 11 Repertoire, technique and performance idioms since 1900

1. Verena Jakobsen Barth, *Die Trompete als Soloinstrument in der Kunstmusik Europas seit 1900: mit besonderer Berücksichtigung der Entwicklung ab 1980 am Beispiel der Solisten Håkan Hardenberger, Ole Edward Antonsen und Reinhold Friedrich* (Gothenburg: University of Gothenburg, 2007), pp. 44–6, 67–71.
2. See Edward H. Tarr, *East Meets West: The Russian Trumpet Tradition from the Time of Peter the Great to the October Revolution* (Hillsdale, NY: Pendragon Press, 2003), pp. 117–18, 331–2.
3. Varèse, *Intégrales*, f.p. New York, 1 March 1925; Ravel, *Boléro*, f.p. Paris Opéra, 22 November 1928.
4. Ernst-Alexandre Ansermet, 'Bechet and Jazz visit Europe, 1919', in *Frontiers of Jazz*, ed. Ralph de Toledano, 3rd rev. edn (Gretna, La: Pelican, 1994), pp. 111–18.
5. This led directly to Stravinsky's Three Pieces for Clarinet of 1919.
6. See Mervyn Cooke, *The Chronicle of Jazz* (London: Thames & Hudson, 1997), p. 44, for more information regarding Ernest Ansermet, who conducted the first performance of *Histoire du soldat*. Ansermet visited the USA in 1916, bringing back sheet music for various rags, which he shared with Stravinsky.
7. Dahlqvist, *The Keyed Trumpet*, p. 20.
8. See Jakobsen Barth, *Die Trompete*, pp. 383–7, for Seifert's repertoire list.
9. For more on Karl Pilss and Helmut Wobisch during this period, see Robert Suggs, 'Brilliant music for a dark era: Karl Pilss, Helmut Wobisch, and the Trompetenchor der Stadt Wien', *International Trumpet Guild Journal* 28/2 (Jan. 2004), 12–16.

10. The concerto's dedicatee was his son Brian Boughton (b.1927), a pupil of Ernest Hall at the Royal College of Music. The concerto had to wait for its first performance until 1989, with John Wallace and The Fife Sinfonia.
11. Jakobsen Barth, *Die Trompete*, pp. 117–18. For a transcript of a list of 177 performances of the Brandenburg Concerto by Scherbaum outside Germany between 1955 and 1983, found on his hand-written copy of the trumpet part, see Edward H. Tarr, 'The "Bach trumpet" in the nineteenth and twentieth centuries', in *Musique Ancienne – Instruments et Imagination: Actes des Rencontres Internationales Harmoniques, Lausanne 2004* (*Music of the Past – Instruments and Imagination: Proceedings of the Harmoniques International Congress, Lausanne 2004*), ed. M. Latcham (Bern: Peter Lang, 2006), pp. 46–7.
12. For more on Scherbaum, see Jakobsen Barth, *Die Trompete*, and Verena Jakobsen, 'Adolf Scherbaum (1909–2000), trailblazer of the classical solo trumpet', *Brass Bulletin* 122 (2003), 62–74.
13. See the Maurice André discography, compiled by Gérard Weber, at <www.maurice-andre.com> (updated 33/2010), accessed 15 November 2010. A discography, compiled by Olivier Delavault, is included in Guy Touvron, *Maurice André: Une Trompette Pour la Renommée* (Monaco: Rocher, 2003).
14. *Baroque Trumpet Concertos*, Maurice André, Riccardo Muti, Philharmonia Orchestra. 1985 (recorded 1984). Compact disc: EMI CDC 7473112.
15. *Trumpet Concertos*, Maurice André, Herbert von Karajan, Berlin Philharmonic Orchestra. 1974. Vinyl record: HMV ASD3044.
16. Giuliano Sommerhalder won second prize, and Guillaume Couloumy and Gabor Richter shared third prize, in the same year.
17. The system of co-principals, or two recognised principal players in strings, wind, brass and percussion sections sharing the annualised work of an orchestra in batches of groups of concerts and recordings with the same conductor, became more widespread as the century progressed. A wide variety of practices exists: sometimes there is implied seniority, as when there is a principal and co-principal (or assistant principal), and sometimes the terminology of equality is used, like joint-principal.
18. Premiered in this complete form by the Ensemble Modern at the Frankfurter Alte Oper in 1996, conducted by Peter Rundel.
19. Written for and performed with the composer by John Wallace.
20. The solo careers of Hardenberger, Friedrich and Antonsen, and the repertoire they engendered, are the main focus of Jakobsen Barth, *Die Trompete*.
21. Composers commissioned include Philip Glass, Ned Rorem, Somei Satoh and Aulis Sallinen.
22. On the PJBE, see Donna McDonald, *The Odyssey of the Philip Jones Brass Ensemble* (Bulle: Editions Bim, 1986).
23. Excerpt from the composer's note, from the Sir Peter Maxwell Davies website, MaxOpus.com. For the complete note, see <http://www.maxopus.com/work_detail.aspx?key=48>, accessed 29 December 2009.
24. Rolf Quinque, *ASA – Atmung–Stütze–Ansatz Methode* (Éditions BIM: Bulle, Switzerland, 1980); Carmine Caruso: *Musical Calisthenics for Brass* (Hollywood, Ca.: Almo, 1979); Jerome Callet, *Trumpet Yoga* (Charles Colin, New York, 1971); Jerome Callet and Robert Civiletti, *The Secrets of the Tongue-Controlled Embouchure – TCE* (New York: Royal Press Printing Company, 2002); Vladimir Pushkarev, *Tongue Aperture Method* (Moscow: The Author, 2000).
25. Jean-Pierre Mathez, *Trumpet Method*, Vienna Instrumental Tutors (Vienna: Universal Edition, 1976).
26. The authors are indebted to the first-hand knowledge of Howard Snell and Elgar Howarth in this regard.

Chapter 12 Jazz and the image of the trumpet

1. Paul E. Bierley, *The Incredible Band of John Philip Sousa* (Urbana: University of Illinois Press, 2006), p. 13.
2. Louis Armstrong, *Satchmo: My Life in New Orleans* (London: Peter Davies, 1955), p. 190.
3. For more on Mortimer and Macintosh, see John Wallace and Trevor Herbert, 'Aspects of performance techniques: the brass band and its influence on other brass-playing', in *The British*

Brass Band: A Musical and Social History, ed. Trevor Herbert (Oxford: Oxford University Press, 2000), pp. 296–9.

4. Good examples are *Il Bacio* and *Carnival of Venice* (Columbia, 1932).
5. *Grove 2*, s.v. 'Beiderbecke, (Leon) Bix'.
6. See the interview with Armstrong from June 1935: 'My chops was beat – but I'm dyin' to swing again', in *Down Beat: 60 Years of Jazz*, ed. Frank Alkyer (Milwaukee, WI: Hal Leonard, 1995).
7. See Krin Gabbard, 'Signifyin(g) the phallus: Mo' Better Blues and representations of the jazz trumpet', in *Representing Jazz*, ed. Krin Gabbard (Durham, NC: Duke University Press, 1995), pp. 104–30, for an interesting viewpoint on the categorisation of 'hot' and 'cool' trumpet playing.
8. See Michael H. Kater, *Different Drummers: Jazz in the Culture of Nazi Germany* (Oxford: Oxford University Press, 1992), p. 23; Alfred Einstein, *A Short History of Music*, revised edn (London: Cassell, 1953), p. 208.
9. See William Russell and Stephen W. Smith, 'New Orleans Music', in *Jazzmen: The Story of Hot Jazz Told in the Lives of the Men Who Created It*, ed. Frederic Ramsey, Jr., and Charles Edward Smith (New York: Harcourt Brace, 1939), pp. 9–18.
10. Frederic Ramsey, Jr., 'King Oliver and his Creole Jazz Band', in *Jazzmen*, ed. F. Ramsey, Jr., and C. E. Smith, p. 69.
11. For more on collective improvisation, see Thomas Brothers, *Louis Armstrong's New Orleans* (New York: Norton, 2007), pp. 284–92.
12. See Mark Hustwitt, '"Caught in a whirlpool of aching sound": the production of dance music in Britain in the 1920s', *Popular Music* 3 (1983), 11.
13. Ibid.
14. Westerberg credits Armstrong with cornet in recordings up to 13 December 1927 (Hot Five), then trumpet from 27 June 1928 (Hot Five), while acknowledging that the switch may have occurred earlier (Hans Westerberg, *Boy from New Orleans: Louis "Satchmo" Armstrong, on Records, Films, Radio and Television* (Copenhagen: Jazzmedia, 1981), p. 3). Willems, on the other hand, lists all recording from the sessions of 28 May 1926 with Erskine Tate's Vendome Orchestra on as being on trumpet (Jos Willems, *All of Me: The Complete Discography of Louis Armstrong*, Studies in Jazz 51 (Lanham, Md.: Scarecrow Press, 2006)).
15. See Chapter 2, where Louis Panico's 1923 tutor, *The Novelty Cornetist*, and muted effects such as *Baby Talk* and *Baby Cry* are referenced.
16. See Inez M. Cavanaugh, 'Three interviews' (1945); and 'Roger Pryor Dodge on Bubber Miley' (1940), in *The Duke Ellington Reader*, ed. Mark Tucker (Oxford: Oxford University Press, 1993), pp. 465–8, 454–8.
17. Trumpeter's jargon, with local variation, generally refers to notes above high F6, as 'super G's, A's, B's', and notes from C7 and above as 'double high C', and so on. Playing loudly in this register is often referred to amongst trumpeters as 'screaming'. Listen to Cat Anderson on *Great Times* (CO–44664–1), recorded New York, 20 November 1950, for 'super A's', and *The Tattooed Bride* (CO–44749–1), recorded New York, 18 December 1950, for 'double high C', both of which sound a tone lower as they are played on B flat trumpet.
18. See 'Roger Pryor Dodge on *Black and Tan Fantasy*, from "Harpsichords and Jazz Trumpets" (1934)', in *The Duke Ellington Reader*, pp. 105–10.
19. See Gunther Schuller, 'The case for Ellington's music as living repertory', in *The Duke Ellington Reader*, pp. 418–21.
20. According to Gunther Schuller, 'Harry James was possibly the most complete trumpet player who ever lived' (spoken introduction to a reconstruction of Harry James's *The Mole*, performed by the Scottish National Jazz Orchestra at the Edinburgh International Festival, 26 August 2010).
21. See André Hodeir, 'A masterpiece: Concerto for Cootie', in *The Duke Ellington Reader*, pp. 276–88.
22. In conversations with John Wallace, from 1977 to the present.
23. The authors are indebted to Andrew Lynn for this insight. Letter dated 10 February 2011.
24. Dan Morgenstern, *Living with Jazz: A Reader Edited by Sheldon Meyer* (New York: Pantheon, 2004), pp. 46–8.
25. The Hays Office, a self-monitoring organization set up by the film industry in 1922, had, by 1930, set up the Motion Picture Production Code, which censored representations of interracial liaisons.
26. Dan Morgenstern, *Living with Jazz*, pp. 38–9.

27. Diegetic music is music that is part of the story that the characters are aware of. Non-diegetic music makes up the musical score of the soundtrack that provides an emotional impact for the audience. See Claudia Gorbman, 'Film Music', in *The Oxford Guide to Film Studies*, ed. John Hill and Pamela Church Gibson (Oxford: Oxford University Press, 1998). This chapter has an excellent bibliography for further reading on music in film.
28. In reality, *Fantasy* had originally been a collaboration between Bubber Miley and Ellington.
29. See Krin Gabbard, *Hotter Than That: The Trumpet, Jazz, and American Culture* (New York: Faber and Faber, 2008), pp. 215–18.
30. For more on this subject, see Claudia Gorbman, *Unheard Melodies: Narrative Film Music* (Bloomington: Indiana University Press; London: British Film Institute, 1987).
31. For more on the trumpet in silent cinema, see Gillian B. Anderson, *Music for Silent Films, 1894–1929: A Guide* (Washington, DC: Library of Congress, 1988).
32. John Williams, as quoted by Barry Millington in his obituary of Maurice Murphy in *The Guardian*, 29 November 2010.
33. See the bibliography in Kenneth M. Cramer, Erin Million and Lynn A. Perreault, 'Perceptions of musicians: gender stereotypes and social role theory', *Psychology of Music* 30 (2002), 164–74.
34. See Betsy G. Miller, 'Anna Teresa Berger, cornet virtuoso', *ITG Journal* 22/3 (Feb. 1998). For more on the position of women musicians in this period, see Margaret Myers, *Blowing her Own Trumpet: European Ladies' Orchestras & Other Women Musicians, 1870–1950 in Sweden* (Göteborg: Advelningen för musikvetenskap, Göteborg Universitet, 1993).
35. Elena Ostleitner and Ursula Simek, *Carole Dawn Reinhart – A Biography*, 2nd edn (Strasshof: Vier-Viertel-Verlag, 2002); Wolfgang Sandner, '"Ich bin kein typischer Trompeter": ein Gespräch mit Carole Dawn Reinhart', *Musik+Medizin* 1 (1979), 46–51.
36. Michel Laplace, 'Ladies in Jazz: Valaida Snow, Queen of the trumpet', *Brass Bulletin* 70 (1990), 48.
37. Candace Allen, *Valaida* (London: Vertigo, 2004); Mark Miller, *High Hat, Trumpet and Rhythm: The Life and Music of Valaida Snow* (Toronto: Mercury Press, 2007); Pascal Rannou, *Noire, La Neige* (Marseille: Editions Parenthèses, 2008).
38. See Richard Harrington, 'The Canon Wars Come to Jazz', *The Washington Post*, 20 February 1994.
39. Thomas Sancton, 'A conversation with Wynton Marsalis', *Jazz Times*, March 1997.
40. Richard B. Woodward, 'Jazz wars: a tale of age, rage, and hash brownies', *Village Voice*, 9 August 1994, 27–34.
41. See Wynton Marsalis, 'A viper in the bosom of the Blues', *The New York Times*, 19 December 1993; and Jeff Taylor, 'Encounters with Jazz', *I.S.A.M. Newsletter* 24 (Fall 1994).
42. Marsalis's tours to the UK were always accompanied by intense media interest. See 'What Marsalis plays isn't jazz – in a rare interview, David Murray tells Stuart Nicholson how Wynton Marsalis is killing the genre's creative spirit', *The Daily Telegraph*, 14 August 1999; and 'And the trumpet shall sound – Wynton Marsalis is a man with a mission to spread the gospel of jazz. Some people are worried his influence will make the music too respectable. The virtuoso trumpeter talks to Adam Sweeting', *The Daily Telegraph*, 6 February 2001.
43. Leslie Gourse, *Wynton Marsalis: Skain's Domain, a Biography* (New York: Schirmer, 1999), p. 158.
44. Wynton Marsalis, liner note to *All Rise*, 2002, 2 Compact Discs. Sony. B00006EXIC.
45. Laurence Begreen, *Louis Armstrong: An Extravagant Life* (London: HarperCollins), 1997, p. 477.

Bibliography

The abbreviation *ITG* refers to *International Trumpet Guild*

Ahrens, Christian, trans. S. Plank, *Valved Brass: The History of an Invention* (Hillsdale, NY: Pendragon Press, 2008).

Alkyer, Frank (ed.), *Down Beat: 60 Years of Jazz* (Milwaukee, WI: Hal Leonard, 1995).

Allen, Candace, *Valaida* (London: Vertigo, 2004).

Allsop, Peter, *Arcangelo Corelli: New Orpheus of our Times* (Oxford: Oxford University Press, 1999).

Altenburg, Johann Ernst, *Essay on an Introduction to the Heroic and Musical Trumpeters' and Kettledrummers' Art: For the Sake of a Wider Acceptance of the Same, Described Historically, Theoretically, and Practically and Illustrated with Examples*, 1795, trans. E. H. Tarr (Nashville, Tenn.: The Brass Press, 1974).

Anderson, Gillian B., *Music for Silent Films, 1894–1929: A Guide* (Washington, DC: Library of Congress, 1988).

Andrews, Frank, *Brass Band Cylinder and Non-Microgroove Disc Recordings, 1903–1960*; with a foreword by Trevor Herbert. (Winchester: Piccolo Press, 1997).

Anglo, Sydney, *The Great Tournament Roll of Westminster: A Collotype Reproduction of the Manuscript* (Oxford: Clarendon Press, 1968).

Ansermet, Ernst-Alexandre, 'Bechet and Jazz visit Europe, 1919', in *Frontiers of Jazz*, ed. Ralph de Toledano, 3rd rev. edn (Gretna, La: Pelican, 1994), pp. 111–18.

Anthony, James R., *French Baroque Music from Beaujoyeulx to Rameau*, revised edn (London: Batsford, 1978).

Anthony, James R., 'Air and aria added to French Opera from the death of Lully to 1720', *Revue de Musicologie* 77 (1991), 201–19.

Anzenberger, Friedrich, 'The earliest French tutor for slide trumpet', *Historic Brass Society Journal* 4 (1992), 106–11.

Anzenberger, Friedrich, 'Method books for natural trumpet in the 19th century: an annotated bibliography', *Historic Brass Society Journal* 5 (1993), 1–21.

Anzenberger, Friedrich, 'Method books for keyed trumpet in the 19th century: an annotated bibliography', *Historic Brass Society Journal* 6 (1994), 1–10.

Anzenberger, Friedrich, 'Method books for trumpet and cornet using stopped notes in the 19th century: an annotated bibliography', *Historic Brass Society Journal* 7 (1995), 1–11.

Anzenberger, Friedrich, 'Method books for slide trumpet: an annotated bibliography', *Historic Brass Society Journal* 8 (1996), 102–14.

Anzenberger, Friedrich, 'Method books for valve trumpet to 1850: an annotated bibliography', *Historic Brass Society Journal* 9 (1997), 50–62.

Arban, Jean–Baptiste, *Cornet Method*, trans. E. Ruch; ed. J. Fitz–Gerald (London: Hawkes & Son, 1907).

Armstrong, Louis, *Swing That Music* (London: Longmans, 1937).

Armstrong, Louis, *Satchmo: My Life in New Orleans* (London: Peter Davies, 1955).

Arnold, Denis, *Giovanni Gabrieli and the Music of the Venetian High Renaissance* (Oxford: Oxford University Press, 1979).

Ashbee, Andrew, *Records of English Court Music*, 9 vols; vols 1–4 (Snodland: Andrew Ashbee, 1986–91); vols 5–9 (Aldershot: Scolar Press, 1991–96).

Ashbee, Andrew, and David Lasocki, assisted by Peter Holman and Fiona Kisby, *A Biographical Dictionary of English Court Musicians, 1485–1714*, 2 vols (Aldershot: Ashgate, 1998).

Baines, Anthony, 'James Talbot's manuscript. (Christ Church Library Music MS 1187). I. Wind instruments', *The Galpin Society Journal* 1 (1948), 9–26.

Baines, Anthony, 'Fifteenth-century instruments in Tinctoris's "De inventione et usu musicae"', *The Galpin Society Journal* 3 (1950), 19–26.

Baines, Anthony, 'The evolution of trumpet music up to Fantini', *Proceedings of the Royal Musical Association* 101 (1974–75), 1–9.

Baines, Anthony, *Brass Instruments: Their History and Development*, 1976 (London: Constable and Co., 1993).

Baldwin, David, '*Arbuckle's Complete Cornet Method* (1866)', *International Trumpet Guild [ITG] Journal* 14/3 (Feb. 1990), 31–7.

Barclay, Robert, *The Art of the Trumpet-Maker: The Materials, Tools, and Techniques of the Seventeenth and Eighteenth Centuries in Nuremberg* (Oxford: Clarendon Press, 1992).

Barclay, Robert, 'Design, technology and manufacture before 1800', in *The Cambridge Companion to Brass Instruments*, ed. T. Herbert and J. Wallace (Cambridge: Cambridge University Press, 1997), pp. 24–37.

Bargans, Karl, 'On the trumpet, as at present employed in the orchestra', *The Harmonicon* (Jan. 1830), 23–5.

Bate, Philip, *The Trumpet and Trombone: An Outline of Their History, Development and Construction*, 2nd edn (London: Ernest Benn, 1978).

Bendinelli, Cesare, *The Entire Art of Trumpet Playing, 1614*, trans. with commentary by E. H. Tarr (Nashville, Tenn.: The Brass Press, 1975).

Berger, Jean, 'Notes on some 17th-century compositions for trumpets and strings in Bologna', *The Musical Quarterly* 37 (1951), 354–67.

Berger, Jean, 'The sacred works of Giacomo Antonio Perti', *Journal of the American Musicological Society* 17 (1964), 370–7.

Bergreen, Laurence, *Louis Armstrong: An Extravagant Life* (London: Harper Collins, 1997).

Bernstein, Leonard, *The Unanswered Question: Six talks at Harvard* (Cambridge, Mass: Harvard University Press, 1976).

Besseler, Heinrich, preface to J. S. Bach, *Sechs Brandenburgische Konzerte* (Kassel: Bärenreiter, 1956).

Bevan, Clifford, 'The (P)Russian trumpet', *The Galpin Society Journal* 41 (1988), 112–14.

Bevan, Clifford, *The Tuba Family*, 2nd edn (Winchester: Piccolo Press, 2000).

Bickley, Diana, 'The trumpet shall sound: some reasons that suggest why Berlioz altered the part for *trompette à pistons* in his overture *Waverley*', *Historic Brass Society Journal* 6 (1994), 61–83.

Bierley, Paul E., *The Incredible Band of John Philip Sousa* (Urbana: University of Illinois Press, 2006).

Bigard, Barney, *With Louis and the Duke: The Autobiography of a Jazz Clarinetist*, ed. Barry Martyn (New York: Oxford University Press, 1986).

Birkemeier, Richard P., 'The history and music of the orchestral trumpet of the nineteenth century, part 1', *ITG Journal* 9/3 (Feb. 1985), 23–39.

Birkemeier, Richard P., 'The history and music of the orchestral trumpet of the nineteenth century, part 2', *ITG Journal* 9/4 (May 1985), 13–27.

Birkemeier, Richard P., 'The F trumpet and its last virtuoso, Walter Morrow', *Brass Bulletin* 65 (1989), 34–45.

Blandford, W. F. H., 'The "Bach trumpet"', *Monthly Musical Record* 65 (1935), 49–51, 73–6, 97–100.

Bockmuehl, Markus N. A., '"The trumpet shall sound": *shofar* symbolism and its reception in early Christianity', in *Templum Amicitiae: Essays on the Second Temple Presented to Ernst Bammel*, ed. William Horbury (Journal for the Study of the New Testament Supplement Series 48, Sheffield: JSOT Press, 1991), pp. 199–225.

Bowles, Edmund A., 'Were musical instruments used in the liturgical service during the Middle Ages?', *The Galpin Society Journal* 10 (1957), 40–56.

Bowles, Edmund A., 'The role of musical instruments in medieval sacred drama', *The Musical Quarterly* 45 (1959), 67–84.

Bowles, Edmund A., 'Musical instruments in civic processions during the Middle Ages', *Acta Musicologica* 33 (1961), 147–61.

Bowles, Edmund A., *La Pratique Musicale au Moyen Age: Musical Performance in the Late Middle Ages* (Geneva: Monkoff, 1983).

Bowles, Edmund A., 'The double, double, double beat of the thundering drum: the timpani in early music', *Early Music* 19 (1991), 419–35.

Boyd, Malcolm, *Bach: The Brandenburg Concertos* (Cambridge: Cambridge University Press, 1993).

Bray, Roger, 'Dryden and Draghi in harmony in the 1687 "Song for St Cecilia's Day"', *Music and Letters* 78 (1997), 319–36.

Bridges, Glenn, *Pioneers in Brass* (Detroit: Sherwood Publications, 1965).

Brofsky, Howard, 'The symphonies of Padre Martini', *The Musical Quarterly* 51 (1965), 649–73.

Brothers, Thomas (ed.), *Louis Armstrong in his Own Words: Selected Writings* (Oxford: Oxford University Press, 1999).

Brothers, Thomas, *Louis Armstrong's New Orleans* (New York: Norton, 2007).

Brown, A. Peter, 'Caldara's trumpet music for the imperial celebrations of Charles VI and Elisabeth Christine', in *Antonio Caldara: Essays on his Life and Times*, ed. B. W. Pritchard (Aldershot: Scolar Press, 1987), pp. 1–48.

Brown, A. Peter, 'The trumpet overture and sinfonia in Vienna (1715–1822)', in *Music in Eighteenth-Century Austria*, ed. David Wyn Jones (Cambridge: Cambridge University Press, 1996), pp. 13–69.

Brown, Howard M., and Stanley Sadie (eds), *Performance Practice: Music Before 1600* (Basingstoke: Macmillan, 1989).

Brownlow, J. Art, *The Last Trumpet: A History of the English Slide Trumpet* (Stuyvesant, NY: Pendragon Press, 1996).

Büchler, Alfred, 'Horns and trumpets in Byzantium: images and texts', *Historic Brass Society Journal* 12 (2000), 23–59.

Buelow, George J., 'Opera in Hamburg 300 years ago', *The Musical Times* 119 (1978), 26–8.

Bukofzer, Manfred F., *Music in the Baroque Era from Monteverdi to Bach* (New York: Norton, 1947).

Burden, Michael (ed.), *Performing the Music of Henry Purcell* (Oxford: Clarendon Press, 1996).

Burgkmair, Hans, *The Triumph of Maximilian I: 137 Woodcuts by Hans Burgkmair and Others. With a Translation of Descriptive Text, Introduction and Notes by Stanley Appelbaum* (New York: Dover 1964).

Burkhart, Raymond David, 'Brass chamber music in Lyceum and Chautauqua' (PhD dissertation, Claremond Graduate University, 2010).

Burney, Charles, *An Account of the Musical Performances in Westminster Abbey and the Pantheon, May 26th, 27th, 29th; and June the 3d, and 5th, 1784 in Commemoration of Handel* (London: Payne, 1785).

Burney, Charles, *A General History of Music: From the Earliest Ages to the Present Period (1789)*, ed. F. Mercer, 2 vols (London: G. T. Foulis, 1935).

Burney, Charles, *An Eighteenth-Century Musical Tour in France and Italy*, ed. Percy A. Scholes, Dr. Burney's Musical Tours in Europe 1 (London: Oxford University Press, 1959).

Burrows, Donald, *Handel* (Oxford: Oxford University Press, 1994).

Burrows, Donald, 'Of Handel, London trumpeters, and trumpet music', *Historic Brass Society Journal* 11 (1999), 1–9.

Busch, Hans (ed. and trans.), *Verdi's "Aida": The History of an Opera in Letters and Documents* (Minneapolis: University of Minnesota Press, 1978).

Butt, John, *Bach: Mass in B Minor* (Cambridge: Cambridge University Press, 1991).

Byrne, Maurice, 'The goldsmith-trumpet-makers of the British Isles', *The Galpin Society Journal* 19 (1966), 71–83.

Byrne, Maurice, 'Instruments for the Goldsmiths Company', *The Galpin Society Journal* 24 (1971), 63–8.

Cairns, David (trans. and ed.), *The Memoirs of Hector Berlioz*, 1870, 2nd revised edn (London: Everyman's Library, 2002).

Cammarota, Robert M., 'On the performance of "Quia respexit . . . omnes generationes" from J. S. Bach's Magnificat', *The Journal of Musicology* 18/3 (2001), 458–89.

Campbell, Murray, Clive Greated, and Arnold Myers, *Musical Instruments: History, Technology, and Performance of Instruments of Western Music* (Oxford: Oxford University Press, 2004).

Carnovale, Norbert A., and Paul F. Doerksen, *Twentieth-Century Music for Trumpet and Orchestra: An Annotated Bibliography*, 2nd rev. edn (Nashville, Tenn.: The Brass Press, 1994).

Carse, Adam, *The Orchestra from Beethoven to Berlioz: A History of the Orchestra in the First Half of the 19th Century, and of the Development of Orchestral Baton-Conducting* (Cambridge: Heffer, 1948).

Carse, Adam, *The Life of Jullien: Adventurer, Showman-Conductor and Establisher of the Promenade Concerts in England, Together with a History of Those Concerts up to 1895* (Cambridge: Heffer, 1951).

Carter, Stewart, 'Trombone obbligatos in Viennese oratorios of the Baroque', *Historic Brass Society Journal* 2 (1990), 52–77.

Carter, Stewart (ed.), *Perspectives in Brass Scholarship: Proceedings of the International Historic Brass Symposium, Amherst, 1995* (Stuyvesant, NY: Pendragon Press, 1997).

Carter, Stewart, review of Saunders, *Cross, Sword, and Lyre*, *Journal of Seventeenth-Century Music* 3/1 (1997) <http://sscm–jscm.press.illinois.edu/v3/no1/carter.html>, accessed 17 July 2009.

Carter, Stewart (ed.), *Brass Scholarship in Review: Proceedings of the Historic Brass Society Conference, Cité de la Musique, Paris 1999* (Hillsdale, NY: Pendragon Press, 2006).
Cazalet, William Wahab, *The History of the Royal Academy of Music* (London: T. Bosworth, 1854).
Cazeaux, Isabelle, *French Music in the Fifteenth and Sixteenth Centuries* (Oxford: Blackwell, 1975).
Cessac, Catherine, *Marc-Antoine Charpentier*, trans. E. T. Glasgow (Portland, Oregon: Amadeus Press, 1995).
Chan, Mary, and Jamie C. Kassler, *Roger North's Cursory Notes of Musicke (c. 1698–c. 1703): A Physical, Psychological and Critical Theory* (Kensington, N.S.W.: Unisearch, University of New South Wales, 1986).
Čížek, Bohuslav, 'Josef Kail (1795–1871), forgotten brass instrument innovator', *Brass Bulletin* 73 (1991), 64–75; 74 (1991), 24–9.
Clagget, Charles, *Musical Phænomena ... No. 1: The Aiuton, and the Chromatic Trumpets and the French Horns, capable of fine tune and regular harmony in all the keys in use, minor as well as major* (London: 'printed for the author and sold at the Musical Museum', 1793).
Clark, Keith C., 'Performances of the Brandenburg Concerto No. 2 in the United States', *ITG Journal* 3/3 (Oct. 1978), 24–6.
Clark, Keith C., 'Trumpet sections of American symphony orchestras: The Boston Symphony Orchestra', *ITG Newsletter* 5/3 (May 1979), 6–9.
Clark, Keith C., 'Trumpet sections of American symphony orchestras: The Chicago Symphony Orchestra', *ITG Journal* 8/2 (Dec. 1983), 17–22.
Collins, Timothy A., 'Gottfried Reiche: a more complete biography', *ITG Journal* 15/3 (Feb. 1991), 4–28.
Collins, Tim, 'So, how many holes is a baroque trumpet supposed to have?', *Historic Brass Society Newsletter* 9 (1996), 11–15.
Collins, Timothy A., '"Of the differences between trumpeters and city tower musicians": the relationship of stadtpfeifer and kammeradschaft trumpeters', *The Galpin Society Journal* 53 (2000), 51–9.
Conforzi, Igino, 'Girolamo Fantini, "monarch of the trumpet": recent additions to his biography', trans. Jesse Rosenberg and Henry Meredith, *Historic Brass Society Journal* 5 (1993), 159–73.
Cooke, Mervyn, *The Chronicle of Jazz* (London: Thames & Hudson, 1997).
Cooper, Stefan, 'The trumpet players of the San Francisco Symphony 1911–1995', *ITG Journal* 20/3 (Feb. 1996), 32–41.
Corder, Frederick, *The Orchestra and How to Write for it: A Practical Guide to Every Branch and Detail of Modern Orchestration*, 5th edn (London: J. Curwen [1896]).
Cron, Matthew, 'In defense of Altenburg: the pitch and form of foreign trumpets', *Historic Brass Society Journal* 8 (1996), 6–41.
Cron, Matthew, and Don Smithers, *A Calendar and Comprehensive Source Catalogue of Georg Philipp Telemann's Vocal and Instrumental Music with Brass* (Tallahassee, FL: International Trumpet Guild, 1995).
Cudworth, Charles, 'The Vauxhall "Lists"', *The Galpin Society Journal* 20 (1967), 24–42.
Cudworth, Charles, and Franklin B. Zimmerman, 'The trumpet voluntary', *Music & Letters* 41 (1960), 342–8.
Dahlqvist, Reine, *The Keyed Trumpet and its Greatest Virtuoso, Anton Weidinger* (Nashville, Tenn.: The Brass Press, 1975).
Dahlqvist, Reine, 'Some notes on the early valve', *The Galpin Society Journal* 33 (1980), 111–24.
R. Dahlqvist, Reine, 'Pitches of German, French, and English trumpets in the 17th and 18th centuries', *Historic Brass Society Journal* 5 (1993), 29–41.
Dahlqvist, Reine, 'A reply to Matthew Cron', *Historic Brass Society Journal* 8 (1996), 142–5.
Dahlqvist, Reine, and Bengt Eklund, 'The Bach renaissance and the trumpet', *Euro-ITG Newsletter* 1 (1995), 12–17.
Dale, Delbert A., *Trumpet Technique* (London: Oxford University Press, 1965).
Dart, Thurston, 'The mock trumpet', *The Galpin Society Journal* 6 (1953), 35–40.
Dart, Thurston, 'Music and musical instruments in Cotgrave's *Dictionarie* (1611)', *The Galpin Society Journal* 21 (1968), 70–80.
Dauverné, François Georges Auguste, 'Method for trumpet', trans. Gaetan Chenier, Ruby Miller Orval, Rebecca Pike and Jeffrey Snedeker, *Historic Brass Society Journal* 3 (1991), 179–261.
Dean, Roger T., 'Jazz, improvisation and brass', in *The Cambridge Companion to Brass Instruments*, ed. T. Herbert and J. Wallace (Cambridge: Cambridge University Press, 1997), pp. 217–35.

Dean, Winton, 'The dramatic element in Handel's oratorios', *Proceedings of the Royal Musical Association* 79 (1952–3), 33–49.

Dean, Winton, *The New Grove Handel* (London: Macmillan, 1982).

Deutsch, Otto Erich, *Handel: A Documentary Biography* (London: A. and C. Black, 1955).

Dick, Alastair, 'The earlier history of the shawm in India', *The Galpin Society Journal* 37 (1984), 80–98.

Dickey, Bruce, 'The cornett', in *The Cambridge Companion to Brass Instruments*, ed. T. Herbert and J. Wallace (Cambridge: Cambridge University Press, 1997), pp. 51–67.

Diprose, Mike, 'Partial success: natural trumpet – the march forward', *Early Music Review* 105 (Feb. 2005), 9–10.

Diprose, Mike, 'Return to the natural trumpet', *Early Music Review* 110 (Dec. 2005), 6–7.

Dournon, Geneviève, 'Organology', in *Ethnomusicology: An Introduction*, ed. H. Myers (London: Macmillan, 1992), pp. 245–300.

Downey, Peter, 'A Renaissance correspondence concerning trumpet music', *Early Music* 9 (1981), 325–9.

Downey, Peter, 'The Trumpet and its Role in Music of the Renaissance and Early Baroque', 3 vols (Ph.D. thesis, The Queen's University of Belfast, 1983).

Downey, Peter, 'The Renaissance slide trumpet: fact or fiction?', *Early Music* 12 (1984), 26–33.

Downey, Peter, 'Adam Drese's 1648 funeral music and the invention of the slide trumpet', in *Irish Musical Studies 1: Musicology in Ireland*, ed. G. Gillen and H. White (Dublin: Irish Academic Press, 1990), pp. 200–17.

Downey, Peter, 'What Samuel Pepys heard on 3 February 1661: English trumpet style under the later Stuart monarchs', *Early Music* 18 (1990), 417–28.

Downey, Peter, 'In tubis ductilibus et voce tubae', in *Irish Musical Studies 2: Music and the Church*, ed. G. Gillen and H. White (Dublin: Irish Academic Press, 1993), pp. 302–32.

Downey, Peter, 'Lip–blown instruments of Ireland before the Norman invasion', *Historic Brass Society Journal* 5 (1993), 75–91.

Downey, Peter, 'Trumpet style in 17th-century France and the music of *Les Trompettes du Roy*', *Historic Brass Society Journal* 7 (1995), 67–99.

Downey, Peter, 'On sounding the trumpet and beating the drum in 17th-century England', *Early Music* 24 (1996), 263–77.

Downey, Peter, 'Performing Mr Purcell's "exotick" trumpet notes', in *Performing the Music of Henry Purcell*, ed. M. Burden (Oxford: Clarendon Press, 1996), pp. 49–60.

Downey, Peter, 'From the rim to the hub: Fortuna's wheel and instrumental music at the German-speaking Renaissance courts', in *Perspectives in Brass Scholarship*, ed. Stewart Carter (Stuyvesant, NY: Pendragon Press, 1997), pp. 1–18.

Dudgeon, Ralph T., *The Keyed Bugle* (Metuchen, NJ, and London: Scarecrow Press, 1993).

Dudgeon, Ralph T., Phillip Eastop, Trevor Herbert and John Wallace, 'Playing, learning and teaching brass', in *The Cambridge Companion to Brass Instruments*, ed. T. Herbert and J. Wallace (Cambridge: Cambridge University Press, 1997), pp. 193–206.

Duffin, Ross W., 'The *trompette des menestrels* in the 15th-century *alta capella*', *Early Music* 17 (1989), 397–402.

Ecklund, Peter, '"Louis Licks" and nineteenth-century cornet etudes: the roots of melodic improvisation as seen in the jazz style of Louis Armstrong', *Historic Brass Society Journal* 13 (2001), 90–101.

Edwards, F. G., 'Bach's music in England', *The Musical Times* 37 (Sep.–Dec. 1896), 585–7, 652–7, 722–6, 797–800.

Ehrlich, Cyril, *First Philharmonic: A History of the Royal Philharmonic Society* (Oxford: Clarendon Press, 1995).

Eichborn, Hermann L., *Die Trompete in alter und neuer Zeit* (Leipzig: Breitkopf & Härtel, 1881).

Eichborn, Hermann L., *Das alte Clarinblasen auf Trompeten*, 1894 (Nashville, Tenn.: The Brass Press, 1973).

Einstein, Alfred, *A Short History of Music*, revised edn (London: Cassell, 1953).

Eisensmith, Kevin, 'Joseph Riepel's Concerto in D à Clarino Principale', *ITG Journal* 27/4 (June 2003), 8–16.

Eklund, Bengt, and Reine Dahlqvist, 'The Brandenburg Concerto No.2', *Euro–ITG Newsletter* 2 (1995), 4–9.

Ellis, Katharine, *Interpreting the Musical Past: Early Music in Nineteenth-Century France* (New York and Oxford: Oxford University Press, 2005).

Fantini, Girolamo, *Modo Per Imparare a Sonare di Tromba Tanto di Guerra Quanto Musicalmente*, 1638; facsimile reprint with English translation and critical commentary by Edward H. Tarr (Nashville, Tenn.: The Brass Press, 1978).

Farmer, Henry G., *The Rise and Development of Military Music* (London: W. Reeves, 1912).

Farmer, Henry G., 'The instruments of music on the Taq-i Bustan bas-reliefs', *The Journal of the Royal Asiatic Society of Great Britain and Ireland* (July 1938), 397–412.

Farmer, Henry G., 'Crusading martial music', *Music & Letters* 30 (1949), 243–9.

Fétis, Francois–Joseph, *Curiosités historiques de la musique, complément nécessaire de La musique mise à la portée de tout le monde* (Paris: Janet et Cotelle, 1830).

Fischer, Henry G., 'The trumpet in ancient Egypt', in *Pyramid Studies and Other Essays Presented to I. E. S. Edwards*, ed. J. Baines [et al.] (London: The Egypt Exploration Society, 1988), pp. 103–9.

Fiske, Roger, *English Theatre Music in the Eighteenth Century*, 2nd edn (Oxford: Oxford University Press, 1986).

Fitzpatrick, Horace, *The Horn and Horn-Playing and the Austro–Bohemian Tradition from 1680 to 1830* (London: Oxford University Press, 1970).

Foster, Myles B., *History of the Philharmonic Society of London: 1813–1912. A Record of a Hundred Years' Work in the Cause of Music* (London: John Lane, 1912).

Foster, Pops, *The Autobiography of Pops Foster: New Orleans Jazzman, as told to Tom Stoddard* (San Francisco, CA: Backbeat Books, 2005).

Franko, Sam, *Chords and Discords: Memoirs and Musings of an American Musician* (New York: Viking Press, 1938).

Franquin, Merri, 'La Trompette et le Cornet', in *Encyclopédie de la Musique et Dictionnaire du Conservatoire*, pt 2, vol. 3 (Paris: Delagrave, 1927), pp. 1597–637.

Frederiksen, Brian, *Arnold Jacobs: Song and Wind*, ed. John Taylor (United States: WindSong Press, 1996).

Fröhlich, Joseph, *Vollständige theoretisch-pracktische Musikschule für alle beym Orchester gebräuchliche wichtigere Instrumente zum Gebrauch für Musikdirectoren–Lehrer und Liebhaber* (Bonn: N. Simrock, 1811).

Gabbard, Krin, 'Signifyin(g) the phallus: Mo' Better Blues and representations of the jazz trumpet', in *Representing Jazz*, ed. Krin Gabbard (Durham, NC: Duke University Press, 1995), pp. 104–30.

Gabbard, Krin, *Hotter Than That: The Trumpet, Jazz, and American Culture* (New York: Faber and Faber, 2008).

Galpin, Francis W., *The Music of the Sumerians and their Immediate Successors the Babylonians & Assyrians* (Cambridge: Cambridge University Press, 1937).

Galpin, Francis W., *Old English Instruments of Music: Their History and Character*, 1910, 4th rev. edn, with supplementary notes by Thurston Dart (London: Methuen, 1965).

Gambassi, Osvaldo, *Il Concerto Palatino della Signoria di Bologna* (Florence: L. S. Olschki, 1989).

Gianturco, Carolyn, 'Music for a Genoese wedding of 1681', *Music & Letters* 63 (1982), 31–43.

Gorbman, Claudia, *Unheard Melodies: Narrative Film Music* (Bloomington: Indiana University Press; London: British Film Institute, 1987).

Gorbman, Claudia, 'Film Music', in *The Oxford Guide to Film Studies*, ed. J. Hill and P. C. Gibson (Oxford: Oxford University Press, 1998).

Gourse, Leslie, *Wynton Marsalis: Skain's Domain, a Biography* (New York: Schirmer, 1999).

Grano, John, *Handel's Trumpeter: The Diary of John Grano*, ed. John Ginger, with a foreword by Crispian Steele-Perkins (Stuyvesant, NY: Pendragon Press, 1997).

Grossmann-Vendrey, Susanna, *Felix Mendelssohn Bartholdy und die Musik der Vergangenheit* (Regensburg: Gustav Bosse, 1969).

Grout, Donald Jay, and Claude V. Palisca, *A History of Western Music*, 6th edn (New York and London: Norton, 2000).

Haar, James, 'Munich at the time of Orlande de Lassus', in *The Renaissance, From the 1470s to the end of the 16th century*, Man and Music 2, ed. I. Fenlon (London: Macmillan, 1989), pp. 243–62.

Haine, Malou, *Adolphe Sax (1814–1894): Sa Vie, Son Œuvre, et Ses Instruments de Musique* (Brussels: University of Brussels, 1980).

Hale, John R., '*Salpinx* and *salpinktes*: trumpet and trumpeter in Ancient Greece', in *Literature, Art, History: Studies on Classical Antiquity and Tradition in Honour of W.J. Henderson*, ed. A. F. Basson and W. J. Dominik (Frankfurt and New York: Peter Lang, 2003), pp. 267–73.

Halfpenny, Eric, 'William Shaw's "Harmonic Trumpet"', *The Galpin Society Journal* 13 (1960), 7–13.

Halfpenny, Eric, 'William Bull and the English baroque trumpet', *The Galpin Society Journal* 15 (1962), 18–24.

Halfpenny, Eric, 'Two Oxford trumpets', *The Galpin Society Journal* 16 (1963), 49–62.

Halfpenny, Eric, 'Early British Trumpet Mouthpieces', *The Galpin Society Journal* 20 (1967), 76–88.

Halfpenny, Eric, 'Four seventeenth-century British trumpets', *The Galpin Society Journal* 22 (1969), 51–7.

Harris, Ellen T., liner note to Kathleen Battle and Wynton Marsalis, *Baroque Duet* (1992). Compact disc. Sony Classical 01-046672-10.

Harris-Warrick, Rebecca, 'Magnificence in motion: stage musicians in Lully's ballets and operas', *Cambridge Opera Journal* 6 (1994), 189–203.

Hartinger, Anselm, 'A "fairly correct copy of the mass"? – Mendelssohn's score of the B-minor Mass as a document of the Romantic's view on matters of performance practice and source criticism', in *International Symposium: Understanding Bach's B-minor Mass* (Discussion Books 1 and 2), ed. Yo Tomita, E. Crean, I. Mills and T. Kovačevič (Belfast: Queen's University, 2007), pp. 322–43.

Hawkins, John, *A General History of the Science and Practice of Music*, 1776, ed. O. Wessely, 2 vols (Graz: Akademische Druck- u. Verlagsanstalt, 1969).

Hazen, Margaret Hindle, and Robert M. Hazen, *The Music Men: An Illustrated History of Brass Bands in America, 1800–1920* (Washington, D.C.: Smithsonian Institution Press, 1987).

Herbert, Trevor, 'Victorian brass bands: the establishment of a "working class musical tradition"', *Historic Brass Society Journal* 4 (1992), 1–11.

Herbert, Trevor (ed.), *The British Brass Band: A Musical and Social History* (Oxford: Oxford University Press, 2000).

Herbert, Trevor, *The Trombone* (New Haven, Conn.; London: Yale University Press, 2006).

Herbert, Trevor (2008), 'The Robert Minter Collection: a handlist of seventeenth- and eighteenth-century trumpet repertoire', <http://www.open.ac.uk/Arts/minter>, accessed 20 August 2009.

Herbert, Trevor, 'Brass playing in the early twentieth century: idioms and cultures of performance'. Introduction to *Early Twentieth-Century Brass Idioms: Art, Jazz, and Other Popular Traditions*, Studies in Jazz 58, ed. Howard T. Weiner (Lanham, MD: Scarecrow Press, 2009), pp. xi–xvii.

Herbert, Trevor, and John Wallace (eds), *The Cambridge Companion to Brass Instruments* (Cambridge: Cambridge University Press, 1997).

Herforth, Harry, Adolph Herseth and Martin Lessen, 'A tribute to George Mager (1885–1950)', *ITG Journal* 10/2 (Dec. 1985), 14–16.

Herissone, Rebecca, 'The origins and contents of the Magdalene College partbooks', *The Royal Musical Association Research Chronicle* 29 (1996), 47–95.

Heyde, Herbert, 'On the early history of valves and valve instruments in Germany (1814–1833)', *Brass Bulletin* 24 (1978), 9–33; 25 (1979), 41–50; 26 (1979), 69–82; 27 (1979), 51–61.

Heyde, Herbert, *Trompeten, Posaunen, Tuben*, Katalog: Musikinstrumenten-Museum der Karl-Marx-Universität Leipzig 3 (Leipzig: Deutscher Verlag für Musik, 1980).

Heyde, Herbert, *Das Ventilblasinstrument: Seine Entwicklung im Deutschsprachingen Raum von den Anfängen bis zur Gegenwart* (Leipzig: Deutscher Verlag fur Musik, 1987).

Hickmann, Hans, *La Trompette dans l'Égypte Ancienne*, 1946; facsimile reprint (Nashville, Tenn.: The Brass Press, 1976).

Hicks, Anthony, 'Handel's "La Resurrezione"', *The Musical Times* 110 (1969), 145–8.

Hiebert, Thomas, 'Virtuosity, experimentation, and innovation in horn writing from early 18th-century Dresden', *Historic Brass Society Journal* 4 (1992), 112–59.

Hiebert, Thomas, 'Early examples of mixed-keyed horns and trumpets in works of C. Graupner', *Historic Brass Society Journal* 6 (1994), 231–43.

Hiller, Albert, *Trompetenmusiken aus drei Jahrhunderten (ca. 1600–nach 1900)* (Cologne: Haas, 1993).

Hitchcock, H. Wiley, *Marc-Antoine Charpentier* (Oxford: Oxford University Press, 1990).

Hodeir, André, 'A masterpiece: Concerto for Cootie', in *The Duke Ellington Reader*, ed. Mark Tucker (Oxford: Oxford University Press, 1993), pp. 276–88.

Holman, Peter, 'The trumpet sonata in England', *Early Music* 4 (1976), 424–9.

Holman, Peter, 'English trumpets – a response', *Early Music* 19 (1991), 443.

Holman, Peter, *Four and Twenty Fiddlers: The Violin at the English Court, 1540–1690* (Oxford: Oxford University Press, 1993).

Holoman, D. Kern, *The Société des Concerts du Conservatoire, 1828–1967* (Berkeley: University of California Press, 2004).

Holoman, D. Kern, 'The Société des Concerts du Conservatoire (1828–1967)', <http://hector.ucdavis.edu/SdC/default.html>, accessed 21 July 2008.

Hoover, Cynthia A., 'A trumpet battle at Niblo's Pleasure Garden', *The Musical Quarterly* 55 (1969), 384–95.

Hornbostel, Erich M. von, and Curt Sachs, 'Classification of musical instruments', 1914, in *Ethnomusicology: An Introduction*, ed. H. Myers (London: Macmillan, 1992), 444–61.

Hosler, Dorothy, *The Sounds and Colors of Power: The Sacred Metallurgical Technology of Ancient West Mexico* (Cambridge, Mass.: MIT Press, 1994).

Howey, Henry, 'The lives of *hoftrompeter* and *stadtpfeiffer* as portrayed in three novels of Daniel Speer', *Historic Brass Society Journal* 3 (1991), 65–78.

Hunter, David, 'The Irish state music from 1716 to 1742 and Handel's band in Dublin', *Göttinger Händel-Beiträge* 11 (2006), 171–98.

Hunter, Fraser, 'About the carnyx: historical background', at <http://www.carnyxscotland.co.uk>, accessed 20 July 2009.

Hurrell, Martin, 'The BBC Symphony Orchestra trumpet section', *ITG Journal* (Sept. 1995), 4–16.

Hustwitt, Mark, '"Caught in a whirlpool of aching sound": the production of dance music in Britain in the 1920s', *Popular Music* 3 (1983), 7–31.

Hyde, John, *A New and Compleat Preceptor for the Trumpet and Bugle Horn, With the Whole of the Cavalry Duty as Approved of and Ordered by His Royal Highness the Duke of York, Commander in Chief* (London: The Author, [1799]).

Izikowitz, Karl Gustav, *Musical and Other Sound Instruments of the South American Indians: A Comparative Ethnographical Study*, 1934 (East Ardsley: S.R. Publishers, 1970).

Jakobsen, Verena, 'Adolf Scherbaum (1909–2000), trailblazer of the classical solo trumpet', *Brass Bulletin* 122 (2003), 62–74.

Jakobsen Barth, Verena, *Die Trompete als Soloinstrument in der Kunstmusik Europas seit 1900: mit besonderer Berücksichtigung der Entwicklung ab 1980 am Beispiel der Solisten Håkan Hardenberger, Ole Edward Antonsen und Reinhold Friedrich* (Gothenburg: University of Gothenburg, 2007).

Johnstone, H. Diack, 'A ringside seat at the Handel Commemoration', *The Musical Times* 125 (Nov. 1984), 632–6.

Jones, Max, John Chilton and Leonard Feather, *Salute to Satchmo* (London: I.P.C. Press, 1970).

Kater, Michael H., *Different Drummers: Jazz in the Culture of Nazi Germany* (Oxford: Oxford University Press, 1992).

Keim, Friedel, *Das Grosse Buch der Trompete: Instrument, Geschichte, Trompeterlexikon* (Mainz: Schott, 2005).

Keim, Friedel, *Das Grosse Buch der Trompete: Band 2* (Mainz: Schott, 2009).

Keller, Jindrich, 'Antique trumpet mutes', *Historic Brass Society Journal* 2 (1990), 97–103.

Kelly, Daniel, 'The competition solos of J. B. Arban', *ITG Journal* 30/3 (March 2006), 17–28.

Kennedy, Michael, *A Catalogue of the Works of Ralph Vaughan Williams*, 2nd edn (Oxford: Oxford University Press, 1996).

Kenyon de Pascual, Beryl, trans. with introduction, 'José de Juan Martínez' *Método de Clarín* (1830)', *Historic Brass Society Journal* 5 (1993), 92–106.

Kernfeld, Barry (ed.), *The New Grove Dictionary of Jazz* (London: Macmillan, 1988).

Kirby, Percival R., 'The trumpets of Tut-Ankh-Amen and their successors', *Journal of the Royal Anthropological Institute* 77 (1950), 33–45.

Kmen, Henry A., *Music in New Orleans: The Formative Years, 1791–1841* (Baton Rouge: Louisiana State University Press, 1966).

Koury, Daniel J., *Orchestral Performance Practices in the Nineteenth Century: Size, Proportions, and Seating* (Ann Arbor, Mich.: UMI Research Press, 1986).

Krause, Sebastian, 'God of the trombone', *Brass Bulletin* 117 (2002), 68–80.

Kreitner, Kenneth, 'Minstrels in Spanish churches, 1400–1600', *Early Music* 20 (1992), 533–46.

Kreitner, Kenneth, 'Music in the Corpus Christi procession of fifteenth-century Barcelona', *Early Music History* 14 (1995), 153–204.

Krentz, Peter, 'The *salpinx* in Greek warfare', in *Hoplites: The Classical Greek Battle Experience*, ed. V. D. Hanson (London: Routledge, 1991), pp. 110–20.

Krüger, Irmtraud, preface to J. W. Hertel, *Concerto per la Tromba in Eb (No. 1)* ([Coburg]: McNaughttan, 1994).

Krumpfer, Hans-Joachim, '1796–1908: the long sleep of the Haydn trumpet concerto', *Brass Bulletin* 75 (1991), 36–9.

Kurtzman, Jeffrey, and Linda Maria Koldau, '*Trombe, trombe d'argento, trombe squarciate, tromboni, and pifferi* in Venetian processions and ceremonies of the sixteenth and seventeenth centuries', *Journal of Seventeenth-Century Music* 8 (2002), <http://www.sscm-jscm.org/jscm/v8/no1/kurtzman.html>, accessed 20 April 2009.

Landels, John G., *Music in Ancient Greece and Rome* (London: Routledge, 1999).

Landon, H. C. Robbins, *The Collected Correspondence and London Notebooks of Joseph Haydn* (London: Barrie and Rockliff, 1959).

Langey, Otto, *Otto Langey's Tutor for the Cornet. Revised, re-arranged & many studies added, selected from works of the great masters, also some exercises & melodious studies with marks of phrasing & expression carefully marked, composed for this tutor by Walter Morrow, Professor of the cornet & trumpet at the Guildhall School of Music & member of the orchestras:- Philharmonic Society, Royal Choral Society, Richter Concerts, London Symphony Concerts etc.* (London: Hawkes & Son; New York: Jos. W. Stern & Co., *c.*1911).

Laplace, Michel, 'A woman and a life in the service of the trumpet: Edna White', *Brass Bulletin* 48 (1984), 10–16.

Laplace, Michel, 'Ladies in Jazz: Valaida Snow, Queen of the trumpet', *Brass Bulletin* 70 (1990), 48–50.

Lasocki, David, with Roger Prior, *The Bassanos: Venetian Musicians and Instrument Makers in England, 1531–1665* (Aldershot: Scolar Press, 1995).

Lawergren, Bo, 'Oxus trumpets, ca. 2200–1800 BCE: material overview, usage, societal role, and catalog', *Iranica Antiqua* 38 (2003), 41–118.

Lawson, Colin, 'The chalumeau in the works of Fux', in *Johann Joseph Fux and the Music of the Austro-Italian Baroque*, ed. H. White (Aldershot: Scolar Press, 1992), pp. 78–94.

Lawson, Graeme, and Geoff Egan, 'Medieval trumpet from the City of London', *The Galpin Society Journal* 41 (1988), 63–6.

Lawson, Graeme, 'Medieval trumpet from the City of London, II', *The Galpin Society Journal* 44 (1991), 150–6.

Leech-Wilkinson, Daniel, *Machaut's Mass: An Introduction* (Oxford: Clarendon Press, 1990).

Leech-Wilkinson, Daniel, *The Modern Invention of Medieval Music: Scholarship, Ideology, Performance* (Cambridge: Cambridge University Press, 2002).

Lewis, H. M., 'Roger Voisin: an orchestral legend', *ITG Newsletter* 6/2 (Feb. 1980), 5–7.

Lewis, Michael, 'Solo Trombone Performances at the Gewandhaus in the Nineteenth Century', *International Trombone Association Journal* 20, No. 3 (Summer 1992), 27–32.

A list of pupils received into the Academy since its foundation in 1822–3; together with a list of the subscribers to the institution and amount of subscriptions to the close of 1837; a general account of the state of the funds up to midsummer, 1838; to which is added the rules and regulations of the establishment (London: Royal Academy of Music, *c.*1838).

The London Stage, 1660–1800. A Calendar of Plays, Entertainments & Afterpieces ... Compiled from the Playbills, Newspapers and Theatrical Diaries of the Period, 5 pts (Carbondale: Southern Illinois University Press, 1960–68).

Luongo, Paul, 'Theodore Thomas's 1902 performance of Bach's Mass in B minor: working within the Grand American Festival', in *International Symposium: Understanding Bach's B-minor Mass* (Discussion Books 1 and 2), ed. Yo Tomita, E. Crean, I. Mills and T. Kovačević (Belfast: Queen's University, 2007), pp. 322–43.

Macaluso, Rosario, 'Brass playing in Belgium: school of trumpet in Liège', *Brass Bulletin* 88, (1994), 38–42; 89 (1995), 74–81; 90 (1995), 8–21; 91 (1995), 60–72.

Macaluso, Rosario, 'A grand master: Théo Charlier', *ITG Journal* 25/4 (June 2001), 30–6.

Macdonald, Hugh, *Berlioz's Orchestration Treatise: A Translation and Commentary* (Cambridge: Cambridge University Press, 2002).

Madeuf, Pierre-Yves, Jean-François Madeuf, and Graham Nicholson, 'The Guitbert trumpet: a remarkable discovery', *Historic Brass Society Journal* 11 (1999), 181–6.

Mahillon, Victor Charles, *éléments D'Acoustique Musicale et Instrumentale: Comprenant L'Examen de la Construction Théorique de Tous les Instruments de Musique en Usage Dans L'Orchestration Moderne* (Brussels: C. Mahillon, 1874).

Manniche, Lise, *Musical Instruments from the Tomb of Tut'ankhamūn* (Oxford: Griffith Institute, 1976).

Marín, Miguel Ángel, 'Corelli in the Spanish provinces: the reception of Corelli's sonatas in Jaca', paper presented at the 9th Biennial Conference on Baroque Music, Trinity College Dublin, July 2000.

Mathez, Jean-Pierre, *Joseph Jean-Baptiste Laurent Arban 1825–1889* (Moudon: Editions BIM, 1977).

Mathez, Jean-Pierre, and G. Bonino, 'The Milan Conservatory (1808–1999)', *Brass Bulletin* 106 (1999), 54–71.

Matthews, Betty, *The Royal Society of Musicians of Great Britain List of Members, 1738–1984* (London: The Royal Society of Musicians, 1985).

MacCracken, Thomas G., 'Die verwendung der blechblasinstrumente bei J.S. Bach unter besonderer berücksichtigung der tromba da tirarsi', *Bach-Jahrbuch* 70 (1984), 59–89.

McCredie, Andrew D., 'Nicola Matteis the younger: Caldara's collaborator and ballet composer in the service of the Emperor, Charles VI', in *Antonio Caldara: Essays on his Life and Times*, ed. B. W. Pritchard (Aldershot: Scolar Press, 1987), pp. 153–82.

McDonald, Donna, *The Odyssey of the Philip Jones Brass Ensemble* (Bulle: Editions Bim, 1986).

McGairl, Pamela, 'The Vauxhall Jubilee, 1786', *The Musical Times* 127 (1986), 611–15.

McGeer, Eric, *Sowing the Dragon's Teeth: Byzantine Warfare in the Tenth Century* (Washington, DC: Dumbarton Oaks Research Library and Collection, 1995).

McGrady, Richard, 'The court trumpeters of Charles I and Charles II', *The Music Review* 35 (1974), 223–30.

McGrattan, Alexander, 'The trumpet in funeral ceremonies in Scotland and England during the 17th Century', *Historic Brass Society Journal* 7 (1995), 168–84.

McGrattan, Alexander, 'The solo trumpet in Scotland, 1695–1800', in *Perspectives in Brass Scholarship*, ed. S. Carter (Stuyvesant, NY: Pendragon Press, 1997), pp. 79–90.

McGrattan, Alexander, 'Italian wind instrumentalists at the Scottish royal court during the 16th century', *Early Music* 24 (2001), 534–51.

McGrattan, Alexander, 'The trumpet in Restoration theatre suites', *Historic Brass Society Journal* 14 (2002), 133–64.

McGrattan, Alexander, 'The first and last blast of the trumpet: ceremonial music in seventeenth-century Scotland', in *Defining Strains: The Musical Life of Scots in the Seventeenth Century*, ed. James Porter. Studies in the History and Culture of Scotland 2 (Oxford: Peter Lang, 2007), pp. 245–67.

McLean, Hugh, 'Krebs's concerted chorales and fantasias', *The Musical Times* 122 (1981), 770–3.

McVeigh, Simon, *Concert Life in London from Mozart to Haydn* (Cambridge: Cambridge University Press, 1993).

Menke, Werner, *History of the Trumpet of Bach and Handel*, trans. G. Abraham, London, 1934, repr. (Nashville, Tenn.: The Brass Press, 1985).

Mercer-Taylor, Peter, 'Mendelssohn and the institution(s) of German art music', in *The Cambridge Companion to Mendelssohn*, ed. Peter Mercer-Taylor (Cambridge: Cambridge University Press, 2004), pp. 11–25.

Merkley, Paul A., and Lora L. M. Merkley, *Music and Patronage in the Sforza Court* (Turnhout: Brepols, 1999).

Mersenne, Marin, *Harmonie universelle* (Paris: Pierre Ballard, 1636).

Meucci, Renato, 'Roman military instruments and the lituus', *The Galpin Society Journal* 42 (1989), 85–97.

Meucci, Renato, 'On the early history of the trumpet in Italy', *Basler Jahrbuch für historische Musikpraxis* 15 (1991), 9–34.

Meucci, Renato, trans. Enrico Pelitti, 'The Pelitti firm: makers of brass instruments in nineteenth-century Milan', *Historic Brass Society Journal* 6 (1994), 304–33.

Miller, Mark, *High Hat, Trumpet and Rhythm: The Life and Music of Valaida Snow* (Toronto: Mercury Press, 2007).

Miller, Mary E., *The Murals of Bonampak* (Princeton, N.J.: Princeton University Press, 1986).

Montagu, Jeremy, 'One of Tutankhamon's Trumpets', *The Galpin Society Journal* 29 (1976), 115–17.

Morgenstern, Dan, *Living with Jazz: A Reader Edited by Sheldon Meyer* (New York: Pantheon, 2004).

Morley-Pegge, Reginald, *The French Horn: Some Notes on the Evolution of the Instrument and of its Technique*, 2nd edn (London: Ernest Benn, 1973).

Morrow, Walter, 'The trumpet as an orchestral instrument', *Proceedings of the Musical Association* 21 (1895), 133–47.

Moule, A. C., *A List of Musical and Other Sound-Producing Instruments of the Chinese*, 1908 (Buren: Frits Knuf, 1989).

Myers, Arnold, 'Design, technology and manufacture since 1800', in *The Cambridge Companion to Brass Instruments*, ed. T. Herbert and J. Wallace (Cambridge: Cambridge University Press, 1997), pp. 115–30.

Myers, Arnold, 'Brasswind innovation and output of Boosey & Co. in the Blaikley era', *Historic Brass Society Journal* 14 (2002), 391–423.

Myers, Arnold, and Frank Tomes, 'PCB cornets and Webster trumpets: Rudall Carte's patent conical bore brasswind', *Historic Brass Society Journal* 7 (1995), 107–22.

Myers, Herbert W., 'Slide trumpet madness: fact or fiction?', *Early Music* 17 (1989), 383–9.

Myers, Herbert W., 'Evidence of the emerging trombone in the late fifteenth century: what iconography may be trying to tell us', *Historic Brass Society Journal* 17 (2005), 7–35.

Myers, Margaret, *Blowing her Own Trumpet: European Ladies' Orchestras & Other Women Musicians 1870–1950 in Sweden*, (Göteborg: Avdelningen för musikvetenskap, Göteborg Universitet, 1993).

Nelson, Janet L., 'The Lord's anointed and the people's choice: Carolingian royal ritual', in *Rituals of Royalty: Power and Ceremonial in Traditional Societies*, ed. D. Cannadine and S. Price (Cambridge: Cambridge University Press, 1987), pp. 137–80.

Newsome, Roy, 'Belle Vue and brass bands', *Manchester Sounds* 2 (2001), 5–31.

Nordquist, Gullög C., 'The *salpinx* as an instrument of Eros and Dionysus', *Imago Musicae* 8 (1991), 61–72.

Nordquist, Gullög C., 'Instrumental music in representations of Greek cult', in *The Iconography of Greek Cult in The Archaic and Classical periods. Proceedings of the First International Seminar on Ancient Greek Cult, Delphi, 1990*, ed. Robin Hägg (Athènes and Liege: Centre d'étude de la Religion Grecque Antique, 1992), pp. 143–68.

Olmstead, Andrea, *Juilliard: A History* (Urbana and Chicago: University of Illinois Press, 1999).

Ostleitner, Elena, and Ursula Simek, *Carole Dawn Reinhart – A Biography*, 2nd edn (Strasshof: Vier-Viertel-Verlag, 2002).

Ottenberg, Hans-Günter, trans. P. J. Whitmore, *C.P.E. Bach* (Oxford: Oxford University Press, 1987).

Owens, Samantha, 'Professional women musicians in early eighteenth-century Württemberg', *Music & Letters* 82 (2001), 32–50.

Panico, Louis, *The Novelty Cornetist: A Complete, Thorough Exposition of how to Execute Every Known Trick on the Cornet Such as Baby Talk, Baby Cry, Blues, Chinese Effect, Flutter Tongue, Horse Neigh, Laugh, Sneeze, Improvisation and Other Effects*, 2nd edn (Chicago: Forster Music Publisher Inc., 1927).

Parker, Maurice, *Sir Thomas Beecham, Bart, C.H. (1879–1961): A Calendar of his Concert and Theatrical Performances* (Westcliff-on-Sea: Sir Thomas Beecham Society, 1985).

Parrott, Andrew, 'Performing Machaut's Mass on record', *Early Music* 5 (1977), 492–5.

Pertl, Brian, 'Some observations on the "dung chen" of the Nechung Monastery', *Asian Music* 23/2 (1992), 89–96.

Peters, Edward (ed.), *The First Crusade: The Chronicle of Fulcher of Chartres and Other Source Materials*, 2nd edn (Philadelphia: University of Pennsylvania Press, 1998).

Peters, Gretchen, 'Urban musical culture in late Medieval Southern France: evidence from private notarial contracts', *Early Music* 25 (1997), 403–10.

Philip, Robert, 'Brass playing before globalization', in *Brass Scholarship in Review*, ed. S. Carter (Hillsdale, NY: Pendragon Press, 2006), pp. 275–88.

Pierre, Constant, *La Facture Instrumentale à l'Exposition Universelle de 1889. Notes d'un Musicien sur les Instruments à Souffle Humain Nouveaux & Perfectionnés* (Paris: Librairie de l'Art Indépendant, 1890).

Pierre, Constant, *Le Conservatoire National de Musique et de Déclamation: Documents Historiques et Administraitifs, Recueillis ou Reconstitués par Constant Pierre; Sous-Chef du Secrétariat* (Paris: Imprimerie nationale, 1900).

Pietzsch, Hermann, 'The natural trumpet and the valve-trumpet and their use in the orchestra', in *The Trumpet as an Orchestral Instrument and its Treatment During the Different Periods of Musical Culture*, trans. J. Bernhoff, rev. edn by C. P. Lillya and R. Schilke (Ann Arbor, Mich.: University Music Press, n.d.).

Piggott, Stuart, 'The carnyx in early Iron Age Britain', *The Antiquaries Journal* 39 (1959), 19–32.

Pinnock, Andrew, 'A wider role for the flat trumpet', *The Galpin Society Journal* 42 (1989), 105–11.

Pinnock, Andrew, and Bruce Wood, 'A counterblast on English trumpets', *Early Music* 19 (1991), 437–43.

Plank, Steven E., '"And now about the cauldron sing": music and the supernatural on the Restoration stage', *Early Music* 18 (1990), 393–407.

Plank, Steven E., '"Knowledge in the making": recent discourse on Bach and the slide trumpet', *Historic Brass Society Journal* 8 (1996), 1–5.

Pöhlmann, Egert, and Martin L. West, *Documents of Ancient Greek Music: The Extant Melodies and Fragments* (Oxford: Clarendon Press, 2001).

Polk, Keith, 'The trombone in archival documents: 1350–1500', *Journal of the International Trombone Association* 15/3 (1987), 24–31.

Polk, Keith, 'Augustein Schubinger and the zinck: innovation in performance practice', *Historic Brass Society Journal* 1 (1989), 83–92.

Polk, Keith, 'The trombone, the slide trumpet and the ensemble tradition of the early Renaissance', *Early Music* 17 (1989), 389–97.

Polk, Keith, 'Patronage and innovation in instrumental music in the 15th century', *Historic Brass Society Journal* 3 (1991), 151–78.

Polk, Keith, *German Instrumental Music of the Late Middle Ages: Players, Patrons, and Performance Practice* (Cambridge: Cambridge University Press, 1992).

Polk, Keith, 'Brass instruments in art music in the Middle Ages', in *The Cambridge Companion to Brass Instruments*, ed. T. Herbert and J. Wallace (Cambridge: Cambridge University Press, 1997), pp. 38–50.

Polk, Keith, 'The invention of the slide principle and the earliest trombone or, the birth of a notion', in *Perspectives in Brass Scholarship*, ed. Stewart Carter (Stuyvesant, NY: Pendragon Press, 1997), pp. 19–27.

Price, Curtis A., *Music in the Restoration Theatre* (Ann Arbor, Mich.: UMI Research Press, 1979).

Price, Curtis A., *Henry Purcell and the London Stage* (Cambridge: Cambridge University Press, 1984).

Pritchard, Brian W. (ed.), *Antonio Caldara: Essays on his Life and Times* (Aldershot: Scolar Press, 1987).

Prout, Ebenezer, *Instrumentation* (London: Novello, Ewer and Co., 1878).

Prout, Ebenezer, *The Orchestra*, 2 vols (London: Augener, 1897/9).

Ramsey, Frederic, Jr., and Charles Edward Smith (ed.), *Jazzmen: The Story of Hot Jazz Told in the Lives of the Men Who Created It* (New York: Harcourt Brace, 1939).

Ramsey, Frederic, Jn., 'King Oliver and his Creole Jazz Band', in *Jazzmen*, ed. F. Ramsey, Jr., and C. E. Smith, pp. 59–91.

Rasmussen, Mary, 'English trumpet concertos in some eighteenth-century printed collections', *Brass Quarterly* 5 (1961), 51–7.

Rastall, Richard, 'Minstrelsy, church and clergy in Medieval England', *Journal of the Royal Musical Association* 97 (1970), 83–98.

Ratner, Leonard G., *Classic Music: Expression, Form, and Style* (New York: Schirmer, 1980).

Reese, Gustave, *Music in the Middle Ages* (New York: Norton, 1940).

Rice, John A., 'The musical bee: references to Mozart and Cherubini in Hummel's "New Year" concerto', *Music & Letters* 77 (1996), 401–24.

Ridgeon, John, *The Physiology of Brass Playing: A Comparative Study of Brass Playing and Teaching Techniques* (Manton: Brass Wind, 1986).

Rimsky-Korsakov, Nikolay, *Principles of Orchestration, With Musical Examples Drawn From His Own Works*, 1913, ed. M. Steinberg, trans. E. Agate, 2 vols (Berlin: Edition Russe de Musique, 1923).

Romero, Frank Edward, '*Morceaux de concours pour trompette et cornet*, contest pieces of the Paris Conservatory 1835–1999' (DMA thesis, University of Oklahoma, 2001).

Rosand, Ellen, *Opera in Seventeenth-Century Venice: The Creation of a Genre* (Berkeley: University of California Press, 1991).

Rose, Algernon, S., *Talks with Bandsmen: A Popular Handbook for Brass Instrumentalists*, 1895; facsimile edn with introduction by Arnold Myers (London: Tony Bingham, 1996).

Rosenberg, Jesse (trans.), '*Il vero modo di diminuir* [by Girolamo dalla Casa]: a translation', *Historic Brass Society Journal* 1 (1989), 109–14.

Russell, William, and Stephen W. Smith, 'New Orleans Music', in *Jazzmen: The Story of Hot Jazz Told in the Lives of the Men Who Created It*, ed. Frederic Ramsey, Jr., and Charles Edward Smith (New York: Harcourt Brace, 1939), pp. 7–37.

Rust, Brian, *Jazz Records, 1897–1942*, 4th edn (New Rochelle, NY: Arlington House, 1978).

Sachs, Curt, *The History of Musical Instruments* (New York: Norton, 1940).

Sachs, Curt, *Handbuch der Musikinstrumentenkunde*, 1920, 2nd edn, repr. (Hildesheim: Olms; Wiesbaden: Breitkopf & Härtel, 1967).

Sachs, Joel, *Kapellmeister Hummel in England and France*, Detroit Monographs in Musicology 6 (Detroit: Information Coordinators Inc., 1977).

Sadler, Graham, 'Rameau and the orchestra', *Proceedings of the Royal Musical Association* 108 (1981–2), 47–68.

Sandner, Wolfgang, '"Ich bin kein typischer Trompeter": ein Gespräch mit Carole Dawn Reinhart', *Musik+Medizin* 1 (1979), 46–51.

Sarkissian, Margaret, 'Lip-vibrated instruments of the ancient and non-western world', in *The Cambridge Companion to Brass Instruments*, ed. T. Herbert and J. Wallace (Cambridge: Cambridge University Press, 1997), pp. 5–18.

Saunders, Steven, 'The Hapsburg court of Ferdinand II and the "Messa, Magnificat et Iubilate Deo a sette chori concertati con le trombe" (1621) of Giovanni Valentini', *Journal of the American Musicological Society* 44 (1991), 359–403.

Saunders, Steven, *Cross, Sword, and Lyre: Sacred Music at the Imperial Court of Ferdinand II of Habsburg (1619–1637)* (Oxford: Clarendon Press, 1995).

Sawkins, Lionel, *A Thematic Catalogue of the Works of Michel–Richard de Lalande (1657–1726); with the Assistance of John Nightingale* (Oxford: Oxford University Press, 2005).

Schmidt, Carl B., 'Antonio Cesti's *Il pomo d'oro*: a reexamination of a famous Hapsburg court spectacle', *Journal of the American Musicological Society* 29 (1976), 381–412.

Schnoebelen, Anne, 'Performance practices at San Petronio in the Baroque', *Acta Musicologica* 41 (1969), 37–55.

Schnoebelen, Anne, 'Bologna, 1580–1700', in *The Early Baroque Era: From the Late 16th Century to the 1660s*, Man and Music 3, ed. C. Price (Basingstoke: Macmillan, 1993), pp. 103–20.

Schuller, Gunther, 'The case for Ellington's music as living repertory', in *The Duke Ellington Reader*, ed. Mark Tucker (Oxford: Oxford University Press, 1993), pp. 418–21

Schulze, Hans-Joachim, 'Johann Sebastian Bach's orchestra: some unanswered questions', *Early Music* 17 (1989), 3–16.

Schwartz, Richard I., *The Cornet Compendium: The History and Development of the Nineteenth-Century Cornet* (2000–2001) at <http://www.angelfire.com/music2/thecornetcompendium>, accessed April 2009.

Scott, J. E., 'Roman Music', in *Ancient and Oriental Music*, ed. E. Wellesz, New Oxford History of Music 1 (London: Oxford University Press, 1957), pp. 404–20.

Scullard, H. H., *Festivals and Ceremonies of the Roman Republic* (London: Thames and Hudson, 1981).

Seifert, Herbert, 'The secular–dramatic compositions of Fux: a general survey', in *Johann Joseph Fux and the Music of the Austro-Italian Baroque*, ed. H. White (Aldershot: Scolar Press, 1992), pp. 138–52.

Seiffert, Max, 'Die chorbibliothek der St. Michaelisschule in Lüneburg', *Sammelbände der Internationalen Musikgesellschaft* 9 (1908), 593–621.

Selfride-Field, Eleanor, 'The Viennese court orchestra in the time of Caldara', in *Antonio Caldara: Essays on his Life and Times*, ed. B. W. Pritchard (Aldershot: Scolar Press, 1987), pp. 115–51.

Sendrey, Alfred, *Music in Ancient Israel* (London: Vision Press, 1969).

Seraphinoff, Richard, Raymond Parks and Robert Barclay, *Making a Natural Trumpet: An Illustrated Workshop Guide* (Edinburgh: EUCHMI, 2003).

Sharp, David B., Arnold Myers, and D. Murray Campbell, 'Using pulse reflectometry to compare the evolution of the cornet and the trumpet in the 19th and 20th centuries', *Proceedings of the International Symposium on Musical Acoustics, Edinburgh, 19–22 August 1997: Institute of Acoustics* 19/5 (1997), 541–8.

Shaw, G. Bernard, ed. Dan H. Laurence, *Shaw's Music: The Complete Musical Criticism in Three Volumes* (London: Bodley Head, 1981).

Sheldon, David A., 'Johann Friedrich Fasch: problems in style classification', *The Musical Quarterly* 58 (1972), 92–116.

Shook, Brian, 'William Vacchiano (1912–2005): a tribute to his life, career, and pedagogical method', *ITG Journal* 30/3 (March 2006), 6–16.

Skeates, Robin, 'Triton's trumpet: a Neolithic symbol in Italy', *Oxford Journal of Archaeology* 10 (1991), 17–31.

Slocum, Kay Brainerd, '*Confrérie, bruderschaft* and guild: the formation of musicians' fraternal organisations in thirteenth- and fourteenth-century Europe', *Early Music History* 14 (1995), 257–74.

Smith, André M., 'Arban in Russia: a memento in the Library of Congress', *ITG Journal* 17/3 (Feb. 1993), 4–11, 34.

Smith, André M., 'The life and work of Vincent Bach (née Vincenz Schrottenbach) 1890–1976: the early years to World War II', *ITG Journal* 19/2 (Dec. 1994), 5–35.

Smith, André M., 'The life and work of Vincent Bach (1890–1976): 1941–1976 (and beyond)', *ITG Journal* 19/3 (Feb. 1995), 4–34.

Smith, André M., 'Max Schlossberg: founder of the American school of trumpet playing in the twentieth century', *ITG Journal* 21/4 (May 1997), 22–48.

Smith, Richard A., 'Recent developments in trumpet design', *ITG Journal* 3 (Oct. 1978), 27–9.

Smithers, Don L., 'The trumpets of J. W. Haas: a survey of four generations of Nuremberg brass instrument makers', *The Galpin Society Journal* 18 (1965), 23–41.

Smithers, Don L., 'Seventeenth-century English trumpet music', *Music & Letters* 48 (1967), 358–65.

Smithers, Don L., 'Music for the Prince–Bishop', *Music and Musicians* 18 (1970), 24–7.

Smithers, Don L., 'The Hapsburg Imperial *Trompeter* and *Heerpaucker* Privileges of 1653', *The Galpin Society Journal* 24 (1971), 84–95.

Smithers, Don L., 'The Baroque trumpet after 1721: some preliminary observations. Part one: science and practice', *Early Music* 5 (1977), 176–9.

Smithers, Don L., 'The Baroque trumpet after 1721: some preliminary observations. Part two: function and use', *Early Music* 6 (1978), 356–61.

Smithers, Don L., 'Gottfried Reiches ansehen und sein einfluss auf die musik Johann Sebastian Bachs', *Bach-Jahrbuch* 73/1 (1987), 113–50.

Smithers, Don L., *The Music and History of the Baroque Trumpet Before 1721*, 2nd edn (Carbondale, Ill.: Southern Illinois University Press, 1988).

Smithers, Don L., 'A new look at the historical, linguistic and taxonomic bases for the evolution of lip-blown instruments from Classical Antiquity until the end of the Middle Ages', *Historic Brass Society Journal* 1 (1989), 3–64.

Smithers, Don L., 'Antique trumpet mutes: a retrospective commentary', *Historic Brass Society Journal* 2 (1990), 104–11.

Smithers, Don L., 'Bach, Reiche and the Leipzig *Collegia Musica*', *Historic Brass Society Journal* 2 (1990), 1–51.

Smithers, Don L., 'Mozart's orchestral brass', *Early Music* 20 (1992), 254–65.

Smithers, Don L., K. Wogram and J. M. Bowsher, 'Playing the baroque trumpet', *Scientific American* 254/4 (1986), 108–15.

Snell, Howard, *The Trumpet: Its Practice and Performance: A Guide for Students* (Hollington: Rakeway Music, 1997).

Snyder, Kerala J., *Dieterich Buxtehude: Organist in Lübeck* (New York: Schirmer, 1987).

Sonneck, Oscar G. T., *Early Opera in America* (New York: Schirmer, 1915).

Sonneck, Oscar G. T., *Early Concert-Life in America (1731–1800)*, 1907 (New York: Da Capo Press, 1978).

Sorenson, Scott P., 'Valentine Snow, Handel's trumpeter', *ITG Journal* 4 (1979), 5–11.

Sorenson, Scott, and John Webb, 'The Harpers and the trumpet', *The Galpin Society Journal* 39 (1986), 35–57.

Speer, Daniel, *Grund-richtiger, kurtz- leicht- und nöthiger, jetzt wol-vermehrter Unterricht der musicalischen Kunst, oder Vierfaches musicalisches Kleblau* (Ulm: Im Verlag G. W. Kuhnen, gedruckt bey C. B. Kuhnen Seel. Erben, 1697).

Spitta, Philipp, trans. C. Bell and J. A. Fuller Maitland, *Johann Sebastian Bach: His Work and Influence on the Music of Germany, 1685–1750*, 3 vols (London: Novello, 1899).

Spitzer, John, 'Improvized ornamentation in a Handel aria with obbligato wind accompaniment', *Early Music* 16 (1988), 514–22.

Spitzer, John and Neal Zaslaw, *The Birth of the Orchestra: History of an Institution, 1650–1815* (Oxford: Oxford University Press, 2004).

Stary, P. F., 'Foreign elements in Etruscan arms and armour: 8th to 3rd centuries B.C.', *Proceedings of the Prehistoric Society* 45 (1979), 179–206.

Steele-Perkins, Crispian, 'Practical observations on natural, slide and flat trumpets', *The Galpin Society Journal* 42 (1989), 122–7.

Steele-Perkins, Crispian, *The Trumpet* (London: Kahn & Averill, 2001).

Steenstrup, Kristian, *Teaching Brass*, 2nd rev. edn (Aarhus: The Royal Academy of Music, 2007).

Sternfeld, Frederick W., 'The dramatic and allegorical function of music in Shakespeare's tragedies: the symbolism of trumpets', *Annales Musicologiques* 3 (1955), 265–82.

Stevenson, Robert, 'Ancient Peruvian instruments', *The Galpin Society Journal* 12 (1959), 17–43.

Stevenson, Robert, *Music in Aztec & Inca Territory* (Berkeley: University of California Press, 1968).

Stewart, M. Dee (ed.), *Arnold Jacobs: The Legacy of a Master: The Personal and Pedagogical Recollections of Thirty-One of his Colleagues, Students, and Friends* (Northfield, Ill.: Instrumentalist Publishing Co., 1987).

Stockigt, Janice B., and Michael Talbot, 'Two more new Vivaldi finds in Dresden', *Eighteenth–Century Music* 3/1 (2006), 35–61.

Strohm, Reinhard, *Music in Late Medieval Bruges* (Oxford: Clarendon Press, 1985).

Suggs, Robert, 'Brilliant music for a dark era: Karl Pilss, Helmut Wobisch, and the Trompetenchor der Stadt Wien', *International Trumpet Guild Journal* 28/2 (Jan. 2004), 12–16.

Suppan, Wolfgang, 'The use of wind instruments (excluding chalumeau) in Fux's music', in *Johann Joseph Fux and the Music of the Austro-Italian Baroque*, ed. H. White (Aldershot: Scolar Press, 1992), pp. 95–108.

Talbot, Michael, *The Sacred Vocal Music of Antonio Vivaldi*, Studi di Musica Veneta 8 (Florence: Olschki, 1995).

Tarr, Edward H., 'The trumpets and music of the Charamela Real', *ITG Journal* 1 (Oct. 1976), 38–9.

Tarr, Edward H., 'Die musik und die instrumente der charamela real in Lissabon', *Forum musicologicum: Basler Studien zur Interpretation der alten Musik* 2 (1980), 181–229.

Tarr, Edward H., *The Trumpet*, trans. S. E. Plank and E. H. Tarr (London: Batsford, 1988).

Tarr, Edward H., 'Two great trumpet virtuosos and their instruments', *ITG Journal* 16/3 (Feb. 1992), 17.

Tarr, Edward H., 'The romantic trumpet', *Historic Brass Society Journal* 5 (1993), 213–61.

Tarr, Edward H., 'The romantic trumpet: part two', *Historic Brass Society Journal* 6 (1994), 110–215.

Tarr, Edward H., 'The trumpet before 1800', in *The Cambridge Companion to Brass Instruments*, ed. T. Herbert and J. Wallace (Cambridge: Cambridge University Press, 1997), pp. 84–102.

Tarr, Edward H., 'Ferdinand Weinschenk (1831–1910), pivotal figure in German trumpet history', *Historic Brass Society Journal* 11 (1999), 10–36.

Tarr, Edward H., 'Bach and the others: eighteenth-century trumpeter-hornists', *Brass Bulletin* 119 (2002), 44–55 (part 1); *Brass Bulletin* 120 (2002), 38–47 (part 2).

Tarr, Edward H., *East Meets West: The Russian Trumpet Tradition from the Time of Peter the Great to the October Revolution* (Hillsdale, NY: Pendragon Press, 2003).

Tarr, Edward H., 'The "Bach trumpet" in the nineteenth and twentieth centuries', in *Musique Ancienne – Instruments et Imagination: Actes des Rencontres Internationales Harmoniques, Lausanne 2004* (*Music of the Past – Instruments and Imagination: Proceedings of the Harmoniques International Congress, Lausanne 2004*), ed. M. Latcham (Bern: Peter Lang, 2006), pp. 17–48.

Tarr, Edward H., 'Oskar Böhme revisited: young musicians' training, instruments, and repertoire in the late nineteenth and early twentieth centuries', in *Brass Scholarship in Review*, ed. S. Carter (Hillsdale, NY: Pendragon Press, 2006), pp. 187–221.

Taube, Karl A., *Aztec and Maya Myths* (London: British Museum Press, 1993).

Taylor, Eric, *Musical Instruments of South-East Asia* (Singapore; Oxford: Oxford University Press, 1989).

Taylor, Jeff, 'Encounters with Jazz', *I.S.A.M. Newsletter* 24 (Fall 1994).

Termini, Olga, '*L'Irene* in Venice and Naples: tyrant and victim, or the *rifacimento* process examined', in *Antonio Caldara: Essays on his Life and Times*, ed. B. W. Pritchard (Aldershot: Scolar Press, 1987), pp. 365–407.

Terry, Charles Sanford, *Bach's Orchestra* (London: Oxford University Press, 1932).

Thomason, Geoffrey, 'Hess, huffs and Hallé facts: staff appointments in the early years of the Royal Manchester College of Music', *Manchester Sounds* 3 (2002), 55–67.

Thrasher, Alan R., *Chinese Musical Instruments* (Oxford: Oxford University Press, 2000).

Tilmouth, Michael, 'A calendar of references to music in newspapers published in London and the provinces (1660–1719)', *Royal Musical Association Research Chronicle* 1 (1961).

Tilmouth, Michael, 'The beginnings of provincial concert life in England', in *Music in Eighteenth-Century England: Essays in Memory of Charles Cudworth*, ed. C. Hogwood and R. Luckett (Cambridge: Cambridge University Press, 1983), pp. 1–17.

Titcomb, Caldwell, 'Baroque court and military trumpets and kettledrums: technique and music', *The Galpin Society Journal*, 9 (1956), 56–81.

Tomes, Frank, 'Flat trumpet experiments', *The Galpin Society Journal* 43 (1990), 164–5.

Tucker, Mark (ed.), *The Duke Ellington Reader* (Oxford: Oxford University Press, 1993).

Turner, Gordon, and Alwyn W. Turner, *The Trumpets Will Sound: The Story of the Royal Military School of Music, Kneller Hall* (Tunbridge Wells: Parapress, 1996).

Turner, Samuel, *An Account of an Embassy to the Court of the Teshoo Lama, in Tibet; Containing a Narrative of a Journey through Bootan, and Part of Tibet* (London: W. Bulmer, 1800).

Turrentine, Edgar, 'Notes on the ancient Olympic trumpet-blowing contests', 1969, in *Brass Anthology: A Compendium of Articles from The Instrumentalist on Playing the Brass Instruments* (Evanston, Ill.: The Instrumentalist Publishing Company, 1980), pp. 497–8.

Vermes, Geza, *The Complete Dead Sea Scrolls in English* (London: Penguin, 1997).

Wallace, John, 'Brass solo and chamber music from 1800', in *The Cambridge Companion to Brass Instruments*, ed. T. Herbert and J. Wallace (Cambridge: Cambridge University Press, 1997), pp. 236–54.

Wallace, John, and Trevor Herbert, 'Aspects of performance practices: the brass band and its influence on other brass–playing styles', in *The British Brass Band: A Musical and Social History*, ed. Trevor Herbert (Oxford: Oxford University Press, 2000), pp. 278–305.

Walter, Rudolf, 'Bemerkungen zu den Kompositionen von Johann Joseph Fux zum *Offertorium*', in *Johann Joseph Fux and the Music of the Austro–Italian Baroque*, ed. H. M. White (Aldershot: Scolar Press, 1992), pp. 231–61.

Waterhouse, William, *The New Langwill Index: A Dictionary of Musical Wind-Instrument Makers and Inventors* (London: Tony Bingham, 1993).

Webb, John, 'The Billingsgate trumpet', *The Galpin Society Journal* 41 (1988), 59–62.

Webb, John, 'The English slide trumpet', *Historic Brass Society Journal* 5 (1993), 262–79.

Webb, John, 'The flat trumpet in perspective', *The Galpin Society Journal* 46 (1993), 154–60.

Webber, Geoffrey, *North German Church Music in the Age of Buxtehude* (Oxford: Clarendon Press, 1996).

Wedgwood, Denis, 'Ovoid? About valves', *Brass Bulletin* 102 (1998), 29–33.

Wegman, Rob C. 'The minstrel school in the late Middle Ages', *Historic Brass Society Journal* 14 (2002), 11–30.

Weimer, Lee J., 'The trumpet as a solo instrument in New York City from 1835 to 1845' (DMA thesis, University of Memphis, 1999).

Werner, Eric, 'Musical aspects of the Dead Sea Scrolls', *The Musical Quarterly* 43 (1957), 21–37.

West, Jeremy, and Susan Smith, *How to Play the Cornett* (London: JW Publications, 1995).

West, Martin L., *Ancient Greek Music* (Oxford: Clarendon Press, 1992).

Westerberg, Hans, *Boy from New Orleans: Louis "Satchmo" Armstrong, on Records, Films, Radio and Television* (Copenhagen: Jazzmedia, 1981).

Wheeler, Joseph, 'Further notes on the classic trumpet', *The Galpin Society Journal* 18 (1965), 14–22.

White, Harry, 'The *Sepolcro* oratorios of Fux: an assessment', in *Johann Joseph Fux and the Music of the Austro–Italian Baroque*, ed. H. White (Aldershot: Scolar Press, 1992), pp. 164–230.

White, Harry (ed.), *Johann Joseph Fux and the Music of the Austro–Italian Baroque* (Aldershot: Scolar Press, 1992).

Whitehead, Lance, and Arnold Myers, 'The Köhler family of brasswind instrument makers', *Historic Brass Society Journal* 16 (2004), 89–123.

Wilkinson, John Gardner, *The Manners and Customs of the Ancient Egyptians*, 3rd edn, 5 vols (London: John Murray, 1847).

Willems, Jos, *All of Me: The Complete Discography of Louis Armstrong*, Studies in Jazz 51 (Lanham, Md.: Scarecrow Press, 2006).

Wills, Simon, 'Brass in the modern orchestra', in *The Cambridge Companion to Brass Instruments*, ed. T. Herbert and J. Wallace (Cambridge: Cambridge University Press, 1997), pp. 157–76.

Wilson, John (ed.), *Roger North on Music: Being a Selection from his Essays Written During the Years c.1695–1728* (London: Novello, 1959).

Wolff, Christoph, *Johann Sebastian Bach: The Learned Musician* (Oxford: Oxford University Press, 2001).

Wood, Bruce, 'The first performance of Purcell's funeral music for Queen Mary', in *Performing the Music of Henry Purcell*, ed. M. Burden (Oxford: Clarendon Press, 1996), pp. 61–81.

Worsthorne, Simon Towneley, *Venetian Opera in the Seventeenth Century* (Oxford: Clarendon Press, 1954).

Wright, Craig M., *Music at the Court of Burgundy, 1364–1419: A Documentary History* (Henryville, Pa.: Institute of Mediaeval Music, 1979).

Wright, Craig M., *Music and Ceremony at Notre Dame of Paris, 500–1550* (Cambridge: Cambridge University Press, 1989).

Wulstan, David, 'The sounding of the shofar', *The Galpin Society Journal* 26 (1973), 29–46.

Xanthoulis, Nikos, 'The salpinx in Greek antiquity', *ITG Journal* (Oct. 2006), 39–45.

Ziolkowski, John, 'The invention of the tuba (trumpet)', *The Classical World* 92/4 (1999), 367–73.

Ziolkowski, John, 'The Roman *bucina*: a distinct musical instrument?', *Historic Brass Society Journal* 14 (2002), 31–58.

Index